6 대화를 듣고, 남자의 마지막 말의 의도로 가장 적절한 것을 고르시오.

① 요청　　　② 항의　　　③ 동의　　　④ 조언　　　⑤ 칭찬

7 대화를 듣고, 남자가 가져올 물건으로 가장 적절한 것을 고르시오.

① 줄자　　　　　② 앞치마　　　　　③ 실내화
④ 종이컵　　　　⑤ 베이킹 소다

8 대화를 듣고, 두 사람이 대화 직후에 할 일로 가장 적절한 것을 고르시오.

① 호텔 예약하기　　　② 시장 구경하기　　　③ 선물 사러 가기
④ 휴대폰 가져오기　　　⑤ 사진 찍으러 가기

9 대화를 듣고, 두 사람이 Meeting with the Webtoon Artist에 대해 언급하지 <u>않은</u> 것을 고르시오.

① 행사 요일　　　② 작가 이름　　　③ 행사 장소
④ 질의응답 시간 여부　　　⑤ 참가 기념품

10 다음을 듣고, 남자가 하는 말의 내용으로 가장 적절한 것을 고르시오.

① 작가와의 만남 행사　　　② 희망 도서 신청 절차
③ 필독 도서 목록 공지　　　④ 도서 대출 연장 방법
⑤ 독서 동아리 활동 안내

11 대화를 듣고, English book club에 대한 내용으로 일치하지 <u>않는</u> 것을 고르시오.

① 영어로 된 시를 읽기도 한다.　　　② 만화책을 읽기도 한다.
③ 김 선생님이 토론을 지도한다.　　　④ 매주 목요일에 모인다.
⑤ 학교 미디어 센터에서 모임이 열린다.

12번~20번 문제는 다음 페이지에 ➡

12 대화를 듣고, 남자가 외출을 하는 목적으로 가장 적절한 것을 고르시오.

① 산책을 하기 위해서　　　　② 심부름을 하기 위해서
③ 책을 대출하기 위해서　　　④ 간식거리를 사기 위해서
⑤ 과제 모임을 하기 위해서

13 대화를 듣고, 두 사람이 만날 시각을 고르시오.

① 8:00 a.m.　　② 9:00 a.m.　　③ 10:00 a.m.　　④ 11:00 a.m.　　⑤ 12:00 p.m.

14 대화를 듣고, 두 사람의 관계로 가장 적절한 것을 고르시오.

① 경찰관 - 시민　　　② 여행사 직원 - 고객　　　③ 호텔 관리인 - 숙박객
④ 기차표 판매원 - 승객　　⑤ 놀이공원 안내원 - 이용객

15 대화를 듣고, 여자가 남자에게 부탁한 일로 가장 적절한 것을 고르시오.

① 배드민턴 채 빌려주기　　　② 오는 길에 양파 사오기
③ 공원에서 만나기　　　　　④ 같이 수프 만들기
⑤ 친구에게 안부 전해주기

16 대화를 듣고, 남자가 재채기를 하는 이유로 가장 적절한 것을 고르시오.

① 감기에 걸려서　　　　　② 알레르기성 비염이 있어서
③ 꽃가루 알레르기가 있어서　　④ 고양이 털이 많은 곳에 가서
⑤ 자극적인 향수 냄새로 인해서

17 다음 그림의 상황에 가장 적절한 대화를 고르시오.

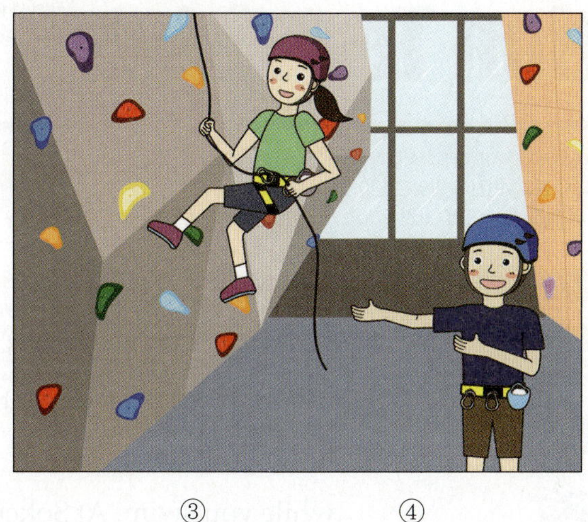

①   ②   ③   ④   ⑤

18 다음을 듣고, 남자가 Sports Day에 대해서 언급하지 <u>않은</u> 것을 고르시오.

① 행사 날짜   ② 스포츠 게임 종류   ③ 경기 시작 시간
④ 점심 식사   ⑤ 옷차림

[19~20] 대화를 듣고, 남자의 마지막 말에 이어질 여자의 말로 가장 적절한 것을 고르시오.

19 Woman: ________________________________

① I'm not hungry now.   ② The waiters were not kind at all.
③ Because it's too hot outside.   ④ The music was so good.
⑤ I'll pay for dinner.

20 Woman: ________________________________

① Sure. I like playing baseball.   ② Thanks. How about you?
③ Would you like to join me?   ④ Well, that sounds boring.
⑤ I don't like exercising.

Dictation Test 01

M2(17)_01_D

Dictation(받아쓰기)은 본문을 받아쓰면서 영어듣기의 집중력을 향상시키고 다양한 표현을 정리하기 위한 영어듣기 학습법입니다. **녹음을 다시 듣고, 빈칸에 알맞은 단어를 써 보세요.**
※Dictation의 정답은 듣기 대본의 밑줄 친 부분을 확인하세요.

📖 정답 p. 1

✏️ 맞은 개수 　 / 총152개

2025 영어듣기능력평가 1회 1번 변형

날씨파악-그림

1. 다음을 듣고, 속초 해변의 날씨로 가장 적절한 것을 고르시오.

① 　② 

③ 　④ 

⑤

01 W: Hello, swimmers. This is the beach weather report. It will be sunny at Daecheon Beach today. You can enjoy a ___________ ___________ while you swim. At Sokcho Beach, there will be ___________ ___________. High waves are forecasted, so I advise you not to swim at Sokcho Beach today. Heavy rain is expected at Haeundae Beach, so it's ___________ ___________ ___________ ___________ to swim there, either.

2025 영어듣기능력평가 1회 2번 변형

그림정보파악

2. 대화를 듣고, 여자가 주문할 레인부츠로 가장 적절한 것을 고르시오.

① 　② 

③ 　④ 

⑤ 

02 W: Jimmy, come here and ___________ ___________ your rain boots on the screen.

M: Sure, Mom.

W: Do you want boots with handles? The ones with handles are easy to ___________ ___________ ___________.

M: Well, I don't want handles on my boots.

W: Okay. How do you like the ones with pointy dinosaur spikes?

M: I love the spikes. They look so cool!

W: Great. Do you want the ones with dinosaurs or just plain ones?

M: I'll ___________ ___________ the plain ones, please.

W: Okay. I'll order those for you.

심정추론

3. 대화를 듣고, 여자의 심정으로 가장 적절한 것을 고르시오.

① 지루함　　② 불안함
③ 신남　　　④ 자랑스러움
⑤ 편안함

03

W: Kevin, ＿＿＿＿ ＿＿＿＿ ＿＿＿＿.

M: What do you mean?

W: I ＿＿＿＿ ＿＿＿＿ ＿＿＿＿ the principal's office, and I don't know why!

M: Well, it could be about something good.

W: How could it be? The principal wants to talk with a student!

M: Relax, Amanda. You don't need to worry ＿＿＿＿ ＿＿＿＿ ＿＿＿＿.

W: What should I do? I have to go now.

M: Calm down. I'll wait here for you until you come back.

한일파악

4. 대화를 듣고, 남자가 주말에 한 일로 가장 적절한 것을 고르시오.

① 집 안 가구 옮기기
② 자전거 청소하기
③ 집 앞 눈 치우기
④ 자전거 타러 가기
⑤ 캠핑 용품 구입하기

04

W: Hi, Eric. How was your weekend?

M: I just stayed home.

W: Well, the weather wasn't very good.

M: Yeah, I wanted to ＿＿＿＿ ＿＿＿＿, but it snowed.

W: I'm sorry to hear that.

M: It's okay. I ＿＿＿＿ ＿＿＿＿ ＿＿＿＿, instead.

W: Nice. Do you like riding your bike?

M: Yes. I ride for hours when the weather is good.

다음 페이지에 계속 ➡

5. 대화를 듣고, 두 사람이 대화하는 장소로 가장 적절한 곳을 고르시오.
① 슈퍼마켓
② 시계 전문점
③ 분실물 보관소
④ 은행
⑤ 휴대폰 수리점

05
M: May I help you?

W: Yes, my watch ___________ ___________. It's not ticking.

M: Let me have a look. (*Pause*) There ___________ to be a problem with the battery.

W: Can you fix it?

M: Yes, it just needs ___________ ___________ ___________.

W: Okay. How long will that take?

M: It should only take about 5 minutes. I'll have it ready for you shortly.

6. 대화를 듣고, 남자의 마지막 말의 의도로 가장 적절한 것을 고르시오.
① 요청　　　　② 항의
③ 동의　　　　④ 조언
⑤ 칭찬

06
M: What are you doing, Fatima?

W: I'm ___________ calligraphy.

M: What's calligraphy?

W: It's the visual art of handwriting. See what I just wrote?

M: It's beautiful. It looks like the ________ ________ ___________.

W: I know! I need more practice, but I really like this design.

M: Would you ________ ________ ________ ________ here in the same design?

W: I know! I need more practice, but I really like this design.

7. 대화를 듣고, 남자가 가져올 물건으로 가장 적절한 것을 고르시오.

① 줄자 ② 앞치마
③ 실내화 ④ 종이컵
⑤ 베이킹 소다

07
M: Emma, are you still helping with the science booth for the school festival?

W: Yes! I'm __________ the "make-your-own-volcano" activity.

M: Sounds fun! Do you have __________ __________ __________ ready?

W: Almost. But we still need some paper cups to hold the baking soda.

M: Oh, I have some __________ __________ __________ at home.

W: Great. Do you think you could bring them tomorrow?

M: Sure! No problem.

8. 대화를 듣고, 두 사람이 대화 직후에 할 일로 가장 적절한 것을 고르시오.

① 호텔 예약하기
② 시장 구경하기
③ 선물 사러 가기
④ 휴대폰 가져오기
⑤ 사진 찍으러 가기

08
W: Eric, it is the last evening of our package tour.

M: Yes. We have some free time. Is there anything you want to do?

W: How about going to a __________ __________? It would be fun.

M: It could be __________ for us to go there on our own.

W: You're right.

M: I saw some beautiful fountains in the hotel lobby. Let's __________ __________ __________!

W: Great. Do you have your phone with you?

M: Of course. Let's go now.

다음 페이지에 계속 ➡

9. 대화를 듣고, 두 사람이 Meeting with the Webtoon Artist에 대해 언급하지 **않은** 것을 고르시오.
① 행사 요일
② 작가 이름
③ 행사 장소
④ 질의응답 시간 여부
⑤ 참가 기념품

09

W: Kevin, did you hear about the Meeting with the Webtoon Artist?

M: Yes! It's this Friday, right? My favorite artist, Jayoon Kim, will be there.

W: That's awesome. Where is it ___________ ___________?

M: At the ___________ ___________ of BookNBook, the big bookstore downtown.

W: Will there be a Q&A ___________ with the artist?

M: Yes, at the end of the event. We can even ask him questions directly.

W: Awesome! I'll get my questions ready.

10. 다음을 듣고, 남자가 하는 말의 내용으로 가장 적절한 것을 고르시오.
① 작가와의 만남 행사
② 희망 도서 신청 절차
③ 필독 도서 목록 공지
④ 도서 대출 연장 방법
⑤ 독서 동아리 활동 안내

10

M: Hello, everyone. This is Mr. Kim, the teacher in charge of the library club. I'd like to inform you about the required reading list for ___________ ___________. All students are expected to read at least three books from the list by the end of June. The list ___________ a variety of Korean and international books. You can find it posted on the library ___________ ___________ and on the school website. If you have any questions, feel free to ___________ ___________ the library after school.

대화내용불일치

11. 대화를 듣고, English book club에 대한 내용으로 일치하지 않는 것을 고르시오.

① 영어로 된 시를 읽기도 한다.
② 만화책을 읽기도 한다.
③ 김 선생님이 토론을 지도한다.
④ 매주 목요일에 모인다.
⑤ 학교 미디어 센터에서 모임이 열린다.

11

M: Kate, will you join our English book club?

W: Yes, I'd love to. Do you also read English poems?

M: Sure. Sometimes we read comic books, too.

W: Sounds fun!

M: Yeah. And our English teacher, Ms. Kim ________ ________ ____________.

W: That's nice. By the way, how many times a week do you meet?

M: ________ ________ ________, every Friday. Why don't you come this Friday?

W: Okay. Where should I go?

M: Come to the school Media Center. We always meet there.

2025 영어듣기능력평가 1회 12번 변형

외출목적파악

12. 대화를 듣고, 남자가 외출을 하는 목적으로 가장 적절한 것을 고르시오.

① 산책을 하기 위해서
② 심부름을 하기 위해서
③ 책을 대출하기 위해서
④ 간식거리를 사기 위해서
⑤ 과제 모임을 하기 위해서

12

M: Mom, I'm going out for a bit.

W: Where are you going, David? Are you going to the library?

M: No, I've finished my homework __________.

W: Then why are you going out?

M: I'm just __________ __________ hungry. I want to get some snacks from the store.

W: Okay. Be careful and don't buy __________ __________ __________!

M: Don't worry. I'll be back soon.

다음 페이지에 계속 ➡

13. 대화를 듣고, 두 사람이 만날 시각을 고르시오.

① 8:00 a.m.   ② 9:00 a.m.
③ 10:00 a.m.   ④ 11:00 a.m.
⑤ 12:00 p.m.

13

W: We finally get to go to Panda World tomorrow! I'm so excited.

M: Me, too! What time does Panda World open?

W: It opens at 9:00 a.m. and closes at 12:00 p.m.

M: ___________ ___________ ___________ meet at 11:00 a.m.?

W: You can ___________ the pandas at 11:00 a.m. Let's get there before then.

M: ___________ ___________ we meet at the bus stop at 10:00 a.m., instead?

W: Sounds perfect. We can catch the shuttle bus to get there.

14. 대화를 듣고, 두 사람의 관계로 가장 적절한 것을 고르시오.

① 경찰관 – 시민
② 여행사 직원 – 고객
③ 호텔 관리인 – 숙박객
④ 기차표 판매원 – 승객
⑤ 놀이공원 안내원 – 이용객

14

(Telephone rings.)

M: Hello. This is Wonder Tours. ___________ ___________ ___________ ___________ ___________?

W: Hi. I'd like to go to London this weekend.

M: OK. Would you like to go by train?

W: Yes. And I'd like a guided bus tour.

M: Sure. How about accommodation? We have some ___________ ___________ ___________ ___________.

W: I'll stay in London for two nights. Could you tell me what the prices are?

M: Sure. Could you ___________ ___________ ___________ ___________?

W: No problem.

부탁(요청)한일파악

15. 대화를 듣고, 여자가 남자에게 부탁한 일로 가장 적절한 것을 고르시오.

① 배드민턴 채 빌려주기
② 오는 길에 양파 사오기
③ 공원에서 만나기
④ 같이 수프 만들기
⑤ 친구에게 안부 전해주기

15

W: What's with the badminton racket, Keith?

M: Oh, Tim wants to ________ ________ from me. I'm meeting him at the park in ten minutes.

W: You're not playing with him?

M: No, I'll just ________ ________ ________ and come back.

W: Could you buy me some onions ________ ________ ________ ________?

M: Sure, Mom. What are you making?

W: Just some soup. Thank you, son.

2024 영어듣기능력평가 2회 16번 변형

이유파악

16. 대화를 듣고, 남자가 재채기를 하는 이유로 가장 적절한 것을 고르시오.

① 감기에 걸려서
② 알레르기성 비염이 있어서
③ 꽃가루 알레르기가 있어서
④ 고양이 털이 많은 곳에 가서
⑤ 자극적인 향수 냄새로 인해서

16

W: Bless you! Are you okay, Noah?

M: Yes, thanks. I'm just sneezing a lot this morning.

W: Oh no, did you __________ __________ __________?

M: No, I don't think so. I feel fine __________ __________ the sneezing.

W: Then maybe it's an allergy.

M: Yeah, I have a pollen allergy, and the trees near my house __________ __________ __________ flowers now.

W: I see. You should take your allergy medicine.

M: I will. I __________ __________ take it today.

다음 페이지에 계속 ➡

17. 다음 그림의 상황에 가장 적절한 대화를 고르시오.

①   ②
③   ④
⑤

17

① M: We finally ___________ ___________ to the top!

W: Yeah, the view is amazing up here!

② M: What are you ___________ ___________?

W: I'm just doing some push-ups.

③ M: ___________ ___________ ___________ that

yellow rock with your left foot.

W: Okay, I'll ___________ ___________ ___________

___________.

④ M: The drone show is really fantastic!

W: Yeah, I'm so glad we came!

⑤ M: Why are you wearing a helmet?

W: I'm going for a bike ride.

18. 다음을 듣고, 남자가 Sports Day에 대해서 언급하지 <u>않은</u> 것을 고르시오.

① 행사 날짜
② 스포츠 게임 종류
③ 경기 시작 시간
④ 점심 식사
⑤ 옷차림

18

M: Hello, students! This Friday, July 12 is Sports Day, one of our biggest events of the year. ___________ ___________, we will ___________ ___________ ___________ such as a marathon, swimming contest, and soccer game. Lunch ___________ ___________ ___________, and snacks will also be provided. Be sure to wear comfortable clothes for the outdoor activities.

알맞은응답찾기

19. 대화를 듣고, 남자의 마지막 말에 이어질 여자의 말로 가장 적절한 것을 고르시오.

Woman: _________________

① I'm not hungry now.
② The waiters were not kind at all.
③ Because it's too hot outside.
④ The music was so good.
⑤ I'll pay for dinner.

19
M: I am starving. Do we have anything to eat?

W: No, I'm afraid we need to go to the grocery store.

M: What about ________ ________ for dinner?

W: That's a good idea. Which ___________ do you want to go to?

M: How about that new sushi restaurant we went to ________ ________?

W: I don't want to go there again.

M: Why? The food was ________ ________.

W: The waiters were not kind at all.

알맞은응답찾기

20. 대화를 듣고, 남자의 마지막 말에 이어질 여자의 말로 가장 적절한 것을 고르시오.

Woman: _________________

① Sure. I like playing baseball.
② Thanks. How about you?
③ Would you like to join me?
④ Well, that sounds boring.
⑤ I don't like exercising.

20
M: What time do you ________ get up in the morning?

W: I get up at 6 o'clock and ________.

M: Wow! You're very diligent.

W: Oh, it's nothing. It's just one of my habits.

M: What kinds of exercises do you do?

W: I go jogging and swimming. I have been feeling ________ ________ ________ since I started some exercising in the morning.

M: That ________ ________. I'm going to start exercising tomorrow.

W: Would you like to join me?

Words & Expressions Review 01

● 다음 단어를 암기하세요.

문제	번호	단어	뜻
1	□ 1	advise	권하다, 조언하다
2	□ 2	pick out	~을 고르다, 선택하다
	□ 3	be in trouble	큰일 나다, 곤경에 처하다
3	□ 4	principal	교장, 학장, 총장
	□ 5	ahead of time	미리, 예정보다 일찍
	□ 6	cycling	사이클링, 자전거 타기
4	□ 7	instead	대신에
	□ 8	for hours	몇 시간 동안
	□ 9	work	작동하다
5	□ 10	appear	~인 것 같다
	□ 11	shortly	곧, 이내
	□ 12	calligraphy	서예
6	□ 13	letter	글자, 문자
	□ 14	write ~ down	~을 적다
	□ 15	still	여전히, 아직(도)
7	□ 16	extra	여분의, 추가의
	□ 17	last	마지막의
8	□ 18	fountain	분수
	□ 19	branch	지점, 지사
9	□ 20	session	(특정한 활동을 위한) 시간[기간]
	□ 21	required	필수의
10	□ 22	a variety of	다양한

문제	번호	단어	뜻
10	□ 23	international	국제의, 국제적인
11	□ 24	lead	이끌다
	□ 25	discussion	토론, 논의
12	□ 26	sweet	단 것, 과자
13	□ 27	feed	먹이를 주다
	□ 28	catch	(버스·기차 등을 시간 맞춰) 타다
	□ 29	weekend	주말
14	□ 30	accommodation	숙소, 숙박 시설
	□ 31	hold on a second	잠시 기다리다
15	□ 32	hand ~ over	~을 건네주다
	□ 33	on one's way back	돌아오는 길에
16	□ 34	sneeze	재채기하다
	□ 35	pollen	꽃가루, 화분
17	□ 36	make it	해내다
	□ 37	give it a try	시도해 보다
	□ 38	hold	개최하다, 열다
18	□ 39	comfortable	편안한
	□ 40	outdoor	야외의
19	□ 41	eat out	외식하다
	□ 42	restaurant	식당
20	□ 43	exercise	운동, 운동하다
	□ 44	feel better	(기분이) 나아지다

● 왼쪽 단어장의 뜻이 보이지 않게 반으로 접고, 학습한 단어의 뜻을 아래 빈칸에 적어주세요.

1	hand ~ over	23	calligraphy
2	for hours	24	restaurant
3	instead	25	be in trouble
4	exercise	26	extra
5	cycling	27	international
6	outdoor	28	work
7	shortly	29	catch
8	write ~ down	30	hold on a second
9	on one's way back	31	make it
10	a variety of	32	give it a try
11	pick out	33	eat out
12	lead	34	session
13	fountain	35	discussion
14	accommodation	36	last
15	principal	37	still
16	appear	38	letter
17	feed	39	ahead of time
18	feel better	40	pollen
19	advise	41	required
20	weekend	42	sweet
21	branch	43	hold
22	comfortable	44	sneeze

02회 중학영어듣기 모의고사

M2(17)_02_US
모두 **미국식 발음(US)**
으로 녹음

M2(17)_02_UK
20문제 중 5문제에 **영국식 발음
(US+UK)**을 포함하여 녹음

정답 및 해석 p. 6

1 다음을 듣고, 현재 부산의 날씨로 가장 적절한 것을 고르시오.

① 　② 　③ 　④ 　⑤ 

2 대화를 듣고, 남자가 구입할 화분으로 가장 적절한 것을 고르시오.

① 　② 　③ 　④ 　⑤ 

3 대화를 듣고, 남자의 심정으로 가장 적절한 것을 고르시오.

① sad　② excited　③ scared　④ bored　⑤ shy

4 대화를 듣고, 남자가 지난달에 한 일로 가장 적절한 것을 고르시오.

① 등산하기　② 수영하기　③ 낚시하기
④ 유적지 탐방하기　⑤ 맛집 방문하기

5 대화를 듣고, 두 사람이 대화하는 장소로 가장 적절한 곳을 고르시오.

① PC방　② 영화관　③ 공항　④ 기차역　⑤ 기념품 가게

6 대화를 듣고, 여자의 마지막 말의 의도로 가장 적절한 것을 고르시오.

① 요청 ② 사과 ③ 축하 ④ 비판 ⑤ 위로

7 대화를 듣고, 여자가 구입할 과일을 고르시오.

① 사과 ② 복숭아 ③ 포도 ④ 수박 ⑤ 배

8 대화를 듣고, 남자가 대화 직후에 할 일로 가장 적절한 것을 고르시오.

① 수영모 사기 ② 준비 운동하기 ③ 집으로 돌아가기
④ 구명조끼 빌리기 ⑤ 수영강습 등록하기

9 대화를 듣고, 두 사람이 댄스 오디션에 대해 언급하지 <u>않은</u> 것을 고르시오.

① 장소 ② 요일 ③ 준비한 장기
④ 접수 마감일 ⑤ 심사위원

10 다음을 듣고, 여자가 하는 말의 내용으로 가장 적절한 것을 고르시오.

① 동아리 규칙 안내 ② 코딩 워크숍 홍보 ③ 사이버 폭력 예방 교육
④ 현장체험학습일 공지 ⑤ 코딩 공모전 소개

11 대화를 듣고, 음악실에 대한 내용과 일치하지 <u>않는</u> 것을 고르시오.

① 음악실은 3층에 있다. ② 신청은 온라인으로 한다.
③ 키보드, 기타, 드럼을 연습할 수 있다. ④ 사용 시간은 1시간 이내이다.
⑤ 사용 후 제자리에 정리해야 한다.

12번~20번 문제는 다음 페이지에 ➡

12 대화를 듣고, 여자가 전화를 건 목적으로 가장 적절한 것을 고르시오.

① 도난 사건을 신고하기 위해서
② 휴대폰 수리를 맡기기 위해서
③ 제품 출시 일정을 알아보기 위해서
④ 지하철 막차 시간을 물어보기 위해서
⑤ 분실물 습득 여부를 확인하기 위해서

13 대화를 듣고, 여자가 지불해야 할 금액으로 가장 적절한 것을 고르시오.

① $17 ② $18 ③ $27 ④ $29 ⑤ $30

14 대화를 듣고, 두 사람의 관계로 가장 적절한 것을 고르시오.

① 부하 직원 – 상관 ② 과학자 – 투자자 ③ 고객 – 수리 기사
④ 의사 – 환자 ⑤ 가게 주인 – 원료 공급업자

15 대화를 듣고, 여자가 남자에게 부탁한 일로 가장 적절한 것을 고르시오.

① 요리사 칭찬해 주기 ② 메뉴판 가져다주기
③ 스테이크 소스 가져다주기 ④ 새 디저트 설명해 주기
⑤ 딸 데려오기

16 대화를 듣고, 여자가 불꽃놀이를 보러 갈 수 <u>없는</u> 이유로 가장 적절한 것을 고르시오.

① 심부름을 가야 해서 ② 친구와 선약이 있어서
③ 장소가 너무 멀어서 ④ 가족 여행을 가야 해서
⑤ 동생을 배웅해야 해서

17 다음 그림의 상황에 가장 적절한 대화를 고르시오.

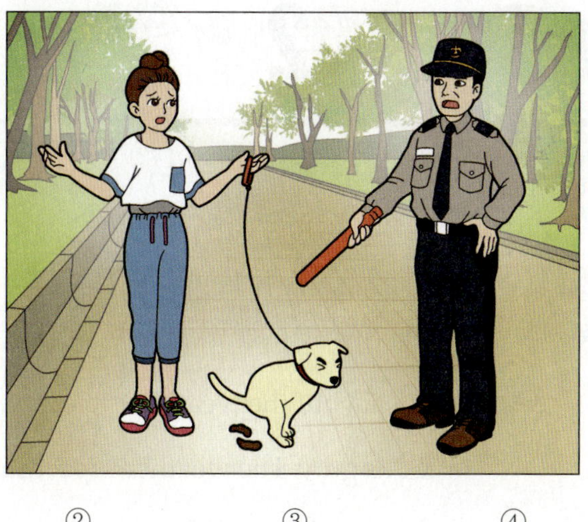

①   ②   ③   ④   ⑤

18 다음을 듣고, 여자가 영화에 대해 언급하지 <u>않은</u> 것을 고르시오.

① 감독   ② 제목   ③ 장르
④ 배우   ⑤ 개봉일

[19~20] 대화를 듣고, 여자의 마지막 말에 이어질 남자의 말로 가장 적절한 것을 고르시오.

19 Man: ___________________________________

① It starts at 8 o'clock.   ② We meet twice a week.
③ It costs 30 dollars a month.   ④ We play at the sports center.
⑤ There are six people in my class.

20 Man: ___________________________________

① I cannot see how.   ② No, it's not your fault.
③ Yes, write it down here.   ④ Please turn to page 19.
⑤ Sure, let me bring it to you.

Dictation Test 02

M2(17)_02_D

Dictation(받아쓰기)은 본문을 받아쓰면서 영어듣기의 집중력을 향상시키고 다양한 표현을 정리하기 위한 영어듣기 학습법입니다. **녹음을 다시 듣고, 빈칸에 알맞은 단어를 써 보세요.**
※Dictation의 정답은 듣기 대본의 밑줄 친 부분을 확인하세요.

정답 p. 6

맞은 개수 / 총149개

2024 영어듣기능력평가 2회 1번 변형

날씨파악–그림

1. 다음을 듣고, 현재 부산의 날씨로 가장 적절한 것을 고르시오.

① ② ③ ④ ⑤

01 W: Hi, Travel Buddies! I ___________ ___________ in Busan, but the weather is cloudy now. The sky looks gray. The weather report says it will rain this evening, so I'll ___________ my umbrella ___________. Tomorrow will be sunny, so I'm excited to go to the beach. But I heard there will be strong winds the day after tomorrow. ___________ ___________ and enjoy!

그림정보파악

2. 대화를 듣고, 남자가 구입할 화분으로 가장 적절한 것을 고르시오.

① ② ③ ④ ⑤

02 W: Hi, how may I help you?

M: I'm ___________ ___________ a houseplant.

W: Then, how about one of these? They're quite ___________.

M: I love the plant with star-shaped leaves. I'll take one of them.

W: Would you like your plant in a ___________ ___________ or a ___________ ___________?

M: I'd like a round pot.

W: Okay!

---

3. 대화를 듣고, 남자의 심정으로 가장 적절한 것을 고르시오.

① sad　　　② excited
③ scared　　④ bored
⑤ shy

03

W: Mike, did you hear the news?

M: What news?

W: Jay's Sandwich Shop is closing.

M: Oh, no! Why? Their sandwiches are the best in town!

W: The owner's parents are ________. So, he is leaving town to ________ ________ ________.

M: I'm sorry to hear that. I ________ ________ ________ ________, too.

W: You really like the place, don't you?

M: Yeah, it's ________ news.

4. 대화를 듣고, 남자가 지난달에 한 일로 가장 적절한 것을 고르시오.

① 등산하기
② 수영하기
③ 낚시하기
④ 유적지 탐방하기
⑤ 맛집 방문하기

04

M: Hey, what are you going to do this weekend?

W: I'm going to Sok-cho resort with my family.

M: That's nice! I ________ ________ ________ ________.

W: Really? Did you go trekking? I've heard there's a famous trekking course there.

M: There is, but I ________ ________ ________. It was really fun.

W: I think I should do that, too.

다음 페이지에 계속 ➡

5. 대화를 듣고, 두 사람이 대화하는 장소로 가장 적절한 곳을 고르시오.
   ① PC방　　② 영화관
   ③ 공항　　④ 기차역
   ⑤ 기념품 가게

05 W: Hi. I ________ ________ ________ online, but I want to change it. Should I do that online?

M: You can change it here, too.

W: Excellent! Could you change it ________ ________ ________ ________, please?

M: Let me see. You are going to Yeosu, right?

W: Yes. And it's for today.

M: There is another one that departs at 4 p.m. Is that OK?

W: That would be great.

M: Here's your new ticket.

6. 대화를 듣고, 여자의 마지막 말의 의도로 가장 적절한 것을 고르시오.
   ① 요청　　② 사과
   ③ 축하　　④ 비판
   ⑤ 위로

06 W: You look so gloomy. ________ ________ ________?

M: Oh, it's awful.

W: What is it? Please, tell me.

M: I was cleaning my classroom. And I broke my teacher's glasses ________ ________.

W: Oh, that's too bad. You must feel awful.

M: He said it was OK, but I couldn't even ________ ________ in the eye.

W: Don't be so depressed. It was just a mistake.

7. 대화를 듣고, 여자가 구입할 과일을 고르시오.
① 사과　　② 복숭아
③ 포도　　④ 수박
⑤ 배

07

M: Hello, ma'am. Are you looking for some fruit?

W: Yes. ________ ________ ________ buy some grapes for my family.

M: Unfortunately, grapes are ________ ________ ________ at the moment.

W: Hmm, then what ________ ________ ________?

M: How about apples or peaches? The peaches are especially sweet these days.

W: Well, my daughter is ________ ________ peaches. Are these watermelons sweet?

M: Sure! Would you like one of these?

W: Yes, please. My kids will love it.

---

8. 대화를 듣고, 남자가 대화 직후에 할 일로 가장 적절한 것을 고르시오.
① 수영모 사기
② 준비 운동하기
③ 집으로 돌아가기
④ 구명조끼 빌리기
⑤ 수영강습 등록하기

08

W: Excuse me, sir. You cannot go into the pool ________ ________ ________ ________.

M: Oh, I know, but I forgot to bring mine today. Can I borrow one here?

W: I'm sorry. But we don't ________ ________.

M: Then what should I do?

W: You'll have to buy one.

M: Is there a store nearby?

W: There's one ________ ________ the pool.

M: Alright. I'll go buy the bathing cap right now.

다음 페이지에 계속 ➡

9. 대화를 듣고, 두 사람이 댄스 오디션에 대해 언급하지 않은 것을 고르시오.
① 장소　　② 요일
③ 준비한 장기　　④ 접수 마감일
⑤ 심사위원

09 W: Steve, I heard you are getting a dance audition. That's awesome!

M: It's always been my dream.

W: Are you ＿＿＿＿＿＿ ＿＿＿＿ the audition being held at DP Entertainment's Culture Center?

M: Exactly. It will ＿＿＿＿ ＿＿＿＿ next Wednesday.

W: What are you going to show them?

M: I'll show them a minute-long dance and some of my special moves.

W: The CEO and some of the DP Entertainment singers will be there, right?

M: Yes, they will be there ＿＿＿＿ ＿＿＿＿. I'm nervous, but I'll do my best.

10. 다음을 듣고, 여자가 하는 말의 내용으로 가장 적절한 것을 고르시오.
① 동아리 규칙 안내
② 코딩 워크숍 홍보
③ 사이버 폭력 예방 교육
④ 현장체험학습일 공지
⑤ 코딩 공모전 소개

10 W: Hi, students. Do you have a ＿＿＿＿ for coding? Then, our coding workshop is the perfect ＿＿＿＿ for you! In this workshop, you'll learn how to create your own programs and games. ＿＿＿＿ ＿＿＿＿ ＿＿＿＿ is necessary—we'll start from the basics. Best of all, it's free to attend, and we have all the resources you need. Come and ＿＿＿＿ the world of coding with us today!

대화내용불일치

11. 대화를 듣고, 음악실에 대한 내용과 일치하지 <u>않는</u> 것을 고르시오.
① 음악실은 3층에 있다.
② 신청은 온라인으로 한다.
③ 키보드, 기타, 드럼을 연습할 수 있다.
④ 사용 시간은 1시간 이내이다.
⑤ 사용 후 제자리에 정리해야 한다.

11

M: Hey, Jiyoon. Do you know anything about using the music room?

W: Yes. It's on the third floor, next to the art room.

M: Do we need to sign up first?

W: Yes. You need to ____________ ____________ a form on the school website.

M: Got it. What ____________ are available?

W: There are keyboards, guitars, and even a violin — but no drums.

M: Okay. And how long can we use the room?

W: For ____________ ____________ an hour. Don't forget to put everything back when you're done.

전화목적파악

12. 대화를 듣고, 여자가 전화를 건 목적으로 가장 적절한 것을 고르시오.
① 도난 사건을 신고하기 위해서
② 휴대폰 수리를 맡기기 위해서
③ 제품 출시 일정을 알아보기 위해서
④ 지하철 막차 시간을 물어보기 위해서
⑤ 분실물 습득 여부를 확인하기 위해서

12

(*Telephone rings.*)

M: Hello, City Metro Service. How may I help you?

W: Hi, I think I lost my cellphone on Metro line 2.

M: Would you like to ________ a lost item?

W: No, I ________ ________ ________ that online.

M: Oh, that's good. What can I do for you, then?

W: Could you check if my phone has ________ ________?

M: Of course. Just give me your report number.

W: I have it here. Just a second.

다음 페이지에 계속 ➡

13. 대화를 듣고, 여자가 지불해야 할 금액으로 가장 적절한 것을 고르시오.

① $17   ② $18
③ $27   ④ $29
⑤ $30

13

M: May I help you?

W: I'd like to buy some grapes. How much are they?

M: Our grapes are ________ ________, so you can get them today for only $6 per kilo instead of $7.

W: That's great. I'll take ________ ________, please.

M: How about melons, ma'am? They only ________ $________ ________.

W: I love melons! I'll take ________.

M: Here you go.

14. 대화를 듣고, 두 사람의 관계로 가장 적절한 것을 고르시오.

① 부하 직원 – 상관
② 과학자 – 투자자
③ 고객 – 수리 기사
④ 의사 – 환자
⑤ 가게 주인 – 원료 공급업자

14

(Telephone rings.)

W: Hello.

M: Ms. Blake, I'm calling from the G.A. Shop.

W: Oh, hi. Is my coffee maker ready?

M: ________ ________ ________. I fixed the heater, but I found ________ ________.

W: What is it?

M: The water tank is ________. This will take another day to fix. It'll ________ ________, too.

W: Well, that's OK. Can I pick it up tomorrow, then?

M: Yes. I'll call you when it's ready.

15. 대화를 듣고, 여자가 남자에게 부탁한 일로 가장 적절한 것을 고르시오.

① 요리사 칭찬해 주기
② 메뉴판 가져다주기
③ 스테이크 소스 가져다주기
④ 새 디저트 설명해 주기
⑤ 딸 데려오기

15

M: How was your food today, ma'am?

W: It was very good. The steak is always delicious at this restaurant.

M: Thank you, ma'am. Our chef will be delighted to hear that. Would you like some more wine?

W: No, thanks, but can I ________ ________ ________ ________ ________, please?

M: Sure. We have a new dessert menu.

W: Oh, I'm too full. I want to ________ ________ ________ for my daughter.

M: Of course. I'll ________ ________ ________ ________.

16. 대화를 듣고, 여자가 불꽃놀이를 보러 갈 수 <u>없는</u> 이유로 가장 적절한 것을 고르시오.

① 심부름을 가야 해서
② 친구와 선약이 있어서
③ 장소가 너무 멀어서
④ 가족 여행을 가야 해서
⑤ 동생을 배웅해야 해서

16

(*Cellphone rings.*)

W: Hi, Dean.

M: Hi, Clair. You know there will be ________ ________, right?

W: Yes, at Central Park.

M: I'm going with Shane. Will you join us?

W: I'd love to, but I can't.

M: Why not? Is the park ________ ________ ________?

W: Oh, no. My sister leaves tonight. ________ ________ ________ ________ ________ with her and my parents.

M: That was today! OK, see you around.

다음 페이지에 계속 ➡

17. 다음 그림의 상황에 가장 적절한 대화를 고르시오.

①   ②
③   ④
⑤

17

① M: You should pick up the dog waste.

W: I know, but I ________ ________ ________

a bag.

② M: Let's walk the dog in the park.

W: I'm afraid dogs ________ ________ ________

________ .

③ M: Don't leave the dog in the car.

W: OK. I guess it is too hot today.

④ M: How can I help you?

W: I think my dog is sick. It's not eating.

⑤ M: What are you doing ________ ________

__________ ?

W: I'm washing my dog. It's so dirty!

2025 영어듣기능력평가 1회 18번 변형

18. 다음을 듣고, 여자가 영화에 대해 언급하지 <u>않은</u> 것을 고르시오.

① 감독   ② 제목
③ 장르   ④ 배우
⑤ 개봉일

18

W: Hello, movie fans! I want to tell you about a new movie made by Karen Wills. The movie __________ __________ *Night Train*. It's a suspense movie with lots of action and many surprises. The story is about a police officer __________ a bad guy on a train that doesn't stop. The movie is very exciting and fun to watch. It will __________ __________ on July 26th. Don't miss it!

19. 대화를 듣고, 여자의 마지막 말에 이어질 남자의 말로 가장 적절한 것을 고르시오.

Man: ________________

① It starts at 8 o'clock.
② We meet twice a week.
③ It costs 30 dollars a month.
④ We play at the sports center.
⑤ There are six people in my class.

19

M: Emily, do you want to go for lunch?

W: Sorry, but I'm going to skip lunch today. I've ________ ________ ________ ________ recently.

M: You know ________ ________ is bad for your health, right?

W: Yes. But it's so hard to exercise regularly.

M: It's easier if you do it with friends. How about joining my tennis class?

W: OK. How ________ do you play?

M: We meet twice a week.

20. 대화를 듣고, 여자의 마지막 말에 이어질 남자의 말로 가장 적절한 것을 고르시오.

Man: ________________

① I cannot see how.
② No, it's not your fault.
③ Yes, write it down here.
④ Please turn to page 19.
⑤ Sure, let me bring it to you.

20

M: May I help you?

W: Yes, please. I'm ________ ________ a small in this sweater.

M: Let me check. *(Pause)* Hmm… We have only medium and large sizes left.

W: That's too bad. Do you have any ________ ________, then?

M: Yes. We have white and gray colors in small.

W: Gray would be good. Can I see it?

M: Sure, let me bring it to you.

Words & Expressions Review 02

● 다음 단어를 암기하세요.

문제	번호	단어	뜻
1	□1	buddy	친구
	□2	arrive	도착하다
2	□3	quite	꽤, 상당히
	□4	popular	인기 있는
	□5	pot	화분
3	□6	look after	~를 보살펴 주다
	□7	feel sorry for ~	~를 안됐다고 생각하다
4	□8	instead	대신에
	□9	fun	재미있는, 재미
5	□10	book	예약하다
6	□11	gloomy	우울한
	□12	awful	끔찍한
	□13	by accident	실수로, 우연히
7	□14	out of stock	품절인
	□15	at the moment	지금
	□16	watermelon	수박
8	□17	bathing cap	수영모
	□18	lend	대여하다, 빌려주다
9	□19	judge	심사위원, 심판
	□20	passion	열정
10	□21	opportunity	기회
	□22	prior	사전의

문제	번호	단어	뜻
	□23	instrument	악기
11	□24	available	사용할 수 있는
	□25	keyboard	(피아노의) 건반
	□26	report	신고하다, 알리다
12	□27	turn up	(잃어버린 물건 등이) 나타나다, 찾게 되다
	□28	Just a second.	잠시만요.
13	□29	on sale	할인[세일] 중인
	□30	ready	준비가 된
14	□31	leak	(액체·기체가) 새다
	□32	cost	비용이 들다
	□33	delicious	맛있는
15	□34	delighted	매우 기뻐하는
	□35	dessert	후식, 디저트
16	□36	fireworks	불꽃놀이
	□37	waste	배설물, 쓰레기
17	□38	I'm afraid ~	(유감이지만) ~ 같다
	□39	allow	허락하다
	□40	suspense	서스펜스, 긴장감
18	□41	chase	뒤쫓다, 추적하다
	□42	miss	놓치다, 지나치다
19	□43	skip	거르다, (정해진 차례를) 건너뛰다
20	□44	look for	~을 찾다

●왼쪽 단어장의 뜻이 보이지 않게 반으로 접고, 학습한 단어의 뜻을 아래 빈칸에 적어주세요.

1	keyboard		23	judge
2	pot		24	buddy
3	bathing cap		25	skip
4	on sale		26	feel sorry for ~
5	look for		27	book
6	suspense		28	gloomy
7	available		29	waste
8	prior		30	by accident
9	ready		31	quite
10	out of stock		32	awful
11	opportunity		33	lend
12	chase		34	watermelon
13	turn up		35	allow
14	instead		36	delicious
15	miss		37	cost
16	arrive		38	popular
17	look after		39	delighted
18	dessert		40	I'm afraid ~
19	at the moment		41	fun
20	passion		42	report
21	Just a second.		43	instrument
22	fireworks		44	leak

03회 중학영어듣기 모의고사

M2(17)_03_US
모두 **미국식 발음(US)** 으로 녹음

M2(17)_03_UK
20문제 중 5문제에 **영국식 발음 (US+UK)**을 포함하여 녹음

정답 및 해석 p. 10

1 다음을 듣고, 내일의 날씨로 가장 적절한 것을 고르시오.

 ①    ②    ③    ④    ⑤

2 대화를 듣고, 남자가 주문할 모자로 가장 적절한 것을 고르시오.

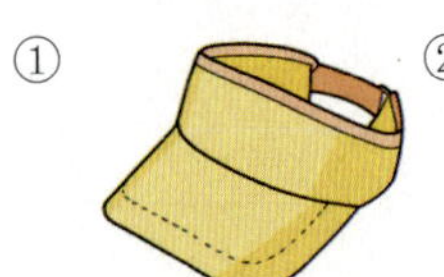 ①    ②    ③    ④    ⑤

3 대화를 듣고, 여자의 심정으로 가장 적절한 것을 고르시오.

① proud   ② bored   ③ sorry   ④ scared   ⑤ relaxed

4 대화를 듣고, 여자가 지난 주말에 한 일로 가장 적절한 것을 고르시오.

① 시험 공부하기   ② 놀이공원 가기
③ 중고책 가게 가기   ④ 택배 물품 보내기
⑤ 자원봉사 활동하기

5 대화를 듣고, 두 사람이 대화하는 장소로 가장 적절한 곳을 고르시오.

① 야구장　　② 축구장　　③ 영화관　　④ 우체국　　⑤ 놀이공원

6 대화를 듣고, 마지막 말에 담긴 여자의 의도로 적절한 것을 고르시오.

① 요청　　② 수락　　③ 거절　　④ 사과　　⑤ 격려

7 대화를 듣고, 두 사람이 이번 주말에 할 일로 가장 적절한 것을 고르시오.

① 등산하기　　② 캠핑하기　　③ 낚시하기
④ 집에서 쉬기　　⑤ 워터파크 가기

8 대화를 듣고, 여자가 대화 직후에 할 일로 가장 적절한 것을 고르시오.

① 가위 가져오기　　② 안내문 만들기　　③ 색종이 오리기
④ 문방구 가기　　⑤ 과제 제출하기

9 대화를 듣고, 두 사람이 TV 프로그램에 대해 언급하지 <u>않은</u> 것을 고르시오.

① 프로그램명　　② 진행자　　③ 교재
④ 시작 시각　　⑤ 재방송 여부

10 다음을 듣고, 무엇에 관한 안내인지 가장 적절한 것을 고르시오.

① 학급 회의 개최　　② 견학 일정 안내　　③ 기계 작동 원리
④ 견학 주의 사항　　⑤ 미아 발생 대처법

11번~20번 문제는 다음 페이지에 ➡

11 대화를 듣고, 동영상에 대한 내용으로 일치하지 <u>않는</u> 것을 고르시오.

① 지구온난화에 대한 영상이다.　　② 학교 웹사이트에서 볼 수 있다.
③ 영상 길이는 15분이다.　　④ 영어로 된 영상이다.
⑤ 영어 자막을 제공한다.

12 대화를 듣고, 여자가 상점을 방문한 이유로 가장 적절한 것을 고르시오.

① 현금 영수증을 발급 받으려고　　② 납품 착오에 대해 사과하려고
③ 누락된 할인 적용을 요청하려고　　④ 하자가 있는 물품을 교환하려고
⑤ 계산 안 된 상품에 대해 지불하려고

13 대화를 듣고, 여자가 받은 거스름돈으로 가장 적절한 것을 고르시오.

① $1　　② $2　　③ $3　　④ $4　　⑤ $5

14 대화를 듣고, 두 사람의 관계로 가장 적절한 것을 고르시오.

① 점원 — 손님　　② 공항 직원 — 입국자　　③ 은행원 — 고객
④ 상담원 — 고객　　⑤ 교사 — 학생

15 대화를 듣고, 남자가 여자에게 부탁한 일로 가장 적절한 것을 고르시오.

① 손님 명단 확인하기　　② 의자 준비하기　　③ 책자 가져오기
④ 동료에게 부탁하기　　⑤ 물병 가져오기

16 대화를 듣고, 여자가 케이크를 구운 이유로 가장 적절한 것을 고르시오.

① 제빵 연습을 하기 위해서　　② 생일을 축하하기 위해서　　③ 대회에 참가하기 위해서
④ 우승을 축하하기 위해서　　⑤ 집필을 응원하기 위해서

17 다음 그림의 상황에 가장 적절한 대화를 고르시오.

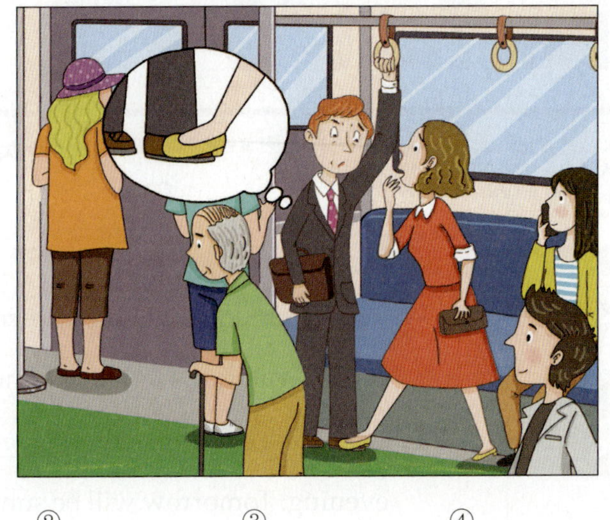

①   ②   ③   ④   ⑤

18 다음을 듣고, 남자가 콘서트에 대해 언급하지 <u>않은</u> 것을 고르시오.

① 연주자   ② 장소   ③ 날짜   ④ 시작 시간   ⑤ 관람 연령

[19~20] 대화를 듣고, 여자의 마지막 말에 이어질 남자의 말로 가장 적절한 것을 고르시오.

19 Man: _______________________________

① Don't worry about that too much.
② I didn't know that you've lived abroad.
③ No, but I hope to visit there someday.
④ I don't like to ride a gondola.
⑤ Venice is in Italy.

20 Man: _______________________________

① I like that restaurant very much.   ② I don't know what you mean.
③ I saw an ad in a magazine.   ④ I had spaghetti, too.
⑤ My favorite food is Mexican.

Dictation Test 03

M2(17)_03_D

Dictation(받아쓰기)은 본문을 받아쓰면서 영어듣기의 집중력을 향상시키고 다양한 표현을 정리하기 위한 영어듣기 학습법입니다. **녹음을 다시 듣고, 빈칸에 알맞은 단어를 써 보세요.**

※Dictation의 정답은 듣기 대본의 밑줄 친 부분을 확인하세요.

정답 p. 10

맞은 개수 / 총139개

날씨파악-그림

1. 다음을 듣고, 내일의 날씨로 가장 적절한 것을 고르시오.

①  ② 

③  ④ 

⑤ 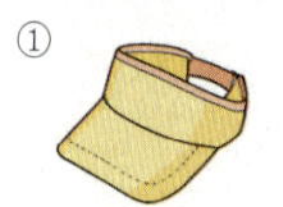

01 W: Good morning. I'm Kelly Green from the weather center. Today, it'll be cloudy and ________ in some areas. The showers will ________ ________ this evening. Tomorrow will be sunny and very hot. I ________ you wear a hat and protect your skin with sunscreen if you go to the beach.

그림정보파악

2025 영어듣기능력평가 1회 2번 변형

2. 대화를 듣고, 남자가 주문할 모자로 가장 적절한 것을 고르시오.

①  ②

③  ④ 

⑤ 

02 M: Amy, come here and check out these hats on the screen.

W: Sure, Dad. *[Pause]* Oh, are you buying a hat for me?

M: Yes. How about this one? It's a visor so it doesn't ________ the top of your head.

W: Well, I don't want a ________ hat.

M: I see. Then, how about the ones with animal faces that do have a top?

W: They're cute. I like the one with ________ ________ ________.

M: Okay. I'll order it.

---

3. 대화를 듣고, 여자의 심정으로 가장 적절한 것을 고르시오.

① proud   ② bored
③ sorry   ④ scared
⑤ relaxed

03

W: How was the model airplane __________ today?

M: Fantastic, Mom! I had so much fun. I saw an air show there.

W: __________ __________! How did your model airplane do?

M: It __________ for about two and a half minutes!

W: That's amazing!

M: Yeah. I won first prize.

W: You did a __________ __________!

🇺🇸🇬🇧

2025 영어듣기능력평가 1회 4번 변형

4. 대화를 듣고, 여자가 지난 주말에 한 일로 가장 적절한 것을 고르시오.

① 시험 공부하기
② 놀이공원 가기
③ 중고책 가게 가기
④ 택배 물품 보내기
⑤ 자원봉사 활동하기

04

M: Lily, why are you __________ all those old books?

W: I'm donating them to the local library.

M: That's really kind of you.

W: Thanks. Last weekend, I __________ at the library and saw they needed more books for kids.

M: Oh, I see. Was the volunteering fun?

W: Yes! I helped kids __________ __________ __________ and read to them. I want to do it again.

다음 페이지에 계속 ➡

5. 대화를 듣고, 두 사람이 대화하는 장소로
   가장 적절한 곳을 고르시오.
   ① 야구장 ② 축구장
   ③ 영화관 ④ 우체국
   ⑤ 놀이공원

05

W: Jung-hoon, _________ _________! I found our seats.

M: Wow, these seats are amazing. I can see all the

    players on the field.

W: Yeah, why did you bring your glove with you?

M: You never know when a foul ball _________

    _________ your way.

W: Are you allowed to keep the ball?

M: Of course! Look, the game is _________ _________

    start.

6. 대화를 듣고, 마지막 말에 담긴 여자의
   의도로 적절한 것을 고르시오.
   ① 요청 ② 수락
   ③ 거절 ④ 사과
   ⑤ 격려

06

W: What _________ _________ _________!

M: Hi, Molly. This is my dog Ali.

W: Hi, Ali. He is so cute! I love fuzzy dogs.

M: Great. Actually, can you _________ _________

    _________ _________?

W: Alright. What is it?

M: I'm going on vacation next week. Could you take

    care of my dog for a week?

W: Oh, _________ _________ _________, _________ my

    parents don't like dogs.

7. 대화를 듣고, 두 사람이 이번 주말에 할 일로 가장 적절한 것을 고르시오.

① 등산하기
② 캠핑하기
③ 낚시하기
④ 집에서 쉬기
⑤ 워터파크 가기

07
M: Chloe, how about going hiking this weekend?

W: Dad, I don't want to go hiking. Can't we just _________ _________ _________?

M: It'd be nice to relax at the top of the mountain and enjoy nature.

W: That's not relaxing for me. And besides, getting to the top is a lot of work.

M: How about _________ _________, then? We can have a relaxing time at the lake.

W: Well, alright. That's much better than _________ _________ _________ _____________.

M: Great.

8. 대화를 듣고, 여자가 대화 직후에 할 일로 가장 적절한 것을 고르시오.

① 가위 가져오기
② 안내문 만들기
③ 색종이 오리기
④ 문방구 가기
⑤ 과제 제출하기

08
M: Our club is _________ a wildlife campaign tomorrow, right?

W: Yes, we need to make some posters for it.

M: We have to buy some _____________ to make the posters.

W: What do we need?

M: We need paperboard, colored paper, scissors, and glue.

W: I have two _________ of scissors, so we don't have to buy them.

M: That's great. Can you bring the scissors?

W: Okay. I'll get them _________ _________.

다음 페이지에 계속 ➡

9. 대화를 듣고, 두 사람이 TV 프로그램에 대해 언급하지 <u>않은</u> 것을 고르시오.

① 프로그램명　　② 진행자
③ 교재　　④ 시작 시각
⑤ 재방송 여부

09 M: Yena, your English __________ ______________ a lot since last year. How did you do it?

W: *Jumping English* helped me a lot.

M: Isn't that a TV program?

W: Yes. It's _________ _________ the famous teacher, Mr. Lee.

M: Really? I want to start watching it, too.

W: You should. It's a great program. It's on every evening at 8.

M: Oh, I can't watch it at that time. Do you know if they have reruns?

W: Sure. They _________ _________ _________ the next morning at 6 a.m.

10. 다음을 듣고, 무엇에 관한 안내인지 가장 적절한 것을 고르시오.

① 학급 회의 개최
② 견학 일정 안내
③ 기계 작동 원리
④ 견학 주의 사항
⑤ 미아 발생 대처법

10 M: Hello, everyone. Welcome to our car factory. Before we start the tour, there are a few things you need to _________ _________ _________. First, you should always wear your hardhat. Second, _________ not to wander away from the group. Finally, _________ _________ _________ any machines. However, you are always welcome to ask questions. Now, shall we start _________ _________?

11. 대화를 듣고, 동영상에 대한 내용으로 일치하지 <u>않는</u> 것을 고르시오.
① 지구온난화에 대한 영상이다.
② 학교 웹사이트에서 볼 수 있다.
③ 영상 길이는 15분이다.
④ 영어로 된 영상이다.
⑤ 영어 자막을 제공한다.

11

M: Kate, did you watch the video clip that I told you about?

W: Sorry, I totally forgot. What was it?

M: A short documentary film about ________ ________.

W: Oh, now I remember. Can I still watch it on our school website?

M: Sure. It's only 15 minutes long.

W: Okay. Is it in English?

M: No, it's ________ ________.

W: Oh, no. That could be a problem.

M: Don't worry. It has English ____________.

방문이유파악

2024 영어듣기능력평가 2회 12번 변형

12. 대화를 듣고, 여자가 상점을 방문한 이유로 가장 적절한 것을 고르시오.
① 현금 영수증을 발급 받으려고
② 납품 착오에 대해 사과하려고
③ 누락된 할인 적용을 요청하려고
④ 하자가 있는 물품을 교환하려고
⑤ 계산 안 된 상품에 대해 지불하려고

12

M: Hello.

W: Hi, I was here __________ and bought some groceries.

M: Is there something wrong?

W: Well, when I got home, I __________ that I hadn't paid for something.

M: Oh, I see. Do you have it with you?

W: Yes, it's these carrots. I don't see them __________ __________ __________.

M: Hmm, you're right. They're not on the receipt. Thank you so much for coming back.

W: No problem. I'll __________ __________ them now.

다음 페이지에 계속 ➡

13. 대화를 듣고, 여자가 받은 거스름돈으로 가장 적절한 것을 고르시오.

① $1 　　② $2
③ $3 　　④ $4
⑤ $5

13

M: May I help you?

W: How much is this __________ __________?

M: It's $1.

W: How about this chocolate donut?

M: It's $2. But you get a $2 __________ if you buy any six donuts.

W: I don't need that many donuts. I'll just get one plain donut and one chocolate donut.

M: Okay, __________ __________ __________ 3 dollars. Do you have any discount coupons?

W: No, here's 5 dollars.

M: Here you are. Thank you.

14. 대화를 듣고, 두 사람의 관계로 가장 적절한 것을 고르시오.

① 점원 — 손님
② 공항 직원 — 입국자
③ 은행원 — 고객
④ 상담원 — 고객
⑤ 교사 — 학생

14

W: Hello, how can I assist you?

M: I want to open a savings account.

W: Have you brought the necessary __________ with you?

M: Yes, I have my __________ __________ and proof of address right here.

W: Perfect. How much would you like to __________ into the account?

M: I'm thinking of starting with $500. Here it is.

W: All right. Let's begin by __________ __________ __________.

15. 대화를 듣고, 남자가 여자에게 부탁한 일로 가장 적절한 것을 고르시오.

① 손님 명단 확인하기
② 의자 준비하기
③ 책자 가져오기
④ 동료에게 부탁하기
⑤ 물병 가져오기

15
M: Here is the ＿＿＿＿ ＿＿＿＿, Carly.

W: Is this final?

M: Yes. We have four more guests now.

W: Then, we'll need more chairs in the meeting room.

M: And more ＿＿＿＿ ＿＿＿＿. I'll ask Sam from Marketing to bring them.

W: Oh, we ＿＿＿＿ ＿＿＿＿ ＿＿＿＿, too. I have some on my desk.

M: Can you go ＿＿＿＿ ＿＿＿＿? I'll get the chairs.

W: OK. I'll be right back.

16. 대화를 듣고, 여자가 케이크를 구운 이유로 가장 적절한 것을 고르시오.

① 제빵 연습을 하기 위해서
② 생일을 축하하기 위해서
③ 대회에 참가하기 위해서
④ 우승을 축하하기 위해서
⑤ 집필을 응원하기 위해서

16
M: Hi, Kate. What's with the box?

W: Hi, Paul. There's a cake in it. I ＿＿＿＿ ＿＿＿＿ ＿＿＿＿.

M: A cake? Is it someone's birthday?

W: No. Yesterday, my sister ＿＿＿＿ ＿＿＿＿ ＿＿＿＿. The cake is for her. We'll have a family party this evening.

M: That's great! What kind of contest was it?

W: It was ＿＿＿＿ ＿＿＿＿ ＿＿＿＿.

다음 페이지에 계속 ➡

17. 다음 그림의 상황에 가장 적절한 대화를 고르시오.

① ②
③ ④
⑤

17

① M: I think you are ______ ______ ______. You should check your ticket.

W: Oh, I was in the wrong seat. Sorry.

② M: Are you excited to go on a family trip?

W: I am so excited that I couldn't sleep last night!

③ M: If you have time, could you ______ ______ a short survey?

W: Yeah, sure. What is it about?

④ M: Do you know where the subway station is?

W: Yes, go straight and ______ ______ ______ when you see the bank.

⑤ M: Ouch, you ______ ______ my foot!

W: Oh my, I am so sorry for doing that!

18. 다음을 듣고, 남자가 콘서트에 대해 언급하지 <u>않은</u> 것을 고르시오.

① 연주자 ② 장소
③ 날짜 ④ 시작 시간
⑤ 관람 연령

18

M: Hello, students. Today, I'd like to invite you to a special concert by one of our ______ ______, violinist Jack Dawson. He will play violin sonatas by Beethoven. It will be ______ ______ City Art Center. The concert is on May 5. It starts at 7 p.m. ______ ______ ______, so come and enjoy the concert. I hope to see you there!

19. 대화를 듣고, 여자의 마지막 말에 이어질 남자의 말로 가장 적절한 것을 고르시오.

Man: _________________

① Don't worry about that too much.
② I didn't know that you've lived abroad.
③ No, but I hope to visit there someday.
④ I don't like to ride a gondola.
⑤ Venice is in Italy.

19
W: Look at this picture from my trip to Italy.

M: Wow, you look _________ _________ in this picture.

W: Thank you. It was taken in Venice last year.

M: Oh, that's why you are _________ a gondola.

W: It was really exciting.

M: Venice is _________ _________ its canals. I love that city.

W: Oh, have you been there, too?

M: No, but I hope to visit there someday.

20. 대화를 듣고, 여자의 마지막 말에 이어질 남자의 말로 가장 적절한 것을 고르시오.

Man: _________________

① I like that restaurant very much.
② I don't know what you mean.
③ I saw an ad in a magazine.
④ I had spaghetti, too.
⑤ My favorite food is Mexican.

20
M: Did you go to the Italian restaurant that I _________ _________ about?

W: Yes, I went there with my family.

M: _________ _________ it?

W: Oh, it was lovely. We had a great time.

M: What about the food? Did you try any of the pizzas?

W: Yes, we had gorgonzola pizza and some spaghetti. They were _________!

M: I'm glad you liked them.

W: How did you _________ _________ that restaurant?

M: I saw an ad in a magazine.

Words & Expressions Review 03

● 다음 단어를 암기하세요.

문제	번호	단어	뜻
1	□ 1	suggest	권하다, 제안하다
	□ 2	sunscreen	자외선 차단 크림
2	□ 3	visor	(모자의) 챙
	□ 4	cover	덮다, 씌우다, 가리다
3	□ 5	fly	날다
4	□ 6	sort	분류하다, 구분하다
	□ 7	donate	기부하다, 기증하다
	□ 8	glove	(야구) 글러브, 장갑
5	□ 9	keep	갖다, 가지고 있다
	□ 10	be about to + 동사	막 ~하려는 참이다
6	□ 11	fuzzy	(털이) 복슬복슬한
	□ 12	take care of ~	~을 돌보다
7	□ 13	relaxing	편안한, 마음을 느긋하게 해 주는
	□ 14	a lot of work	힘든 일, 손이 많이 가는 일
8	□ 15	wildlife	야생 동물
	□ 16	material	재료
9	□ 17	improve	향상시키다, 개선되다
	□ 18	host	(방송을) 진행하다, 사회자 역할을 하다
	□ 19	rerun	재방송
	□ 20	factory	공장
10	□ 21	keep in mind	명심하다
	□ 22	look around	구경하다, 둘러보다

문제	번호	단어	뜻
	□ 23	film	영화
11	□ 24	global warming	지구온난화
	□ 25	subtitle	자막
12	□ 26	earlier	전에, 앞서
	□ 27	realize	깨닫다
13	□ 28	plain	있는 그대로의, 꾸미지 않은
14	□ 29	assist	돕다
	□ 30	deposit	예금하다
	□ 31	guest	손님
15	□ 32	bring	가져오다, 가져가다
	□ 33	booklet	소책자
16	□ 34	bake	(음식을) 굽다
	□ 35	win a contest	대회에서 우승하다
	□ 36	participate in	~에 참여하다
17	□ 37	survey	설문 조사
	□ 38	step on one's foot	~의 발을 밟다
18	□ 39	invite	초대하다
	□ 40	former	예전의, 과거의
	□ 41	exciting	신나는, 흥미로운
19	□ 42	be famous for ~	~으로 유명하다
	□ 43	canal	운하, 수로
20	□ 44	magazine	잡지

03
회
단어

● 왼쪽 단어장의 뜻이 보이지 않게 반으로 접고, 학습한 단어의 뜻을 아래 빈칸에 적어주세요.

1	assist		23	take care of ~
2	keep		24	material
3	canal		25	participate in
4	host		26	a lot of work
5	earlier		27	factory
6	fly		28	survey
7	be famous for ~		29	subtitle
8	invite		30	improve
9	fuzzy		31	film
10	visor		32	suggest
11	rerun		33	booklet
12	former		34	bring
13	cover		35	keep in mind
14	deposit		36	step on one's foot
15	donate		37	win a contest
16	guest		38	look around
17	exciting		39	global warming
18	magazine		40	glove
19	realize		41	be about to + 동사
20	sort		42	relaxing
21	sunscreen		43	wildlife
22	plain		44	bake

04회 중학영어듣기 모의고사

M2(17)_04_US
모두 **미국식 발음(US)**
으로 녹음

M2(17)_04_UK
20문제 중 5문제에 **영국식 발음**
(US+UK)을 포함하여 녹음

정답 및 해석 p. 15

1 다음을 듣고, 뉴욕의 날씨로 가장 적절한 것을 고르시오.

① 　② 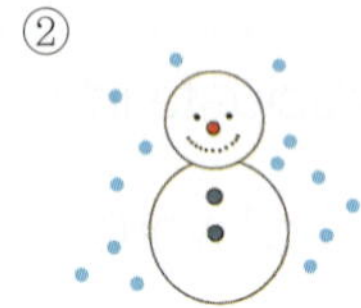　③ 　④ 　⑤ 

2 대화를 듣고, 테이블 매트 위의 물건 배치로 가장 적절한 것을 고르시오.

① 　② 　③ 　④ 　⑤ 

3 대화를 듣고, 여자의 심정으로 가장 적절한 것을 고르시오.

① proud　② bored　③ angry　④ happy　⑤ thankful

4 대화를 듣고, 여자가 Sports Day에 한 일로 가장 적절한 것을 고르시오.

① 축구 하기
② 사진 전시하기
③ 운동기구 설치하기
④ 얼굴에 그림 그려주기
⑤ 개인 물병 사용 홍보하기

5 대화를 듣고, 대화가 이루어지는 장소를 고르시오.

① 백화점
② 우체국
③ 식당
④ 버스 정류장
⑤ 분실물 보관소

6 대화를 듣고, 남자의 마지막 말의 의도로 가장 적절한 것을 고르시오.

① 칭찬 ② 격려 ③ 항의 ④ 수락 ⑤ 용서

7 대화를 듣고, 여자가 만든 것으로 가장 적절한 것을 고르시오.

① 계란말이 ② 잡채 ③ 김치 ④ 미역국 ⑤ 고기전

8 대화를 듣고, 남자가 대화 직후에 할 일로 가장 적절한 것을 고르시오.

① 친구 만나기 ② 교실 청소하기
③ 휴지통 비우기 ④ 방향제 뿌리기
⑤ 에어컨 가동하기

9 대화를 듣고, 두 사람이 동아리 신설에 대해 언급하지 않은 것을 고르시오.

① 지도 교사 ② 신청서 작성 ③ 활동 교실
④ 부원 모집 ⑤ 활동비 지원

10 다음을 듣고, 여자가 하는 말의 내용으로 가장 적절한 것을 고르시오.

① 여행 일정 ② 식사 예절 ③ 안전 수칙
④ 예약 방법 ⑤ 문화재 보호

11번~20번 문제는 다음 페이지에 ➡

11 대화를 듣고, English Essay Contest에 대한 내용과 일치하지 <u>않는</u> 것을 고르시오.

① 이번 주 목요일에 진행된다.   ② 오후 4시에 시작한다.
③ 이메일로 대회 신청서를 제출해야 한다.   ④ 에세이 주제는 대회 전날에 공지된다.
⑤ 1시간 동안 진행된다.

12 대화를 듣고, 남자가 전화를 건 목적으로 가장 적절한 것을 고르시오.

① 휴대폰을 찾기 위해서   ② 데이트 약속을 잡기 위해서
③ 습득 분실물을 신고하기 위해서   ④ 가구 배송 시간을 확인하기 위해서
⑤ 부모님께 외출 허락을 받기 위해서

13 대화를 듣고, 두 사람이 만날 시각을 고르시오.

① 5:00 p.m.   ② 5:30 p.m.   ③ 6:00 p.m.   ④ 6:30 p.m.   ⑤ 7:00 p.m.

14 대화를 듣고, 두 사람의 관계로 가장 적절한 것을 고르시오.

① 신발가게 직원 — 고객   ② 자동차 판매원 — 고객
③ 디자이너 — 고객   ④ 미술 선생님 — 학생
⑤ 옷가게 점원 — 고객

15 대화를 듣고, 여자가 남자에게 부탁한 일로 가장 적절한 것을 고르시오.

① 전화 걸어주기   ② 핸드폰 구매하기
③ 분실물 신고하기   ④ 영화 초대권 교환하기
⑤ 영화관 위치 알려주기

16 대화를 듣고, 여자가 기타 강습을 중단한 이유로 가장 적절한 것을 고르시오.

① 손가락이 아파서   ② 강습비가 올라서
③ 연습할 시간이 없어서   ④ 강습 수준이 맞지 않아서
⑤ 수업 시간 변경이 어려워서

17 다음 그림의 상황에 가장 적절한 대화를 고르시오.

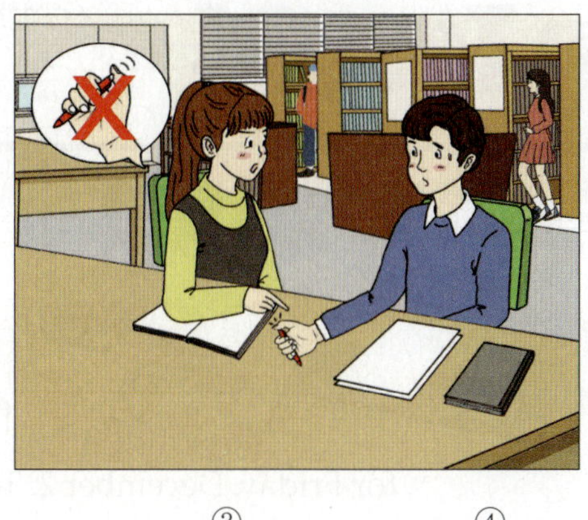

①   ②   ③   ④   ⑤

18 대화를 듣고, 두 사람이 테마 파크에 대해 언급하지 <u>않은</u> 것을 고르시오.

① 이용 나이   ② 체험 가능 직업   ③ 티켓 가격
④ 티켓 구매 방법   ⑤ 위치

[19~20] 대화를 듣고, 남자의 마지막 말에 이어질 여자의 말로 가장 적절한 것을 고르시오.

19 Woman: ______________________________________

① I think it is 10 meters long.
② I don't know what time it is.
③ It is too late to play outside.
④ I'll show you how to paint the wall.
⑤ I've been taking the class for a month.

20 Woman: ______________________________________

① Definitely, I'd love to.   ② Oh, I'm sorry to hear that.
③ Then, you should eat more.   ④ No. Roller coasters scare me.
⑤ Please check out the website.

Dictation Test 04

M2(17)_04_D

Dictation(받아쓰기)은 본문을 받아쓰면서 영어듣기의 집중력을 향상시키고 다양한 표현을 정리하기 위한 영어듣기 학습법입니다. **녹음을 다시 듣고, 빈칸에 알맞은 단어를 써 보세요.**
※Dictation의 정답은 듣기 대본의 밑줄 친 부분을 확인하세요.

정답 p. 15

맞은 개수 / 총155개

날씨파악–그림

1. 다음을 듣고, 뉴욕의 날씨로 가장 적절한 것을 고르시오.

①  ② 

③  ④ (해)

⑤ 

01 M: Good evening. Here's the world weather report for Friday, December 2. Tokyo will have cloudy skies and ________ ____________. In Shanghai, it will be sunny, but the air quality will be bad. In Berlin, the ________ will be heavy all day. New York will have its first ________ of the year, so be careful of the slippery roads. Thank you.

고난도 **그림정보파악**

2. 대화를 듣고, 테이블 매트 위의 물건 배치로 가장 적절한 것을 고르시오.

①  ② 

③  ④ 

⑤ 

02 M: Molly, can you ________ ________ ________ the table setting? Our guests will be here soon.

W: Sure. You already ________ ________ ________ on the mat.

M: Yup. Please put the fork on the left side of it.

W: Done. Shall I put the knife on ________ ________ ________?

M: Yes, please. And the spoon goes to the right side of the knife.

W: How about this small spoon?

M: Put it on the upper side of the plate.

W: OK. I'll set the rest ________ ________.

---

3. 대화를 듣고, 여자의 심정으로 가장 적절한 것을 고르시오.
   ① proud   ② bored
   ③ angry   ④ happy
   ⑤ thankful

03

M: What's wrong, Mina?

W: Minho ________ ________ ________ on my textbook!

M: Don't be ________. He's only five years old.

W: But Dad, this is not the first time!

M: You know he's young. I guess you need to keep your things out of his reach.

W: Oh, you always ________ ________ ________.

4. 대화를 듣고, 여자가 Sports Day에 한 일로 가장 적절한 것을 고르시오.
   ① 축구 하기
   ② 사진 전시하기
   ③ 운동기구 설치하기
   ④ 얼굴에 그림 그려주기
   ⑤ 개인 물병 사용 홍보하기

04

W: Hey, Bill. What are you ________ ________?

M: I'm just looking at some photos. They're from our school's Sports Day.

W: Let me see. (*Pause*) Oh, here you are ________ ________.

M: Yes, I ran as a mid-fielder. Which sport did you play?

W: I didn't play any sports.

M: Then, what did you do?

W: I did ________ ________ for students with my art group members.

다음 페이지에 계속 ➡

5. 대화를 듣고, 대화가 이루어지는 장소를
고르시오.
① 백화점
② 우체국
③ 식당
④ 버스 정류장
⑤ 분실물 보관소

05
W: How can I help you?

M: I lost my wallet. I came here to ________ ________

someone turned it in.

W: What does it ________ ________?

M: It's red and there is a zipper ________ ________

________.

W: A red wallet? Oh, is this yours?

M: Yes, that's it! Thank you so much.

W: You're welcome. If you lose something again, you

can use our website, www.lost112.go.kr.

6. 대화를 듣고, 남자의 마지막 말의 의도로
가장 적절한 것을 고르시오.
① 칭찬　　　② 격려
③ 항의　　　④ 수락
⑤ 용서

06
W: Hi, Tim. How are you doing these days?

M: Hey, Jina. I am not ________ ________.

W: Oh, what's wrong?

M: I can't score any points in my soccer game these

days. It's __________.

W: It's probably ________ ________ ________. You

were always a great soccer player.

M: Thank you. It is very nice of you to say so.

W: How about I help you __________ your shooting?

I can be the ball girl.

M: Oh, that would be great!

7. 대화를 듣고, 여자가 만든 것으로 가장 적절한 것을 고르시오.
① 계란말이　② 잡채
③ 김치　④ 미역국
⑤ 고기전

07
M: Sue, how was school today?

W: Good. We learned how to ________ ________ ________ today.

M: What is that?

W: It's cooked with mi-yuk.

M: Ah! I know the soup. Your mom made it for your birthday, remember?

W: Of course. We put ________ ________ ________, too. It was very tasty.

M: Wasn't it difficult to make?

W: Not at all. I'll make it for you next time.

M: Thanks. That's ________ ________ ________ ________.

8. 대화를 듣고, 남자가 대화 직후에 할 일로 가장 적절한 것을 고르시오.
① 친구 만나기
② 교실 청소하기
③ 휴지통 비우기
④ 방향제 뿌리기
⑤ 에어컨 가동하기

08
W: Jacob, what's that ________ smell coming from your room?

M: I don't know, Mom. I cleaned my room yesterday.

W: I know, but did you ________ ________ ________ as you promised?

M: Oops, I forgot. I think that's where the smell is coming from.

W: You should ________ ________ ________ right now.

M: Yes, I'll do it right away.

다음 페이지에 계속 ➡

9. 대화를 듣고, 두 사람이 동아리 신설에
    대해 언급하지 <u>않은</u> 것을 고르시오.
    ① 지도 교사 　② 신청서 작성
    ③ 활동 교실 　④ 부원 모집
    ⑤ 활동비 지원

09

M: Hello, Ms. Collin. Could you tell me how I can start a new club?

W: Sure, what club do you want to create?

M: A singing club. Mr. Han has agreed to be our ___________ teacher.

W: Great. Then, you need to fill out this form and get it _________ _________ Mr. Han.

M: Thank you. Can we use the music room for our club?

W: Sure. But, you ___________ _________ _________ get some club members first.

M: I already have eight members _________ _________ _________ to join.

10. 다음을 듣고, 여자가 하는 말의 내용으로
    가장 적절한 것을 고르시오.
    ① 여행 일정 　② 식사 예절
    ③ 안전 수칙 　④ 예약 방법
    ⑤ 문화재 보호

10

W: Hello, everyone. Let me tell you about today's ___________. Now, we're going to Tiananmen, _________ _________ The Gate of Heavenly Peace. Next, we'll visit Beijing's Palace Museum, _________ _________ as the Forbidden City. After that, we'll come back here to have dinner. I hope you _________ ___________ in Beijing. Thank you.

11. 대화를 듣고, English Essay Contest에 대한 내용과 일치하지 <u>않는</u> 것을 고르시오.

① 이번 주 목요일에 진행된다.
② 오후 4시에 시작한다.
③ 이메일로 대회 신청서를 제출해야 한다.
④ 에세이 주제는 대회 전날에 공지된다.
⑤ 1시간 동안 진행된다.

11

W: Mr. Kim, I'm hoping to enter the school English Essay Contest.

M: Great! It's this Thursday.

W: It starts at 4 p.m., right?

M: Yes. You ________ ________ ________ your contest entry form to me by e-mail.

W: Sure, I'll send it today.

M: The essay topic ________ ________ ________ right before the start of the contest.

W: Okay. How much time will I have to ________ my essay?

M: Oh, the contest will be one-hour long.

W: Thank you!

12. 대화를 듣고, 남자가 전화를 건 목적으로 가장 적절한 것을 고르시오.

① 휴대폰을 찾기 위해서
② 데이트 약속을 잡기 위해서
③ 습득 분실물을 신고하기 위해서
④ 가구 배송 시간을 확인하기 위해서
⑤ 부모님께 외출 허락을 받기 위해서

12

(*Cellphone rings.*)

M: Hey, Grace. It's me, Jay.

W: Hey, Jay. Whose number is this?

M: I'm ________ ________ my dad's phone. I think I left mine at your place.

W: Really? I'm at home. I'll ________ ________ ________.

M: Could you check your desk first?

W: [*Pause*] Oh, here's your cellphone! You left it on the chair.

M: Great. Thanks. Can I come and ________ ________ ________ now?

W: Sure. I'll wait.

다음 페이지에 계속 ➡

13. 대화를 듣고, 두 사람이 만날 시각을 고르시오.

① 5:00 p.m.
② 5:30 p.m.
③ 6:00 p.m.
④ 6:30 p.m.
⑤ 7:00 p.m.

13

W: I'm really excited about the concert this Saturday.

M: Same here! It starts at 7 p.m., right?

W: Yes, how about meeting at 5 p.m.?

M: That __________ __________ __________ early. What about 6:30 p.m.?

W: There's a pre-concert __________ __________ __________ with the band. Wouldn't you like to meet them?

M: That sounds fantastic! Let's meet at 6 p.m. then.

W: Perfect. See you __________ __________ __________ to the stadium!

14. 대화를 듣고, 두 사람의 관계로 가장 적절한 것을 고르시오.

① 신발가게 직원 — 고객
② 자동차 판매원 — 고객
③ 디자이너 — 고객
④ 미술 선생님 — 학생
⑤ 옷가게 점원 — 고객

14

W: This __________ __________ __________ but I don't like the color. Do you have this in green?

M: No, I'm sorry. That style only __________ __________ blue and red.

W: Hmm… May I try the blue one?

M: Of course. Here you are.

W: I would like __________ __________ __________, please. This one is too big.

M: Oh, I'm sorry. Here's a medium.

W: Thank you.

M: How about a pair of jeans __________ __________ __________ that shirt? All jeans are on sale until tomorrow.

W: That's great! I was thinking of getting new jeans.

15. 대화를 듣고, 여자가 남자에게 부탁한 일로 가장 적절한 것을 고르시오.

① 전화 걸어주기
② 핸드폰 구매하기
③ 분실물 신고하기
④ 영화 초대권 교환하기
⑤ 영화관 위치 알려주기

15
W: Ryan, I'm going out to a movie with Emily.

M: Okay, have fun, you two!

W: Hmm… Honey, ________ ________ ________ my phone? I can't find it.

M: Nope, I haven't seen it. Have you ________ ________ ________?

W: Yes, it isn't here.

M: Where could it have gone?

W: I'm sorry, but can you ________ ________ ________ so that I can find it?

M: No problem. I'm calling it right now.

W: Oh, I think I can hear it ringing in our bedroom.

2024 영어듣기능력평가 2회 16번 변형

16. 대화를 듣고, 여자가 기타 강습을 중단한 이유로 가장 적절한 것을 고르시오.

① 손가락이 아파서
② 강습비가 올라서
③ 연습할 시간이 없어서
④ 강습 수준이 맞지 않아서
⑤ 수업 시간 변경이 어려워서

16
M: Hi, Lisa. Are you still taking guitar lessons these days?

W: Oh, didn't I tell you? I __________ __________ to the lessons last week.

M: Really? Was it because the lesson __________ went up?

W: No, the cost wasn't a problem.

M: Then, why did you stop going?

W: I wanted to change my class time, but they couldn't __________ __________ __________ I wanted.

M: Oh, okay. That's too bad.

다음 페이지에 계속 ➡

17. 다음 그림의 상황에 가장 적절한 대화를 고르시오.

①   ②
③   ④
⑤

17

① W: Can you help me _________ this problem?

M: Of course. Let me see.

② W: Can I borrow your eraser _________ _________

_________?

M: Sure. Here you are.

③ W: Where can I find the library?

M: It's next to the post office.

④ W: Excuse me. Could you _________ _________ your

pen?

M: Oh, I'm really sorry.

⑤ W: You look nice today. I like your new haircut.

M: Thank you for the kind words!

18. 대화를 듣고, 두 사람이 테마 파크에 대해 언급하지 <u>않은</u> 것을 고르시오.

① 이용 나이
② 체험 가능 직업
③ 티켓 가격
④ 티켓 구매 방법
⑤ 위치

18

W: _________ _________ we go to the Children's

Job Experience Theme Park together?

M: The Children's Job Experience Theme Park? What

is it _________?

W: It's a special job experience program for kids from

36 months old to 16 years old. You can _________

_________ different jobs like a firefighter, a cook,

and a doctor.

M: That's cool! How can I get a ticket?

W: You can buy the ticket online.

M: Great. Where is it _________?

W: It's _________ _________ the Nature Park Zoo.

19. 대화를 듣고, 남자의 마지막 말에 이어질 여자의 말로 가장 적절한 것을 고르시오.

Woman: ________________

① I think it is 10 meters long.
② I don't know what time it is.
③ It is too late to play outside.
④ I'll show you how to paint the wall.
⑤ I've been taking the class for a month.

19

M: Hi, Jessica! You've been in such a good mood lately. What's going on?

W: Thank you for __________. I've got a new hobby.

M: Oh, what is it?

W: I've been going to a painting class. It helps me relax and __________ __________ __________ __________ things.

M: Good for you! I'm glad you found __________ __________.

W: I never knew how much fun it could be to play with colors.

M: How long have you been doing it?

W: I've been taking the class for a month.

20. 대화를 듣고, 남자의 마지막 말에 이어질 여자의 말로 가장 적절한 것을 고르시오.

Woman: ________________

① Definitely, I'd love to.
② Oh, I'm sorry to hear that.
③ Then, you should eat more.
④ No. Roller coasters scare me.
⑤ Please check out the website.

20

W: Glen, I haven't __________ __________ for any after-school programs yet. Have you?

M: Yes, I have __________ __________ the science class.

W: Science class? What is it about?

M: We are going to do a lot of __________ __________.

W: That sounds fun! What kind of experiments?

M: We'll be making things __________ __________ mini volcanoes and paper roller coasters.

W: Wow, that sounds pretty exciting!

M: Why don't you join me? The class is not __________ yet.

W: Definitely, I'd love to.

Words & Expressions Review 04

● 다음 단어를 암기하세요.

문제	번호	단어	뜻
1	☐ 1	temperature	기온, 온도
	☐ 2	air quality	대기질, 공기의 질
2	☐ 3	soon	곧
3	☐ 4	draw a picture	그림을 그리다
	☐ 5	take one's side	~의 편을 들다
4	☐ 6	Sports Day	운동회 날
	☐ 7	mid-fielder	미드필더
	☐ 8	face painting	페이스 페인팅
5	☐ 9	lose	잃어버리다
	☐ 10	turn ~ in	~을 돌려주다
6	☐ 11	frustrating	불만스러운, 좌절감을 주는
	☐ 12	phase	(변화·발달 과정상의 한) 단계
7	☐ 13	seaweed	미역, 해초
	☐ 14	tasty	맛있는
	☐ 15	sweet	다정한, 상냥한
8	☐ 16	awful	지독한, 끔찍한
	☐ 17	empty	비우다
	☐ 18	wastebasket	휴지통
9	☐ 19	agree	승낙하다, 동의하다
	☐ 20	fill out	~을 작성하다
	☐ 21	be willing to + 동사	기꺼이 ~하다
10	☐ 22	schedule	일정

문제	번호	단어	뜻
10	☐ 23	known as ~	~으로 알려진
	☐ 24	enjoy oneself	즐겁게 보내다
	☐ 25	contest	대회, 시합
11	☐ 26	entry form	참가 신청서
	☐ 27	announce	발표하다, 알리다
12	☐ 28	leave	~을 두고 오다[가다]
	☐ 29	place	(개인의) 집, 살 곳
13	☐ 30	entrance	입구, 출입구
	☐ 31	fit	(크기가) 맞다
14	☐ 32	go with ~	~과 어울리다
	☐ 33	on sale	할인[세일] 중인
	☐ 34	go out	나가다, 외출하다
15	☐ 35	purse	손가방
	☐ 36	ring	(벨이) 울리다
16	☐ 37	fee	요금
	☐ 38	cost	비용, 값
	☐ 39	experience	경험
18	☐ 40	exactly	정확히
	☐ 41	try out	시도해 보다
19	☐ 42	notice	알아차리다
	☐ 43	register	등록하다, 신청하다
20	☐ 44	experiment	실험

M2(17)_W_04

●왼쪽 단어장의 뜻이 보이지 않게 반으로 접고, 학습한 단어의 뜻을 아래 빈칸에 적어주세요.

1	go with ~	23	ring
2	notice	24	place
3	try out	25	agree
4	exactly	26	purse
5	experiment	27	contest
6	frustrating	28	register
7	fill out	29	entrance
8	experience	30	tasty
9	known as ~	31	entry form
10	announce	32	sweet
11	mid-fielder	33	lose
12	leave	34	be willing to + 동사
13	Sports Day	35	temperature
14	cost	36	on sale
15	wastebasket	37	phase
16	face painting	38	fit
17	soon	39	empty
18	enjoy oneself	40	go out
19	seaweed	41	schedule
20	fee	42	take one's side
21	turn ~ in	43	draw a picture
22	air quality	44	awful

05회 중학영어듣기 모의고사

M2(17)_05_US
모두 **미국식 발음(US)**
으로 녹음

M2(17)_05_UK
20문제 중 5문제에 **영국식 발음
(US+UK)**을 포함하여 녹음

정답 및 해석 p.20

1 다음을 듣고, 목요일의 날씨로 가장 적절한 것을 고르시오.

①  ② 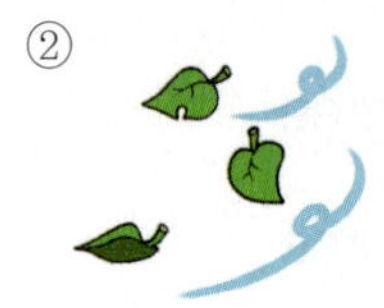 ③  ④  ⑤ 

2 대화를 듣고, 남자가 주문할 수건으로 가장 적절한 것을 고르시오.

①  ②  ③  ④  ⑤ 

3 대화를 듣고, 남자의 심정으로 가장 적절한 것을 고르시오.

① worried　　② cheerful　　③ upset　　④ bored　　⑤ surprised

4 대화를 듣고, 남자가 학교 연극에서 맡은 일로 가장 적절한 것을 고르시오.

① 연기하기　　② 대본 쓰기　　③ 세트 만들기
④ 음식 준비하기　　⑤ 의상 제작하기

5 대화를 듣고, 두 사람이 대화하는 장소로 가장 적절한 곳을 고르시오.

① 우체국　　② 세탁소　　③ 기차역
④ 분실물 센터　　⑤ 옷 가게

6 대화를 듣고, 여자의 마지막 말의 의도로 적절한 것을 고르시오.

① 충고　　　　② 감사　　　　③ 동의　　　　④ 제안　　　　⑤ 거절

7 대화를 듣고, 여자가 소풍에 가져가지 <u>않을</u> 물건을 고르시오.

① 청재킷　　　　② 머리띠　　　　③ 선글라스
④ 점심 도시락　　⑤ 물병

8 대화를 듣고, 두 사람이 대화 직후에 할 일로 가장 적절한 것을 고르시오.

① 영화 표 구입하기　　② 친구에게 전화하기　　③ 배터리 충전하기
④ 버스 노선 확인하기　　⑤ 버스 표 예약하기

9 대화를 듣고, 남자가 저자 사인회에 대해 언급하지 <u>않은</u> 것을 고르시오.

① 행사 일시　　　　② 장소　　　　③ 소요 시간
④ 인원 수 제한　　　⑤ 사진 촬영

10 다음을 듣고, 여자가 하는 말의 내용으로 가장 적절한 것을 고르시오.

① 온라인 수업 접속 안내　　　② 홈페이지 제작 방법
③ 영화관 이용 예절　　　　　④ 컴퓨터 조립 과정
⑤ 인터넷 이용 주의사항

11번~20번 문제는 다음 페이지에 ➡

11 대화를 듣고, 자전거 투어에 대한 내용과 일치하지 <u>않는</u> 것을 고르시오.

① 자전거 한 대당 10유로에 빌려준다.　② 다섯 곳의 관광지를 방문한다.
③ 3시간이 소요된다.　④ 아침과 오후 투어가 있다.
⑤ 예약을 해야 한다.

12 대화를 듣고, 여자가 전화를 건 목적으로 가장 적절한 것을 고르시오.

① 수강 신청을 하기 위해서　② 수강 신청을 취소하기 위해서
③ 수업 시간을 변경하기 위해서　④ 수강 과목을 변경하기 위해서
⑤ 수업 준비물을 물어보기 위해서

13 대화를 듣고, 남자가 지불해야 할 금액으로 가장 적절한 것을 고르시오.

① $8　② $10　③ $20　④ $24　⑤ $30

14 대화를 듣고, 두 사람의 관계로 적절한 것을 고르시오.

① 선생님 — 학생　② 식당 직원 — 손님
③ 요리사 — 견습생　④ 아빠 — 딸
⑤ 사장 — 비서

15 대화를 듣고, 남자가 여자에게 부탁한 일로 가장 적절한 것을 고르시오.

① 이삿짐 싸기　② 책 구매하기　③ 가위 전해주기
④ 서재 청소하기　⑤ 책꽂이 조립하기

16 대화를 듣고, 남자가 밤에 잠을 잘 <u>못</u> 자는 이유로 가장 적절한 것을 고르시오.

① 종종 낮잠을 자서　② 공부할 것이 너무 많아서
③ 마음에 걱정거리가 있어서　④ 아기인 동생이 울어서
⑤ 이웃집이 소란스러워서

17 다음 그림의 상황에 가장 적절한 대화를 고르시오.

①   ②   ③   ④   ⑤

18 다음을 듣고, 여자가 책에 대해 언급하지 <u>않은</u> 것을 고르시오.

① 제목   ② 작가   ③ 내용   ④ 가격   ⑤ 판매 순위

[19~20] 대화를 듣고, 여자의 마지막 말에 이어질 남자의 말로 가장 적절한 것을 고르시오.

19 Man: _______________________________________

① It's fine. I like to run.   ② You can't miss it.
③ Don't worry. It's not far.   ④ Okay. I'll take the number 20.
⑤ I should walk then. Thank you.

20 Man: _______________________________________

① Dinner is at seven.   ② I have to go to school.
③ I'll be home for dinner.   ④ The movie is two hours long.
⑤ No, I don't have any homework.

Dictation Test 05 

M2(17)_05_D

Dictation(받아쓰기)은 본문을 받아쓰면서 영어듣기의 집중력을 향상시키고 다양한 표현을 정리하기 위한
영어듣기 학습법입니다. **녹음을 다시 듣고, 빈칸에 알맞은 단어를 써 보세요.**
※Dictation의 정답은 듣기 대본의 밑줄 친 부분을 확인하세요.

정답 p. 20

맞은 개수 / 총178개

날씨파악–그림

1. 다음을 듣고, 목요일의 날씨로 가장 적절
한 것을 고르시오.

① ② ③ ④ ⑤

01 W: Good morning. Here's the weekly weather

forecast. On Monday, it'll be _________ all day.

On Tuesday and Wednesday, it'll be cloudy and

windy. On Thursday, _________ _________

_________ and the rain will continue until early

Saturday morning. After the rain, we can expect

_________ _________ for the rest of the weekend.

Thank you.

그림정보파악

2. 대화를 듣고, 남자가 주문할 수건으로 가
장 적절한 것을 고르시오.

① ② ③ ④ ⑤

02 M: Honey, we need to decide on a towel design.

W: It's a gift for the guests coming to Peggy's first

birthday party, isn't it?

M: Right. How about the one with a rabbit?

W: I think a towel _________ _________ _________ is

better. She was born in the Year of the Pig.

M: Okay. Why don't we _________ _________ _________

_________, July 30, on it?

W: Good idea. Let's put the date _________ the pig.

M: Great. I'll place an order, then.

---

3. 대화를 듣고, 남자의 심정으로 가장 적절한 것을 고르시오.
  ① worried   ② cheerful
  ③ upset   ④ bored
  ⑤ surprised

03

W: Gary, I heard you hurt your finger.

M: Oh, yeah. It's okay, though. It'll heal.

W: But, you won't be able to play the guitar at the festival. ________ ________ ________?

M: I'm not. Because I got to ________ ________ ________ in the school play instead!

W: Really? That's amazing!

M: I'm still part of the school festival. So I'm fine.

W: You're right. I'm happy for you.

M: Thanks. Life isn't ________ ________ ________!

4. 대화를 듣고, 남자가 학교 연극에서 맡은 일로 가장 적절한 것을 고르시오.
  ① 연기하기
  ② 대본 쓰기
  ③ 세트 만들기
  ④ 음식 준비하기
  ⑤ 의상 제작하기

04

M: Hi, Sarah. Will you be coming to the school play tonight?

W: Of course. How are you feeling right now?

M: I'm fine, but I'm also ________ ________ ________.

W: Yeah, it's a big responsibility. What is your role in the play?

M: I'm not participating as an actor this time.

W: Oh, then how are you ________ ________ the play?

M: I made costumes for all of the actors.

W: That's amazing! I'll ________ ________ ________ ________ ________ the costumes tonight.

다음 페이지에 계속 ➡

5. 대화를 듣고, 두 사람이 대화하는 장소로 가장 적절한 곳을 고르시오.

① 우체국
② 세탁소
③ 기차역
④ 분실물 센터
⑤ 옷 가게

05
M: Hello. How may I help you?

W: Hi. I'm here to __________ __________ __________

__________ . My name is Sarah Cho.

M: It's four blouses and two coats, right?

W: That's right! How do you remember all that?

M: Well, one of your coats has such a unique design.

W: Thank you. Oh, my blouses look brand new!

M: Our __________ __________ __________ works like magic.

W: Thank you so much. I should __________ __________

more clothes.

M: Any time.

6. 대화를 듣고, 여자의 마지막 말의 의도로 적절한 것을 고르시오.

① 충고　　② 감사
③ 동의　　④ 제안
⑤ 거절

06
W: Hello, Johnny, fancy meeting you here! What did you buy?

M: Oh, hi, Ellen! I just bought something for dinner. How about you? Wow, that's __________ __________

__________ __________ .

W: Yeah, it's for Dad's birthday celebration tomorrow.

M: I see. Hmm… Can you carry all of those __________

__________ ? Let me __________ __________ of them for you.

W: No, thanks. Don't worry, __________ __________

__________ .

7. 대화를 듣고, 여자가 소풍에 가져가지 <u>않</u>을 물건을 고르시오.

① 청재킷　② 머리띠
③ 선글라스　④ 점심 도시락
⑤ 물병

07

M: Are you excited about the school picnic tomorrow?

W: Of course, Dad! My friends and I will ________ ________ ________ ________ in front of the class.

M: Oh, wow. Did you pack the costume, then?

W: Yeah, a jean jacket and a red hairband.

M: What about sunglasses?

W: No, we decided not to wear them.

M: Should you ________ ________ ________?

W: Yes. Mom will pack it for me.

M: Good. ________ ________ ________ put a water bottle in the bag now?

W: OK, Dad.

8. 대화를 듣고, 두 사람이 대화 직후에 할 일로 가장 적절한 것을 고르시오.

① 영화 표 구입하기
② 친구에게 전화하기
③ 배터리 충전하기
④ 버스 노선 확인하기
⑤ 버스 표 예약하기

08

M: Suji, I'm so sorry that I'm late.

W: What happened, Jiho? The movie ________ ________ ________.

M: I know. I took the wrong bus, and had to take another one to get here.

W: I see. But why didn't you call me?

M: My battery died. I'm so sorry. ________ ________ ________ ________.

W: Well, let's just get tickets for the next ________.

M: Sure. Let's do that.

다음 페이지에 계속 ➡

9. 대화를 듣고, 남자가 저자 사인회에 대해 언급하지 <u>않은</u> 것을 고르시오.
　① 행사 일시
　② 장소
　③ 소요 시간
　④ 인원 수 제한
　⑤ 사진 촬영

09 *(Telephone rings.)*

M: Hello, Barnes Books.

W: Hello, I heard Chris Bunner has a book signing this week. _________ _________ _________ exactly?

M: It's this Sunday at 3 p.m.

W: I see. Where is it going to be held?

M: _________ _________ _________ at the café inside our bookstore.

W: Great. How long will the event be?

M: It's _________ _________ _________ two hours.

W: Can I take a picture with the author?

M: Of course, you can.

W: That's great. Thanks.

10. 다음을 듣고, 여자가 하는 말의 내용으로 가장 적절한 것을 고르시오.
　① 온라인 수업 접속 안내
　② 홈페이지 제작 방법
　③ 영화관 이용 예절
　④ 컴퓨터 조립 과정
　⑤ 인터넷 이용 주의사항

10 W: Hello, students. I am going to tell you how to _________ _________ _________, so listen carefully. Each of your __________ is already created. All you need to do is to log in. Your ID is your student email address. The password is randomly created and _________ _________ your email. So, when you first _________ _________, don't forget to change your password.

11. 대화를 듣고, 자전거 투어에 대한 내용과 일치하지 <u>않는</u> 것을 고르시오.
   ① 자전거 한 대당 10유로로 빌려 준다.
   ② 다섯 곳의 관광지를 방문한다.
   ③ 3시간이 소요된다.
   ④ 아침과 오후 투어가 있다.
   ⑤ 예약을 해야 한다.

11

W: Honey, why don't we take a bike tour tomorrow?

M: Good idea. We can enjoy Barcelona in a special way.

W: According to this website, we can ________ ________ ________ for €10.

M: That's nice! A guide ________ ________ ________ to five different sights.

W: The tour takes three hours and it's free.

M: Wonderful! They have morning and afternoon tour times.

W: Let's take a morning tour. Do we need to ________ ________ ________?

M: No, we just need to be at the meeting point at 9 a.m.

12. 대화를 듣고, 여자가 전화를 건 목적으로 가장 적절한 것을 고르시오.
   ① 수강 신청을 하기 위해서
   ② 수강 신청을 취소하기 위해서
   ③ 수업 시간을 변경하기 위해서
   ④ 수강 과목을 변경하기 위해서
   ⑤ 수업 준비물을 물어보기 위해서

12

(*Telephone rings.*)

M: Hello. Joy Community Center.

W: Hi. I ________ ________ ________ the morning aerobics program, but I'd like to change it.

M: ________ ________ ________ your name?

W: Becky Han.

M: Okay. (*Typing sound*) How would you like to change it?

W: I signed up for the 10 a.m. class and I'd like to ________ ________ ________ the 8 p.m. class.

M: Sure. (*Pause*) ________ ________. Now you're in the evening class for the aerobics program.

W: Thank you.

다음 페이지에 계속 ➡

13. 대화를 듣고, 남자가 지불해야 할 금액으로 가장 적절한 것을 고르시오.

① $8
② $10
③ $20
④ $24
⑤ $30

13

W: Welcome to the Baek Art Gallery. May I help you?

M: Hi, I'd like to buy three tickets, please.

W: Okay. The tickets are 10 dollars each.

M: Can I use these 20% __________ coupons?

W: Of course you can. That'll ________ ________ ________ ________ each ticket.

M: Then, it's 8 dollars each, right?

W: Right. So, it'll be 24 dollars ________ ________.

M: Okay. Here you are.

14. 대화를 듣고, 두 사람의 관계로 적절한 것을 고르시오.

① 선생님 — 학생
② 식당 직원 — 손님
③ 요리사 — 견습생
④ 아빠 — 딸
⑤ 사장 — 비서

14

M: Good evening, ma'am. Can I ________ ________ ________?

W: Yes. I'll have the cranberry salad and the beef steak.

M: How would you like your steak?

W: I want it medium.

M: Okay. Would you like ____________ ________ ________?

W: Just water with lemon, please.

M: Alright. ____________ ________ I can get you?

W: No, thanks. That's all.

15. 대화를 듣고, 남자가 여자에게 부탁한 일
로 가장 적절한 것을 고르시오.

① 이삿짐 싸기
② 책 구매하기
③ 가위 전해주기
④ 서재 청소하기
⑤ 책꽂이 조립하기

15

W: Honey, we should finish unpacking our stuff today.

M: Good idea. Let's start with our study then.

W: Okay. These boxes ________ ________ ________ books, right?

M: Yeah. Let's start __________ ________ ________.

W: If you open the boxes, I'll put the books on the bookshelf.

M: Okay. These boxes are heavily wrapped with tape. Could you ________ ________ ________ ________?

W: Yes. Here you go.

16. 대화를 듣고, 남자가 밤에 잠을 잘 못 자
는 이유로 가장 적절한 것을 고르시오.

① 종종 낮잠을 자서
② 공부할 것이 너무 많아서
③ 마음에 걱정거리가 있어서
④ 아기인 동생이 울어서
⑤ 이웃집이 소란스러워서

16

M: Ms. Choi is ________ ________ ________ because I'm late.

W: Again? Why are you often late these days?

M: I can't sleep well at night.

W: Why? Do you ________ ________ ________ during the daytime?

M: After school? No. You know we both don't have time. We have to study.

W: Then, what is it? Is there something that's __________ you?

M: No. It's my baby brother. He ________ ________ ________ ________ and cries.

W: Oh, dear.

다음 페이지에 계속 ➡

17. 다음 그림의 상황에 가장 적절한 대화를 고르시오.

①   ②
③   ④
⑤

17

① W: How are we going to get there?

M: Let's take the subway. It'll be fast.

② W: Music is too loud in this café.

M: ________ ________. Shall we speak to the waiter?

③ W: Excuse me. Is this seat taken?

M: No, I'm sorry. I'll ________ ________ ____________.

④ W: Let's sit down and listen to some music.

M: OK. I'll take my earphones out.

⑤ W: Can you ________ ________ the music?

M: Of course. I'm sorry it was too loud.

---

18. 다음을 듣고, 여자가 책에 대해 언급하지 **않은** 것을 고르시오.

① 제목   ② 작가
③ 내용   ④ 가격
⑤ 판매 순위

18

W: Good morning, listeners! Today I want to introduce a new book. The title is *Talking to the Moon*. The book was ________ ________ a best-selling writer, Sujan Lee. The story is about children's friendship and courage, just like her previous books. It's already at number five on the Amazon ________ ________ ________. This book will make an excellent present for your children. So, don't ________ ________!

19. 대화를 듣고, 여자의 마지막 말에 이어질 남자의 말로 가장 적절한 것을 고르시오.

Man: ________________

① It's fine. I like to run.
② You can't miss it.
③ Don't worry. It's not far.
④ Okay. I'll take the number 20.
⑤ I should walk then. Thank you.

19

M: Excuse me. Are you a local here?

W: Yes, why do you ask?

M: I'm looking for a hospital. Is there a hospital near here?

W: There is. ________ ________ ________ ________ and turn left when you get to the end.

M: Oh, ________ ________? How long will it take?

W: About 20 minutes. It's only ________ ________ ________ ________.

M: Is there a bus, too?

W: Yes, but you're going to have to wait for 20 minutes for it.

M: I should walk then. Thank you.

20. 대화를 듣고, 여자의 마지막 말에 이어질 남자의 말로 가장 적절한 것을 고르시오.

Man: ________________

① Dinner is at seven.
② I have to go to school.
③ I'll be home for dinner.
④ The movie is two hours long.
⑤ No, I don't have any homework.

20

M: Mom, can I go out to the movies with my friends?

W: Sure you can, but have you finished your homework?

M: Of course! I finished it earlier ________ ________ I could go out.

W: Then, did you clean your room like I ________ ________ ________?

M: Yes, Mom. I've done everything you told me to.

W: Good job! Well, in that case, ________ ________ ________ at the movies then.

M: Thanks, Mom. I'll be leaving in a minute.

W: Okay. When will you ________ ________ home?

M: I'll be home for dinner.

Words & Expressions Review 05

●다음 단어를 암기하세요.

문제	번호	단어	뜻	문제	번호	단어	뜻
1	☐ 1	continue	계속하다, 지속시키다	10	☐ 23	randomly	무작위로
	☐ 2	expect	예상하다, 기대하다	11	☐ 24	make a reservation	예약하다
2	☐ 3	below	밑에	12	☐ 25	sign up for ~	~에 등록하다
	☐ 4	place an order	주문하다		☐ 26	art gallery	미술관, 화랑
	☐ 5	upset	속상한, 마음이 상한	13	☐ 27	discount	할인
3	☐ 6	play a role	역할을 맡다		☐ 28	in total	총, 모두 합하여
	☐ 7	part	구성원, 일원		☐ 29	take an order	주문을 받다
	☐ 8	nervous	긴장한, 불안한	14	☐ 30	anything else	그 밖에 다른 것
4	☐ 9	responsibility	책임, 책임감		☐ 31	unpack	(짐을) 풀다
	☐ 10	connected to	~과 관련된	15	☐ 32	heavily	아주 많이, 심하게
5	☐ 11	unique	독특한		☐ 33	be wrapped with ~	~으로 싸여 있다
	☐ 12	brand new	완전히 새 것인		☐ 34	angry at ~	~에게 화난
	☐ 13	grocery	식료품	16	☐ 35	daytime	낮 (시간)
6	☐ 14	by oneself	혼자서		☐ 36	take A out	A를 꺼내다
	☐ 15	manage	감당하다, 처리하다	17	☐ 37	turn down	(소리·온도 등을) 줄이다
7	☐ 16	costume	의상, 복장		☐ 38	friendship	우정
8	☐ 17	another	다른, 또 하나의	18	☐ 39	courage	용기, 용감
	☐ 18	fault	잘못, 결함		☐ 40	previous	이전의, 앞선
9	☐ 19	be held	~이 열리다, 개최되다		☐ 41	local	(특정 지역에 사는) 주민, 현지인
	☐ 20	be scheduled to + 동사	~할 예정이다	19	☐ 42	on foot	걸어서, 도보로
10	☐ 21	access	접속하다		☐ 43	You can't miss it.	쉽게 찾을 거예요.
	☐ 22	account	계정	20	☐ 44	in that case	그렇다면, 그런 경우에는

● 왼쪽 단어장의 뜻이 보이지 않게 반으로 접고, 학습한 단어의 뜻을 아래 빈칸에 적어주세요.

1	on foot	23	fault
2	connected to	24	heavily
3	friendship	25	expect
4	responsibility	26	access
5	brand new	27	costume
6	below	28	in that case
7	previous	29	take an order
8	nervous	30	play a role
9	unpack	31	manage
10	part	32	by oneself
11	local	33	art gallery
12	angry at ~	34	grocery
13	turn down	35	discount
14	anything else	36	in total
15	unique	37	another
16	sign up for ~	38	be wrapped with ~
17	place an order	39	upset
18	take A out	40	be scheduled to + 동사
19	courage	41	randomly
20	be held	42	daytime
21	make a reservation	43	account
22	You can't miss it.	44	continue

06회 중학영어듣기 모의고사

M2(17)_06_US
모두 **미국식 발음(US)**
으로 녹음

M2(17)_06_UK
20문제 중 5문제에 **영국식 발음**
(US+UK)을 포함하여 녹음

정답 및 해석 p.25

1
다음을 듣고, 목요일의 날씨로 가장 적절한 것을 고르시오.

①  ②  ③  ④  ⑤ 

2
대화를 듣고, 남자가 만든 장난감 상자를 고르시오.

①  ②  ③ 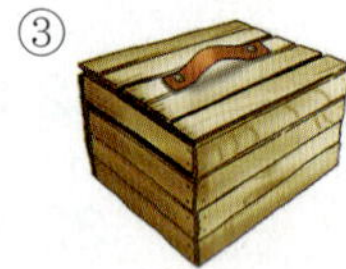 ④  ⑤ 

3
대화를 듣고, 여자의 심정으로 가장 적절한 것을 고르시오.

① scared ② thankful ③ bored ④ cheerful ⑤ peaceful

4
대화를 듣고, 여자가 City Music Festival에서 한 일로 가장 적절한 것을 고르시오.

① 공연 관람하기　　② 춤추기　　③ 사진 찍기
④ 축제 진행 돕기　　⑤ 봉사자 인솔하기

5 대화를 듣고, 두 사람이 대화하는 장소로 가장 적절한 곳을 고르시오.

① 미용실   ② 사진촬영 스튜디오   ③ 의류 매장
④ 미술관   ⑤ 박물관

6 대화를 듣고, 남자의 마지막 말의 의도로 가장 적절한 것을 고르시오.

① 제안   ② 충고   ③ 사과   ④ 확신   ⑤ 칭찬

7 대화를 듣고, 여자가 만든 것으로 가장 적절한 것을 고르시오.

① 공   ② 모자   ③ 인형
④ 목도리   ⑤ 신발

8 대화를 듣고, 여자가 대화 직후에 할 일로 가장 적절한 것을 고르시오.

① 운동하기   ② 쓰레기 버리기   ③ 신발 주문하기
④ 점심 메뉴 고르기   ⑤ 쿠폰 출력하기

9 대화를 듣고, 두 사람이 TV 프로그램에 대해 언급하지 <u>않은</u> 것을 고르시오.

① 제목   ② 장르   ③ 주연 배우
④ 방영 채널   ⑤ 작가

10 다음을 듣고, 남자가 하는 말의 내용으로 가장 적절한 것을 고르시오.

① 스포츠 경기 관람 예절   ② 층간 소음 협조 안내문
③ 전자제품 사용법   ④ 시험 유의사항
⑤ 지진 시 대처 방법

11번~20번 문제는 다음 페이지에 ➡

11 대화를 듣고, 한국 요리 강좌에 대한 내용으로 일치하지 <u>않는</u> 것을 고르시오.

① 토요일에 열린다.　　　　　　　　② 초급자를 위한 강좌이다.
③ 떡볶이 만드는 법을 배운다.　　　 ④ 수강료는 무료이다.
⑤ 수강 가능 인원은 최대 20명이다.

12 대화를 듣고, 여자가 전화를 건 목적으로 가장 적절한 것을 고르시오.

① 결혼식 불참을 알리기 위해서　　　 ② 뉴욕행 비행기를 예약하기 위해서
③ 결혼식장을 예약하기 위해서　　　 ④ 사업상 회의에 함께 가기 위해서
⑤ 약속을 잡기 위해서

13 대화를 듣고, 남자가 지불해야 할 금액으로 가장 적절한 것을 고르시오.

① $4　　　　② $5　　　　③ $6　　　　④ $7　　　　⑤ $8

14 대화를 듣고, 두 사람의 관계로 가장 적절한 것을 고르시오.

① 보험설계사 — 고객　　　　　② 정육점 직원 — 손님
③ 요리사 — 학원 수강생　　　　④ 호텔 지배인 — 투숙객
⑤ 웨이터 — 손님

15 대화를 듣고, 남자가 여자에게 부탁한 일로 가장 적절한 것을 고르시오.

① 창문 열기　　　　② 컴퓨터 고치기　　　　③ 숙제 도와주기
④ 선풍기 틀어 주기　　 ⑤ 영어 가르쳐 주기

16 대화를 듣고, 남자가 주말에 전주에 간 이유로 가장 적절한 것을 고르시오.

① 관광하기 좋은 곳이라서
② 교통 사정을 알아보기 위해서
③ 친척을 방문하기 위해서
④ 봉사활동을 하기 위해서
⑤ 맛있는 먹거리가 많아서

17 다음 그림의 상황에 가장 적절한 대화를 고르시오.

①　　②　　③　　④　　⑤

18 다음을 듣고, 여자가 콘서트에 대해 언급하지 <u>않은</u> 것을 고르시오.

① 특별 출연자　② 장소　③ 날짜　④ 티켓 가격　⑤ 티켓 구입 방법

[19~20] 대화를 듣고, 남자의 마지막 말에 이어질 여자의 말로 가장 적절한 것을 고르시오.

19 Woman: ____

① You can stay if you want.
② He is not coming with us.
③ My flight leaves at 10 a.m.
④ Our neighbor will take care of him.
⑤ There's a good restaurant in Thailand.

20 Woman: ____

① Turn right, please.
② You don't have to.
③ I'll drop by a café.
④ Where did he send it?
⑤ Skateboarding could be fun.

Dictation Test 06  

M2(17)_06_D

Dictation(받아쓰기)은 본문을 받아쓰면서 영어듣기의 집중력을 향상시키고 다양한 표현을 정리하기 위한 영어듣기 학습법입니다. **녹음을 다시 듣고, 빈칸에 알맞은 단어를 써 보세요.**
※Dictation의 정답은 듣기 대본의 밑줄 친 부분을 확인하세요. 📖 정답 p. 25

맞은 개수 / 총153개

날씨파악–그림

1. 다음을 듣고, 목요일의 날씨로 가장 적절한 것을 고르시오.

①  ②
③ ④
⑤  

01 W: Good evening. This is the ________ ________ ________ of Sunday. Tomorrow, it will continue to rain, so don't forget your umbrella. We'll have clear skies from Tuesday to Wednesday. But on Thursday, we're expecting ________ ________ ________. The wind will be over by Friday morning, and it will get chilly with ________ ________ ________ snow.

그림정보파악

2. 대화를 듣고, 남자가 만든 장난감 상자를 고르시오.

①  ② 
③  ④ 
⑤ 

02 M: Honey, I made this wooden box for Noah to store his toys.
W: Great! I can see ________ ________ ________ on top of the box.
M: Yes, the handle will ________ ________ ________ to open the box.
W: Wow! You even carved his name on the front of the box!
M: Yes. I thought about putting the word 'Toys' there, but I ________ ________ ________ his name 'Noah' onto it instead.
W: I think that's better. Noah will like it.

---

3. 대화를 듣고, 여자의 심정으로 가장 적절한 것을 고르시오.
① scared　② thankful
③ bored　④ cheerful
⑤ peaceful

03

M: Rita, did you hear the news about the fire?

W: What fire?

M: The diner on Bernard Street ________ ________ last night.

W: Oh, dear. Did anybody get hurt?

M: Thankfully, no. But, the police say the fire was ________ ________ __________.

W: Someone set the fire? That's horrible!

M: Yeah. The house fire that happened last month could have been set by the same person.

W: That's _____________. It means there's a ________ in our town!

4. 대화를 듣고, 여자가 City Music Festival에서 한 일로 가장 적절한 것을 고르시오.
① 공연 관람하기
② 춤추기
③ 사진 찍기
④ 축제 진행 돕기
⑤ 봉사자 인솔하기

04

M: Mindy, I heard you went to City Music Festival last weekend.

W: Yes! There were so many people dancing and taking pictures.

M: That sounds like ________ ________ ________ ________. Did you see any bands playing?

W: Sadly, no. I was too busy.

M: Doing what?

W: I ________ ________ safety flyers to people and took out trash.

M: Oh! You weren't there to enjoy. You were there to help.

W: Yeah. I _____________ ________ ________.

다음 페이지에 계속 ➡

5. 대화를 듣고, 두 사람이 대화하는 장소로 가장 적절한 곳을 고르시오.
   ① 미용실
   ② 사진촬영 스튜디오
   ③ 의류 매장
   ④ 미술관
   ⑤ 박물관

05
W: May I help you?

M: Hello. I'm here for the 2 o'clock session.

W: Oh, are you Mr. Simmonds?

M: Yes. My wife and the kids are __________ __________ __________.

W: Is this your first time having a __________ __________ __________?

M: No, we've done it before.

W: Great. The photographer is experienced with kids, so it'll be a fun session.

M: That's nice. Can I go __________ __________? I've brought my suit.

W: Sure. The changing room is over there.

6. 대화를 듣고, 남자의 마지막 말의 의도로 가장 적절한 것을 고르시오.
   ① 제안   ② 충고
   ③ 사과   ④ 확신
   ⑤ 칭찬

06
W: I'm so glad a lot of people came today.

M: Oh, a lot of people here __________ __________ __________ antique exhibits.

W: It seems like it. I'm just happy my efforts __________ __________.

M: Did you organize this event?

W: I did. It took a lot of time and energy, but it was worth it.

M: It sure was! You did a __________ __________.

7. 대화를 듣고, 여자가 만든 것으로 가장 적절한 것을 고르시오.

① 공   ② 모자
③ 인형   ④ 목도리
⑤ 신발

07

M: Sofia, how was the volunteer work today?

W: Good. It ________ ________ ________ ________,

   Dad.

M: Really? What did you do?

W: I made dolls for ________ ________ ________.

M: I didn't know you could make dolls.

W: I couldn't, really. But, there was a manual and it

   was easy to follow.

M: That's good. Did you make anything else?

W: Not me, but the others made hats and scarves, too.

M: That sounds wonderful.

8. 대화를 듣고, 여자가 대화 직후에 할 일로 가장 적절한 것을 고르시오.

① 운동하기
② 쓰레기 버리기
③ 신발 주문하기
④ 점심 메뉴 고르기
⑤ 쿠폰 출력하기

08

M: Mom, my running shoes are ________ ________.

W: Oh, are they?

M: Yes. Look at them. I think I need to ________

   ________ ________.

W: You're right. Shall we go shopping after lunch?

M: Actually, I already found the perfect ones on the

   Internet.

W: Really? Can you show them to me?

M: Here. They're even offering a ________ ________

   for purchases made today.

W: They look nice. I'll ________ the shoes for you

   right away.

다음 페이지에 계속 ➡

9. 대화를 듣고, 두 사람이 TV 프로그램에 대해 언급하지 <u>않은</u> 것을 고르시오.

① 제목
② 장르
③ 주연 배우
④ 방영 채널
⑤ 작가

09

W: Hey, Jim. Did you watch the new show, *Love Forever*?

M: Yeah. I don't like romances, but I actually watched this one.

W: If you don't like romances, why did you ________ ________ ________ ________ ________ this one?

M: I really like the main actor in it, Park Soo Jung.

W: Oh, really? Is she your ________?

M: Kind of? Anyway, I hope that the writer, Kim Nam Su, does not ________ ________ ________ ________ like he did with his last show.

W: Well, we will have to see about that.

10. 다음을 듣고, 남자가 하는 말의 내용으로 가장 적절한 것을 고르시오.

① 스포츠 경기 관람 예절
② 층간 소음 협조 안내문
③ 전자제품 사용법
④ 시험 유의사항
⑤ 지진 시 대처 방법

10

M: Attention, everybody. Before we start the test, I would like to ________ ________ ________. First, all cell phones must be turned off and placed inside your bags. If you are ________ ________ ________ ________ to other people, you will get an automatic zero for this test. Also, if you have a question, raise your hand quietly. Thank you.

11. 대화를 듣고, 한국 요리 강좌에 대한 내용으로 일치하지 <u>않는</u> 것을 고르시오.

① 토요일에 열린다.
② 초급자를 위한 강좌이다.
③ 떡볶이 만드는 법을 배운다.
④ 수강료는 무료이다.
⑤ 수강 가능 인원은 최대 20명이다.

11

M: Kate, do you have any plans for this Saturday?

W: Not really.

M: Then why don't we take a one-day Korean food cooking class at the community center?

W: Sounds fun! But I'm not good at cooking. Is that okay?

M: Sure. It's a course for ___________. They will teach us how to make *tteokbokki*.

W: Oh, I love *tteokbokki*. How much is the _______?

M: It's only 5,000 won. But the class is ________ _______ twenty people.

W: Oh, then we should hurry and register.

---

12. 대화를 듣고, 여자가 전화를 건 목적으로 가장 적절한 것을 고르시오.

① 결혼식 불참을 알리기 위해서
② 뉴욕행 비행기를 예약하기 위해서
③ 결혼식장을 예약하기 위해서
④ 사업상 회의에 함께 가기 위해서
⑤ 약속을 잡기 위해서

12

(Telephone rings.)

W: Hello. Can I speak to Mr. Walton?

M: Sorry. He is out _______ _______. Can I take a message?

W: Yes. This is Ms. Holmes. Please tell him that I'm going to New York this evening _______ _______.

M: Then, you won't be able to _______ his wedding _______ _________, will you?

W: No. Could you tell him that I'm really sorry about that?

M: All right. I'll tell him when he gets back.

다음 페이지에 계속 ➡

13. 대화를 듣고, 남자가 지불해야 할 금액으로 가장 적절한 것을 고르시오.

① $4 ② $5
③ $6 ④ $7
⑤ $8

13
W: Good morning. Would you like to order?

M: Yes. I'd like a ham and egg sandwich, please.

W: OK. _________ _________ _________. Would you like anything to drink?

M: Umm… How much is a coffee?

W: It's 2 dollars, but with the sandwich, you _________ _________ _________ _________.

M: Then the coffee is just 1 dollar. I'll have one, please.

W: Sure. It's 6 dollars _________ _________. Anything else?

M: No, that's all. Here's my credit card.

14. 대화를 듣고, 두 사람의 관계로 가장 적절한 것을 고르시오.

① 보험설계사 — 고객
② 정육점 직원 — 손님
③ 요리사 — 학원 수강생
④ 호텔 지배인 — 투숙객
⑤ 웨이터 — 손님

14
M: Hello. What would you like today?

W: Hello. I'd like _________ _________ for soup.

M: OK. I'll _________ _________ _________ for you. How much would you like?

W: 200g, please. And can I have _________ _________ _________ _________?

M: Yes. You can choose from the packets in front of you.

W: OK. Let me see. *(pause)* I'd like this one.

M: Sure. That'll be $32 in total.

W: Here's my credit card.

M: Thank you.

15. 대화를 듣고, 남자가 여자에게 부탁한 일로 가장 적절한 것을 고르시오.

① 창문 열기
② 컴퓨터 고치기
③ 숙제 도와주기
④ 선풍기 틀어 주기
⑤ 영어 가르쳐 주기

15
W: Are you doing your English homework, Minho?

M: Yes, I am. It's so difficult.

W: Do you _________ _________ _________ help you?

M: Thanks, but I will try to do it _________ _________

_________.

W: OK. Is there anything I can do for you?

M: Well, can you open the windows for me?

W: Sure. It's very hot _________ _________.

16. 대화를 듣고, 남자가 주말에 전주에 간 이유로 가장 적절한 것을 고르시오.

① 관광하기 좋은 곳이라서
② 교통 사정을 알아보기 위해서
③ 친척을 방문하기 위해서
④ 봉사활동을 하기 위해서
⑤ 맛있는 먹거리가 많아서

16
W: What did you do _________ _________

_________?

M: I visited Jeon-ju. The weekend traffic was awful,

but I love the city.

W: Yeah. There are so many things to see, right?

M: Yes. But, I wasn't there for sightseeing. My granny

lives there.

W: So, you were _________ _________ _________?

M: That's right. I do that _________ _________

_________.

W: You are a good boy.

다음 페이지에 계속 ➡

17. 다음 그림의 상황에 가장 적절한 대화를 고르시오.

① ②
③ ④
⑤

17
① M: What happened to your leg?

W: I _________ _________ and broke it.

② M: What do you want to be in the future?

W: I want to be a doctor.

③ M: Can I _________ _________ _________ for this?

W: Sure. May I see your receipt?

④ M: How can I help you?

W: I need something for _________ _____________,

please.

⑤ M: Can I try this shirt on?

W: Of course. The fitting room is over there.

18. 다음을 듣고, 여자가 콘서트에 대해 언급 하지 <u>않은</u> 것을 고르시오.

① 특별 출연자   ② 장소
③ 날짜   ④ 티켓 가격
⑤ 티켓 구입 방법

18
W: Green Art Center would like to invite you to our summer concert. You can meet the world-famous musician, Olivia Sharp, who will be our _________ _________. It will be held in our main hall. The concert is on July 2 at 7 p.m. All the _________ from ticket sales _________ _____ _____________ to children's charities. You can buy your tickets online on our website. We hope to see you at the concert.

19. 대화를 듣고, 남자의 마지막 말에 이어질 여자의 말로 가장 적절한 것을 고르시오.

Woman: _______________

① You can stay if you want.
② He is not coming with us.
③ My flight leaves at 10 a.m.
④ Our neighbor will take care of him.
⑤ There's a good restaurant in Thailand.

19
M: Alice, do you have any special plans for summer vacation?
W: Well, I'm going to ________ ________ ________ ________ at a resort in Thailand with my family.
M: Sounds like a perfect way to enjoy the vacation.
W: Yes, I'm so excited about it.
M: How long are you going to stay there?
W: I'm going to stay for a week.
M: Then, who's going to take care of your dog Max ________ ________ ________?
W: Our neighbor will take care of him.

20. 대화를 듣고, 남자의 마지막 말에 이어질 여자의 말로 가장 적절한 것을 고르시오.

Woman: _______________

① Turn right, please.
② You don't have to.
③ I'll drop by a café.
④ Where did he send it?
⑤ Skateboarding could be fun.

20
M: Hannah, what do you do in your free time?
W: I usually ________ ________. How about you?
M: I play games. But I'm getting a little ________ ________ that.
W: Maybe it's time to ________ ________ something new.
M: I think so, too. I just don't know what to do.
W: How about something active? Do you like sports?
M: I'm not sure. Can you ________ something?
W: Skateboarding could be fun.

Words & Expressions Review 06

● 다음 단어를 암기하세요.

문제	번호	단어	뜻	문제	번호	단어	뜻
1	□ 1	expect	~을 예상하다, 기대하다	12	□ 23	on business	사업상, 업무로
2	□ 2	store	보관하다		□ 24	attend	참석하다
	□ 3	carve	새기다, 조각하다	13	□ 25	get a discount	할인을 받다
3	□ 4	diner	작은 식당		□ 26	credit card	신용카드
	□ 5	burn down	타버리다		□ 27	cut up	~을 (잘게) 자르다
	□ 6	set a fire	불 지르다, 방화하다	14	□ 28	roasting	굽기, 볶기
	□ 7	frightening	무서운, 깜짝 놀라게 하는		□ 29	packet	(포장용) 곽, 통
	□ 8	criminal	범인, 범죄자	15	□ 30	on one's own	스스로, 혼자서
4	□ 9	hand out	나눠주다	16	□ 31	awful	끔찍한, 지독한
5	□ 10	experienced	경험 있는, 숙련된		□ 32	sightseeing	관광
6	□ 11	antique	골동품		□ 33	fall down	넘어지다
	□ 12	exhibit	전시물, 전시하다	17	□ 34	break	부러지다, 부서지다
7	□ 13	in need	도움이 필요한		□ 35	refund	환불
8	□ 14	worn out	낡은, 닳아 해진		□ 36	world-famous	세계적으로 유명한
	□ 15	throw away	버리다	18	□ 37	profit	수익, 이익
	□ 16	purchase	구매, 구입		□ 38	charity	자선 단체, 구호 단체
	□ 17	make an exception for	~을 예외로 하다		□ 39	take a rest	쉬다
9	□ 18	mess up	~을 망치다, 엉망으로 만들다	19	□ 40	gone	가버린
	□ 19	last	지난, 가장 최근의		□ 41	neighbor	이웃
10	□ 20	instruction	지시(사항)		□ 42	get tired of	~에 싫증이 나다
11	□ 21	course	강의, 강좌	20	□ 43	active	활동적인
	□ 22	beginner	초보자, 초급자		□ 44	drop by	잠깐 들르다

●왼쪽 단어장의 뜻이 보이지 않게 반으로 접고, 학습한 단어의 뜻을 아래 빈칸에 적어주세요.

1	neighbor		23	diner
2	on business		24	mess up
3	refund		25	carve
4	gone		26	credit card
5	break		27	charity
6	get tired of		28	take a rest
7	experienced		29	throw away
8	antique		30	worn out
9	instruction		31	fall down
10	store		32	get a discount
11	attend		33	burn down
12	active		34	on one's own
13	last		35	exhibit
14	packet		36	drop by
15	sightseeing		37	set a fire
16	make an exception for		38	hand out
17	profit		39	course
18	awful		40	beginner
19	world-famous		41	cut up
20	purchase		42	expect
21	in need		43	roasting
22	criminal		44	frightening

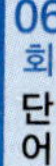

06
회
단어

07회 중학영어듣기 모의고사

M2(17)_07_US
모두 **미국식 발음(US)**
으로 녹음

M2(17)_07_UK
20문제 중 5문제에 **영국식 발음
(US+UK)**을 포함하여 녹음

정답 및 해석 p.30

1 다음을 듣고, 토요일의 날씨로 가장 적절한 것을 고르시오.

①  ②  ③  ④  ⑤ 

2 대화를 듣고, 남자가 만든 표지판으로 가장 적절한 것을 고르시오.

① 

② 

③ 

④ 

⑤ 

3 대화를 듣고, 여자의 심정으로 가장 적절한 것을 고르시오.

① calm ② happy ③ scared ④ angry ⑤ disappointed

4 대화를 듣고, 남자가 지난 주말에 한 일로 가장 적절한 것을 고르시오.

① 식당에 가기 ② 부엌 청소하기 ③ 생일 선물 사기
④ 케이크 주문하기 ⑤ 베이킹 수업 듣기

5 대화를 듣고, 두 사람이 대화하는 장소로 가장 적절한 곳을 고르시오.

① 사진관　　　　② 극장 매표소　　　　③ 학교 양호실
④ 영화 세트장　　⑤ 옷 가게

6 대화를 듣고, 여자의 마지막 말의 의도로 가장 적절한 것을 고르시오.

① 격려　　② 설득　　③ 칭찬　　④ 동의　　⑤ 충고

7 대화를 듣고, 두 사람이 준비할 선물이 무엇인지 고르시오.

① 넥타이　　② 양말　　③ 잠옷　　④ 카드　　⑤ 케이크

8 대화를 듣고, 두 사람이 대화 직후에 할 일로 가장 적절한 것을 고르시오.

① 산책하기　　　　② 식당에 가기　　　　③ 피자 배달시키기
④ 전시회 관람하기　⑤ 보드 게임 구매하기

9 대화를 듣고, 두 사람이 복싱 체육관에 대해 언급하지 않은 것을 고르시오.

① 체육관 이름　　② 초보자용 강좌　　③ 수강료
④ 주말 강좌　　　⑤ 글러브 대여

10 다음을 듣고, 여자가 하는 말의 내용으로 가장 적절한 것을 고르시오.

① 도서관 이용수칙　　　　② 과제물 제출 기한
③ 설문조사 참여 방법　　　④ 홈페이지 제작 과정
⑤ 온라인 수강신청 안내

11번~20번 문제는 다음 페이지에 ➡

11 대화를 듣고, balcony concert에 대한 내용으로 일치하지 <u>않는</u> 것을 고르시오.

① 오늘 공연이 예정되어 있다.　　　　② 15명만 무대 앞에서 관람할 수 있다.
③ 3명의 연주자가 출연한다.　　　　④ 1시간짜리 공연이다.
⑤ 오후 2시에 시작한다.

12 대화를 듣고, 남자가 전화를 건 목적으로 가장 적절한 것을 고르시오.

① 음식을 주문하기 위해서　　　　② 기차 표를 예약하기 위해서
③ 예약 시간을 변경하기 위해서　　　　④ 구독 서비스를 해지하기 위해서
⑤ 에어컨 수리를 요청하기 위해서

13 대화를 듣고, 여자가 받은 거스름돈으로 가장 적절한 것을 고르시오.

① $1　　　② $2　　　③ $3　　　④ $4　　　⑤ $5

14 대화를 듣고, 두 사람의 관계로 가장 적절한 것을 고르시오.

① 약사 – 손님　　　② 요리사 – 음식 평론가　　　③ 안내 데스크 직원 – 고객
④ 치과의사 – 환자　　　⑤ 수영강사 – 수강생

15 대화를 듣고, 여자가 남자에게 부탁한 일로 가장 적절한 것을 고르시오.

① 박람회에 함께 가기　　　② 웹사이트 주소 알려주기　　　③ 결혼식 참석하기
④ 입장권 교환하기　　　⑤ 게임 용품 사다 주기

16 대화를 듣고, 여자가 레스토랑을 예약하지 <u>못한</u> 이유로 가장 적절한 것을 고르시오.

① 예약이 다 차서　　　　② 정기 휴무일이어서
③ 레스토랑이 폐업을 해서　　　　④ 온라인 예약만 가능해서
⑤ 레스토랑이 보수 공사중이어서

17 다음 그림의 상황에 가장 적절한 대화를 고르시오.

①   ②   ③   ④   ⑤

18 다음을 듣고, 여자가 방과 후 요리 수업에 대해 언급하지 <u>않은</u> 것을 고르시오.

① 교사 이름   ② 수업 내용   ③ 준비물   ④ 수업 시간   ⑤ 모집 인원

[19~20] 대화를 듣고, 여자의 마지막 말에 이어질 남자의 말로 가장 적절한 것을 고르시오.

19 Man: _______________________________________

① Ask me anything.   ② I liked the food best.
③ The vacation was boring.   ④ I went to Seoul during the summer.
⑤ The best things are worth waiting for.

20 Man: _______________________________________

① Enjoy your trip to our city.   ② Okay, I'll buy the white one.
③ Yes, my favorite color is black.   ④ The fitting room is over there.
⑤ This T-shirt is too small for me.

Dictation Test 07

M2(17)_07_D

Dictation(받아쓰기)은 본문을 받아쓰면서 영어듣기의 집중력을 향상시키고 다양한 표현을 정리하기 위한 영어듣기 학습법입니다. **녹음을 다시 듣고, 빈칸에 알맞은 단어를 써 보세요.**
※Dictation의 정답은 듣기 대본의 밑줄 친 부분을 확인하세요.

정답 p. 30

맞은 개수 / 총133개

날씨파악–그림

1. 다음을 듣고, 토요일의 날씨로 가장 적절한 것을 고르시오.

① ② ③ ④ ⑤

01 W: Good morning. This is the weekly weather report. Starting on Monday, we'll see ________ ________ and beautiful sunshine for three days. On Thursday and Friday, it'll be ________ all day. On Saturday, there will be ________ ________, which will continue through Sunday. So, I'm afraid your weekend picnic will have to wait until next week. Have a great week, everyone!

그림정보파악

2. 대화를 듣고, 남자가 만든 표지판으로 가장 적절한 것을 고르시오.

①  ② 
③  ④ 
⑤ 

02 W: Tyler, what's this? Is this sign for you?

M: Yes, I made it to ________ ________ my car. I'm a beginner driver.

W: Oh, that's why you wrote "New Driver" in big letters in the center of the sign.

M: Yeah, I'm not used to driving yet.

W: I see. I like that you put a wing on ________ ________ of the word.

M: Thanks. I hope other drivers will be ________ with me.

W: Don't worry. Every driver knows what it is like to be a beginner on the road.

---

3. 대화를 듣고, 여자의 심정으로 가장 적절한 것을 고르시오.

① calm　　② happy
③ scared　　④ angry
⑤ disappointed

03
W: Honey, did you _________ the movie tickets?

M: No, not yet.

W: Oh, you need to hurry. I don't want to see a movie sitting right _________ _________ _________ the screen like last time.

M: Don't worry. I am buying the tickets on my smart phone right now.

W: Are there any seats left?

M: Yes. There are a few seats left. We can sit in row G.

W: _________ _________!

2025 영어듣기능력평가 1회 4번 변형

4. 대화를 듣고, 남자가 지난 주말에 한 일로 가장 적절한 것을 고르시오.

① 식당에 가기
② 부엌 청소하기
③ 생일 선물 사기
④ 케이크 주문하기
⑤ 베이킹 수업 듣기

04
W: Eric, why are you so busy in the kitchen?

M: I'm making a cake for my mom's birthday.

W: That's so sweet! Did you learn __________ __________ __________?

M: Yes. Last weekend, I took a baking class to __________ __________ for today.

W: Wow! That's really ____________ of you.

M: I hope she'll like it. It's my first homemade cake.

다음 페이지에 계속 ➡

5. 대화를 듣고, 두 사람이 대화하는 장소로 가장 적절한 곳을 고르시오.

① 사진관
② 극장 매표소
③ 학교 양호실
④ 영화 세트장
⑤ 옷 가게

05
W: Wow, this place looks so real!

M: You're right. It's amazing!

W: Hey, do you ____________ that school?

M: Oh, is that the setting of the movie, *Rising Youth*?

W: That's right! This is the very place that movie ________ ________.

M: Cool! Let's take some pictures.

W: Wait, there's a school uniform rental shop over there. Let's ____________ uniforms and then take pictures.

M: Sounds great!

6. 대화를 듣고, 여자의 마지막 말의 의도로 가장 적절한 것을 고르시오.

① 격려   ② 설득
③ 칭찬   ④ 동의
⑤ 충고

06
W: Hey, Greg. I heard you are going to be on a Science Quiz Show.

M: Oh, no. It ________ ________ ________ ________.

W: But, you are trying out, right?

M: Yes. I have to pass ________ ________ ________ first.

W: When you pass that, do I get to see you on TV?

M: On the show, yes.

W: When is the test?

M: Next week.

W: Well, good luck! ____________ ____________!

7. 대화를 듣고, 두 사람이 준비할 선물이 무엇인지 고르시오.

① 넥타이　　② 양말
③ 잠옷　　　④ 카드
⑤ 케이크

07

M: What are you going to buy for Daddy's birthday present?

W: I am ___________ _________. Do you have anything _________ _________?

M: How about a tie or a pair of socks?

W: Well, he _____________ has many of those.

M: How about pajamas?

W: Umm, I am not sure about his size.

M: Then, _________ _________ _________ ask Mom about his size?

W: That's a good idea.

할일파악(대화직후)

8. 대화를 듣고, 두 사람이 대화 직후에 할 일로 가장 적절한 것을 고르시오.

① 산책하기
② 식당에 가기
③ 피자 배달시키기
④ 전시회 관람하기
⑤ 보드 게임 구매하기

08

W: Wow, the exhibition was amazing!

M: What's the plan now, honey?

W: Let's ___________ some pizza at your favorite restaurant downtown.

M: That place is always crowded. Let's ___________ ___________ ___________ ___________ over the phone and eat at home instead.

W: Sure. Afterwards, why don't we play some board games?

M: Sounds like a plan! What kind of pizza do you want?

W: I want a pepperoni pizza. ___________ ___________ ___________ right now.

다음 페이지에 계속 ➡

9. 대화를 듣고, 두 사람이 복싱 체육관에 대해 언급하지 <u>않은</u> 것을 고르시오.

① 체육관 이름　② 초보자용 강좌
③ 수강료　　　④ 주말 강좌
⑤ 글러브 대여

09

W: Mark, where do you _________ _________ these days?

M: I work out at the Lucky Punch boxing gym. You should come work out there, too.

W: But I've never tried boxing before.

M: Don't worry. There are classes _________ _________ just like you.

W: Oh, do they also offer those classes _________ _________?

M: Of course. There are a lot of weekend classes.

W: Great! Do I need to buy boxing gloves right away?

M: Only if you want to. You can actually borrow them for free at the gym.

10. 다음을 듣고, 여자가 하는 말의 내용으로 가장 적절한 것을 고르시오.

① 도서관 이용수칙
② 과제물 제출 기한
③ 설문조사 참여 방법
④ 홈페이지 제작 과정
⑤ 온라인 수강신청 안내

10

W: Hello, students. Today, I'll tell you how to _________ in the survey for the new library for teenagers. First, _________ _________ _________ provided on our school website. It will lead you directly to the online survey. Second, _________ _________ _________ by clicking on the answers of your choice. They will be kept completely secret. Finally, _________ your answers online.

11. 대화를 듣고, balcony concert에 대한 내용으로 일치하지 <u>않는</u> 것을 고르시오.

① 오늘 공연이 예정되어 있다.
② 15명만 무대 앞에서 관람할 수 있다.
③ 3명의 연주자가 출연한다.
④ 1시간짜리 공연이다.
⑤ 오후 2시에 시작한다.

11

W: Look at this notice, Dad. There's a balcony concert in our apartment complex.

M: Oh, it's today. It's ___________ ________ allow people to listen from their own balconies.

W: Can't we watch from in front of the stage?

M: Yes, but only 15 people are ________ to watch from there.

W: It says a pianist and two violinists will play.

M: The concert ________ ________ an hour and a half. Do you want to go?

W: No, let's watch from our balcony. It starts at 2 p.m.

M: OK. Let's go home.

12. 대화를 듣고, 남자가 전화를 건 목적으로 가장 적절한 것을 고르시오.

① 음식을 주문하기 위해서
② 기차 표를 예약하기 위해서
③ 예약 시간을 변경하기 위해서
④ 구독 서비스를 해지하기 위해서
⑤ 에어컨 수리를 요청하기 위해서

12

(Telephone rings.)

W: Hello. Best Korean Restaurant. How may I help you?

M: Hi. I'd ________ ________ ________ my dinner reservation.

W: __________, sir. May I have your name?

M: Yes. Gordon Lee.

W: Okay. You __________ a table for two tonight at 6 p.m.

M: Right. Would it be possible to change my reservation to 8 p.m.?

W: Let me see. *(pause)* Yes, I can ________ that for you. Can I help you with anything else?

M: No, that's all. Thank you.

다음 페이지에 계속 ➡

13. 대화를 듣고, 여자가 받은 거스름돈으로 가장 적절한 것을 고르시오.

① $1   ② $2
③ $3   ④ $4
⑤ $5

13

M: Hi, would you like to order?

W: Yes. I would like this box of macaroons.

M: That's 15 dollars. Would you like ________ ________?

W: Ooh! Those egg tarts ________ ________. I'll have two of those.

M: Sure, they're 2 dollars each.

W: What is ________ ________ ________?

M: That'll be 19 dollars in total.

W: Here's 20 dollars.

M: Thank you. Here's your ________.

14. 대화를 듣고, 두 사람의 관계로 가장 적절한 것을 고르시오.

① 약사 – 손님
② 요리사 – 음식 평론가
③ 안내 데스크 직원 – 고객
④ 치과의사 – 환자
⑤ 수영강사 – 수강생

14

M: Good morning, Ms. Jackson. What can I do for you?

W: My ________ ________ hurts so badly.

M: Okay. Let's take a look at your tooth.

W: Oh, I'm scared. I'm always ________ ________ the dentist.

M: Take a deep ________ first.

W: Okay. I'm ready now.

M: If you're ready, open your mouth please.

15. 대화를 듣고, 여자가 남자에게 부탁한 일로 가장 적절한 것을 고르시오.

① 박람회에 함께 가기
② 웹사이트 주소 알려주기
③ 결혼식 참석하기
④ 입장권 교환하기
⑤ 게임 용품 사다 주기

15

W: Mark, are you going to the Game Fair this Saturday?

M: Yeah, I'm __________ __________ for the day. You're going as well, right?

W: I can't. I forgot my cousin's wedding is on that day.

M: But, you said you had already bought the ticket.

W: I did. So, could you __________ __________ __________ __________?

M: Sure! What is it?

W: Could you change my ticket for Sunday? You can only do it __________ __________.

M: Of course! No problem.

16. 대화를 듣고, 여자가 레스토랑을 예약하지 못한 이유로 가장 적절한 것을 고르시오.

① 예약이 다 차서
② 정기 휴무일이어서
③ 레스토랑이 폐업을 해서
④ 온라인 예약만 가능해서
⑤ 레스토랑이 보수 공사중이어서

16

W: Jaden, do you remember the Korean restaurant we went to last month?

M: Hmm… You mean the place that __________ Korean beef?

W: Yeah, I'm trying to make a dinner reservation, but they're not __________ __________ the phone.

M: Maybe they're __________ today.

W: Let me check their website. *(pause)* Oh, no!

M: What? Is something wrong?

W: It seems that the restaurant __________ __________ __________ __________ last week.

M: What? That's too bad.

다음 페이지에 계속 ➡

17. 다음 그림의 상황에 가장 적절한 대화를 고르시오.

① ②
③ ④
⑤

17

① W: Why are you up so early?

M: I have to go to the airport.

② W: How much is this umbrella?

M: I'm sorry, but it's __________ __________ __________ .

③ W: I think it's going to rain in the afternoon.

M: Okay, I'll __________ __________ __________ with me.

④ W: Can we make a snowman today?

M: Sure, __________ __________ your gloves first.

⑤ W: What sports do you like to watch?

M: I like watching football.

18. 다음을 듣고, 여자가 방과 후 요리 수업에 대해 언급하지 <u>않은</u> 것을 고르시오.

① 교사 이름 ② 수업 내용
③ 준비물 ④ 수업 시간
⑤ 모집 인원

18

W: Hello, students. Let me tell you about the new after-school cooking class. The teacher, Mrs. Jane Parker, is an _____________ cook. In the class, you'll learn __________ __________ __________ Italian food. The class will be on Tuesdays from 3 p.m. to 5 p.m. Only 10 students can __________ __________ __________ , so sign up soon!

19. 대화를 듣고, 여자의 마지막 말에 이어질 남자의 말로 가장 적절한 것을 고르시오.

Man: _______________

① Ask me anything.
② I liked the food best.
③ The vacation was boring.
④ I went to Seoul during the summer.
⑤ The best things are worth waiting for.

19

W: Hi, Kevin. How was your winter vacation?

M: Hi, Claire. It was great. I ________ ________ ________ ________ ________ Seoul with my parents.

W: Really? I'm going there next month!

M: Oh, you'll love it. I enjoyed it a lot.

W: I ________ ________ ________ about the city before I go on my trip.

M: Of course. Ask me anything.

W: What did you like the best?

M: I liked the food best.

2025 영어듣기능력평가 1회 20번 변형

20. 대화를 듣고, 여자의 마지막 말에 이어질 남자의 말로 가장 적절한 것을 고르시오.

Man: _______________

① Enjoy your trip to our city.
② Okay, I'll buy the white one.
③ Yes, my favorite color is black.
④ The fitting room is over there.
⑤ This T-shirt is too small for me.

20

M: Excuse me. What's the best-selling T-shirt in your store?

W: This black T-shirt with our city logo on it is __________ __________ __________.

M: I like the design. It's so __________.

W: It's __________ popular with tourists.

M: Do you have it in different colors?

W: Yes. We have it in white and gray.

M: I have many black and gray T-shirts.

W: Then you should try a different color.

M: Okay, I'll buy the white one.

07
회
딕
테
이
션

Words & Expressions Review 07

●다음 단어를 암기하세요.

문제	번호	단어	뜻
1	□ 1	bright	밝은
2	□ 2	be used to + 동명사	~하는 것에 익숙하다
	□ 3	patient	참을성 있는, 인내심 있는
3	□ 4	book	예약하다, 책
	□ 5	row	열, 줄
4	□ 6	bake	굽다, 구워지다
	□ 7	thoughtful	사려 깊은, 배려심 있는, 친절한
	□ 8	homemade	수제의, 손수 만든, 집에서 만든
5	□ 9	recognize	알아보다
	□ 10	setting	배경, 무대 장치
	□ 11	film	촬영하다, 찍다
6	□ 12	decide	결정하다
	□ 13	try out	시도하다
	□ 14	Fingers crossed!	행운을 빌어!
7	□ 15	have A in mind	A를 생각해두다
8	□ 16	exhibition	전시회
	□ 17	grab	(음식, 물건 등을) 빠르게 사다, 잡다
9	□ 18	work out	운동하다
	□ 19	offer	제공하다
	□ 20	participate in + 명사	~에 참여하다
10	□ 21	survey	설문조사
	□ 22	teenager	10대, 청소년

문제	번호	단어	뜻
10	□ 23	directly	바로, 즉시
	□ 24	submit	제출하다
	□ 25	notice	공지, 공고문
11	□ 26	complex	(건물) 단지, 복합 건물
	□ 27	be designed to + 동사	~하도록 고안되다
	□ 28	last	지속되다
12	□ 29	reservation	예약
	□ 30	arrange	조정하다, 해결하다
13	□ 31	order	주문하다
	□ 32	take a look at ~	~을 (한번) 보다
14	□ 33	be afraid of ~	~을 두려워하다
	□ 34	take a deep breath	심호흡하다
15	□ 35	save	(돈을) 모으다, 저축하다
	□ 36	on site	현장에서
16	□ 37	serve	(식당 등에서 음식을) 제공하다
	□ 38	go out of business	폐업하다
17	□ 39	not for sale	판매하지 않는, 비매품
18	□ 40	experienced	능숙한, 경력 있는
	□ 41	sign up	등록하다, 신청하다
19	□ 42	go on a trip	여행을 가다
	□ 43	worth -ing	~할 가치가 있는
20	□ 44	especially	특히

● 왼쪽 단어장의 뜻이 보이지 않게 반으로 접고, 학습한 단어의 뜻을 아래 빈칸에 적어주세요.

1	homemade		23	film
2	bright		24	Fingers crossed!
3	notice		25	directly
4	grab		26	be used to + 동명사
5	save		27	last
6	take a deep breath		28	bake
7	offer		29	thoughtful
8	decide		30	especially
9	submit		31	reservation
10	setting		32	order
11	work out		33	complex
12	worth -ing		34	try out
13	not for sale		35	row
14	experienced		36	sign up
15	teenager		37	have A in mind
16	participate in + 명사		38	be afraid of ~
17	recognize		39	survey
18	go on a trip		40	serve
19	exhibition		41	be designed to + 동사
20	arrange		42	book
21	take a look at ~		43	patient
22	on site		44	go out of business

08회 중학영어듣기 모의고사

M2(17)_08_US
모두 **미국식 발음(US)** 으로 녹음

M2(17)_08_UK
20문제 중 5문제에 **영국식 발음 (US+UK)**을 포함하여 녹음

정답 및 해석 p. 35

1 다음을 듣고, 금요일의 날씨로 가장 적절한 것을 고르시오.

① 　② 　③ 　④ 　⑤ 

2 대화를 듣고, 남자가 구입할 손목시계로 가장 적절한 것을 고르시오.

① 　② 　③ 　④ 　⑤ 

3 대화를 듣고, 남자의 심정으로 가장 적절한 것을 고르시오.

① shy　② proud　③ bored　④ pleased　⑤ upset

4 대화를 듣고, 여자가 오늘 한 일로 가장 적절한 것을 고르시오.

① 마당 청소하기　② 학교 숙제하기　③ 병원 방문하기
④ 개 사료 구입하기　⑤ 강아지 목욕 시키기

5 대화를 듣고, 두 사람의 대화가 이루어지는 장소로 적절한 것을 고르시오.

① 대사관　　　② 공항　　　③ 음식점　　　④ 호텔　　　⑤ 기차역

6 대화를 듣고, 여자의 마지막 말의 의도로 가장 적절한 것을 고르시오.

① 감사　　　② 불평　　　③ 공감　　　④ 제안　　　⑤ 충고

7 대화를 듣고, 남자가 신청할 수업으로 가장 적절한 것을 고르시오.

① 수영　　　② 요가　　　③ 볼링　　　④ 탁구　　　⑤ 테니스

8 대화를 듣고, 남자가 대화 직후에 할 일로 가장 적절한 것을 고르시오.

① 옷 가게 방문하기　　　② 미술 과제 제출하기　　　③ 회의록 작성하기
④ 카메라 찾아보기　　　⑤ 웹사이트 검색하기

9 대화를 듣고, 여자가 Jenny's Steak House에 대해 언급하지 <u>않은</u> 것을 고르시오.

① 영업 마감 시간　　　② 식당 위치　　　③ 주차장
④ 예약 가능 여부　　　⑤ 생일 할인 혜택

10 다음을 듣고, 여자가 하는 말의 내용으로 가장 적절한 것을 고르시오.

① 도로 공사 안내　　　　　　② 스쿨존 운전 수칙
③ 횡단보도 안전 수칙　　　　④ 자동차 자가 진단법
⑤ 운전면허시험 응시 안내

11번~20번 문제는 다음 페이지에 ➡

11 대화를 듣고, 주말 체육의 날에 관한 정보로 일치하지 <u>않는</u> 것을 고르시오.

① 토요일마다 운영한다.　　　　② 볼링과 골프 수업이 있다.
③ 초보자를 대상으로 한다.　　　④ 온라인으로 접수해야 한다.
⑤ 수강료는 15달러이다.

12 대화를 듣고, 남자가 전화를 건 목적으로 가장 적절한 것을 고르시오.

① 재검진을 받기 위해서　　　　② 진료 예약을 하기 위해서
③ 예약 시간을 변경하기 위해서　④ 분실물에 대해 문의하기 위해서
⑤ 진료 가능 시간을 물어보기 위해서

13 대화를 듣고, 두 사람이 만날 시각을 고르시오.

① 1:00 p.m.　　② 1:30 p.m.　　③ 2:00 p.m.　　④ 2:30 p.m.　　⑤ 3:00 p.m.

14 대화를 듣고, 두 사람의 관계로 적절한 것을 고르시오.

① 서점 직원 — 손님　　② 계산원 — 손님　　③ 학교 직원 — 선생님
④ 도서관 사서 — 학생　　⑤ 과학 선생님 — 학생

15 대화를 듣고, 여자가 남자에게 부탁한 일로 가장 적절한 것을 고르시오.

① 출석 체크하기　　　　　② 가정 통신문 배부하기
③ 체육대회 응원 준비하기　④ 반 친구들 이름표 나눠주기
⑤ 시간표 변경 내용 전달하기

16 대화를 듣고, 남자가 안경을 새로 맞춘 이유로 가장 적절한 것을 고르시오.

① 안경이 낡아서　　　　　　② 안경이 자꾸 흘러내려서
③ 렌즈 도수가 맞지 않아서　　④ 머리 모양과 어울리지 않아서
⑤ 컴퓨터 작업할 때 쓸 안경이 필요해서

17 다음 그림의 상황에 가장 적절한 대화를 고르시오.

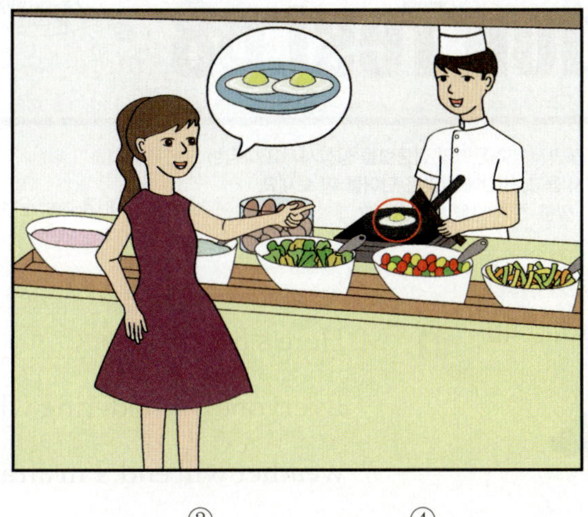

①   ②   ③   ④   ⑤

18 다음을 듣고, 여자가 전시회에 대해 언급하지 <u>않은</u> 것을 고르시오.

① 화가 이름   ② 전시 기간   ③ 관람 시간   ④ 티켓 가격   ⑤ 티켓 할인

[19~20] 대화를 듣고, 남자의 마지막 말에 이어질 여자의 말로 가장 적절한 것을 고르시오.

19 Woman: ________________________________

① The documentary was worth watching.
② Brush your teeth after every meal.
③ Choose water over sugary drinks.
④ Earth's surface is mostly water.
⑤ Shorten your shower time.

20 Woman: ________________________________

① Oh, your bag is so dirty.
② Oh, I see. I'll keep that in mind.
③ Have you ever tried Indian food?
④ How often do you wash your hands?
⑤ My hotel room has a large bathroom.

Dictation Test 08

M2(17)_08_D

Dictation(받아쓰기)은 본문을 받아쓰면서 영어듣기의 집중력을 향상시키고 다양한 표현을 정리하기 위한 영어듣기 학습법입니다. **녹음을 다시 듣고, 빈칸에 알맞은 단어를 써 보세요.**

※Dictation의 정답은 듣기 대본의 밑줄 친 부분을 확인하세요.

정답 p. 35

맞은 개수 / 총151개

 날씨파악-그림

1. 다음을 듣고, 금요일의 날씨로 가장 적절한 것을 고르시오.

①  ② 

③  ④ 

⑤ 

01 M: Here's this week's ＿＿＿＿ ＿＿＿＿. Everyone's wondering when this freezing weather will end. I'm afraid the snow ＿＿＿＿ ＿＿＿＿ until Tuesday. On Wednesday, the temperature will be very low, but it will be sunny. On Thursday, we will have rain ＿＿＿＿ ＿＿＿＿ snow, as the temperature will finally go up. This rain will continue for two days, before it starts snowing again on Saturday. On Sunday, it will be cloudy.

그림정보파악

2. 대화를 듣고, 남자가 구입할 손목시계로 가장 적절한 것을 고르시오.

①  ② 

③  ④ 

⑤ 

02 W: How may I help you?

M: I'm ＿＿＿＿ ＿＿＿＿ a watch.

W: How about this square one?

M: No, I think ＿＿＿＿ ＿＿＿＿ look fancier.

W: Then, what about this digital watch?

M: Well, I wish it had hour and minute ＿＿＿＿ along with digital numbers.

W: Then, you might like this one with both digital and analog ＿＿＿＿.

M: It looks great! I'll take it.

---

3. 대화를 듣고, 남자의 심정으로 가장 적절한 것을 고르시오.
① shy   ② proud
③ bored   ④ pleased
⑤ upset

03
M: Shannon, I can't go to the park with you today.

W: Why not?

M: I don't have my bike. Somebody _________

_________.

W: Oh, no! I'm so sorry to hear that, Jake.

M: I can't believe it. I thought our ____________

_________ _________.

W: Me, too. You got the bike from your parents, right?

M: Yeah, I really don't know _________ _________

_________ _________.

W: Cheer up. They'll understand.

4. 대화를 듣고, 여자가 오늘 한 일로 가장 적절한 것을 고르시오.
① 마당 청소하기
② 학교 숙제하기
③ 병원 방문하기
④ 개 사료 구입하기
⑤ 강아지 목욕 시키기

04
M: Hi, Mina. You look happy. What's up?

W: _________ _________! My parents finally got me a
puppy!

M: Great! I know that _________ _________ _________ a
dog.

W: Yeah, I've got a lot to prepare, though. I actually
visited the pet shop a minute ago.

M: What did you do there?

W: I bought some dog food.

M: Oh, I see. I want to see your dog.

W: Come over to my place on Saturday!

M: OK. _________ _________ _________.

다음 페이지에 계속 ➡

5. 대화를 듣고, 두 사람의 대화가 이루어지는 장소로 적절한 것을 고르시오.

① 대사관   ② 공항
③ 음식점   ④ 호텔
⑤ 기차역

05
W: How can I help you?

M: I'd like to check in for ________ ________.

W: May I see your passport, please?

M: Here it is.

W: We have only an ________ ________ left. Would this be OK?

M: Sure. No problem.

6. 대화를 듣고, 여자의 마지막 말의 의도로 가장 적절한 것을 고르시오.

① 감사   ② 불평
③ 공감   ④ 제안
⑤ 충고

06
W: Hey, Jeff. Can I share something that's been __________ __________?

M: Of course, what's up?

W: Being the older sister sucks. I'm always __________ __________ __________ my little brother's demands.

M: That sounds really annoying. What happened?

W: Today, I wanted to watch my show, but he __________ __________ playing his game, so I gave up.

M: It seems like you're always putting his wants first.

W: Exactly! It's just too much for me.

특정정보파악

7. 대화를 듣고, 남자가 신청할 수업으로 가장 적절한 것을 고르시오.
① 수영　② 요가
③ 볼링　④ 탁구
⑤ 테니스

07

W: Liam, what are you doing?

M: I'm ___________ __________ sports programs on the cultural complex center's website.

W: I took a swimming class there last summer and it was really good. Are you going to __________ __________ for a class?

M: Yes, I'm thinking of taking either tennis or bowling.

W: Oh, I'm interested in tennis. __________ __________ __________ take the tennis class together?

M: That would be great!

할일파악(대화직후)

8. 대화를 듣고, 남자가 대화 직후에 할 일로 가장 적절한 것을 고르시오.
① 옷 가게 방문하기
② 미술 과제 제출하기
③ 회의록 작성하기
④ 카메라 찾아보기
⑤ 웹사이트 검색하기

08

W: Our school sports day is coming soon.

M: Right. What should we do to _______ for it?

W: We need to _______ _______ a design for our class T-shirts.

M: Let's discuss it at our class meeting tomorrow.

W: Sure, but I think we should show some sample designs to our classmates.

M: Good idea. Let's pick some designs _______ _______ _______.

W: Then, can you find me some websites where we can buy the T-shirts?

M: No problem. I'll _______ _______ _______ right away.

다음 페이지에 계속 ➡

9. 대화를 듣고, 여자가 Jenny's Steak House에 대해 언급하지 <u>않은</u> 것을 고르시오.

① 영업 마감 시간
② 식당 위치
③ 주차장
④ 예약 가능 여부
⑤ 생일 할인 혜택

09 *(Telephone rings.)*

W: Hello, Jenny's Steak House. How may I help you?

M: Hello, what time do you close today?

W: We ________ ________ 11 p.m.

M: I see. Where is the restaurant ________ ________?

W: It's on the second floor of the Madison Building.

M: Is there a parking lot nearby?

W: Yes, there's an underground parking lot in the same building.

M: Thanks. Do you have ________ ________ ________ ________?

W: If you present your ID, you'll get a 30 percent discount.

10. 다음을 듣고, 여자가 하는 말의 내용으로 가장 적절한 것을 고르시오.

① 도로 공사 안내
② 스쿨존 운전 수칙
③ 횡단보도 안전 수칙
④ 자동차 자가 진단법
⑤ 운전면허시험 응시 안내

10 W: Hello, Drivers Radio listeners. Today I am going to talk about how to drive safely in a ________ ________. First, reduce your speed when you drive through a school zone. The speed limit is 30km/h. Second, stop and wait at crosswalks even if you don't see anyone ________ ________ ________. Finally, stopping and parking in a school zone is ________ ________.

11. 대화를 듣고, 주말 체육의 날에 관한 정보로 일치하지 <u>않는</u> 것을 고르시오.

① 토요일마다 운영한다.
② 볼링과 골프 수업이 있다.
③ 초보자를 대상으로 한다.
④ 온라인으로 접수해야 한다.
⑤ 수강료는 15달러이다.

11

M: Julie, your school newsletter says _________ _________ a Weekend Sports Day.

W: Yes, Dad. We can enjoy sports _________ _____________.

M: You can choose from bowling and golf.

W: Those are both for beginners. I know how to bowl, so I'll take golf class.

M: Good choice! You need to _________ _________.

W: How much does it cost to take a program?

M: It's only $10 for 15 weeks.

W: Wow! I'll sign up right away.

12. 대화를 듣고, 남자가 전화를 건 목적으로 가장 적절한 것을 고르시오.

① 재검진을 받기 위해서
② 진료 예약을 하기 위해서
③ 예약 시간을 변경하기 위해서
④ 분실물에 대해 문의하기 위해서
⑤ 진료 가능 시간을 물어보기 위해서

12

(Telephone rings.)

W: Doctor's office. How may I help you?

M: I'm Max Parsons. I had an _____________ _________ Dr. Brown yesterday.

W: Hello, Mr. Parsons. Are you not _________ _________ again?

M: No, I'm fine, but I think I left my jacket in the waiting room yesterday.

W: Oh, yes. We found a jacket that had been _________ _________.

M: Does it happen to be a leather jacket?

W: Yes. Feel free to come pick it up _________ _________ _________.

다음 페이지에 계속 ➡

13. 대화를 듣고, 두 사람이 만날 시각을 고르시오.

① 1:00 p.m.   ② 1:30 p.m.
③ 2:00 p.m.   ④ 2:30 p.m.
⑤ 3:00 p.m.

13

W: I'm so excited for the e-sports __________ __________ this Sunday!

M: Me, too! It starts at 3 p.m., right?

W: Yes, how about we meet at 2 p.m.?

M: You know what? There are __________ __________ we can visit before the match. Let's __________ __________ than that.

W: Then, how about 1:30 p.m.?

M: If the match is long, we'll get hungry. Let's meet at 1 p.m. and __________ __________ together first.

W: Sounds good.

---

14. 대화를 듣고, 두 사람의 관계로 적절한 것을 고르시오.

① 서점 직원 — 손님
② 계산원 — 손님
③ 학교 직원 — 선생님
④ 도서관 사서 — 학생
⑤ 과학 선생님 — 학생

14

W: How can I help you today?

M: I'm __________ __________ __________ __________ on thunderstorms and lightning.

W: Do you have a particular title in mind?

M: No, not really. I just need to know how thunderstorms create lightning.

W: Well, we have __________ __________ __________ about weather in the Science section.

M: That's great. Thank you so much!

W: Wait, you have to leave your bag before you enter and show __________ __________ __________.

M: Oops. Sorry. I almost forgot.

부탁(요청)한일파악

15. 대화를 듣고, 여자가 남자에게 부탁한 일로 가장 적절한 것을 고르시오.

① 출석 체크하기
② 가정 통신문 배부하기
③ 체육대회 응원 준비하기
④ 반 친구들 이름표 나눠주기
⑤ 시간표 변경 내용 전달하기

15

M: Hello, Ms. Lee.

W: Hi, Minho. I ___________ __________ __________ call you. Can I ask a ___________ __________?

M: Sure. What is it?

W: Tomorrow's __________ has changed. The second and third periods will __________ __________.

M: Oh, I see.

W: Could you ___________ __________ in our class group chat so everyone knows?

M: Of course. I'll do it right away.

이유파악

16. 대화를 듣고, 남자가 안경을 새로 맞춘 이유로 가장 적절한 것을 고르시오.

① 안경이 낡아서
② 안경이 자꾸 흘러내려서
③ 렌즈 도수가 맞지 않아서
④ 머리 모양과 어울리지 않아서
⑤ 컴퓨터 작업할 때 쓸 안경이 필요해서

16

W: Mike, you look different today.

M: Maybe it's because I got a haircut yesterday.

W: Yeah, but I think something else __________ __________ as well.

M: Oh, I got a new pair of glasses.

W: Ah, that's it. Why did you change your glasses?

M: I had to, because they __________ __________ me all the time.

W: Your glasses? What was the problem?

M: They kept __________ __________.

다음 페이지에 계속 ➡

17. 다음 그림의 상황에 가장 적절한 대화를 고르시오.

①   ②

③   ④

⑤

17

① M: Do you need anything else?

    W: Yes, can I have some napkins, please?

② M: Have you finished all your food?

    W: Yes, that was __________. Thank you.

③ M: How do you want your eggs?

    W: Two eggs ________ ________ ________, please.

④ M: Would you like to see a dessert menu?

    W: No, thanks. ________ ________.

⑤ M: There will be a bit of a wait. We have a lot of orders.

    W: That's okay. I'll wait.

18. 다음을 듣고, 여자가 전시회에 대해 언급하지 <u>않은</u> 것을 고르시오.

① 화가 이름   ② 전시 기간
③ 관람 시간   ④ 티켓 가격
⑤ 티켓 할인

18

W: Welcome to the Modern Art Gallery. I'd like to invite you to a ________ __________ of paintings by the famous artist, Hillary Palmer. The exhibition will ________ ________ ________ 3 weeks starting today. Tickets are 10 dollars each. If you're a student, you can get a 20% ________. Don't miss this great __________ to see the world-class artworks in person.

19. 대화를 듣고, 남자의 마지막 말에 이어질 여자의 말로 가장 적절한 것을 고르시오.

Woman: _______________

① The documentary was worth watching.
② Brush your teeth after every meal.
③ Choose water over sugary drinks.
④ Earth's surface is mostly water.
⑤ Shorten your shower time.

19

M: What did you do yesterday?

W: I saw a documentary about ________ ________ yesterday.

M: Oh, I think it's important to ________ ________ the water on our planet.

W: Yes. I learned that we can save water in many ways.

M: What ways?

W: First, ________ ________ the water while you brush your teeth.

M: Well, that ________ ________ ________. What else?

W: Shorten your shower time.

20. 대화를 듣고, 남자의 마지막 말에 이어질 여자의 말로 가장 적절한 것을 고르시오.

Woman: _______________

① Oh, your bag is so dirty.
② Oh, I see. I'll keep that in mind.
③ Have you ever tried Indian food?
④ How often do you wash your hands?
⑤ My hotel room has a large bathroom.

20

W: I'm going to India next month. I heard you ________ ________ ________. Can you give me some ________?

M: Sure. There are some ________ ________ that you should know about.

W: Can you tell me one that is important?

M: Okay. You should use your right hand when you eat a meal.

W: Really? My right hand? But I'm ________-________.

M: They use the left hand in the bathroom. So they think the left hand is ________.

W: Oh, I see. I'll keep that in mind.

Words & Expressions Review 08

● 다음 단어를 암기하세요.

문제	번호	단어	뜻
1	1	wonder	궁금해하다
	2	temperature	기온, 온도
2	3	fancy	근사한
	4	hand	(시계) 바늘, (시/분/초) 침
3	5	steal	훔치다, 도둑질하다
	6	neighborhood	동네, 이웃 사람들
4	7	prepare	준비하다
	8	actually	사실은, 실제로
5	9	check in	탑승 수속을 밟다
	10	passport	여권
	11	aisle seat	통로 쪽 좌석
6	12	share	공유하다
	13	bug	괴롭히다
	14	demand	요구
7	15	look through	살펴보다, 훑어보다
	16	cultural	문화와 관련된, 문화의
	17	either A or B	A이거나 B
8	18	discuss	토의하다, 토론하다
9	19	exactly	정확히
	20	present	제시하다
10	21	reduce	줄이다, 감소하다
	22	limit	제한, 한계

문제	번호	단어	뜻
11	23	register	등록하다
	24	sign up	등록하다
12	25	appointment	예약, 약속
	26	leave behind	두고 가다, 남겨 두다
13	27	booth	부스
	28	visit	방문하다
14	29	thunderstorm	뇌우
	30	section	부문, 부분, 구역
15	31	favor	부탁, 호의
16	32	as well	또한
	33	annoy	짜증 나게 하다
17	34	a bit of	약간의
	35	discount	할인
18	36	opportunity	기회
	37	world-class	세계적인, 세계 최상급의
	38	care for	관심을 가지다, 돌보다
19	39	turn off	잠그다, 끄다
	40	shorten	단축하다, 짧게 하다
	41	advice	조언, 충고
20	42	cultural difference	문화적 차이
	43	left-handed	왼손잡이의
	44	keep in mind	명심하다

● 왼쪽 단어장의 뜻이 보이지 않게 반으로 접고, 학습한 단어의 뜻을 아래 빈칸에 적어주세요.

1	steal		23	demand
2	left-handed		24	temperature
3	shorten		25	as well
4	cultural difference		26	passport
5	present		27	a bit of
6	bug		28	neighborhood
7	wonder		29	aisle seat
8	look through		30	share
9	hand		31	leave behind
10	favor		32	fancy
11	prepare		33	visit
12	actually		34	thunderstorm
13	reduce		35	world-class
14	cultural		36	advice
15	discuss		37	booth
16	register		38	opportunity
17	section		39	care for
18	discount		40	check in
19	either A or B		41	keep in mind
20	turn off		42	appointment
21	exactly		43	annoy
22	sign up		44	limit

09회 중학영어듣기 모의고사

M2(17)_09_US
모두 **미국식 발음(US)**
으로 녹음

M2(17)_09_UK
20문제 중 5문제에 **영국식 발음**
(US+UK)을 포함하여 녹음

정답 및 해석 p. 40

1 다음을 듣고, 런던의 날씨로 가장 적절한 것을 고르시오.

①  ②  ③ 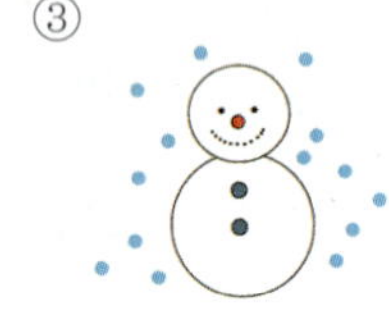 ④  ⑤ 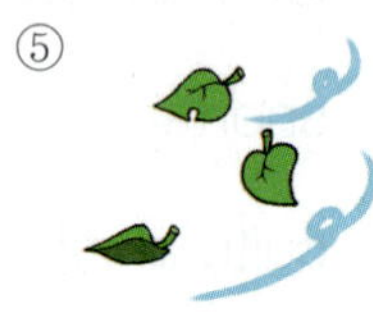

2 대화를 듣고, 여자가 구입한 가방으로 가장 적절한 것을 고르시오.

①  ②  ③  ④  ⑤ 

3 대화를 듣고, 여자의 심정으로 가장 적절한 것을 고르시오.

① 지루함　　② 침착함　　③ 걱정스러움　　④ 놀람　　⑤ 슬픔

4 대화를 듣고, 여자가 발표 준비에서 맡은 일로 가장 적절한 것을 고르시오.

① PPT 만들기　　② 사진 촬영하기　　③ 영상 편집하기
④ 발표 대본 쓰기　　⑤ 자료 조사하기

5 대화를 듣고, 두 사람이 대화하는 장소로 가장 적절한 곳을 고르시오.

① 체육관 ② 문구점 ③ 캠핑용품 판매점
④ 자전거 대여소 ⑤ 분실물센터

6 대화를 듣고, 여자의 마지막 말의 의도로 가장 적절한 것을 고르시오.

① 칭찬 ② 격려 ③ 승낙 ④ 거절 ⑤ 꾸중

7 대화를 듣고, 남자가 가져온 음식으로 가장 적절한 것을 고르시오.

① 김밥 ② 핫도그 ③ 컵라면
④ 샐러드 ⑤ 햄버거

8 대화를 듣고, 남자가 대화 직후 할 일로 가장 적절한 것을 고르시오.

① 농구 경기 보기 ② 참가 신청서 내기 ③ 구인 포스터 만들기
④ 학교 홈페이지 살펴보기 ⑤ 체육 선생님께 여쭤보기

9 대화를 듣고, 두 사람이 만화책에 대해 언급하지 <u>않은</u> 것을 고르시오.

① 제목 ② 장르 ③ 주인공 이름 ④ 판매 부수 ⑤ 작가

10 다음을 듣고, 여자가 하는 말의 내용으로 가장 적절한 것을 고르시오.

① 대회 참가자 모집 ② 운동 경기 소개 ③ 행사 일정 안내
④ 동아리 가입 홍보 ⑤ 학교 축제 공고

11번~20번 문제는 다음 페이지에 ➡

11 대화를 듣고, Night with Stars Event에 대한 내용과 일치하지 <u>않는</u> 것을 고르시오.

① 이번 주 금요일에 개최된다.　② 학교 운동장에서 열린다.

③ 밤 9시에 시작된다.　④ 담요 대여료가 있다.

⑤ 사전 신청을 해야 참여 가능하다.

12 대화를 듣고, 여자가 도서관을 방문한 이유로 가장 적절한 것을 고르시오.

① 책을 예약하려고　② 책을 반납하려고

③ 반납일을 연장하려고　④ 주문한 책이 도착했는지 확인하려고

⑤ 대여도서 분실을 알리려고

13 대화를 듣고, 여자가 받을 거스름돈으로 가장 적절한 것을 고르시오.

① \$2　② \$3　③ \$4　④ \$5　⑤ \$6

14 대화를 듣고, 두 사람의 관계로 가장 적절한 것을 고르시오.

① 미술관 직원 – 화가　② 사진 작가 – 모델　③ 제빵사 – 손님

④ 웨딩플래너 – 고객　⑤ 컴퓨터 수리기사 – 고객

15 대화를 듣고, 여자가 남자에게 부탁한 일로 가장 적절한 것을 고르시오.

① 숙제 제출해주기　② 수학 숙제 도와주기　③ 과학 실험 도와주기

④ 교무실 위치 알려주기　⑤ 수학 선생님 모셔오기

16 대화를 듣고, 남자가 마라톤에 참가할 수 <u>없는</u> 이유로 가장 적절한 것을 고르시오.

① 달리기를 잘하지 못해서　② 참가 신청 기간을 놓쳐서　③ 다른 일정이 있어서

④ 발목을 다쳐서　⑤ 일이 바빠서

17 다음 그림의 상황에 가장 적절한 대화를 고르시오.

①   ②   ③   ④   ⑤

18 다음을 듣고, 여자가 학교 도서관에 대해 언급하지 <u>않은</u> 것을 고르시오.

① 도서 대여 방법   ② 대여 가능 권수   ③ 도서 반납 기한
④ 운영 시간   ⑤ 위치

[19~20] 대화를 듣고, 남자의 마지막 말에 이어질 여자의 말로 가장 적절한 것을 고르시오.

19 Woman: _______________________________________

① I'll buy the guitar right away.   ② I will try not to miss your class.
③ I take lessons three times a week.   ④ I go to piano class every weekend.
⑤ You should listen to music more often.

20 Woman: _______________________________________

① I like comedies.   ② I prefer taking a taxi.
③ Since last Wednesday.   ④ How about in the afternoon?
⑤ Let's meet in front of the school.

Dictation Test 09

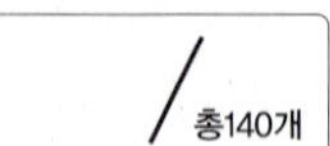

M2(17)_09_D

Dictation(받아쓰기)은 본문을 받아쓰면서 영어듣기의 집중력을 향상시키고 다양한 표현을 정리하기 위한 영어듣기 학습법입니다. **녹음을 다시 듣고, 빈칸에 알맞은 단어를 써 보세요.**
※Dictation의 정답은 듣기 대본의 밑줄 친 부분을 확인하세요.

📖 정답 p. 40

✍ 맞은 개수　／총140개

날씨파악-그림

1. 다음을 듣고, 런던의 날씨로 가장 적절한 것을 고르시오.

① 　②

③ 　④

⑤

01 M: Good morning. Here is today's world weather forecast. In New York, there will be some strong winds, so be ＿＿＿＿＿＿＿＿ for it when you go outside. Shanghai will see some sunshine after many days of cloudy weather. In London, there will be ＿＿＿＿＿＿＿＿ ＿＿＿＿＿＿＿＿, so be careful of the ＿＿＿＿＿＿＿＿ ＿＿＿＿＿＿. Thank you.

그림정보파악

2. 대화를 듣고, 여자가 구입한 가방으로 가장 적절한 것을 고르시오.

① 　② 

③ 　④

⑤

02 M: Sally, you ＿＿＿＿＿＿＿＿ a new bag.

W: Yes, I did. What do you think of it?

M: It's nice. I ＿＿＿＿＿＿ like the pockets.

W: They are good for ＿＿＿＿ ＿＿＿＿ ＿＿＿＿. How about the butterfly?

M: I like it, too. You like butterflies, don't you?

W: Yes, I do.

심정추론

3. 대화를 듣고, 여자의 심정으로 가장 적절한 것을 고르시오.
① 지루함　　② 침착함
③ 걱정스러움　　④ 놀람
⑤ 슬픔

03
M: Hey Sarah, did you see the school writing contest results?

W: I thought the results would be announced next week. Are they out already?

M: Yes! And you ___________ ___________ ___________ with your story about friendship!

W: What? Really? I can't believe it!

M: I just saw the list. Your name is ___________ ___________ ___________.

W: Wow! I never thought I would win! This is amazing!

한일파악

4. 대화를 듣고, 여자가 발표 준비에서 맡은 일로 가장 적절한 것을 고르시오.
① PPT 만들기
② 사진 촬영하기
③ 영상 편집하기
④ 발표 대본 쓰기
⑤ 자료 조사하기

04
W: Justin, how did you like my group's presentation on Korean culture?

M: I thought it was a very ________-________ -__________ presentation. Great job!

W: You really think so?

M: Yes. I thought your PowerPoint slides were very ________ ________.

W: Right? Jane did a great job on them.

M: Also, whoever did the research really ________ ________ ________ into it.

W: That was me!

M: Really? You are such a ________ ________.

다음 페이지에 계속 ➡

5. 대화를 듣고, 두 사람이 대화하는 장소로 가장 적절한 곳을 고르시오.

① 체육관
② 문구점
③ 캠핑용품 판매점
④ 자전거 대여소
⑤ 분실물센터

05

M: May I help you?

W: Hi. I'd like two bicycles for adults, please.

M: Sure. How long would you like to ________ them for?

W: Just for an hour. How much is it?

M: It's 6 dollars in total and you need to ________ your ID card here.

W: Here you are. Do I get it back when I ________ the bicycles?

M: That's right. Take these tickets downstairs and you'll get your bicycles there.

W: Thanks.

6. 대화를 듣고, 여자의 마지막 말의 의도로 가장 적절한 것을 고르시오.

① 칭찬　　② 격려
③ 승낙　　④ 거절
⑤ 꾸중

06

W: Nick, did you ask Alice to see a movie ________ ________ this weekend?

M: No, I didn't.

W: Why not? You ________ her yesterday, didn't you?

M: Yes. But I was ________ she might say no.

W: Don't worry. I think she likes you.

M: Do you really ________ ________?

W: Sure. Go and ask her now.

7. 대화를 듣고, 남자가 가져온 음식으로 가장 적절한 것을 고르시오.

① 김밥 ② 핫도그
③ 컵라면 ④ 샐러드
⑤ 햄버거

07

M: Sujin, what are you having for lunch today?

W: I bought some gimbap __________ __________ __________ to work this morning.

M: Will that be enough?

W: No, that's why I also bought cup noodles. What are you having?

M: I'm __________ __________ __________ with shrimp and avocado.

W: Wow, that sounds delicious! Where did you buy it?

M: I made it at home. It's really simple to make.

W: It sounds __________ __________ than my lunch!

8. 대화를 듣고, 남자가 대화 직후 할 일로 가장 적절한 것을 고르시오.

① 농구 경기 보기
② 참가 신청서 내기
③ 구인 포스터 만들기
④ 학교 홈페이지 살펴보기
⑤ 체육 선생님께 여쭤보기

08

W: Did you hear the news? The basketball team __________ __________ __________ players.

M: Yes, I heard about it. I'm so excited. You know how much I've wanted to join the team.

W: Yeah. You are the first one __________ I thought of when I heard the news.

M: Do you know how I can __________ __________?

W: Maybe you can check the school website.

M: Oh, I can't wait. I __________ __________ our gym teacher about it right now.

다음 페이지에 계속 ➡

9. 대화를 듣고, 두 사람이 만화책에 대해 언급하지 <u>않은</u> 것을 고르시오.
   ① 제목　　　　② 장르
   ③ 주인공 이름　④ 판매 부수
   ⑤ 작가

09

M: Hey, Suzy. Do you read any comic books?

W: Yeah. My favorite comic book is *The Thunder: Storm is Coming.*

M: Oh, I know that one. That is an action comic book, right?

W: Yes, that's right. The main character fights bad guys and saves the city.

M: Was the main character ________ Storm?

W: Yeah! He is ________ ________ ________ character!

M: By the way, who is ________ ________ of this comic book?

W: It's by Andrew River. You should read some of ________ ________.

M: Okay, I will.

10. 다음을 듣고, 여자가 하는 말의 내용으로 가장 적절한 것을 고르시오.
   ① 대회 참가자 모집
   ② 운동 경기 소개
   ③ 행사 일정 안내
   ④ 동아리 가입 홍보
   ⑤ 학교 축제 공고

10

W: Good morning, everyone! The school cheerleading team ________ ________ ________ talented new members. You can learn a variety of skills on our team. We attend all our school's games. And, we ________ ________ ________ last year in a cheerleading competition. You can join ________ ________ your name on the notice board. We will contact you for a tryout and interview.

11. 대화를 듣고, Night with Stars Event에 대한 내용과 일치하지 <u>않는</u> 것을 고르시오.
   ① 이번 주 금요일에 개최된다.
   ② 학교 운동장에서 열린다.
   ③ 밤 9시에 시작된다.
   ④ 담요 대여료가 있다.
   ⑤ 사전 신청을 해야 참여 가능하다.

11

W: Dustin, do you know ________ ________ the Night with Stars Event?

M: Yeah. It's a popular school event. It's this Friday.

W: I heard it will ________ ________ on the school playground.

M: Right. Let's go together. It ________ at 9 p.m.

W: Great. It will be cold, so we should bring a blanket.

M: We don't have to. Blankets are available ________ ________.

W: Great! Do we need to sign up?

M: Yes. Only students who sign up ________ ________ can come.

W: I see.

12. 대화를 듣고, 여자가 도서관을 방문한 이유로 가장 적절한 것을 고르시오.
   ① 책을 예약하려고
   ② 책을 반납하려고
   ③ 반납일을 연장하려고
   ④ 주문한 책이 도착했는지 확인하려고
   ⑤ 대여도서 분실을 알리려고

12

M: Hello. How may I help you?

W: I borrowed a book ________ ________ ________, and there's a problem.

M: Can I first have your name and membership number?

W: It's Jina Park and the number is 3342-7645.

M: OK, you borrowed *The Ten Steps* on July 10.

W: That's right. And it seems ________ ________ ________.

M: I see. If ________ ________ it, you must purchase the same book for us.

W: OK, I'll do that as soon as possible.

다음 페이지에 계속 ➡

수치계산(거스름돈)

13. 대화를 듣고, 여자가 받을 거스름돈으로 가장 적절한 것을 고르시오.

① $2 ② $3
③ $4 ④ $5
⑤ $6

13

M: Welcome to Mega Art Supply! What can I help you with today?

W: Hi, I'm ___________ ___________ buy two sketchbooks and one paintbrush.

M: Okay. Each sketchbook costs 6 dollars and the paintbrush costs 4 dollars.

W: Then, how much does it all ___________ ___________ ___________?

M: It's 16 dollars in total. Do you need anything else?

W: That's okay, I'll just buy these three items. Here's 20 dollars.

M: Thank you. Here's your ___________.

대화자관계추론

14. 대화를 듣고, 두 사람의 관계로 가장 적절한 것을 고르시오.

① 미술관 직원 – 화가
② 사진 작가 – 모델
③ 제빵사 – 손님
④ 웨딩플래너 – 고객
⑤ 컴퓨터 수리기사 – 고객

14

W: Hello. Can I help you?

M: I'd like to order a ________ cake for my parents.

W: Do you have any special design ________ ________?

M: Yes. I want to put their picture on the cake.

W: Okay, anything else?

M: And write "Happy Wedding _____________" below the picture, please.

W: All right. Send the picture to this email address.

M: Thank you. Also, I need it next Thursday.

W: Don't worry. I'll ________ you when it is ready.

15. 대화를 듣고, 여자가 남자에게 부탁한 일
    로 가장 적절한 것을 고르시오.

    ① 숙제 제출해주기
    ② 수학 숙제 도와주기
    ③ 과학 실험 도와주기
    ④ 교무실 위치 알려주기
    ⑤ 수학 선생님 모셔오기

15
W: Hi, Sam! Where are you going?

M: I'm going to the Math teacher's office.

W: Oh, good. Can you do me a ________?

M: What is it?

W: Could you give my ____________ to Ms. Kim? I

have to go to the ____________ lab now.

M: Sure. But don't forget that you ________ me one!

W: Okay. Thanks a lot.

16. 대화를 듣고, 남자가 마라톤에 참가할 수
    없는 이유로 가장 적절한 것을 고르시오.

    ① 달리기를 잘하지 못해서
    ② 참가 신청 기간을 놓쳐서
    ③ 다른 일정이 있어서
    ④ 발목을 다쳐서
    ⑤ 일이 바빠서

16
W: Jim, did you hear about our city marathon?

M: Yes, I did. Are you going to register?

W: Yes, and it would be nice if ________ ________

________ too.

M: Oh, I don't think that's possible.

W: Why? I thought you were a good runner.

M: I like running, but I ________ ________ my left

ankle.

W: Really? Are you okay?

M: It's getting better, but I don't think running in a

marathon is a good idea.

W: Okay, I'll find another partner, then.

다음 페이지에 계속 ➡

17. 다음 그림의 상황에 가장 적절한 대화를 고르시오.

① ②
③ ④
⑤

17
① M: Have you finished doing your homework?

W: Yes, can I go play now?

② M: Do you know where the restroom is?

W: It's at the end of this ___________.

③ M: Can I have ___________ ___________ ___________

water?

W: Sure. Here you go.

④ M: The floor is still wet, so ___________ ___________.

W: Okay. I'll try to ___________ ___________

___________.

⑤ M: This brush is too short for me.

W: Let's go buy a new one.

18. 다음을 듣고, 여자가 학교 도서관에 대해 언급하지 <u>않은</u> 것을 고르시오.
① 도서 대여 방법
② 대여 가능 권수
③ 도서 반납 기한
④ 운영 시간
⑤ 위치

18
W: Hello, new students. I'd like to introduce our school library. If you want to ________ ________ books, just bring them and show your student ID to the front desk. Each student can check out ten books ________ ________ ________. The ________ ________ to return the book to the library is in two weeks. Opening hours are from 10 a.m. to 6 p.m. Thanks.

09 **회 딕테이션**

19. 대화를 듣고, 남자의 마지막 말에 이어질 여자의 말로 가장 적절한 것을 고르시오.

Woman: _________________

① I'll buy the guitar right away.
② I will try not to miss your class.
③ I take lessons three times a week.
④ I go to piano class every weekend.
⑤ You should listen to music more often.

19

M: Hi, Sora! You look so ___________ these days.

W: Hello, Mr. Simon. I've just started a guitar class.

M: That sounds so cool.

W: I'm still a beginner, but I've always wanted to learn and finally decided to __________ __________ __________ __________.

M: I'm sure you're having a lot of fun.

W: Yes. Playing music makes me feel __________ __________ __________.

M: I didn't know __________ __________ __________ music. How often do you go to class?

W: I take lessons three times a week.

---

20. 대화를 듣고, 남자의 마지막 말에 이어질 여자의 말로 가장 적절한 것을 고르시오.

Woman: _________________

① I like comedies.
② I prefer taking a taxi.
③ Since last Wednesday.
④ How about in the afternoon?
⑤ Let's meet in front of the school.

20

W: Tom, did you hear about the ________ ________ in our neighborhood?

M: Yes! My favorite actor Daniel Park will be here.

W: You must be very excited.

M: Of course. I'm going to ________ ________ ________ the movie shoot later.

W: Can I ________ ________ you? I want to see it, too.

M: Sure. I heard that they're shooting ________ ________ today. When do you want to go?

W: How about in the afternoon?

Words & Expressions Review 09

● 다음 단어를 암기하세요.

문제	번호	단어	뜻
1	☐ 1	be prepared for	~을 대비하다
	☐ 2	slippery	미끄러운
2	☐ 3	especially	특히
	☐ 4	butterfly	나비
3	☐ 5	announce	발표하다
	☐ 6	win first place	우승하다, 일등을 하다
4	☐ 7	well-put-together	잘 구성된, 잘 정리된
	☐ 8	whoever	누구든 ~하는 사람(들)
	☐ 9	put effort into	~에 공을 들이다, 노력을 기울이다
5	☐ 10	rent	빌리다, 대여하다
	☐ 11	in total	통틀어, 모두 합하여
7	☐ 12	on one's way	도중에
	☐ 13	delicious	맛있는
8	☐ 14	excited	신나는, 흥분되는
	☐ 15	try out (for) ~	(선발 등을 위한 경쟁에) 지원하다
	☐ 16	check	확인하다
9	☐ 17	main character	주인공
	☐ 18	author	작가, 저자
	☐ 19	work	작품, 일, 저작물
	☐ 20	talented	재능 있는
10	☐ 21	attend	참석하다
	☐ 22	notice board	게시판

문제	번호	단어	뜻
11	☐ 23	be held	~이 열리다, 개최되다
	☐ 24	available	이용할 수 있는
12	☐ 25	in advance	미리, 사전에
	☐ 26	seem	~인 것 같다
	☐ 27	purchase	사다, 구매하다
13	☐ 28	cost	(값·비용이) ~이다
	☐ 29	add up to	총 ~가 되다
	☐ 30	change	거스름돈
	☐ 31	custom	주문 제작한, 맞춤의
14	☐ 32	have ~ in mind	~을 생각해 두다, 염두에 두다
	☐ 33	anniversary	기념일
15	☐ 34	science lab	과학 실험실
	☐ 35	owe	~에게 신세 지다, 빚지다
16	☐ 36	injure	다치다, 부상을 입다
	☐ 37	ankle	발목
18	☐ 38	check out	(책을) 대출하다
	☐ 39	due	~하기로 되어 있는, 예정된
	☐ 40	cheerful	기분 좋은, 쾌활한
19	☐ 41	give it a try	한번 해보다
	☐ 42	creative	창의적인
20	☐ 43	movie shooting	영화 촬영
	☐ 44	favorite	매우 좋아하는

M2(17)_W_09

●왼쪽 단어장의 뜻이 보이지 않게 반으로 접고, 학습한 단어의 뜻을 아래 빈칸에 적어주세요.

1	slippery		23	favorite
2	main character		24	work
3	on one's way		25	check
4	put effort into		26	in advance
5	notice board		27	excited
6	talented		28	science lab
7	cheerful		29	have ~ in mind
8	whoever		30	seem
9	movie shooting		31	give it a try
10	well-put-together		32	check out
11	cost		33	ankle
12	author		34	add up to
13	change		35	win first place
14	especially		36	creative
15	be prepared for		37	purchase
16	rent		38	available
17	be held		39	delicious
18	try out (for) ~		40	due
19	injure		41	in total
20	announce		42	anniversary
21	butterfly		43	attend
22	owe		44	custom

10회 중학영어듣기 모의고사

M2(17)_10_US
모두 **미국식 발음(US)** 으로 녹음

M2(17)_10_UK
20문제 중 5문제에 **영국식 발음** **(US+UK)**을 포함하여 녹음

정답 및 해석 p. 45

1 다음을 듣고, 금요일의 날씨로 가장 적절한 것을 고르시오.

① 
② 
③ 
④ 
⑤ 

2 대화를 듣고, 두 사람이 구입할 실내용 슬리퍼로 가장 적절한 것을 고르시오.

① 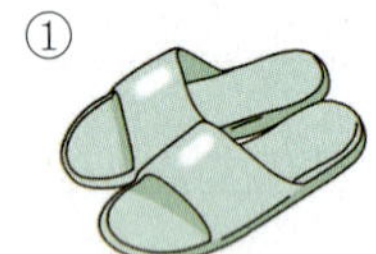
② 
③ 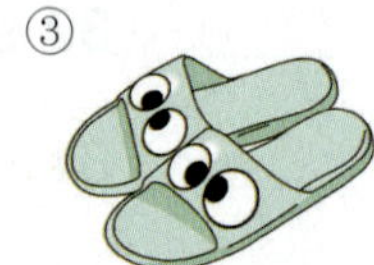
④ 
⑤ 

3 대화를 듣고, 남자의 심정으로 가장 적절한 것을 고르시오.

① excited ② anxious ③ proud ④ calm ⑤ surprised

4 대화를 듣고, 여자가 과학 전람회에서 맡은 일로 가장 적절한 것을 고르시오.

① 청소하기 ② 티켓 팔기 ③ 강당 꾸미기
④ 전단지 만들기 ⑤ 행사 기획하기

5 대화를 듣고, 두 사람이 대화하는 장소로 가장 적절한 곳을 고르시오.

① 비행기 ② 영화관 ③ 버스 ④ 화장실 ⑤ 식당

6 대화를 듣고, 여자의 마지막 말의 의도로 가장 적절한 것을 고르시오.

① 축하　　　② 허가　　　③ 위로　　　④ 동의　　　⑤ 충고

7 대화를 듣고, 남자가 벼룩시장에 가져갈 물건을 고르시오.

① 만화책　　　② 티셔츠　　　③ 책가방　　　④ 농구공　　　⑤ 모자

8 대화를 듣고, 두 사람이 대화 직후에 할 일로 가장 적절한 것을 고르시오.

① 짐 챙기기　　　　　　② 자전거 타기
③ 호수 산책하기　　　　④ 휴가 계획 세우기
⑤ 박물관 방문하기

9 대화를 듣고, 두 사람이 중간고사에 대해 언급하지 <u>않은</u> 것을 고르시오.

① 시험 기간　　　② 수학 시험일　　　③ 교실 이동
④ 책상 재정렬　　　⑤ 휴대전화 반납

10 다음을 듣고, 남자가 하는 말의 내용으로 가장 적절한 것을 고르시오.

① 대중교통 이용 예절　　　　② 자전거 대여 안내
③ 올바른 헬멧 착용법　　　　④ 빗길 교통사고 예방
⑤ 전동 킥보드 안전 수칙

11번~20번 문제는 다음 페이지에 ➡

11 대화를 듣고, 교내 만화대회에 대한 내용과 일치하지 <u>않는</u> 것을 고르시오.

① 학생당 한 개의 작품을 제출한다.
② 만화는 학교 홈페이지에 게시된다.
③ 만화를 그린 학생의 이름은 게시되지 않는다.
④ '좋아요'를 가장 많이 받은 사람이 우승한다.
⑤ 총 5명이 상을 받을 것이다.

12 대화를 듣고, 남자가 전화를 건 목적으로 가장 적절한 것을 고르시오.

① 배드민턴 치는 데 초대하기 위해서　　② 그들이 만날 시각을 묻기 위해서
③ 그의 사촌을 소개하기 위해서　　④ 라켓을 빌리기 위해서
⑤ 돈을 갚기 위해서

13 대화를 듣고, 여자가 지불해야 할 금액으로 가장 적절한 것을 고르시오.

① $9　　② $11　　③ $14　　④ $15　　⑤ $17

14 대화를 듣고, 두 사람의 관계로 가장 적절한 것을 고르시오.

① 입국 심사관 — 관광객　　② 경찰관 — 운전자　　③ 비행기 승무원 — 승객
④ 관광객 — 여행 가이드　　⑤ 택시 기사 — 승객

15 대화를 듣고, 여자가 남자에게 부탁한 일로 가장 적절한 것을 고르시오.

① 샌드위치 싸기　　② 음료수 사 오기
③ 공원에 자리 잡기　　④ 피크닉 매트 가져오기
⑤ 모자 빌려주기

16 대화를 듣고, 여자가 Mozart의 음악을 좋아하는 이유로 가장 적절한 것을 고르시오.

① 세계적으로 유명해서　　② 연주 형태가 다양해서　　③ 이해하기 쉬워서
④ 유쾌하고 재미있어서　　⑤ Mozart의 삶이 묻어나서

17 다음 그림의 상황에 가장 적절한 대화를 고르시오.

①   ②   ③   ④   ⑤

18 다음을 듣고, 여자가 영화에 대해 언급하지 <u>않은</u> 것을 고르시오.

① 감독   ② 제목   ③ 내용   ④ 촬영지   ⑤ 개봉일

[19~20] 대화를 듣고, 여자의 마지막 말에 이어질 남자의 말로 가장 적절한 것을 고르시오.

19 Man: _________________________________

① Well, just a little bit.
② Spanish is a pretty language.
③ I've never been to Spain before.
④ No, I don't listen to Latin music.
⑤ I didn't know you were from Spain.

20 Man: _________________________________

① I'm not an active person.   ② I have a few friends to play with.
③ What kind of sports do you like?   ④ Welcome to our badminton club.
⑤ Definitely! I'll teach you some moves.

Dictation Test 10

M2(17)_10_D

Dictation(받아쓰기)은 본문을 받아쓰면서 영어듣기의 집중력을 향상시키고 다양한 표현을 정리하기 위한 영어듣기 학습법입니다. **녹음을 다시 듣고, 빈칸에 알맞은 단어를 써 보세요.**
※Dictation의 정답은 듣기 대본의 밑줄 친 부분을 확인하세요.

📖 정답 p. 45

맞은 개수 / 총158개

 날씨파악-그림

1. 다음을 듣고, 금요일의 날씨로 가장 적절한 것을 고르시오.

① 　② 

③ 　④ 

⑤ 

01 M: Good evening! This is Tom, and I'm back with another ________ weather report. Monday will be clear and sunny. From Tuesday to Thursday, it will be a bit ________. Friday will be ________, so you might ________ ________ ________. If you're planning outdoor activities, the coming weekend might not be the best time. Heavy rain is expected from Saturday morning through Sunday evening. Thank you.

그림정보파악

2. 대화를 듣고, 두 사람이 구입할 실내용 슬리퍼로 가장 적절한 것을 고르시오.

① 　② 

③ 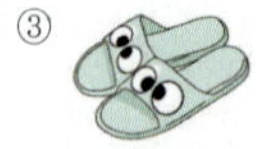　④ 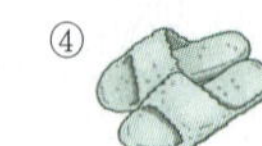

⑤ 

02 W: Honey, I feel like our living room floor is a bit cold these days.

M: Me, too. We should get some ___________ ___________. Let's buy them online.

W: Hmm... *(Pause)* How about this furry pair?

M: I think those will make my feet ___________. Let's buy a pair that isn't furry.

W: Sure. How about these ones which have ___________ ___________ ___________?

M: Yeah, let's buy those ones with rabbits. They also ___________ ___________.

---

3. 대화를 듣고, 남자의 심정으로 가장 적절한 것을 고르시오.

① excited ② anxious
③ proud ④ calm
⑤ surprised

03

W: Sean, why don't you eat _________ _________?

M: I'm sorry, Mom, but I just can't eat any more.

W: Is there ____________ _________?

M: Well, I'm worried because I didn't study _________

   for the test today.

W: Oh, just do your best, son.

M: Yes, I will. But now I feel like _________ _________

   just thinking about the test.

4. 대화를 듣고, 여자가 과학 전람회에서 맡은 일로 가장 적절한 것을 고르시오.

① 청소하기
② 티켓 팔기
③ 강당 꾸미기
④ 전단지 만들기
⑤ 행사 기획하기

04

W: Hi, Jack. Have you heard about the science fair

   tomorrow?

M: Yes. It's going to be a big event, isn't it?

W: Exactly. Our science club is _________ _________

   _________ __________ the fair.

M: Really? That's great! Did you plan the science

   events, too?

W: No, our club ____________ is in charge of that.

M: Oh, then what did you do?

W: I ____________ the auditorium.

M: I see. I'm sure the fair will be a success.

다음 페이지에 계속 ➡

대화장소추론

5. 대화를 듣고, 두 사람이 대화하는 장소로 가장 적절한 곳을 고르시오.
① 비행기 ② 영화관
③ 버스 ④ 화장실
⑤ 식당

05 W: Good evening. ____________ ____________ ____________?

M: Yes, please. Can we sit by the window?

W: Of course. How about this table?

M: It's perfect.

W: All right. Here's the menu. Take your time, and let me know when you are ____________ ____________ ____________.

M: Thank you. Um, can I use the bathroom?

W: Of course. The bathroom is right ____________ ____________ ____________.

마지막말의도파악

6. 대화를 듣고, 여자의 마지막 말의 의도로 가장 적절한 것을 고르시오.
① 축하 ② 허가
③ 위로 ④ 동의
⑤ 충고

06 W: Congratulations, Marty! I ____________ ____________ ____________. You ran really fast.

M: Thanks, Celia. I'm happy that I won.

W: But, ____________ ____________ ____________ ____________?

M: My leg has been hurting a little since the race ended.

W: That can't be good. Did you ____________ ____________ ____________?

M: No. It doesn't hurt that much.

W: I really think you should see the doctor.

7. 대화를 듣고, 남자가 벼룩시장에 가져갈 물건을 고르시오.

① 만화책　　② 티셔츠
③ 책가방　　④ 농구공
⑤ 모자

07

W: Alex, what will you ________ to the flea market?

M: I haven't ________ ________, Mom.

W: How about these comic books?

M: I'm still reading them, plus these are my ________. Can I take this T-shirt?

W: Sure. I'll ________ it for you.

M: Thanks. I'm also thinking of selling this basketball at the market.

W: It's too old. The T-shirt will be enough.

8. 대화를 듣고, 두 사람이 대화 직후에 할 일로 가장 적절한 것을 고르시오.

① 짐 챙기기
② 자전거 타기
③ 호수 산책하기
④ 휴가 계획 세우기
⑤ 박물관 방문하기

08

W: What's your plan for today? It's the first day of our vacation.

M: Yeah, we have so much __________ __________.

W: How about we start with a bike ride around the lake?

M: Actually, I'd like to visit the __________ __________.

W: That sounds interesting! Is there __________ __________ you want to see?

M: Yes, I want to check out the exhibit on local history. Want to join me?

W: Yes! Let's __________ __________ the museum now.

다음 페이지에 계속 ➡

9. 대화를 듣고, 두 사람이 중간고사에 대해
   언급하지 **않은** 것을 고르시오.
   ① 시험 기간　　② 수학 시험일
   ③ 교실 이동　　④ 책상 재정렬
   ⑤ 휴대전화 반납

09
W: Hey, George. The mid-term schedule has come out. Did you see it?

M: Yes. It's from April 28 to 30.

W: I'm glad that the math test is on the last day of exams. There are so many chapters to cover.

M: ＿＿＿＿ ＿＿＿＿ ＿＿＿＿ ＿＿＿＿. Do we need to ＿＿＿＿ ＿＿＿＿ other classrooms like we did last time?

W: Yes, some of us will take tests in different classrooms.

M: Oh, we need to ＿＿＿＿ ＿＿＿＿ the desks for the exams, as well.

W: Our teacher will tell us ＿＿＿＿ ＿＿＿＿ ＿＿＿＿ the desks later.

10. 다음을 듣고, 남자가 하는 말의 내용으로
    가장 적절한 것을 고르시오.
    ① 대중교통 이용 예절
    ② 자전거 대여 안내
    ③ 올바른 헬멧 착용법
    ④ 빗길 교통사고 예방
    ⑤ 전동 킥보드 안전 수칙

10
M: Hello, *Traffic Radio* listeners. Today, I'm going to tell you how to ride an electric kickboard safely. First, ＿＿＿＿ ＿＿＿＿ ＿＿＿＿ including a helmet and knee pads. Second, don't ride the kickboard when it is snowing or raining. The road can be ＿＿＿＿ ＿＿＿＿. Finally, when you are on a ride, hold the handle tight and don't ＿＿＿＿ ＿＿＿＿ ＿＿＿＿ ＿＿＿＿ the road.

11. 대화를 듣고, 교내 만화대회에 대한 내용
과 일치하지 <u>않는</u> 것을 고르시오.
① 학생당 한 개의 작품을 제출한다.
② 만화는 학교 홈페이지에 게시된다.
③ 만화를 그린 학생의 이름은 게시
되지 않는다.
④ '좋아요'를 가장 많이 받은 사람이
우승한다.
⑤ 총 5명이 상을 받을 것이다.

11

M: Janet, look at this poster.

W: Oh, it's about the school __________ contest.

M: Each student will __________ one cartoon.

W: And then, the cartoons will __________

__________ on the school website.

M: Students' names will not be posted. So, we won't

know who drew what.

W: That sounds fair. So, the student who gets the

most "likes" will win, right?

M: That's right. __________ __________ __________

will be the winners.

12. 대화를 듣고, 남자가 전화를 건 목적으로
가장 적절한 것을 고르시오.
① 배드민턴 치는 데 초대하기 위해서
② 그들이 만날 시각을 묻기 위해서
③ 그의 사촌을 소개하기 위해서
④ 라켓을 빌리기 위해서
⑤ 돈을 갚기 위해서

12

(Telephone rings.)

W: Hello?

M: Hello, Sandy. It's me, Paul. Are you busy?

W: Not really. __________ __________?

M: My cousin wants to play badminton with me

today, but __________ __________ __________ __________.

So, I'm wondering if I could __________ __________.

W: Sure. Just come over here and get it.

M: Okay, thanks. I'll come there now. Bye.

다음 페이지에 계속 ➡

13. 대화를 듣고, 여자가 지불해야 할 금액으로 가장 적절한 것을 고르시오.

① $9 ② $11
③ $14 ④ $15
⑤ $17

13
M: Hello. How may I help you?

W: My 5-year-old son has __________ __________ __________.
Do you have anything for children?

M: Yes. We have __________ __________. The powder is
6 dollars, and the liquid is 8 dollars.

W: The __________ type would be better.

M: OK. Here you are.

W: And can I have some __________ __________ masks for
adults?

M: Sure. They're 1 dollar each. How many would you
like?

W: I'd like three.

M: OK. One moment, please.

14. 대화를 듣고, 두 사람의 관계로 가장 적절한 것을 고르시오.

① 입국 심사관 — 관광객
② 경찰관 — 운전자
③ 비행기 승무원 — 승객
④ 관광객 — 여행 가이드
⑤ 택시 기사 — 승객

14
M: Hi. Welcome to Korea. May I have your
__________, please?

W: Sure, __________ __________ __________.

M: Thank you. How long will you stay in Korea?

W: I will be here for ten days.

M: Are you here __________ __________?

W: No. I am here __________ __________.

M: I see. Enjoy your stay in Korea.

W: I will. Thank you very much.

15. 대화를 듣고, 여자가 남자에게 부탁한 일로 가장 적절한 것을 고르시오.

① 샌드위치 싸기
② 음료수 사 오기
③ 공원에 자리 잡기
④ 피크닉 매트 가져오기
⑤ 모자 빌려주기

15 (*Cellphone rings.*)

M: Hello, Emily.

W: Hi, Alex. Remember our picnic plans for today?

M: Yes, ___________ _________ some sandwiches and drinks.

W: That's great. I'm ___________ _________ the park near your house.

M: OK, I'll be there soon.

W: Perfect, but there's a little problem. I __________ __________ _________ the picnic mat.

M: Oh, no worries. I'll ___________ _________ from home.

W: Thanks a lot, Alex. See you soon.

M: No problem. I'll see you shortly.

16. 대화를 듣고, 여자가 Mozart의 음악을 좋아하는 이유로 가장 적절한 것을 고르시오.

① 세계적으로 유명해서
② 연주 형태가 다양해서
③ 이해하기 쉬워서
④ 유쾌하고 재미있어서
⑤ Mozart의 삶이 묻어나서

16 M: Hey, Melanie. What did you do ________ _________ _________?

W: I went to a concert with my parents.

M: What kind of concert?

W: It was a concert by ________ _________ _________. They played a lot of Mozart.

M: Did you like it?

W: Yes! I'm a big fan of Mozart's music.

M: I think his work is difficult to ___________.

W: Maybe. But, his music is ________ _________ _________. That's why I like it.

다음 페이지에 계속 ➡

17. 다음 그림의 상황에 가장 적절한 대화를 고르시오.

①   ②
③   ④
⑤

17

① W: What is your favorite animal?

   M: I love cats! What about you?

② W: What do you want for breakfast?

   M: I would like some cereal.

③ W: How was the movie?

   M: It was really scary. I _________ _________ _________

         _________ my seat!

④ W: Are you ready for your final exams?

   M: Yeah! I studied really hard.

⑤ W: Can you _________ _________ _________ for me?

    My hands are full.

   M: Sure! Here you go.

---

18. 다음을 듣고, 여자가 영화에 대해 언급하지 <u>않은</u> 것을 고르시오.

① 감독   ② 제목
③ 내용   ④ 촬영지
⑤ 개봉일

18

W: Good morning, students. I'd like to tell you about a new documentary movie _________ _________ Nate Young. The title is *You Are Not Alone*. This movie tells the stories of teenagers who have _________ a variety of different problems in life. It will _________ _________ on February 4. I hope that after watching this movie you will _________ that you are not alone. There will always be somebody to _________ _________ _________.

19. 대화를 듣고, 여자의 마지막 말에 이어질 남자의 말로 가장 적절한 것을 고르시오.

Man: ______________

① Well, just a little bit.
② Spanish is a pretty language.
③ I've never been to Spain before.
④ No, I don't listen to Latin music.
⑤ I didn't know you were from Spain.

19

W: What are you doing, Clark?

M: Oh. Hi, Gina! I'm ________ ________ ________.

W: Do you like listening to music?

M: Yes, I do.

W: What music are you listening to?

M: It's Spanish music.

W: Really? Can you __________ Spanish?

M: Well, just a little bit.

20. 대화를 듣고, 여자의 마지막 말에 이어질 남자의 말로 가장 적절한 것을 고르시오.

Man: ______________

① I'm not an active person.
② I have a few friends to play with.
③ What kind of sports do you like?
④ Welcome to our badminton club.
⑤ Definitely! I'll teach you some moves.

20

W: Hey, I heard you've been playing badminton lately.

M: Yeah, I've been playing with some friends at the park.

W: Awesome! What do you like about badminton?

M: I love how fast-paced it is, and it's a great way to __________ __________.

W: Is badminton __________ __________ __________?

M: Not really! It's __________ __________ to learn the basics, like hitting the shuttlecock with the racket.

W: I've __________ __________ badminton before. Do you think I could learn?

M: Definitely! I'll teach you some moves.

Words & Expressions Review 10

● 다음 단어를 암기하세요.

문제	번호	단어	뜻		문제	번호	단어	뜻
1	☐ 1	outdoor activities	야외 활동		11	☐ 23	submit	제출하다
	☐ 2	expect	예상하다, 기대하다			☐ 24	post	게시하다
2	☐ 3	sweaty	땀나게 하는			☐ 25	fair	공평한, 공정한
3	☐ 4	worried	걱정하는, 걱정스러운		12	☐ 26	wonder	궁금하다
	☐ 5	do one's best	최선을 다하다			☐ 27	borrow	빌리다
	☐ 6	throw up ~	~을 토하다		13	☐ 28	mild fever	미열
4	☐ 7	be in charge of	~을 담당하다, 주관하다			☐ 29	liquid	액체
	☐ 8	organize	준비하다, 조직하다		14	☐ 30	passport	여권
	☐ 9	decorate	장식하다, 꾸미다			☐ 31	on vacation	휴가로
5	☐ 10	order	주문하다			☐ 32	pack	(짐을) 챙기다, 싸다, 꾸리다
	☐ 11	around	~를 돈 곳에		15	☐ 33	head to	~로 가다, 향하다
6	☐ 12	limp	절뚝거리다, 기운이 없는			☐ 34	shortly	곧, 얼마 안 되어
	☐ 13	hurt	아프다		16	☐ 35	orchestra	관현악단
7	☐ 14	decide	결정하다			☐ 36	cheery	유쾌한, 쾌활한
8	☐ 15	explore	탐험하다		17	☐ 37	nearly	거의
	☐ 16	actually	사실은			☐ 38	overcome	극복하다, 이겨내다
	☐ 17	local	지역의, 현지의		18	☐ 39	a variety of	여러 가지의
9	☐ 18	set up	준비하다, 설립하다			☐ 40	be released	개봉하다
	☐ 19	arrange	배열하다, 정리하다			☐ 41	realize	깨닫다, 알아차리다
10	☐ 20	slippery	미끄러운		19	☐ 42	listen to ~	~을 듣다
	☐ 21	tight	꽉, 단단히		20	☐ 43	lately	최근에
	☐ 22	take one's eyes off	~에서 눈을 떼다			☐ 44	definitely	그렇고 말고, 확실히, 분명히, 틀림없이

M2(17)_W_10

●왼쪽 단어장의 뜻이 보이지 않게 반으로 접고, 학습한 단어의 뜻을 아래 빈칸에 적어주세요.

1	realize	23	decorate
2	post	24	do one's best
3	be in charge of	25	throw up ~
4	lately	26	orchestra
5	actually	27	local
6	limp	28	sweaty
7	decide	29	worried
8	head to	30	borrow
9	fair	31	definitely
10	wonder	32	submit
11	overcome	33	on vacation
12	listen to ~	34	slippery
13	expect	35	around
14	order	36	arrange
15	explore	37	tight
16	hurt	38	outdoor activities
17	be released	39	cheery
18	pack	40	organize
19	liquid	41	set up
20	nearly	42	passport
21	a variety of	43	take one's eyes off
22	shortly	44	mild fever

정답 및 해석 p. 50

1 다음을 듣고, 오늘 오후의 날씨로 가장 적절한 것을 고르시오.

①  ② 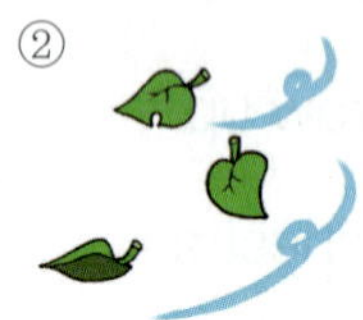 ③  ④ 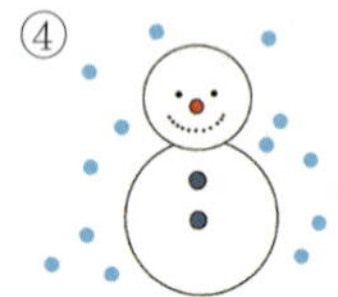 ⑤ 

2 대화를 듣고, 여자가 주문한 텀블러로 가장 적절한 것을 고르시오.

①  ②  ③  ④ 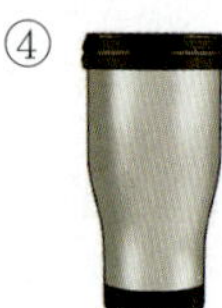 ⑤ 

3 대화를 듣고, 남자의 심정으로 가장 적절한 것을 고르시오.

① angry　　② bored　　③ proud　　④ nervous　　⑤ thankful

4 대화를 듣고, 남자가 오늘 한 일로 가장 적절한 것을 고르시오.

① 자전거 수리하기　　② 친구들과 놀러 가기　　③ 부모님 마중 나가기
④ 생일 선물 사기　　⑤ 자전거 분실 신고하기

5 대화를 듣고, 두 사람이 대화하는 장소로 가장 적절한 곳을 고르시오.

① 영화관　　② 식료품점　　③ 스케이트장
④ 악기 수리점　　⑤ 자동차 대여점

6 대화를 듣고, 여자의 마지막 말의 의도로 가장 적절한 것을 고르시오.

① 칭찬　　　② 사과　　　③ 경고　　　④ 의심　　　⑤ 후회

7 대화를 듣고, 여자가 가져올 물건으로 가장 적절한 것을 고르시오.

① 헬멧　　　② 물통　　　③ 선글라스　　　④ 간식　　　⑤ 장갑

8 대화를 듣고, 두 사람이 대화 직후에 할 일로 가장 적절한 것을 고르시오.

① 친구 집에 가기　　　② 파티 준비하기　　　③ 요리하기
④ 백화점 가기　　　⑤ 친구에게 전화하기

9 대화를 듣고, 두 사람이 영화에 대해 언급하지 <u>않은</u> 것을 고르시오.

① 제목　　　② 감독　　　③ 개봉일　　　④ 주연 배우　　　⑤ 관객수

10 다음을 듣고, 여자가 하는 말의 내용으로 가장 적절한 것을 고르시오.

① 학교 행사 안내　　　② 학급 규칙 설명　　　③ 지역 음식 축제 홍보
④ 미술 수업 소개　　　⑤ 교실 환경미화 일정 공지

11 대화를 듣고, 남자가 예약한 내용과 일치하지 <u>않는</u> 것을 고르시오.

① 다음 주 토요일 점심 식사 예약이다.　　　② 예약자는 Kevin Park이다.
③ 예약 인원은 총 8명이다.　　　④ 창가 자리를 요청했다.
⑤ 식당에서 케이크를 준비할 것이다.

12번~20번 문제는 다음 페이지에 ➡

12 대화를 듣고, 여자가 전화를 건 목적으로 가장 적절한 것을 고르시오.

① 결혼식에 초대하기 위해서
② 식물원에 가자고 제안하기 위해서
③ 이사에 대한 조언을 구하기 위해서
④ 식물을 돌봐달라고 부탁하기 위해서
⑤ 감사의 의미로 식사를 대접하기 위해서

13 대화를 듣고, 여자가 받은 거스름돈으로 가장 적절한 것을 고르시오.

① $1   ② $2   ③ $3   ④ $4   ⑤ $5

14 대화를 듣고, 두 사람의 관계로 가장 적절한 것을 고르시오.

① 감독 – 운동선수
② 디자이너 – 모델
③ 여행 가이드 – 여행객
④ 헬스 트레이너 – 수강생
⑤ 전자 제품 판매원 – 손님

15 대화를 듣고, 남자가 여자에게 요청한 일로 가장 적절한 것을 고르시오.

① 주문 내역 조회하기   ② 수리 기사 보내주기   ③ 배송 날짜 확인하기
④ 배송지 변경하기   ⑤ 재고 확인하기

16 대화를 듣고, 남자가 카페에 가는 이유로 가장 적절한 것을 고르시오.

① 과외를 받기 위해서
② 할인 쿠폰을 쓰기 위해서
③ 조별 과제를 하기 위해서
④ 아르바이트를 하기 위해서
⑤ 혼자 시험 공부를 하기 위해서

17 다음 그림의 상황에 가장 적절한 대화를 고르시오.

①   ②   ③   ④   ⑤

18 다음을 듣고, 남자가 학교 행사에 대해 언급하지 <u>않은</u> 것을 고르시오.

① 장소   ② 일시   ③ 참가 방법

④ 참가 마감 날짜   ⑤ 우승 상품

[19~20] 대화를 듣고, 여자의 마지막 말에 이어질 남자의 말로 가장 적절한 것을 고르시오.

19   **Man:** _______________________________

① I don't like Chinese food, either.   ② Of course, we can.

③ I can speak Japanese.   ④ Yes. I often go to the shopping mall.

⑤ I'm going to Tokyo next week.

20   **Man:** _______________________________

① I've never baked anything.   ② I don't like cheesecake.

③ I want to learn it from her.   ④ I didn't know that she liked it.

⑤ Chocolate cake is my favorite.

Dictation Test 11

M2(17)_11_D

Dictation(받아쓰기)은 본문을 받아쓰면서 영어듣기의 집중력을 향상시키고 다양한 표현을 정리하기 위한 영어듣기 학습법입니다. **녹음을 다시 듣고, 빈칸에 알맞은 단어를 써 보세요.**
※Dictation의 정답은 듣기 대본의 밑줄 친 부분을 확인하세요.

정답 p. 50

맞은 개수 / 총153개

---

1. 다음을 듣고, 오늘 오후의 날씨로 가장 적절한 것을 고르시오.

①  ② 

③  ④ 

⑤ 

01 M: Hello, everyone! This is your daily weather report. This morning, it is expected to be cloudy with a ________ ________ ________ of rain. So, be sure to bring an umbrella. In the afternoon, the temperature will start to ________, and the rain will ________ ________ snow. Be careful when you are driving this afternoon because the road ________ ________ ________.

2. 대화를 듣고, 여자가 주문한 텀블러로 가장 적절한 것을 고르시오.

①  ② 

③  ④ 

⑤ 

02 M: Judy, what are you looking at on your computer?

W: It's the final design of ________ ________ I am ordering for my sister, Tina.

M: Wow, is it a custom order? It looks really cool.

W: Yeah, I ________ ________ ________ on it.

M: That's nice. I think ________ ________ will be very useful, too.

W: That's why I chose this design. I hope Tina likes it.

---

3. 대화를 듣고, 남자의 심정으로 가장 적절한 것을 고르시오.

① angry
② bored
③ proud
④ nervous
⑤ thankful

03

M: Guess what, Nina. I ________ ________ ________ ________!

W: Really? You lost it days ago!

M: Somebody found it and ________ ________ at the school.

W: At the school? Oh, was your student ID in the wallet?

M: Yes. I got back everything that was inside the wallet. How can ________ ________ ________ be so kind?

W: You are lucky.

M: I really am. I want to find the stranger. I want to ________ him or her.

4. 대화를 듣고, 남자가 오늘 한 일로 가장 적절한 것을 고르시오.

① 자전거 수리하기
② 친구들과 놀러 가기
③ 부모님 마중 나가기
④ 생일 선물 사기
⑤ 자전거 분실 신고하기

04

W: Hello, Yong-soo. What's up? You look angry.

M: I'm mad because somebody ________ ________ ________.

W: What? Wasn't your bicycle brand new?

M: Yeah, my parents ________ ________ ________ ________ last week.

W: I'm really sorry to hear that. Is there any way to find it?

M: I just went to the police station and ________ ________ ________.

W: I really hope that you get your bicycle back.

M: Thank you.

다음 페이지에 계속 ➡

5. 대화를 듣고, 두 사람이 대화하는 장소로
   가장 적절한 곳을 고르시오.
   ① 영화관
   ② 식료품점
   ③ 스케이트장
   ④ 악기 수리점
   ⑤ 자동차 대여점

05

W: Welcome to Ice World.

M: Hi. I bought tickets online for ice skating.

W: The rink is this way. Just scan your ticket _________ _________ _________ _________.

M: Thanks. How many hours can we use the rink for?

W: With this ticket, up to three hours.

M: Where is the skate rental?

W: It's right inside, on your right. Just make sure you _________ _________ _________ _________ outside the rink.

M: We won't. Thank you.

6. 대화를 듣고, 여자의 마지막 말의 의도로
   가장 적절한 것을 고르시오.
   ① 칭찬   ② 사과
   ③ 경고   ④ 의심
   ⑤ 후회

06

M: Bye, Mom. I'm going out to play basketball with my friends.

W: _________ _________ _________, young man. Did you finish your homework?

M: Err… Not exactly, but don't worry. I've got it _________ _________.

W: What do you mean that you've got it under control?

M: It means that I can finish it by today. After I come back home!

W: You'd better come back home before 9 o'clock. If you come later than that, _________ _________ for a week!

7. 대화를 듣고, 여자가 가져올 물건으로 가장 적절한 것을 고르시오.
① 헬멧　　② 물통
③ 선글라스　　④ 간식
⑤ 장갑

07
M: Hey, Jasmine. You didn't ________ ________ our bike ride this afternoon, right?

W: No, of course not. Did you bring everything you need for the bike ride?

M: Yeah. I brought my helmet, sunglasses, gloves… Oh, I even brought a snack for us!

W: __________! So, meet me in front of the school at 5 o'clock.

M: Sounds good. Oh, no. I ________ ________ bring my water bottle with me.

W: I have two of them. You can borrow ________ ________ ________. I will bring them with me.

M: Really? Thank you so much.

8. 대화를 듣고, 두 사람이 대화 직후에 할 일로 가장 적절한 것을 고르시오.
① 친구 집에 가기
② 파티 준비하기
③ 요리하기
④ 백화점 가기
⑤ 친구에게 전화하기

08
W: Are you going to Jack's ____________ ________?

M: Yes. It's on Saturday, right?

W: Yes. He said he's going to cook Italian dishes for the guests. He's also going to hold a barbecue party in his garden.

M: Sounds great. ________ ________ ________, have you bought a gift for his housewarming party?

W: ________ ________. How about going to the mall together?

M: That's a good idea, but let's ask Jack ________ ________ ________ first for his new house.

W: Okay. ________ ________ his number.

다음 페이지에 계속 ➡

9. 대화를 듣고, 두 사람이 영화에 대해 언급하지 <u>않은</u> 것을 고르시오.

① 제목　　　② 감독
③ 개봉일　　④ 주연 배우
⑤ 관객수

09
W: Hey, Jack. Did you see the latest *Cat Hero* movie?

M: Yeah, I saw it. Oh, what was the ________ title of it?

W: *Cat Hero: to the Rescue.*

M: Right! Was it ________ by Jane Dickinson?

W: Yeah, I think so.

M: I heard the movie was __________ on February 22nd and is already a huge hit.

W: Really? How many people have seen the movie?

M: I heard that about ten million people have seen that movie!

W: That's a lot! ________ ________ go watch it, too.

M: Yeah, you should. It's a good movie.

10. 다음을 듣고, 여자가 하는 말의 내용으로 가장 적절한 것을 고르시오.

① 학교 행사 안내
② 학급 규칙 설명
③ 지역 음식 축제 홍보
④ 미술 수업 소개
⑤ 교실 환경미화 일정 공지

10
W: Hi, everyone. Did you know that our school's Cultural Diversity Day is next Wednesday? It's a __________ of different cultures around the world. Before the event, we'll __________ our classrooms with flags, traditional crafts, and artwork __________ __________ __________. Then, on Cultural Diversity Day, we'll share stories, music, and food from different cultures. Don't forget to wear something representing your cultural heritage, like traditional clothing or accessories.

대화내용불일치

11. 대화를 듣고, 남자가 예약한 내용과 일치하지 <u>않는</u> 것을 고르시오.
① 다음 주 토요일 점심 식사 예약이다.
② 예약자는 Kevin Park이다.
③ 예약 인원은 총 8명이다.
④ 창가 자리를 요청했다.
⑤ 식당에서 케이크를 준비할 것이다.

11 *(Telephone rings.)*

W: Hello, River View Restaurant.

M: Hi, I'd like to make a __________ __________ for next Saturday.

W: Sure. May I have your name, please?

M: Kevin Park.

W: Okay. How many people will be coming?

M: Eight __________ __________.

W: Got it. Do you have any __________ __________?

M: Yes, we'd like a table by the window. Can we bring our own cake?

W: Sure. Your reservation __________ __________ __________ 12 p.m. next Saturday.

전화목적파악

12. 대화를 듣고, 여자가 전화를 건 목적으로 가장 적절한 것을 고르시오.
① 결혼식에 초대하기 위해서
② 식물원에 가자고 제안하기 위해서
③ 이사에 대한 조언을 구하기 위해서
④ 식물을 돌봐달라고 부탁하기 위해서
⑤ 감사의 의미로 식사를 대접하기 위해서

12 *(Cellphone rings.)*

M: Hello, Sarah. What's up?

W: Hi, Alex. Do you have any plans for this Saturday?

M: Not really. What's going on?

W: My cousin's wedding is this Saturday, and I need someone to __________ __________ __________ while I'm away.

M: Sure, I can take care of them for you.

W: Oh, thank you so much! I really __________ it.

M: No problem at all. I'll make sure they get __________ __________ water.

W: You're a __________!

M: Happy to help!

다음 페이지에 계속 ➡

13. 대화를 듣고, 여자가 받은 거스름돈으로 가장 적절한 것을 고르시오.

① $1　　　② $2
③ $3　　　④ $4
⑤ $5

13

M: Hello. How can I help you?

W: Do you have ＿＿＿＿＿ ＿＿＿＿＿ ＿＿＿＿＿ for the 4D movie *Hero*, starting in ten minutes?

M: Yes, but only ＿＿＿＿＿ ＿＿＿＿＿ ＿＿＿＿＿ ＿＿＿＿＿. Would you still like those seats?

W: Yes, that's no problem.

M: Okay. How many seats?

W: Two, please. They're 14 dollars each, right?

M: Yes. So, it'll be 28 dollars ＿＿＿＿＿ ＿＿＿＿＿.

W: Here is 30 dollars.

M: Thank you. Here are your tickets and change. Enjoy the movie!

14. 대화를 듣고, 두 사람의 관계로 가장 적절한 것을 고르시오.

① 감독 – 운동선수
② 디자이너 – 모델
③ 여행 가이드 – 여행객
④ 헬스 트레이너 – 수강생
⑤ 전자 제품 판매원 – 손님

14

M: Good afternoon. How may I help you?

W: Hi. I'm ＿＿＿＿＿ ＿＿＿＿＿ a new washing machine.

M: Okay. How about this one with a dryer?

W: I don't need the ＿＿＿＿＿ ＿＿＿＿＿, but I want a big washer.

M: Do you want something ＿＿＿＿＿ ＿＿＿＿＿ 20kg?

W: Actually, 20kg sounds perfect.

M: Then, you're lucky! That size is ＿＿＿＿＿ ＿＿＿＿＿ this week.

W: Great! I'm glad I came today.

15. 대화를 듣고, 남자가 여자에게 요청한 일로 가장 적절한 것을 고르시오.

① 주문 내역 조회하기
② 수리 기사 보내주기
③ 배송 날짜 확인하기
④ 배송지 변경하기
⑤ 재고 확인하기

15 (*Telephone rings.*)

W: Mango Computers.

M: Hello. I'm calling from Mr. Kim's office.

W: Yes. How may I help you?

M: I ________ ________ ________ ________, and tomorrow is the delivery day.

W: Do you want to change the date?

M: No. We ________ ________ ________ this week. Can you send them to the ________ ________, please?

W: No problem. Is the same date OK?

M: Yes. I'll give you the address.

16. 대화를 듣고, 남자가 카페에 가는 이유로 가장 적절한 것을 고르시오.

① 과외를 받기 위해서
② 할인 쿠폰을 쓰기 위해서
③ 조별 과제를 하기 위해서
④ 아르바이트를 하기 위해서
⑤ 혼자 시험 공부를 하기 위해서

16 M: Hey, Meg!

W: Hi, Milo. Where are you going?

M: I'm going to the café. I have an ____________ there.

W: Oh, are you going to meet your friends?

M: No, I'm not. Actually, I'm going to ________ ________ ________ ________ from my tutor.

W: I see. What ________ are you learning?

M: I study math with him. It is too hard for me to study alone.

W: I agree. Good luck to you.

다음 페이지에 계속 ➡

17. 다음 그림의 상황에 가장 적절한 대화를 고르시오.

① ②
③ ④
⑤

17

① M: This cake tastes great.

W: I'm glad you like it.

② M: Where should we put this painting?

W: Let's ___________ ___________ above the sofa.

③ M: I love this music.

W: So do I. ___________ ___________ is amazing.

④ M: Would you like some cheese on your pasta?

W: Yes, I'd like a lot, please.

⑤ M: Can I pay with my credit card?

W: Sorry. This line is ___________ ___________

___________.

18. 다음을 듣고, 남자가 학교 행사에 대해 언급하지 <u>않은</u> 것을 고르시오.

① 장소   ② 일시
③ 참가 방법   ④ 참가 마감 날짜
⑤ 우승 상품

18

M: Good afternoon, students. Your favorite school event, the Talent Show is coming next month! It will be held in our school auditorium. The Talent Show is on Friday, February 21 at 7:00 p.m. Please ________ ________ the form on the school website to register as a participant. Registration forms ________ ________ on Monday, February 10. There will be an ________ for participants.

19. 대화를 듣고, 여자의 마지막 말에 이어질 남자의 말로 가장 적절한 것을 고르시오.

Man: _________________

① I don't like Chinese food, either.
② Of course, we can.
③ I can speak Japanese.
④ Yes. I often go to the shopping mall.
⑤ I'm going to Tokyo next week.

19

M: Hi, Mary. What are you going to do _________ _____________?

W: I don't have any plans.

M: Then, how about going to the newly opened Chinese restaurant?

W: You mean the restaurant _________ the shopping mall?

M: Yes. I heard that it is very good.

W: Well, _________ I don't like Chinese food. Can we go to the Japanese restaurant _________?

M: Of course, we can.

---

20. 대화를 듣고, 여자의 마지막 말에 이어질 남자의 말로 가장 적절한 것을 고르시오.

Man: _________________

① I've never baked anything.
② I don't like cheesecake.
③ I want to learn it from her.
④ I didn't know that she liked it.
⑤ Chocolate cake is my favorite.

20

M: Melody, I heard that you're _________ _________ baking.

W: I'm not too bad.

M: Do you know _________ _________ _________ a cheesecake?

W: Yes, I do. Do you want to _________?

M: Yes. My _________ likes cheesecake very much.

W: Well, have you ever baked bread or a cake before?

M: I've never baked anything.

Words & Expressions Review 11

●다음 단어를 암기하세요.

문제	번호	단어	뜻
1	1	be sure to + 동사	반드시 ~하다
	2	turn into	~으로 변하다
2	3	tumbler	텀블러, 큰 컵
	4	custom order	맞춤 주문, 주문 제작
	5	handle	손잡이
3	6	Guess what.	있잖아., 맞혀 봐.
	7	get back	되찾다
	8	repay	보답하다, 갚다
4	9	file a report	신고하다
	10	rink	스케이트장
5	11	up to	~까지
	12	rental	대여
6	13	under control	잘 관리되는
	14	mean	뜻하다, 의미하다
7	15	bring	가져오다, 가져다주다
	16	awesome	아주 멋진, 엄청난
8	17	housewarming party	집들이
	18	by the way	그런데, 그나저나
9	19	exact	정확한
	20	direct	연출하다, 감독하다
	21	release	개봉하다
10	22	cultural	문화의

문제	번호	단어	뜻
10	23	diversity	다양성
	24	craft	공예
11	25	in total	총, 전부 합쳐서
	26	seating	좌석, 자리
13	27	row	줄, 열
	28	dryer	건조기
14	29	function	기능
	30	on sale	할인[세일] 중인
15	31	delivery	배달, 배송
	32	address	주소
16	33	appointment	약속
	34	tutor	과외 선생님, 가정교사
17	35	taste	맛이 나다
	36	hang	걸다
18	37	auditorium	강당
	38	fill out	작성하다, 기입하다
	39	participant	참가자
	40	registration form	신청서
19	41	newly	새로, 새롭게
	42	actually	사실, 실제로
20	43	be good at -ing	~을 잘하다
	44	bake	굽다

●왼쪽 단어장의 뜻이 보이지 않게 반으로 접고, 학습한 단어의 뜻을 아래 빈칸에 적어주세요.

1	function		23	mean
2	under control		24	get back
3	craft		25	fill out
4	handle		26	bring
5	up to		27	exact
6	tumbler		28	custom order
7	in total		29	turn into
8	address		30	direct
9	rink		31	participant
10	taste		32	repay
11	be good at -ing		33	rental
12	file a report		34	registration form
13	on sale		35	release
14	delivery		36	dryer
15	actually		37	hang
16	row		38	tutor
17	Guess what.		39	by the way
18	seating		40	awesome
19	diversity		41	housewarming party
20	bake		42	newly
21	auditorium		43	cultural
22	be sure to + 동사		44	appointment

12회 중학영어듣기 모의고사

M2(17)_12_US
모두 **미국식 발음(US)** 으로 녹음

M2(17)_12_UK
20문제 중 5문제에 **영국식 발음 (US+UK)**을 포함하여 녹음

정답 및 해석 p. 55

1 다음을 듣고, 예상되는 내일의 날씨를 고르시오.

①  ②  ③ 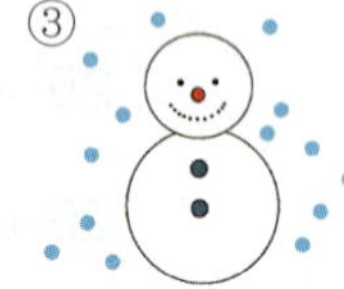 ④  ⑤ 

2 대화를 듣고, 여자가 구입할 도시락 통으로 가장 적절한 것을 고르시오.

①  ②  ③  ④  ⑤ 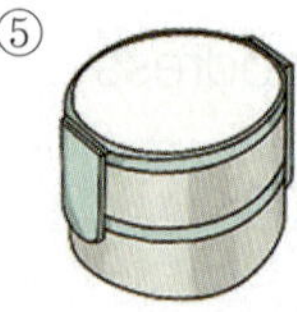

3 대화를 듣고, 여자의 심정으로 가장 적절한 것을 고르시오.

① curious　② tired　③ relieved　④ sad　⑤ angry

4 대화를 듣고, 여자가 어제 한 일로 가장 적절한 것을 고르시오.

① 책 읽기　② 영화 보기　③ 노래 부르기
④ 사촌 보러 가기　⑤ 비디오 게임하기

5 대화를 듣고, 대화가 이루어지는 장소로 가장 적절한 곳을 고르시오.

① 우체국　② 교실　③ 치과 진료실
④ 미용실　⑤ 상담실

6 대화를 듣고, 남자의 마지막 말의 의도로 가장 적절한 것을 고르시오.

① 격려　　　② 축하　　　③ 부탁　　　④ 사과　　　⑤ 허락

7 대화를 듣고, 남자가 기부할 물건으로 가장 적절한 것을 고르시오.

① 책　　　② 장난감　　　③ 농구공　　　④ 청바지　　　⑤ 야구 모자

8 대화를 듣고, 두 사람이 대화 직후에 할 일로 가장 적절한 것을 고르시오.

① 수영하기　　　② 스노클링 하기　　　③ 시장 구경하기
④ 점심 식사하기　　　⑤ 선물 포장하기

9 대화를 듣고, 이 책에 대해서 언급되지 <u>않은</u> 것을 고르시오.

① 제목　　　② 작가　　　③ 출판 시기　　　④ 페이지 수　　　⑤ 가격

10 다음을 듣고, 남자가 하는 말의 내용으로 가장 적절한 것을 고르시오.

① 새로 온 교사 소개　　　② 컴퓨터실 수리 공지
③ 학교 홈페이지 홍보　　　④ 학교 도서관 새 단장 안내
⑤ 도서 대출기기 사용법 설명

11번~20번 문제는 다음 페이지에 ➡

11 대화를 듣고, Korea Guitar Exhibition에 대한 내용과 일치하지 <u>않는</u> 것을 고르시오.

① 이번 주 화요일에 시작한다.　　② 악기를 구입할 수 있다.

③ 기타리스트와 대화할 수 있다.　　④ 미니 콘서트가 열릴 예정이다.

⑤ 학생은 무료 입장이 가능하다.

12 대화를 듣고, 남자가 전화를 건 목적으로 가장 적절한 것을 고르시오.

① 안부를 묻기 위해서

② 택배 보관을 부탁하기 위해서

③ 휴가 일정을 변경하기 위해서

④ 도착 날짜를 알려주기 위해서

⑤ 택배가 왔는지 확인하기 위해서

13 대화를 듣고, 여자가 지불해야 할 금액으로 가장 적절한 것을 고르시오.

① $10　　② $30　　③ $50　　④ $70　　⑤ $80

14 대화를 듣고, 두 사람의 관계로 가장 적절한 것을 고르시오.

① 의사 — 환자　　② 헬스 트레이너 — 고객　　③ 간호사 — 환자

④ 감독 — 운동선수　　⑤ 댄스 강사 — 수강생

15 대화를 듣고, 남자가 여자에게 부탁한 일로 가장 적절한 것을 고르시오.

① 저녁 준비하기　　② 꽃 사 오기

③ 오븐 예열하기　　④ 화단에 물 주기

⑤ 선물 포장하기

16 대화를 듣고, 여자가 옥상에 가는 이유로 가장 적절한 것을 고르시오.

① 청소하기 위해서　　② 카페에서 일하기 위해서

③ 영화 촬영을 돕기 위해서　　④ 전망을 카메라에 담기 위해서

⑤ 좋아하는 연예인을 보기 위해서

17 다음 그림의 상황에 가장 적절한 대화를 고르시오.

①   ②   ③   ④   ⑤

18 다음을 듣고, 여자가 whale shark에 대해 언급하지 <u>않은</u> 것을 고르시오.

① 몸길이   ② 몸무게   ③ 먹이   ④ 수명   ⑤ 서식지

[19~20] 대화를 듣고, 여자의 마지막 말에 이어질 남자의 말로 가장 적절한 것을 고르시오.

19 Man: _______________________________

① I can't eat spicy food.
② I don't like vegetables.
③ Thanks! I'll give it a try.
④ This is my family recipe.
⑤ No, I'm not good at cooking.

20 Man: _______________________________

① She is going there on a boat.
② We are eating seafood for dinner.
③ The island has beautiful mountains.
④ His plane will be leaving in two hours.
⑤ I am flying back to Seoul on Sunday night.

Dictation Test 12

M2(17)_12_D

Dictation(받아쓰기)은 본문을 받아쓰면서 영어듣기의 집중력을 향상시키고 다양한 표현을 정리하기 위한 영어듣기 학습법입니다. **녹음을 다시 듣고, 빈칸에 알맞은 단어를 써 보세요.**
※Dictation의 정답은 듣기 대본의 밑줄 친 부분을 확인하세요.

정답 p. 55

맞은 개수 / 총153개

날씨파악–그림

1. 다음을 듣고, 예상되는 내일의 날씨를 고르시오.

①  ② 

③  ④ 

⑤

01 W: This is the weather forecast for this week. The rain will ________ ________ some wind today. Tomorrow, the rain will stop but it will ________ be cloudy. The temperature will be a little ________ ________ today, ranging from 16 to 18 degrees Celsius.

그림정보파악

2. 대화를 듣고, 여자가 구입할 도시락 통으로 가장 적절한 것을 고르시오.

①  ② 

③  ④ 

⑤ 

02 M: May I help you?

W: Oh, yes. I'm looking for a ________ ________ for my son.

M: Please come this way. How about the one with a dog on it?

W: Hmm... I think Fred would like the one ________ ________ ________ more.

M: Excellent choice. There are two types with a dinosaur. Which one do you like the best?

W: I ________ the round one to the square one. It will be easier to wash. I'll take it.

3. 대화를 듣고, 여자의 심정으로 가장 적절한 것을 고르시오.

① curious ② tired
③ relieved ④ sad
⑤ angry

03
W: You don't look good, Matt. Are you OK?

M: I've ________ ________ ________. I'm going to the doctor after school.

W: Oh, no. You can't come to band practice today, then.

M: Don't worry, I can. I just need the practice to start ________ ________ later.

W: Oh, sure. We can't practice without a drummer, after all.

M: Thanks.

W: I'm glad ________ ________ ________.

4. 대화를 듣고, 여자가 어제 한 일로 가장 적절한 것을 고르시오.

① 책 읽기 ② 영화 보기
③ 노래 부르기 ④ 사촌 보러 가기
⑤ 비디오 게임하기

04
M: Hey, Mina. What did you do yesterday?

W: My ________ came to visit me.

M: Oh, really? Did you ________ ________ with your cousin?

W: Yeah. I played video games with her.

M: I thought you didn't like video games.

W: I don't. I wanted to watch a movie but my cousin wanted to play games.

M: So, you just ________ ________ ________ ________?

W: Yeah. I actually quite enjoyed playing them.

다음 페이지에 계속 ➡

5. 대화를 듣고, 대화가 이루어지는 장소로 가장 적절한 곳을 고르시오.
   ① 우체국　　　② 교실
   ③ 치과 진료실　④ 미용실
   ⑤ 상담실

05
W: When did you start feeling the pain?

M: Two weeks ago.

W: On a scale of one to ten, how would you _________ _________ _________ it is?

M: A two, I guess. It's not really that bad, but it's such a bother because it keeps on coming back.

W: I see. How long does the _________ _________ when you get it?

M: About ten to fifteen minutes, but sometimes it lasts for an hour or so.

W: Alright, let's get started. Let me _________ _________ _________.

6. 대화를 듣고, 남자의 마지막 말의 의도로 가장 적절한 것을 고르시오.
   ① 격려　　　② 축하
   ③ 부탁　　　④ 사과
   ⑤ 허락

06
M: Laura, I have some good news for you.

W: What is it, Mr. Kennedy?

M: You've been _________ _________ _________ our school at the English debating contest.

W: Really? I can't believe it.

M: Congratulations. How do you feel?

W: I'm very happy, but I'm not sure if I'm good enough to represent our school.

M: You'll be fine. And you can always let me know if you need some advice.

W: That'll be very helpful.

M: _________ _________ and do your best. I'm sure _________ _________ _________ _________ _________.

7. 대화를 듣고, 남자가 기부할 물건으로 가장 적절한 것을 고르시오.

① 책 ② 장난감
③ 농구공 ④ 청바지
⑤ 야구 모자

07
W: Lucas, look at this poster. Our school is having a charity event.

M: It says ________ ________ ________ ________ will be given to local charities.

W: The charity event is this Friday in the school gym. Why don't we ___________?

M: Sure! Do you have any useful items ________ ________?

W: I have some books that I don't need anymore. How about you?

M: Hmm... I think I'm going to donate some baseball caps I don't wear.

W: Great!

8. 대화를 듣고, 두 사람이 대화 직후에 할 일로 가장 적절한 것을 고르시오.

① 수영하기
② 스노클링 하기
③ 시장 구경하기
④ 점심 식사하기
⑤ 선물 포장하기

08
M: What do you want to do today? It's our last day on the island.

W: Yeah, ___________ ___________.

M: How about we go snorkeling ___________ ___________ ___________?

W: Actually, I want to explore the local market and buy some ___________.

M: That sounds like a fun idea! Do you need any help finding gifts?

W: Yeah, will you come with me?

M: Of course! Let's go ___________ ___________ the market together now.

다음 페이지에 계속 ➡

9. 대화를 듣고, 이 책에 대해서 언급되지
    않은 것을 고르시오.

    ① 제목   ② 작가
    ③ 출판 시기   ④ 페이지 수
    ⑤ 가격

09

W: Hello. How may I help you?

M: Yes, I'm looking for a book. _________ _________
   The Right.

W: Do you know _________ _________ _________?

M: Marcus Herman. It's new. It was _________ just
   last April.

W: Okay, let me check into the computer. Mmmmh.
   Ahh, yeah, we have that book.

M: Great! How much is it?

W: _________ $_________, sir. It's actually our last copy.
   Let me get it for you.

10. 다음을 듣고, 남자가 하는 말의 내용으로
    가장 적절한 것을 고르시오.

    ① 새로 온 교사 소개
    ② 컴퓨터실 수리 공지
    ③ 학교 홈페이지 홍보
    ④ 학교 도서관 새 단장 안내
    ⑤ 도서 대출기기 사용법 설명

10

M: Hello, everyone. I'm Randy, your school librarian.
   Over the summer vacation, our school library
   _________ _________ some big changes. First, there is
   more room for laptops and tablets. You can easily
   _________ _________ _________, too. Second, the
   librarian's desk was moved to the west side of the
   room. There are also new check-out and check-in
   machines. These will _________ _________ your
   school life.

11. 대화를 듣고, Korea Guitar Exhibition에 대한 내용과 일치하지 <u>않는</u> 것을 고르시오.
① 이번 주 화요일에 시작한다.
② 악기를 구입할 수 있다.
③ 기타리스트와 대화할 수 있다.
④ 미니 콘서트가 열릴 예정이다.
⑤ 학생은 무료 입장이 가능하다.

11
W: Mr. Lee, can you give me some information on the Korea Guitar Exhibition?

M: Oh, the guitar exhibition? It starts this Thursday.

W: Will I be able to ___________ _____________ there?

M: Yes. You'll also _________ _________ _________ to meet and talk to some guitarists.

W: Great! What else will I be able to do there?

M: There's going to be a mini concert at the exhibition. You should _________ _________ _________.

W: Awesome! How much is the admission price?

M: The exhibition is _________ for students.

12. 대화를 듣고, 남자가 전화를 건 목적으로 가장 적절한 것을 고르시오.
① 안부를 묻기 위해서
② 택배 보관을 부탁하기 위해서
③ 휴가 일정을 변경하기 위해서
④ 도착 날짜를 알려주기 위해서
⑤ 택배가 왔는지 확인하기 위해서

12
(*Telephone rings.*)

W: Hello.

M: Hello, Mrs. Jones. This is Sam, your neighbor.

W: Oh, hi. I thought you were _________ ___________ in Busan. Have you come back?

M: No, I'm still in Busan. Actually, I'm calling to _________ you _________ _________.

W: Okay, what is it?

M: Tomorrow, a package will _________ ___________ _________ my place. Could you keep the package until I get home?

W: No problem. I'll _________ _________ _________.
Enjoy your vacation.

M: Thank you so much!

다음 페이지에 계속 ➡

13. 대화를 듣고, 여자가 지불해야 할 금액으로 가장 적절한 것을 고르시오.

① $10 ② $30
③ $50 ④ $70
⑤ $80

13

M: Welcome to Grand Ice Rink. How can I help you?

W: Hi. I'd like to buy two tickets for today's show.

M: An adult ticket is $50 and a student ticket is $30.

W: One adult and one student, please. And I have a

___________ ___________. Can I use it now?

M: Let me ___________ ___________ ___________.

W: Here it is.

M: *(Pause)* Okay. You can use it now. It's a $10

discount coupon, so ___________ ___________ is $70.

W: Great! Here you are.

14. 대화를 듣고, 두 사람의 관계로 가장 적절한 것을 고르시오.

① 의사 — 환자
② 헬스 트레이너 — 고객
③ 간호사 — 환자
④ 감독 — 운동선수
⑤ 댄스 강사 — 수강생

14

M: You're doing great. You look like you've ___________

___________.

W: Thank you. I have been ___________ ___________ just like

you told me.

M: Good. I hope you're drinking plenty of water

after.

W: Yes, I am. I'm eating ___________ ___________

___________, too.

M: That's really good to hear. Keep that up and you'll

soon reach your goal.

W: I'm really glad I hired you. I feel better after all

those exercises you've taught me.

15. 대화를 듣고, 남자가 여자에게 부탁한 일로 가장 적절한 것을 고르시오.

① 저녁 준비하기
② 꽃 사 오기
③ 오븐 예열하기
④ 화단에 물 주기
⑤ 선물 포장하기

15

W: Dad, happy ____________ ______________!

M: Thank you, sweetie.

W: What shall we have for dinner tonight?

M: I'm cooking meat pie, your mom's favorite.

W: Did you ________ ________ ________ for Mom?

M: Yes, I bought earrings for her. But I think I'm

________ __________.

W: Oh, how about buying her some flowers? She'll

love them.

M: Great. Then, can you go and ________ ________

________ now? I'll give you the money.

W: Sure. No problem.

16. 대화를 듣고, 여자가 옥상에 가는 이유로 가장 적절한 것을 고르시오.

① 청소하기 위해서
② 카페에서 일하기 위해서
③ 영화 촬영을 돕기 위해서
④ 전망을 카메라에 담기 위해서
⑤ 좋아하는 연예인을 보기 위해서

16

M: Anna, good to see you. Where are you going?

W: I'm going to the ____________ of this building.

M: Oh, are you going to the new rooftop café?

W: No. My favorite singer Dave Campion is

__________ his first movie here.

M: On the rooftop?

W: Yeah. It's an action film. I just want to watch him

__________ __________.

M: I see. Can I go with you?

W: Sure.

다음 페이지에 계속 ➡

17. 다음 그림의 상황에 가장 적절한 대화를 고르시오.

① ②
③ ④
⑤

17 ① M: Can you take a picture of me?

W: Sure, ________ me your phone.

② M: How can I help you?

W: I want two student tickets.

③ M: You are not ________ ________ ________ a selfie

stick here.

W: Oh, I see. I won't use it.

④ M: Excuse me. Where is the restroom?

W: It's ________ the corner.

⑤ M: What's your favorite painting?

W: I like the Mona Lisa best.

고난도 담화미언급

18. 다음을 듣고, 여자가 whale shark에 대해 언급하지 <u>않은</u> 것을 고르시오.

① 몸길이 ② 몸무게
③ 먹이 ④ 수명
⑤ 서식지

18 W: Hello, everyone. For today's lesson, I want to talk

about whale sharks. Whale sharks are the largest

fish in the sea. On average, they ________ ________

________ ________ between 5 and 10 meters.

They can weigh up to 19 tons. ________ ________

________ of whale sharks is about 70 years. They

like warmer areas and are ________ ________

________ ________ all over the world.

19. 대화를 듣고, 여자의 마지막 말에 이어질 남자의 말로 가장 적절한 것을 고르시오.

Man: _________________

① I can't eat spicy food.
② I don't like vegetables.
③ Thanks! I'll give it a try.
④ This is my family recipe.
⑤ No, I'm not good at cooking.

19

M: What are you making for lunch?

W: I'm cooking bibimbap.

M: That sounds yummy. How do you make bibimbap?

W: First, I cook ___________ ___________ like carrots and spinach. Then, I make beef bulgogi and fry eggs sunny-side up.

M: Cool! What else goes in bibimbap?

W: I also make seasoned soybean sprouts and a spicy sauce with gochujang ___________ ___________ ___________ everything.

M: Sounds great! Can you ___________ ___________ ___________?

W: Sure thing, I'll write it down for you.

M: Thanks! I'll give it a try.

20. 대화를 듣고, 여자의 마지막 말에 이어질 남자의 말로 가장 적절한 것을 고르시오.

Man: _________________

① She is going there on a boat.
② We are eating seafood for dinner.
③ The island has beautiful mountains.
④ His plane will be leaving in two hours.
⑤ I am flying back to Seoul on Sunday night.

20

W: Hi, James. Are you doing anything special this weekend?

M: Yes, I'm visiting my cousin Paul for a ________ ________ ________.

W: Oh, that's nice! Where does he live?

M: He lives on Jeju Island and it's my first time going there.

W: Awesome! It must be really nice there this time of the year.

M: Yes, I'm really excited to see the ___________ ________ on the island.

W: I hope you have a good trip. When are you ________ ________?

M: I am flying back to Seoul on Sunday night.

Words & Expressions Review 12

● 다음 단어를 암기하세요.

문제	번호	단어	뜻
1	1	continue	계속되다
	2	range from A to B	A부터 B까지 이르다
2	3	dinosaur	공룡
	4	excellent	탁월한, 훌륭한
3	5	after all	어쨌든, 결국에는
4	6	cousin	사촌
	7	play along with ~	~에 동의[동조]하는 척하다
	8	quite	꽤, 상당히
5	9	describe	묘사하다
	10	painful	고통스러운
	11	keep on -ing	계속 ~하다
6	12	select	선발하다
	13	represent	대표하다
7	14	charity	자선, 자선 단체
	15	raise	모금하다, 모으다
	16	donate	기부하다, 기증하다
8	17	island	섬
	18	publish	출판하다
9	19	actually	사실은, 실제로
	20	copy	(책·신문 등의) 한 부
10	21	go through	~을 겪다, 거치다
	22	charge	충전하다

문제	번호	단어	뜻
11	23	instrument	악기, 기구, 도구
	24	check out	~을 확인하다
12	25	neighbor	이웃
	26	on vacation	휴가로
13	27	ask A a favor	A에게 부탁을 하다
	28	take a look	(한번) 보다
	29	total	총액, 합계
14	30	lose weight	살이 빠지다, 살을 빼다
	31	work out	운동하다
	32	suggest	제안하다
15	33	wedding anniversary	결혼 기념일
	34	miss	놓치다
16	35	rooftop	옥상
17	36	pass	건네주다
	37	allow	허용하다, 허락하다
	38	selfie stick	셀카봉
	39	around	(모퉁이 따위를) 돌아서
18	40	on average	평균적으로, 대개
	41	lifespan	수명
19	42	give it a try	한번 해보다
20	43	awesome	굉장한, 어마어마한
	44	nature	자연

●왼쪽 단어장의 뜻이 보이지 않게 반으로 접고, 학습한 단어의 뜻을 아래 빈칸에 적어주세요.

1	describe	23	give a try
2	raise	24	on average
3	awesome	25	dinosaur
4	continue	26	donate
5	take a look	27	suggest
6	check out	28	charge
7	wedding anniversary	29	cousin
8	allow	30	selfie stick
9	copy	31	represent
10	select	32	on vacation
11	after all	33	play along with ~
12	charity	34	miss
13	total	35	nature
14	go through	36	pass
15	excellent	37	island
16	rooftop	38	around
17	painful	39	lifespan
18	range from A to B	40	work out
19	keep on -ing	41	ask A a favor
20	publish	42	neighbor
21	actually	43	lose weight
22	quite	44	instrument

13 회 중학영어듣기 모의고사

M2(17)_13_US
모두 **미국식 발음(US)**
으로 녹음

M2(17)_13_UK
20문제 중 5문제에 **영국식 발음**
(US+UK)을 포함하여 녹음

정답 및 해석 p. 60

1 다음을 듣고, 일요일의 날씨로 가장 적절한 것을 고르시오.

①  ②  ③  ④  ⑤ 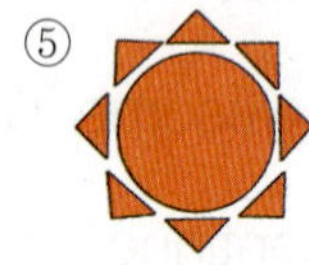

2 대화를 듣고, 여자가 구입할 메모지로 가장 적절한 것을 고르시오.

①  ②  ③  ④  ⑤ 

3 대화를 듣고, 여자의 심정으로 가장 적절한 것을 고르시오.

① 수줍음   ② 화남   ③ 신남
④ 만족함   ⑤ 감사함

4 대화를 듣고, 남자가 어제 한 일로 가장 적절한 것을 고르시오.

① 집안일 돕기   ② 쇼핑몰 가기   ③ 모자 주문하기
④ 컴퓨터 수리하기   ⑤ 야구 경기 관람하기

5 대화를 듣고, 두 사람이 대화하는 장소로 가장 적절한 곳을 고르시오.

① 세탁소   ② 주유소   ③ 식당   ④ 소방서   ⑤ 기차역

6 대화를 듣고, 남자의 마지막 말의 의도로 가장 적절한 것을 고르시오.

① 거절   ② 항의   ③ 요청   ④ 동의   ⑤ 사과

7 대화를 듣고, 남자가 가져올 물건으로 가장 적절한 것을 고르시오.

① 케이크   ② 초   ③ 풍선   ④ 선물   ⑤ 보드게임

8 대화를 듣고, 두 사람이 대화 직후에 할 일로 가장 적절한 것을 고르시오.

① 사진 촬영하기   ② 피자 가게에 가기   ③ 음악 연주하기
④ 티켓 구매하기   ⑤ 콘서트장에 들어가기

9 대화를 듣고, 두 사람이 봉사활동 프로그램에 대해 언급하지 <u>않은</u> 것을 고르시오.

① 봉사 장소   ② 봉사 시간   ③ 신청 방법
④ 모집 인원   ⑤ 신청 마감일

10 다음을 듣고, 남자가 하는 말의 내용으로 가장 적절한 것을 고르시오.

① 텐트 조립 과정   ② 게임 규칙 설명   ③ 시험 주의 사항
④ 현장 학습 준비물   ⑤ 놀이 기구 안전 수칙

11번~20번 문제는 다음 페이지에 ➡

11 대화를 듣고, 한국어 강좌에 대한 내용으로 일치하지 <u>않는</u> 것을 고르시오.

① 시립 문화 센터에서 열린다.　　② 초급반이 있다.
③ 오전에 강좌가 있다.　　④ 레벨 테스트를 받아야 한다.
⑤ 반별 수강 인원은 10명이다.

12 대화를 듣고, 여자가 전화를 건 목적으로 가장 적절한 것을 고르시오.

① 못 간다고 말하기 위해서　　② 길을 물어보기 위해서
③ 늦을 것이라고 말하기 위해서　　④ 갈 곳을 결정하기 위해서
⑤ 만나기로 한 시각을 물어보기 위해서

13 대화를 듣고, 여자가 지불할 금액을 고르시오.

① $41　　② $56　　③ $61　　④ $66　　⑤ $71

14 대화를 듣고, 두 사람의 관계로 가장 적절한 것을 고르시오.

① 배송업체 사장 – 운전사　　② 꽃가게 점원 – 손님
③ 안과의사 – 환자　　④ 정원사 – 집주인
⑤ 교사 – 학생

15 대화를 듣고, 여자가 남자에게 부탁한 일로 가장 적절한 것을 고르시오.

① 택시 예약하기　　② 식물에 물 주기
③ 문단속 확인하기　　④ 역에 데려다주기
⑤ 기차표 예약 변경하기

16 대화를 듣고, 남자가 집까지 걸어간 이유로 가장 적절한 것을 고르시오.

① 버스를 놓쳐서　　② 운동을 하려고　　③ 지갑을 놓고 가서
④ 도서관에 들르려고　　⑤ 친구와 함께 걸어가려고

17 다음 그림의 상황에 가장 적절한 대화를 고르시오.

①　　②　　③　　④　　⑤

18 다음을 듣고, 여자가 Sports Day에 대해 언급하지 <u>않은</u> 것을 고르시오.

① 장소　　② 종료 시각　　③ 점심 메뉴　　④ 대회 종목　　⑤ 준비물

[19~20] 대화를 듣고, 남자의 마지막 말에 이어질 여자의 말로 가장 적절한 것을 고르시오.

19 Woman: _______________________________

① I need to return some science books.　② I need to meet the teacher at 3.
③ Go to the science room.　④ You need your paints.
⑤ Let's make a poster.

20 Woman: _______________________________

① Set a time limit on playing games.　② It's a team-based online game.
③ I'm good at the second one.　④ I've been to the PC room.
⑤ Yeah, I would love that!

Dictation Test 13

M2(17)_13_D

Dictation(받아쓰기)은 본문을 받아쓰면서 영어듣기의 집중력을 향상시키고 다양한 표현을 정리하기 위한 영어듣기 학습법입니다. **녹음을 다시 듣고, 빈칸에 알맞은 단어를 써 보세요.**
※Dictation의 정답은 듣기 대본의 밑줄 친 부분을 확인하세요.

📖 정답 p. 60

맞은 개수 / 총166개

 날씨파악–그림

1. 다음을 듣고, 일요일의 날씨로 가장 적절한 것을 고르시오.

①  ② 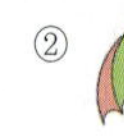

③  ④ 

⑤ 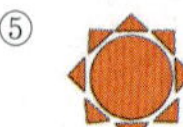

01 M: Good morning, I'm Alan Brown. This is your weekend weather report. It's going to be ________ cloudy during the day today. Light rain showers _______ __________ in the evening. However, on Sunday, the rain will clear and it's going to be sunny all day ________ ________ ________. The daytime temperature is going to ________ 25 degrees Celsius. Thank you.

그림정보파악

2. 대화를 듣고, 여자가 구입할 메모지로 가장 적절한 것을 고르시오.

①  ② 

③  ④

⑤ 

02 M: Hello. Can I help you?

W: Yes. I'm looking for a memo pad ________ __________ my diary.

M: Oh, look over here. These are our best sellers.

W: They all look nice. It's ________ ________ ________ just one.

M: How about this round one with a bear?

W: Well, I prefer the ________ ________.

M: Okay. We have two types of square memo pads.

W: I like the one ________ ________. It looks cute.

M: All right. It's 3,000 won.

심정추론

3. 대화를 듣고, 여자의 심정으로 가장 적절한 것을 고르시오.
   ① 수줍음   ② 화남
   ③ 신남   ④ 만족함
   ⑤ 감사함

03

W: Ugh, I can't believe this!

M: What's wrong, Emily?

W: Dad, look! I bought tickets to this concert and it got canceled at the __________ __________!

M: Oh, no! That's really disappointing. You were so excited about the concert.

W: I had everything planned, and now it's __________.

M: I'm sorry, honey. Maybe you can find another event to go to?

W: It won't be the same. I have been looking forward to this __________ __________!

한일파악

4. 대화를 듣고, 남자가 어제 한 일로 가장 적절한 것을 고르시오.
   ① 집안일 돕기
   ② 쇼핑몰 가기
   ③ 모자 주문하기
   ④ 컴퓨터 수리하기
   ⑤ 야구 경기 관람하기

04

W: Jack, did you buy the baseball cap you wanted?

M: You mean ________ ________ ________ ________ at the mall last weekend?

W: Yes, you said you would ask your mother if you could buy it.

M: Actually, I found out that I can buy it online ________ ________ ________ ________ ________.

W: Oh, really?

M: So I ________ ________ online yesterday.

W: Good for you! I ________ ________ to see you wearing it.

다음 페이지에 계속 ➡

5. 대화를 듣고, 두 사람이 대화하는 장소로
    가장 적절한 곳을 고르시오.
    ① 세탁소   ② 주유소
    ③ 식당   ④ 소방서
    ⑤ 기차역

05 M: Hello, what can I do for you?

W: I'd like to ________ ________ my car. I'll open the

oil tank right away.

M: OK, coming right up. *(Pause)* All done.

W: Thank you. How much is it?

M: It'll be 80,000 won. And you can ________

________ ________ ________ for free.

W: That sounds good. Here is my credit card.

M: All right. Please wait ________ ________ ________.

2025 영어듣기능력평가 1회 6번 변형

6. 대화를 듣고, 남자의 마지막 말의 의도로
    가장 적절한 것을 고르시오.
    ① 거절   ② 항의
    ③ 요청   ④ 동의
    ⑤ 사과

06 W: Daniel, __________ __________ __________

__________ the new science teacher?

M: Well, I've only had one class with him so far.

W: He explains things so clearly and makes the class

really interesting.

M: Oh, I remember he showed us some fun

__________ yesterday.

W: I honestly think he's the best teacher we've had

__________ __________ __________.

M: That's true. I agree with you.

7. 대화를 듣고, 남자가 가져올 물건으로 가장 적절한 것을 고르시오.
① 케이크　　② 초
③ 풍선　　　④ 선물
⑤ 보드게임

07
M: Hey, today is Heesoo's birthday. _________ _________ a surprise party?

W: Sounds great! What should we _________?

M: Jaemin said he'll buy a cake and candles. Do we need anything else?

W: I think _________ _________ _________ balloons would be good.

M: Good idea! Then you _________ the balloons.

W: What about you?

M: I have a board game that everyone can play together. I'll bring that.

W: Okay. See you after school then.

8. 대화를 듣고, 두 사람이 대화 직후에 할 일로 가장 적절한 것을 고르시오.
① 사진 촬영하기
② 피자 가게에 가기
③ 음악 연주하기
④ 티켓 구매하기
⑤ 콘서트장에 들어가기

08
M: Grace, thanks for __________ me to this music concert.

W: You're welcome. I'm glad you could join me.

M: Many of my favorite bands are __________ tonight. Shall we go in?

W: Actually, I'm hungry. Can we __________ __________ __________ to eat before we go in?

M: Of course. What do you feel like eating?

W: How about some pizza? There's a pizzeria just __________ __________ __________.

M: Sounds good. Let's go grab some pizza.

다음 페이지에 계속 ➡

9. 대화를 듣고, 두 사람이 봉사활동 프로그램에 대해 언급하지 <u>않은</u> 것을 고르시오.

① 봉사 장소　② 봉사 시간
③ 신청 방법　④ 모집 인원
⑤ 신청 마감일

09

W: Roy, have you ＿＿＿＿＿ ＿＿＿＿＿ the volunteer program on our school website?

M: Not yet. What are the details?

W: Volunteers will be helping senior citizens at the community center.

M: I see. When does the volunteer program ＿＿＿＿＿ ＿＿＿＿＿?

W: It is every Saturday from 2 to 4 p.m.

M: Do you know ＿＿＿＿＿ ＿＿＿＿＿ ＿＿＿＿＿?

W: Yes. You should download the form and return it by email.

M: That's easy.

W: ＿＿＿＿＿ ＿＿＿＿＿ ＿＿＿＿＿ ＿＿＿＿＿ is June 29th. So, you should hurry and apply if you are interested.

10. 다음을 듣고, 남자가 하는 말의 내용으로 가장 적절한 것을 고르시오.

① 텐트 조립 과정
② 게임 규칙 설명
③ 시험 주의 사항
④ 현장 학습 준비물
⑤ 놀이 기구 안전 수칙

10

M: Hello, class! Let me explain ＿＿＿＿＿ ＿＿＿＿＿ ＿＿＿＿＿ the game, *Blind Square*. You will divide into groups of four. I will give each group a long rope and four blindfolds. ＿＿＿＿＿ ＿＿＿＿＿ a blindfold, hold onto the rope, and try to ＿＿＿＿＿ ＿＿＿＿＿ ＿＿＿＿＿ within 5 minutes with your group members. When your group agrees you've made a square, put the rope down on the floor. The group that makes a square first within ＿＿＿＿＿ ＿＿＿＿＿ ＿＿＿＿＿ wins!

11. 대화를 듣고, 한국어 강좌에 대한 내용으로 일치하지 <u>않는</u> 것을 고르시오.

① 시립 문화 센터에서 열린다.
② 초급반이 있다.
③ 오전에 강좌가 있다.
④ 레벨 테스트를 받아야 한다.
⑤ 반별 수강 인원은 10명이다.

11

M: Martha, do you have any special plans for this summer?

W: _________ _________.

M: Then, why don't we take a Korean course at City Cultural Center?

W: Oh, I would like to learn Korean. Are there any courses for beginners?

M: Yes, there is one in the morning. And there's no level test.

W: Great! How many people can _________ _________ _________ _________?

M: The class is limited to ten people. I guess we should hurry.

W: Okay, let's _________ _________.

12. 대화를 듣고, 여자가 전화를 건 목적으로 가장 적절한 것을 고르시오.

① 못 간다고 말하기 위해서
② 길을 물어보기 위해서
③ 늦을 것이라고 말하기 위해서
④ 갈 곳을 결정하기 위해서
⑤ 만나기로 한 시각을 물어보기 위해서

12

(*Cell phone rings.*)

M: Hello?

W: Hello, this is Cherry.

M: Oh, hi, Cherry. I'm already _________ _________ _________ to the mall. How about you?

W: Me too, but I got stuck _________ _________. I _________ _________ say I cannot make it on time.

M: It's okay, I understand. See you _________ _________ _________!

W: Thanks!

다음 페이지에 계속 ➡

13. 대화를 듣고, 여자가 지불할 금액을 고르시오.

① $41　　② $56
③ $61　　④ $66
⑤ $71

13

M: Welcome to our flower shop.

W: Hello. Do you have purple tulips?

M: Yes, ma'am. Purple tulips cost $________ ________ ________.

W: Okay, I'll buy ________ ________.

M: Would you like a vase to match the flowers? We have a pink vase available for $13. We also sell a red vase ________ $________.

W: Hmm... Okay, I'll take one red vase. Here's my payment.

---

14. 대화를 듣고, 두 사람의 관계로 가장 적절한 것을 고르시오.

① 배송업체 사장 − 운전사
② 꽃가게 점원 − 손님
③ 안과의사 − 환자
④ 정원사 − 집주인
⑤ 교사 − 학생

14

W: Welcome to Suzie's Garden. What can I do for you?

M: Hi. I want to buy some flowers for my mom.

W: How about this basket? ________ ________ ________ popular flowers.

M: Good. Do you ________ ________________, too?

W: Of course. When do you want it?

M: Can you deliver it on May 8th?

W: Sure. ________ ________ will be 35 dollars.

M: Here you are.

부탁(요청)한일파악

15. 대화를 듣고, 여자가 남자에게 부탁한 일로 가장 적절한 것을 고르시오.

① 택시 예약하기
② 식물에 물 주기
③ 문단속 확인하기
④ 역에 데려다주기
⑤ 기차표 예약 변경하기

15

W: Dad, I'm leaving for the trip now.

M: All right. Did you change your train ticket __________ __________ __________?

W: Yes, I changed it to 10 a.m.

M: Good. Then, is everything ready?

W: I guess so. Would you __________ __________ __________ __________?

M: Of course. What is it?

W: Could you book a taxi for me?

M: No problem. I'll __________ __________ __________ it right away.

이유파악

16. 대화를 듣고, 남자가 집까지 걸어간 이유로 가장 적절한 것을 고르시오.

① 버스를 놓쳐서
② 운동을 하려고
③ 지갑을 놓고 가서
④ 도서관에 들르려고
⑤ 친구와 함께 걸어가려고

16

M: Mom, I'm home.

W: Jeff, you're later __________ __________. Why are you sweating so much?

M: Oh, I walked here from school.

W: Why didn't you take a bus? Did you __________ the bus?

M: No, I didn't.

W: Then, why did you walk home? Our home is __________ __________ from your school.

M: I had to __________ __________ the library to return some books on my way home.

W: I see. Next time, call me if you're going to be late.

다음 페이지에 계속 ➡

17. 다음 그림의 상황에 가장 적절한 대화를 고르시오.

① ②
③ ④
⑤

17

① M: I've baked this cake for you.

　W: Thank you so much! It looks delicious.

② M: How may I help you?

　W: I'd like to buy an ＿＿＿＿＿＿ ＿＿＿＿＿＿＿.

③ M: This is not what I ordered.

　W: I'm sorry. I'll check your ＿＿＿＿＿＿.

④ M: I'm so hot and tired.

　W: Then let's go to a café and have a drink.

⑤ M: Could you ＿＿＿＿＿＿ ＿＿＿＿＿＿ the air

　conditioner?

　W: Sure. No problem.

18. 다음을 듣고, 여자가 Sports Day에 대해 언급하지 않은 것을 고르시오.

① 장소　　② 종료 시각
③ 점심 메뉴　④ 대회 종목
⑤ 준비물

18

W: Hello, class. Before you leave for home, I ＿＿＿＿＿＿

＿＿＿＿＿＿ ＿＿＿＿＿＿ ＿＿＿＿＿＿ some important

information about Sports Day tomorrow. You

should come to the Central Field by 9:30 a.m.

The events will start at 10 a.m., and will ＿＿＿＿＿＿

＿＿＿＿＿＿＿ ＿＿＿＿＿＿ 4 p.m. You don't have to

bring your lunch. Hamburgers will be provided.

According to the weather forecast, tomorrow will

be very hot, so ＿＿＿＿＿＿ ＿＿＿＿＿＿ ＿＿＿＿＿＿ and

cold water. See you tomorrow.

19. 대화를 듣고, 남자의 마지막 말에 이어질 여자의 말로 가장 적절한 것을 고르시오.

Woman: _______________

① I need to return some science books.
② I need to meet the teacher at 3.
③ Go to the science room.
④ You need your paints.
⑤ Let's make a poster.

19
M: Hi, Selena. Science Day is this Friday.
W: Hi, Nick. Did you _______ _______ _______ you are going to enter on Friday?
M: Not yet. There is a drawing contest and a writing contest, right?
W: Yes. How about _______ the drawing contest with me?
M: Hmm… What do I need to do for the drawing contest?
W: You need to draw a picture about a science principle and _______ _______ _______ for it.
M: I can do that. Is there anything I should bring to the contest?
W: You need your paints.

---

20. 대화를 듣고, 남자의 마지막 말에 이어질 여자의 말로 가장 적절한 것을 고르시오.

Woman: _______________

① Set a time limit on playing games.
② It's a team-based online game.
③ I'm good at the second one.
④ I've been to the PC room.
⑤ Yeah, I would love that!

20
W: Hey, Drake! You play the game *Underclock*, right?
M: Yeah. Why? Do you play it?
W: Yes. I am a _______ that just started playing.
M: Oh, really? Did you know that they are making *Underclock 2*?
W: I didn't know that. Will it _______ _______ _______ the original?
M: Yes. I heard it will be more difficult to play than the first one.
W: I am already _______ _______ _______ the first one… I wish I were good at playing games.
M: Do you want to go to the PC room with me? I can teach you.
W: Yeah, I would love that!

Words & Expressions Review 13

● 다음 단어를 암기하세요.

문제	번호	단어	뜻	문제	번호	단어	뜻
1	☐ 1	mostly	대체로	11	☐ 23	enroll in ~	~에 등록하다
	☐ 2	expect	예상하다		☐ 24	on one's way (to)	(~로) 가는 길에
	☐ 3	temperature	기온, 온도	12	☐ 25	get stuck	옴짝달싹 못하다, 갇히다
2	☐ 4	look over	~을 살펴보다, 훑어보다		☐ 26	in a while	이따가, 곧
	☐ 5	prefer	선호하다, 좋아하다	13	☐ 27	available	구할[이용할] 수 있는
3	☐ 6	cancel	취소하다		☐ 28	payment	지불, 금액
	☐ 7	ruin	망치다	14	☐ 29	be filled with ~	~으로 가득 차다
4	☐ 8	find out	알게 되다, 알아내다		☐ 30	make a delivery	배달하다
	☐ 9	can't wait to + 동사	빨리 ~하고 싶다, ~이 너무 기대된다	15	☐ 31	do ~ a favor	~의 부탁을 들어주다
5	☐ 10	fill up	(차의 기름 탱크를) 가득 채우다		☐ 32	than usual	평소보다
	☐ 11	for free	무료로	16	☐ 33	sweat	땀을 흘리다
6	☐ 12	so far	지금까지		☐ 34	miss	(탈것을) 놓치다
	☐ 13	clearly	명확하게, 분명히		☐ 35	stop by ~	~에 잠시 들르다
	☐ 14	experiment	실험	17	☐ 36	bill	계산서, 청구서
7	☐ 15	How about ~?	(제안) ~은 어때?		☐ 37	have a drink	(음료 등을) 한 잔 마시다
	☐ 16	a couple of ~	몇 개의, 두서너 개의	18	☐ 38	leave for ~	~로 떠나다
8	☐ 17	invite	초대하다		☐ 39	according to ~	~에 따르면
	☐ 18	perform	공연하다, 연주하다	19	☐ 40	enter	(대회 등에) 참가하다, 출전하다
9	☐ 19	detail	세부사항		☐ 41	principle	(물리·자연의) 법칙
	☐ 20	deadline	마감		☐ 42	newbie	초보자
	☐ 21	application	지원, 신청	20	☐ 43	be different from ~	~과 다르다
10	☐ 22	blindfold	눈가리개		☐ 44	have trouble with ~	~하는 데 어려움을 겪다

● 왼쪽 단어장의 뜻이 보이지 않게 반으로 접고, 학습한 단어의 뜻을 아래 빈칸에 적어주세요.

1	payment		23	be filled with ~
2	bill		24	find out
3	invite		25	so far
4	have trouble with ~		26	cancel
5	prefer		27	deadline
6	ruin		28	experiment
7	have a drink		29	expect
8	available		30	temperature
9	can't wait to + 동사		31	than usual
10	leave for ~		32	a couple of ~
11	stop by ~		33	in a while
12	perform		34	newbie
13	make a delivery		35	for free
14	on one's way (to)		36	detail
15	principle		37	look over
16	according to ~		38	miss
17	sweat		39	clearly
18	blindfold		40	enter
19	fill up		41	application
20	be different from ~		42	do ~ a favor
21	How about ~?		43	get stuck
22	mostly		44	enroll in ~

정답 및 해석 p. 65

1
다음을 듣고, 서울의 내일 날씨로 가장 적절한 것을 고르시오.

① 
② 
③ 
④ 
⑤ 

2
대화를 듣고, 남자가 구입할 운동복으로 가장 적절한 것을 고르시오.

① 
② 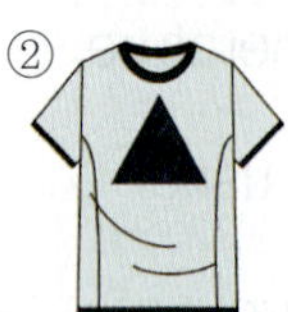
③ 
④ 
⑤ 

3
대화를 듣고, 남자의 심정으로 가장 적절한 것을 고르시오.

① bored　　② scared　　③ excited　　④ relaxed　　⑤ nervous

4
대화를 듣고, 여자가 신문 제작에서 맡은 일로 가장 적절한 것을 고르시오.

① 번역하기　　② 기사 쓰기　　③ 삽화 그리기
④ 인터뷰하기　　⑤ 주제 정하기

5
대화를 듣고, 대화가 이루어지고 있는 장소를 고르시오.

① 서점　　② 도서관　　③ 소방서　　④ 약국　　⑤ 경찰서

6 대화를 듣고, 여자의 마지막 말의 의도로 가장 적절한 것을 고르시오.

① 감사　　　② 거절　　　③ 위로　　　④ 요청　　　⑤ 충고

7 대화를 듣고, 두 사람이 휴가 때 할 일로 가장 적절한 것을 고르시오.

① 캠핑 가기　　　② 영화 보기　　　③ 쇼핑하기
④ 집에서 쉬기　　　⑤ 워터 파크 가기

8 대화를 듣고, 남자가 대화 직후에 할 일로 가장 적절한 것을 고르시오.

① 케이크 가져오기　　　② 테이블 정돈하기
③ 휴식 취하기　　　④ 파티 장식하기
⑤ 장 보러 가기

9 대화를 듣고, 여자가 Science Camp에 대해 언급하지 <u>않은</u> 것을 고르시오.

① 캠프 기간　　　② 참가 대상　　　③ 주최 기관
④ 활동 내용　　　⑤ 참가 비용

10 다음을 듣고, 여자가 하는 말의 내용으로 가장 적절한 것을 고르시오.

① 도서관 위치 설명　　　② 현장체험학습 소개
③ 동아리 축제 일정 공지　　　④ 신규 방과후 프로그램 홍보
⑤ 학교 도서관 이용 규칙 안내

11 대화를 듣고, Green Park Campground에 대한 내용과 일치하지 <u>않는</u> 것을 고르시오.

① 지난달에 개장했다.　　　② 아름다운 호숫가에 위치해 있다.
③ 바비큐를 즐길 수 있다.　　　④ 반려동물 동반이 가능하다.
⑤ 무료 와이파이를 제공한다.

12번~20번 문제는 다음 페이지에 ➡

12 대화를 듣고, 여자가 전화를 건 목적으로 가장 적절한 것을 고르시오.

① 재킷 수선을 맡기기 위해서
② 가게 위치를 문의하기 위해서
③ 구매한 옷을 환불하기 위해서
④ 운영 시간을 확인하기 위해서
⑤ 주문한 옷의 입고 일정을 묻기 위해서

13 대화를 듣고, 남자가 받은 거스름돈으로 가장 적절한 것을 고르시오.

① $1　　② $2　　③ $3　　④ $4　　⑤ $5

14 대화를 듣고, 두 사람의 관계로 가장 적절한 것을 고르시오.

① 의사 – 환자　　② 부동산 중개업자 – 고객
③ 배관공 – 부품 공급업자　　④ 아파트 관리인 – 거주민
⑤ 설계업체 직원 – 시공 기술자

15 대화를 듣고, 여자가 남자에게 부탁한 일로 가장 적절한 것을 고르시오.

① 스트레칭하는 법 알려주기　　② 운동화 챙기기
③ 선글라스 가져오기　　④ 운동복 착용하기
⑤ 도착 시간 알려주기

16 대화를 듣고, 여자가 연습에 나갈 수 <u>없는</u> 이유를 고르시오.

① 감기에 걸려서　　② 늦잠을 자서
③ 어머니 병문안을 가야 해서　　④ 훈련을 받아야 해서
⑤ 동생을 병원에 데려가야 해서

17 다음 그림의 상황에 가장 적절한 대화를 고르시오.

①   ②   ③   ④   ⑤

18 다음을 듣고, 여자가 학교 현장 학습에 대해 언급하지 <u>않은</u> 것을 고르시오.

① 목적지   ② 교통 수단   ③ 집합 시각   ④ 준비물   ⑤ 종료 시각

[19~20] 대화를 듣고, 여자의 마지막 말에 이어질 남자의 말로 가장 적절한 것을 고르시오.

19 Man: _______________________________

① How about this restaurant?
② Plastic is cheaper and lighter.
③ Sorry. I have to do my homework.
④ We can bring our own shopping bags.
⑤ Plastics are no good for the environment.

20 Man: _______________________________

① It's the yellow button.   ② Let's print a test page.
③ We used up all the paper.   ④ We should call in a technician.
⑤ The printer is in the next room.

Dictation Test 14

M2(17)_14_D

Dictation(받아쓰기)은 본문을 받아쓰면서 영어듣기의 집중력을 향상시키고 다양한 표현을 정리하기 위한 영어듣기 학습법입니다. **녹음을 다시 듣고, 빈칸에 알맞은 단어를 써 보세요.**

※Dictation의 정답은 듣기 대본의 밑줄 친 부분을 확인하세요.

정답 p. 65

맞은 개수 / 총184개

날씨파악–그림

1. 다음을 듣고, 서울의 내일 날씨로 가장 적절한 것을 고르시오.

①    ② 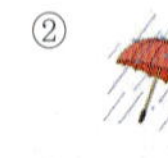

③    ④ 

⑤

01 M: Here is the weather _________ for Seoul. Tonight _________ _________ wet and windy. However, the rain will stop before tomorrow morning. There will be clear and beautiful skies tomorrow. But the _________ _________ _________, you should be _________ when you go out. Yellow dust will come to Seoul with strong winds.

그림정보파악

2. 대화를 듣고, 남자가 구입할 운동복으로 가장 적절한 것을 고르시오.

①    ② 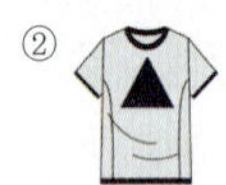

③    ④ 

⑤ 

02 W: How can I help you?

M: I'd like to buy a shirt to wear when I _________ _________ _________ _________.

W: This T-shirt here is quite popular.

M: It's getting cold these days, so I'd like one with _________ _________.

W: Okay, what about this one which has _________?

M: Well, I'd like something more simple.

W: Then how about this one which has a _________ on the chest?

M: That looks great! I'll take it.

---

3. 대화를 듣고, 남자의 심정으로 가장 적절한 것을 고르시오.

① bored　　② scared
③ excited　④ relaxed
⑤ nervous

03

W: Junha, why are you smiling?

M: Hi, Mina. _______ _________ _______ information about Tokyo Disneyland.

W: Why? Are you planning to go there?

M: Yes! Guess what? I _______ _______ _______ _______ there.

W: Really? How did you win it?

M: Well, I won the Japan Introduction Video Contest. I _______ _______ _______ I could do it.

W: You're amazing!

4. 대화를 듣고, 여자가 신문 제작에서 맡은 일로 가장 적절한 것을 고르시오.

① 번역하기
② 기사 쓰기
③ 삽화 그리기
④ 인터뷰하기
⑤ 주제 정하기

04

W: Look, Dad. My classmates and I _______ ___________ this newspaper.

M: It looks great! Was it a school project?

W: Yeah. Elly _______ _______ _______ _______ _______ of Korean history.

M: Nice. Which article did you write?

W: I didn't write any.

M: Then, what did you do?

W: I drew the pictures. They help the reader ___________ _______ ___________.

M: Oh, really? You drew them so well! I think you could be an artist someday.

다음 페이지에 계속 ➡

5. 대화를 듣고, 대화가 이루어지고 있는 장소를 고르시오.
① 서점　　　② 도서관
③ 소방서　　④ 약국
⑤ 경찰서

05
M: Excuse me. Can you tell me where the books about space science are?

W: You can ________ ________ ________ the fourth floor.

M: Thank you. How many books can I ________ ________?

W: Four at a time. You can keep them for five days. After that, you ________ ________ ________ if you don't return the books on time.

M: How much is the fine?

W: 200 won a day per book.

6. 대화를 듣고, 여자의 마지막 말의 의도로 가장 적절한 것을 고르시오.
① 감사　　　② 거절
③ 위로　　　④ 요청
⑤ 충고

06
M: Hey, Jane! You have a ________ ________. What's wrong?

W: Hi, Mike. I was ________ ________ my mom because I didn't get a good grade.

M: Oh, I'm sorry to hear that. You can do better next time!

W: Thanks, Mike. I don't have any energy to take the classes.

M: Did you have lunch?

W: No, I have ________ ____________ so I didn't eat anything.

M: No way! You should eat something! Let's grab some sandwiches.

W: Thank you, but I don't ________ ________ ________ right now.

7. 대화를 듣고, 두 사람이 휴가 때 할 일로 가장 적절한 것을 고르시오.

① 캠핑 가기
② 영화 보기
③ 쇼핑하기
④ 집에서 쉬기
⑤ 워터 파크 가기

07

M: Sarah, we should go camping over the holiday weekend.

W: I'm not sure. How about we ________ ________ ________ or go to the movies instead?

M: I was hoping we could ________ ________ ________ and have a barbecue.

W: It's too hot outside and what if there are bugs?

M: Then what about going to the water park? It will be cool and ________ ________ ________ ________.

W: That does sound like a good idea. Let's go!

M: Good.

8. 대화를 듣고, 남자가 대화 직후에 할 일로 가장 적절한 것을 고르시오.

① 케이크 가져오기
② 테이블 정돈하기
③ 휴식 취하기
④ 파티 장식하기
⑤ 장 보러 가기

08

M: Now, the party decorations are done. ________ ________ ________ do next?

W: Thank you for being so helpful, Matt.

M: You're welcome. Do you want me to ________ ________ ________?

W: We can do that later. Why don't you ________ ________ ________?

M: It's okay. I'm not tired.

W: Then could you ________ ________ the birthday cake from the bakery?

M: No problem. I can go now.

다음 페이지에 계속 ➡

9. 대화를 듣고, 여자가 Science Camp에 대해 언급하지 <u>않은</u> 것을 고르시오.

① 캠프 기간　② 참가 대상
③ 주최 기관　④ 활동 내용
⑤ 참가 비용

09

M: Ms. Wilson, I want to join the Science Camp this year.

W: Sure! I think that's a good idea.

M: How long is the Science Camp?

W: It will be from August 8 to August 15.

M: Can anyone ___________ ________ the Science Camp?

W: Only second-year students can participate this year.

M: I see. What kind of activities are done at the camp?

W: You will do ________ ________ ____________.

M: That sounds fun. How much is the fee?

W: The ________ ________ is 150 dollars.

---

10. 다음을 듣고, 여자가 하는 말의 내용으로 가장 적절한 것을 고르시오.

① 도서관 위치 설명
② 현장체험학습 소개
③ 동아리 축제 일정 공지
④ 신규 방과후 프로그램 홍보
⑤ 학교 도서관 이용 규칙 안내

10

W: Good afternoon, students. I'm here to tell you about a new after-school program we are starting at our school. It's ________ the Reading Buddies Program. This program pairs older students with younger students ________ ________ ________ their reading skills. This will be ________ ________ ____________ for everyone to learn and grow together. If you are interested, please ________ ________ at the library by Friday.

11. 대화를 듣고, Green Park Campground
    에 대한 내용과 일치하지 <u>않는</u> 것을 고르
    시오.
    ① 지난달에 개장했다.
    ② 아름다운 호숫가에 위치해 있다.
    ③ 바비큐를 즐길 수 있다.
    ④ 반려동물 동반이 가능하다.
    ⑤ 무료 와이파이를 제공한다.

11

M: Sandra, do you know Green Park Campground? It just __________ __________ __________.

W: Yes. I heard it's on a beautiful lake.

M: Right. My family and I went there last week. We enjoyed a barbeque.

W: Did you bring your dogs, too?

M: No. You __________ __________ __________ there.

W: I see. Did you rent a tent?

M: Yes, __________ __________ __________ __________ to rent a tent. They even have free wi-fi.

W: That's great.

12. 대화를 듣고, 여자가 전화를 건 목적으로
    가장 적절한 것을 고르시오.
    ① 재킷 수선을 맡기기 위해서
    ② 가게 위치를 문의하기 위해서
    ③ 구매한 옷을 환불하기 위해서
    ④ 운영 시간을 확인하기 위해서
    ⑤ 주문한 옷의 입고 일정을 묻기 위
       해서

12

(Telephone rings.)

M: Hello, Comet Clothing. How may I help you?

W: Hi, I ordered a jacket through your store last week, and I'm __________ when it will be in stock.

M: Sure, may I __________ __________ __________, please?

W: Yes, it's Hannah Kim.

M: *(Typing sound)* I found your order. Your jacket should be __________ __________ this Saturday.

W: Great! Then can I pick it up at the store that day?

M: Sure. We'll notify you __________ __________ __________ it arrives.

W: Okay. Thank you.

다음 페이지에 계속 ➡

13. 대화를 듣고, 남자가 받은 거스름돈으로 가장 적절한 것을 고르시오.

① $1   ② $2
③ $3   ④ $4
⑤ $5

13

W: Hi, welcome to Minute Mini Golf.

M: Hi, I would like to play ________ ________ of mini golf, please.

W: Sure, it's 9 dollars for a round of mini golf. Anything else?

M: I ________ ________ ________ two golf clubs as well.

W: Okay, it's 4 dollars per golf club.

M: Great, how much is that in total?

W: ________ ________ ________ ________ 17 dollars.

M: Okay, here's a 20-dollar bill.

W: Thank you. Here's your ________.

14. 대화를 듣고, 두 사람의 관계로 가장 적절한 것을 고르시오.

① 의사 − 환자
② 부동산 중개업자 − 고객
③ 배관공 − 부품 공급업자
④ 아파트 관리인 − 거주민
⑤ 설계업체 직원 − 시공 기술자

14

M: Hello. Can I help you?

W: Hi. I live in apartment 305, and I think I have a problem.

M: ________ ________ ________ problem?

W: I didn't get any hot water ________ ________.

M: Really? I'm so sorry. Is the problem in the kitchen or bathroom?

W: Both. Can you send someone to ________ ________ it?

M: Of course. I'll send up a repair person ________ ________ ________ ________.

15. 대화를 듣고, 여자가 남자에게 부탁한 일
로 가장 적절한 것을 고르시오.
① 스트레칭하는 법 알려주기
② 운동화 챙기기
③ 선글라스 가져오기
④ 운동복 착용하기
⑤ 도착 시간 알려주기

15 *(Cellphone rings.)*

M: Hello, Emma.

W: Hi, James. Remember our plan to __________ __________ in the park?

M: Yes, I've already put on my running shoes and stretched.

W: That's great. I'm __________ __________ __________ to the park near your house.

M: OK, I'll be there in a few minutes.

W: Perfect, but there's a minor problem. I __________ my sunglasses at home.

M: No worries, I'll bring __________ __________ __________ for you.

W: Thanks a lot, James. See you soon.

16. 대화를 듣고, 여자가 연습에 나갈 수
없는 이유를 고르시오.
① 감기에 걸려서
② 늦잠을 자서
③ 어머니 병문안을 가야 해서
④ 훈련을 받아야 해서
⑤ 동생을 병원에 데려가야 해서

16 *(Telephone rings.)*

W: Hello. Coach Roberts? It's me, Jane.

M: Hello, Jane. How are you?

W: I am all right. But my brother has a __________ __________ and my mom is very busy. So, I'll have to __________ __________ to the doctor.

M: I am sorry to hear that. So, you can't come to the training session this afternoon, can you?

W: No, __________ __________ __________ I can't.

다음 페이지에 계속 ➡

17. 다음 그림의 상황에 가장 적절한 대화를 고르시오.

① ②
③ ④
⑤

17
① W: Do you want to ________ ________ ________ with me?

M: Okay! Let's go to the hardware store afterwards.

② W: Do you like eating cereal?

M: Not really. I ________ pancakes ________ cereal.

③ W: Remind me to buy some cereal later.

M: Okay, I will try not to forget.

④ W: Excuse me, where can I find the cereal?

M: Oh, that would be in ________ number 5.

⑤ W: Do you want to eat steak for dinner?

M: Of course! I will never ________ ________ ________ steak!

18. 다음을 듣고, 여자가 학교 현장 학습에 대해 언급하지 <u>않은</u> 것을 고르시오.

① 목적지　　② 교통 수단
③ 집합 시각　　④ 준비물
⑤ 종료 시각

18
W: Hello, students. Our ________ ________ ________ is tomorrow. As you know, we will visit Newton Science Center. We will use our school buses for the trip. The buses will leave at 9 a.m., so I expect ________ ________ ________ ________ by 8:30. You don't need to bring your lunch, but please don't forget to bring your ________ ________ ________. See you tomorrow, then!

19. 대화를 듣고, 여자의 마지막 말에 이어질 남자의 말로 가장 적절한 것을 고르시오.

Man: _______________

① How about this restaurant?
② Plastic is cheaper and lighter.
③ Sorry. I have to do my homework.
④ We can bring our own shopping bags.
⑤ Plastics are no good for the environment.

19

W: Henry, what are you searching on the Internet?

M: I'm looking for information on _______ _______ _______ _______, Mom.

W: Is it for homework?

M: Yes. I need to find ways to _______ the use of plastic.

W: Right. How about bringing a food container from home when _______ _______ food from a restaurant?

M: Yes. I've discovered that's one of the ways to _______ _______ _______.

W: What other things can we do?

M: We can bring our own shopping bags.

20. 대화를 듣고, 여자의 마지막 말에 이어질 남자의 말로 가장 적절한 것을 고르시오.

Man: _______________

① It's the yellow button.
② Let's print a test page.
③ We used up all the paper.
④ We should call in a technician.
⑤ The printer is in the next room.

20

W: Oh, the printer is _______ _______ _______.

M: Let's _______ the empty cartridge with a new one.

W: Isn't that difficult? Do you know how to do it?

M: It's _______ _______ _______ _______. Open the cover and pull the cartridge out.

W: All right, and then?

M: Remove the protective strip from the new cartridge and _______ _______.

W: All done. What next?

M: Let's print a test page.

Words & Expressions Review 14

● 다음 단어를 암기하세요.

문제	번호	단어	뜻
1	1	weather forecast	일기 예보
	2	day after tomorrow	내일모레
	3	yellow dust	황사
2	4	quite	꽤, 상당히
	5	popular	인기 있는
3	6	search for ~	~을 검색하다
	7	introduction	소개
	8	amazing	대단한, 놀라운
4	9	put together	(이것저것을 모아) 만들다
	10	come up with	~을 생각해 내다, 제안하다
	11	theme	주제, 테마
5	12	check out	(도서관 등에서) 대출하다
	13	fine	벌금을 과하다, 벌금
	14	return	반납하다
6	15	scold	꾸짖다
	16	appetite	식욕
7	17	outdoors	야외에서, 야외로
	18	What if ~?	~이면 어쩌지?
8	19	set the table	식탁을 차리다
	20	take a break	잠시 휴식을 취하다
9	21	participate in ~	~에 참가하다
	22	fee	요금, 가입비

문제	번호	단어	뜻
10	23	buddy	친구
	24	opportunity	기회
11	25	campground	캠핑장, 야영장
	26	rent	빌리다, 대여하다
	27	cost	비용
12	28	pick ~ up	(어디에서) ~을 찾다
	29	notify	알리다
	30	as soon as	~하자마자
13	31	come to	(총계가) ~이 되다
14	32	look into ~	~을 조사하다, 주의 깊게 살펴보다
	33	repair person	수리공
15	34	minor	작은, 가벼운
16	35	be sorry to + 동사	~하게 되어 유감이다
	36	session	시간, 기간
17	37	hardware store	철물점
	38	aisle	통로
18	39	approval	승인
	40	slip	쪽지
19	41	container	용기, 그릇
	42	discover	알아내다, 찾다
20	43	be out of ~	~이 다 떨어지다, ~을 다 써서 없다
	44	use up	다 써버리다

●왼쪽 단어장의 뜻이 보이지 않게 반으로 접고, 학습한 단어의 뜻을 아래 빈칸에 적어주세요.

1	amazing		23	participate in ~
2	appetite		24	introduction
3	opportunity		25	use up
4	day after tomorrow		26	popular
5	set the table		27	campground
6	approval		28	theme
7	pick ~ up		29	weather forecast
8	buddy		30	discover
9	notify		31	look into ~
10	search for ~		32	What if ~?
11	be out of ~		33	outdoors
12	put together		34	be sorry to + 동사
13	fine		35	scold
14	as soon as		36	quite
15	check out		37	container
16	repair person		38	hardware store
17	return		39	rent
18	come to		40	come up with
19	yellow dust		41	session
20	aisle		42	fee
21	take a break		43	slip
22	cost		44	minor

14
회
단
어

15회 중학영어듣기 모의고사

M2(17)_15_US
모두 **미국식 발음(US)** 으로 녹음

M2(17)_15_UK
20문제 중 5문제에 **영국식 발음 (US+UK)**을 포함하여 녹음

정답 및 해석 p. 70

1 다음을 듣고, 대구의 내일 날씨로 가장 적절한 것을 고르시오.

①  ②  ③  ④ 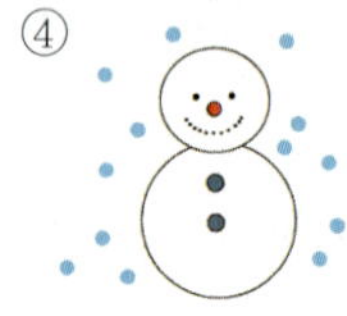 ⑤ 

2 대화를 듣고, 여자가 산 케이크로 가장 적절한 것을 고르시오.

①  ②  ③  ④  ⑤ 

3 대화를 듣고, 여자의 심정으로 가장 적절한 것을 고르시오.

① calm ② upset ③ excited ④ thankful ⑤ disappointed

4 대화를 듣고, 남자가 어제 한 일로 가장 적절한 것을 고르시오.

① 운동하기 ② 농장 가기 ③ 쓰레기 줍기
④ 사과잼 만들기 ⑤ 놀이공원 가기

5 대화를 듣고, 두 사람이 대화하는 장소로 가장 적절한 곳을 고르시오.

① 병원 ② 호텔 ③ 공항 ④ 우체국 ⑤ 장난감 가게

6 대화를 듣고, 여자의 마지막 말에 담긴 의도를 고르시오.

① 동의　　　② 사과　　　③ 제안　　　④ 용서　　　⑤ 항의

7 대화를 듣고, 남자가 만들 물건으로 가장 적절한 것을 고르시오.

① 필통　　　② 쓰레기통　　　③ 치마　　　④ 목도리　　　⑤ 가방

8 대화를 듣고, 두 사람이 대화 직후에 할 일로 가장 적절한 것을 고르시오.

① 농구하기　　　② 음식 주문하기　　　③ 체육관 청소하기
④ 보드게임 챙기기　　　⑤ 친구들에게 물어보기

9 대화를 듣고, 두 사람이 다큐멘터리에 대해 언급하지 <u>않은</u> 것을 고르시오.

① 내레이터　　　② 제목　　　③ 내용
④ 장르　　　⑤ 수상 여부

10 다음을 듣고, 남자가 하는 말의 내용으로 가장 적절한 것을 고르시오.

① 여행 일정 짜는 요령　　　② 외국어 공부하는 방법　　　③ 통역 앱 사용하는 방법
④ 교내 영어 말하기 대회　　　⑤ 외국인 친구 사귀는 법

11 대화를 듣고, Mega Shopping Mall에 대한 내용과 일치하지 <u>않는</u> 것을 고르시오.

① 지난주 토요일에 개장했다.
② 도시에서 가장 큰 복합 쇼핑몰이다.
③ 학교로부터 지하철로 10분 거리에 있다.
④ 쇼핑몰 안에 워터파크가 있다.
⑤ 10달러 이상 구매 고객에게 사은품을 준다.

12번~20번 문제는 다음 페이지에 ➡

12 대화를 듣고, 남자가 전화를 건 목적으로 가장 적절한 것을 고르시오.

① 식사에 초대하기 위해서　　　　② 행사 연기를 요청하기 위해서
③ 예약 인원을 확인하기 위해서　　④ 식사 메뉴를 변경하기 위해서
⑤ 식당의 위치를 물어보기 위해서

13 대화를 듣고, 두 사람이 만날 시각을 고르시오.

① 5:00 p.m.　　② 5:15 p.m.　　③ 5:30 p.m.　　④ 5:45 p.m.　　⑤ 6:00 p.m.

14 대화를 듣고, 두 사람의 관계로 가장 적절한 것을 고르시오.

① 교사 — 학부모　　② 상담원 — 학생　　③ 의사 — 환자 보호자
④ 서점 주인 — 손님　　⑤ 학원 강사 — 수강생

15 대화를 듣고, 여자가 남자에게 부탁한 일로 가장 적절한 것을 고르시오.

① 설거지하기　　② 쓰레기 버리기　　③ 동생 숙제 도와주기
④ 함께 축구 경기 보기　　⑤ 경기 내용 설명하기

16 대화를 듣고, 여자가 친구의 집에 가는 이유로 가장 적절한 것을 고르시오.

① 영화를 보기 위해서　　　　② 저녁을 먹기 위해서
③ 자전거를 빌리기 위해서　　④ 빌린 책을 돌려주기 위해서
⑤ 과제 조사를 같이 하기 위해서

17 다음 그림의 상황에 가장 적절한 대화를 고르시오.

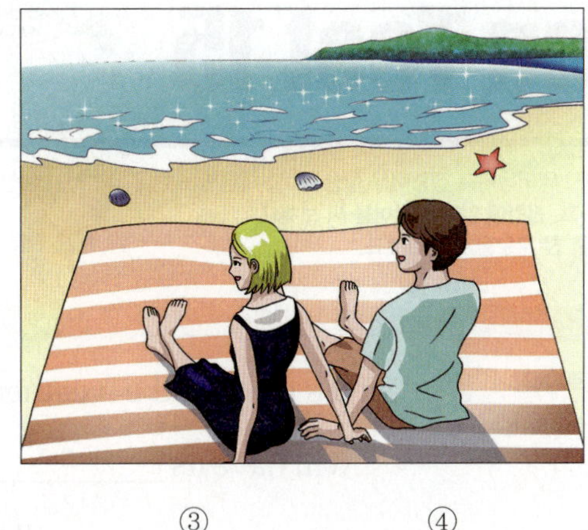

①   ②   ③   ④   ⑤

18 다음을 듣고, 여자가 자신에 대해 언급하지 <u>않은</u> 것을 고르시오.

① 이름   ② 사는 곳   ③ 전공   ④ 직업   ⑤ 수상 경력

[19~20] 대화를 듣고, 남자의 마지막 말에 이어질 여자의 말로 가장 적절한 것을 고르시오.

19 Woman: ________________________________

① I want to adopt two dogs.   ② We need some volunteers.

③ What did you do last Saturday?   ④ Yes. I want to be an animal doctor.

⑤ Wonderful. Let's start this weekend.

20 Woman: ________________________________

① Let's eat pizza for dinner tonight.

② My dream is to become a firefighter.

③ I have to get home by at least 7 o'clock.

④ I heard that it's going to start at 3 o'clock.

⑤ What do you have to do when a fire breaks out?

Dictation Test 15

M2(17)_15_D

Dictation(받아쓰기)은 본문을 받아쓰면서 영어듣기의 집중력을 향상시키고 다양한 표현을 정리하기 위한 영어듣기 학습법입니다. **녹음을 다시 듣고, 빈칸에 알맞은 단어를 써 보세요.**
※Dictation의 정답은 듣기 대본의 밑줄 친 부분을 확인하세요.

정답 p. 70

맞은 개수 / 총163개

---

1. 다음을 듣고, 대구의 내일 날씨로 가장 적절한 것을 고르시오.

①  ② 

③  ④ 

⑤

01 M: It's time for the weather forecast. Tomorrow, Seoul will have its ＿＿＿ ＿＿＿ ＿＿＿ ＿＿＿ ＿＿＿. Daejeon will be rainy. In Gangneung, there will be a lot of snow ＿＿＿ ＿＿＿ strong winds, so when you drive, be extra cautious. And in Daegu, it will be clear and sunny, but it will be cold, so ＿＿＿ ＿＿＿.

---

2. 대화를 듣고, 여자가 산 케이크로 가장 적절한 것을 고르시오.

①  ② 

③  ④ 

⑤ 

02 M: May I help you?

W: Yes, I'd like to buy a cake.

M: Sure. What do you have ＿＿＿ ＿＿＿?

W: I'd like one with flowers ＿＿＿ ＿＿＿. But, I don't want any writing on it.

M: Then, ＿＿＿ ＿＿＿ this heart-shaped cake? It's very ＿＿＿ these days.

W: It's nice. I'll take it.

---

3. 대화를 듣고, 여자의 심정으로 가장 적절한 것을 고르시오.
   ① calm   ② upset
   ③ excited   ④ thankful
   ⑤ disappointed

03

M: Bad news, Ava. Dad can't take us to the beach. He has to work.

W: I heard. Well, it ____________ ____________ ____________.

M: But you really wanted to go there this weekend.

W: I did. But you and I can't go ____________ ____________ ____________, can we?

M: True. You seem pretty ____________ about this.

W: ____________ ____________? There's always another day.

M: All right. If you say so.

4. 대화를 듣고, 남자가 어제 한 일로 가장 적절한 것을 고르시오.
   ① 운동하기
   ② 농장 가기
   ③ 쓰레기 줍기
   ④ 사과잼 만들기
   ⑤ 놀이공원 가기

04

M: Jasmine, I've brought some apples for you.

W: Oh, thanks. Where did you get them?

M: I went to my grandparents' farm yesterday and ____________ ____________ ____________.

W: Wow! That's cool!

M: It was hard ____________ ____________, but I had so much fun.

W: That sounds very exciting.

M: It's not ____________ ____________ ____________. Why don't you join me next weekend?

W: Great! I'd love to go there and try it.

다음 페이지에 계속 ➡

5. 대화를 듣고, 두 사람이 대화하는 장소로 가장 적절한 곳을 고르시오.

① 병원　　　② 호텔
③ 공항　　　④ 우체국
⑤ 장난감 가게

05

M: Hello. How may I help you?

W: I'd like to send this ___________ to Korea.

M: OK. Can you put it here, please?

W: Sure. I'd like to send it _______ _______ _______.

M: OK. Then it will be 17 dollars. _______ _______

the package?

W: Some toys for my cousins in Korea.

M: I see.

6. 대화를 듣고, 여자의 마지막 말에 담긴 의도를 고르시오.

① 동의　　　② 사과
③ 제안　　　④ 용서
⑤ 항의

06

M: Mom, I have something to tell you. Please don't
_______ _______ _______ me.

W: What happened, my dear? Why do you look so
worried?

M: I was watching TV and I ___________ _______
grape juice on the new carpet.

W: Oh no! That carpet was a gift from your aunt!

M: I know, Mom. I'm really sorry.

W: It's all right. I'm glad you told me. Just _______
_______ _______ next time.

7. 대화를 듣고, 남자가 만들 물건으로 가장 적절한 것을 고르시오.

① 필통　　　　② 쓰레기통
③ 치마　　　　④ 목도리
⑤ 가방

07

M: Jimin, your jeans _________ _________ _________ _________ on you.

W: You're right, Dad. Maybe I should put them in the recycling bin.

M: Can't you get them _______?

W: I think it's better to just buy a new pair. These ones are too old.

M: Well, why don't I make something out of them?

W: Great! What can you make?

M: Hmm…You already have many bags. So, I'll _________ _________ _________ _________.

W: That's fantastic!

8. 대화를 듣고, 두 사람이 대화 직후에 할 일로 가장 적절한 것을 고르시오.

① 농구하기
② 음식 주문하기
③ 체육관 청소하기
④ 보드게임 챙기기
⑤ 친구들에게 물어보기

08

W: Phew, that gym class was _____________!

M: Tell me about it, Emma. I'm ready to relax.

W: What do you want to do after school, Jack?

M: Let's go to the basketball court and __________ __________ __________.

W: It's a bit far. How about we play some board games in the cafeteria instead?

M: Okay. Then, how about we invite Sarah and Matt __________ __________ __________?

W: That sounds like fun! Let's go ask them now.

다음 페이지에 계속 ➡

9. 대화를 듣고, 두 사람이 다큐멘터리에 대해 언급하지 **않은** 것을 고르시오.

① 내레이터
② 제목
③ 내용
④ 장르
⑤ 수상 여부

09

W: Peter, what are you watching on your laptop?

M: I'm watching a documentary. It's narrated by my favorite actor, Ben Parker.

W: Oh, I love his voice. It's __________ __________ __________ documentaries. What's the title?

M: The title is *The World's Deadliest Spiders*.

W: Ah, let me guess. The documentary is about venomous spiders, isn't it?

M: You're right. Spiders are __________ __________.

W: That sounds like a __________ documentary.

M: Yes, it is. Actually, nature documentaries are my favorite.

2024 영어듣기능력평가 2회 10번 변형

10. 다음을 듣고, 남자가 하는 말의 내용으로 가장 적절한 것을 고르시오.

① 여행 일정 짜는 요령
② 외국어 공부하는 방법
③ 통역 앱 사용하는 방법
④ 교내 영어 말하기 대회
⑤ 외국인 친구 사귀는 법

10

M: Hello, travelers. Today, I want to give you some tips on using __________ __________ during your trip abroad. First, download the app and check __________ __________ __________ without the Internet. Second, try speaking into the app so it can translate your voice. Third, save some __________ __________ before your trip. That way, you can find them quickly. These apps can really __________ __________ __________ in a foreign country.

11. 대화를 듣고, Mega Shopping Mall에 대한 내용과 일치하지 <u>않는</u> 것을 고르시오.

① 지난주 토요일에 개장했다.
② 도시에서 가장 큰 복합 쇼핑몰이다.
③ 학교로부터 지하철로 10분 거리에 있다.
④ 쇼핑몰 안에 워터파크가 있다.
⑤ 10달러 이상 구매 고객에게 사은품을 준다.

11

M: Tiffany, have you been to the Mega Shopping Mall? It opened last Saturday.

W: Not yet. I heard it's now the biggest shopping mall in the city.

M: That's right. It only takes 10 minutes by subway ________ ________ ________ from our school.

W: Wow! It's near our school.

M: I heard that one of the major hot spots is Aquafield, ________ ____________ ________ a spa and waterpark.

W: Great! We should go check it out.

M: Sure. There's an opening event that offers a gift ________ __________ ________ $100 until next week.

W: That's great.

12. 대화를 듣고, 남자가 전화를 건 목적으로 가장 적절한 것을 고르시오.

① 식사에 초대하기 위해서
② 행사 연기를 요청하기 위해서
③ 예약 인원을 확인하기 위해서
④ 식사 메뉴를 변경하기 위해서
⑤ 식당의 위치를 물어보기 위해서

12

(Telephone rings.)

W: Hello. Noah's Restaurant.

M: Hi. I __________ __________ __________ for three people this Saturday. My name is Harry Wilson.

W: Let me see... Yes, I have your name here, sir. How may I help you?

M: I __________ Dinner Course A. Can I change it to Course B?

W: Sure. So, Dinner Course B for three people, right?

M: That's right.

W: I've made the change. Is there __________ __________?

M: No, that's all. Thank you.

다음 페이지에 계속 ➡

13. 대화를 듣고, 두 사람이 만날 시각을 고르시오.

① 5:00 p.m. ② 5:15 p.m.
③ 5:30 p.m. ④ 5:45 p.m.
⑤ 6:00 p.m.

13

M: I'm really ___________ ___________ ___________ the movie premiere this Friday.

W: Me, too! It's at 6 p.m., isn't it?

M: Yes, how about we meet at 5 p.m.?

W: That's ___________ ___________ ___________ for me. What about 5:30 p.m.?

M: There's a red carpet event before the premiere. Wouldn't you like to see ___________ ___________?

W: Oh, absolutely! Let's meet at 5:15 p.m.

M: Sounds good. See you outside the theater!

14. 대화를 듣고, 두 사람의 관계로 가장 적절한 것을 고르시오.

① 교사 — 학부모
② 상담원 — 학생
③ 의사 — 환자 보호자
④ 서점 주인 — 손님
⑤ 학원 강사 — 수강생

14

W: Hello, Mr. Kim. Thank you ___________ ___________.

M: No problem, Mrs. Han. So, how is my son doing?

W: He's doing great, especially in English, but he ___________ ___________ ___________ ___________.

M: I see. How is he in your class?

W: He's very good. He likes history, and he's a great student.

M: ___________ ___________ ___________ ___________. He also said that he likes your class very much.

W: Thank you. I'm glad to hear that.

15. 대화를 듣고, 여자가 남자에게 부탁한 일로 가장 적절한 것을 고르시오.

① 설거지하기
② 쓰레기 버리기
③ 동생 숙제 도와주기
④ 함께 축구 경기 보기
⑤ 경기 내용 설명하기

15
W: Giho, can you ________ ________ ________ ________?

You have to do your homework.

M: Mom, this is my favorite soccer team. Can I

________ ________ ________ ________?

W: OK. But you must do your homework later.

M: I promise. And I'll also do the dishes.

W: I've already done that. Can you ________ ________

________ ________ instead?

M: Of course. Come and watch, Mom.

W: OK. Oh, your favorite player is playing.

M: Yes! I'm so excited.

16. 대화를 듣고, 여자가 친구의 집에 가는 이유로 가장 적절한 것을 고르시오.

① 영화를 보기 위해서
② 저녁을 먹기 위해서
③ 자전거를 빌리기 위해서
④ 빌린 책을 돌려주기 위해서
⑤ 과제 조사를 같이 하기 위해서

16
W: Dad, I'm going to Jenny's.

M: Jenny? Who is Jenny?

W: I've told you about her, Dad. She is my new

friend.

M: Oh, I see. But it's almost 5 p.m. Why are you going

to Jenny's now?

W: We have to ________ ________ ________

together for a science report.

M: Okay. Do you want me to ________ ________

________ ________?

W: It's okay. I will just ride my bike.

M: Will it take long?

W: No, Dad. I'll ________ ________ before dinner.

다음 페이지에 계속 ➡

17. 다음 그림의 상황에 가장 적절한 대화를 고르시오.

① ②
③ ④
⑤

17

① M: Do you want some more cake?

W: Yes, please. It's delicious.

② M: __________ __________ ____________ to your ear.

W: It seems like I'm hearing the sea.

③ M: I'd like two tickets to Busan, please.

W: Okay. That will be 20 dollars.

④ M: Would you help me __________ __________ _________?

W: Sure. No problem.

⑤ M: Isn't it ____________ here, honey?

W: Yes, it is. I love the sound of the waves.

2023 영어듣기능력평가 1회 18번 변형

18. 다음을 듣고, 여자가 자신에 대해 언급하지 <u>않은</u> 것을 고르시오.

① 이름　　　② 사는 곳
③ 전공　　　④ 직업
⑤ 수상 경력

18

W: Hello, everyone. Let me introduce myself to you. My name is Vicki Johnson. I live in London, England. Since ____________, I've always wanted to work in the field of fashion and beauty. So, I studied jewelry design at university. I'm a __________ __________ designer now. I design rings, earrings, and necklaces __________ __________ gold, silver, and bronze. Today, I'm going to tell you __________ __________ _________ a jewelry designer.

19. 대화를 듣고, 남자의 마지막 말에 이어질 여자의 말로 가장 적절한 것을 고르시오.

Woman: ________________

① I want to adopt two dogs.
② We need some volunteers.
③ What did you do last Saturday?
④ Yes. I want to be an animal doctor.
⑤ Wonderful. Let's start this weekend.

19

M: Monica, we should decide where to do ________ ________.

W: I know. Have you found anything?

M: Look at this website for volunteer work at an ________ ________.

W: An animal shelter? What are we supposed to do there?

M: We help to ________ the cats and dogs and ________ ________.

W: That's interesting. But we only have time on weekends. Are they open on Saturdays?

M: Let me check. *(Pause)* Yes, they are.

W: Wonderful. Let's start this weekend.

20. 대화를 듣고, 남자의 마지막 말에 이어질 여자의 말로 가장 적절한 것을 고르시오.

Woman: ________________

① Let's eat pizza for dinner tonight.
② My dream is to become a firefighter.
③ I have to get home by at least 7 o'clock.
④ I heard that it's going to start at 3 o'clock.
⑤ What do you have to do when a fire breaks out?

20

W: I heard that there's going to be a fire drill at school today.

M: What's a fire drill?

W: It's when you practice getting out of the building in case ________ ________ ________ ________.

M: Oh, is that really necessary? I don't feel like running around.

W: It's to help prepare for an actual fire, so we should ________ ________ ________.

M: Okay. When is the drill going to start?

W: I heard that it's going to start at 3 o'clock.

Words & Expressions Review 15

● 다음 단어를 암기하세요.

문제	번호	단어	뜻	문제	번호	단어	뜻
1	1	along with	~과 함께	10	23	translation	통역, 번역
	2	extra	각별히, 특별히		24	abroad	해외로
	3	cautious	조심스러운, 신중한		25	save	저장하다
2	4	have A in mind	A를 마음에 두다	11	26	check out	~을 확인하다, 조사하다
	5	-shaped	~ 모양의	12	27	book	예약하다
3	6	It can't be helped.	어쩔 수 없다.	13	28	celebrity	유명인, 유명인사
	7	on our own	단독으로, 우리끼리		29	Absolutely.	물론이지., 그럼.
	8	seem	~처럼 보이다	14	30	difficult	어려운
4	9	pick	(과일 등을) 따다		31	do the dishes	설거지하다
	10	at first	처음에는	15	32	take out	내놓다, 꺼내다
	11	join	(행위 등을) 함께 하다		33	trash	쓰레기
5	12	package	소포	16	34	give ~ a ride	~를 태워주다
	13	air mail	항공 우편		35	take long	(시간이) 오래 걸리다
6	14	get mad at ~	~에게 화내다	17	36	carry	나르다, 들고 있다
	15	accidentally	실수로, 우연히		37	peaceful	평화로운
7	16	alter	(옷을) 고치다	18	38	childhood	어린 시절
	17	out of	(수단·재료) ~로, ~에 의해		39	field	분야
8	18	exhausting	진을 빼는, 기진맥진하는	19	40	be supposed to + 동사	~해야 한다, ~할 의무가 있다
	19	Tell me about it.	내 말이 (그 말이야).		41	adopt	입양하다
	20	instead	대신에		42	drill	훈련
9	21	deadly	치명적인, 생명을 앗아가는	20	43	break out	발생하다
	22	venomous	독이 있는		44	actual	실제의

M2(17)_W_15

●왼쪽 단어장의 뜻이 보이지 않게 반으로 접고, 학습한 단어의 뜻을 아래 빈칸에 적어주세요.

1	package	23	take out
2	pick	24	take long
3	Absolutely.	25	book
4	seem	26	difficult
5	trash	27	alter
6	extra	28	drill
7	cautious	29	instead
8	abroad	30	give ~ a ride
9	field	31	translation
10	at first	32	actual
11	save	33	deadly
12	peaceful	34	out of
13	do the dishes	35	on our own
14	It can't be helped.	36	adopt
15	Tell me about it.	37	along with
16	venomous	38	exhausting
17	childhood	39	get mad at ~
18	-shaped	40	celebrity
19	break out	41	join
20	have A in mind	42	air mail
21	be supposed to + 동사	43	accidentally
22	check out	44	carry

15
회
단
어

정답 및 해석 p. 75

1 다음을 듣고, 오늘 오후의 날씨로 가장 적절한 것을 고르시오.

① 　② ③ ④ ⑤

2 대화를 듣고, 여자가 구입할 컵받침으로 가장 적절한 것을 고르시오.

① 　② ③ 　④ 　⑤ 

3 대화를 듣고, 여자의 심정으로 가장 적절한 것을 고르시오.

① proud　② excited　③ envious　④ worried　⑤ disappointed

4 대화를 듣고, 남자가 지난 주말에 한 일로 가장 적절한 것을 고르시오.

① 아르바이트하기　② 중고 물품 팔기
③ 영화 관람하기　④ 배낭 주문하기
⑤ 자전거 타기

5 대화를 듣고, 두 사람이 대화하는 장소로 가장 적절한 곳을 고르시오.

① 은행　② 버스　③ 학교
④ 공연장　⑤ 기차역

6 대화를 듣고, 여자의 마지막 말의 의도로 가장 적절한 것을 고르시오.

① 항의　　　　② 거절　　　　③ 제안　　　　④ 요청　　　　⑤ 감탄

7 대화를 듣고, 남자가 조카들을 위해 한 일이 <u>아닌</u> 것을 고르시오.

① 공원 가기　　　　② 요리하기　　　　③ 영화관 가기
④ 보드게임 하기　　⑤ 비디오게임 하기

8 대화를 듣고, 여자가 대화 직후에 할 일로 가장 적절한 것을 고르시오.

① 우산 사 오기　　　　② 간식 사 오기　　　　③ 배달 주문하기
④ 돗자리 가져오기　　⑤ 휴대폰 충전하기

9 대화를 듣고, 두 사람이 사진집에 대해 언급하지 <u>않은</u> 것을 고르시오.

① 작가 이름　　② 출간일　　③ 주제　　④ 가격　　⑤ 판매 부수

10 다음을 듣고, 남자가 하는 말의 내용으로 가장 적절한 것을 고르시오.

① 행사 일정 안내　　② 축제 참가자 소개　　③ 자원봉사자 모집
④ 학교 교칙 안내　　⑤ 교원 채용 공고

11 대화를 듣고, Power Center에 대한 내용과 일치하지 <u>않는</u> 것을 고르시오.

① 노란색이다.　　　　　　　　② 시청 옆에 있다.
③ Erica Johnson이 설계했다.　④ 디자인상을 받았다.
⑤ 정상 회담이 진행 중이다.

12번~20번 문제는 다음 페이지에 ➡

12 대화를 듣고, 남자가 전화를 건 목적으로 가장 적절한 것을 고르시오.

① 주문을 변경하기 위해서
② 룸서비스 주문을 위해서
③ 숙박비용을 문의하기 위해서
④ 호텔 체류 기간을 연장하기 위해서
⑤ 호텔 체크인 시간을 물어보기 위해서

13 대화를 듣고, 남자가 받은 거스름돈으로 가장 적절한 것을 고르시오.

① $1 ② $2 ③ $3 ④ $8 ⑤ $9

14 대화를 듣고, 두 사람의 관계로 가장 적절한 것을 고르시오.

① 은행원 – 고객 ② 경찰관 – 시민 ③ 판매원 – 손님
④ 부하 직원 – 상사 ⑤ 학부모 – 교사

15 대화를 듣고, 여자가 남자에게 부탁한 일로 가장 적절한 것을 고르시오.

① 피자 주문하기 ② 거실 조명 끄기 ③ 탁자에 접시 놓기
④ 컵 가져오기 ⑤ 안경 가져오기

16 대화를 듣고, 남자가 늦게 귀가한 이유로 가장 적절한 것을 고르시오.

① 친구들과 놀다가 ② 교실을 청소하다가 ③ 추가 수업을 받다가
④ 대체 버스를 기다리다가 ⑤ 영화 촬영을 구경하다가

17 다음 그림의 상황에 가장 적절한 대화를 고르시오.

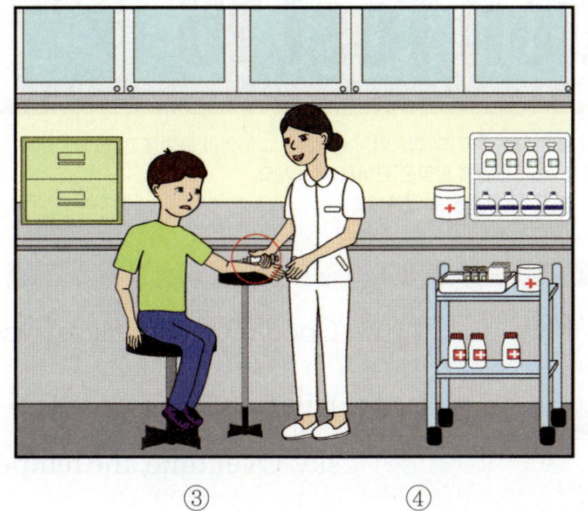

①   ②   ③   ④   ⑤

18 다음을 듣고, 여자가 오페라에 대해 언급하지 <u>않은</u> 것을 고르시오.

① 작곡가   ② 제목   ③ 출연진
④ 공연 장소   ⑤ 티켓 가격

[19~20] 대화를 듣고, 여자의 마지막 말에 이어질 남자의 말로 가장 적절한 것을 고르시오.

19 Man: _______________________________________

① I'd love to, but I have other plans.
② I would like to see your family.
③ There are many art galleries in New York.
④ You have a wonderful plan.
⑤ New York is a big city.

20 Man: _______________________________________

① I don't like mobile games.
② Yes, the story is really good.
③ Really? It's my favorite book.
④ Then, I will read the novel, too.
⑤ I can tell you about the kingdom.

Dictation Test 16

M2(17)_16_D

Dictation(받아쓰기)은 본문을 받아쓰면서 영어듣기의 집중력을 향상시키고 다양한 표현을 정리하기 위한 영어듣기 학습법입니다. **녹음을 다시 듣고, 빈칸에 알맞은 단어를 써 보세요.**
※Dictation의 정답은 듣기 대본의 밑줄 친 부분을 확인하세요.

📖 정답 p. 75

✏️ 맞은 개수 ／ 총170개

날씨파악–그림

1. 다음을 듣고, 오늘 오후의 날씨로 가장 적절한 것을 고르시오.

①  ② 

③  ④ 

⑤

01 W: Good morning. Here's today's weather. Today will ____________ ____________ with thick clouds in the sky. Over time, the temperature will drop, and there will be snow in the afternoon. The snow is ____________ ____________ ____________ until midnight, and then the sky will clear up tomorrow morning. So, if you are out this afternoon, you'll have to ____________ ____________ ____________ snow on the roads.

그림정보파악

2. 대화를 듣고, 여자가 구입할 컵받침으로 가장 적절한 것을 고르시오.

①  ② 

③  ④ 

⑤ 

02 W: Excuse me, I'm ____________ ____________ a coaster.

M: Oh, they're here. These are the popular ones.

W: They're all cute. I don't know ____________ ____________ ____________ ____________.

M: How about the one with a whale?

W: Well, I prefer pandas more than whales.

M: Okay. There are two coasters with a panda. Which one do you like more?

W: I like ____________ ____________ ____________. I'll take that one.

3. 대화를 듣고, 여자의 심정으로 가장 적절한 것을 고르시오.
① proud ② excited
③ envious ④ worried
⑤ disappointed

03
W: You look happy, Andy. ___________ ___________ ?

M: I'm going to go *sea walking next week. I ___________ ___________ !

W: Sea walking? But you can't even swim, can you?

M: No, but it ___________ ___________ . I'll wear a special air helmet.

W: Are you sure it will be safe?

M: Of course! Just imagine walking around at the bottom of the sea!

W: But that sounds ___________ ___________ to me.

M: I'll be fine. There will be lifeguards around, too.

W: OK, just ___________ ___________ you remember all the safety rules and follow them.

*sea walking: 산소 공급 호스가 달린 헬멧을 쓰고 바닷속을 걷는 여가 활동

---

4. 대화를 듣고, 남자가 지난 주말에 한 일로 가장 적절한 것을 고르시오.
① 아르바이트하기
② 중고 물품 팔기
③ 영화 관람하기
④ 배낭 주문하기
⑤ 자전거 타기

04
W: Do you want to go to the movies?

M: I can't. I have to ___________ ___________ .

W: Why?

M: I want to buy a bicycle. And I promised my dad I would pay for ___________ ___________ ___________ .

W: That's nice of you! It'll take some time to save that much money, ___________ .

M: So, I started a part-time job last weekend.

W: Maybe I should ___________ ___________ ___________ ___________ , too. I want a new backpack, but I don't want to ask my parents for money.

다음 페이지에 계속 ➡

5. 대화를 듣고, 두 사람이 대화하는 장소로
가장 적절한 곳을 고르시오.
① 은행　　② 버스
③ 학교　　④ 공연장
⑤ 기차역

05

M: Hey, Maggie. Glad to see you here.

W: Hi, Jim. Where are you going?

M: I'm _________ _________ _________ _________ my piano lesson. It's three stops away.

W: Yeah? I'm on my way home. Whoa, _________ _________ is bumpy today.

M: The driver looks mad. I hope he doesn't _________ _________ anything.

W: Maybe it's just the road. Can you push that button? I'm _________ _________ at the next stop.

M: Sure. See you tomorrow.

6. 대화를 듣고, 여자의 마지막 말의 의도로
가장 적절한 것을 고르시오.
① 항의　　② 거절
③ 제안　　④ 요청
⑤ 감탄

06

W: What are you doing, Harry?

M: I'm _________ _________ _________ on dental clinics for children.

W: Is it for your daughter?

M: Yes. She needs to get a dental check-up, but she hates going to the dentist.

W: So, you're looking for a place that will be _________ _________ for her?

M: Yes. It would be nice to find a clinic that is child-friendly.

W: Then how about _________ _________ _________ about it on the community website?

7. 대화를 듣고, 남자가 조카들을 위해 한 일이 <u>아닌</u> 것을 고르시오.

① 공원 가기
② 요리하기
③ 영화관 가기
④ 보드게임 하기
⑤ 비디오게임 하기

07
W: How was your weekend? What did you do?

M: I spent some time with my nephews. It was a lot of fun.

W: Really? What did you ________ ________ ________?

M: We went ________ ________ ________. I cooked *tteokbokki* for lunch, too.

W: I didn't know you could cook. What else did you do?

M: We also played a board game and ________ ________ ________ together at home.

W: What a nice uncle you are!

M: We played a new video game, too. It was so much fun.

할일파악(대화직후)

2025 영어듣기능력평가 1회 8번 변형

8. 대화를 듣고, 여자가 대화 직후에 할 일로 가장 적절한 것을 고르시오.

① 우산 사 오기
② 간식 사 오기
③ 배달 주문하기
④ 돗자리 가져오기
⑤ 휴대폰 충전하기

08
W: Jake, this __________ __________ is so nice! It's so beautiful and quiet here.

M: Yeah, I'm glad we found this place.

W: But the ground is __________ __________ __________.

M: Should we just sit on the grass?

W: No, I'll get the picnic mat from the car.

M: Do you want me __________ __________ __________ you?

W: It's fine. I'll be right back with it.

다음 페이지에 계속 ➡

9. 대화를 듣고, 두 사람이 사진집에 대해 언급하지 <u>않은</u> 것을 고르시오.

① 작가 이름
② 출간일
③ 주제
④ 가격
⑤ 판매 부수

09

W: Hey, David! Do you know the photographer named Tommy Shipman?

M: I do! Didn't he _________ a new photograph collection?

W: He did! It came out two days ago on June 3rd.

M: Really? So, what's the overall theme of it?

W: It is a collection of photos of fashionable people from _________ _________ _________ _________!

M: Cool! I bet a lot of people want to see this collection.

W: Definitely! I heard 25,500 copies _________ _________ _________ already!

10. 다음을 듣고, 남자가 하는 말의 내용으로 가장 적절한 것을 고르시오.

① 행사 일정 안내
② 축제 참가자 소개
③ 자원봉사자 모집
④ 학교 교칙 안내
⑤ 교원 채용 공고

10

(Chime bell rings.)

M: Hello, everyone. The school festival is _________ _________ next Friday! We need forty _________ for that day. Everyone is welcome. If you're interested, please _________ _________. You can register either on the list in the school office or school website. You must sign up _________ next Tuesday. Don't miss your _________ to become a volunteer!

11. 대화를 듣고, Power Center에 대한 내용과 일치하지 <u>않는</u> 것을 고르시오.
① 노란색이다.
② 시청 옆에 있다.
③ Erica Johnson이 설계했다.
④ 디자인상을 받았다.
⑤ 정상 회담이 진행 중이다.

11

W: Matt, what's that big yellow building?

M: The one next to City Hall? It's a new convention center called Power Center.

W: Ah, that's the one! I heard a famous _________ designed it.

M: Yes, it _________ _________ _________ Erica Johnson.

W: Right. It's really beautiful.

M: Isn't it? It also won a design award.

W: That's amazing. Look! There's an _____________ _________ _________ going on right now.

M: Do you want to go check it out?

W: Yes!

12. 대화를 듣고, 남자가 전화를 건 목적으로 가장 적절한 것을 고르시오.
① 주문을 변경하기 위해서
② 룸서비스 주문을 위해서
③ 숙박비용을 문의하기 위해서
④ 호텔 체류 기간을 연장하기 위해서
⑤ 호텔 체크인 시간을 물어보기 위해서

12

(Telephone rings.)

W: Hello. Nature Hotel.

M: Hi, I booked four nights in a suite starting on August 8th, but I'd like to _________ _________ _____________.

W: Sure, may I have your name, please?

M: It's Eddie Carpenter.

W: All right. How would you like to change your reservation?

M: I would like to stay until the 15th _________ _________ the 12th.

W: Okay, your reservation _________ _________ _____________. Anything else?

M: No, that's all. Thank you.

다음 페이지에 계속 ➡

13. 대화를 듣고, 남자가 받은 거스름돈으로 가장 적절한 것을 고르시오.

① $1　　② $2
③ $3　　④ $8
⑤ $9

13

W: Welcome to Burger House. How may I help you?

M: Could I get one chicken burger combo?

W: That will be 11 dollars. What kind of drink would you like?

M: Coke, please. Oh, can I ________ ________ ________ as well?

W: Yes. That will be ________ ________ ________. Is that okay?

M: Yes. It's fine.

W: Your total is 12 dollars.

M: Here is a 20-dollar bill.

W: ________ ________ ________ ________. Thank you.

14. 대화를 듣고, 두 사람의 관계로 가장 적절한 것을 고르시오.

① 은행원 – 고객
② 경찰관 – 시민
③ 판매원 – 손님
④ 부하 직원 – 상사
⑤ 학부모 – 교사

14

M: How can I help you, ma'am?

W: I picked up this wallet on the street ________ ________ the police station.

M: Oh, that's kind of you. Did you look inside the wallet?

W: No, I trust that you will find the owner.

M: Of course. ________ ________ ________ your name, please?

W: It's Violet Carter.

M: Thank you. Could you also ________ ________ ________ ________?

W: Sure! I hope you find the owner soon.

15. 대화를 듣고, 여자가 남자에게 부탁한 일로 가장 적절한 것을 고르시오.

① 피자 주문하기
② 거실 조명 끄기
③ 탁자에 접시 놓기
④ 컵 가져오기
⑤ 안경 가져오기

15

M: Honey, hurry up! The movie's starting.

W: OK. Have you ordered the pizza?

M: Yes, I have. Do you want me to ________ ________ the light?

W: No, let's leave it on. Thanks for ________ ________ ________ on the table. Oh, but we don't have any cups for the Coke.

M: I'll go get some. Is there ________ ________ ________ ________?

W: I forgot my glasses. Can you bring them from the bedroom?

M: No problem.

16. 대화를 듣고, 남자가 늦게 귀가한 이유로 가장 적절한 것을 고르시오.

① 친구들과 놀다가
② 교실을 청소하다가
③ 추가 수업을 받다가
④ 대체 버스를 기다리다가
⑤ 영화 촬영을 구경하다가

16

W: Ben, you got home late today.

M: I'm sorry, Mom. I didn't know how much time ________ ________.

W: Did you play with your friends?

M: Not today. I left school right after class.

W: Then, did the bus ________ ________ again?

M: No. I saw people filming a movie on the way home.

W: Oh, did you watch them?

M: Yes. I ________ ________ ________ for almost two hours. It was fun.

다음 페이지에 계속 ➡

17. 다음 그림의 상황에 가장 적절한 대화를 고르시오.

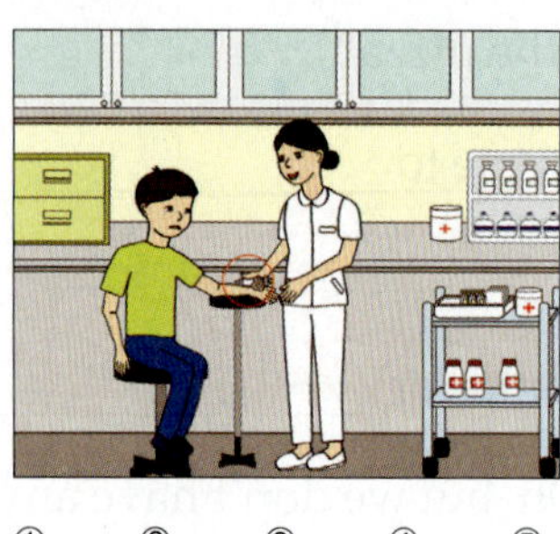

① ② ③ ④ ⑤

17

① M: I ________ ________ my bike.

W: Let me put some medicine on the wound.

② M: Can I open the window?

W: Sure, ________ ________.

③ M: How long does it take to get to the hospital?

W: It takes about 10 minutes by car.

④ M: It's going to hurt, isn't it? I hate ________ ________.

W: I'll do my best to ________ the pain.

⑤ M: What is your favorite ice cream flavor?

W: I like vanilla the best.

18. 다음을 듣고, 여자가 오페라에 대해 언급하지 <u>않은</u> 것을 고르시오.

① 작곡가
② 제목
③ 출연진
④ 공연 장소
⑤ 티켓 가격

18

W: Hello, everyone. Today, I'd like to tell you about a new opera ________ ________ ________ ________ Hilda Woo. It's called *My Luck* and it is about the lives of six people who win the lottery. The characters will be played by ________ ________ ________, including the famous baritone, Sebastian Vale. The opera will be playing at Star Art Center ________ ________ ________. Buy your tickets online now!

19. 대화를 듣고, 여자의 마지막 말에 이어질 남자의 말로 가장 적절한 것을 고르시오.

Man: ______________________

① I'd love to, but I have other plans.
② I would like to see your family.
③ There are many art galleries in New York.
④ You have a wonderful plan.
⑤ New York is a big city.

19

M: What are you doing, Jessica?

W: I'm ________ ________ a book on modern art.

M: Modern art? Why?

W: I'm ________ to go to a modern art gallery in New York this weekend. So I want to study about it first.

M: Wow! What a ____________ ________! Are you going there with your family?

W: No. I'm going there ________. Do you want to come with me?

M: <u>I'd love to, but I have other plans.</u>

20. 대화를 듣고, 여자의 마지막 말에 이어질 남자의 말로 가장 적절한 것을 고르시오.

Man: ______________________

① I don't like mobile games.
② Yes, the story is really good.
③ Really? It's my favorite book.
④ Then, I will read the novel, too.
⑤ I can tell you about the kingdom.

20

W: What are you doing?

M: I'm playing a mobile game. ____________ ____________ *The Next Kingdom.*

W: Really? Did you read the novel ____________ ____________?

M: What do you mean?

W: The game ____________ ____________ ____________ a fantasy novel titled, *The Next Kingdom.*

M: I didn't know that! I wonder if the book is ____________ ____________ ____________ the game.

W: Oh, I'm sure it is. I enjoyed reading it.

M: <u>Then, I will read the novel, too.</u>

Words & Expressions Review 16

● 다음 단어를 암기하세요.

문제	번호	단어	뜻
1	□ 1	start off	(~하는 것으로) 시작하다
	□ 2	over time	시간이 지나면서
	□ 3	last	(특정한 시간 동안) 지속되다
2	□ 4	coaster	컵받침
3	□ 5	matter	문제가 되다, 중요하다
	□ 6	bottom	바닥
4	□ 7	save	저축하다, 절약하다
	□ 8	look for	~을 찾다
	□ 9	ask A for B	A에게 B를 요구하다
5	□ 10	on one's way to ~	~로 가는 길에
	□ 11	stop	정거장, 정류장
	□ 12	run into ~	~에 들이받다, 충돌하다
	□ 13	get off	내리다, 하차하다
6	□ 14	search for	~을 찾다
	□ 15	nephew	남자 조카
7	□ 16	what else	그 밖에 다른 것
	□ 17	watch a film	영화를 보다
8	□ 18	spot	(특정한) 곳, 장소
	□ 19	ground	땅, 지면
	□ 20	publish	출판하다, 발행하다
9	□ 21	overall	전반적인, 종합적인
	□ 22	theme	주제, 테마

문제	번호	단어	뜻
9	□ 23	bet	~이 틀림없다, (돈을) 걸다
	□ 24	volunteer	자원봉사자
10	□ 25	sign up	(강좌 등에) 등록하다
	□ 26	register	등록하다, 기록부
11	□ 27	architect	건축가
	□ 28	fair	박람회
12	□ 29	extend	연장하다
13	□ 30	upsize	양을 늘리다
	□ 31	as well	~도, 또한
14	□ 32	across from	~의 건너편에
	□ 33	fill in	(서식을) 작성하다
15	□ 34	turn off ~	~을 끄다
	□ 35	leave	그대로 두다
16	□ 36	pass	흐르다, 지나가다
	□ 37	break down	고장 나다
	□ 38	fall off ~	~에서 떨어지다
17	□ 39	reduce	줄이다
	□ 40	flavor	맛, 풍미
18	□ 41	composer	작곡가
19	□ 42	gallery	전시관
20	□ 43	be called	~으로 불리다
	□ 44	be based on	~에 기초하다, ~을 바탕으로 하다

M2(17)_W_16

● 왼쪽 단어장의 뜻이 보이지 않게 반으로 접고, 학습한 단어의 뜻을 아래 빈칸에 적어주세요.

1	leave		23	break down
2	be based on		24	last
3	theme		25	register
4	ask A for B		26	composer
5	gallery		27	what else
6	run into ~		28	bottom
7	volunteer		29	across from
8	fair		30	on one's way to ~
9	search for		31	publish
10	bet		32	stop
11	spot		33	over time
12	get off		34	overall
13	ground		35	fall off ~
14	fill in		36	look for
15	sign up		37	matter
16	upsize		38	turn off ~
17	reduce		39	architect
18	extend		40	as well
19	start off		41	pass
20	watch a film		42	save
21	coaster		43	nephew
22	be called		44	flavor

16회 단어

17회 중학영어듣기 모의고사

M2(17)_17_US
모두 **미국식 발음(US)** 으로 녹음

M2(17)_17_UK
20문제 중 5문제에 **영국식 발음 (US+UK)**을 포함하여 녹음

정답 및 해석 p. 80

1 다음을 듣고, 마카오의 내일 날씨로 적절한 것을 고르시오.

① 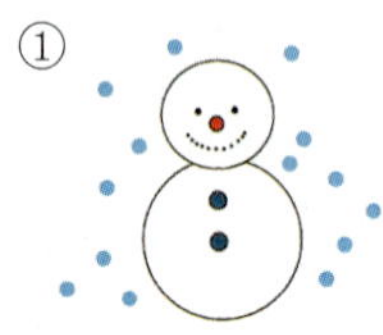 ②  ③  ④  ⑤ 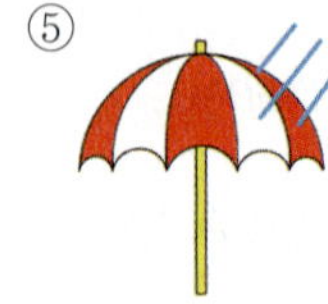

2 대화를 듣고, 남자가 구입할 공으로 가장 적절한 것을 고르시오.

①  ②  ③  ④  ⑤ 

3 대화를 듣고, 남자의 심정으로 가장 적절한 것을 고르시오.

① disappointed　　② angry　　③ jealous
④ nervous　　⑤ excited

4 대화를 듣고, 남자가 오늘 한 일로 가장 적절한 것을 고르시오.

① 사진 정리하기　　② 동네 산책하기　　③ 농구 경기 관람하기
④ 할머니 댁 방문하기　　⑤ 친구 병원 데려다주기

5 대화를 듣고, 두 사람이 대화하는 장소로 가장 적절한 곳을 고르시오.
① 호텔　　　② 서점　　　③ 공항　　　④ 영화관　　　⑤ 음식점

6 대화를 듣고, 남자의 마지막 말의 의도로 가장 적절한 것을 고르시오.
① 승낙　　　② 위로　　　③ 칭찬
④ 감사　　　⑤ 사과

7 대화를 듣고, 남자가 새로 만들자고 제안할 동아리를 고르시오.
① 영화 감상반　　　② 비디오 게임반　　　③ 패션 디자인반
④ 요리반　　　⑤ 수영반

8 대화를 듣고, 여자가 대화 직후에 할 일로 가장 적절한 것을 고르시오.
① 조깅하기　　　② 병원에 가기　　　③ 식품점 가기
④ 집에서 쉬기　　　⑤ 감기약 사오기

9 대화를 듣고, 두 사람이 드라마에 대해 언급하지 <u>않은</u> 것을 고르시오.
① 제목　　　② 주연 배우　　　③ 내용
④ 방영 시간　　　⑤ 방영 채널

10 다음을 듣고, 여자가 하는 말의 내용으로 가장 적절한 것을 고르시오.
① 미아 안내　　　② 분실물 공지　　　③ 직원 회의 일정 변경
④ 층별 판매품목 소개　　　⑤ 장난감 할인 행사 홍보

11번~20번 문제는 다음 페이지에 ➡

11 대화를 듣고, Spring Flower Festival에 대한 내용과 일치하지 <u>않는</u> 것을 고르시오.

① Orion 공원에서 개최된다.　　　　② 5월 5일에 시작했다.
③ 누구나 무료로 참여 가능하다.　　④ 사진 콘테스트를 하고 있다.
⑤ 매주 화요일은 휴무이다.

12 대화를 듣고, 여자가 전화를 건 목적으로 가장 적절한 것을 고르시오.

① 약속 시간을 변경하기 위해서　　　② 모임 장소를 확인하기 위해서
③ 약속 장소를 변경하기 위해서　　　④ 모임 참석자를 확인하기 위해서
⑤ 약속을 취소하기 위해서

13 대화를 듣고, 여자가 지불해야 할 금액으로 가장 적절한 것을 고르시오.

① $5　　　　② $10　　　　③ $15　　　　④ $20　　　　⑤ $30

14 대화를 듣고, 두 사람의 관계로 가장 적절한 것을 고르시오.

① 경찰관 — 시민　　　　　② 은행원 — 고객
③ 역무원 — 관광객　　　　④ 편의점 직원 — 손님
⑤ 휴대폰 수리기사 — 고객

15 대화를 듣고, 여자가 남자에게 부탁한 일로 가장 적절한 것을 고르시오.

① 주문 취소하기　　　② 메뉴 변경하기　　　③ 구매 내용 확인하기
④ 주문 추가하기　　　⑤ 배송 시간 변경하기

16 대화를 듣고, 남자가 동물 보호소에 가지 <u>못하는</u> 이유로 가장 적절한 것을 고르시오.

① 봄맞이 대청소를 해야 해서　　　② 할머니를 뵈러 가야 해서
③ 고양이 알레르기가 있어서　　　④ 가족 모임이 있어서
⑤ 동물병원에 가야 해서

17 다음 그림의 상황에 가장 적절한 대화를 고르시오.

①   ②   ③   ④   ⑤

18 다음을 듣고, 여자가 현장학습에 대해 언급하지 <u>않은</u> 것을 고르시오.

① 실시 날짜   ② 모임 장소   ③ 버스 출발 시간
④ 목적지   ⑤ 복장 규정

[19~20] 대화를 듣고, 남자의 마지막 말에 이어질 여자의 말로 가장 적절한 것을 고르시오.

19 Woman: _______________________________________

① Then I'll have that.   ② You can order milk.
③ Take this medicine now.   ④ These oranges look fresh.
⑤ My favorite fruit is strawberries.

20 Woman: _______________________________________

① Happy birthday to her!   ② Don't forget to write a letter.
③ It's next to the post office.   ④ Sure, let me show you some.
⑤ Why don't you buy a necklace?

Dictation Test 17

M2(17)_17_D

Dictation(받아쓰기)은 본문을 받아쓰면서 영어듣기의 집중력을 향상시키고 다양한 표현을 정리하기 위한 영어듣기 학습법입니다. **녹음을 다시 듣고, 빈칸에 알맞은 단어를 써 보세요.**
※Dictation의 정답은 듣기 대본의 밑줄 친 부분을 확인하세요.　　📖 정답 p. 80

맞은 개수　　／ 총165개

날씨파악–그림

1. 다음을 듣고, 마카오의 내일 날씨로 적절한 것을 고르시오.

① 　② 

③ 　④ 

⑤ 

01 W: Today, in Macao, we had _________ cloudy skies.
The temperature ____________ 21 degrees Celsius.
Tomorrow's forecast will be sunny with clear
skies. The temperature will be around 25 degrees.
It should be a _________ _________ _________ go to
the beach.

그림정보파악

2. 대화를 듣고, 남자가 구입할 공으로 가장 적절한 것을 고르시오.

① 　② 

③ 　④ 

⑤

02 W: May I help you?
M: I want to buy a ball _________ _________ _________.
W: How about this one with the bear on it? It's
popular.
M: Well, my nephew isn't that young. I _________
_________ _________ _________.
W: Boys like it. This one has Pele's name, too.
M: It's nice, but I'll take this ball _________ _________
_________ on it.
W: Sure.

---

3. 대화를 듣고, 남자의 심정으로 가장 적절한 것을 고르시오.

① disappointed ② angry
③ jealous　　　 ④ nervous
⑤ excited

03

M: Mom, Uncle Dennis __________ __________ a letter.

W: Oh, really? Let me see it.

M: What does it say?

W: It's an invitation.

M: __________ __________?

W: To a baby shower.

M: Really? I'm gonna have a baby __________?

W: Yes. That's why Aunt Wendy's belly keeps growing. She's pregnant.

M: I can't wait to play with my little cousin! I __________ __________ it will be a boy or a girl.

4. 대화를 듣고, 남자가 오늘 한 일로 가장 적절한 것을 고르시오.

① 사진 정리하기
② 동네 산책하기
③ 농구 경기 관람하기
④ 할머니 댁 방문하기
⑤ 친구 병원 데려다주기

04

M: Mom, I'm home from school.

W: You're home early. I thought you __________ __________ __________ play basketball after school today.

M: Logan __________ his ankle at school, so we couldn't play.

W: Oh, did he get __________ hurt?

M: No, but he had trouble walking on his own so I helped him to the hospital.

W: Ah, that's sweet of you. Good job!

M: It wasn't a big deal.

다음 페이지에 계속 ➡

5. 대화를 듣고, 두 사람이 대화하는 장소로
   가장 적절한 곳을 고르시오.

   ① 호텔　　② 서점
   ③ 공항　　④ 영화관
   ⑤ 음식점

05

M: Good afternoon. How may I help you?

W: Hi, I ＿＿＿＿＿ ＿＿＿＿＿ ＿＿＿＿＿＿ for today.

   My name is Julie Kim.

M: Let me check. Can you show me your passport,

   please?

W: Sure, here you go.

M: Mrs. Kim, ＿＿＿＿＿ ＿＿＿＿＿＿ a standard

   room for you for two nights. Is that correct?

W: Yes, it is.

M: We've upgraded your room so it now has an

   ocean view. Here's your key card to room 701.

W: That's great! Thank you very much.

M: You're welcome. Please ＿＿＿＿＿ ＿＿＿＿＿

   ＿＿＿＿＿!

6. 대화를 듣고, 남자의 마지막 말의 의도로
   가장 적절한 것을 고르시오.

   ① 승낙　　② 위로
   ③ 칭찬　　④ 감사
   ⑤ 사과

06

M: Wow, what happened to you, Avery?

W: I ＿＿＿＿＿ ＿＿＿＿＿ ＿＿＿＿＿ ＿＿＿＿＿ and broke

   my leg.

M: That must have hurt. How long do you have to

   ＿＿＿＿＿ ＿＿＿＿＿ ＿＿＿＿＿ ＿＿＿＿＿?

W: The doctor said to keep it on for a month.

M: So, you have to be on crutches for a month?

W: Unfortunately, yes. I guess this is what I get for

   ＿＿＿＿＿ ＿＿＿＿＿ ＿＿＿＿＿ on the stairs.

M: No, don't say that. Does your leg still hurt?

W: Yeah, a little bit.

M: I hope you feel better soon.

7. 대화를 듣고, 남자가 새로 만들자고 제안
   할 동아리를 고르시오.
   ① 영화 감상반
   ② 비디오 게임반
   ③ 패션 디자인반
   ④ 요리반
   ⑤ 수영반

07
W: Did you know that our school is ________ ___________ for a new club?

M: Yes, I've heard that someone suggested a video games club or a fashion design club.

W: I don't think the teachers will choose ________ ________ ________.

M: Do you have an idea for one?

W: I was thinking about a cooking club. How about you?

M: I'm ________ ________ ___________ a swimming club.

W: Oh, that's nice!

8. 대화를 듣고, 여자가 대화 직후에 할 일
   로 가장 적절한 것을 고르시오.
   ① 조깅하기
   ② 병원에 가기
   ③ 식품점 가기
   ④ 집에서 쉬기
   ⑤ 감기약 사오기

08
W: Honey, let's go jogging.

M: Sorry, but I can't go out today. I'm not ________ ________.

W: Why don't you see a doctor?

M: Well, I think I just need to ________ ________ ________ at home.

W: Okay. I'll make chicken soup for you. What do you think?

M: I like chicken soup. Thank you, honey.

W: I'm going to the __________ ________ now. Get some sleep, then.

다음 페이지에 계속 ➡

9. 대화를 듣고, 두 사람이 드라마에 대해 언급하지 <u>않은</u> 것을 고르시오.
① 제목　　　② 주연 배우
③ 내용　　　④ 방영 시간
⑤ 방영 채널

09
W: Jaehoon, _________ _________ _________ this video clip?

M: Oh, is this the one that's been popular online recently?

W: Yes! It's a trailer for a new TV show, *The Prize*.

M: I haven't seen it yet. Is it good?

W: It's _________ _________. The beloved actor, Kim Sung Hyun, stars as the main character, Namsoo.

M: Oh, I love him, too. What is it about?

W: _________ _________ _________ a survival story of some kind.

M: Sounds interesting. Where is it going to be aired?

W: It will _________ _________ _________ ONBC.

10. 다음을 듣고, 여자가 하는 말의 내용으로 가장 적절한 것을 고르시오.
① 미아 안내
② 분실물 공지
③ 직원 회의 일정 변경
④ 층별 판매품목 소개
⑤ 장난감 할인 행사 홍보

10
W: May I have your attention, please? We have a lost boy here named Jimmy Mulligan and he _________ _________ _________ his father. He was found at the toy section this afternoon. He is six years old and he is wearing a _________ _________ _________ _________ shirt, black pants and a red baseball cap. If you know this child, please come to the customer service office. Thank you.

11. 대화를 듣고, Spring Flower Festival에 대한 내용과 일치하지 <u>않는</u> 것을 고르시오.

① Orion 공원에서 개최된다.
② 5월 5일에 시작했다.
③ 누구나 무료로 참여 가능하다.
④ 사진 콘테스트를 하고 있다.
⑤ 매주 화요일은 휴무이다.

11

M: Maggie, have you heard about the Spring Flower Festival that's ________ ________ ________ Orion Park?

W: Yes. Actually, I went to the festival last weekend. It started on May fifth.

M: Is there an ____________ ________?

W: It's only $2 per person and children under 8 are free.

M: I heard they are having a photo contest!

W: Yes, you can ________ the photos that you take at the festival online ________ ________ ________ in the contest.

M: Sounds fun!

W: Oh, you should know it's closed on Tuesdays.

M: I see. Thanks for the information.

---

12. 대화를 듣고, 여자가 전화를 건 목적으로 가장 적절한 것을 고르시오.

① 약속 시간을 변경하기 위해서
② 모임 장소를 확인하기 위해서
③ 약속 장소를 변경하기 위해서
④ 모임 참석자를 확인하기 위해서
⑤ 약속을 취소하기 위해서

12

(Telephone rings.)

M: Hello.

W: Hello, Travis. Are we still meeting at two o'clock?

M: Yes. Why do you ask?

W: I don't think I can ________ ________.

M: Are you busy? Do you want to cancel?

W: No, I have ________ ________ ________ to do, but I really want to see a movie. How about meeting at five o'clock?

M: Okay. Five o'clock ________ ________ ________ the theater, right?

W: Yes. See you then.

다음 페이지에 계속 ➡

13. 대화를 듣고, 여자가 지불해야 할 금액으로 가장 적절한 것을 고르시오.

① $5　　　② $10
③ $15　　④ $20
⑤ $30

13
W: Hello, ________ ________ ________ ________ some bicycles.

M: Okay. How many do you need?

W: I want one for me and one for my 10-year-old son.

M: The price is the same for adults and children.

W: Okay. How much is it?

M: It's $________ ________ ________. How long do you need them?

W: I think we need them for 3 hours.

M: If you rent them for a half day, you will only pay $10 for each.

W: That's great. Then, I'd like to rent two bikes for a half day.

M: Sure! I'll ________ ________ ________. One moment, please.

14. 대화를 듣고, 두 사람의 관계로 가장 적절한 것을 고르시오.

① 경찰관 — 시민
② 은행원 — 고객
③ 역무원 — 관광객
④ 편의점 직원 — 손님
⑤ 휴대폰 수리기사 — 고객

14
M: Hi, what can I help you with?

W: My cell phone battery ________ ________ ________.

M: Let me see. How long have you been using this phone?

W: Around three years. What can I do about it?

M: Well, if you don't want to get a new phone, I think it's best to ________ ________ ________.

W: How much will that cost?

M: It costs $49 for this model.

W: Okay. Please change it for me.

M: No problem. Please ________ ________ this form.

15. 대화를 듣고, 여자가 남자에게 부탁한 일로 가장 적절한 것을 고르시오.

① 주문 취소하기
② 메뉴 변경하기
③ 구매 내용 확인하기
④ 주문 추가하기
⑤ 배송 시간 변경하기

15

(*Telephone rings.*)

M: Charlie's Cupcakes.

W: Hello. This is Hollie Jenkins. I ________ ________ ________ yesterday.

M: Let me see. You ordered twelve vanilla cupcakes.

W: Yes. Can I ________ ________ ________?

M: Would you like to change the original order?

W: No. I want to ________ ________ ________ cupcakes. Mint chocolate, this time.

M: No problem. When do you want to pick them up?

W: At 2 p.m. Thank you.

16. 대화를 듣고, 남자가 동물 보호소에 가지 못하는 이유로 가장 적절한 것을 고르시오.

① 봄맞이 대청소를 해야 해서
② 할머니를 뵈러 가야 해서
③ 고양이 알레르기가 있어서
④ 가족 모임이 있어서
⑤ 동물병원에 가야 해서

16

M: Karen, you look excited. What's up?

W: I'm actually ________ ________ ________ ________ the animal shelter to volunteer.

M: That sounds exciting! What kind of work do you do there?

W: I usually walk the dogs and ________ ________ ________.

M: Wow, that's amazing. I love animals, too.

W: Why don't you ________ ________ this weekend?

M: I wish I could, but I have to visit my sick grandmother.

W: No problem. Family always ________ ________.

다음 페이지에 계속 ➡

17. 다음 그림의 상황에 가장 적절한 대화를 고르시오.

① ② ③ ④ ⑤

17 ① M: How much is this bag?

W: I'll go and ________ ________ ________ for you.

② M: It looks delicious! Did you do all the cooking?

W: Yes, I did. Help yourself.

③ M: The sun is strong. Why don't you wear a hat?

W: Okay, I will. Thanks.

④ M: He's ________ ________ ________ on the phone.

W: Yes. Let's move to another table.

⑤ M: It's so cold.

W: Right. Let's go inside and ________ __________ ________.

18. 다음을 듣고, 여자가 현장학습에 대해 언급하지 <u>않은</u> 것을 고르시오.

① 실시 날짜
② 모임 장소
③ 버스 출발 시간
④ 목적지
⑤ 복장 규정

18 W: Hello, students. The grade two class field trip will be held this Saturday, August 9. ________ ________ ________ is the front yard of the school. Boarding time is 7 a.m. and the bus will ________ __________ at 7:15 a.m. Please don't be late so that we can depart on time. ________ ________ ________ ________ your school shirt and jogging pants. I hope everyone enjoys the trip!

알맞은응답찾기

19. 대화를 듣고, 남자의 마지막 말에 이어질 여자의 말로 가장 적절한 것을 고르시오.

Woman: _______________

① Then I'll have that.
② You can order milk.
③ Take this medicine now.
④ These oranges look fresh.
⑤ My favorite fruit is strawberries.

19

M: Hello. Welcome to Juice Wonderland! How can I help you?

W: Hi. What's __________ __________ __________ drink in this store?

M: The strawberry smoothie is our __________ __________.

W: Does it have any milk in it?

M: Yes, it's __________ __________ milk and yogurt.

W: Milk gives me a _______________. Do you have a drink without any milk in it?

M: Yes. We have orange juice. It's made with oranges only.

W: Then I'll have that.

알맞은응답찾기

20. 대화를 듣고, 남자의 마지막 말에 이어질 여자의 말로 가장 적절한 것을 고르시오.

Woman: _______________

① Happy birthday to her!
② Don't forget to write a letter.
③ It's next to the post office.
④ Sure, let me show you some.
⑤ Why don't you buy a necklace?

20

M: Hey, I didn't _______ _______ _______ you at the book store.

W: Hi, Pierce. I'm here to buy some books for my friends.

M: Oh, is it someone's birthday?

W: No, I'm going to give books as a gift for World Book Day.

M: That's a good idea. Maybe I'll buy a _______ book for my mom, too.

W: Good for you. Does she like poetry?

M: Yes, but I don't know much about it. Can you _____________ one?

W: Sure, let me show you some.

Words & Expressions Review 17

● 다음 단어를 암기하세요.

문제	번호	단어	뜻
1	1	partly	부분적으로
	2	reach	~에 달하다, 이르다
2	3	nephew	남자 조카
	4	thunder	천둥
	5	text	글, 문서
3	6	invitation	초대장, 초대
	7	belly	배
	8	pregnant	임신한
4	9	badly	심하게, 몹시
	10	on one's own	혼자서, 단독으로
5	11	reservation	예약
	12	standard	일반적인, 보통의
6	13	fall down	넘어지다
	14	crutch	목발
	15	unfortunately	불행하게도, 유감스럽게도
7	16	take a suggestion	제안을 받아들이다
	17	either	(둘 중) 어느 한쪽
8	18	feel well	건강 상태가 좋다
	19	get some rest	약간의 휴식을 취하다
	20	grocery store	식료품점
9	21	trailer	(영화, 텔레비전 프로그램의) 예고편
	22	air	방송하다, 방송되다

문제	번호	단어	뜻
10	23	attention	주목, 집중
	24	striped	줄무늬의
11	25	take place	열리다, 개최되다
	26	submit	제출하다
12	27	cancel	취소하다
13	28	rent	대여하다, 빌리다
14	29	replace	교체하다, 대체하다
	30	fill out	~을 작성하다, 기입하다
15	31	place an order	주문하다
	32	make a change	변경하다
16	33	come along	함께 가다[오다]
	34	come first	가장 먼저다, 최우선 고려 사항이다
17	35	Help yourself.	마음껏 드세요.
	36	speak on the phone	통화하다
	37	loudly	큰 소리로, 크게
18	38	promptly	정확히, 즉각
	39	depart	출발하다, 떠나다
	40	on time	정시에
19	41	be made with	~으로 만들어지다
	42	stomachache	복통
20	43	poetry	시
	44	recommend	추천하다

●왼쪽 단어장의 뜻이 보이지 않게 반으로 접고, 학습한 단어의 뜻을 아래 빈칸에 적어주세요.

1 promptly		23 text	
2 standard		24 crutch	
3 reservation		25 depart	
4 place an order		26 be made with	
5 cancel		27 on one's own	
6 stomachache		28 come along	
7 air		29 Help yourself.	
8 pregnant		30 poetry	
9 replace		31 make a change	
10 nephew		32 either	
11 partly		33 fall down	
12 get some rest		34 badly	
13 thunder		35 grocery store	
14 come first		36 on time	
15 loudly		37 attention	
16 striped		38 recommend	
17 belly		39 reach	
18 speak on the phone		40 invitation	
19 take place		41 feel well	
20 fill out		42 unfortunately	
21 trailer		43 rent	
22 take a suggestion		44 submit	

18회 중학영어듣기 모의고사

M2(17)_18_US
모두 **미국식 발음(US)**
으로 녹음

M2(17)_18_UK
20문제 중 5문제에 **영국식 발음**
(US+UK)을 포함하여 녹음

정답 및 해석 p.85

1 다음을 듣고, 내일 아침의 날씨로 가장 적절한 것을 고르시오.

2 대화를 듣고, 여자가 주문할 우산으로 가장 적절한 것을 고르시오.

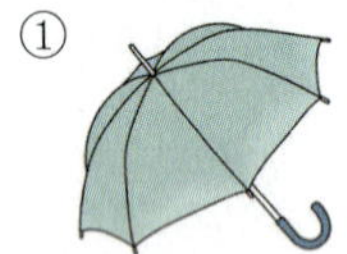  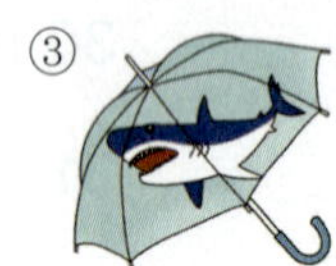 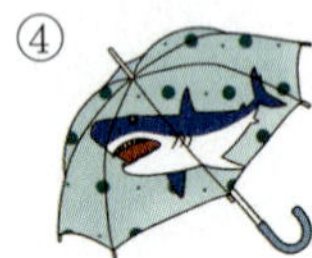 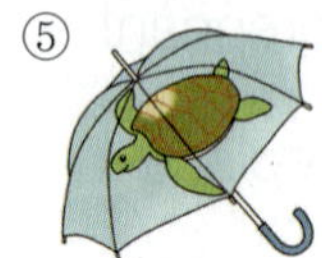

3 대화를 듣고, 남자의 심정으로 가장 적절한 것을 고르시오.

① worried　　② excited　　③ nervous　　④ bored　　⑤ angry

4 대화를 듣고, 여자가 주말에 한 일로 가장 적절한 것을 고르시오.

① 조개 줍기　　② 바다 수영하기　　③ 영화배우 사인회 참석하기
④ 해변 주변 청소하기　　⑤ 영화 촬영장 방문하기

5 대화를 듣고, 두 사람이 대화하는 장소로 가장 적절한 곳을 고르시오.

① 병원　　② 공원　　③ 영화관　　④ 지하철　　⑤ 버스 정류장

6 대화를 듣고, 남자의 마지막 말의 의도로 가장 적절한 것을 고르시오.

① 격려　　　　　② 후회　　　　　③ 설득
④ 동의　　　　　⑤ 경고

7 대화를 듣고, 여자의 계획을 고르시오.

① 머리 자르기　　　② 머리 염색하기　　　③ 가발 사기
④ 파마하기　　　　⑤ 미용실에서 일하기

8 대화를 듣고, 남자가 대화 직후에 할 일로 가장 적절한 것을 고르시오.

① 설문지 복사하기　　② 발표 촬영하기　　③ 교실 청소하기
④ 책상 정리하기　　　⑤ 문자 전송하기

9 대화를 듣고, 두 사람이 가수에 대해 언급하지 <u>않은</u> 것을 고르시오.

① 이름　　　　　② 데뷔 시기　　　③ 곡 제목
④ 장르　　　　　⑤ 음원 성적

10 다음을 듣고, 여자가 하는 말의 내용으로 가장 적절한 것을 고르시오.

① 체육관 공사 예고　　② 특별 강연 소개　　③ 학교 행사 안내
④ 신설 동아리 홍보　　⑤ 시간표 변경 공지

11번~20번 문제는 다음 페이지에 ➡

11 대화를 듣고, Summer Dance Class에 대한 내용과 일치하지 <u>않는</u> 것을 고르시오.

① 7월 1일부터 시작한다.　　　　　　② 힙합 댄스를 가르친다.
③ 매주 토요일 오전 10시에 열린다.　　④ 강좌는 두 시간 동안 진행된다.
⑤ 수강신청은 주민센터에서 해야 한다.

12 대화를 듣고, 여자가 상점을 방문한 이유로 가장 적절한 것을 고르시오.

① 쿠폰을 사용하려고　　　　　　② 결제 수단을 바꾸려고
③ 구매한 상품을 교환하려고　　　④ 영수증을 재발급 받으려고
⑤ 고장 난 물건을 수리하려고

13 대화를 듣고, 여자가 받은 거스름돈으로 가장 적절한 것을 고르시오.

① $1　　　　② $2　　　　③ $3　　　　④ $4　　　　⑤ $5

14 대화를 듣고, 두 사람의 관계로 가장 적절한 것을 고르시오.

① 선원 – 승객　　　　② 선장 – 선원　　　　③ 경찰관 – 시민
④ 일기예보관 – 기자　　⑤ 수상 안전요원 – 시설 관리자

15 대화를 듣고, 남자가 여자에게 부탁한 일로 가장 적절한 것을 고르시오.

① 음악 교사 소개해주기　　② 피아노 연주해주기　　③ 웹사이트 주소 알려주기
④ 같이 보고서 쓰기　　　　⑤ 문자 알림 신청하기

16 대화를 듣고, 여자가 공원에 가는 이유로 가장 적절한 것을 고르시오.

① 운동을 하기 위해서　　　　② 봉사활동을 하기 위해서
③ 야간 사진을 찍기 위해서　　④ 클래식 공연을 보기 위해서
⑤ 강아지를 산책시키기 위해서

17 다음 그림의 상황에 가장 적절한 대화를 고르시오.

①   ②   ③   ④   ⑤

18 다음을 듣고, 여자가 미술 대회에 대해 언급하지 <u>않은</u> 것을 고르시오.

① 주최자   ② 날짜   ③ 입상 상품

④ 참가 신청 기한   ⑤ 심사자

[19~20]   대화를 듣고, 남자의 마지막 말에 이어질 여자의 말로 가장 적절한 것을 고르시오.

19   Woman: _______________________________________

① Sorry, I'm busy at the moment.

② Okay, I'll take care of it right away.

③ Thank you for cleaning up the room.

④ Let's order some curtains and cushions.

⑤ I'll call the guests and cancel the meeting.

20   Woman: _______________________________________

① Oh, that's too bad.   ② Don't mention it.

③ Nice to see you.   ④ That's a good idea.

⑤ It sounds like you had a great time.

Dictation Test 18

M2(17)_18_D

Dictation(받아쓰기)은 본문을 받아쓰면서 영어듣기의 집중력을 향상시키고 다양한 표현을 정리하기 위한 영어듣기 학습법입니다. **녹음을 다시 듣고, 빈칸에 알맞은 단어를 써 보세요.**
※Dictation의 정답은 듣기 대본의 밑줄 친 부분을 확인하세요.

정답 p. 85

맞은 개수 / 총166개

날씨파악-그림

1. 다음을 듣고, 내일 아침의 날씨로 가장 적절한 것을 고르시오.

① 
② (눈사람)
③ 
④ (깃발)
⑤ 

01 W: Good morning! You are listening to Everyday Weather. We are expecting snow this morning along with ________ _______ ____________ ________. Also, it will be quite windy. So, remember to dress warmly. Looking ahead, tomorrow morning, it is expected to be sunny. ________ _______ for any new weather updates!

2025 영어듣기능력평가 1회 2번 변형

그림정보파악

2. 대화를 듣고, 여자가 주문할 우산으로 가장 적절한 것을 고르시오.

① 
② 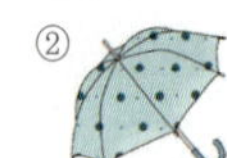
③ 
④ 
⑤ 

02 W: Danny, do you want to look at these umbrellas on my screen?

M: Sure, Mom. You're going to ___________ ___________ ___________ ___________, right?

W: Yes. I think the polka-dotted one ___________ ___________.

M: Hmm. I don't want polka dots on my umbrella.

W: Okay. Then, how about these ones with sea animals on them?

M: They're cool. I'll go for the one ___________ ___________ ___________.

W: Great. I'll order that one.

---

3. 대화를 듣고, 남자의 심정으로 가장 적절한 것을 고르시오.

① worried ② excited
③ nervous ④ bored
⑤ angry

03

W: You ________ ________ today. What's up?

M: I'm ________ ________ a picnic with my family tomorrow.

W: That sounds like a lot of fun.

M: Yes. And the weather forecast said that it would be a beautiful day.

W: Oh, really? I ________ ________ ________ a great time.

M: Thanks.

4. 대화를 듣고, 여자가 주말에 한 일로 가장 적절한 것을 고르시오.

① 조개 줍기
② 바다 수영하기
③ 영화배우 사인회 참석하기
④ 해변 주변 청소하기
⑤ 영화 촬영장 방문하기

04

M: Mary, you ________ ________ ________!

W: Thanks. I went to the beach last weekend.

M: Good. Did you go swimming?

W: No, I didn't swim. The water was still too cold.

M: Then, what did you do? Oh, let me guess. You collected clams?

W: Actually, there was ________ ________ ________ on the beach.

M: Wow, you went there just to see the shoot?

W: Yes! I watched my favorite actor __________ and ________ for three hours!

다음 페이지에 계속 ➡

5. 대화를 듣고, 두 사람이 대화하는 장소로 가장 적절한 곳을 고르시오.

① 병원
② 공원
③ 영화관
④ 지하철
⑤ 버스 정류장

05

M: Hello, how can I help you?

W: Hi, I'd like to buy two tickets for *Toy Adventures*.

M: Sure! For what time?

W: 6:30, please.

M: Let me check. *(pause)* Um… We only have

________ ________ ________ ________. Is that okay

with you?

W: Hmm… Can we at least get seats that are in the

center?

M: Sure! I'll ________ ________ ________ that are in

the center. That will be 30 dollars, please.

W: Here's my credit card.

M: Please wait for a minute while I ________ ________

________ ________.

6. 대화를 듣고, 남자의 마지막 말의 의도로 가장 적절한 것을 고르시오.

① 격려
② 후회
③ 설득
④ 동의
⑤ 경고

06

W: I'm so happy that the exam ________ ________!

M: Yes. I really want to sleep all day.

W: Didn't you sleep well? So, ________ ________

________ ________.

M: Of course not! I studied science until late, but the

exam was still very hard.

W: I think I did science all right, but English was very

difficult for me.

M: ________ ________ ________ ________. It was hard

for me, too.

7. 대화를 듣고, 여자의 계획을 고르시오.

① 머리 자르기
② 머리 염색하기
③ 가발 사기
④ 파마하기
⑤ 미용실에서 일하기

07
W: I'm ________ ________ ________ my hairstyle.

I want to try a different look.

M: What do you have in mind?

W: Hmm… Do you think blonde hair will ________

________ ________ me?

M: No, I don't think so. Your hair will look like a wig.

W: Okay. I'll just ________ ________ ________ at the

salon then.

M: That's a good idea. You'll look cute with curly

hair.

2024 영어듣기능력평가 2회 8번 변형

8. 대화를 듣고, 남자가 대화 직후에 할 일로 가장 적절한 것을 고르시오.

① 설문지 복사하기
② 발표 촬영하기
③ 교실 청소하기
④ 책상 정리하기
⑤ 문자 전송하기

08
W: Hi, Kevin. Did you __________ __________

__________ for your project?

M: Yes, Ms. Park. I prepared the survey questions last

night.

W: Good job! Did you bring __________ __________

for the class?

M: Oh! I only brought one copy with me.

W: You'll need to __________ __________ copies to

everyone.

M: Right. Can I use the copy machine now?

W: Sure. It's in the teachers' room.

M: Okay. I'll go and __________ __________

__________ my survey right now.

다음 페이지에 계속 ➡

9. 대화를 듣고, 두 사람이 가수에 대해 언급하지 <u>않은</u> 것을 고르시오.

① 이름
② 데뷔 시기
③ 곡 제목
④ 장르
⑤ 음원 성적

09

W: Daniel, what are you listening to?

M: It's a song by a new singer, Paula Dawson. Do you want to hear it?

W: Yes, I do! (*pause*) Oh, it's good. She just ________ ________ ________ this month, right?

M: That's right. This song is ________ "Crash."

W: Strong name. And it sounds like a rock ballad.

M: Yes, it is. I like rock ballads very much.

W: I like them, too. I should ____________ ________ ________.

M: Yeah, you should.

10. 다음을 듣고, 여자가 하는 말의 내용으로 가장 적절한 것을 고르시오.

① 체육관 공사 예고
② 특별 강연 소개
③ 학교 행사 안내
④ 신설 동아리 홍보
⑤ 시간표 변경 공지

10

W: Hello, students. Future Career Week has finally arrived! The event will ____________ ____________ between 3 and 5 p.m. for five days starting next Monday. After class, go to the gym and ____________ ____________ as many programs as possible. You will be ____________ ____________ how many exciting future jobs there are, and you can ____________ them all with your friends. For more information, check out the school website. Have fun!

11. 대화를 듣고, Summer Dance Class에 대한 내용과 일치하지 <u>않는</u> 것을 고르시오.

① 7월 1일부터 시작한다.
② 힙합 댄스를 가르친다.
③ 매주 토요일 오전 10시에 열린다.
④ 강좌는 두 시간 동안 진행된다.
⑤ 수강신청은 주민센터에서 해야 한다.

11

M: Amy, do you have any plans for the summer?

W: Yes! I'm going to take a dance class. It'll _________ _________ July 1.

M: That's cool. What kind of dance?

W: Hip-hop. Are you interested?

M: Yeah, I've always wanted to learn hip-hop. When is the class held?

W: Every Saturday at 10 a.m. It's _________ _________ _________.

M: All right. I'll _________ _________ for it.

W: Great! You need to sign up at the community center.

2024 영어듣기능력평가 2회 12번 변형

12. 대화를 듣고, 여자가 상점을 방문한 이유로 가장 적절한 것을 고르시오.

① 쿠폰을 사용하려고
② 결제 수단을 바꾸려고
③ 구매한 상품을 교환하려고
④ 영수증을 재발급 받으려고
⑤ 고장 난 물건을 수리하려고

12

M: Hello. Can I help you?

W: Yes. I bought this electric fan here this morning.

M: I see. Is there a problem with it?

W: No, the fan _________ _________. I just want to cancel the payment I made and _________ _________ a different credit card.

M: Sure. Do you have your receipt and the card you used?

W: Yes, I _________ _________.

M: Great. I'll help you with that.

다음 페이지에 계속 ➡

13. 대화를 듣고, 여자가 받은 거스름돈으로 가장 적절한 것을 고르시오.

① $1 ② $2
③ $3 ④ $4
⑤ $5

13
M: Welcome to Juice World. May I __________ __________ __________?

W: Yes. I would like to order one ABC juice.

M: Okay. What size would you like? If you __________, it will cost one dollar more.

W: I'll upsize, please.

M: Okay, that will be 5 dollars. __________ __________ __________ __________ for today?

W: Oh, could I also get __________ __________ __________ rice crisps?

M: Including the rice crisps, your total will be 7 dollars.

W: Here is 10 dollars for you.

M: Thank you. Here is your change.

2025 영어듣기능력평가 1회 14번 변형

14. 대화를 듣고, 두 사람의 관계로 가장 적절한 것을 고르시오.

① 선원 — 승객
② 선장 — 선원
③ 경찰관 — 시민
④ 일기예보관 — 기자
⑤ 수상 안전요원 — 시설 관리자

14
W: Excuse me. Why hasn't boarding started? The ferry is supposed to leave in a minute.

M: I'm sorry. The captain has __________ __________. The waves are too high right now.

W: Oh, no. I really have to cross the channel tonight.

M: It __________ __________ the weather, but I'm sure we will be able to leave tonight.

W: Are you one of the crew?

M: Yes. I'll __________ __________ __________ as soon as we are ready to leave.

W: Thank you.

15. 대화를 듣고, 남자가 여자에게 부탁한 일로 가장 적절한 것을 고르시오.

① 음악 교사 소개해주기
② 피아노 연주해주기
③ 웹사이트 주소 알려주기
④ 같이 보고서 쓰기
⑤ 문자 알림 신청하기

15

W: Fred, you look tired.

M: I ___________ ___________ ___________ trying to write a song.

W: The music homework? But, you are good at playing the piano.

M: Well, writing a song is a ___________ ___________ ___________.

W: Oh… I know what you mean. Well, I know a website that might help.

M: What kind of website is it?

W: It shows simple steps to song writing.

M: Can you give me the website address?

W: Sure. I'll ___________ ___________ to you.

16. 대화를 듣고, 여자가 공원에 가는 이유로 가장 적절한 것을 고르시오.

① 운동을 하기 위해서
② 봉사활동을 하기 위해서
③ 야간 사진을 찍기 위해서
④ 클래식 공연을 보기 위해서
⑤ 강아지를 산책시키기 위해서

16

M: Hey, Jenny. Where are you ___________?

W: I'm going to Central Park.

M: Why are you going there at this hour? It's ___________ ___________.

W: There's going to be a free concert there tonight.

M: You mean at Central Park?

W: Yeah. The concert ___________ ___________ ___________ the Korea Symphony Orchestra.

M: Oh, so it's a classical music concert. Can I ___________ ___________ ___________?

W: Of course! Let's go.

다음 페이지에 계속 ➡

17. 다음 그림의 상황에 가장 적절한 대화를 고르시오.

① ②
③ ④
⑤

17

① W: Can I borrow your bicycle on the weekend?

M: I'm sorry, but mine is broken.

② W: Excuse me. Where can I find cereal?

M: That would be _________ _________ _________, ma'am.

③ W: I think the steak is undercooked. Could you _________ _________ _________?

M: Certainly. I'll have the chef cook it more.

④ W: How would you like your one thousand dollars, sir?

M: In fifties, please.

⑤ W: How often should I take this medicine?

M: Take it once a day _________ _________ _________.

18. 다음을 듣고, 여자가 미술 대회에 대해 언급하지 <u>않은</u> 것을 고르시오.

① 주최자
② 날짜
③ 입상 상품
④ 참가 신청 기한
⑤ 심사자

18

W: Hello, students! For art lovers, Washington Middle School _________ _________ _________ _________. It will be _________ next month, on the 21st at the school. First prize will be a tablet PC. There are other prizes for winners, so sign up now! Students' work _________ _________ _________ by local artists. Your art teachers are expecting many talented students to enter the contest!

알맞은응답찾기

19. 대화를 듣고, 남자의 마지막 말에 이어질 여자의 말로 가장 적절한 것을 고르시오.

Woman: ___________________

① Sorry, I'm busy at the moment.
② Okay, I'll take care of it right away.
③ Thank you for cleaning up the room.
④ Let's order some curtains and cushions.
⑤ I'll call the guests and cancel the meeting.

19

M: Angela, we need to get things ready.

W: What's going on, Dad?

M: Don't you remember that we have guests today? They will be here soon.

W: Oh, right. I've already ___________ ___________ my room like you asked.

M: You have? Great! Then, can you ___________ ___________ ___________ ___________ with the living room?

W: Sure. What do you need me to do?

M: Please open the curtains and ___________ the cushions on the sofa.

W: Okay, I'll take care of it right away.

알맞은응답찾기

20. 대화를 듣고, 남자의 마지막 말에 이어질 여자의 말로 가장 적절한 것을 고르시오.

Woman: ___________________

① Oh, that's too bad.
② Don't mention it.
③ Nice to see you.
④ That's a good idea.
⑤ It sounds like you had a great time.

20

W: How was your trip, Mike?

M: ___________ ___________ ___________.

W: Why? What happened?

M: Most of the time, I ___________ ___________ the hotel.

W: Why? Were you sick?

M: No, I wasn't. It was ___________ ___________ the bad weather. It rained ___________ ___________.

W: Oh, that's too bad.

Words & Expressions Review 18

● 다음 단어를 암기하세요.

문제	번호	단어	뜻
1	☐ 1	drop	(수량·정도의) 하락, 감소
	☐ 2	look ahead	(앞일, 미래 등을) 내다보다
	☐ 3	stay tuned	채널을 고정하다
2	☐ 4	screen	화면
	☐ 5	polka-dotted	물방울무늬의
3	☐ 6	go on a picnic	소풍을 가다
	☐ 7	hope	바라다, 희망
4	☐ 8	collect	모으다, 수집하다
	☐ 9	clam	조개
	☐ 10	movie shooting	영화 촬영
5	☐ 11	front	앞의
	☐ 12	row	줄, 열
	☐ 13	at least	적어도, 최소한
	☐ 14	print out	인쇄하다
6	☐ 15	be over	끝나다
7	☐ 16	get tired of ~	~이 지겨워지다
	☐ 17	look good on ~	~와 잘 어울리다
8	☐ 18	survey	설문조사
9	☐ 19	debut	~을 최초로 공개하다
	☐ 20	title	제목을 붙이다
10	☐ 21	event	행사
	☐ 22	be amazed at	~에 깜짝 놀라다

문제	번호	단어	뜻
10	☐ 23	explore	탐색하다
11	☐ 24	sign up for ~	~에 등록하다
	☐ 25	electric	전기의, 전기를 이용하는
12	☐ 26	work	(기계·장치 등이) 작동하다, 기능하다
	☐ 27	payment	결제, 지불
13	☐ 28	take an order	주문을 받다
14	☐ 29	delay	지연시키다, 지체하게 하다
	☐ 30	departure	출발
15	☐ 31	totally	완전히, 전적으로
	☐ 32	step	단계
16	☐ 33	be headed	(특정 방향으로) 가다, 향하다
	☐ 34	feature	~을 출연시키다, ~에 출연하다
	☐ 35	come with	~와 같이 가다
	☐ 36	aisle	통로
17	☐ 37	undercooked	덜 익은
	☐ 38	take a medicine	약을 먹다
18	☐ 39	hold	개최하다, 열다
	☐ 40	judge	심사하다, 평가하다
19	☐ 41	give ~ a hand	~에게 도움을 주다
	☐ 42	arrange	정리하다, 배열하다
20	☐ 43	stay	머무르다
	☐ 44	bad weather	안 좋은 날씨

M2(17)_W_18

●왼쪽 단어장의 뜻이 보이지 않게 반으로 접고, 학습한 단어의 뜻을 아래 빈칸에 적어주세요.

1	work		23	judge
2	debut		24	undercooked
3	event		25	clam
4	front		26	get tired of ~
5	hold		27	stay
6	go on a picnic		28	look good on ~
7	row		29	departure
8	give ~ a hand		30	be headed
9	arrange		31	title
10	payment		32	come with
11	collect		33	be amazed at
12	stay tuned		34	electric
13	drop		35	totally
14	bad weather		36	movie shooting
15	hope		37	be over
16	sign up for ~		38	delay
17	aisle		39	feature
18	at least		40	take a medicine
19	step		41	print out
20	polka-dotted		42	explore
21	survey		43	look ahead
22	take an order		44	screen

18
회
단
어

정답 및 해석 p. 90

1 다음을 듣고, 일요일의 날씨로 적절한 것을 고르시오.

①  ②  ③ 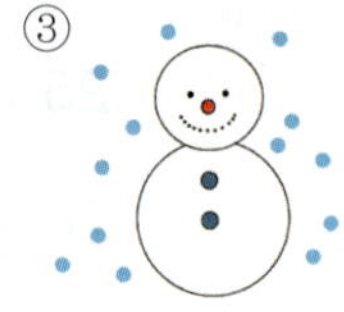 ④  ⑤ 

2 대화를 듣고, 두 사람이 구입할 발매트로 가장 적절한 것을 고르시오.

①  ②  ③  ④  ⑤ 

3 대화를 듣고, 남자의 심정으로 가장 적절한 것을 고르시오.

① shy ② proud ③ worried
④ thankful ⑤ disappointed

4 대화를 듣고, 남자가 지난 주말에 한 일로 가장 적절한 것을 고르시오.

① 강아지 용품 구매하기 ② 동물 병원에 가기
③ 공원에 산책 가기 ④ 시험 공부하기
⑤ 봉사활동 하기

5 대화를 듣고, 두 사람이 대화하는 장소로 가장 적절한 곳을 고르시오.

① 세차장 ② 귀금속 가게 ③ 박람회장
④ 자동차 정비소 ⑤ 분실물 보관소

6 대화를 듣고, 여자의 마지막 말의 의도로 가장 적절한 것을 고르시오.

① 확인 ② 사과 ③ 제안 ④ 초대 ⑤ 불평

7 대화를 듣고, Steve의 고민이 무엇인지 고르시오.

① 선물 전달 방법 ② 지갑을 잃어버린 일 ③ 친구와의 다툼
④ 형의 결혼 준비 ⑤ 부모님 선물

8 대화를 듣고, 여자가 대화 직후에 할 일로 가장 적절한 것을 고르시오.

① 음료수 사기 ② 기념품 사기 ③ 선글라스 사기
④ 입장권 구매하기 ⑤ 모자 가지러 가기

9 대화를 듣고, 두 사람이 수영 강좌에 대해 언급하지 <u>않은</u> 것을 고르시오.

① 초급 강좌 유무 ② 강좌당 인원 ③ 수강료
④ 수건 제공 여부 ⑤ 사물함 이용 가격

10 다음을 듣고, 여자가 하는 말의 내용으로 가장 적절한 것을 고르시오.

① 화상 응급처치법 ② 물놀이 사고 예방법
③ 수분 섭취의 중요성 ④ 폭염 대비 건강 수칙
⑤ 자외선 차단제의 종류

11번~20번 문제는 다음 페이지에 ➡

11 대화를 듣고, 오디션에 대한 내용으로 일치하지 <u>않는</u> 것을 고르시오.

① TV 프로그램을 위한 것이다.
② 최종 우승자는 뮤지컬에 출연한다.
③ 전국에서 100명을 뽑는다.
④ 신청하려면 동영상을 보내야 한다.
⑤ 3주 후에 신청이 마감된다.

12 대화를 듣고, 여자가 전화를 건 목적으로 가장 적절한 것을 고르시오.

① 주말 약속을 취소하기 위해서
② 동아리에 가입 신청하기 위해서
③ 청소 업체를 추천받기 위해서
④ 봉사 활동 참여를 권유하기 위해서
⑤ 봉사 활동 일정을 알아보기 위해서

13 대화를 듣고, 여자가 지불할 금액으로 가장 적절한 것을 고르시오.

① $4   ② $6   ③ $8   ④ $10   ⑤ $12

14 대화를 듣고, 두 사람의 관계로 가장 적절한 것을 고르시오.

① 작가 — 독자
② 배우 — 매니저
③ 연주자 — 기자
④ 공항 직원 — 탑승객
⑤ 공연장 관리인 — 관람객

15 대화를 듣고, 여자가 남자에게 부탁한 일로 가장 적절한 것을 고르시오.

① 방 청소하기
② 달걀 사 오기
③ 음식 주문하기
④ 연필 빌려주기
⑤ 강아지 산책시키기

16 대화를 듣고, 여자가 쇼핑몰에 가는 이유로 가장 적절한 것을 고르시오.

① 행사를 준비하기 위해서
② 인형을 사기 위해서
③ 구매물품을 환불하기 위해서
④ 아르바이트를 하기 위해서
⑤ 팬 사인회에 참여하기 위해서

17 다음 그림의 상황에 가장 적절한 대화를 고르시오.

①   ②   ③   ④   ⑤

18 다음을 듣고, 남자가 Yellow Waffles에 대해 언급하지 <u>않은</u> 것을 고르시오.

① 개업일   ② 판매 상품   ③ 개업 사은품

④ 좌석 수   ⑤ 배달 서비스

[19~20]   대화를 듣고, 남자의 마지막 말에 이어질 여자의 말로 가장 적절한 것을 고르시오.

19   **Woman:** _______________________________________

① Okay, I'll see you then.   ② We're going out for dinner.

③ No, I don't like playing basketball.   ④ Thank you for lending me your book.

⑤ I prefer tennis to basketball.

20   **Woman:** _______________________________________

① Don't hang out for too long.

② The park is quite far from here.

③ The rain isn't going to stop anytime soon.

④ You and your friends have made good plans.

⑤ It's dangerous to ride a bike these days.

Dictation Test 19

M2(17)_19_D

Dictation(받아쓰기)은 본문을 받아쓰면서 영어듣기의 집중력을 향상시키고 다양한 표현을 정리하기 위한 영어듣기 학습법입니다. **녹음을 다시 듣고, 빈칸에 알맞은 단어를 써 보세요.**
※Dictation의 정답은 듣기 대본의 밑줄 친 부분을 확인하세요.

정답 p. 90

맞은 개수 / 총151개

날씨파악–그림

1. 다음을 듣고, 일요일의 날씨로 적절한 것을 고르시오.

①  ② 

③  ④ 

⑤ 

01 M: Good morning. This is the Friday ______________ report. Today, it will be ________ in the afternoon, and it's going to rain at night. On Saturday, it will be colder, and the rain will ________ ________ snow. The snowy weather will __________ until Monday. Thank you.

그림정보파악

2. 대화를 듣고, 두 사람이 구입할 발매트로 가장 적절한 것을 고르시오.

①  ② 

③  ④ 

⑤ 

02 M: Which one of these mats do you like most for our bathroom?

W: I like the bright, ________-________ mat.

M: But the bright one will ________ ________ ________.

W: You're right. Then, which mat do you like?

M: I think a dark mat would be best. Let's choose one of these cloud-shaped ones.

W: Okay. How about the dark, cloud-shaped mat with __________ ________ ________?

M: The smiley face looks cute. Let's buy that one.

---

3. 대화를 듣고, 남자의 심정으로 가장 적절한 것을 고르시오.

① shy
② proud
③ worried
④ thankful
⑤ disappointed

03
M: This painting is amazing! What a little artist our daughter is!

W: I know. She's __________ her skills a lot ________.

M: No one will believe this is the work of a 10-year-old.

W: You're right. She's ________ ________ ________ ________ ________.

M: Let me take a picture of her painting.

W: What are you going to do with it?

M: I want to show everyone ________ ____________ our daughter is.

4. 대화를 듣고, 남자가 지난 주말에 한 일로 가장 적절한 것을 고르시오.

① 강아지 용품 구매하기
② 동물 병원에 가기
③ 공원에 산책 가기
④ 시험 공부하기
⑤ 봉사활동 하기

04
W: I really want a dog, but I ________ ________ ________.

M: You can still play with dogs even if you don't own one.

W: How can I do that?

M: I ____________ at an ________ ________ last weekend and played with the dogs there. You can do the same.

W: Really? Volunteer work sounds like a great idea.

M: Yes, and it's good for the dogs, too. They need love and __________.

W: I'll definitely check it out.

다음 페이지에 계속 ➡

5. 대화를 듣고, 두 사람이 대화하는 장소로 가장 적절한 곳을 고르시오.

① 세차장
② 귀금속 가게
③ 박람회장
④ 자동차 정비소
⑤ 분실물 보관소

05
M: Welcome. How may I help you?

W: I'm here to ________ ________ my earrings.

M: Did you pre-order a new pair?

W: No. I left my old earrings here for repair. The hooks ________ ________ ________.

M: Right. Are you Amanda Peet? Here they are.

W: That's right. (pause) Oh, they are shining like new!

M: The cleaning service is included.

W: Thanks a lot. I'll ________ ________ to buy new ones some other time.

6. 대화를 듣고, 여자의 마지막 말의 의도로 가장 적절한 것을 고르시오.

① 확인   ② 사과
③ 제안   ④ 초대
⑤ 불평

06
W: Why do you ________ ________ ________?

M: My dog is missing.

W: I'm so sorry. How did it happen?

M: I think she left when the door was open.

W: Why was the door open?

M: I guess I ________ ________ ________ when I went to the convenience store.

W: Oh, no! Well, did you check the ________ ________?

M: I did. She wasn't there.

W: Then, why don't you make some ________?

7. 대화를 듣고, Steve의 고민이 무엇인지 고르시오.
① 선물 전달 방법
② 지갑을 잃어버린 일
③ 친구와의 다툼
④ 형의 결혼 준비
⑤ 부모님 선물

07
W: You _________ _________ _________ today. What's the matter?

M: I'm worried.

W: What is it, Steve?

M: Next Friday is my parents' _________ anniversary. But I don't have enough money to _________ _________ a nice present.

W: Don't worry too much. Your parents will like whatever you give them.

M: Do you really think so?

W: Sure. A small gift from your heart will _________ _________ happy.

2025 영어듣기능력평가 1회 8번 변형

8. 대화를 듣고, 여자가 대화 직후에 할 일로 가장 적절한 것을 고르시오.
① 음료수 사기
② 기념품 사기
③ 선글라스 사기
④ 입장권 구매하기
⑤ 모자 가지러 가기

08
W: Ben, the zoo is ___________ ___________ I thought!

M: Yeah, it's really sunny today, too. You'd better put on your hat.

W: You're right. I should've brought my hat from the car.

M: Do you want me to get it for you?

W: No, it's okay. ___________ ___________ ___________ it myself.

M: Are you sure?

W: Yes, I'll be right back with my hat.

다음 페이지에 계속 ➡

9. 대화를 듣고, 두 사람이 수영 강좌에 대해 언급하지 <u>않은</u> 것을 고르시오.

① 초급 강좌 유무
② 강좌당 인원
③ 수강료
④ 수건 제공 여부
⑤ 사물함 이용 가격

09 (*Telephone rings.*)

W: Hello, Blue Swimming Center. How may I help you?

M: Hi, I want to learn to swim. Do you have classes ________ ____________?

W: Yes. We offer a beginner's class every morning.

M: Oh, good. ________ ________ ____________ are in each class?

W: We take up to six people in each class.

M: Do I need to ________ ________ ________ ________?

W: No, we have towels for you here.

M: Can I use the lockers?

W: Sure. It's 10 dollars per month.

M: Okay. Thank you.

10. 다음을 듣고, 여자가 하는 말의 내용으로 가장 적절한 것을 고르시오.

① 화상 응급처치법
② 물놀이 사고 예방법
③ 수분 섭취의 중요성
④ 폭염 대비 건강 수칙
⑤ 자외선 차단제의 종류

10 W: Hello, students. Today, I'm going to tell you how to stay healthy ________ ________ ________. First, try to keep out of the sun between 11 a.m. and 3 p.m. Second, ________ plenty of water often. Lastly, ________ __________ __________ and wear a hat, if you have to go out in the heat. Please be careful in hot weather.

11. 대화를 듣고, 오디션에 대한 내용으로 일치하지 <u>않는</u> 것을 고르시오.

① TV 프로그램을 위한 것이다.
② 최종 우승자는 뮤지컬에 출연한다.
③ 전국에서 100명을 뽑는다.
④ 신청하려면 동영상을 보내야 한다.
⑤ 3주 후에 신청이 마감된다.

11

M: Emily, look at this website. They're _________ __________ for a singing contest.

W: It's for a TV program.

M: Yes. The winners will _________ _________ a famous musical. Why don't you try out? It would be your dream come true!

W: They only select 100 people from the whole country.

M: You just have to _________ _________ _________ _________ of your singing to apply. There's nothing to lose.

W: When is the deadline?

M: It's December 1st.

W: That's _________ _________ from today.

M: That's plenty of time!

12. 대화를 듣고, 여자가 전화를 건 목적으로 가장 적절한 것을 고르시오.

① 주말 약속을 취소하기 위해서
② 동아리에 가입 신청하기 위해서
③ 청소 업체를 추천받기 위해서
④ 봉사 활동 참여를 권유하기 위해서
⑤ 봉사 활동 일정을 알아보기 위해서

12

(*Cellphone rings.*)

M: Hello?

W: Hello! It's Ruth. Are you busy this weekend?

M: No, not really. Why?

W: Mark and I are ____________ this Saturday. Do you want to join us?

M: Cool! What kind of volunteer work are you guys thinking of doing?

W: Well, we were thinking about volunteering for a river clean-up group. The members of the group _________ _________ _________ by the riverside.

M: Sounds great. Can you _________ _________ _________ as well?

W: Sure.

다음 페이지에 계속 ➡

13. 대화를 듣고, 여자가 지불할 금액으로 가장 적절한 것을 고르시오.

① $4 ② $6
③ $8 ④ $10
⑤ $12

13

M: May I take your order?

W: Yes. I'd like to have an egg sandwich, please.

M: That will be 5 dollars. Do you want ________ ________ ________ potato chips, too?

W: Yes, please. Can I have ________ ________ ________ orange juice as well?

M: Sure. The orange juice is 3 dollars. And the potato chips are 2 dollars.

W: Okay. How much is ________ ________?

M: Your total is 10 dollars. Do you want to ________ ________ ________?

W: Yes. I'll pay in cash.

14. 대화를 듣고, 두 사람의 관계로 가장 적절한 것을 고르시오.

① 작가 — 독자
② 배우 — 매니저
③ 연주자 — 기자
④ 공항 직원 — 탑승객
⑤ 공연장 관리인 — 관람객

14

M: Hello, Ms. Davidson. I'm Jinsu Han from *The Monthly Pianist* magazine.

W: It's nice to meet you, Mr. Han.

M: Thank you for giving your time ________ ________ ____________.

W: My pleasure.

M: So, are you here in Korea for your concert tomorrow?

W: That's right. This is my second visit.

M: I guess you ________ __________ here the last time you came.

W: Yes. Korean audiences are very ____________.

M: Tell me more about it.

15. 대화를 듣고, 여자가 남자에게 부탁한 일로 가장 적절한 것을 고르시오.

① 방 청소하기
② 달걀 사 오기
③ 음식 주문하기
④ 연필 빌려주기
⑤ 강아지 산책시키기

15
M: Mom, I'm a bit hungry. Can I have a snack?

W: Sure, what do you want? We can make some pancakes, _________ ________ ________.

M: That sounds great! Let's make pancakes, then.

W: Okay. We'll need milk, ________, and some eggs.

M: I'll go check. (pauses) I only see milk and flour.

W: Then, can you go and ________ ________ ________ now?

M: Okay. I'll be back in a few minutes.

16. 대화를 듣고, 여자가 쇼핑몰에 가는 이유로 가장 적절한 것을 고르시오.

① 행사를 준비하기 위해서
② 인형을 사기 위해서
③ 구매물품을 환불하기 위해서
④ 아르바이트를 하기 위해서
⑤ 팬 사인회에 참여하기 위해서

16
M: Hello, Lisa. Where are you __________?

W: I'm on my way to the shopping mall.

M: Oh, do you have __________ ________ _______?

W: No. I'm going to meet my favorite boy group there. I ________ ________ for their fan signing event.

M: Wow! Lucky you. That's why you look so awesome today.

W: Thank you. I even brought some dolls ________ ___________ for them.

M: Good for you. I hope you have a wonderful time there.

W: Thank you so much.

다음 페이지에 계속 ➡

17. 다음 그림의 상황에 가장 적절한 대화를 고르시오.

①   ②
③   ④
⑤

17
① W: I'm looking for a guitar for beginners.

M: How about this one? It's $100.

② W: Are you going to ____________ _________ the talent show?

M: Yes, I'm going to play the piano.

③ W: Could you turn down the music, please?

M: Oh, sorry. I'll ________ _________ _________.

④ W: Look! That guy is busking over there.

M: Let's go and take a look.

⑤ W: It's so ____________ _________ here. All the benches are full.

M: We should have come earlier.

18. 다음을 듣고, 남자가 Yellow Waffles에 대해 언급하지 <u>않은</u> 것을 고르시오.

① 개업일
② 판매 상품
③ 개업 사은품
④ 좌석 수
⑤ 배달 서비스

18
M: Hello, everyone. Friday, May 19 is the grand opening of Yellow Waffles, our new store. Our store will have more than 20 ________ ________ delicious waffles, coffees, and many other ice drinks. Anyone who buys a waffle-coffee combo will ________ ________ __________ as a welcome gift. We also make __________ for orders of 30 dollars or more. Please download our app for more information.

19. 대화를 듣고, 남자의 마지막 말에 이어질
여자의 말로 가장 적절한 것을 고르시오.

Woman: ____________________

① Okay, I'll see you then.
② We're going out for dinner.
③ No, I don't like playing
basketball.
④ Thank you for lending me
your book.
⑤ I prefer tennis to basketball.

19

W: Hey, Anthony. Can I ask you a favor?

M: Sure! What is it?

W: Can you teach me how to throw free throws?

M: Yeah, no problem. ________ ________ ________
your PE exams, right?

W: You're right. I've practiced a lot, but I don't
________ ________ ________ ________ ________.

M: I see... Then, how about meeting at the school
basketball court at 8 p.m.?

W: Okay, I'll see you then.

---

20. 대화를 듣고, 남자의 마지막 말에 이어질
여자의 말로 가장 적절한 것을 고르시오.

Woman: ____________________

① Don't hang out for too long.
② The park is quite far from
here.
③ The rain isn't going to stop
anytime soon.
④ You and your friends have
made good plans.
⑤ It's dangerous to ride a bike
these days.

20

W: Where are you going, Peter?

M: I'm going out to ride my bike, Mom.

W: Look out the window. It's raining hard.

M: Oh, no! I ____________ ________ ________ my
friends at the park.

W: Well, maybe you should call them and change
your plans.

M: Will it rain for long? I really want to ________
________ ________ ________.

W: The rain isn't going to stop anytime soon.

Words & Expressions Review 19

● 다음 단어를 암기하세요.

문제	번호	단어	뜻
1	1	weather report	날씨 보도
2	2	bright	밝은
	3	cloud	구름
3	4	improve	향상시키다
	5	lately	최근에
	6	for one's age	나이에 비해
	7	talented	(타고난) 재능이 있는
4	8	animal shelter	동물 보호소
	9	attention	관심, 주의
	10	definitely	반드시, 분명히
5	11	repair	수리, 보수, 수선
	12	fall off	떨어지다
6	13	missing	없어진, 실종된
	14	convenience store	편의점
	15	flyer	전단지
7	16	look down	기운 없어 보이다
	17	enough	충분한
	18	gift	선물
9	19	beginner	초보자, 초급자
	20	up to ~	~까지
	21	locker	사물함
10	22	extreme	극도의

문제	번호	단어	뜻
10	23	keep out of ~	~을 피하다
	24	apply	바르다
	25	star	주연을 맡다
11	26	deadline	기한
	27	plenty of	많은
12	28	riverside	강변
	29	sign up	신청하다, 등록하다
13	30	cash	현금
	31	perform	연주하다
14	32	audience	청중, 관중
	33	enthusiastic	열광적인
15	34	a bit	조금, 약간
	35	flour	밀가루
16	36	head	(특정 방향으로) 가다, 향하다
	37	turn down	(소리·온도 등을) 줄이다, 낮추다
17	38	busk	길거리에서 연주하다
	39	crowded	(사람들이) 붐비는, 복잡한
	40	sort	종류
18	41	make deliveries	배달하다
	42	information	정보
19	43	get better	나아지다, 좋아지다
20	44	hang out	어울려 시간을 보내다

● 왼쪽 단어장의 뜻이 보이지 않게 반으로 접고, 학습한 단어의 뜻을 아래 빈칸에 적어주세요.

1	talented	23	turn down
2	repair	24	definitely
3	head	25	flyer
4	enthusiastic	26	information
5	a bit	27	apply
6	fall off	28	up to ~
7	flour	29	convenience store
8	hang out	30	audience
9	star	31	locker
10	bright	32	deadline
11	crowded	33	make deliveries
12	extreme	34	for one's age
13	cloud	35	enough
14	attention	36	weather report
15	plenty of	37	animal shelter
16	cash	38	riverside
17	sign up	39	look down
18	get better	40	sort
19	beginner	41	missing
20	gift	42	improve
21	keep out of ~	43	lately
22	perform	44	busk

19 회 단어

20회 중학영어듣기 모의고사

M2(17)_20_US
모두 **미국식 발음(US)**
으로 녹음

M2(17)_20_UK
20문제 중 5문제에 **영국식 발음**
(US+UK)을 포함하여 녹음

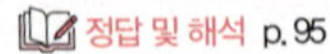 정답 및 해석 p. 95

1 다음을 듣고, Athens의 날씨로 가장 적절한 것을 고르시오.

①  ②  ③  ④  ⑤ 

2 대화를 듣고, 여자가 구입할 커튼으로 가장 적절한 것을 고르시오.

①  ②  ③  ④  ⑤ 

3 대화를 듣고, 여자의 심정으로 가장 적절한 것을 고르시오.

① relieved   ② shy   ③ bored
④ disappointed   ⑤ thankful

4 대화를 듣고, 남자가 학교 홍보영상 프로젝트에서 맡은 일로 가장 적절한 것을 고르시오.

① 촬영하기   ② 대본 쓰기   ③ 자막 쓰기
④ 배경음악 넣기   ⑤ 영상 업로드하기

5 대화를 듣고, 두 사람이 대화하는 장소로 가장 적절한 곳을 고르시오.

① 서점   ② 헬스장   ③ 볼링장   ④ 야구장   ⑤ 도서관

6 대화를 듣고, 남자의 마지막 말의 의도로 가장 적절한 것을 고르시오.

① 제안　　　② 조언　　　③ 요청　　　④ 거절　　　⑤ 칭찬

7 대화를 듣고, 두 사람이 생일 파티에 가지고 갈 것을 고르시오.

① 곰 인형　　　② 요리책　　　③ 생일 카드　　　④ 케이크　　　⑤ 목걸이

8 대화를 듣고, 남자가 대화 직후에 할 일로 가장 적절한 것을 고르시오.

① 영상 편집하기　　　　　　② 교실 청소하기
③ 선생님 사진 찍기　　　　　④ 영화 감상문 제출하기
⑤ 학교 웹사이트 방문하기

9 대화를 듣고, 두 사람이 모바일 앱에 대해 언급하지 <u>않은</u> 것을 고르시오.

① 이름　　　② 추천 문제　　　③ 동영상 자료　　　④ 평점　　　⑤ 가격

10 다음을 듣고, 남자가 하는 말의 내용으로 가장 적절한 것을 고르시오.

① 식순 안내　　　　② 친구 소개　　　　③ 결혼 축사
④ 경기 초대　　　　⑤ 팀 홍보

11 대화를 듣고, 가방에 대한 내용과 일치하지 <u>않는</u> 것을 고르시오.

① 할인 중이다.　　　　　　　② 주머니가 많이 있다.
③ 용량이 15리터다.　　　　　④ 구매 시 비가림막을 1달러에 살 수 있다.
⑤ 두 가지 색의 제품이 있다.

12번~20번 문제는 다음 페이지에 ➡

12 대화를 듣고, 여자가 전화를 건 목적으로 가장 적절한 것을 고르시오.

① 컴퓨터 모델을 추천받으려고
② 노트북을 빌리려고
③ 몇 시에 방문할지 물어보려고
④ 컴퓨터 수리점을 추천받으려고
⑤ 컴퓨터를 수리하는 데 도움을 요청하려고

13 대화를 듣고, 여자가 지불해야 할 금액으로 가장 적절한 것을 고르시오.

① $4　　② $7　　③ $11　　④ $15　　⑤ $18

14 대화를 듣고, 두 사람의 관계로 가장 적절한 것을 고르시오.

① 미용사 — 손님
② 의사 — 환자
③ 재단사 — 디자이너
④ 옷가게 주인 — 손님
⑤ 호텔 직원 — 투숙객

15 대화를 듣고, 남자가 여자에게 부탁한 일로 가장 적절한 것을 고르시오.

① 피아노 가르쳐주기
② 함께 콘서트에 가기
③ 학교에 포스터 게시하기
④ 콘서트 표 디자인하기
⑤ 연습실로 데리러 오기

16 대화를 듣고, 여자가 놀이공원에 가지 <u>않은</u> 이유로 가장 적절한 것을 고르시오.

① 피로가 쌓여서
② 비가 많이 와서
③ 입장료가 너무 비싸서
④ 화재로 교통 체증이 심해서
⑤ 셔틀버스 운행이 중단되어서

17 다음 그림의 상황에 가장 적절한 대화를 고르시오.

①   ②   ③   ④   ⑤

18 다음을 듣고, 여자가 자신에 대해 언급하지 <u>않은</u> 것을 고르시오.

① 이름   ② 출신   ③ 나이   ④ 전공   ⑤ 직업

[19~20]   대화를 듣고, 남자의 마지막 말에 이어질 여자의 말로 가장 적절한 것을 고르시오.

19 Woman: _______________________________

① Dinner is on me.   ② That is a nice belt.
③ I don't like shopping.   ④ I prefer tea to coffee.
⑤ You should call that store now.

20 Woman: _______________________________

① It's all about creativity.   ② It's 5 dollars for students.
③ He didn't win the contest.   ④ I am very tired right now.
⑤ You should go to bed early.

Dictation Test 20

M2(17)_20_D

Dictation(받아쓰기)은 본문을 받아쓰면서 영어듣기의 집중력을 향상시키고 다양한 표현을 정리하기 위한 영어듣기 학습법입니다. **녹음을 다시 듣고, 빈칸에 알맞은 단어를 써 보세요.**
※Dictation의 정답은 듣기 대본의 밑줄 친 부분을 확인하세요.

 정답 p. 95

맞은 개수 / 총167개

날씨파악-그림

1. 다음을 듣고, Athens의 날씨로 가장 적절한 것을 고르시오.

①  ② 
③  ④ 
⑤ 

01 W: Good morning. Here is the weather forecast for today. Beijing will have a __________ __________, while Tokyo will have __________ __________. Melbourne will have rain showers. __________ Athens will experience snow, it will be sunny in London.

그림정보파악

2. 대화를 듣고, 여자가 구입할 커튼으로 가장 적절한 것을 고르시오.

①  ② 
③  ④ 
⑤ 

02 W: Excuse me. I'm looking for a curtain for my children's room.
M: Oh, look over here. These styles are popular for children.
W: Oh, they all look so cute!
M: How about this one __________ __________ __________ on it?
W: Well, my children love dogs.
M: All right. There are two curtains __________ __________ __________. Which one do you prefer?
W: I like the one with the __________ __________. I'll take it.

---

3. 대화를 듣고, 여자의 심정으로 가장 적절한 것을 고르시오.
① relieved   ② shy
③ bored   ④ disappointed
⑤ thankful

03

M: Hi, Susan. What did you do yesterday?

W: I attended a dance competition.

M: How did it go?

W: Not great. I didn't ____________ __________ to the final round.

M: Oh, I'm sorry to hear that. What happened?

W: I __________ during my routine and __________ my rhythm.

M: You practiced so hard for this competition.

W: Yes, I did. I had expected to __________ __________.

4. 대화를 듣고, 남자가 학교 홍보영상 프로젝트에서 맡은 일로 가장 적절한 것을 고르시오.
① 촬영하기
② 대본 쓰기
③ 자막 쓰기
④ 배경음악 넣기
⑤ 영상 업로드하기

04

W: Jake, how's your school promotion video project going?

M: It's finished, Mom. Mr. Park will ________ the video on the school website today.

W: Great. Did your project group do all the ________ ________ ________ yourselves?

M: Yes, we did.

W: Wow. What was your role in the project?

M: I ________ ________ __________.

W: Oh, transcribing all the words people say in the video ________ ________ ________ hard work.

M: Yes, it was. But it was fun.

다음 페이지에 계속 ➡

5. 대화를 듣고, 두 사람이 대화하는 장소로
   가장 적절한 곳을 고르시오.
   ① 서점
   ② 헬스장
   ③ 볼링장
   ④ 야구장
   ⑤ 도서관

05

W: Wow, you got a strike! Good job!

M: Thanks. It's your turn now. Try to ________
   ________ ________ ________ at the end of the lane!

W: Okay, but I think this ball is too heavy for me.

M: Try using this ball ________.

W: Thank you. *(pause)* Did you see that? I ________
   ________ nine pins!

M: Good job!

6. 대화를 듣고, 남자의 마지막 말의 의도로
   가장 적절한 것을 고르시오.
   ① 제안   ② 조언
   ③ 요청   ④ 거절
   ⑤ 칭찬

06

M: Emily, what are you doing?

W: I'm ________ ________ this online form to
   participate in a recycling event.

M: A recycling event? What's that all about?

W: You wash used plastic bottles and return them,
   and then you ________ ________ ________ ________.

M: Wow. I want to participate, too. Does everyone get
   a prize?

W: No, they'll pick 100 people ________. But you
   should try it.

M: Would you ________ ________ ________ ________
   to the online event?

7. 대화를 듣고, 두 사람이 생일 파티에 가지고 갈 것을 고르시오.

① 곰 인형　　② 요리책
③ 생일 카드　　④ 케이크
⑤ 목걸이

07

M: Are you ________ ________ come to Yumi's birthday party?

W: Yes, I am.

M: I'm ________ ________ buying a teddy bear for her. What about you?

W: I don't buy presents. I usually make them.

M: Then shall we make a gift ________?

W: Let's see. Maybe we can make her a necklace.

M: A necklace will be ________!

8. 대화를 듣고, 남자가 대화 직후에 할 일로 가장 적절한 것을 고르시오.

① 영상 편집하기
② 교실 청소하기
③ 선생님 사진 찍기
④ 영화 감상문 제출하기
⑤ 학교 웹사이트 방문하기

08

W: We've finally finished ________ the videos for our school website.

M: Yes. Now we need to ________ them.

W: I can do that, but can you help me with something else?

M: Sure. What is it?

W: I need some photos of our teachers to ________ to the videos.

M: OK. What do you want me to do?

W: Can you ________ ________ ________ the teachers in their classrooms?

M: No problem. I'll go and do it right away.

다음 페이지에 계속 ➡

9. 대화를 듣고, 두 사람이 모바일 앱에 대해 언급하지 <u>않은</u> 것을 고르시오.

① 이름
② 추천 문제
③ 동영상 자료
④ 평점
⑤ 가격

09

W: Wow! Fred, how did you get a perfect score on our math quiz?

M: I got a lot of help by using Math Master.

W: Oh, isn't that ________ ________ __________?

M: Yes. It ____________ daily math problems for you to study.

W: Oh, really? Is it helpful?

M: Of course! It also provides lots of video content which is ________ ________ ________.

W: Wow! I think I should download it.

M: You really should! ________ ________ ________ about it is that it's free!

10. 다음을 듣고, 남자가 하는 말의 내용으로 가장 적절한 것을 고르시오.

① 식순 안내
② 친구 소개
③ 결혼 축사
④ 경기 초대
⑤ 팀 홍보

10

M: Hi, everyone. As the Best Man, I want to thank you for coming today. It was a beautiful wedding. I've never seen my friend Matthew so happy. ________ ________ we were rookie basketball players, he has helped me ________ ________ ________. I'm sure his kind, generous heart will make his bride very happy. Please join me in wishing the couple ________ ________ ________ ________, health, and joy.

11. 대화를 듣고, 가방에 대한 내용과 일치하지 <u>않는</u> 것을 고르시오.

① 할인 중이다.
② 주머니가 많이 있다.
③ 용량이 15리터다.
④ 구매 시 비가림막을 1달러에 살 수 있다.
⑤ 두 가지 색의 제품이 있다.

11

M: Hey, check out this new backpack. It's __________ __________.

W: Oh, that's a good price. And it has so many pockets and sections!

M: Yeah, it's __________ __________ for everything I need.

W: And it's spacious. It can hold up to 15 liters.

M: Plus, they're including a __________ __________ __________ with it.

W: That's awesome. It __________ __________ two colors, blue or gray.

M: I think I prefer the gray one.

12. 대화를 듣고, 여자가 전화를 건 목적으로 가장 적절한 것을 고르시오.

① 컴퓨터 모델을 추천받으려고
② 노트북을 빌리려고
③ 몇 시에 방문할지 물어보려고
④ 컴퓨터 수리점을 추천받으려고
⑤ 컴퓨터를 수리하는 데 도움을 요청하려고

12 *(Telephone rings.)*

M: Hello?

W: Hi, Mike. It's Jenny. Is this __________ __________ __________ to call?

M: Hi, Jenny. Not at all. What's going on?

W: I was hoping you could help me with my laptop.

M: What's wrong with it?

W: I'm not sure. It __________ __________. And all these errors come up.

M: I see. Well, sure, I can __________ __________ __________ at it.

다음 페이지에 계속 ➡

13. 대화를 듣고, 여자가 지불해야 할 금액으로 가장 적절한 것을 고르시오.

① $4 ② $7
③ $11 ④ $15
⑤ $18

13

M: Hi, are you ___________ ___________ ___________?

W: Yes, I want a large popcorn and a hotdog, please.

M: It's 11 dollars. Anything else?

W: Um… I'd like two Diet Cokes, please.

M: Okay. ___________ ___________ ___________ ___________

15 dollars.

W: Oh, I got this free popcorn coupon for my

birthday. Can I use it now?

M: Of course. The popcorn is 8 dollars so ___________

___________ ___________ from your total.

W: All right. Here's my credit card.

14. 대화를 듣고, 두 사람의 관계로 가장 적절한 것을 고르시오.

① 미용사 — 손님
② 의사 — 환자
③ 재단사 — 디자이너
④ 옷가게 주인 — 손님
⑤ 호텔 직원 — 투숙객

14

W: Hello, I ___________ ___________ ___________ yesterday.

M: Yes, come in. What can I do for you?

W: I would like to change my hair color.

M: ___________ ___________ ___________ and we'll take a look.

W: Will I look good in black?

M: Yes, you are very fair. Black would ___________

___________ ___________ you.

W: My hair has grown so long. I also want to have it

cut.

M: Okay. What do you have in mind?

W: I would like it to be shorter.

M: Hmm… a shoulder-length cut would be better for

the shape of your face.

15. 대화를 듣고, 남자가 여자에게 부탁한 일로 가장 적절한 것을 고르시오.
① 피아노 가르쳐주기
② 함께 콘서트에 가기
③ 학교에 포스터 게시하기
④ 콘서트 표 디자인하기
⑤ 연습실로 데리러 오기

15 (Cellphone rings.)

M: Hello.

W: Hi, Junho. It's Dabin. How's your ___________ _________ for the school concert?

M: Not too bad. I was just practicing the piano.

W: Have you finished _________ _________ _________?

M: Yes. It was really hard, and took a lot of time.

W: I see. Is there anything I can do to help?

M: Can you _________ _________ the posters at school? Then I can practice some more.

W: Sure. I'll come to _________ _________ _________ later.

16. 대화를 듣고, 여자가 놀이공원에 가지 않은 이유로 가장 적절한 것을 고르시오.
① 피로가 쌓여서
② 비가 많이 와서
③ 입장료가 너무 비싸서
④ 화재로 교통 체증이 심해서
⑤ 셔틀버스 운행이 중단되어서

16 M: Leona, how was the amusement park?

W: Oh, I didn't go.

M: Were you ___________ ___________ ___________ ___________?

W: No. I was going to take the shuttle bus anyway.

M: Then, why didn't you go? It wasn't raining, was it?

W: No. There was a big fire near the park. I heard about it on the morning news.

M: What? I didn't know that. So, ___________ _________ _________ _________.

W: Really bad. I didn't want to arrive late. So, I just stayed home. _________ _________ _________.

다음 페이지에 계속 ➡

17. 다음 그림의 상황에 가장 적절한 대화를 고르시오.

① ②
③ ④
⑤

17
① W: I don't think he should eat here.

M: You're right. Everyone ________ ________ his food.

② W: Do you have this shirt ________ ________ ________ ________?

M: Sure. I'll go get it for you.

③ W: Dinner's ready.

M: Wow. Everything looks so delicious.

④ W: It's ________ ________ ________.

M: Yes. I think we should get inside.

⑤ W: Are you ready to order?

M: Not yet. Do you have any ________________?

18. 다음을 듣고, 여자가 자신에 대해 언급하지 않은 것을 고르시오.

① 이름 ② 출신
③ 나이 ④ 전공
⑤ 직업

18
W: Hello, everyone. Let me introduce myself to you. My name is Chelsea Collins. I'm from California, USA. I've been ________ ________ ________ since childhood. So, I studied nursing science at university. I'm a nurse now. I ________ ________ a big university hospital, and help many sick people there. Today, I'm going to tell you about ________ ________ ________ in the life of a nurse.

19. 대화를 듣고, 남자의 마지막 말에 이어질
여자의 말로 가장 적절한 것을 고르시오.

Woman: ___________________

① Dinner is on me.
② That is a nice belt.
③ I don't like shopping.
④ I prefer tea to coffee.
⑤ You should call that store now.

19

M: Shannon, I can't find my _________.

W: What? Did you check _________ _________?

M: Yes, but it's not there.

W: You used it when we were at the coffee house.

M: No, you paid for the coffee.

W: Right. Where did you go before we met?

M: Umm… I went to a clothing store and _________
_________ _________.

W: You should call that store now.

20. 대화를 듣고, 남자의 마지막 말에 이어질
여자의 말로 가장 적절한 것을 고르시오.

Woman: ___________________

① It's all about creativity.
② It's 5 dollars for students.
③ He didn't win the contest.
④ I am very tired right now.
⑤ You should go to bed early.

20

M: Hi, Dahyun. What are you looking at?

W: Hey, Minwoo. I'm _________ _________ the website
for the Teen Invention Contest.

M: Teen Invention Contest? Tell me more about it.

W: At the contest, you need to _________ _____________
_________.

M: Something new? Can I make anything?

W: No, you will be given materials. You can use only
_________ _________ _________.

M: Oh, then it will not be easy.

W: It's all about creativity.

Words & Expressions Review 20

● 다음 단어를 암기하세요.

문제	번호	단어	뜻
1	1	while	~이긴 하지만, 반면에
	2	rain shower	소나기
2	3	prefer	~을 더 좋아하다
	4	checkered	체크무늬의
3	5	stumble	발을 헛디디다
	6	expect	기대하다
4	7	promotion	홍보[판촉] (활동)
	8	subtitle	자막
	9	transcribe	(연설 등을) 문자화하다, 필기하다
5	10	focus on ~	~에 집중하다
	11	knock down	쓰러뜨리다
6	12	fill in a form	서식을 작성하다
	13	participate in	~에 참여하다
	14	randomly	무작위로
7	15	plan to + 동사	~할 계획이다
	16	think of -ing	~하는 것을 생각하다
8	17	edit	편집하다, 수정하다
	18	take a photo of ~	~의 사진을 찍다, ~을 촬영하다
9	19	recommend	추천하다
	20	helpful	도움이 되는
10	21	generous	넉넉한, 관대한
	22	bride	신부

문제	번호	단어	뜻
11	23	section	구획, 부분, 부문
	24	spacious	널찍한
12	25	up to	~까지
	26	Not at all.	전혀.
13	27	The total comes to ~	총액은 ~이다
	28	deduct	빼다, 제하다
14	29	make a reservation	예약하다
	30	look good on ~	~와 잘 어울리다
15	31	shape	모양, 형태
	32	preparation	준비
	33	put up	붙이다, 게시하다
16	34	traffic	교통(량)
17	35	heavily	많이, 심하게
18	36	medicine	의학
	37	childhood	어린 시절
	38	typical	전형적인, 보통의
19	39	pay for ~	~의 값을 지불하다
	40	Dinner is on me.	저녁은 내가 살게.
20	41	check out	~을 확인하다
	42	invention	발명
	43	material	(물건의) 재료
	44	It's all about ~	~이 핵심이다, 가장 중요하다

●왼쪽 단어장의 뜻이 보이지 않게 반으로 접고, 학습한 단어의 뜻을 아래 빈칸에 적어주세요.

1	fill in a form	23	expect
2	bride	24	rain shower
3	up to	25	section
4	traffic	26	spacious
5	participate in	27	Not at all.
6	pay for ~	28	transcribe
7	Dinner is on me.	29	stumble
8	recommend	30	helpful
9	childhood	31	put up
10	The total comes to ~	32	plan to + 동사
11	typical	33	focus on ~
12	edit	34	randomly
13	think of -ing	35	deduct
14	while	36	promotion
15	subtitle	37	take a photo of ~
16	heavily	38	It's all about ~
17	make a reservation	39	invention
18	prefer	40	generous
19	medicine	41	shape
20	material	42	preparation
21	knock down	43	check out
22	checkered	44	look good on ~

20
회
단
어

21회 중학영어듣기 모의고사

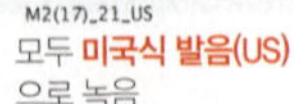

M2(17)_21_US
모두 **미국식 발음(US)** 으로 녹음

M2(17)_21_UK
20문제 중 5문제에 **영국식 발음 (US+UK)**을 포함하여 녹음

정답 및 해석 p. 100

1 다음을 듣고, 목요일의 날씨로 적절한 것을 고르시오.

① 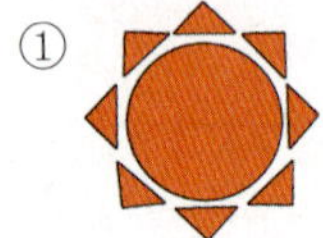 ②  ③  ④  ⑤ 

2 대화를 듣고, 여자가 만든 필통으로 가장 적절한 것을 고르시오.

① ② ③ ④ ⑤

3 대화를 듣고, 남자의 심정으로 가장 적절한 것을 고르시오.

① sad　　② jealous　　③ surprised　　④ excited　　⑤ nervous

4 대화를 듣고, 여자가 지난 주말에 한 일로 가장 적절한 것을 고르시오.

① 빨래하기　　② 가방 구매하기　　③ 봉사활동 하기
④ 옷장 정리하기　　⑤ 목재 가구 만들기

5 대화를 듣고, 두 사람이 대화하는 장소로 가장 적절한 곳을 고르시오.

① 강당　　② 꽃집　　③ 마당　　④ 식물원　　⑤ 결혼식장

6 대화를 듣고, 여자의 마지막 말의 의도로 가장 적절한 것을 고르시오.

① 축하 ② 용서 ③ 허락 ④ 제안 ⑤ 거절

7 대화를 듣고, 여자가 주문한 음식을 고르시오.

① chicken stew ② beef curry ③ clam chowder
④ fish fillet ⑤ beef steak

8 대화를 듣고, 두 사람이 대화 직후에 할 일로 가장 적절한 것을 고르시오.

① 매점 가기 ② 교실 청소하기 ③ 방학 숙제 하기
④ 사물함 정리하기 ⑤ 학교 도서관에 가기

9 대화를 듣고, 두 사람이 라디오 프로그램에 대해 언급하지 <u>않은</u> 것을 고르시오.

① 이름 ② 시간 ③ 주파수 ④ 진행자 ⑤ 재방송

10 다음을 듣고, 남자가 하는 말의 내용으로 가장 적절한 것을 고르시오.

① 교통규칙 준수 ② 산불 대피 요령 ③ 캠핑장 이용수칙
④ 반려동물 산책 예절 ⑤ 층간소음 방지 방법

11번~20번 문제는 다음 페이지에 ➡

11 대화를 듣고, Nature Walk 행사에 대한 내용과 일치하지 <u>않는</u> 것을 고르시오.

① 가이드가 다양한 동식물에 대해 알려준다.　② 쌍안경을 대여해준다.
③ 이번 주 일요일 오후 2시에 진행된다.　④ 온라인으로 신청해야 한다.
⑤ 숲 지도가 제공된다.

12 대화를 듣고, 남자가 전화를 건 목적으로 가장 적절한 것을 고르시오.

① 진료 시간을 문의하기 위해서　　② 예약 날짜를 변경하기 위해서
③ 주차 등록을 요청하기 위해서　　④ 병원의 위치를 물어보기 위해서
⑤ 약 복용 방법을 확인하기 위해서

13 대화를 듣고, 남자가 받은 거스름돈으로 가장 적절한 것을 고르시오.

① $2　　　② $3　　　③ $4　　　④ $5　　　⑤ $6

14 대화를 듣고, 두 사람의 관계로 가장 적절한 것을 고르시오.

① 중고물품 판매자 – 구매자　　② 매표소 직원 – 관람객
③ 우체국 직원 – 손님　　　　④ 은행원 – 고객
⑤ 승무원 – 승객

15 대화를 듣고, 여자가 남자에게 부탁한 일로 가장 적절한 것을 고르시오.

① 리뷰 확인하기　　② 식당 찾아보기　　③ 회원 가입하기
④ 영화표 예매하기　　⑤ 저녁식사 준비하기

16 대화를 듣고, 여자가 해산물을 먹지 <u>않는</u> 이유를 고르시오.

① 이탈리아 음식을 먹고 싶어서　　② 해산물 요리가 비싸서
③ 해산물을 좋아하지 않아서　　④ 해산물에 알레르기가 있어서
⑤ 배가 고프지 않아서

17 대화를 듣고, 그림의 상황에 가장 적절한 대화를 고르시오.

①   ②   ③   ④   ⑤

18 다음을 듣고, 여자가 연극에 대해 언급하지 않은 것을 고르시오.

① 제목   ② 내용   ③ 작가   ④ 공연 장소   ⑤ 공연 기간

[19~20] 대화를 듣고, 여자의 마지막 말에 이어질 남자의 말로 가장 적절한 것을 고르시오.

19 Man: _______________________________

① Where did you buy your bag?
② Okay. Wait here while I get your bag.
③ No, I didn't make a call to my mom.
④ Yes, Mrs. Hudson is our school nurse.
⑤ Can you tell me where the nearest hospital is?

20 Man: _______________________________

① Don't worry. She'll be fine.   ② Please say hello to her for me.
③ Can you come to my birthday party?   ④ I didn't buy her a birthday present.
⑤ She played with me when she was young.

Dictation Test 21

M2(17)_21_D

Dictation(받아쓰기)은 본문을 받아쓰면서 영어듣기의 집중력을 향상시키고 다양한 표현을 정리하기 위한 영어듣기 학습법입니다. **녹음을 다시 듣고, 빈칸에 알맞은 단어를 써 보세요.**
※Dictation의 정답은 듣기 대본의 밑줄 친 부분을 확인하세요.

📖 정답 p. 100

맞은 개수 / 총160개

 날씨파악–그림

1. 다음을 듣고, 목요일의 날씨로 적절한 것을 고르시오.

01 M: Good morning. Today is Monday, March 4, and here is the weather forecast for this week. It will be sunny today and tomorrow, Tuesday. The weather will ___________ ___________ ___________ from Wednesday until Friday. Finally, there will be ___________ ___________ on Saturday and Sunday.

그림정보파악

2. 대화를 듣고, 여자가 만든 필통으로 가장 적절한 것을 고르시오.

02 M: Allison, what's this? Is it a pencil case?

W: Yes, I made it at school. I took ___________ lessons.

M: Wow, nice work! I like the ___________ ___________.

W: Thanks. I picked the cloth myself.

M: There's even a tag ___________ ___________ ___________ on it! Did you make the tag, too?

W: Yeah, I wanted to mark it as mine.

M: I see. You are really good with your hands.

---

3. 대화를 듣고, 남자의 심정으로 가장 적절한 것을 고르시오.

① sad   ② jealous
③ surprised   ④ excited
⑤ nervous

03
M: Hey, my brother and I are going to the __________ __________.

W: Wow, that's great. Have you ever been to a soccer match before?

M: No. ________, this is my first time.

W: I'm sure you will like it.

M: Yes, I'm really ________ ________ to it.

W: Oh, I envy you. Let's go together ________ ________.

2025 영어듣기능력평가 1회 4번 변형

한일파악 🇺🇸🇬🇧

4. 대화를 듣고, 여자가 지난 주말에 한 일로 가장 적절한 것을 고르시오.

① 빨래하기
② 가방 구매하기
③ 봉사활동 하기
④ 옷장 정리하기
⑤ 목재 가구 만들기

04
M: Chloe, what are you carrying in that big bag?

W: Some old clothes. I'm taking them to the __________ __________.

M: That's nice of you. What made you decide to do that?

W: Last weekend, I cleaned out my closet and found so many clothes I __________ __________ __________.

M: Good idea! I should do that, too.

W: Yeah, it feels good to give clothes to people __________ __________ them.

다음 페이지에 계속 ➡

5. 대화를 듣고, 두 사람이 대화하는 장소로 가장 적절한 곳을 고르시오.

① 강당　　② 꽃집
③ 마당　　④ 식물원
⑤ 결혼식장

05
W: Hello. How can I help you?

M: I'd like to buy some flowers for my daughter's __________ __________.

W: Okay. Let me see. How about this ________ ________?

M: I don't think my daughter likes roses. What else do you have?

W: This tulip bouquet is also popular for ________ ________ ________ __________.

M: I like that bouquet. How much is it?

W: It's 50 dollars.

6. 대화를 듣고, 여자의 마지막 말의 의도로 가장 적절한 것을 고르시오.

① 축하　　② 용서
③ 허락　　④ 제안
⑤ 거절

06
W: What are you doing, Jake?

M: Hi, Luna. I'm ________ ________ ________ ________ for a while.

W: Are you going on a family trip? You did that last year for summer vacation.

M: No. I'm going to a two-week training program for the school cycling team.

W: Oh, you ________ ________ ________! I know how much you wanted to be a member.

M: I know! I still can't believe I'm ________ ________ ________.

W: It's great news. I'm so happy for you.

7. 대화를 듣고, 여자가 주문한 음식을 고르시오.

① chicken stew
② beef curry
③ clam chowder
④ fish fillet
⑤ beef steak

07

M: Good evening. What can I get you?

W: What are ________ ________ ________ tonight?

M: Well, we have chicken stew and beef curry as our specials.

W: I've had them before. Do you have ________ ____________?

M: Yes, we do. We also have clam chowder or fish fillet, if you like.

W: On second thought, can you just get me ________ ________ ________ with plenty of onions, please?

M: How do you want your steak cooked?

W: Medium will be fine, thanks.

2023 영어듣기능력평가 2회 8번 변형

8. 대화를 듣고, 두 사람이 대화 직후에 할 일로 가장 적절한 것을 고르시오.

① 매점 가기
② 교실 청소하기
③ 방학 숙제 하기
④ 사물함 정리하기
⑤ 학교 도서관에 가기

08

W: What are you doing today? It's our last day before our summer vacation.

M: Yeah, we're finally ____________ ____________ __________ from school.

W: Do you want to __________ __________ __________ at the cafeteria?

M: No, I actually need to go to the school library.

W: Do you have some books __________ __________?

M: Yes, the books I borrowed are __________ __________. Want to come along?

W: Sure, let's head there now.

21
회
딕
테
이
션

다음 페이지에 계속 ➡

9. 대화를 듣고, 두 사람이 라디오 프로그램에 대해 언급하지 <u>않은</u> 것을 고르시오.
① 이름　　② 시간
③ 주파수　④ 진행자
⑤ 재방송

09

W: Woosung, are the ＿＿＿＿＿＿ for your trip to China going well?

M: Yes. I am listening to the radio to practice speaking Chinese these days.

W: What's the name of the program?

M: *Chinese Exploration*! ＿＿＿＿ ＿＿＿＿ ＿＿＿＿ at 6 a.m. every morning.

W: I'd like to listen to it. Where can I hear the program?

M: On 95 FM.

W: Cool! But it's on too early. I'm not a ＿＿＿＿ ＿＿＿＿.

M: Don't worry! It's being rerun twice every afternoon.

W: That's great. I'll ＿＿＿＿＿＿ check it out!

10. 다음을 듣고, 남자가 하는 말의 내용으로 가장 적절한 것을 고르시오.
① 교통규칙 준수
② 산불 대피 요령
③ 캠핑장 이용수칙
④ 반려동물 산책 예절
⑤ 층간소음 방지 방법

10

M: Welcome to Little Forest Campsite! For everyone's ＿＿＿＿＿＿, please remember these rules when using the campsite. First, do not make a fire ＿＿＿＿ on the ground without fire tools. Between 11 p.m. and 7 a.m., ＿＿＿＿ the noise ＿＿＿＿ so everyone can have a peaceful night. Finally, no pets ＿＿＿＿ ＿＿＿＿ in the campsite. Thank you.

11. 대화를 듣고, Nature Walk 행사에 대한 내용과 일치하지 <u>않는</u> 것을 고르시오.

① 가이드가 다양한 동식물에 대해 알려준다.
② 쌍안경을 대여해준다.
③ 이번 주 일요일 오후 2시에 진행된다.
④ 온라인으로 신청해야 한다.
⑤ 숲 지도가 제공된다.

11

M: Esther, look! There's going to be a Nature Walk at Central Forest this weekend.

W: Oh, it's ________ ________ ________ where you can learn about different plants and animals.

M: Doesn't it sound fun?

W: Yeah, they will ________ ________ binoculars so we can ________ the wildlife up close.

M: Great! It's this Saturday at 2 p.m.

W: Good. We'll need to ________ ________ online.

M: Okay. Is there anything else we need to know?

W: Yes, they will ________ ________ ________ a map of the forest.

12. 대화를 듣고, 남자가 전화를 건 목적으로 가장 적절한 것을 고르시오.

① 진료 시간을 문의하기 위해서
② 예약 날짜를 변경하기 위해서
③ 주차 등록을 요청하기 위해서
④ 병원의 위치를 물어보기 위해서
⑤ 약 복용 방법을 확인하기 위해서

12

(Telephone rings.)

W: Hello. Dr. Kim's Dental Clinic.

M: Hi. I ________ ________ ________ on May 7th, but I'd like to change it.

W: May I have your name?

M: It's Kevin Park.

W: Please hold. *(Pause)* Your appointment is at 2 p.m. Would you like to come ________ ________ ________ ________?

M: No, 2 p.m. is good, but can I come on the 8th ________ ________ the 7th?

W: Sure. I'll change your appointment to the next day.

M: Thank you.

다음 페이지에 계속 ➡

13. 대화를 듣고, 남자가 받은 거스름돈으로 가장 적절한 것을 고르시오.

① $2　　　　② $3
③ $4　　　　④ $5
⑤ $6

13

W: Good morning. How may I help you today?

M: The sandwiches look great. How much are they?

W: They are usually $7 each, but we are having a sale today. Every sandwich is $6 _________ _________.

M: That's great. I'd like two tuna sandwiches and one bacon sandwich please.

W: Is it for _________ _________ _________ _________?

M: To go please.

W: Okay. It's $18 in total.

M: Here's a 20 dollar _________.

W: Here's your _________.

14. 대화를 듣고, 두 사람의 관계로 가장 적절한 것을 고르시오.

① 중고물품 판매자 – 구매자
② 매표소 직원 – 관람객
③ 우체국 직원 – 손님
④ 은행원 – 고객
⑤ 승무원 – 승객

14

W: Hi. I want to send this _________ to Singapore.

M: Okay. Do you want to send it by air or ship?

W: The ship _________ _________ _________, doesn't it?

M: Yes, much longer.

W: Then, please send it by air.

M: Okay. If you pay the _________ on the post office app, you'll get a 10% discount.

W: That's great! I'll pay on my phone now.

M: _________ _________ _________.

부탁(요청)한일파악

15. 대화를 듣고, 여자가 남자에게 부탁한 일로 가장 적절한 것을 고르시오.
① 리뷰 확인하기
② 식당 찾아보기
③ 회원 가입하기
④ 영화표 예매하기
⑤ 저녁식사 준비하기

15
M: Hi, Betty. Do you want to watch a movie with me?

W: Of course. I'm __________ on Friday.

M: Me, too. Let's book tickets now. [Pause] How about this action movie?

W: I'd like to see it. I have a membership at the theater, so I'll __________ __________ __________.

M: Okay. The movie starts at 8 p.m. How about having dinner before watching the movie?

W: That's a good idea. Can you __________ __________ __________ around the theater?

M: Sure.

이유파악

16. 대화를 듣고, 여자가 해산물을 먹지 <u>않는</u> 이유를 고르시오.
① 이탈리아 음식을 먹고 싶어서
② 해산물 요리가 비싸서
③ 해산물을 좋아하지 않아서
④ 해산물에 알레르기가 있어서
⑤ 배가 고프지 않아서

16
M: __________ __________ that Italian restaurant in town!

W: I want to, but I can't.

M: Why not? I thought you liked Italian food.

W: I heard the food there is expensive. I don't have __________ __________ __________ __________.

M: How about that seafood restaurant nearby? I heard their crab dish is delicious.

W: Sorry, I don't eat crabs.

M: Oh, I forgot. You __________ __________ __________ seafood.

W: Let's just eat at my place. I'm not very hungry now anyway.

다음 페이지에 계속 ➡

17. 대화를 듣고, 그림의 상황에 가장 적절한 대화를 고르시오.

① ② ③ ④ ⑤

17

① M: What do you think of my tie?

W: Pink _________ you very well.

② M: What would you _________ _________ have?

W: One burger and a Coke, please.

③ M: Would you like to watch a movie?

W: Yes, that would be great!

④ M: We have an _________ _________ to Brazil.

W: Thank you, I'll take that then.

⑤ M: Would you like me to _________ - _________ these?

W: No, thank you.

18. 다음을 듣고, 여자가 연극에 대해 언급하지 **않은** 것을 고르시오.

① 제목   ② 내용
③ 작가   ④ 공연 장소
⑤ 공연 기간

18

W: Hello, everyone. Today, I'd like to tell you about a play. The title is *A Man Next Door*. The story is about a small neighborhood and the people _________ _________ _________ _________ who live there. It is written by Nora Jung, and the main role will be _________ by Dan Nolan. It will be _________ at Blue Art Center. You can buy tickets both online and offline. Students _________ _________ _________ on their tickets.

19. 대화를 듣고, 여자의 마지막 말에 이어질 남자의 말로 가장 적절한 것을 고르시오.

Man: _________________

① Where did you buy your bag?
② Okay. Wait here while I get your bag.
③ No, I didn't make a call to my mom.
④ Yes, Mrs. Hudson is our school nurse.
⑤ Can you tell me where the nearest hospital is?

19

M: Cathy, you don't look so good. Are you feeling alright?

W: I feel sick. I think I _________ _______ _________.

M: Oh, no! Do you want to go see the school nurse?

W: No, I think I should go to the hospital.

M: Okay. Is there anything that I can _________ _________ _________?

W: Well, can you _________ _________ _________ _________ for me, please? I have to call my mom.

M: Okay. Wait here while I get your bag.

20. 대화를 듣고, 여자의 마지막 말에 이어질 남자의 말로 가장 적절한 것을 고르시오.

Man: _________________

① Don't worry. She'll be fine.
② Please say hello to her for me.
③ Can you come to my birthday party?
④ I didn't buy her a birthday present.
⑤ She played with me when she was young.

20

W: Matt, you're not _________ _________. Why?

M: I'm afraid I can't go to Mary's birthday party. My grandfather is sick. I have to stay home with him.

W: Really? That's _________ _________. Does he have a serious illness?

M: No, he's just not _________ _________ today.

W: I see. Then, I guess I'll have to _________ _________.

M: Please say hello to her for me.

Words & Expressions Review 21

● 다음 단어를 암기하세요.

문제	번호	단어	뜻
1	1	partly	부분적으로
	2	rain shower	소나기
2	3	sewing	바느질, 재봉
	4	striped pattern	줄무늬
3	5	actually	사실, 실제로
	6	look forward to ~	~을 기대하다
4	7	carry	들고 가다, 나르다
	8	donation	기부, 기증
	9	decide	결심하다, 결정하다
5	10	graduation ceremony	졸업식
6	11	pack	(짐을) 싸다, 꾸리다
	12	go away	집을 떠나다, 어디를 가다
	13	make the team	팀에 들어가다
7	14	dish	요리, 접시
	15	on second thought	다시 생각해보니
	16	plenty of ~	충분한, 많은
	17	grab a snack	간단히 뭐 좀 먹다, 간식을 먹다
8	18	due	반납일이 ~인
	19	head	~로 향하다
9	20	broadcast	방송하다
	21	rerun	재방송하다
10	22	convenience	편의, 편리

문제	번호	단어	뜻
10	23	keep ~ down	~을 줄이다, 낮추다
11	24	binoculars	쌍안경
	25	up close	바로 가까이에(서)
12	26	appointment	(진찰 등의) 예약
	27	instead of	~ 대신에
13	28	noon	낮 12시, 정오
	29	change	거스름돈
14	30	package	소포
	31	postage	우편 요금
	32	take one's time	천천히 하다, 여유를 가지다
15	33	free	한가한, 다른 계획[약속]이 없는
	34	book	예매하다, 예약하다
16	35	nearby	근처에, 가까이에
	36	be allergic to ~	~에 알레르기가 있다
	37	suit	어울리다
17	38	flight	비행기, 항공편
	39	gift-wrap	선물용으로 포장하다
18	40	past	과거
	41	role	(배우의) 역할, 배역
19	42	go get	가서 가져오다
	43	dress up	(옷을) 차려 입다
20	44	serious	심각한, 진지한

● 왼쪽 단어장의 뜻이 보이지 않게 반으로 접고, 학습한 단어의 뜻을 아래 빈칸에 적어주세요.

1	pack		23	free
2	postage		24	on second thought
3	take one's time		25	flight
4	binoculars		26	nearby
5	be allergic to ~		27	package
6	dress up		28	grab a snack
7	carry		29	change
8	gift-wrap		30	look forward to ~
9	go get		31	decide
10	book		32	graduation ceremony
11	broadcast		33	dish
12	donation		34	go away
13	make the team		35	actually
14	appointment		36	suit
15	head		37	partly
16	noon		38	plenty of ~
17	serious		39	due
18	convenience		40	up close
19	striped pattern		41	rain shower
20	keep ~ down		42	past
21	instead of		43	sewing
22	role		44	rerun

22회 중학영어듣기 모의고사

M2(17)_22_US
모두 **미국식 발음(US)**
으로 녹음

M2(17)_22_UK
20문제 중 5문제에 **영국식 발음
(US+UK)**을 포함하여 녹음

정답 및 해석 p. 105

1 다음을 듣고, 수요일의 날씨로 가장 적절한 것을 고르시오.

①  ②  ③  ④  ⑤ 

2 대화를 듣고, 여자가 구입할 장갑으로 가장 적절한 것을 고르시오.

① 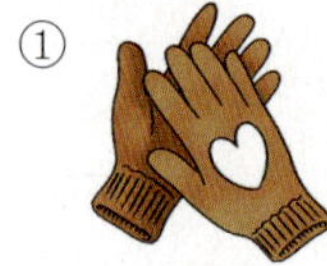 ②  ③ 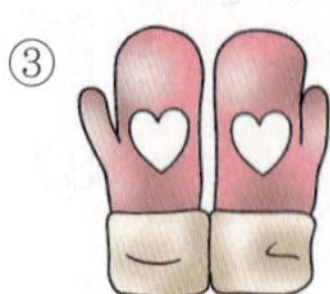 ④ 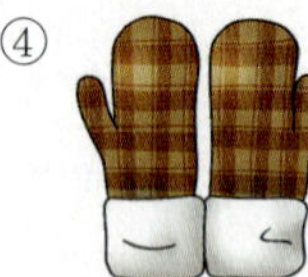 ⑤ 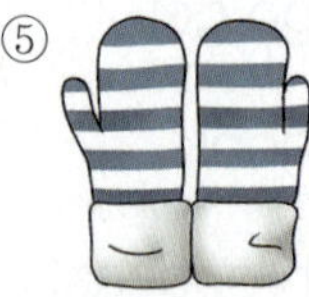

3 대화를 듣고, 남자의 심정으로 가장 적절한 것을 고르시오.

① sad   ② proud   ③ nervous   ④ relieved   ⑤ cheerful

4 대화를 듣고, 여자가 어제 한 일로 가장 적절한 것을 고르시오.

① 책 구입하기   ② 옷장 정리하기   ③ 자전거 수리하기
④ 물건 가격표 붙이기   ⑤ 벼룩시장 방문하기

5 대화를 듣고, 두 사람이 대화하는 장소로 가장 적절한 곳을 고르시오.

① 은행　　② 식당　　③ 서점　　④ 미술관　　⑤ 옷가게

6 대화를 듣고, 여자의 마지막 말의 의도로 가장 적절한 것을 고르시오.

① 불평　　② 사과　　③ 허락　　④ 감사　　⑤ 거절

7 대화를 듣고, 남자가 살 물건으로 가장 적절한 것을 고르시오.

① 칼　　② 재킷　　③ 의자　　④ 손전등　　⑤ 식료품

8 대화를 듣고, 남자가 대화 직후에 할 일로 가장 적절한 것을 고르시오.

① 할인쿠폰 찾아보기　　② 친구에게 전화하기
③ 중고상품 판매하기　　④ 인터넷에서 제품 검색하기
⑤ 다른 색상의 신발 신어보기

9 대화를 듣고, 두 사람이 대회에 대해 언급하지 <u>않은</u> 것을 고르시오.

① 명칭　　② 주최 기관　　③ 개최 기간
④ 지원 자격　　⑤ 우승 상품

10 다음을 듣고, 여자가 하는 말의 내용으로 가장 적절한 것을 고르시오.

① 신규 교사 소개　　② 학생회장 선거 공지　　③ 화재 시 대피 요령
④ 교내 건의함 위치 안내　　⑤ 급식실 이용 규칙 안내

11번~20번 문제는 다음 페이지에 ➡

11 대화를 듣고, 뮤지컬에 관한 정보로 일치하지 <u>않는</u> 것을 고르시오.

① 제목이 '라이온 킹'이다.　　　　② Lakewood 극장에서 공연한다.
③ 이번 주 일요일 저녁 7시 공연이다.　④ 상연 시간은 3시간이다.
⑤ 좌석은 앞에서 두 번째 줄에 있다.

12 대화를 듣고, 남자가 전화를 건 목적으로 가장 적절한 것을 고르시오.

① 병원 예약을 미루기 위해서　　　　② 결석 사유를 물어보기 위해서
③ 아들의 입원을 알리기 위해서　　　④ 학생의 안부를 확인하기 위해서
⑤ 자녀의 조퇴를 요청하기 위해서

13 대화를 듣고, 남자가 받은 거스름돈으로 가장 적절한 것을 고르시오.

① $1　　　　② $2　　　　③ $3　　　　④ $4　　　　⑤ $5

14 대화를 듣고, 두 사람의 관계로 가장 적절한 것을 고르시오.

① 호텔 직원 ― 손님　　　　② 관광 가이드 ― 관광객
③ 여행사 직원 ― 고객　　　④ 관광 가이드 ― 버스 기사
⑤ 택시 기사 ― 손님

15 대화를 듣고, 남자가 여자에게 제안한 것으로 가장 적절한 것을 고르시오.

① 음식 만들기　　　② 봉사활동 하기　　　③ 학원 등록하기
④ 집 안 청소하기　　⑤ 교복 수선하기

16 대화를 듣고, Derek이 토요일에 테니스 레슨을 받지 <u>못하는</u> 이유를 고르시오.

① 보충 수업이 있어서　　　　　② 식료품점에서 쇼핑을 해야 해서
③ 형과 함께 테니스를 쳐야 해서　④ 공부를 해야 해서
⑤ 형의 가게에서 일을 도와야 해서

 다음 그림의 상황에 가장 적절한 대화를 고르시오.

①   ②   ③   ④   ⑤

18 다음을 듣고, 여자가 게임에 대해 언급하지 <u>않은</u> 것을 고르시오.

① 제목   ② 장르   ③ 내용   ④ 발매일   ⑤ 가격

[19~20] 대화를 듣고, 남자의 마지막 말에 이어질 여자의 말로 가장 적절한 것을 고르시오.

19 Woman: _______________________________________

① It will cost us 30 dollars.
② I think the white one is better.
③ Let's order a Christmas cake.
④ We should wrap all the presents.
⑤ I want to buy a black coat for myself.

20 Woman: _______________________________________

① I'm not interested in clubs.
② Think it over before quitting.
③ I hope you'll get better soon.
④ There are too many meetings.
⑤ Why don't you take math lessons?

Dictation Test 22

M2(17)_22_D

Dictation(받아쓰기)은 본문을 받아쓰면서 영어듣기의 집중력을 향상시키고 다양한 표현을 정리하기 위한 영어듣기 학습법입니다. **녹음을 다시 듣고, 빈칸에 알맞은 단어를 써 보세요.**
※Dictation의 정답은 듣기 대본의 밑줄 친 부분을 확인하세요.

📖 정답 p. 105

맞은 개수 / 총174개

---

1. 다음을 듣고, 수요일의 날씨로 가장 적절한 것을 고르시오.

①  ② 

③  ④ 

⑤ 

01 W: Good evening! This is Peggy with your three-day weather report. Monday will be mainly _________ and hot, but it will be _________ in the evening. On Tuesday, the temperature will go down and _________ _________ are expected. On Wednesday, there is a strong chance of _________. So, don't forget to _________ _________ _________ with you on Wednesday. Thank you.

---

2. 대화를 듣고, 여자가 구입할 장갑으로 가장 적절한 것을 고르시오.

①  ② 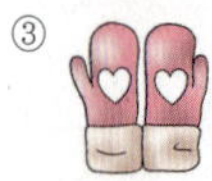

③  ④ 

⑤ 

02 M: May I help you?

W: Hi, I'm looking for gloves to wear for the winter.

M: We have _________ _________ _________.

W: I like mittens better.

M: Okay. How about these _________ _________?

W: I don't like checkered designs.

M: Then, what about these mittens with hearts?

W: They look pretty. I'll buy _________ _________ _________.

심정추론

3. 대화를 듣고, 남자의 심정으로 가장 적절한 것을 고르시오.

① sad
② proud
③ nervous
④ relieved
⑤ cheerful

03
W: When is your student concert at the community center?

M: It was yesterday.

W: Oh, no! I missed it. I really wanted to see you play the piano.

M: Don't worry. You didn't ________ ________.

W: What do you mean?

M: I made a ________ ________ at the beginning and played ________ afterwards.

W: Oh, I see. Are you okay?

M: Not really. I still ________ ________ ________.

한일파악

4. 대화를 듣고, 여자가 어제 한 일로 가장 적절한 것을 고르시오.

① 책 구입하기
② 옷장 정리하기
③ 자전거 수리하기
④ 물건 가격표 붙이기
⑤ 벼룩시장 방문하기

04
M: Are you going to the flea market tomorrow, Jia?

W: Yes. I will be ________ ________ ________ there.

M: Really?

W: Yes. I want to ________ ________ ________ ________ and buy a new bicycle.

M: Great. What are you selling?

W: Some clothes I don't wear anymore and some books. I ________ all of them yesterday.

M: You labeled all your things with the prices?

W: Right. I have some books you might like, so come and ________ ________ ________!

다음 페이지에 계속 ➡

5. 대화를 듣고, 두 사람이 대화하는 장소로 가장 적절한 곳을 고르시오.

① 은행
② 식당
③ 서점
④ 미술관
⑤ 옷가게

05

M: Honey, this place is huge!

W: It is. Why don't we ________ ________ the floor plan first?

M: Good idea. We are here at the counter… Oh, the ________ ________ are on the second floor.

W: Let's go there and find the book you're looking for.

M: Aren't you going to buy anything?

W: I'll ________ ________ ____________. That section is on the second floor, too.

6. 대화를 듣고, 여자의 마지막 말의 의도로 가장 적절한 것을 고르시오.

① 불평　　② 사과
③ 허락　　④ 감사
⑤ 거절

06

W: Excuse me. May I ask what you're doing here?

M: We're ________ ________ ________ ________.

W: Well, I live next door and it's a little ________.

M: Oh, I'm sorry. There wasn't enough room in the kitchen to unpack it.

W: So, you're doing it in the corridor?

M: Yes. We'll try to be as quiet as possible.

W: How long do you think it'll take?

M: About 5 more minutes. Is it OK if we ________ ________ here?

W: Only 5 minutes? Then you can ________ ________ ________.

7. 대화를 듣고, 남자가 살 물건으로 가장 적절한 것을 고르시오.

① 칼
② 재킷
③ 의자
④ 손전등
⑤ 식료품

07

M: Helen, have you finished packing for camping tomorrow?

W: Yes, Dad. I ________________ ________ ________ a flashlight and a warm jacket.

M: Good! By the way, I found the camping chairs that we thought ________ ________ ________.

W: Cool! We're all set.

M: One little problem. I can't find the camping knife, so I'm ________ ________ to buy one.

W: Oh, I see. Do you want me to come with you?

M: No need. Why don't you help your mom with her packing?

W: Okay, I will.

8. 대화를 듣고, 남자가 대화 직후에 할 일로 가장 적절한 것을 고르시오.

① 할인쿠폰 찾아보기
② 친구에게 전화하기
③ 중고상품 판매하기
④ 인터넷에서 제품 검색하기
⑤ 다른 색상의 신발 신어보기

08

W: Honey, those shoes look really ________ ________ ________.

M: Thanks. This is the last pair they have. I think I'll buy them.

W: But they are quite ________.

M: If I don't buy them now, they could be sold out.

W: Why don't you ________ the product online first? The price could be lower.

M: Good idea. I'll search ________ ________ ________ with my phone right now.

다음 페이지에 계속 ➡

9. 대화를 듣고, 두 사람이 대회에 대해 언급하지 **않은** 것을 고르시오.

① 명칭
② 주최 기관
③ 개최 기간
④ 지원 자격
⑤ 우승 상품

09
W: Jinho, have you heard about the Global Science Fair Competition?

M: Yes, I have. Google hosts that international competition, right?

W: Yeah. I ________ ________ ________ to the final competition.

M: Really? Congratulations! When is it?

W: It's from March 1st to May 15th.

M: Oh, it ________ a long time. Do you have to ________ ________ the competition?

W: Yes. Only students who won the regional science competition can ________ ________ ________.

M: I see. I'm sure you will do well.

10. 다음을 듣고, 여자가 하는 말의 내용으로 가장 적절한 것을 고르시오.

① 신규 교사 소개
② 학생회장 선거 공지
③ 화재 시 대피 요령
④ 교내 건의함 위치 안내
⑤ 급식실 이용 규칙 안내

10
W: Hello, students. I'm Ms. Kim, your head teacher. Before using the cafeteria, please ________ ________ ________ these rules. First, your safety is very important, so do not run. ________ ________ ________ and don't push others. Second, again for your safety, ________ your hands before eating. Third, help yourself to the food, but ________ ________ ________ ________ it. I hope you enjoy your lunch.

11. 대화를 듣고, 뮤지컬에 관한 정보로 일치하지 <u>않는</u> 것을 고르시오.

① 제목이 '라이온 킹'이다.
② Lakewood 극장에서 공연한다.
③ 이번 주 일요일 저녁 7시 공연이다.
④ 상연 시간은 3시간이다.
⑤ 좌석은 앞에서 두 번째 줄에 있다.

11

M: Kelly, I have two tickets to a musical. Do you want to go?

W: I'd love to! Which musical is it?

M: *The Lion King*. It's playing at Lakewood Theater.

W: Great. When is the show?

M: This Sunday at 7 p.m. And _______ _______ _______ is two hours.

W: I see. Are we going to sit close to the stage?

M: Yeah, our seats are _______ _______ _______ _______.

W: That's awesome! I can't wait to see it.

12. 대화를 듣고, 남자가 전화를 건 목적으로 가장 적절한 것을 고르시오.

① 병원 예약을 미루기 위해서
② 결석 사유를 물어보기 위해서
③ 아들의 입원을 알리기 위해서
④ 학생의 안부를 확인하기 위해서
⑤ 자녀의 조퇴를 요청하기 위해서

12

(*Telephone rings.*)

W: Hello.

M: Hi, Mrs. Morris. I'm Hank Moore, John's homeroom teacher.

W: Oh, hi, Mr. Moore. Thanks again for bringing my son to the hospital earlier today.

M: No problem. I called to _______ _______ _______ John. How is he doing?

W: He's doing fine. The doctor __________ him. He's resting in his room now.

M: I'm glad to hear it. So, was it a stomach _______?

W: Yes. Nothing serious. He'll be up and _______ _______ soon.

M: That's good news.

다음 페이지에 계속 ➡

13. 대화를 듣고, 남자가 받은 거스름돈으로 가장 적절한 것을 고르시오.

① $1   ② $2
③ $3   ④ $4
⑤ $5

13
W: Hello, are you ________ ________ ________?

M: Yes. I want two cups of black coffee, please.

W: Okay, it's 4 dollars ________ ________ ________.

   Anything else?

M: Um, I would like a piece of strawberry cake, please.

W: Okay, that will be 5 dollars.

M: How much is ________ ________?

W: The total will be 13 dollars. For here or to go?

M: To go. Here's 15 dollars.

W: Thank you. Here is ________ ________.

14. 대화를 듣고, 두 사람의 관계로 가장 적절한 것을 고르시오.

① 호텔 직원 — 손님
② 관광 가이드 — 관광객
③ 여행사 직원 — 고객
④ 관광 가이드 — 버스 기사
⑤ 택시 기사 — 손님

14
W: Can you tell me ________ ________ we'll leave?

M: We'll leave in a few minutes, ma'am, but we're still waiting for the other members of the group to arrive.

W: I wonder why they're late.

M: They're probably tired and overslept at the hotel.

W: You can say that again! Do you think our tour today will be ________ ________ ________ yesterday's?

M: Well, I'll be taking your group to some historical places. However, since ________ ________ ________ them mostly from the bus, I don't think it will be too tiring.

W: That's good news! I'm ________ ________ ________ today's tour.

15. 대화를 듣고, 남자가 여자에게 제안한 것으로 가장 적절한 것을 고르시오.

① 음식 만들기
② 봉사활동 하기
③ 학원 등록하기
④ 집 안 청소하기
⑤ 교복 수선하기

15

M: Candice, what are you going to do this Sunday?

W: I'm going to ________ ________ ________. What about you?

M: I'm volunteering at the ________ ________.

W: Oh, I didn't know you volunteered. What do you do there?

M: I clean the kitchen and ________ ________ ________ ________.

W: How kind of you!

M: Will you join me? They need more volunteers.

W: Okay, I'll join you.

16. 대화를 듣고, Derek이 토요일에 테니스 레슨을 받지 <u>못하는</u> 이유를 고르시오.

① 보충 수업이 있어서
② 식료품점에서 쇼핑을 해야 해서
③ 형과 함께 테니스를 쳐야 해서
④ 공부를 해야 해서
⑤ 형의 가게에서 일을 도와야 해서

16

W: Hi, Derek. Long time ________ ________. How have you been?

M: Great. Thank you. And you?

W: I'm fine. Are you still ________ tennis lessons on Saturdays?

M: No, I'm not. I can't take lessons because I'm ________ ________ at my brother's store.

W: The grocery store near your school?

M: Yes. I usually ________ ________ on Saturdays.

다음 페이지에 계속 ➡

17. 다음 그림의 상황에 가장 적절한 대화를 고르시오.

①   ②
③   ④
⑤

17

① M: Can you ________ ________ ________ ________ for me?

W: Sure. No problem.

② M: Excuse me, where is the Hanjin apartment building?

W: It's that tall building you see right there.

③ M: It's so hot today.

W: Right. Let's get ____________ ________ ________.

④ M: Do you need help with that box?

W: Oh, it's fine. I can handle it myself.

⑤ M: This bottle goes in with the plastics, right?

W: Yes, but ________ ________ ________ ________ first.

18. 다음을 듣고, 여자가 게임에 대해 언급하지 <u>않은</u> 것을 고르시오.

① 제목   ② 장르
③ 내용   ④ 발매일
⑤ 가격

18

W: Hello, All About Games subscribers! Today, I will introduce a fun game to you. The title is *Story of Seasons*. It is a role-playing simulation game. In this game, ________ ________ ________ your grandfather's farm after his death, so you need to ________ ________ and raise animals. The price is 20 dollars. If you are a fan of these kinds of games, I'm sure you will ________ ________ ________, too!

19. 대화를 듣고, 남자의 마지막 말에 이어질 여자의 말로 가장 적절한 것을 고르시오.

Woman: _________________

① It will cost us 30 dollars.
② I think the white one is better.
③ Let's order a Christmas cake.
④ We should wrap all the presents.
⑤ I want to buy a black coat for myself.

19
M: Honey, I think we _________ _________ _________ _________ on our list for Christmas.

W: Let's see… We didn't buy a present for your mother.

M: What should we get for her?

W: How about this sweater? It looks _________ _________ _________.

M: Didn't we buy one for her last Christmas?

W: Oh, you're right. Then, how about giving her a scarf?

M: Okay. _________ _________ _________ this red scarf or that white one?

W: I think the white one is better.

20. 대화를 듣고, 남자의 마지막 말에 이어질 여자의 말로 가장 적절한 것을 고르시오.

Woman: _________________

① I'm not interested in clubs.
② Think it over before quitting.
③ I hope you'll get better soon.
④ There are too many meetings.
⑤ Why don't you take math lessons?

20
W: Did you join any clubs this semester?

M: I joined the school newsletter club.

W: School newsletter club? That sounds interesting. How do you like it?

M: It's _________ _________. But, there is one problem.

W: What is it?

M: Sometimes it _________ too much of my _________. Meetings, interviews, writing…

W: Oh, I'm sorry to hear that.

M: Maybe I'll just _________ _________ next semester.

W: Think it over before quitting.

Words & Expressions Review 22

● 다음 단어를 암기하세요.

문제	번호	단어	뜻
1	1	mainly	주로
	2	chance	가능성
2	3	mitten	벙어리장갑
	4	checkered	체크무늬의
3	5	terribly	형편없이, 몹시, 심각하게
	6	afterwards	그 뒤에, 나중에
4	7	flea market	벼룩 시장
	8	have a look	구경하다, (한번) 보다
5	9	huge	엄청난, 거대한
	10	floor plan	평면도
	11	counter	판매대, 계산대
6	12	unpack	(짐을) 풀다
	13	corridor	복도
	14	carry on ~	~을 계속하다
7	15	all set	준비가 다 된
	16	head out	~로 향하다
8	17	look good on ~	~와 잘 어울리다
9	18	host	주최하다
	19	make it through	진출하다, 통과하다
	20	regional	지역의, 지방의
10	21	head teacher	교장
	22	stay in line	줄을 서다

문제	번호	단어	뜻
11	23	row	줄
	24	can't wait to + 동사	빨리[매우] ~하고 싶어 하다
	25	check in on ~	~의 안부를 확인하다, 상태를 살피다
12	26	discharge	(병원에서) 퇴원시키다
	27	run around	(이리저리) 뛰어다니다
	28	arrive	도착하다
14	29	oversleep	늦잠 자다
	30	look forward to ~	~을 기대하다
15	31	soup kitchen	무료 급식소
	32	throw out the garbage	쓰레기를 버리다
	33	lesson	강습, 수업
16	34	be busy -ing	~하느라 바쁘다
	35	grocery store	식료품점
17	36	handle	처리하다, 다루다
	37	subscriber	구독자
18	38	manage	관리하다, 운영하다
	39	crop	농작물
19	40	wrap	포장하다, 싸다
	41	comfortable	편한, 안락한
	42	semester	학기
20	43	drop	그만두다, 중단하다
	44	quit	그만두다

●왼쪽 단어장의 뜻이 보이지 않게 반으로 접고, 학습한 단어의 뜻을 아래 빈칸에 적어주세요.

1	row	23	terribly
2	mainly	24	host
3	floor plan	25	head teacher
4	semester	26	manage
5	corridor	27	throw out the garbage
6	soup kitchen	28	grocery store
7	checkered	29	be busy -ing
8	unpack	30	check in on ~
9	lesson	31	counter
10	huge	32	mitten
11	afterwards	33	flea market
12	drop	34	oversleep
13	have a look	35	comfortable
14	carry on ~	36	look forward to ~
15	wrap	37	can't wait to + 동사
16	quit	38	crop
17	all set	39	head out
18	regional	40	chance
19	look good on ~	41	make it through
20	subscriber	42	handle
21	arrive	43	discharge
22	stay in line	44	run around

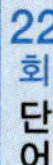

23회 중학영어듣기 모의고사

M2(17)_23_US
모두 **미국식 발음(US)**
으로 녹음

M2(17)_23_UK
20문제 중 5문제에 **영국식 발음**
(US+UK)을 포함하여 녹음

정답 및 해석 p. 110

1 다음을 듣고, 예상되는 뉴욕의 날씨로 가장 적절한 것을 고르시오.

①  ②  ③  ④  ⑤ 

2 대화를 듣고, 두 사람이 구입할 액자로 가장 적절한 것을 고르시오.

① 

② 

③ 

④ 

⑤ 

3 대화를 듣고, 남자의 심정으로 가장 적절한 것을 고르시오.

① nervous　② anxious　③ proud　④ relaxed　⑤ angry

4 대화를 듣고, 남자가 어제 한 일로 가장 적절한 것을 고르시오.

① 수학 숙제　② 교실 청소　③ 친구 병문안
④ 컴퓨터 게임　⑤ 부모님 심부름

5 대화를 듣고, 두 사람이 대화하는 장소로 가장 적절한 곳을 고르시오.

① 은행　　②학교　　③옷가게　　④카페　　⑤기념품점

6 대화를 듣고, 남자의 마지막 말의 의도로 가장 적절한 것을 고르시오.

① 요청　　②항의　　③거절　　④감사　　⑤칭찬

7 대화를 듣고, 여자가 구입할 기념품으로 가장 적절한 것을 고르시오.

① 냉장고 자석　　　　② 현지 예술품
③ 초콜릿　　　　　　④ 머그잔
⑤ 열쇠고리

8 대화를 듣고, 두 사람이 대화 직후에 할 일로 가장 적절한 것을 고르시오.

① 쿠키 굽기　　　② 스카프 고르기　　　③ 할머니 선물 사기
④ 케이크 주문하기　⑤ 레시피 찾아보기

9 대화를 듣고, 두 사람이 사진 대회에 대해 언급하지 않은 것을 고르시오.

① 제출 기한　　　② 주제　　　③ 제출 방법
④ 우승 상품　　　⑤ 심사 위원

10 다음을 듣고, 여자가 하는 말의 내용으로 가장 적절한 것을 고르시오.

① 학교 차량 정기검사　　　② 공중 화장실 이용 예절
③ 수학여행 관련 공지사항　④ 여름철 피서지 안전사고
⑤ 기말고사 시험 범위 공지

11번~20번 문제는 다음 페이지에 ➡

11 대화를 듣고, 학교 독서 모임에 대한 내용으로 일치하지 <u>않는</u> 것을 고르시오.

① 회원이 현재 10명이다.　　　　　② 무료 가입이 가능하다.
③ 2주에 한 권씩 책을 읽는다.　　　④ 책을 읽은 후에 모임을 갖는다.
⑤ 독후감을 작성해야 한다.

12 대화를 듣고, 남자가 전화를 건 목적으로 가장 적절한 것을 고르시오.

① 비용을 묻기 위해서　　　　　② 방을 예약하기 위해서
③ 방을 변경하기 위해서　　　　④ 예약을 취소하기 위해서
⑤ 분실물을 신고하기 위해서

13 대화를 듣고, 여자가 지불해야 할 금액으로 가장 적절한 것을 고르시오.

① $10　　　② $13　　　③ $20　　　④ $26　　　⑤ $30

14 대화를 듣고, 두 사람의 관계로 가장 적절한 것을 고르시오.

① 경찰관 — 운전자　　② 카페 직원 — 손님　　③ 버스 기사 — 승객
④ 환경미화원 — 보행자　　⑤ 공연장 관리인 — 관객

15 대화를 듣고, 여자가 남자에게 부탁한 일로 가장 적절한 것을 고르시오.

① 자료 복사하기　　② 점심 요리하기　　③ 병원에 함께 가기
④ 먹을 것 사다 주기　　⑤ 회의 시간 변경하기

16 대화를 듣고, 여자가 스페인어 회화 수업을 중단한 이유로 가장 적절한 것을 고르시오.

① 강사가 자주 결석해서　　　　② 학원 위치가 바뀌어서
③ 수강생이 너무 많아져서　　　④ 해외 출장을 가게 되어서
⑤ 강습 수준이 맞지 않아서

17 다음 그림의 상황에 가장 적절한 대화를 고르시오.

①   ②   ③   ④   ⑤

18 다음을 듣고, 남자가 역사 박물관에 대해 언급하지 <u>않은</u> 것을 고르시오.

① 전시품   ② 특별 전시   ③ 개관 시간
④ 휴관일   ⑤ 입장료

[19~20]   대화를 듣고, 남자의 마지막 말에 이어질 여자의 말로 가장 적절한 것을 고르시오.

19 Woman: ________________________________

① They like to live in caves.   ② They are native to Australia.
③ They are known to eat leaves.   ④ They have no natural predators.
⑤ They sleep up to 22 hours a day.

20 Woman: ________________________________

① What a sad story!   ② That sounds unbelievable.
③ I couldn't believe my eyes.   ④ I hope you see dolphins next time.
⑤ It was lucky that you were on a boat.

Dictation Test 23

M2(17)_23_D

Dictation(받아쓰기)은 본문을 받아쓰면서 영어듣기의 집중력을 향상시키고 다양한 표현을 정리하기 위한 영어듣기 학습법입니다. **녹음을 다시 듣고, 빈칸에 알맞은 단어를 써 보세요.**
※Dictation의 정답은 듣기 대본의 밑줄 친 부분을 확인하세요.

📖 정답 p. 110

맞은 개수 / 총149개

 날씨파악–그림 🇺🇸🇬🇧

1. 다음을 듣고, 예상되는 뉴욕의 날씨로 가장 적절한 것을 고르시오.

①  ② 

③  ④ 

⑤ 

01

W: Hello. Here's today's weather report for cities ________ ________ ________. In Seoul, there will be thunderstorms and the temperature will drop. On the other hand, it ________ ________ ________ in Hong Kong as the sunshine continues through this week. Tokyo will be very cloudy. In New York, showers are expected as the temperature rises and days of heavy snow end. London will be ________ ________ ________. Thank you very much.

그림정보파악

2. 대화를 듣고, 두 사람이 구입할 액자로 가장 적절한 것을 고르시오.

①  ② 

③  ④ 

⑤ 

02

M: Leah, what are you looking at on the Internet?

W: I think we need a ____________ ____________ as a decoration in the living room.

M: That's a great idea! *[Pause]* How about these double photo frames?

W: Well, I think single frames are ____________ ____________ to look at.

M: I see. Then, check out this square one. It looks simple and nice.

W: I love it. Let's buy that ____________ ____________ photo frame.

3. 대화를 듣고, 남자의 심정으로 가장 적절
   한 것을 고르시오.
   ① nervous   ② anxious
   ③ proud   ④ relaxed
   ⑤ angry

03
M: That's amazing! When did our daughter learn to skateboard like that?

W: She ___________ ____________ __________ about four months ago.

M: Did you know about this?

W: Yeah, but she asked me to __________ __________ __________. She wanted to surprise you.

M: She's ____________! Everyone here is clapping and shouting for her cool moves.

W: She __________ every day after school.

M: I want everyone to know she's our daughter.

4. 대화를 듣고, 남자가 어제 한 일로 가장
   적절한 것을 고르시오.
   ① 수학 숙제
   ② 교실 청소
   ③ 친구 병문안
   ④ 컴퓨터 게임
   ⑤ 부모님 심부름

04
W: Dong-hyun, you look very tired.

M: Yeah, I didn't get enough sleep last night.

W: Did you play computer games again?

M: No, I _________ _________ ________ doing my homework.

W: Really? What homework?

M: Our math homework. Aren't we supposed to __________ __________ ________ today?

W: No, I'm sure it's not due until next week.

M: Oh… That means I stayed up late ________ ________!

W: Look on the bright side. At least you finished your homework.

다음 페이지에 계속 ➡

5. 대화를 듣고, 두 사람이 대화하는 장소로
가장 적절한 곳을 고르시오.

① 은행　　　　② 학교
③ 옷가게　　　④ 카페
⑤ 기념품점

05
M: Hi, Lucy. What can I get you?

W: Hi, Tim. I'm not ________ ________ ________
anything.

M: Is something wrong?

W: No, no. You see, I bought a cup of coffee and some
cookies here this morning.

M: Yes, I remember.

W: I found that you gave me a dollar more ________
________.

M: Oh, so you came back?

W: Yeah, here's a dollar. Sorry I didn't come back
right away.

M: I know how ________ ________ ________
________ your clothing shop. Thank you for this.
You are so kind.

W: You are welcome. See you tomorrow!

마지막말의도파악

6. 대화를 듣고, 남자의 마지막 말의 의도로
가장 적절한 것을 고르시오.

① 요청　　　　② 항의
③ 거절　　　　④ 감사
⑤ 칭찬

06
M: Sia, what are you building?

W: These are ________ airplanes.

M: Model airplanes? What do you do with them?

W: Some people collect them, others enjoy building
and painting them.

M: That sounds interesting. Do you collect them?

W: No, I build them ________ ________
________. It's fun and challenging.

M: Can you show me ________ ________
________ one?

7. 대화를 듣고, 여자가 구입할 기념품으로 가장 적절한 것을 고르시오.

① 냉장고 자석　② 현지 예술품
③ 초콜릿　④ 머그잔
⑤ 열쇠고리

07
W: Can you come here and ___________ ___________ ___________?

M: Sure thing. What's up?

W: I'm trying to choose between these two ___________ for my friends back home.

M: The refrigerator magnet and the ___________ artwork?

W: Yeah, I like both of them, but I can't decide which one to buy.

M: Hmm... I think the local artwork would be a unique and ___________ gift.

W: Do you really think so? Okay, then I'll buy it.

8. 대화를 듣고, 두 사람이 대화 직후에 할 일로 가장 적절한 것을 고르시오.

① 쿠키 굽기
② 스카프 고르기
③ 할머니 선물 사기
④ 케이크 주문하기
⑤ 레시피 찾아보기

08
M: Matt, today is Grandma's 80th birthday.

W: Right. I ___________ a scarf for her.

M: That's ___________. We can give her the scarf at the party.

W: What else can we do ___________ ___________?

M: Let's bake some cookies before the party.

W: Good idea. What type of cookies should we make?

M: How about chocolate chip cookies? Grandma loves them.

W: Sounds perfect. Let's ___________ ___________ a recipe.

다음 페이지에 계속 ➡

9. 대화를 듣고, 두 사람이 사진 대회에 대해 언급하지 <u>않은</u> 것을 고르시오.

① 제출 기한　　② 주제
③ 제출 방법　　④ 우승 상품
⑤ 심사 위원

09

W: Carl, are you going to ___________ __________ the photography contest?

M: I haven't ___________ __________ my mind yet.

W: Don't forget the deadline for submission is October 20th.

M: I know. And the theme of the photo contest is family.

W: Yes. Do you have the email address?

M: Of course. I'm ___________ __________ submit my photo with a short introduction __________ __________, right?

W: Right! Do you know the prize for the winner?

M: Sure. The winner will receive a gift certificate.

10. 다음을 듣고, 여자가 하는 말의 내용으로 가장 적절한 것을 고르시오.

① 학교 차량 정기검사
② 공중 화장실 이용 예절
③ 수학여행 관련 공지사항
④ 여름철 피서지 안전사고
⑤ 기말고사 시험 범위 공지

10

W: Class, please ________ ________. I have some important announcements to make, so listen carefully. As you are ________ ________ ________, tomorrow we will be going on a school trip. We will be leaving at 8 o'clock tomorrow morning, so everybody must be on board the school bus by 7:50 a.m. Please, don't be late! We will be staying there for two nights, so don't forget to bring your ________ ________ and __________. Lastly, at all times please be safe.

11. 대화를 듣고, 학교 독서 모임에 대한 내용으로 일치하지 <u>않는</u> 것을 고르시오.

① 회원이 현재 10명이다.
② 무료 가입이 가능하다.
③ 2주에 한 권씩 책을 읽는다.
④ 책을 읽은 후에 모임을 갖는다.
⑤ 독후감을 작성해야 한다.

11
W: Mark, you ________ ________ ________ me at the school book club. You'll love it.

M: Hmm… I'm not sure. How many members are there?

W: Currently, we have 10 members, and you can join for free.

M: Okay, how many books do you read?

W: We read one book every two weeks.

M: So, you have __________ ________ ________ ________ after reading the book?

W: You're right. We also don't write any book reports. So, no pressure.

M: That sounds okay. ________ ________ ________, then.

12. 대화를 듣고, 남자가 전화를 건 목적으로 가장 적절한 것을 고르시오.

① 비용을 묻기 위해서
② 방을 예약하기 위해서
③ 방을 변경하기 위해서
④ 예약을 취소하기 위해서
⑤ 분실물을 신고하기 위해서

12
(*Telephone rings.*)

W: Good morning, Grand Hotel. How may I ________ you?

M: Hi, I have a reservation for a room tomorrow night, but I ________ ________ ________ ________.

W: I'm sorry to hear that. May I have your name and reservation number, please?

M: It's Brandon Lee and my reservation number is 3672.

W: Thank you. May I know why you are cancelling?

M: There was a sudden change of plans.

W: I see. Your reservation ________ ________.

M: Thank you.

다음 페이지에 계속 ➡

13. 대화를 듣고, 여자가 지불해야 할 금액으로 가장 적절한 것을 고르시오.

① $10   ② $13
③ $20   ④ $26
⑤ $30

13

M: Good morning. Welcome to Central Museum.

W: Good morning. I would like two tickets, please.

M: Sure. The tickets are 13 dollars __________ __________.

W: Oh, I heard there's a __________ for students.

M: Yes, there's a 3-dollar discount if you show me your student card.

W: Here are two student cards. That means it's 10 dollars each, right?

M: Yes. Your __________ __________ __________ 20 dollars.

W: Here's my credit card.

14. 대화를 듣고, 두 사람의 관계로 가장 적절한 것을 고르시오.

① 경찰관 – 운전자
② 카페 직원 – 손님
③ 버스 기사 – 승객
④ 환경미화원 – 보행자
⑤ 공연장 관리인 – 관객

14

W: Excuse me, sir. You can't have that drink here.

M: What do you mean?

W: Drinks in disposable containers are not allowed on the bus.

M: Oh, I didn't know. Why is that?

W: If a drink __________ __________, it can be dangerous.

M: I see. But can't I __________ __________ just this once?

W: I'm afraid not. It's the rule. I can't start the bus unless you get off.

M: OK, it looks like I __________ __________ __________.

15. 대화를 듣고, 여자가 남자에게 부탁한 일로 가장 적절한 것을 고르시오.
① 자료 복사하기
② 점심 요리하기
③ 병원에 함께 가기
④ 먹을 것 사다 주기
⑤ 회의 시간 변경하기

15

M: Jessica, let's go eat lunch.

W: I'm sorry, but I think you should go alone today.

M: Why? Are you feeling all right?

W: Actually, I'm ________ ________ ________ the materials for the meeting at 2 p.m. this afternoon.

M: Oh, do you need any help? Like ________ ________ ________ ________?

W: That's okay. Instead, can you buy me something to eat?

M: Sure! What about a sandwich?

W: ________ ________ ________. Thank you.

M: No problem.

2025 영어듣기능력평가 1회 16번 변형

16. 대화를 듣고, 여자가 스페인어 회화 수업을 중단한 이유로 가장 적절한 것을 고르시오.
① 강사가 자주 결석해서
② 학원 위치가 바뀌어서
③ 수강생이 너무 많아져서
④ 해외 출장을 가게 되어서
⑤ 강습 수준이 맞지 않아서

16

M: Hi, Rachael. Are you still taking that Spanish ____________ class?

W: Oh, I thought I told you. I'm not taking it anymore.

M: Really? Why? I thought you really liked it. Was the textbook ____________ ____________?

W: No, the materials were fine.

M: Then what happened?

W: I'm going on a long business trip overseas, so I ____________ ____________ ____________ going to the class.

M: I see. Are you planning to join the class again when you return?

W: Yes, definitely.

다음 페이지에 계속 ➡

23
회
딕테이션

17. 다음 그림의 상황에 가장 적절한 대화를 고르시오.

① 　　　　②
③ 　　　　④
⑤

17

① M: Excuse me, where is the bank?

W: It's next to the police office.

② M: Hi, I'd like to order a coffee, please.

W: Of course! ___________ __________ or to go?

③ M: Look at the waiting line.

W: ___________ __________ __________ go

somewhere else?

④ M: What do you want to drink?

W: ___________ __________ a soda.

⑤ M: This music is so good.

W: Right? I love every song of theirs.

18. 다음을 듣고, 남자가 역사 박물관에 대해 언급하지 <u>않은</u> 것을 고르시오.

① 전시품　　② 특별 전시
③ 개관 시간　　④ 휴관일
⑤ 입장료

18　M: Hello, everyone. Welcome to Central History Museum. Our museum introduces our country's history through pictures, art works, and many other items from the past. We also have a ________ ________ on the second floor. We are open from 10 a.m. to 6 p.m., on Tuesday and Thursday through Sunday, and to 7 p.m. on Wednesdays. Please ________ ________ that we are closed on Mondays. Please check our website for more details.

19. 대화를 듣고, 남자의 마지막 말에 이어질 여자의 말로 가장 적절한 것을 고르시오.

Woman: _______________

① They like to live in caves.
② They are native to Australia.
③ They are known to eat leaves.
④ They have no natural predators.
⑤ They sleep up to 22 hours a day.

19

W: Hi, Tim. Did you watch the nature documentary on TV last night?

M: No, what was it about?

W: It was about interesting _______ _______.

M: Can you tell me one?

W: Sure. Do you know what animal _______ _______ _______?

M: I don't know. Is it the bat?

W: No. It's koalas!

M: Really? How much time do they _______ _______?

W: They sleep up to 22 hours a day.

---

20. 대화를 듣고, 남자의 마지막 말에 이어질 여자의 말로 가장 적절한 것을 고르시오.

Woman: _______________

① What a sad story!
② That sounds unbelievable.
③ I couldn't believe my eyes.
④ I hope you see dolphins next time.
⑤ It was lucky that you were on a boat.

20

W: Hi, Somin. How was your trip to Jeju-do?

M: It was fantastic. I had so much fun.

W: How did you get there, _______ _______ _______ or by plane?

M: I went there by plane. Then my parents rented a car and drove us around.

W: What is the _______ _______ thing from your trip?

M: It's seeing dolphins in the sea. We were so lucky.

W: Wow. Did you _______ _______ _______ _______ to see them?

M: No. We were in our car and suddenly, we spotted dolphins out in the sea.

W: That sounds unbelievable.

Words & Expressions Review 23

● 다음 단어를 암기하세요.

문제	번호	단어	뜻
1	1	on the other hand	반면에
	2	frame	액자
2	3	as	~으로(서)
	4	decoration	장식품
3	5	pick up	(습관·재주 등을) 익히게 되다
	6	unbelievable	놀랄 만한, 믿을 수 없는
4	7	hand in	제출하다
	8	Look on the bright side.	긍정적으로 생각해.
	9	get A B	A에게 B를 주다
5	10	change	거스름돈
	11	busy with ~	~으로 바쁜
6	12	collect	수집하다
	13	challenging	도전의식을 불러일으키는, 도전적인
	14	souvenir	기념품
7	15	artwork	예술품
	16	unique	특별한, 독특한
8	17	knit	(실로 옷을) 뜨다, 짜다
	18	thoughtful	사려 깊은
9	19	make up one's mind	결정하다, 결심하다
	20	submission	(서류 등의) 제출
10	21	announcement	공지, 발표
	22	carefully	주의하여, 신중히

문제	번호	단어	뜻
10	23	aware of	~을 아는
11	24	gathering	모임
	25	Count me in.	나도 끼워줘.
	26	assist	돕다
12	27	cancel	취소하다
	28	sudden	갑작스러운
13	29	each	각자, 각각
	30	come to	(합계가) 되다, (정도, 범위 등에) 이르다
14	31	disposable	일회용의
	32	unless	만약 ~하지 않는다면
	33	actually	사실
15	34	work on	작업하다
	35	material	자료, 재료
16	36	conversation	회화, 대화
	37	overseas	해외로, 해외의
	38	definitely	(강조의 의미로 쓰여) 절대(로), 분명히[틀림없이]
18	39	floor	(건물의) 층, 바닥
	40	details	세부 사항
19	41	native to A	A가 원산지인, A 고유의
	42	natural predator	천적, 자연적 포식자
20	43	memorable	기억할 만한
	44	suddenly	갑자기

● 왼쪽 단어장의 뜻이 보이지 않게 반으로 접고, 학습한 단어의 뜻을 아래 빈칸에 적어주세요.

1	assist	23	carefully
2	challenging	24	unbelievable
3	submission	25	Look on the bright side.
4	pick up	26	collect
5	frame	27	aware of
6	get A B	28	unless
7	details	29	gathering
8	cancel	30	overseas
9	artwork	31	make up one's mind
10	suddenly	32	disposable
11	announcement	33	actually
12	decoration	34	change
13	come to	35	each
14	souvenir	36	busy with ~
15	material	37	hand in
16	unique	38	as
17	memorable	39	definitely
18	on the other hand	40	conversation
19	work on	41	floor
20	knit	42	thoughtful
21	Count me in.	43	native to A
22	sudden	44	natural predator

1 다음을 듣고, 목요일의 날씨로 가장 적절한 것을 고르시오.

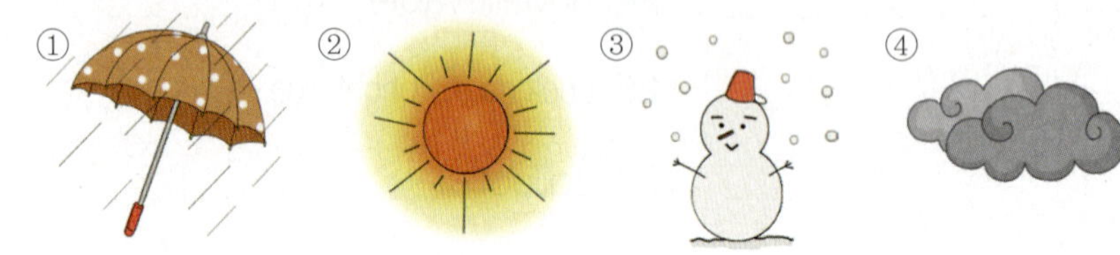

2 대화를 듣고, 남자가 구입할 열쇠고리를 고르시오.

3 대화를 듣고, 남자의 심정으로 가장 적절한 것을 고르시오.

① proud
② bored
③ nervous
④ sad
⑤ happy

4 대화를 듣고, 남자가 지난 주말에 한 일로 가장 적절한 것을 고르시오.

① 영화 촬영장 방문하기
② 제빵 수업 수강하기
③ 축구 경기 관람하기
④ 초콜릿 구매하기
⑤ 오븐 수리하기

5 대화를 듣고, 두 사람이 대화하는 장소로 가장 적절한 곳을 고르시오.

① 미용실　　② 사진관　　③ 안경점　　④ 미술관　　⑤ 공항

6 대화를 듣고, 남자의 마지막 말의 의도로 가장 적절한 것을 고르시오.

① 경고　　② 격려　　③ 거절　　④ 제안　　⑤ 사과

7 대화를 듣고, 여자가 파티를 위해 준비할 음식으로 가장 적절한 것을 고르시오.

① 타코　　② 과일 샐러드　　③ 브라우니
④ 파스타　　⑤ 레모네이드

8 대화를 듣고, 남자가 대화 직후에 할 일로 가장 적절한 것을 고르시오.

① 제과점에 가기　　② 초콜릿 사기　　③ 부엌 청소하기
④ 오븐에 반죽 넣기　　⑤ 쿠키 반죽 만들기

9 대화를 듣고, 두 사람이 과학 경진대회에 대해 언급하지 <u>않은</u> 것을 고르시오.

① 날짜　　② 장소　　③ 신청 가능 대상
④ 발표 주제　　⑤ 발표 제한 시간

10 다음을 듣고, 여자가 하는 말의 내용으로 가장 적절한 것을 고르시오.

① 수영 대회 준비　　② 경기장행 버스 이용 안내
③ 축구 관람 에티켓　　④ 스쿨버스 운행 시간 변경 공지
⑤ 운동부 가입 방법

11번~20번 문제는 다음 페이지에 ➡

11 대화를 듣고, 두 사람이 구입할 제품에 대한 내용으로 일치하지 <u>않는</u> 것을 고르시오.

① 미취학 아동용이다.   ② 바퀴가 두 개이다.
③ 두 가지 색상으로 나온다.   ④ 30달러이다.
⑤ 배송료는 무료이다.

12 대화를 듣고, 남자가 전화를 건 목적으로 가장 적절한 것을 고르시오.

① 식당 예약을 하기 위해서   ② 배달 주문을 하기 위해서
③ 메뉴에 대해 문의하기 위해서   ④ 예약 시간을 변경하기 위해서
⑤ 식당의 위치를 물어보기 위해서

13 대화를 듣고, 두 사람이 만날 시각을 고르시오.

① 12:00 p.m.   ② 12:30 p.m.   ③ 1:00 p.m.   ④ 1:30 p.m.   ⑤ 2:00 p.m.

14 대화를 듣고, 두 사람의 관계로 가장 적절한 것을 고르시오.

① 시장 – 기자   ② 버스 기사 – 손님
③ 기차 승무원 – 기사   ④ 공항 직원 – 탑승객
⑤ 지하철 역무원 – 승객

15 대화를 듣고, 남자가 여자에게 부탁한 일로 가장 적절한 것을 고르시오.

① 냉장고 청소하기   ② 에어컨 수리하기
③ 종이컵 버려 주기   ④ 예약 시간 변경하기
⑤ 벌레 퇴치 약 뿌리기

16 대화를 듣고, 여자가 수영장에 갈 수 <u>없는</u> 이유로 가장 적절한 것을 고르시오.

① 감기에 걸려서   ② 학교에 가야 해서
③ 내부 수리 중이어서   ④ 회원제로만 운영돼서
⑤ 조모임에 참석해야 해서

17 다음 그림의 상황에 가장 적절한 대화를 고르시오.

①   ②   ③   ④   ⑤

18 다음을 듣고, 뮤지컬 'Hide'에 대해 언급하지 <u>않은</u> 것을 고르시오.

① 공연 장소   ② 출연 배우   ③ 공연 기간
④ 티켓 가격   ⑤ 티켓 판매 시작일

[19~20] 대화를 듣고, 남자의 마지막 말에 이어질 여자의 말로 가장 적절한 것을 고르시오.

19 Woman: _______________________________________

① Don't worry. You're an excellent pianist.
② Sorry, but I'm in the middle of my lunch break.
③ Great news! I'm glad you bought a new piano.
④ Of course! Thanks for giving me the heads up.
⑤ No problem. I enjoy listening to classical music, too.

20 Woman: _______________________________________

① I'm good at swimming.
② That's a beautiful beach.
③ I'm really sorry about that.
④ I think I'll go there every day.
⑤ We go camping every summer.

Dictation Test 24

M2(17)_24_D

Dictation(받아쓰기)은 본문을 받아쓰면서 영어듣기의 집중력을 향상시키고 다양한 표현을 정리하기 위한 영어듣기 학습법입니다. **녹음을 다시 듣고, 빈칸에 알맞은 단어를 써 보세요.**

※Dictation의 정답은 듣기 대본의 밑줄 친 부분을 확인하세요.

정답 p. 115

맞은 개수 / 총154개

날씨파악–그림

1. 다음을 듣고, 목요일의 날씨로 가장 적절한 것을 고르시오.

①  ② 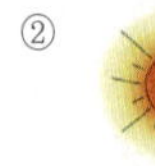

③  ④ 

⑤ 

01 M: Good morning. Let's __________ __________ __________ __________ the weather for this week. On Monday, it will be sunny all day. But on Tuesday, __________ __________ __________ __________. So, get your umbrella ready. It will be cloudy on Wednesday. Again, you will see some rain on Thursday. But on Friday, you will have a sunny day.

그림정보파악

2023 영어듣기능력평가 2회 2번 변형

2. 대화를 듣고, 남자가 구입할 열쇠고리를 고르시오.

02 W: Welcome to Ocean Gift Shop. How can I help you?

M: Hi. I'm looking for a keychain for my friend.

W: Sure. We have seashell and __________-__________ keychains. Both are quite popular.

M: I'll choose the starfish-shaped keychain.

W: Good choice. They come in two styles, __________ and polka-dotted. Which do you prefer?

M: I think the polka-dotted one looks nice.

W: All right. Then, how about this one with the word "SEA" on it? It reminds you of the __________ __________.

M: Great! I'll take it.

---

3. 대화를 듣고, 남자의 심정으로 가장 적절
   한 것을 고르시오.
   ① proud   ② bored
   ③ nervous   ④ sad
   ⑤ happy

03

M: Mom, can we leave now?

W: Not yet, honey. We need some onions.

M: We've ________ ________ so much stuff, though.

W: Not that much. What's wrong? Are you feeling unwell?

M: No. I just want to ________ ________ ________ here. This market is not fun.

W: You promised to help me, Dave.

M: Yeah, but we've ________ ________ too long.

W: It's only been twenty minutes. You really need to learn some ____________.

4. 대화를 듣고, 남자가 지난 주말에 한 일
   로 가장 적절한 것을 고르시오.
   ① 영화 촬영장 방문하기
   ② 제빵 수업 수강하기
   ③ 축구 경기 관람하기
   ④ 초콜릿 구매하기
   ⑤ 오븐 수리하기

04

W: Alex, what's that smell?

M: I __________ a chocolate cake. I just took it out of the oven.

W: It smells really good! I've never baked one. Can I __________ __________ __________?

M: Sure, but I'm not sure if it turned out well.

W: Thanks. *(Pause)* It tastes amazing!

M: Thanks. I actually __________ a baking class last weekend.

W: That's interesting. Maybe I should join one, too.

다음 페이지에 계속 ➡

5. 대화를 듣고, 두 사람이 대화하는 장소로 가장 적절한 곳을 고르시오.
① 미용실 ② 사진관
③ 안경점 ④ 미술관
⑤ 공항

05
M: Hello. How may I help you?

W: I'd like to get a ________________ __________ ________.

M: Okay. Here is a mirror so you can check your appearance before I take the picture.

W: Do I have to ________ ________ my glasses?

M: They are allowed as long as your eyes are clearly visible and there is no glare on the lenses.

W: All right. Then, I'll just wear them.

M: ________ ________ ________ behind your ears so that the ears can be seen.

W: Okay. Now, I am ready.

M: Keep your mouth closed and ________ ________ ____________!

6. 대화를 듣고, 남자의 마지막 말의 의도로 가장 적절한 것을 고르시오.
① 경고 ② 격려
③ 거절 ④ 제안
⑤ 사과

06
W: Oh, no! It's almost ________ ________ ________ ____________! Can we just leave?

M: Don't even think of backing out. Just relax, okay?

W: I'm sorry, Coach, but I can't do this.

M: I don't understand why ________ ________ ____________, Megan.

W: The other contestants are so good! I don't stand a chance!

M: That's not true. You have what it takes to win this contest.

W: Do you really think so?

M: I'm positive. ____________ ________ yourself.

7. 대화를 듣고, 여자가 파티를 위해 준비할 음식으로 가장 적절한 것을 고르시오.

① 타코　　　② 과일 샐러드
③ 브라우니　　④ 파스타
⑤ 레모네이드

07
W: Robin, could you help me?

M: Of course. How can I help you?

W: What should I bring to the potluck party? I'm __________ __________ choose between pasta and tacos with assorted fillings.

M: __________ __________ them are good options.

W: Yes. That's why I can't decide.

M: Hmm… I think tacos would be better. They are __________ to eat, and people can customize them according to their preferences.

W: You're right. I'll make sure to bring __________ __________ like meat, beans and veggies.

8. 대화를 듣고, 남자가 대화 직후에 할 일로 가장 적절한 것을 고르시오.

① 제과점에 가기
② 초콜릿 사기
③ 부엌 청소하기
④ 오븐에 반죽 넣기
⑤ 쿠키 반죽 만들기

08
M: Mia, can you come to the kitchen and __________ __________ __________ __________?

W: Sure, Dad. What do you need me to do?

M: Can you __________ __________ some chocolate chips from the cupboard?

W: Okay. Oh! Are you baking cookies? Can I help you make them?

M: Sure! Why don't you take this dough and shape it into a cookie?

W: Okay. (*pause*) Hmm… This is harder than I thought.

M: You __________ __________ __________ __________! Now, I'll put these in the oven for you.

다음 페이지에 계속 ➡

9. 대화를 듣고, 두 사람이 과학 경진대회에 대해 언급하지 <u>않은</u> 것을 고르시오.
① 날짜　　　　② 장소
③ 신청 가능 대상　④ 발표 주제
⑤ 발표 제한 시간

09 W: Hey, Max. Have you heard about the __________ _________ next month?

M: No, I didn't know about it. When is it?

W: It's on February 15th. __________ __________ _________ all middle schoolers.

M: Cool! What kind of projects can we do?

W: Anything __________ __________ science — from biology to physics!

M: Awesome! How long do we have to present our projects?

W: Each ___________ should be about 5 minutes long.

M: Sounds fun! I'll start thinking of ideas now!

10. 다음을 듣고, 여자가 하는 말의 내용으로 가장 적절한 것을 고르시오.
① 수영 대회 준비
② 경기장행 버스 이용 안내
③ 축구 관람 에티켓
④ 스쿨버스 운행 시간 변경 공지
⑤ 운동부 가입 방법

10 W: Hello, students. Our school football team's ________ ________ is tomorrow. I know a lot of you want to see the game. So, the school has booked a bus. If you want to ________ ________ ________ to the stadium, please tell your teacher. The bus will leave the school at 5 p.m. Come to the game, and show your support. See you tomorrow!

11. 대화를 듣고, 두 사람이 구입할 제품에 대한 내용으로 일치하지 <u>않는</u> 것을 고르시오.

① 미취학 아동용이다.
② 바퀴가 두 개이다.
③ 두 가지 색상으로 나온다.
④ 30달러이다.
⑤ 배송료는 무료이다.

11

W: Honey, look at this website! This toy scooter is on sale.

M: Yeah, and it's for preschool children __________ __________ __________ __________.

W: Right. It's perfect for Billy. And it's three-wheeled for safety.

M: That's nice! __________ __________ __________ two colors. Which color do you like?

W: I prefer the blue one. Is the price okay?

M: It's only 30 dollars. That's good.

W: Yeah, it's also __________ __________ __________.

M: Okay. Let's order it now.

12. 대화를 듣고, 남자가 전화를 건 목적으로 가장 적절한 것을 고르시오.

① 식당 예약을 하기 위해서
② 배달 주문을 하기 위해서
③ 메뉴에 대해 문의하기 위해서
④ 예약 시간을 변경하기 위해서
⑤ 식당의 위치를 물어보기 위해서

12

(*Telephone rings.*)

W: Hello, this is Jolly Bistro.

M: Hi. I'm __________ __________ __________ at your restaurant tonight, but I have some questions __________ your menu.

W: Yes, how may I help you?

M: So, my daughter is a vegetarian. Do you have any __________ __________ on the menu?

W: Oh, yes, we do. We have vegetarian burgers, mushroom pasta, and various salad __________.

M: That's great. Thank you so much.

W: Is there anything else I can help you with?

M: No. That will be all. Thanks.

다음 페이지에 계속 ➡

13. 대화를 듣고, 두 사람이 만날 시각을 고르시오.

① 12:00 p.m. ② 12:30 p.m.
③ 1:00 p.m. ④ 1:30 p.m.
⑤ 2:00 p.m.

13

M: I have good news, Wanda. A new Mexican restaurant ________ ________ ________.

W: Wow, I love Mexican food! When do they open?

M: This Saturday. Do you want to go there together?

W: Sure! Can we meet at 12 p.m. on Saturday?

M: I'm sorry! I have a tennis lesson until 1 p.m.

W: Then, how about meeting at 1:30?

M: If a late lunch is ________ ________ ________, it's okay with me.

W: Alright. I'll see you at the restaurant, then. I hope there's a grand opening event!

2024 영어듣기능력평가 2회 14번 변형

14. 대화를 듣고, 두 사람의 관계로 가장 적절한 것을 고르시오.

① 시장 – 기자
② 버스 기사 – 손님
③ 기차 승무원 – 기사
④ 공항 직원 – 탑승객
⑤ 지하철 역무원 – 승객

14

M: Excuse me. Is the subway on Line 4 __________ now?

W: I'm afraid not. It is temporarily __________ __________ __________ due to a signal problem.

M: Oh no. I need to get to City Hall Station soon.

W: In that case, take Line 3 to Union Station and __________ __________ a bus there.

M: Got it. Thanks for the information.

W: You're welcome. Let me know if you need any more help.

15. 대화를 듣고, 남자가 여자에게 부탁한 일로 가장 적절한 것을 고르시오.

① 냉장고 청소하기
② 에어컨 수리하기
③ 종이컵 버려 주기
④ 예약 시간 변경하기
⑤ 벌레 퇴치 약 뿌리기

15

M: Mom, can you come here for a minute?

W: Sure. What's the matter?

M: You know how much I hate cockroaches, right?

W: Yeah, I know that you're ______________ __________

__________.

M: Well, I managed to ________ one underneath that

paper cup over there.

W: Good job! I'm proud of you! Is it still alive?

M: Yes, Mom. Could you ________ ________ that

paper cup for me? I'm too scared to touch it again.

W: Okay, leave it to me.

---

16. 대화를 듣고, 여자가 수영장에 갈 수 없는 이유로 가장 적절한 것을 고르시오.

① 감기에 걸려서
② 학교에 가야 해서
③ 내부 수리 중이어서
④ 회원제로만 운영돼서
⑤ 조모임에 참석해야 해서

16

W: Dad, I'm going swimming. I need to ________

________ ______________.

M: Honey, is that a good idea? I thought you had a

cold.

W: No need to worry. I feel fine today.

M: Okay, but don't exercise too hard.

W: Thanks, I'll be home before dinner.

M: __________ __________ ________ ________ ________,

isn't the swimming pool closed for repairs?

W: Err… I'm not sure.

M: Yes, it says here on their website.

W: Oh, it seems that they aren't open until next

month.

M: I guess you should just ________ ________

________ ________ instead.

다음 페이지에 계속 ➡

17. 다음 그림의 상황에 가장 적절한 대화를
고르시오.

① ② ③ ④ ⑤

17

① W: You look so excited. What's up?

M: I've bought a new cell phone.

② W: It's ___________. Can I close the window?

M: Sure. Go ahead.

③ W: Get up now, or you will be _________ _________ school.

M: OK, Mom. I will.

④ W: Would you like some more spaghetti?

M: No, thank you. I'm ___________.

⑤ W: It's going to rain according to the weather forecast.

M: I'd ___________ ____________ forget to take an umbrella, then.

18. 다음을 듣고, 뮤지컬 'Hide'에 대해 언급
하지 <u>않은</u> 것을 고르시오.

① 공연 장소　　② 출연 배우
③ 공연 기간　　④ 티켓 가격
⑤ 티켓 판매 시작일

18

W: Dear musical fans, our musical company is

_________ _______ ____________ the opening of

the musical *Hide* playing at the Roseville Theater.

The musical is about the tragic love between a

doctor called Hide and his fiancée Emma. We are

proud to introduce _________ _________ ________,

David Choi who will be playing the main

character. The musical will be on stage from

September 14th to December 21st. You can

______________ ________ starting on August 20th.

We hope you don't miss it!

19. 대화를 듣고, 남자의 마지막 말에 이어질
    여자의 말로 가장 적절한 것을 고르시오.

Woman: _________________

① Don't worry. You're an
   excellent pianist.
② Sorry, but I'm in the middle of
   my lunch break.
③ Great news! I'm glad you
   bought a new piano.
④ Of course! Thanks for giving
   me the heads up.
⑤ No problem. I enjoy listening
   to classical music, too.

19 *(Telephone rings.)*

M: Hello, Mrs. Hudson? This is Michael.

W: Hi, Michael. How are you?

M: Not so great. I'm actually calling to tell you that
   I ________ ________ ________ ________ make it to
   my piano lesson this week.

W: Oh, I hope nothing's wrong!

M: I ____________ ________ ________ yesterday
   while playing basketball, so I can't play the piano
   this week.

W: I'm sorry to hear that. I hope you ________
   ________ soon.

M: Thank you. So, may I reschedule my lesson to next
   week?

W: Of course! Thanks for giving me the heads up.

20. 대화를 듣고, 남자의 마지막 말에 이어질
    여자의 말로 가장 적절한 것을 고르시오.

Woman: _________________

① I'm good at swimming.
② That's a beautiful beach.
③ I'm really sorry about that.
④ I think I'll go there every day.
⑤ We go camping every
   summer.

20 M: Jane, is it true that ________ ________ ________
   Sok-cho?

W: Yes. My family will stay there for two weeks.

M: That long? Where will you stay?

W: My parents ____________ ________ ________.
   I can't wait to try all the famous food there.

M: Will you go sea bathing, too? That's a beach area.

W: No, I don't like water. But, there's a big traditional
   market!

M: Right, you ________ ____________.

W: I think I'll go there every day.

Words & Expressions Review 24

● 다음 단어를 암기하세요.

문제	번호	단어	뜻
1	☐ 1	take a look at ~	~을 (한번) 보다
	☐ 2	cloudy	흐린
2	☐ 3	remind	떠올리게 하다
	☐ 4	stuff	것, 물건
3	☐ 5	feel unwell	몸이 안 좋다
	☐ 6	patience	인내심, 참을성
4	☐ 7	turn out	(결과가) ~으로 되다, 되어 가다
	☐ 8	attend	참석하다
5	☐ 9	appearance	외모
	☐ 10	as long as ~	~하는 한
6	☐ 11	back out	내빼다, 철회하다
	☐ 12	contestant	참가자
	☐ 13	stand a chance	가능성이 있다
	☐ 14	I'm positive.	확실해.
7	☐ 15	convenient	간편한, 편리한
	☐ 16	customize	원하는 대로 만들다, 바꾸다
8	☐ 17	give ~ a hand	~를 돕다
9	☐ 18	related to	~과 관련 있는
	☐ 19	present	발표하다
	☐ 20	final game	결승 경기
10	☐ 21	catch a bus	버스를 (잡아) 타다
	☐ 22	support	지지, 응원

문제	번호	단어	뜻
11	☐ 23	preschool children	미취학 아동
	☐ 24	safety	안전, 안전성
	☐ 25	bistro	(편안한 분위기의) 작은 식당
12	☐ 26	regarding	~에 관하여
	☐ 27	vegetarian	채식주의자, 채식(주의자)의
	☐ 28	choice	선택 가능한 수[범위]
14	☐ 29	temporarily	일시적으로
	☐ 30	out of service	서비스가 중단된, 사용이 중지된
15	☐ 31	capture	포획하다
	☐ 32	have a cold	감기에 걸리다
16	☐ 33	come to think of it	그러고 보니
	☐ 34	go for a run	달리다
	☐ 35	chilly	쌀쌀한, 추운
17	☐ 36	go ahead	(승인, 인가) ~하세요
	☐ 37	according to	~에 따르면, ~에 의하면
	☐ 38	announce	발표하다
18	☐ 39	tragic	비극적인
	☐ 40	miss	놓치다
19	☐ 41	actually	실은
	☐ 42	sprain	삐다
20	☐ 43	sea bathing	해수욕
	☐ 44	traditional	전통적인

● 왼쪽 단어장의 뜻이 보이지 않게 반으로 접고, 학습한 단어의 뜻을 아래 빈칸에 적어주세요.

1	actually	23	stand a chance
2	I'm positive.	24	give ~ a hand
3	attend	25	miss
4	patience	26	take a look at ~
5	according to	27	as long as ~
6	capture	28	customize
7	preschool children	29	out of service
8	convenient	30	chilly
9	go ahead	31	stuff
10	turn out	32	support
11	vegetarian	33	have a cold
12	final game	34	temporarily
13	contestant	35	appearance
14	come to think of it	36	sea bathing
15	cloudy	37	sprain
16	present	38	traditional
17	bistro	39	safety
18	remind	40	go for a run
19	catch a bus	41	feel unwell
20	regarding	42	choice
21	related to	43	tragic
22	announce	44	back out

24
회
단
어

2026 17차 개정판

마더텅 100% 실전대비
MP3 중학영어듣기
24회 모의고사 2학년

MOTHERTONGUE
마더텅출판사
since 1999.4.1.

발행 17차 개정판 3쇄(2026년 1월 16일)

Chief Editorial Director 서은숙 **Editorial Directors** 이혜빈, 최민정, 최은조, 박상우, 신준기, 김현수, 이윤정, 강수민, 김다영

English Editors Christopher Swafford, Jordan Sanders **책임 원고 검수** 서은숙 **감수** 강산(EBSi 수능영어 강사)

Writers 김경미, 박선주, 신재진, 유예슬, 박상우, 최은조, 김다영, 이용진, 장정문, 박헌준, 신주희, 이천우, 최동렬, 김선혜, 이장원, 김두리, 김유한, 김창범, 노영선, 민희성, 박근혜, 박재민, 손은진, 이찬희, 이상미, 조아라, 허혜경, 손필헌, 호현, 박희나, 정수지, 신은경, 김지야, 남현정, 박석완, 유현주, 김현지, 조승희, 박현정, 김현정, 탁나희, 안명은, 이수안, Steve McLeod, Arvin Adams, Janine Davis, Iris James, Lorelei Rivers, Tristan Hughes, Liz Stewart

단어 및 해석 집필 정하은, 김현수, 이은영, 박상우, 선대훈, 황희진, 이정현, 김택

원어민 감수 Kathy O'Handley

Audio 녹음 김지야, 이영재, 백찬솔, 손정은, 이승아, 이승민 **Audio 편집** 와이알미디어, Netiline, 이형구

Audio 감수 신소미, 이미경, 차선화, 김송이, 김현수, 이은영, 선대훈, 변선영, 신의진, 박새미, 신재진, 한기범, 장지현, 허은혜, 황혜진, 손정은, 이혜경, 김수정, 김주현, 조재윤, 이상미, 백경빈, 장시은, 정다혜, 문은아, 이슬기, 이한주, 신진실, 유윤정

Voice Actors 임승미, April Lynn, Laura-Leigh, Margaret Chung, Tony Ruse, Peter Bint, Monique Dami Lee, Janet Lee, Shane Hahm, Josh Smith, Anna Sue, 이지나, Alexander Jensen, Josh Schwartzy

교정 이은영, 정하은, 이혜빈, 최민정, 신재진, 박상우, 신소미, 신준기, 조수성, 최은조, 정은주, 유지원, 차선화, 윤숙경, 김효진, 김하나, 김단, 장정문, 임홍일, 이영재, 임하람, 장지현, 김현, 하은옥, 김주현, 선대훈, 이승민, 신영은, 최소영, 오정훈, 성은혜, 홍성경, 남현정, 양희송, 정새로나, 이한주, 신진실, 정현희, 신순화, 장신혜, 변선영, 이윤정, 박혜미

표지디자인 김연실 **내지디자인** 김연실, 양은선, 양정혜 **인디자인편집** 고연화, 최송실, 양은선, 정은영, 박경아

Illustrators 정제욱, 이혜승, 박현주, 이은경, 이지은, 박우선, 양은선

제작 이주영 **발행인** 문숙영 **발행처** ㈜ 마더텅 (Mother Tongue Co., Ltd.)

주소 서울시 금천구 가마산로 96 708호 **팩스** 02-3142-9126 **홈페이지** www.toptutor.co.kr

등록번호 제1-2423호 (1999년 1월 8일)

마더텅 교재를 풀면서 궁금한 점이 생기셨나요?

교재 관련 내용 문의나 오류신고 사항이 있으면 아래 문의처로 보내 주세요!
문의하신 내용에 대해 성심성의껏 답변해 드리겠습니다.

또한 교재의 **내용 오류** 또는 **오·탈자, 그 외 수정이 필요한 사항**에 대해 가장 먼저 신고해 주신 분께는 감사의 마음을 담아 네이버페이 포인트 1천 원 을 보내 드립니다!

＊기한: 2026년 12월 31일 ＊오류신고 이벤트는 당사 사정에 따라 조기 종료될 수 있습니다. ＊홈페이지에 게시된 정오표 기준으로 최초 신고된 오류에 한하여 상품권을 보내 드립니다.

● **카카오톡** mothertongue @ **이메일** mothert1004@toptutor.co.kr ⌂ **홈페이지** www.toptutor.co.kr □ **교재Q&A게시판**

🎧 **고객센터 전화** 1661-1064(07:00~22:00) ✉ **문자** 010-6640-1064(문자수신전용)

 ## 📱》 모바일로 교재 MP3 재생 방법 마더텅의 교재 MP3는 모바일 스트리밍/다운로드를 지원합니다.

1 아래의 QR 코드 접속

2 스타플레이어 어플 설치

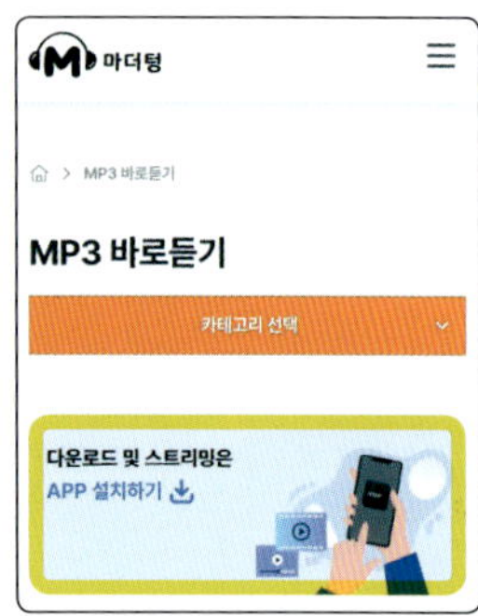

▶▶ SKIP (특정 부분을 건너 뛰어 뒤로 가거나 앞으로 다시 가서 듣고 싶은 경우)

1

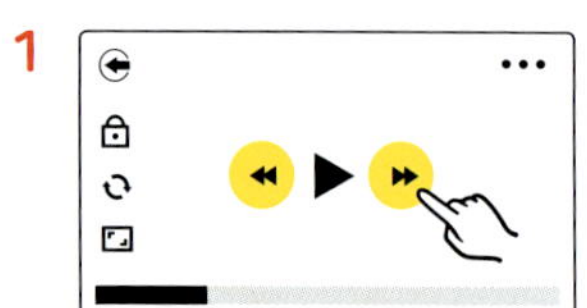

재생 버튼 양쪽의 화살표를 누르면 앞으로 가거나 뒤로 갈 수 있습니다.

2

우측 상단의 점 세 개 버튼을 누르면 REW/FF시간 설정 (안드로이드) 건너 뛰기 설정 (iOS) 가능

구간반복 (특정 구간을 반복 재생하고 싶은 경우)

1. 좌측 또는 우측 하단 구간반복 아이콘 누르면 빨간 선 활성화
2. 선의 양쪽 끝점을 이동하여 원하는 반복재생 구간 설정 가능

마더텅 학습 교재 이벤트에 참여해 주세요. 참여해 주신 분께 선물을 드립니다.

이벤트 1 1분 간단 교재 사용 후기 이벤트

마더텅은 고객님의 소중한 의견을 반영하여 보다 좋은 책을 만들고자 합니다.
교재 구매 후, <교재 사용 후기 이벤트>에 참여해 주신 모든 분께는 감사의 마음을 담아
네이버페이 포인트 1천 원 을 보내 드립니다. 지금 바로 QR 코드를 스캔해 소중한 의견을 보내 주세요!

이벤트 2 중학영어듣기 인증샷 이벤트

SNS에 <중학영어듣기> 인증샷을 올려 주시면 참여해 주신 모든 분께 감사의 마음을 담아
네이버페이 포인트 2천 원 을 보내 드립니다. 지금 바로 QR 코드를 스캔해 작성한 게시물의 URL을 입력해 주세요!

필수 태그 #마더텅 #중학영어듣기

이벤트 3 마더텅 우편 이벤트

본 교재의 24회 고난도 모의고사 페이지를 오려서 마더텅으로 보내 주세요!
추첨을 통해 소정의 상품을 보내 드립니다.

참여 방법 24회 고난도 모의고사(p.368~371) 풀이 및 채점 완료
→ 해당 페이지를 모두 오려서 마더텅에 발송(우편, 택배 등) → QR 코드를 스캔하고 발송 인증

주소 (08501) 서울특별시 금천구 가마산로 96, 대륭테크노타운 8차 708호, 마더텅 이벤트 담당자 앞 / 010-6640-1064

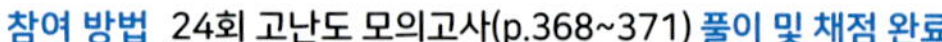

※ 이벤트 기간: 2026년 12월 31일까지 (•해당 이벤트는 당사 사정에 따라 조기 종료될 수 있습니다.) ※ 자세한 사항은 해당 QR 코드를 스캔하거나 홈페이지 이벤트 공지 글을 참고해 주세요. ※ 당사 사정에 따라 이벤트의 내용이나 상품이 변경될 수 있으며 변경 시 홈페이지에 공지합니다. ※ 만 14세 미만은 부모님께서 신청해 주셔야 합니다. ※ 상품은 이벤트 참여일로부터 4~5일(영업일 기준) 내에 발송됩니다. (단, 이벤트 3은 예외) ※ 동일 교재로 세 가지 이벤트 모두 참여 가능합니다. (단, 같은 이벤트 중복 참여는 불가합니다.)

2026 17차 개정판

마더텅 100% 실전대비 MP3 중학 영어듣기 24회 모의고사 2학년

정답과 해석

MOTHERTONGUE
마더텅출판사
since 1999.4.1.

학습계획표 24회 완성

✔ 100% 실전대비 MP3 중학영어듣기 24회 모의고사를 100% 활용할 수 있도록 도와주는 학습계획표입니다. 계획표를 활용하여 학습 일정을 계획하고
자신의 성적을 체크해 보세요. 스스로 학습 현황을 체크하면서 공부하는 습관은 문제집을 끝까지 푸는 데 도움을 줍니다.

✔ 계획은 도중에 틀어질 수 있습니다. 하지만 계획을 세우고 지키는 과정은 그 자체로 효율적인 학습에 큰 도움이 됩니다.
학습 중 계획이 변경될 경우에 대비해 마더텅 홈페이지에서 학습계획표 PDF 파일을 제공하고 있습니다.

회	학습날짜	문항수	학습결과		딕테이션 맞은 갯수
1회		20	맞음	개	
2회		20	맞음	개	
3회		20	맞음	개	
4회		20	맞음	개	
5회		20	맞음	개	
6회		20	맞음	개	
7회		20	맞음	개	
8회		20	맞음	개	
9회		20	맞음	개	
10회		20	맞음	개	
11회		20	맞음	개	
12회		20	맞음	개	
13회		20	맞음	개	
14회		20	맞음	개	
15회		20	맞음	개	
16회		20	맞음	개	
17회		20	맞음	개	
18회		20	맞음	개	
19회		20	맞음	개	
20회		20	맞음	개	
21회		20	맞음	개	
22회		20	맞음	개	
23회		20	맞음	개	
24회		20	맞음	개	

Listening Test
영어듣기 모의고사 **01**회

|정답|

01 ④	02 ③	03 ②	04 ②	05 ②
06 ①	07 ④	08 ⑤	09 ⑤	10 ③
11 ①	12 ④	13 ③	14 ③	15 ②
16 ③	17 ③	18 ③	19 ②	20 ③

01   날씨파악-그림   ▶정답 ④

들·기·대·본

W: Hello, swimmers. This is the beach weather report. It will be sunny at Daecheon Beach today. You can enjoy a clear sky while you swim. At Sokcho Beach, there will be strong winds. High waves are forecasted, so I advise you not to swim at Sokcho Beach today. Heavy rain is expected at Haeundae Beach, so it's not a good day to swim there, either.

우·리·말·해·석

여: 안녕하세요, 수영하러 가시는 여러분. 해변 날씨 예보입니다. 오늘 대천 해변은 맑겠습니다. 수영하는 동안 맑은 하늘을 즐기실 수 있습니다. 속초 해변에는 강한 바람이 불겠습니다. 높은 파도가 예상되므로, 오늘은 속초 해변에서 수영하지 않으시길 권합니다. 해운대 해변에는 폭우가 예상되므로, 그곳 역시 수영하기에 좋은 날은 아닙니다.

단·어·및·표·현

forecast[fɔ́ːrkæst] ⑧ 예상하다, 예보하다
advise[ədváiz] ⑧ 권하다, 조언하다
expect[ikspékt] ⑧ 예상하다, 기대하다

02   그림정보파악   ▶정답 ③

들·기·대·본

W: Jimmy, come here and pick out your rain boots on the screen.
M: Sure, Mom.
W: Do you want boots with handles? The ones with handles are easy to get on and off.
M: Well, I don't want handles on my boots.
W: Okay. How do you like the ones with pointy dinosaur spikes?
M: I love the spikes. They look so cool!
W: Great. Do you want the ones with dinosaurs or just plain ones?
M: I'll go with the plain ones, please.
W: Okay. I'll order those for you.

우·리·말·해·석

여: Jimmy, 이리 와서 화면에 있는 네 장화를 골라보렴.
남: 네, 엄마.
여: 너는 손잡이가 달린 장화를 원하니? 손잡이가 있는 것들이 신고 벗기 편해.
남: 음, 저는 제 장화에 손잡이가 있는 것을 원하지 않아요.
여: 그래. 뾰족한 공룡 돌기가 달린 것들은 어때?
남: 전 돌기가 너무 좋아요. 그것들은 엄청 멋져 보여요!
여: 좋아. 너는 공룡이 있는 것들을 원하니 아니면 그냥 무늬 없는 것들을 원하니?
남: 전 무늬 없는 걸로 할게요.

여: 알겠어. 내가 널 위해 그것들을 주문할게.

단·어·및·표·현

pick out ~을 고르다, 선택하다
get on ~을 신다, 착용하다
get off ~을 벗다
pointy[pɔ́inti] ⑱ 뾰족한
dinosaur spike 공룡(등 지느러미에 솟은) 돌기

03   심정추론   ▶정답 ②

들·기·대·본

W: Kevin, I'm in trouble.
M: What do you mean?
W: I was called to the principal's office, and I don't know why!
M: Well, it could be about something good.
W: How could it be? The principal wants to talk with a student!
M: Relax, Amanda. You don't need to worry ahead of time.
W: What should I do? I have to go now.
M: Calm down. I'll wait here for you until you come back.

우·리·말·해·석

여: Kevin, 나 큰일 났어.
남: 무슨 일이야?
여: 나를 교장실에서 불렀는데 이유를 모르겠어!
남: 음, 그것은 무언가 좋은 것에 대한 것일 수도 있잖아.
여: 그럴 리가 있겠어? 교장선생님이 학생과 얘기하고 싶어 한다고!
남: 진정해, Amanda. 너는 미리 걱정할 필요 없어.
여: 내가 어떻게 해야 하지? 나는 지금 가야 해.
남: 진정해. 네가 돌아올 때까지 내가 여기서 너를 기다릴게.

단·어·및·표·현

be in trouble 큰일 나다, 곤경에 처하다
principal[prínsəpəl] ⑱ 교장, 학장, 총장
ahead of time 미리, 예정보다 일찍

04   한일파악   ▶정답 ②

들·기·대·본

W: Hi, Eric. How was your weekend?
M: I just stayed home.
W: Well, the weather wasn't very good.
M: Yeah, I wanted to go cycling, but it snowed.
W: I'm sorry to hear that.
M: It's okay. I cleaned my bike, instead.
W: Nice. Do you like riding your bike?
M: Yes. I ride for hours when the weather is good.

우·리·말·해·석

여: 안녕, Eric. 네 주말은 어땠어?
남: 나는 그냥 집에 있었어.
여: 글쎄, 날씨가 그리 좋지 않았어.
남: 맞아, 난 사이클링을 하러 가고 싶었는데 눈이 왔어.
여: 안됐다.
남: 괜찮아. 대신에 나는 자전거를 청소했어.
여: 잘했어. 너는 네 자전거 타는 것을 좋아해?
남: 응. 난 날씨가 좋을 때 몇 시간 동안 (자전거를) 타.

단·어·및·표·현

cycling[sáikliŋ] ⑱ 사이클링, 자전거 타기
instead[instéd] ⑨ 대신에
for hours 몇 시간 동안

05 대화장소추론 ▶정답 ②

듣·기·대·본

M: May I help you?
W: Yes, my watch isn't working. It's not ticking.
M: Let me have a look. (*Pause*) There appears to be a problem with the battery.
W: Can you fix it?
M: Yes, it just needs a new battery.
W: Okay. How long will that take?
M: It should only take about 5 minutes. I'll have it ready for you shortly.

우·리·말·해·석

남: 도와드릴까요?
여: 네, 제 손목시계가 작동하지 않아요. 똑딱거리지 않아요.
남: 제가 한번 볼게요. (잠시 후) 건전지에 문제가 있는 것 같아요.
여: 당신이 그것을 고칠 수 있나요?
남: 네, 그저 새로운 건전지가 필요할 뿐이에요.
여: 알겠어요. 그건 얼마나 걸릴까요?
남: 5분 정도만 걸릴 거예요. 제가 그것을 당신을 위해 곧 준비해드릴게요.

단·어·및·표·현

work [wəːrk] 동 작동하다
tick [tik] 동 똑딱[째깍]거리다
appear [əpíər] 동 ~인 것 같다
about [əbáut] 부 ~정도, 약, ~쯤
shortly [ʃɔ́ːrtli] 부 곧

06 마지막말의도파악 ▶정답 ①

듣·기·대·본

M: What are you doing, Fatima?
W: I'm practicing calligraphy.
M: What's calligraphy?
W: It's the visual art of handwriting. See what I just wrote?
M: It's beautiful. It looks like the letters are dancing.
W: I know! I need more practice, but I really like this design.
M: Would you write my name down here in the same design?

우·리·말·해·석

남: 너 뭐 하고 있니, Fatima?
여: 난 서예를 연습하고 있어.
남: 서예가 뭐야?
여: 그건 손글씨의 시각 예술이야. 내가 방금 쓴 거 보여?
남: 아름다워. 글자들이 춤추고 있는 것처럼 보여.
여: 맞아! 난 더 많은 연습이 필요하지만, 이 디자인이 정말 마음에 들어.
남: 같은 디자인으로 내 이름을 여기에 적어줄 수 있어?

단·어·및·표·현

practice [præktis] 동 연습하다 명 연습
calligraphy [kəlígrəfi] 명 서예
visual art 시각 예술
handwriting [hændràitiŋ] 명 손글씨, (개인의) 필적
letter [létər] 명 글자, 문자
write ~ down ~을 적다

07 특정정보파악 ▶정답 ④

듣·기·대·본

M: Emma, are you still helping with the science booth for the school festival?
W: Yes! I'm preparing the "make-your-own-volcano"

activity.
M: Sounds fun! Do you have all the materials ready?
W: Almost. But we still need some paper cups to hold the baking soda.
M: Oh, I have some extra paper cups at home.
W: Great. Do you think you could bring them tomorrow?
M: Sure! No problem.

우·리·말·해·석

남: Emma, 너는 여전히 학교 축제를 위한 과학 부스를 돕고 있니?
여: 응! 나는 '나만의 화산 만들기' 활동을 준비하고 있어.
남: 재미있겠다! 재료들은 모두 다 준비했어?
여: 거의 다 했어. 그런데 베이킹소다를 담을 종이컵이 아직 좀 더 필요해.
남: 아, 우리 집에 여분의 종이컵이 좀 있어.
여: 잘 됐다. 너는 내일 그걸 가져올 수 있니?
남: 물론이지! 문제없어.

단·어·및·표·현

still [stil] 부 여전히, 아직(도)
prepare [pripέər] 동 준비하다
material [mətíəriəl] 명 재료
hold [hould] 동 담다, 수용하다
extra [ékstrə] 형 여분의, 추가의

08 할일파악(대화직후) ▶정답 ⑤

듣·기·대·본

W: Eric, it is the last evening of our package tour.
M: Yes. We have some free time. Is there anything you want to do?
W: How about going to a local market? It would be fun.
M: It could be dangerous for us to go there on our own.
W: You're right.
M: I saw some beautiful fountains in the hotel lobby. Let's take some pictures!
W: Great. Do you have your phone with you?
M: Of course. Let's go now.

우·리·말·해·석

여: Eric, 우리 패키지 여행의 마지막 저녁이야.
남: 응. 우리에겐 자유 시간이 좀 있어. 너는 하고 싶은 것이 있니?
여: 현지 시장을 가보는 건 어때? 재밌을 거야.
남: 우리끼리 단독으로 그곳에 가는 것은 위험할 수 있어.
여: 맞아.
남: 나는 호텔 로비에서 어떤 아름다운 분수를 봤어. 우리 사진들을 좀 찍자!
여: 좋아. 너는 (휴대) 전화를 가지고 있어?
남: 물론이지. 지금 가자.

단·어·및·표·현

last [læst] 형 마지막의
package tour 패키지 여행
local market 현지 시장
on one's own 단독으로, 혼자서
fountain [fáuntən] 명 분수

09 대화미언급 ▶정답 ⑤

듣·기·대·본

W: Kevin, did you hear about the Meeting with the Webtoon Artist?
M: Yes! It's this Friday, right? My favorite artist, Jayoon Kim, will be there.

W: That's awesome. Where is it being held?
M: At the main branch of BookNBook, the big bookstore downtown.
W: Will there be a Q&A session with the artist?
M: Yes, at the end of the event. We can even ask him questions directly.
W: Awesome! I'll get my questions ready.

우·리·말·해·석

여: Kevin, 너는 웹툰 작가와의 만남에 대해 들었어?
남: 응! 이번 금요일이지, 맞지? 내가 제일 좋아하는 작가, Jayoon Kim이 거기 올 거야.
여: 멋지다. 그건 어디에서 열려?
남: 시내에 있는 큰 서점인 BookNBook의 본점에서.
여: 작가와의 질의응답 시간도 있을까?
남: 응, 행사 마지막에. 우리는 그한테 직접 질문도 할 수 있어.
여: 대박! 나는 내 질문들을 미리 준비할 거야.

단·어·및·표·현

branch [bræntʃ] 몡 지점, 지사
session [séʃən] 몡 (특정한 활동을 위한) 시간[기간]

10 담화화제추론 ▶정답 ③

듣·기·대·본

M: Hello, everyone. This is Mr. Kim, the teacher in charge of the library club. I'd like to inform you about the required reading list for this semester. All students are expected to read at least three books from the list by the end of June. The list includes a variety of Korean and international books. You can find it posted on the library bulletin board and on the school website. If you have any questions, feel free to stop by the library after school.

우·리·말·해·석

남: 안녕하세요, 여러분. 저는 독서 동아리를 담당하고 있는 교사 김 선생님입니다. 저는 이번 학기의 필독 도서 목록에 대해 알려드리려고 합니다. 모든 학생은 6월 말까지 이 목록에 있는 책 중에서 최소 세 권을 읽을 것이 요구됩니다(읽어야 합니다). 이 목록에는 다양한 한국 도서와 외국 도서가 포함되어 있습니다. 여러분은 이 목록을 도서관 게시판과 학교 홈페이지에서 확인하실 수 있습니다. 궁금한 점이 있으시면 방과 후에 도서관에 들러 주세요.

단·어·및·표·현

in charge of ~을 담당하다, 맡다
required [rikwáiərd] 몡 필수의
semester [siméstər] 몡 학기
expect [ikspékt] 동 (~할 것을) 요구하다, 기대하다
include [inklúːd] 동 포함하다
a variety of 다양한
international [ìntərnǽʃənəl] 몡 국제의, 국제적인
bulletin board 게시판
stop by (~에) 잠시 들르다

11 대화내용불일치 ▶정답 ④

듣·기·대·본

M: Kate, will you join our English book club?
W: Yes, I'd love to. Do you also read English poems?
M: Sure. Sometimes we read comic books, too.
W: Sounds fun!
M: Yeah. And our English teacher, Ms. Kim leads the discussion.

W: That's nice. By the way, how many times a week do you meet?
M: Once a week, every Friday. Why don't you come this Friday?
W: Okay. Where should I go?
M: Come to the school Media Center. We always meet there.

우·리·말·해·석

남: Kate, 너 우리 영어 독서 동아리에 가입할래?
여: 그래, 좋아. 너희 영어 시도 읽니?
남: 그럼. 우리는 때때로 만화책도 읽어.
여: 재미있겠다!
남: 응. 그리고 우리 영어 선생님인 김 선생님께서 토론을 이끌어주셔.
여: 그거 좋다. 그런데, 너희 일주일에 몇 번 만나니?
남: 일주일에 한 번, 매주 금요일에 만나. 이번 주 금요일에 오는 게 어때?
여: 알았어. 어디로 가야 해?
남: 학교 미디어 센터로 와. 우리는 항상 거기서 만나.

단·어·및·표·현

join [dʒɔin] 동 가입하다
poem [póuəm] 몡 시
lead [liːd] 동 이끌다
discussion [diskʌ́ʃən] 몡 토론, 논의

12 외출목적파악 ▶정답 ④

듣·기·대·본

M: Mom, I'm going out for a bit.
W: Where are you going, David? Are you going to the library?
M: No, I've finished my homework already.
W: Then why are you going out?
M: I'm just a little hungry. I want to get some snacks from the store.
W: Okay. Be careful and don't buy too many sweets!
M: Don't worry. I'll be back soon.

우·리·말·해·석

남: 엄마, 저 잠깐 밖에 나갔다 올게요.
여: 어디 가는데, David? 너 도서관에 가는 거니?
남: 아뇨, 저는 이미 숙제를 끝냈어요.
여: 그럼 왜 나가는데?
남: 저는 그냥 조금 배가 고파서요. 저는 가게에 가서 간식 좀 사고 싶어요.
여: 그래. 조심하고 단 것 너무 많이 사지 마!
남: 걱정 마세요. 저 금방 돌아올게요.

단·어·및·표·현

sweet [swiːt] 몡 단 것, 과자

13 수치파악 ▶정답 ③

듣·기·대·본

W: We finally get to go to Panda World tomorrow! I'm so excited.
M: Me, too! What time does Panda World open?
W: It opens at 9:00 a.m. and closes at 12:00 p.m.
M: Why don't we meet at 11:00 a.m.?
W: You can feed the pandas at 11:00 a.m. Let's get there before then.
M: How about we meet at the bus stop at 10:00 a.m., instead?
W: Sounds perfect. We can catch the shuttle bus to get there.

우·리·말·해·석
여: 우리 드디어 내일 판다 월드에 갈 수 있게 됐어! 나 너무 신나.
남: 나도! 판다 월드는 몇 시에 문을 열지?
여: 오전 9시에 열고, 오후 12시에 닫아.
남: 우리 오전 11시에 만나는 게 어때?
여: 오전 11시에 판다에게 먹이를 줄 수 있어. 우리 그 전에 거기에 도착하
   도록 하자.
남: 대신, 우리 오전 10시에 버스 정류장에서 만나는 건 어때?
여: 완벽하다. 우리 그곳(판다 월드)으로 가는 셔틀 버스를 탈 수 있어.

단·어·및·표·현
feed [fiːd] 통 먹이를 주다
instead [instéd] 튀 대신에
catch [kætʃ] 통 (버스·기차 등을 시간 맞춰) 타다

14 대화자관계추론 ▶ 정답 ②
듣·기·대·본
(Telephone rings.)
M: Hello. This is Wonder Tours. How may I help you?
W: Hi. I'd like to go to London this weekend.
M: OK. Would you like to go by train?
W: Yes. And I'd like a guided bus tour.
M: Sure. How about accommodation? We have some
   good offers on hotels.
W: I'll stay in London for two nights. Could you tell me what
   the prices are?
M: Sure. Could you hold on a second?
W: No problem.
우·리·말·해·석
(전화벨이 울린다.)
남: 여보세요. Wonder Tours입니다. 무엇을 도와드릴까요?
여: 안녕하세요. 이번 주말에 런던에 가고 싶은데요.
남: 알겠습니다. 열차로 가고 싶으신가요?
여: 네. 그리고 가이드 버스 투어도 하고 싶어요.
남: 물론이죠. 숙소는 어떻게 하실 건가요? 저희가 좋은 호텔 할인도 제공
   하고 있어요.
여: 런던에서 2박을 할 예정인데요. 가격이 얼마인지 알려주실 수 있나요?
남: 당연하죠. 잠시만 기다려주실래요?
여: 그럼요.
단·어·및·표·현
guided bus tour 가이드 버스 투어
offer [ɔ́(ː)fər] 명 (짧은 기간 동안의) 할인, 특가

15 부탁(요청)한일파악 ▶ 정답 ②
듣·기·대·본
W: What's with the badminton racket, Keith?
M: Oh, Tim wants to borrow it from me. I'm meeting him at
   the park in ten minutes.
W: You're not playing with him?
M: No, I'll just hand this over and come back.
W: Could you buy me some onions on your way back?
M: Sure, Mom. What are you making?
W: Just some soup. Thank you, son.
우·리·말·해·석
여: 배드민턴 채는 왜 들고 있는 거야, Keith?
남: 아, Tim이 제게서 그것을 빌리고 싶어 해요. 십 분 후에 공원에서 그를
   만날 거예요.
여: 그와 함께 치는 건 아니고?
남: 네, 저는 그냥 이걸 건네주고 돌아올 거예요.

여: 돌아오는 길에 양파를 좀 사다 주겠니?
남: 물론이죠. 엄마. 무엇을 만드세요?
여: 그냥 수프 조금. 고맙다. 아들아.
단·어·및·표·현
on one's way back 돌아오는 길에

16 이유파악 ▶ 정답 ③
듣·기·대·본
W: Bless you! Are you okay, Noah?
M: Yes, thanks. I'm just sneezing a lot this morning.
W: Oh no, did you catch a cold?
M: No, I don't think so. I feel fine except for the sneezing.
W: Then maybe it's an allergy.
M: Yeah, I have a pollen allergy, and the trees near my
   house are full of flowers now.
W: I see. You should take your allergy medicine.
M: I will. I forgot to take it today.
우·리·말·해·석
여: 몸 조심해! 너 괜찮니, Noah?
남: 응, 고마워. 나는 오늘 아침에 재채기를 많이 하고 있어.
여: 어머, 너 감기 걸린 거니?
남: 아니, 그런 것 같진 않아. 나는 재채기하는 것 제외하고는 괜찮아.
여: 그럼 그건 아마 알레르기일지도 몰라.
남: 응. 나는 꽃가루 알레르기가 있는데 우리 집 근처에 있는 나무들에 지
   금 꽃이 가득 피었어.
여: 그렇구나. 너는 네 알레르기 약을 먹어야 해.
남: 그러려고. 나는 오늘 그것을 먹는 걸 깜빡했어.

단·어·및·표·현
bless you (재채기한 사람에게) 몸 조심하세요
sneeze [sniːz] 통 재채기하다
except for ~을 제외하고
pollen [pálən] 명 꽃가루, 화분

17 그림상황에적절한대화찾기 ▶ 정답 ③
듣·기·대·본
① M: We finally made it to the top!
   W: Yeah, the view is amazing up here!
② M: What are you working on?
   W: I'm just doing some push-ups.
③ M: Try stepping on that yellow rock with your left foot.
   W: Okay, I'll give it a try.
④ M: The drone show is really fantastic!
   W: Yeah, I'm so glad we came!
⑤ M: Why are you wearing a helmet?
   W: I'm going for a bike ride.
우·리·말·해·석
① 남: 우리가 드디어 정상에 도착했어!
   여: 그래, 여기 위에서 보이는 경치가 정말 멋지다!
② 남: 너 뭐 하고 있어?
   여: 나는 그냥 팔굽혀펴기를 좀 하고 있어.
③ 남: 왼발로 저 노란 돌을 밟으려고 해봐.
   여: 알겠어, 시도해 볼게.
④ 남: 이 드론 쇼 정말 환상적이다!
   여: 응, 우리가 (여기) 왔다는 게 정말 기뻐!
⑤ 남: 너는 왜 헬멧을 쓰고 있어?
   여: 나는 자전거를 타러 갈 거야.
단·어·및·표·현
make it 해내다

step on ~을 밟다
give it a try 시도해 보다

18 담화미언급　▶정답 ③

듣·기·대·본
M: Hello, students! This Friday, July 12 is Sports Day, one of our biggest events of the year. This year, we will hold different activities such as a marathon, swimming contest, and soccer game. Lunch will be served, and snacks will also be provided. Be sure to wear comfortable clothes for the outdoor activities.

우·리·말·해·석
남: 안녕하세요, 학생 여러분! 이번 금요일, 7월 12일은 스포츠의 날로, 한 해의 가장 큰 행사들 중 하나입니다. 올해에는, 우리는 마라톤, 수영 대회, 그리고 축구 경기 같은 다른 활동들을 개최할 것입니다. 점심이 제공될 것이고, 간식 또한 제공될 것입니다. 꼭 야외 활동을 위한 편안한 옷을 입도록 하세요.

단·어·및·표·현
hold [hould] 통 개최하다, 열다
outdoor [áutdɔ̀:r] 형 야외의

19 알맞은응답찾기　▶정답 ②

듣·기·대·본
M: I am starving. Do we have anything to eat?
W: No, I'm afraid we need to go to the grocery store.
M: What about eating out for dinner?
W: That's a good idea. Which restaurant do you want to go to?
M: How about that new sushi restaurant we went to last week?
W: I don't want to go there again.
M: Why? The food was really good.
W: The waiters were not kind at all.

우·리·말·해·석
① 지금은 배고프지 않아.
② 종업원들이 전혀 친절하지 않았어.
③ 밖이 너무 덥기 때문이야.
④ 음악이 아주 좋았지.
⑤ 저녁은 내가 살게.

남: 난 너무 배가 고파. 우리 먹을 것 좀 있어?
여: 아니, 유감이지만 우리는 식료품점에 가야 할 것 같아.
남: 저녁에 외식하는 거 어때?
여: 좋은 생각이야. 어느 식당에 가고 싶니?
남: 지난주에 갔던 그 새로 생긴 초밥 식당은 어때?
여: 난 거기 다시 가고 싶지 않아.
남: 왜? 음식은 엄청 맛있었잖아.
여: 종업원들이 전혀 친절하지 않았어.

단·어·및·표·현
starving [stɑ́:rviŋ] 형 너무 배고픈, 굶주린
eat out 외식하다
not at all 전혀 ~하지 않다 (= never)

20 알맞은응답찾기　▶정답 ③

듣·기·대·본
M: What time do you usually get up in the morning?
W: I get up at 6 o'clock and exercise.
M: Wow! You're very diligent.
W: Oh, it's nothing. It's just one of my habits.
M: What kinds of exercises do you do?
W: I go jogging and swimming. I have been feeling a lot better since I started some exercising in the morning.
M: That sounds good. I'm going to start exercising tomorrow.
W: Would you like to join me?

우·리·말·해·석
① 물론이지. 난 야구하는 걸 좋아해.
② 고마워. 너는?
③ 나랑 같이 할래?
④ 저런, 지루할 것 같은데.
⑤ 난 운동하는 것이 싫어.

남: 아침에 보통 몇 시에 일어나니?
여: 나는 아침 6시에 일어나서 운동을 해.
남: 왜! 너는 정말 부지런하구나.
여: 오, 그건 별거 아냐. 그것은 단지 내 습관 중에 하나야.
남: 어떤 종류의 운동을 하니?
여: 조깅이랑 수영을 해. 아침에 운동을 하기 시작한 이후로 컨디션이 훨씬 많이 좋아졌어.
남: 좋은데. 나도 내일부터 운동 시작할 거야.
여: 나랑 같이 할래?

단·어·및·표·현
exercise [éksərsàiz] 명 운동 통 운동하다
diligent [dílidʒənt] 형 부지런한
a lot 많이

Words & Expressions Review

1. ~을 건네주다	2. 몇 시간 동안	3. 대신에
4. 운동, 운동하다	5. 사이클링, 자전거 타기	6. 야외의
7. 곧, 이내	8. ~을 적다	9. 돌아오는 길에
10. 다양한	11. ~을 고르다, 선택하다	12. 이끌다
13. 분수	14. 숙소, 숙박 시설	15. 교장, 학장, 총장
16. ~인 것 같다	17. 먹이를 주다	18. (기분이) 나아지다
19. 권하다, 조언하다	20. 주말	21. 지점, 지사
22. 편안한	23. 서예	24. 식당
25. 큰일 나다, 곤경에 처하다	26. 여분의, 추가의	27. 국제의, 국제적인
28. 작동하다	29. (버스·기차 등을 시간 맞춰) 타다	30. 잠시 기다리다
31. 해내다	32. 시도해 보다	33. 외식하다
34. (특정한 활동을 위한) 시간[기간]	35. 토론, 논의	36. 마지막의
37. 여전히, 아직(도)	38. 글자, 문자	39. 미리, 예정보다 일찍
40. 꽃가루, 화분	41. 필수의	42. 단 것, 과자
43. 개최하다, 열다	44. 재채기하다	

영어듣기 모의고사 02회

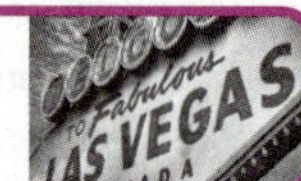

|정답|

01 ⑤	02 ①	03 ①	04 ③	05 ④
06 ⑤	07 ④	08 ①	09 ④	10 ②
11 ③	12 ⑤	13 ③	14 ③	15 ②
16 ⑤	17 ①	18 ④	19 ②	20 ⑤

01 　날씨파악-그림　　　　　　▶정답 ⑤

듣·기·대·본

W: Hi, Travel Buddies! I just arrived in Busan, but the weather is cloudy now. The sky looks gray. The weather report says it will rain this evening, so I'll keep my umbrella ready. Tomorrow will be sunny, so I'm excited to go to the beach. But I heard there will be strong winds the day after tomorrow. Stay safe and enjoy!

우·리·말·해·석

여: 안녕하세요, Travel Buddies(여행 친구들)! 저는 방금 막 부산에 도착했는데, 지금은 날씨가 흐려요. 하늘은 회색으로 보여요(하늘이 회색빛이에요). 일기 예보에 따르면 오늘 저녁에 비가 올 거라 했으니 전 제 우산을 준비해 둘게요. 내일은 맑을 예정이라서 저는 해변에 가는 게 기대돼요. 그런데 모레는 강풍이 불 것이라고 들었어요. 다들 안전하고 즐거운 시간 보내세요!

단·어·및·표·현

buddy[bʌ́di] ⑲ 친구
arrive[əráiv] ⑧ 도착하다
weather report 일기 예보
keep ~ ready ~을 준비해 두다
the day after tomorrow 모레

02 　그림정보파악　　　　　　▶정답 ①

듣·기·대·본

W: Hi, how may I help you?
M: I'm looking for a houseplant.
W: Then, how about one of these? They're quite popular.
M: I love the plant with star-shaped leaves. I'll take one of them.
W: Would you like your plant in a square pot or a round pot?
M: I'd like a round pot.
W: Okay!

우·리·말·해·석

여: 안녕하세요, 어떻게 도와드릴까요?
남: 저는 실내용 화초를 찾고 있어요.
여: 그렇다면, 이것들 중 하나는 어떠세요? 그것들은 꽤 인기 있어요.
남: 저는 별 모양 잎을 가진 저 식물이 마음에 들어요. 저는 저것들 중 하나를 살게요.
여: 당신의 식물을 네모난 화분에 넣어드릴까요, 아니면 동그란 화분에 넣어드릴까요?
남: 저는 동그란 화분을 원해요.
여: 알겠습니다!

단·어·및·표·현

quite[kwait] ⑨ 꽤, 상당히
popular[pɑ́pjələr] ⑲ 인기 있는

pot[pɑt] ⑲ 화분, 병, 항아리

03 　심정추론　　　　　　▶정답 ①

듣·기·대·본

W: Mike, did you hear the news?
M: What news?
W: Jay's Sandwich Shop is closing.
M: Oh, no! Why? Their sandwiches are the best in town!
W: The owner's parents are ill. So, he is leaving town to look after them.
M: I'm sorry to hear that. I feel sorry for myself, too.
W: You really like the place, don't you?
M: Yeah, it's terrible news.

우·리·말·해·석

① 슬픈　　② 신남　　③ 겁이 난　　④ 지루한　　⑤ 수줍은

여: Mike, 너 그 소식 들었어?
남: 무슨 소식?
여: Jay's Sandwich Shop이 문을 닫는대.
남: 아, 이런! 왜? 그들의 샌드위치는 도시에서 최고인데!
여: (가게) 주인의 부모님께서 편찮으시대. 그래서, 그는 그들을 보살피기 위해서 도시를 떠난대.
남: 그렇다니 유감이야. 나는 나 자신도 안됐다고 생각해.
여: 너 그곳을 정말 좋아하는구나, 그렇지 않아?
남: 맞아, 끔찍한 소식이야.

단·어·및·표·현

ill[il] ⑲ 아픈, 병든
look after ~를 보살펴 주다
feel sorry for ~ ~를 안됐다고 생각하다, 애처롭게 여기다
terrible[térəbl] ⑲ 끔찍한, 무서운

04 　한일파악　　　　　　▶정답 ③

듣·기·대·본

M: Hey, what are you going to do this weekend?
W: I'm going to Sok-cho resort with my family.
M: That's nice! I went there last month.
W: Really? Did you go trekking? I've heard there's a famous trekking course there.
M: There is, but I went fishing instead. It was really fun.
W: I think I should do that, too.

우·리·말·해·석

남: 야, 이번 주말에 뭐 할 거야?
여: 가족들과 속초 리조트에 갈 거야.
남: 멋지다! 나는 지난달에 거기에 갔어.
여: 정말? 트레킹 하러 갔어? 거기에 유명한 트레킹 코스가 있다고 들었어.
남: 있어, 하지만 나는 대신에 낚시하러 갔어. 정말 재미있었어.
여: 나도 그렇게 해야겠다.

단·어·및·표·현

fun[fʌn] ⑲ 재미있는

05 　대화장소추론　　　　　　▶정답 ④

듣·기·대·본

W: Hi. I booked this ticket online, but I want to change it. Should I do that online?
M: You can change it here, too.
W: Excellent! Could you change it for a later train, please?
M: Let me see. You are going to Yeosu, right?
W: Yes. And it's for today.

M: There is another one that departs at 4 p.m. Is that OK?

W: That would be great.

M: Here's your new ticket.

우·리·말·해·석

여: 안녕하세요. 제가 온라인으로 이 티켓을 예약했는데, 변경하고 싶어서
요. 온라인으로 변경을 해야 할까요?

남: 여기에서도 변경하실 수 있어요.

여: 좋네요! 나중에 출발하는 기차로 변경해주실 수 있으세요?

남: 한번 볼게요. 여수로 가시는 거네요, 맞죠?

여: 네. 그리고 오늘 기차예요.

남: 오후 4시에 출발하는 게 하나 있네요. 괜찮으세요?

여: 아주 좋아요.

남: 여기 새 티켓이요.

단·어·및·표·현

book[buk] ⑧ 예약하다

06   마지막말의도파악   ▶ 정답 ⑤

듣·기·대·본

W: You look so gloomy. What's the matter?

M: Oh, it's awful.

W: What is it? Please, tell me.

M: I was cleaning my classroom. And I broke my teacher's
glasses by accident.

W: Oh, that's too bad. You must feel awful.

M: He said it was OK, but I couldn't even look him in the eye.

W: Don't be so depressed. It was just a mistake.

우·리·말·해·석

여: 너 우울해 보인다. 무슨 일이야?

남: 오, 끔찍해.

여: 뭔데? 이야기해봐.

남: 난 교실 청소를 하고 있었어. 그리고 실수로 선생님의 안경을 깨뜨렸어.

여: 오, 정말 안됐구나. 정말 기분 안 좋겠다.

남: 선생님은 괜찮다고 하셨지만, 난 차마 눈도 못 보겠더라고.

여: 너무 낙심하지 마. 그건 단지 실수였잖아.

단·어·및·표·현

gloomy[glúːmi] ⑱ 우울한

by accident 실수로, 우연히

🔊 LISTENING ADVICE

'Don't be so depressed.'에서 'Don't'는 단어가 'nt'로 끝날 때 끝
소리 [t]가 탈락되거나 약하게 발음되기 때문에 [도운]으로 들립니다.
또한 'ed'로 끝나는 동사의 과거형이나 과거분사형은 'ed' 앞이 'b, g,
z, j, l, r, m, n, w'이면 [d]로, 'p, k, s, f, ch, sh, ks'이면 [t]로 't, d'
이면 [id]로 발음되기 때문에 'depressed'는 [디프레스트]라고 발음
됩니다.

---

07   특정정보파악   ▶ 정답 ④

듣·기·대·본

M: Hello, ma'am. Are you looking for some fruit?

W: Yes. I'd love to buy some grapes for my family.

M: Unfortunately, grapes are out of stock at the moment.

W: Hmm, then what would you recommend?

M: How about apples or peaches? The peaches are
especially sweet these days.

W: Well, my daughter is allergic to peaches. Are these
watermelons sweet?

M: Sure! Would you like one of these?

W: Yes, please. My kids will love it.

우·리·말·해·석

남: 안녕하세요, 부인. 과일을 찾고 계세요?

여: 네. 가족들을 위해 포도를 좀 사고 싶은데요.

남: 안타깝게도, 포도는 지금 품절이에요.

여: 흠, 그러면 어떤 걸 추천해주시겠어요?

남: 사과나 복숭아는 어떠세요? 특히 복숭아가 요즘 아주 달아요.

여: 글쎄요, 제 딸이 복숭아에 알레르기가 있어요. 이 수박들은 단가요?

남: 물론이죠! 이것들 중 하나 하시겠어요?

여: 네, 부탁해요. 아이들이 좋아할 거예요.

단·어·및·표·현

out of stock 품절인

08   할일파악(대화직후)   ▶ 정답 ①

듣·기·대·본

W: Excuse me, sir. You cannot go into the pool without a
bathing cap.

M: Oh, I know, but I forgot to bring mine today. Can I
borrow one here?

W: I'm sorry. But we don't lend any.

M: Then what should I do?

W: You'll have to buy one.

M: Is there a store nearby?

W: There's one right outside the pool.

M: Alright. I'll go buy the bathing cap right now.

우·리·말·해·석

여: 실례합니다, 손님. 수영모 없이 수영장에 들어가실 수 없습니다.

남: 오, 알아요, 하지만 오늘 제가 제 것을 가져오는 것을 잊어버렸어요. 여
기서 하나 빌려도 될까요?

여: 죄송합니다. 하지만 저희는 대여는 하지 않습니다.

남: 그러면 저는 어떻게 해야 하죠?

여: 하나 사셔야 합니다.

남: 근처에 가게가 있나요?

여: 수영장 바로 밖에 하나 있습니다.

남: 알겠어요. 지금 바로 수영모를 사러 갈게요.

단·어·및·표·현

bathing cap 수영모

lend[lend] ⑧ 대여하다, 빌려주다

09   대화미언급   ▶ 정답 ④

듣·기·대·본

W: Steve, I heard you are getting a dance audition. That's
awesome!

M: It's always been my dream.

W: Are you participating in the audition being held at DP
Entertainment's Culture Center?

M: Exactly. It will be held next Wednesday.

W: What are you going to show them?

M: I'll show them a minute-long dance and some of my
special moves.

W: The CEO and some of the DP Entertainment singers will
be there, right?

M: Yes, they will be there as judges. I'm nervous, but I'll do
my best.

우·리·말·해·석

여: Steve, 난 네가 댄스 오디션을 본다고 들었어. 굉장한걸!

남: 그건 항상 내 꿈이었어.

여: 넌 DP 엔터테인먼트의 문화 센터에서 열리는 오디션에 참가하는 거야?

남: 정확해. 그건 다음 주 수요일에 열릴 거야.

여: 너는 그들에게 무엇을 보여줄 거야?

남: 나는 그들에게 1분짜리 춤과 내 특별한 동작들 몇몇을 보여줄 거야.

여: CEO와 DP 엔터테인먼트 가수들 몇몇이 그곳에 있을 거야, 그렇지?

남: 응, 그들은 그곳에 심사위원으로서 있을 거야. 나는 불안하지만, 최선을 다할 거야.

단·어·및·표·현

get an audition 오디션을 보다
participate in ~에 참가하다
hold [hould] ⑧ 열다, 개최하다
move [muːv] ⑲ 동작
judge [dʒʌdʒ] ⑲ 심사위원, 심판
nervous [nə́ːrvəs] ⑱ 불안한
do one's best 최선을 다하다

10 담화화제추론 ▶정답 ②

듣·기·대·본

W: Hi, students. Do you have a passion for coding? Then, our coding workshop is the perfect opportunity for you! In this workshop, you'll learn how to create your own programs and games. No prior experience is necessary — we'll start from the basics. Best of all, it's free to attend, and we have all the resources you need. Come and explore the world of coding with us today!

우·리·말·해·석

여: 학생 여러분, 안녕하세요. 여러분은 코딩에 대한 열정이 있나요? 그렇다면, 우리의 코딩 워크숍은 여러분에게 완벽한 기회입니다! 이 워크숍에서, 여러분은 어떻게 여러분만의 프로그램과 게임을 만드는지 배우게 될 것입니다. 우리는 기초부터 시작할 것이므로 사전 경험은 필요하지 않습니다. 무엇보다도, 그것은 참석하는 데 무료이고, 저희는 여러분이 필요한 모든 자원을 가지고 있습니다. 오늘 와서 저희와 함께 코딩의 세계를 탐험해 보세요!

단·어·및·표·현

passion [pǽʃən] ⑲ 열정
opportunity [àpərtjúːnəti] ⑲ 기회
create [kriéit] ⑧ 만들어 내다, 창조하다
prior [práiər] ⑱ 사전의
best of all 무엇보다도, 특히
attend [əténd] ⑧ 참석하다
explore [iksplɔ́ːr] ⑧ 탐험하다

11 대화내용불일치 ▶정답 ③

듣·기·대·본

M: Hey, Jiyoon. Do you know anything about using the music room?

W: Yes. It's on the third floor, next to the art room.

M: Do we need to sign up first?

W: Yes. You need to fill out a form on the school website.

M: Got it. What instruments are available?

W: There are keyboards, guitars, and even a violin — but no drums.

M: Okay. And how long can we use the room?

W: For up to an hour. Don't forget to put everything back when you're done.

우·리·말·해·석

남: 안녕, 지윤아. 너 음악실 사용하는 것에 대해서 아는 거 있어?

여: 응. 그건 3층에 있고 미술실 옆에 있어.

남: 우리 신청을 먼저 해야 돼?

여: 응. 학교 홈페이지에서 신청서를 작성해야 해.

남: 알겠어. 어떤 악기들을 사용할 수 있어?

여: 건반, 기타, 그리고 바이올린도 있지만 드럼은 없어.

남: 그렇구나. 그리고 우리는 그 방을 얼마나 오래 쓸 수 있어?

여: 최대 한 시간까지. 네가 끝났을 때 모든 것을 제자리에 돌려놓는 것을 잊지 마.

단·어·및·표·현

fill out 작성하다
instrument [ínstrəmənt] ⑲ 악기
available [əvéiləbl] ⑱ 사용할 수 있는
keyboard [kíːbɔ̀ːrd] ⑲ (피아노의) 건반
up to ~까지

12 전화목적파악 ▶정답 ⑤

듣·기·대·본

(Telephone rings.)

M: Hello, City Metro Service. How may I help you?

W: Hi, I think I lost my cellphone on Metro line 2.

M: Would you like to report a lost item?

W: No, I have already done that online.

M: Oh, that's good. What can I do for you, then?

W: Could you check if my phone has turned up?

M: Of course. Just give me your report number.

W: I have it here. Just a second.

우·리·말·해·석

(전화벨이 울린다.)

남: 안녕하세요, 도시철도 서비스입니다. 어떻게 도와드릴까요?

여: 안녕하세요, 저는 2호선에서 제 휴대폰을 잃어버린 것 같아요.

남: 분실물 신고를 하시겠어요?

여: 아뇨, 저는 이미 온라인으로 그것을 했어요.

남: 오, 좋습니다. 그럼, 제가 무엇을 해드릴 수 있을까요?

여: 제 폰이 나타났는지 확인해 주실 수 있나요?

남: 물론이죠. 당신의 신고 번호만 알려주세요.

여: 제가 여기에 그것을 가지고 있어요. 잠시만요.

단·어·및·표·현

report [ripɔ́ːrt] ⑧ 신고하다, 알리다
turn up (잃어버린 물건 등이) 나타나다, 찾게 되다

13 수치계산 ▶정답 ③

듣·기·대·본

M: May I help you?

W: I'd like to buy some grapes. How much are they?

M: Our grapes are on sale, so you can get them today for only $6 per kilo instead of $7.

W: That's great. I'll take two kilos, please.

M: How about melons, ma'am? They only cost $5 each.

W: I love melons! I'll take three.

M: Here you go.

우·리·말·해·석

남: 도와드릴까요?

여: 전 포도를 좀 사고 싶어요. 그것들은 얼마인가요?

남: 포도는 할인 중이라서 오늘은 1킬로에 7달러 대신 고작 6달러에 살 수 있어요.

여: 정말 잘됐네요. 2킬로를 구입하겠습니다.

남: 멜론은 어때요, 부인? 그것들은 개당 겨우 5달러예요.

여: 저는 멜론을 정말 좋아해요! 3개를 사겠어요.

남: 여기 있습니다.

instead of ~ ~ 대신에

14 대화자관계추론　▶ 정답 ③

듣·기·대·본

(Telephone rings.)
W: Hello.
M: Ms. Blake, I'm calling from the G.A. Shop.
W: Oh, hi. Is my coffee maker ready?
M: Not quite yet. I fixed the heater, but I found another problem.
W: What is it?
M: The water tank is leaking. This will take another day to fix. It'll cost more, too.
W: Well, that's OK. Can I pick it up tomorrow, then?
M: Yes. I'll call you when it's ready.

우·리·말·해·석

(전화벨이 울린다.)
여: 여보세요.
남: Blake 씨, G.A. 숍입니다.
여: 아, 안녕하세요. 제 커피 메이커가 준비되었나요?
남: 아직 아닙니다. 히터는 고쳤지만, 다른 문제를 발견했습니다.
여: 뭐지요?
남: 물 탱크가 샙니다. 이것을 수리하는 데 하루가 더 걸리겠습니다. 비용도 더 들고요.
여: 음, 괜찮습니다. 그러면 내일 가지러 가도 되나요?
남: 네. 준비되면 전화 드리겠습니다.

단·어·및·표·현
leak [liːk] 통 (액체·기체가) 새다

15 부탁(요청)한일파악　▶ 정답 ②

듣·기·대·본

M: How was your food today, ma'am?
W: It was very good. The steak is always delicious at this restaurant.
M: Thank you, ma'am. Our chef will be delighted to hear that. Would you like some more wine?
W: No, thanks, but can I look at the menu again, please?
M: Sure. We have a new dessert menu.
W: Oh, I'm too full. I want to take out something for my daughter.
M: Of course. I'll bring it right away.

우·리·말·해·석

남: 오늘 음식이 어떠셨나요, 부인?
여: 아주 좋았어요. 이 레스토랑은 스테이크가 항상 맛있어요.
남: 감사합니다. 부인. 그 말씀을 들으면 저희 주방장이 매우 기뻐할 것입니다. 포도주를 더 드시겠습니까?
여: 아니요, 고맙습니다만, 메뉴를 다시 볼 수 있을까요?
남: 물론입니다. 새로운 후식 메뉴가 있습니다.
여: 아, 저는 배가 너무 불러요. 제 딸을 위해 무엇을 좀 포장해 가려고요.
남: 물론입니다. 바로 가져다 드리겠습니다.

단·어·및·표·현
delighted [diláitid] 형 매우 기뻐하는

16 이유파악　▶ 정답 ⑤

듣·기·대·본

(Cellphone rings.)
W: Hi, Dean.
M: Hi, Clair. You know there will be fireworks tonight, right?
W: Yes, at Central Park.
M: I'm going with Shane. Will you join us?
W: I'd love to, but I can't.
M: Why not? Is the park too far away?
W: Oh, no. My sister leaves tonight. I'm going to the airport with her and my parents.
M: That was today! OK, see you around.

우·리·말·해·석

(휴대전화가 울린다.)
여: 안녕, Dean.
남: 안녕, Clair. 오늘 밤에 불꽃놀이가 있다는 거 알고 있지, 그렇지?
여: 응, Central 공원에서.
남: 나 Shane하고 갈 거야. 우리랑 같이 갈래?
여: 그러고 싶지만, 그럴 수 없어.
남: 왜 안 돼? 공원이 너무 멀어?
여: 아, 아니. 내 동생이 오늘 밤에 떠나. 동생과 부모님이랑 함께 공항에 갈 거야.
남: 그게 오늘이었구나! 알았어, 조만간 보자.

단·어·및·표·현
far away 멀리, 멀리 떨어져

🦻 LISTENING ADVICE

'I'm going to the airport with her and my parents.'에서 'the airport'의 발음을 들어보면 'the'가 [디]라고 발음되는 걸 들을 수 있습니다. 'the'는 모음 앞에서는 이렇게 [디]라고 발음되고, 자음 앞에서는 [더]라고 발음됩니다.

17 그림상황에적절한대화찾기　▶ 정답 ①

듣·기·대·본

① M: You should pick up the dog waste.
  W: I know, but I forgot to bring a bag.
② M: Let's walk the dog in the park.
  W: I'm afraid dogs are not allowed there.
③ M: Don't leave the dog in the car.
  W: OK. I guess it is too hot today.
④ M: How can I help you?
  W: I think my dog is sick. It's not eating.
⑤ M: What are you doing in the bathroom?
  W: I'm washing my dog. It's so dirty!

우·리·말·해·석

① 남: 당신은 강아지 배설물을 주워야 해요.
  여: 알아요, 하지만 봉투를 가져오는 걸 잊어버렸어요.
② 남: 공원에서 강아지를 산책시키자.
  여: 그곳에 강아지들이 들어가지 못하는 것 같아.
③ 남: 강아지를 차 안에 남겨 두지 마.
  여: 알았어. 오늘은 너무 더운 것 같네.
④ 남: 무엇을 도와드릴까요?
  여: 저희 강아지가 아픈 것 같아요. 먹지를 않아요.
⑤ 남: 화장실에서 뭐해?
  여: 강아지를 씻기고 있어. 너무 더러워!

단·어·및·표·현
waste [weist] 명 배설물, 쓰레기

18 담화미언급　▶ 정답 ④

듣·기·대·본

W: Hello, movie fans! I want to tell you about a new movie

made by Karen Wills. The movie is called *Night Train*. It's a suspense movie with lots of action and many surprises. The story is about a police officer chasing a bad guy on a train that doesn't stop. The movie is very exciting and fun to watch. It will come out on July 26th. Don't miss it!

우·리·말·해·석

여: 안녕하세요, 영화 팬 여러분! 저는 Karen Wills가 만든 새 영화에 대해 여러분께 말씀드리고 싶습니다. 그 영화의 제목은 "Night Train"입니다. 그것은 많은 액션과 많은 놀라움이 있는 서스펜스 영화(긴장감 가득한 영화)입니다. 이야기는 멈추지 않는 기차에서 나쁜 사람을 쫓는 경찰관에 대한 내용입니다. 그 영화는 매우 흥미진진하고, 보기에도 재미있습니다. 그것은 7월 26일에 개봉될 것입니다. 놓치지 마세요!

단·어·및·표·현

suspense[səspéns] 명 서스펜스, 긴장감
chase[tʃeis] 동 뒤쫓다, 추적하다
miss[mis] 동 놓치다, 지나치다

19 알맞은응답찾기 ▶ 정답 ②

들·기·대·본

M: Emily, do you want to go for lunch?
W: Sorry, but I'm going to skip lunch today. I've gained too much weight recently.
M: You know skipping meals is bad for your health, right?
W: Yes. But it's so hard to exercise regularly.
M: It's easier if you do it with friends. How about joining my tennis class?
W: OK. How often do you play?
M: We meet twice a week.

우·리·말·해·석

① 그것은 8시에 시작해.
② 우리는 일주일에 두 번 만나.
③ 그것은 한 달에 30달러야.
④ 우리는 스포츠센터에서 해.
⑤ 내 반에는 여섯 명이 있어.

남: Emily, 점심 먹으러 갈래?
여: 미안하지만, 난 오늘 점심은 거를 거야. 나 최근에 몸무게가 너무 많이 늘었거든.
남: 식사를 거르는 게 너의 건강에 좋지 않다는 것을 알잖아, 그렇지?
여: 응. 하지만 규칙적으로 운동하는 건 너무 힘들어.
남: 친구들과 같이 하면 더 쉬워. 내 테니스 수업에 가입하는 건 어때?
여: 좋아. 얼마나 자주 하는데?
남: **우리는 일주일에 두 번 만나.**

단·어·및·표·현

skip[skip] 동 거르다, (정해진 차례를) 건너뛰다
gain weight 몸무게가 늘다
meal[mi:l] 명 (특히 아침·점심·저녁의) 식사

20 알맞은응답찾기 ▶ 정답 ⑤

들·기·대·본

M: May I help you?
W: Yes, please. I'm looking for a small in this sweater.
M: Let me check. (*Pause*) Hmm… We have only medium and large sizes left.
W: That's too bad. Do you have any different colors, then?
M: Yes. We have white and gray colors in small.
W: Gray would be good. Can I see it?
M: Sure, let me bring it to you.

우·리·말·해·석

① 어떻게 하는지 모르겠습니다.
② 아니요, 당신의 잘못이 아닙니다.
③ 네, 여기에 적어주세요.
④ 19페이지를 펴세요.
⑤ 물론이죠, 제가 가져다 드릴게요.

남: 도와드릴까요?
여: 네, 부탁드려요. 저는 이 스웨터의 작은 사이즈를 찾고 있어요.
남: 확인해보겠습니다. (잠시 후) 흠… 저희는 오직 중간과 큰 사이즈만 남아있네요.
여: 유감이네요. 다른 색은 없나요, 그러면?
남: 있습니다. 흰색과 회색은 작은 사이즈가 있네요.
여: 회색이 좋을 것 같아요. 제가 볼 수 있을까요?
남: **물론이죠, 제가 가져다 드릴게요.**

단·어·및·표·현

look for ~ ~을 찾다
fault[fɔːlt] 명 잘못, 책임

Words & Expressions Review

1. (피아노의) 건반	2. 화분	3. 수영모
4. 할인[세일] 중인	5. ~을 찾다	6. 서스펜스, 긴장감
7. 사용할 수 있는	8. 사전의	9. 준비가 된
10. 품절인	11. 기회	12. 뒤쫓다, 추적하다
13. (잃어버린 물건 등이) 나타나다, 찾게 되다	14. 대신에	15. 놓치다, 지나치다
16. 도착하다	17. ~를 보살펴 주다	18. 후식, 디저트
19. 지금	20. 열정	21. 잠시만요.
22. 불꽃놀이	23. 심사위원, 심판	24. 친구
25. 거르다, (정해진 차례를) 건너뛰다	26. ~를 안됐다고 생각하다	27. 예약하다
28. 우울한	29. 배설물, 쓰레기	30. 실수로, 우연히
31. 꽤, 상당히	32. 끔찍한	33. 대여하다, 빌려주다
34. 수박	35. 허락하다	36. 맛있는
37. 비용이 들다	38. 인기 있는	39. 매우 기뻐하는
40. (유감이지만) ~ 같다	41. 재미있는, 재미	42. 신고하다, 알리다
43. 악기	44. (액체·기체가) 새다	

Listening Test
영어듣기 모의고사 03회

|정|답|

01 ③	02 ⑤	03 ①	04 ⑤	05 ①
06 ③	07 ③	08 ①	09 ③	10 ④
11 ④	12 ⑤	13 ②	14 ③	15 ③
16 ④	17 ⑤	18 ⑤	19 ③	20 ③

01 날씨파악-그림　▶정답 ③

듣·기·대·본

W: Good morning. I'm Kelly Green from the weather center. Today, it'll be cloudy and rainy in some areas. The showers will stop by this evening. Tomorrow will be sunny and very hot. I suggest you wear a hat and protect your skin with sunscreen if you go to the beach.

우·리·말·해·석

여: 좋은 아침입니다. 기상센터의 Kelly Green입니다. 오늘은 구름이 끼고 일부 지역에는 비가 오겠습니다. 소나기는 오늘 저녁까지 그칠 것입니다. 내일은 화창하고 매우 덥겠습니다. 해변에 가시게 되면 모자를 착용하시고 자외선 차단 크림으로 피부를 보호하시길 권합니다.

단·어·및·표·현

sunscreen [sʌ́nskrìːn] 명 자외선 차단 크림

02 그림정보파악　▶정답 ⑤

듣·기·대·본

M: Amy, come here and check out these hats on the screen.

W: Sure, Dad. [Pause] Oh, are you buying a hat for me?

M: Yes. How about this one? It's a visor so it doesn't cover the top of your head.

W: Well, I don't want a topless hat.

M: I see. Then, how about the ones with animal faces that do have a top?

W: They're cute. I like the one with the sheep face.

M: Okay. I'll order it.

우·리·말·해·석

남: Amy, 이리 와서 화면에 있는 이 모자들을 확인해보렴.

여: 네, 아빠. [잠시 후] 아, 저를 위해 모자를 사 주시려는 거예요?

남: 응. 이건 어떠니? 이건 챙 형태라 네 머리의 위쪽은 덮지 않아.

여: 음, 저는 윗부분이 없는 모자를 원하지 않아요.

남: 그렇구나. 그러면, (머리) 위쪽이 있는 동물 얼굴이 있는 것들은 어떠니?

여: 그것들은 귀엽네요. 전 양 얼굴이 있는 것이 좋아요.

남: 좋아. 내가 그걸로 주문할게.

단·어·및·표·현

check out 확인하다, 살펴보다
visor [váizər] 명 (모자의) 챙
cover [kʌ́vər] 동 덮다, 씌우다, 가리다
topless [táplis] 형 윗부분이 없는

03 심정추론　▶정답 ①

듣·기·대·본

W: How was the model airplane contest today?

M: Fantastic, Mom! I had so much fun. I saw an air show there.

W: Sounds great! How did your model airplane do?

M: It flew for about two and a half minutes!

W: That's amazing!

M: Yeah. I won first prize.

W: You did a great job!

우·리·말·해·석

① 자랑스러운　② 지루한　③ 미안한　④ 겁먹은　⑤ 느긋한

여: 오늘 모형 비행기 대회는 어땠니?

남: 환상적이었어요, 엄마! 무척 재미있었어요. 저는 거기서 에어쇼도 봤어요.

여: 재미있었겠구나! 너의 모형 비행기는 어땠니?

남: 그것은 약 2분 30초를 날았어요!

여: 그것 놀랍구나!

남: 네. 저는 1등 상을 탔어요.

여: 정말 잘했구나!

단·어·및·표·현

fly [flai] 동 날다
prize [praiz] 명 상, 상품

04 한일파악　▶정답 ⑤

듣·기·대·본

M: Lily, why are you sorting all those old books?

W: I'm donating them to the local library.

M: That's really kind of you.

W: Thanks. Last weekend, I volunteered at the library and saw they needed more books for kids.

M: Oh, I see. Was the volunteering fun?

W: Yes! I helped kids pick out books and read to them. I want to do it again.

우·리·말·해·석

남: Lily, 넌 왜 저 오래된 책들을 모두 분류하고 있는 거야?

여: 나는 그것들을 지역 도서관에 기부할 거야.

남: 넌 정말 친절하구나.

여: 고마워. 지난 주말에, 나는 도서관에서 자원봉사를 했는데, 그들에게 아이들을 위한 더 많은 책들이 필요하다는 것을 알게 됐어.

남: 아, 그렇구나. 자원봉사는 재미있었어?

여: 응! 나는 아이들이 책들을 고르는 것을 도와주고 그들에게 (책을) 읽어 줬어. 나는 그것을 또 하고 싶어.

단·어·및·표·현

sort [sɔːrt] 동 분류하다, 구분하다
donate [dóuneit] 동 기부하다, 기증하다
volunteer [vὰləntíər] 동 자원봉사를 하다
pick out 고르다, 선택하다

05 대화장소추론　▶정답 ①

듣·기·대·본

W: Jung-hoon, over here! I found our seats.

M: Wow, these seats are amazing. I can see all the players on the field.

W: Yeah, why did you bring your glove with you?

M: You never know when a foul ball might come your way.

W: Are you allowed to keep the ball?

M: Of course! Look, the game is about to start.

우·리·말·해·석

여: 정훈아, 이쪽이야! 내가 우리 자리를 찾았어.

남: 와, 이 자리들 굉장하다. 경기장에 있는 모든 선수들을 볼 수 있어.

여: 응, 너 야구 글러브는 왜 가지고 왔니?

남: 파울 볼이 언제 내 쪽으로 올지 모르잖아.

여: 공을 가지는 게 허용되니?

남: 물론이야! 봐, 경기가 막 시작하려고 해.

단·어·및·표·현

you never know ~ ~를 알 수 없다
keep [kiːp] 동 갖다, 가지고 있다

06 마지막말의도파악　▶정답 ③

듣·기·대·본

W: What a lovely dog!

M: Hi, Molly. This is my dog Ali.

W: Hi, Ali. He is so cute! I love fuzzy dogs.
M: Great. Actually, can you do me a favor?
W: Alright. What is it?
M: I'm going on vacation next week. Could you take care of my dog for a week?
W: Oh, I'd love to, but my parents don't like dogs.

우·리·말·해·석
여: 정말 귀여운 강아지구나!
남: 안녕, Molly. 내 강아지 Ali야.
여: 안녕, Ali. 정말 귀엽다! 난 복슬복슬한 강아지들을 좋아해.
남: 잘됐다. 저 있잖아, 내가 부탁 하나만 해도 될까?
여: 좋아. 뭔데?
남: 내가 다음 주에 휴가를 가는데, 한 주 동안 내 강아지를 돌봐 줄 수 있을까?
여: 오, 나도 그러고 싶지만 부모님께서 강아지를 좋아하시지 않으셔(서 안 될 거 같아).

단·어·및·표·현
fuzzy [fʌ́zi] 형 (털이) 복슬복슬한
take care of ~ ~을 돌보다

07 특정정보파악 ▶정답 ③

듣·기·대·본
M: Chloe, how about going hiking this weekend?
W: Dad, I don't want to go hiking. Can't we just relax at home?
M: It'd be nice to relax at the top of the mountain and enjoy nature.
W: That's not relaxing for me. And besides, getting to the top is a lot of work.
M: How about going fishing, then? We can have a relaxing time at the lake.
W: Well, alright. That's much better than hiking up a mountain.
M: Great.

우·리·말·해·석
남: Chloe, 이번 주말에 등산 가는 거 어때?
여: 아빠, 저는 등산 가고 싶지 않아요. 우리 그냥 집에서 쉬면 안 될까요?
남: 산꼭대기에서 휴식을 취하고 자연을 즐기면 좋을 거야.
여: 그건 저에게 휴식을 취하는 게 아니에요. 게다가, 정상에 오르는 건 힘든 일이에요.
남: 그러면 낚시하러 가는 건 어떠니? 우리는 호수에서 편안한 시간을 보낼 수 있어.
여: 음, 좋아요. 그게 산 오르는 것보다 훨씬 더 나아요.
남: 좋아.

단·어·및·표·현
relaxing [rilǽksiŋ] 형 편안한, 마음을 느긋하게 해 주는
a lot of work 힘든 일, 손이 많이 가는 일

08 할일파악(대화직후) ▶정답 ①

듣·기·대·본
M: Our club is holding a wildlife campaign tomorrow, right?
W: Yes, we need to make some posters for it.
M: We have to buy some materials to make the posters.
W: What do we need?
M: We need paperboard, colored paper, scissors, and glue.
W: I have two pairs of scissors, so we don't have to buy them.
M: That's great. Can you bring the scissors?

W: Okay. I'll get them right away.

우·리·말·해·석
남: 우리 동아리는 내일 야생 동물 캠페인을 열어, 그렇지?
여: 응, 우리는 그것을 위한 포스터를 만들어야 해.
남: 우리는 포스터를 만들기 위해 재료들을 사야 해.
여: 우리에게 무엇이 필요하지?
남: 우리는 판지, 색종이, 가위, 그리고 풀이 필요해.
여: 내게 가위 두 개가 있어, 그러니 그건 안 사도 돼.
남: 잘됐네. 가위 좀 가져다 줄래?
여: 알겠어. 바로 가져올게.

단·어·및·표·현
hold [hould] 동 열다, 개최하다
wildlife [wáildlàif] 명 야생 동물
poster [póustər] 명 (안내, 홍보용) 포스터, 벽보
material [mətíəriəl] 명 재료
paperboard [péipərbɔ̀ːrd] 명 판지, 두꺼운 종이

09 대화미언급 ▶정답 ③

듣·기·대·본
M: Yena, your English has improved a lot since last year. How did you do it?
W: *Jumping English* helped me a lot.
M: Isn't that a TV program?
W: Yes. It's hosted by the famous teacher, Mr. Lee.
M: Really? I want to start watching it, too.
W: You should. It's a great program. It's on every evening at 8.
M: Oh, I can't watch it at that time. Do you know if they have reruns?
W: Sure. They repeat the program the next morning at 6 a.m.

우·리·말·해·석
남: 예나야, 작년 이후로 너의 영어가 많이 향상됐더라. 어떻게 한 거야?
여: "Jumping English"가 나에게 큰 도움이 됐어.
남: 그거 텔레비전 프로그램 아니야?
여: 맞아. 그건 유명한 선생님인 Mr. Lee가 진행하셔.
남: 진짜? 나도 그걸 보기 시작하고 싶다.
여: 꼭 그렇게 해. 그건 정말 좋은 프로그램이야. 그건 매일 저녁 8시에 해.
남: 오, 난 그 시간엔 그걸 볼 수 없어. 혹시 재방송도 하는지 알고 있어?
여: 그럼. 다음 날 오전 6시에 프로그램을 반복해 줘.

단·어·및·표·현
improve [imprúːv] 동 향상시키다, 개선되다
host [houst] 동 (방송을) 진행하다, 사회자 역할을 하다
rerun [ríːrʌ̀n] 명 재방송
repeat [ripíːt] 동 반복하다

10 담화화제추론 ▶정답 ④

듣·기·대·본
M: Hello, everyone. Welcome to our car factory. Before we start the tour, there are a few things you need to keep in mind. First, you should always wear your hardhat. Second, try not to wander away from the group. Finally, do not touch any machines. However, you are always welcome to ask questions. Now, shall we start looking around?

우·리·말·해·석
남: 안녕하세요, 여러분. 저희 자동차 공장에 오신 것을 환영합니다. 투어를 시작하기 전에, 여러분들이 명심해야 할 몇 가지 사항들이 있습니다. 첫 번째로, 항상 안전모를 써야 합니다. 두 번째로, 그룹에서 떨어져

돌아다니지 않도록 합니다. 마지막으로, 어떤 기계도 만지지 말아 주세요. 하지만 질문하는 것은 언제나 환영합니다. 이제, 구경을 시작해 볼까요?

단·어·및·표·현
keep in mind 명심하다

11 대화내용불일치 ▶정답 ④

듣·기·대·본

M: Kate, did you watch the video clip that I told you about?
W: Sorry, I totally forgot. What was it?
M: A short documentary film about global warming.
W: Oh, now I remember. Can I still watch it on our school website?
M: Sure. It's only 15 minutes long.
W: Okay. Is it in English?
M: No, it's in French.
W: Oh, no. That could be a problem.
M: Don't worry. It has English subtitles.

우·리·말·해·석

남: Kate, 내가 말했던 그 영상 봤니?
여: 미안해, 나 완전히 잊어버렸어. 그게 뭐였지?
남: 지구온난화에 대한 짧은 다큐멘터리 영화야.
여: 아, 이제 기억난다. 아직도 우리 학교 웹사이트에서 볼 수 있어?
남: 그럼. 그건 겨우 15분짜리야.
여: 알겠어. 그거 영어로 되어 있니?
남: 아니, 프랑스어로 되어 있어.
여: 오, 이런. 그건 문제가 될 수 있겠어.
남: 걱정하지 마. 영어 자막이 있어.

단·어·및·표·현
film [film] 명 영화
global warming 지구온난화
subtitle [sʌ́btàitl] 명 자막

12 방문이유파악 ▶정답 ⑤

듣·기·대·본

M: Hello.
W: Hi, I was here earlier and bought some groceries.
M: Is there something wrong?
W: Well, when I got home, I realized that I hadn't paid for something.
M: Oh, I see. Do you have it with you?
W: Yes, it's these carrots. I don't see them on the receipt.
M: Hmm, you're right. They're not on the receipt. Thank you so much for coming back.
W: No problem. I'll pay for them now.

우·리·말·해·석

남: 안녕하세요.
여: 안녕하세요, 저는 (아까) 전에 여기 왔었고 식료품을 좀 샀어요.
남: 무슨 문제가 있나요?
여: 음, 집에 갔을 때, 제가 어떤 물건에 대해 계산을 하지 않았다는 것을 깨달았어요.
남: 아, 그렇군요. 그것을 가지고 계신가요?
여: 네, 이 당근들이에요. 영수증에서 이것들이 보이지 않아요.
남: 흠, 당신이 맞네요. 그것들은 영수증에 없어요. 다시 와 주셔서 정말 감사합니다.
여: 천만에요. 지금 그것들의 값을 지불할게요.

단·어·및·표·현
earlier [ə́ːrliər] 부 전에, 앞서

grocery [gróusəri] 명 식료품, 잡화
realize [ríːəlàiz] 동 깨닫다
receipt [risíːt] 명 영수증

13 수치계산 ▶정답 ②

듣·기·대·본

M: May I help you?
W: How much is this plain donut?
M: It's $1.
W: How about this chocolate donut?
M: It's $2. But you get a $2 discount if you buy any six donuts.
W: I don't need that many donuts. I'll just get one plain donut and one chocolate donut.
M: Okay, your total is 3 dollars. Do you have any discount coupons?
W: No, here's 5 dollars.
M: Here you are. Thank you.

우·리·말·해·석

남: 도와드릴까요?
여: 이 플레인 도넛은 얼마인가요?
남: 그것은 1달러예요.
여: 이 초콜릿 도넛은요?
남: 그것은 2달러예요. 하지만 손님이 아무 도넛이나 여섯 개를 사면 2달러 할인을 받아요.
여: 저는 그렇게 많은 도넛은 필요 없어요. 저는 그냥 플레인 도넛 한 개와 초콜릿 도넛 한 개를 살게요.
남: 알겠습니다. 총 3달러입니다. 할인 쿠폰이 있으세요?
여: 아니요, 여기 5달러요.
남: 여기 있습니다. 감사합니다.

단·어·및·표·현
plain [plein] 형 있는 그대로의, 꾸미지 않은

14 대화자관계추론 ▶정답 ③

듣·기·대·본

W: Hello, how can I assist you?
M: I want to open a savings account.
W: Have you brought the necessary documents with you?
M: Yes, I have my ID card and proof of address right here.
W: Perfect. How much would you like to deposit into the account?
M: I'm thinking of starting with $500. Here it is.
W: All right. Let's begin by opening your account.

우·리·말·해·석

여: 안녕하세요, 어떻게 도와드릴까요?
남: 저는 보통 예금 계좌를 개설하고 싶어요.
여: 필요한 서류들을 가지고 오셨나요?
남: 네, 저는 여기 제 신분증과 주소 증명서를 갖고 왔어요.
여: 완벽해요. 계좌에 얼마나 예금하고 싶으세요?
남: 저는 500달러로 시작하려고 생각하고 있어요. 여기 있어요.
여: 알겠습니다. 당신의 계좌를 개설하는 것부터 시작합시다.

단·어·및·표·현
assist [əsíst] 동 돕다
open [óupən] 동 (계좌를) 개설하다
savings account 보통 예금 계좌
document [dɑ́kjumənt] 명 서류
ID card 신분증

proof of address 주소 증명
deposit [dipázit] ⑧ 예금하다

15 부탁(요청)한일파악 ▶ 정답 ③

듣·기·대·본

M: Here is the guest list, Carly.
W: Is this final?
M: Yes. We have four more guests now.
W: Then, we'll need more chairs in the meeting room.
M: And more water bottles. I'll ask Sam from Marketing to bring them.
W: Oh, we need more booklets, too. I have some on my desk.
M: Can you go bring them? I'll get the chairs.
W: OK. I'll be right back.

우·리·말·해·석

남: 손님 명단 여기 있어요, Carly.
여: 이게 최종이에요?
남: 네. 현재 4명의 손님이 추가되었어요.
여: 그러면, 회의실에 의자가 더 필요할 거예요.
남: 그리고 물병도요. 마케팅 팀의 Sam에게 가져오라고 부탁할게요.
여: 아, 소책자들도 더 필요해요. 제 책상에 몇 개 있어요.
남: 가서 그것들을 가져올 수 있어요? 저는 의자들을 가져올게요.
여: 알았어요. 곧 돌아올게요.

단·어·및·표·현

bring [briŋ] ⑧ 가져오다, 가져가다

16 이유파악 ▶ 정답 ④

듣·기·대·본

M: Hi, Kate. What's with the box?
W: Hi, Paul. There's a cake in it. I just baked it.
M: A cake? Is it someone's birthday?
W: No. Yesterday, my sister won a contest. The cake is for her. We'll have a family party this evening.
M: That's great! What kind of contest was it?
W: It was a writing contest.

우·리·말·해·석

남: 안녕, Kate. 웬 박스야?
여: 안녕, Paul. 이 안에 케이크가 들어 있어. 내가 방금 구웠어.
남: 케이크? 누구 생일이야?
여: 아니. 어제 내 여동생이 대회에서 우승했어. 이 케이크는 그녀를 위한 거야. 우리는 오늘 저녁에 가족 파티를 할 거야.
남: 멋지다! 무슨 대회였는데?
여: 글짓기 대회였어.

단·어·및·표·현

win a contest 대회에서 우승하다

17 그림상황에적절한대화찾기 ▶ 정답 ⑤

듣·기·대·본

① M: I think you are in my seat. You should check your ticket.
　W: Oh, I was in the wrong seat. Sorry.
② M: Are you excited to go on a family trip?
　W: I am so excited that I couldn't sleep last night!
③ M: If you have time, could you participate in a short survey?
　W: Yeah, sure. What is it about?

④ M: Do you know where the subway station is?
　W: Yes, go straight and take a left when you see the bank.
⑤ M: Ouch, you stepped on my foot!
　W: Oh my, I am so sorry for doing that!

우·리·말·해·석

① 남: 당신은 제 자리에 앉아있는 것 같아요. 당신의 표를 확인해 보세요.
　여: 오, 제가 잘못된 자리에 앉아있었네요. 죄송합니다.
② 남: 너는 가족여행을 가게 되어 신나니?
　여: 나는 너무 신나서 어젯밤에 잠을 못 잤어!
③ 남: 만약 시간이 있으시면, 짧은 설문에 참여해주실 수 있으세요?
　여: 네, 그러죠. 무엇에 관한 건가요?
④ 남: 당신은 지하철역이 어디 있는지 아시나요?
　여: 네, 직진한 다음 은행이 보이면 좌회전하세요.
⑤ 남: 아야, 당신은 제 발을 밟았어요!
　여: 오 이런, 그렇게 해서 정말 죄송합니다!

단·어·및·표·현

participate in ~에 참여하다
survey [sə́rvei] ⑲ 설문 조사
step on one's foot ~의 발을 밟다

18 담화미언급 ▶ 정답 ⑤

듣·기·대·본

M: Hello, students. Today, I'd like to invite you to a special concert by one of our former students, violinist Jack Dawson. He will play violin sonatas by Beethoven. It will be held at City Art Center. The concert is on May 5. It starts at 7 p.m. Admission is free, so come and enjoy the concert. I hope to see you there!

우·리·말·해·석

남: 안녕하세요, 학생 여러분. 오늘 저는 여러분을 우리의 예전 학생들 중 한 명인 바이올린 연주자 Jack Dawson의 특별한 공연으로 초대하고 싶습니다. 그는 베토벤의 바이올린 소나타들을 연주할 것입니다. 그것은 시 예술 센터에서 개최될 것입니다. 공연은 5월 5일에 있습니다. 그것은 저녁 7시에 시작합니다. 입장료는 무료이므로 와서 공연을 즐기세요. 저는 그곳에서 여러분을 뵙기 바랍니다!

단·어·및·표·현

invite [inváit] ⑧ 초대하다
former [fɔ́ːrmər] ⑱ 예전의, 과거의
hold [hould] ⑧ 개최하다
admission [ədmíʃən] ⑲ 입장료

19 알맞은응답찾기 ▶ 정답 ③

듣·기·대·본

W: Look at this picture from my trip to Italy.
M: Wow, you look so cute in this picture.
W: Thank you. It was taken in Venice last year.
M: Oh, that's why you are riding a gondola.
W: It was really exciting.
M: Venice is famous for its canals. I love that city.
W: Oh, have you been there, too?
M: No, but I hope to visit there someday.

우·리·말·해·석

① 그건 너무 걱정하지 마.
② 네가 해외에서 살았던 건 몰랐어.
③ 아니, 하지만 언젠가 가보고 싶어.
④ 난 곤돌라 타는 걸 좋아하지 않아.
⑤ 베니스는 이탈리아에 있어.

여: 내 이탈리아 여행에서의 이 사진을 봐봐.
남: 와, 너 이 사진에서 굉장히 귀여워 보인다.
여: 고마워. 작년에 베니스에서 찍은 거야.
남: 오, 그래서 네가 곤돌라를 타고 있구나.
여: 굉장히 신났었어.
남: 베니스는 운하들로 유명하지. 난 그 도시가 정말 좋아.
여: 아, 너도 거기 가 봤니?
남: **아니, 하지만 언젠가 가보고 싶어.**

단·어·및·표·현

be famous for ~ ~로 유명하다
canal [kənǽl] 명 운하, 수로

20 알맞은응답찾기 ▶ 정답 ③

듣·기·대·본

M: Did you go to the Italian restaurant that I told you about?
W: Yes, I went there with my family.
M: How was it?
W: Oh, it was lovely. We had a great time.
M: What about the food? Did you try any of the pizzas?
W: Yes, we had gorgonzola pizza and some spaghetti. They were delicious!
M: I'm glad you liked them.
W: How did you know about that restaurant?
M: I saw an ad in a magazine.

우·리·말·해·석

① 나는 그 레스토랑을 아주 좋아해.
② 네가 의미하는 게 뭔지 모르겠어.
③ 잡지에서 광고를 보았어.
④ 나도 스파게티를 먹었어.
⑤ 내가 가장 좋아하는 음식은 멕시코 음식이야.

남: 내가 이야기해 준 이탈리아 식당에 갔었니?
여: 응. 나는 내 가족들과 함께 거기에 갔어.
남: 어땠어?
여: 오, 그건 아주 좋았어. 우리는 멋진 시간을 가졌어.
남: 음식은 어땠어? 피자들 중에 먹어본 것이 있니?
여: 응. 우리는 고르곤졸라 피자와 스파게티를 좀 먹었어. 그것들은 맛있었어!
남: 네가 그것들을 좋아했다니 나도 기뻐.
여: 너는 그 식당에 대해 어떻게 알았니?
남: **잡지에서 광고를 보았어.**

단·어·및·표·현

lovely [lʌ́vli] 형 아주 좋은, 사랑스러운
try [trai] 동 먹어보다, ~을 시험 삼아 써보다

👂 LISTENING ADVICE

문장 혹은 단어 내에서 'd' 다음에 'y'가 오면, [d] 소리는 [y] 소리의 영향을 받아 [ㄷ] 소리보다는 [ㅈ]과 유사한 소리로 변합니다. 따라서 'told you'는 [톨드 유]가 아닌 [톨쥬], 'glad you'는 [글래드 유]가 아닌 [글래쥬], 'did you'는 [디드 유]가 아닌 [디쥬]로 발음됩니다. 이러한 발음의 동화현상에 유의하여 20번을 다시 한번 들어보세요.

Words & Expressions Review

1. 돕다	2. 갖다, 가지고 있다	3. 운하, 수로
4. (방송을) 진행하다, 사회자 역할을 하다	5. 전에, 앞서	6. 날다
7. ~으로 유명하다	8. 초대하다	9. (털이) 복슬복슬한
10. (모자의) 챙	11. 재방송	12. 예전의, 과거의
13. 덮다, 씌우다, 가리다	14. 예금하다	15. 기부하다, 기증하다
16. 손님	17. 신나는, 흥미로운	18. 잡지
19. 깨닫다	20. 분류하다, 구분하다	21. 자외선 차단 크림
22. 있는 그대로의, 꾸미지 않은	23. ~을 돌보다	24. 재료
25. ~에 참여하다	26. 힘든 일, 손이 많이 가는 일	27. 공장
28. 설문 조사	29. 자막	30. 향상시키다, 개선되다
31. 영화	32. 권하다, 제안하다	33. 소책자
34. 가져오다, 가져가다	35. 명심하다	36. ~의 발을 밟다
37. 대회에서 우승하다	38. 구경하다, 둘러보다	39. 지구온난화
40. (야구) 글러브, 장갑	41. 막 ~하려는 참이다	42. 편안한, 마음을 느긋하게 해 주는
43. 야생 동물	44. (음식을) 굽다	

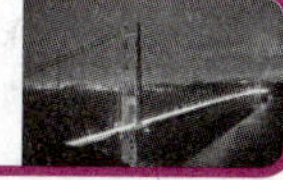

Listening Test

영어듣기 모의고사 04회

|정|답|

01 ②	02 ③	03 ③	04 ④	05 ⑤
06 ④	07 ④	08 ③	09 ⑤	10 ①
11 ④	12 ①	13 ③	14 ⑤	15 ①
16 ⑤	17 ④	18 ③	19 ⑤	20 ①

01 날씨파악-그림 ▶ 정답 ②

듣·기·대·본

M: Good evening. Here's the world weather report for Friday, December 2. Tokyo will have cloudy skies and low temperatures. In Shanghai, it will be sunny, but the air quality will be bad. In Berlin, the fog will be heavy all day. New York will have its first snow of the year, so be careful of the slippery roads. Thank you.

우·리·말·해·석

남: 안녕하세요. 12월 2일, 금요일의 세계 일기 예보입니다. 도쿄는 구름이 많이 끼고 기온이 낮을 것입니다. 상하이는 화창하겠으나, 대기질이 나쁠 것입니다. 베를린은 온종일 안개가 짙게 낄 것입니다. 뉴욕에는 올해의 첫눈이 내릴 것이니, 미끄러운 길 조심하세요. 감사합니다.

단·어·및·표·현

weather report 일기 예보
temperature [témpərətʃər] 명 기온, 온도
air quality 대기질, 공기의 질
fog [fɔ(:)g] 명 안개

02 그림정보파악 ▶ 정답 ③

듣·기·대·본

M: Molly, can you help me with the table setting? Our guests will be here soon.

W: Sure. You already <u>put the plate</u> on the mat.
M: Yup. Please put the fork on the left side of it.
W: Done. Shall I put the knife on <u>the other side</u>?
M: Yes, please. And the spoon goes to the right side of the knife.
W: How about this small spoon?
M: Put it on the upper side of the plate.
W: OK. I'll set the rest <u>the same</u>.

우·리·말·해·석

남: Molly, 너 내가 테이블 세팅하는 거 도와줄 수 있니? 우리 손님들이 곧 여기 올 거야.
여: 물론이지. 너는 이미 접시를 매트 위에 놓았네.
남: 응. 포크를 그것의 왼쪽에 놓아 줘.
여: 됐어. 다른 쪽에 나이프를 놓을까?
남: 응, 그렇게 해 줘. 그리고 숟가락은 나이프의 오른쪽에 놓여.
여: 이 작은 숟가락은?
남: 그것은 접시의 위쪽에 둬.
여: 좋아. 내가 나머지를 똑같이 세팅할게.

단·어·및·표·현
soon [suːn] ⊕ 곧
plate [pleit] ⑲ 접시

03 심정추론 ▶정답 ③

듣·기·대·본

M: What's wrong, Mina?
W: Minho <u>drew a picture</u> on my textbook!
M: Don't be <u>upset</u>. He's only five years old.
W: But Dad, this is not the first time!
M: You know he's young. I guess you need to keep your things out of his reach.
W: Oh, <u>you always take his side</u>.

우·리·말·해·석
① 자랑스러운   ② 지루한   ③ 화난
④ 행복한   ⑤ 감사한

남: 무슨 일이니, 미나야?
여: 민호가 제 교과서에 그림을 그렸어요!
남: 속상해하지 마라. 그 애는 겨우 5살이잖니.
여: 하지만 아빠, 이번이 처음이 아니라고요!
남: 너도 그가 어리다는 거 알잖니. 내 생각엔 너는 너의 물건들을 그의 손이 닿지 않는 곳에 보관해야 할 것 같구나.
여: 아, 아빠는 항상 그 아이 편을 들어요.

단·어·및·표·현
upset [ʌpsét] ⑲ 속상한, 마음이 상한
take one's side ~의 편을 들다

04 한일파악 ▶정답 ④

듣·기·대·본

W: Hey, Bill. What are you <u>looking at</u>?
M: I'm just looking at some photos. They're from our school's Sports Day.
W: Let me see. (*Pause*) Oh, here you are <u>playing soccer</u>.
M: Yes, I ran as a mid-fielder. Which sport did you play?
W: I didn't play any sports.
M: Then, <u>what did you do</u>?
W: I did <u>face painting</u> for students with my art group members.

우·리·말·해·석
여: 안녕, Bill. 무엇을 보고 있니?
남: 그냥 사진들을 좀 보고 있어. 우리 학교 운동회 날에 찍힌 것들이야.
여: 어디 보자. (잠시 후) 오, 여기 네가 축구를 하고 있어.
남: 맞아. 나 미드필더로 뛰었어. 너는 어느 운동을 했니?
여: 나는 어떤 운동도 안 했어.
남: 그럼, 넌 무엇을 했니?
여: 나는 내 미술부원들과 함께 학생들의 얼굴에 그림을 그려줬어.

단·어·및·표·현
Sports Day 운동회 날
mid-fielder 미드필더

05 대화장소추론 ▶정답 ⑤

듣·기·대·본

W: How can I help you?
M: I lost my wallet. I came here to <u>check if</u> someone turned it in.
W: What does it <u>look like</u>?
M: It's red and there is a zipper <u>on the side</u>.
W: A red wallet? Oh, is this yours?
M: Yes, that's it! Thank you so much.
W: You're welcome. If you lose something again, you can use our website, www.lost112.go.kr.

우·리·말·해·석
여: 어떻게 도와드릴까요?
남: 제 지갑을 잃어버렸어요. 누군가가 돌려주었는지 확인하고 싶어서 왔는데요.
여: 어떻게 생겼나요?
남: 그건 빨간색이고, 옆에 지퍼가 있어요.
여: 빨간 지갑이라고요? 오, 이게 당신 것인가요?
남: 네, 맞아요! 정말 고맙습니다.
여: 천만에요. 다시 무언가를 잃어버리신다면 우리 웹사이트 www.lost112. go.kr을 이용할 수 있어요.

단·어·및·표·현
turn ~ in ~을 돌려주다, ~을 제출하다

06 마지막말의도파악 ▶정답 ④

듣·기·대·본

W: Hi, Tim. How are you doing these days?
M: Hey, Jina. I am not <u>doing great</u>.
W: Oh, what's wrong?
M: I can't score any points in my soccer game these days. It's <u>frustrating</u>.
W: It's probably <u>just a phase</u>. You were always a great soccer player.
M: Thank you. It is very nice of you to say so.
W: How about I help you <u>practice</u> your shooting? I can be the ball girl.
M: Oh, that would be great!

우·리·말·해·석
여: 안녕, Tim. 요즘 너 어떻게 지내?
남: 안녕, Jina. 난 잘 지내지 못해.
여: 저런, 무슨 일 있니?
남: 나는 요즘 축구 경기에서 한 골도 못 넣어. 불만스러워.
여: 그것은 그저 (변화, 발전의) 한 단계일 거야. 너는 항상 뛰어난 축구선수였어.
남: 고마워. 그렇게 말해주다니 너는 참 친절하구나.

여: 내가 너의 슈팅 연습을 도와주는 건 어떠니? 내가 볼걸(시합에서 밖으로 나간 공을 잡아 건네주는 일을 하는 소녀)이 되어 줄 수 있어.
남: 오, 그거 정말 좋다!

단·어·및·표·현

frustrating [frʌ́strèitiŋ] ⑧ 불만스러운, 좌절감을 주는
phase [feiz] ⑨ (변화·발달 과정상의 한) 단계

07 특정정보파악 ▶ 정답 ④

듣·기·대·본

M: Sue, how was school today?
W: Good. We learned how to make seaweed soup today.
M: What is that?
W: It's cooked with mi-yuk.
M: Ah! I know the soup. Your mom made it for your birthday, remember?
W: Of course. We put beef in it, too. It was very tasty.
M: Wasn't it difficult to make?
W: Not at all. I'll make it for you next time.
M: Thanks. That's very sweet of you.

우·리·말·해·석

남: Sue, 오늘 학교는 어땠어?
여: 좋았어. 우리는 오늘 미역국을 만드는 법을 배웠어.
남: 그것이 뭐야?
여: 그것은 미역으로 조리되는 거야.
남: 아! 나는 그 국을 알아. 너희 어머니께서 네 생일을 위해 만드셨잖아, 기억해?
여: 물론이지. 우리는 그 안에 소고기도 넣었어. 그것은 매우 맛있었어.
남: 그것은 만들기 어렵지 않았어?
여: 전혀. 내가 다음에 너에게 그것을 만들어 줄게.
남: 고마워. 너는 아주 다정하구나.

단·어·및·표·현

seaweed [síːwìd] ⑨ 미역, 해초

08 할일파악(대화직후) ▶ 정답 ③

듣·기·대·본

W: Jacob, what's that awful smell coming from your room?
M: I don't know, Mom. I cleaned my room yesterday.
W: I know, but did you empty your wastebasket as you promised?
M: Oops, I forgot. I think that's where the smell is coming from.
W: You should take it out right now.
M: Yes, I'll do it right away.

우·리·말·해·석

여: Jacob, 네 방에서 나는 지독한 냄새는 뭐니?
남: 저도 모르겠어요, 엄마. 저 어제 방 청소를 했어요.
여: 나도 알아, 하지만 휴지통은 약속한 대로 비웠니?
남: 이런, 잊어버렸어요. 제 생각에 그곳으로부터 냄새가 나는 것 같아요.
여: 지금 바로 밖에 내다 버려야 한다.
남: 네, 바로 할게요.

단·어·및·표·현

awful [ɔ́ːfəl] ⑧ 지독한, 끔찍한
empty [émpti] ⑧ 비우다
wastebasket [wéistbæ̀skit] ⑨ 휴지통

09 대화미언급 ▶ 정답 ⑤

듣·기·대·본

M: Hello, Ms. Collin. Could you tell me how I can start a new club?
W: Sure, what club do you want to create?
M: A singing club. Mr. Han has agreed to be our guidance teacher.
W: Great. Then, you need to fill out this form and get it signed by Mr. Han.
M: Thank you. Can we use the music room for our club?
W: Sure. But, you probably need to get some club members first.
M: I already have eight members who are willing to join.

우·리·말·해·석

남: 안녕하세요, Collin 선생님. 신규 동아리를 어떻게 만드는지 제게 알려 주실 수 있나요?
여: 물론이지, 무슨 동아리를 만들고 싶니?
남: 노래 부르기 동아리요. 한 선생님이 저희 지도 선생님이 되어주시기로 승낙했어요.
여: 잘됐다. 그러면 이 양식을 작성해서 한 선생님의 서명을 받으면 돼.
남: 감사합니다. 저희 동아리에서 음악실을 사용해도 될까요?
여: 물론이지. 하지만, 아마 너는 우선 동아리 구성원들을 모아야 할 거야.
남: 동아리에 기꺼이 가입하고 싶어 하는 사람이 이미 8명이나 있어요.

단·어·및·표·현

fill out 작성하다

10 담화화제추론 ▶ 정답 ①

듣·기·대·본

W: Hello, everyone. Let me tell you about today's schedule. Now, we're going to Tiananmen, which means The Gate of Heavenly Peace. Next, we'll visit Beijing's Palace Museum, better known as the Forbidden City. After that, we'll come back here to have dinner. I hope you enjoy yourselves in Beijing. Thank you.

우·리·말·해·석

여: 안녕하세요, 여러분. 오늘의 일정에 대해 말씀드리겠습니다. 이제, 우리는 '천국 같은 평화의 문'이라는 뜻의 천안문으로 가겠습니다. 다음에는 우리는 '금단의 도시(자금성)'로 더 잘 알려진, 북경 고궁 박물관을 방문하겠습니다. 그런 후에, 우리는 저녁을 먹으러 여기로 돌아오겠습니다. 북경에서 즐겁게 보내시길 바랍니다. 감사합니다.

단·어·및·표·현

schedule [skédʒuːl] ⑨ 일정
enjoy oneself 즐겁게 보내다, 즐기다

11 대화내용불일치 ▶ 정답 ④

듣·기·대·본

W: Mr. Kim, I'm hoping to enter the school English Essay Contest.
M: Great! It's this Thursday.
W: It starts at 4 p.m., right?
M: Yes. You need to send your contest entry form to me by e-mail.
W: Sure, I'll send it today.
M: The essay topic will be announced right before the start of the contest.
W: Okay. How much time will I have to complete my essay?
M: Oh, the contest will be one-hour long.
W: Thank you!

우·리·말·해·석

여: 김 선생님, 저는 학교 영어 에세이 대회에 참가하고 싶어요.
남: 훌륭하구나! 그건 이번 주 목요일이란다.

04 회 모의고사

여: 그건 오후 4시에 시작하죠?

남: 그래. 너는 나에게 이메일로 대회 참가 신청서를 제출해야 해.

여: 네, 오늘 그걸 보낼게요.

남: 에세이 주제는 대회 시작 바로 직전에 발표될 거야.

여: 알겠어요. 제가 에세이를 완성하는 데 시간을 얼마나 갖게 될까요?

남: 오, 대회는 한 시간 동안이란다.

여: 감사합니다!

단·어·및·표·현
contest [kάntest] 명 대회, 시합
entry form 참가 신청서
announce [ənάuns] 동 발표하다, 알리다
complete [kəmplíːt] 동 완성하다, 끝마치다

12 전화목적파악 ▶정답 ①

듣·기·대·본

(*Cellphone rings.*)

M: Hey, Grace. It's me, Jay.

W: Hey, Jay. Whose number is this?

M: I'm calling from my dad's phone. I think I left mine at your place.

W: Really? I'm at home. I'll look for it.

M: Could you check your desk first?

W: [*Pause*] Oh, here's your cellphone! You left it on the chair.

M: Great. Thanks. Can I come and pick it up now?

W: Sure. I'll wait.

우·리·말·해·석

(휴대폰이 울린다.)

남: 안녕, Grace. 나야, Jay.

여: 안녕, Jay. 이건 누구 번호야?

남: 나는 아빠의 휴대폰으로 전화하고 있어. 내 생각에 내가 내 것을 너희 집에 두고 온 것 같아.

여: 정말? 나 집에 있어. 내가 그것을 찾아볼게.

남: 네 책상을 먼저 확인해 줄 수 있어?

여: [잠시 후] 오, 여기 네 휴대폰이 있다! 너는 그것을 의자 위에 두고 갔어.

남: 좋아. 고마워. 내가 지금 가서 그것을 찾아와도 될까?

여: 물론이지. 기다릴게.

단·어·및·표·현
leave [liːv] 동 ~을 두고 오다[가다]
place [pleis] 명 (개인의) 집, 살 곳
pick ~ up (어디에서) ~을 찾다[찾아오다]

13 수치파악 ▶정답 ③

듣·기·대·본

W: I'm really excited about the concert this Saturday.

M: Same here! It starts at 7 p.m., right?

W: Yes, how about meeting at 5 p.m.?

M: That seems a bit early. What about 6:30 p.m.?

W: There's a pre-concert meet and greet with the band. Wouldn't you like to meet them?

M: That sounds fantastic! Let's meet at 6 p.m. then.

W: Perfect. See you at the entrance to the stadium!

우·리·말·해·석

여: 나는 이번 토요일에 있을 콘서트가 너무 기대돼.

남: 나도 그래! 오후 7시에 시작하잖아, 맞지?

여: 응, 오후 5시에 만나는 거 어때?

남: 약간 이른 것 같아. 오후 6시 30분은 어때?

여: 콘서트 시작 전 밴드와 팬미팅이 있어. 넌 그들을 만나고 싶지 않아?

남: 굉장하게 들리는걸! 그러면 오후 6시에 만나자.

여: 완벽해. 경기장 입구에서 보자!

단·어·및·표·현
a bit 약간, 조금, 다소
pre- ~ 전의, 미리
meet and greet 팬미팅
entrance [éntrəns] 명 입구, 출입구
stadium [stéidiəm] 명 경기장

14 대화자관계추론 ▶정답 ⑤

듣·기·대·본

W: This fits me nicely but I don't like the color. Do you have this in green?

M: No, I'm sorry. That style only comes in blue and red.

W: Hmm… May I try the blue one?

M: Of course. Here you are.

W: I would like a smaller size, please. This one is too big.

M: Oh, I'm sorry. Here's a medium.

W: Thank you.

M: How about a pair of jeans to go with that shirt? All jeans are on sale until tomorrow.

W: That's great! I was thinking of getting new jeans.

우·리·말·해·석

여: 이건 제게 잘 맞지만 색이 마음에 들지 않아요. 이거 녹색이 있나요?

남: 죄송하지만, 없습니다. 그 스타일은 파랑과 빨강으로만 나와요.

여: 음… 파란색을 입어봐도 될까요?

남: 물론이죠, 여기 있습니다.

여: 좀 더 작은 사이즈 부탁해요. 이건 너무 크네요.

남: 아, 죄송합니다. 여기 중간 사이즈 있습니다.

여: 감사합니다.

남: 그 셔츠와 어울리는 청바지는 어떠세요? 내일까지 모든 청바지가 할인됩니다.

여: 그거 좋네요! 전 새 청바지를 사려고 생각 중이었거든요.

단·어·및·표·현
fit [fit] 동 (모양·크기가) 맞다

15 부탁(요청)한일파악 ▶정답 ①

듣·기·대·본

W: Ryan, I'm going out to a movie with Emily.

M: Okay, have fun, you two!

W: Hmm… Honey, have you seen my phone? I can't find it.

M: Nope, I haven't seen it. Have you checked your purse?

W: Yes, it isn't here.

M: Where could it have gone?

W: I'm sorry, but can you call my phone so that I can find it?

M: No problem. I'm calling it right now.

W: Oh, I think I can hear it ringing in our bedroom.

우·리·말·해·석

여: Ryan, 나 Emily와 함께 영화 보러 나가요.

남: 알겠어요, 즐거운 시간 보내세요, 두 분!

여: 흠… 여보, 내 전화기 봤어요? 나 못 찾겠어요.

남: 아뇨, 난 못 봤어요. 손가방은 확인해 봤어요?

여: 네, 그것은 여기에 없어요.

남: 그게 어디로 갔을까요?

여: 미안하지만, 내 전화기로 전화해서 내가 그것을 찾을 수 있게 해줄래요?

남: 그럼요. 지금 바로 전화할게요.

여: 아, 내 생각에 우리 침실에서 그것이 울리는 소리가 들리는 것 같아요.

단·어·및·표·현

go out 나가다, 외출하다
purse[pəːrs] 몡 손가방, (특히 여성용의 작은) 지갑
ring[ríŋ] 통 (벨이) 울리다

16 이유파악 ▶정답 ⑤

듣·기·대·본

M: Hi, Lisa. Are you still taking guitar lessons these days?
W: Oh, didn't I tell you? I <u>stopped going</u> to the lessons last week.
M: Really? Was it because the lesson <u>fees</u> went up?
W: No, the cost wasn't a problem.
M: Then, why did you stop going?
W: I wanted to change my class time, but they couldn't match the time I wanted.
M: Oh, okay. That's too bad.

우·리·말·해·석

남: 안녕, Lisa. 너 요즘에도 기타 수업을 계속 듣고 있니?
여: 아, 내가 말 안 했니? 나는 지난주에 그 수업에 가는 것을 그만뒀어.
남: 정말? 수업료가 올랐기 때문이니?
여: 아니, 비용은 문제가 아니었어.
남: 그럼, 왜 가는 걸 그만뒀어?
여: 나는 수업 시간을 바꾸고 싶었는데, 그들이 내가 원하는 시간에 맞춰 줄 수 없었어.
남: 아, 그렇구나. 그거 안타깝다.

단·어·및·표·현

fee[fiː] 몡 요금
cost[kɔ(ː)st] 몡 비용, 값
match[mætʃ] 통 ~와 맞추다

17 그림상황에적절한대화찾기 ▶정답 ④

듣·기·대·본

① W: Can you help me <u>solve</u> this problem?
  M: Of course. Let me see.
② W: Can I borrow your eraser <u>for a moment</u>?
  M: Sure. Here you are.
③ W: Where can I find the library?
  M: It's next to the post office.
④ W: Excuse me. Could you <u>stop clicking</u> your pen?
  M: Oh, I'm really sorry.
⑤ W: You look nice today. I like your new haircut.
  M: Thank you for the kind words!

우·리·말·해·석

① 여: 내가 이 문제 해결하는 것을 도와줄 수 있어?
  남: 물론이지. 어디 보자.
② 여: 잠깐 네 지우개를 빌려도 될까?
  남: 물론이지. 여기 있어.
③ 여: 어디서 도서관을 찾을 수 있나요?
  남: 그것은 우체국 옆에 있어요.
④ 여: 실례합니다. 펜을 딸깍거리는 것을 멈춰주시겠어요?
  남: 오, 정말 죄송해요.
⑤ 여: 너 오늘 멋져 보인다. 네 새로운 머리 모양이 마음에 들어.
  남: 친절한 말 고마워!

단·어·및·표·현

solve[sɑlv] 통 해결하다, 풀다
for a moment 잠깐, 잠시 동안
click[klik] 통 찰칵[딸깍]하는 소리를 내다, 클릭하다

18 대화미언급 ▶정답 ③

듣·기·대·본

W: <u>How about</u> we go to the Children's Job Experience Theme Park together?
M: The Children's Job Experience Theme Park? What is it <u>exactly</u>?
W: It's a special job experience program <u>for kids from 36 months old to 16 years old.</u> You can <u>try out</u> different jobs like a firefighter, a cook, and a doctor.
M: That's cool! How can I get a ticket?
W: You can buy the ticket online.
M: Great. Where is it <u>located</u>?
W: It's <u>next to the Nature Park Zoo.</u>

우·리·말·해·석

여: 우리 같이 어린이 직업 체험 테마파크에 가는 게 어때?
남: 어린이 직업 체험 테마파크? 그게 정확히 뭐야?
여: 그건 36개월부터 16살까지의 아이들을 위한 특별한 직업 체험 프로그램이야. 너는 소방관, 요리사, 그리고 의사 같은 다양한 직업들을 시도해 볼 수 있어.
남: 그거 멋지다! 티켓은 어떻게 구해?
여: 너는 온라인으로 티켓을 살 수 있어.
남: 좋네. 그건 어디에 있어?
여: 그건 자연 공원 동물원 옆에 위치해 있어.

단·어·및·표·현

experience[ikspí(ː)əriəns] 몡 경험
exactly[igzǽktli] 뿐 정확히
try out 시도해 보다
be located 위치해 있다

19 알맞은응답찾기 ▶정답 ⑤

듣·기·대·본

M: Hi, Jessica! You've been in such a good mood lately. What's going on?
W: Thank you for <u>noticing</u>. I've got a new hobby.
M: Oh, what is it?
W: I've been going to a painting class. It helps me relax and <u>take my mind off</u> things.
M: Good for you! I'm glad you found <u>something interesting</u>.
W: I never knew how much fun it could be to play with colors.
M: <u>How long have you been doing it?</u>
W: <u>I've been taking the class for a month.</u>

우·리·말·해·석

① 내 생각에 그것은 10미터 길이야.
② 나는 몇 시인지 모르겠어.
③ 밖에서 놀기엔 너무 늦었어.
④ 내가 벽을 칠하는 법을 보여줄게.
⑤ 나는 그 수업을 한 달 동안 듣고 있어.

남: 안녕, Jessica! 너 요즘 기분이 아주 좋아 보여. 무슨 일 있어?
여: 알아차려줘서 고마워. 나 새로운 취미가 생겼어.
남: 오, 그게 뭐야?
여: 나는 그림 수업에 다니고 있었어. 그건 내가 긴장을 풀고 일들을 잠시 잊어버리게 하는 데 도움이 돼.
남: 잘됐네! 난 네가 흥미 있어 하는 것을 찾아서 기뻐.
여: 나는 색을 가지고 노는 게 이렇게 재미있을 줄은 전혀 몰랐어.
남: 그것을 얼마나 오래 해 왔어?
여: <u>나는 그 수업을 한 달 동안 듣고 있어.</u>

mood[muːd] 몡 기분
notice[nóutis] 통 알아차리다
take one's mind off ~을 (잠시) 잊어버리다, ~에서 마음을 돌리다

20 알맞은응답찾기　　　　▶정답 ①

듣·기·대·본

W: Glen, I haven't signed up for any after-school programs yet. Have you?
M: Yes, I have registered for the science class.
W: Science class? What is it about?
M: We are going to do a lot of science experiments.
W: That sounds fun! What kind of experiments?
M: We'll be making things such as mini volcanoes and paper roller coasters.
W: Wow, that sounds pretty exciting!
M: Why don't you join me? The class is not full yet.
W: Definitely, I'd love to.

우·리·말·해·석

① 물론, 그리고 싶어.
② 오, 안타깝게 됐어.
③ 그러면, 너는 더 먹어야 해.
④ 아니. 롤러코스터는 날 무섭게 해. (난 롤러코스터가 무서워.)
⑤ 웹사이트를 확인해 봐.

여: Glen, 나는 아직 어떤 방과 후 학교 프로그램도 신청하지 못했어. 너는 했니?
남: 응, 나는 과학 수업에 등록했어.
여: 과학 수업? 그건 무엇에 관한 거야?
남: 우리는 많은 과학 실험들을 할 거야.
여: 재밌겠는걸! 어떤 종류의 실험?
남: 우리는 작은 화산이나 종이 롤러코스터 같은 것들을 만들 거야.
여: 와, 매우 신나겠는걸!
남: 나와 함께하는 게 어때? 수업은 아직 가득 차지 않았어.
여: **물론, 그리고 싶어.**

단·어·및·표·현

sign up for ~을 신청하다
yet[jet] 뿐 아직
register[rédʒistər] 통 등록하다, 신청하다
experiment[ikspérəmənt] 몡 실험
such as ~ 같은
volcano[vɑlkéinou] 몡 화산
pretty[príti] 뿐 매우, 아주
full[ful] 혱 가득 찬, 만원의

Words & Expressions Review

1. ~과 어울리다	2. 알아차리다	3. 시도해 보다
4. 정확히	5. 실험	6. 불만스러운, 좌절감을 주는
7. ~을 작성하다	8. 경험	9. ~으로 알려진
10. 발표하다, 알리다	11. 미드필더	12. ~을 두고 오다 [가다]
13. 운동회 날	14. 비용, 값	15. 휴지통
16. 페이스 페인팅	17. 곧	18. 즐겁게 보내다
19. 미역, 해초	20. 요금	21. ~을 돌려주다
22. 대기질, 공기의 질	23. (벨이) 울리다	24. (개인의) 집, 살 곳
25. 승낙하다, 동의하다	26. 손가방	27. 대회, 시합
28. 등록하다, 신청하다	29. 입구, 출입구	30. 맛있는
31. 참가 신청서	32. 다정한, 상냥한	33. 잃어버리다
34. 기꺼이 ~하다	35. 기온, 온도	36. 할인[세일] 중인
37. (변화·발달 과정상의 한) 단계	38. (크기가) 맞다	39. 비우다
40. 나가다, 외출하다	41. 일정	42. ~의 편을 들다
43. 그림을 그리다	44. 지독한, 끔찍한	

Listening Test
영어듣기 모의고사 05회

|정답|

01 ③	02 ⑤	03 ②	04 ⑤	05 ②
06 ⑤	07 ③	08 ①	09 ④	10 ①
11 ⑤	12 ③	13 ④	14 ②	15 ③
16 ④	17 ⑤	18 ④	19 ⑤	20 ③

01 날씨파악-그림　　　　▶정답 ③

듣·기·대·본

W: Good morning. Here's the weekly weather forecast. On Monday, it'll be sunny all day. On Tuesday and Wednesday, it'll be cloudy and windy. On Thursday, it'll start raining and the rain will continue until early Saturday morning. After the rain, we can expect clear skies for the rest of the weekend. Thank you.

우·리·말·해·석

여: 좋은 아침입니다. 주간 일기 예보입니다. 월요일에는 하루 종일 맑을 것입니다. 화요일과 수요일에는 흐리고 바람이 불 것입니다. 목요일은 비가 오기 시작할 것이고 그 비는 토요일 이른 아침까지 계속될 것입니다. 비가 온 후에는 남은 주말 동안 맑은 하늘이 예상됩니다. 감사합니다.

단·어·및·표·현

weekly weather forecast 주간 일기 예보
continue[kəntínju(ː)] 통 계속하다, 지속시키다
expect[ikspékt] 통 예상하다, 기대하다

02 그림정보파악　　　　▶정답 ⑤

듣·기·대·본

M: Honey, we need to decide on a towel design.
W: It's a gift for the guests coming to Peggy's first birthday party, isn't it?
M: Right. How about the one with a rabbit?
W: I think a towel with a pig is better. She was born in the Year of the Pig.
M: Okay. Why don't we put her birth date, July 30, on it?
W: Good idea. Let's put the date below the pig.

M: Great. I'll place an order, then.

우·리·말·해·석

남: 여보, 우리는 수건 디자인에 대해 결정해야 해요.

여: 그것은 Peggy의 돌잔치에 오는 손님들을 위한 선물이죠, 그렇지 않아요?

남: 맞아요. 토끼가 있는 것이 어때요?

여: 나는 돼지가 있는 수건이 더 좋다고 생각해요. 그녀는 돼지 해에 태어났어요.

남: 좋아요. 그녀의 생일인 7월 30일을 그것에 표시하는 것이 어때요?

여: 좋은 생각이에요. 날짜를 돼지 밑에 두어요.

남: 좋아요. 그러면 내가 주문을 할게요.

단·어·및·표·현

below [bilóu] 전 ~ 밑에

place an order 주문하다

03 심정추론 ▶정답 ②

듣·기·대·본

W: Gary, I heard you hurt your finger.

M: Oh, yeah. It's okay, though. It'll heal.

W: But, you won't be able to play the guitar at the festival. Aren't you upset?

M: I'm not. Because I got to play a role in the school play instead!

W: Really? That's amazing!

M: I'm still part of the school festival. So I'm fine.

W: You're right. I'm happy for you.

M: Thanks. Life isn't all that bad!

우·리·말·해·석

① 걱정하는 　　② 즐거운 　　③ 속상한
④ 지루한 　　⑤ 놀란

여: Gary, 나 네가 네 손가락을 다쳤다고 들었어.

남: 오, 맞아. 근데, 괜찮아. 나을 거야.

여: 하지만, 너는 축제에서 기타를 연주할 수 없잖아. 너 속상하지 않아?

남: 속상하지 않아. 왜냐하면 나는 대신에 학교 연극에서 역할을 맡았거든!

여: 정말? 그거 멋지다!

남: 나는 아직 학교 축제의 구성원이야. 그래서 나는 괜찮아.

여: 네 말이 맞아. 네가 잘 되어 기쁘다.

남: 고마워. 인생은 모두 그렇게 나쁘지는 않아!

단·어·및·표·현

upset [ʌpsét] 형 속상한, 마음이 상한

play a role 역할을 맡다

play [plei] 명 연극

part [pɑːrt] 명 구성원, 일원

04 한일파악 ▶정답 ⑤

듣·기·대·본

M: Hi, Sarah. Will you be coming to the school play tonight?

W: Of course. How are you feeling right now?

M: I'm fine, but I'm also a bit nervous.

W: Yeah, it's a big responsibility. What is your role in the play?

M: I'm not participating as an actor this time.

W: Oh, then how are you connected to the play?

M: I made costumes for all of the actors.

W: That's amazing! I'll take a close look at the costumes tonight.

우·리·말·해·석

남: 안녕, Sarah. 너는 오늘 밤 학교 연극에 올 거니?

여: 물론이지. 지금 기분이 어때?

남: 괜찮지만 약간 긴장되기도 해.

여: 응, 책임감이 크구나. 연극에서 너의 역할은 뭐야?

남: 이번에 난 배우로 참여하지 않아.

여: 오, 그러면 넌 연극과 어떻게 관련되어 있어?

남: 난 모든 배우들의 의상을 만들었어.

여: 놀라운걸! 오늘 밤 의상들을 주의 깊게 볼게.

단·어·및·표·현

responsibility [rispɑ̀nsəbíləti] 명 책임, 책임감

connected to ~과 관련된

costume [kɑ́stjuːm] 명 (연극·영화 등에서) 의상

take a close look at ~을 주의 깊게 보다

05 대화장소추론 ▶정답 ②

듣·기·대·본

M: Hello. How may I help you?

W: Hi. I'm here to pick up my laundry. My name is Sarah Cho.

M: It's four blouses and two coats, right?

W: That's right! How do you remember all that?

M: Well, one of your coats has such a unique design.

W: Thank you. Oh, my blouses look brand new!

M: Our new washing machine works like magic.

W: Thank you so much. I should bring in more clothes.

M: Any time.

우·리·말·해·석

남: 안녕하세요. 어떻게 도와드릴까요?

여: 안녕하세요. 제 세탁물을 가지러 왔어요. 제 이름은 Sarah Cho예요.

남: 블라우스 네 개와 코트 두 개, 맞죠?

여: 맞아요! 어떻게 그 모든 것을 기억하세요?

남: 음, 손님의 코트 중 하나가 매우 독특한 디자인이기 때문이죠.

여: 감사합니다. 아, 제 블라우스가 완전히 새 것처럼 보여요!

남: 저희의 새 세탁기가 마법처럼 작동합니다.

여: 정말 감사합니다. 제가 옷들을 더 가져와야겠어요.

남: 언제든지요.

단·어·및·표·현

unique [juːníːk] 형 독특한

brand new 완전히 새 것인

06 마지막말의도파악 ▶정답 ⑤

듣·기·대·본

W: Hello, Johnny, fancy meeting you here! What did you buy?

M: Oh, hi, Ellen! I just bought something for dinner. How about you? Wow, that's a lot of groceries.

W: Yeah, it's for Dad's birthday celebration tomorrow.

M: I see. Hmm… Can you carry all of those by yourself? Let me take some of them for you.

W: No, thanks. Don't worry, I can manage.

우·리·말·해·석

여: 안녕, Johnny, 여기서 널 만나니 좋다! 너 무엇을 샀니?

남: 오, 안녕, Ellen! 나 저녁거리를 좀 샀어. 넌 어때? 와, 정말 많은 식료품이구나.

여: 응, 이것들은 내일 아빠 생신 축하를 위한 것들이야.

남: 그렇구나. 흠… 너 혼자서 그거 다 가져갈 수 있어? 내가 너를 위해 좀 들어줄게.

여: 아니, 고맙지만 됐어. 걱정 마, 나 혼자 감당할 수 있어.

단·어·및·표·현

by oneself 혼자서
manage [mǽnidʒ] (동) 감당하다, 처리하다, 다루다

07 특정정보파악 ▶정답 ③

듣·기·대·본

M: Are you excited about the school picnic tomorrow?
W: Of course, Dad! My friends and I will do a dance cover in front of the class.
M: Oh, wow. Did you pack the costume, then?
W: Yeah, a jean jacket and a red hairband.
M: What about sunglasses?
W: No, we decided not to wear them.
M: Should you bring your lunch?
W: Yes. Mom will pack it for me.
M: Good. Why don't you put a water bottle in the bag now?
W: OK, Dad.

우·리·말·해·석

남: 내일 학교 소풍 때문에 신이 나니?
여: 당연하죠, 아빠! 제 친구들이랑 저는 반 친구들 앞에서 커버 댄스를 할 거예요.
남: 오, 우와. 그러면 의상도 챙겼니?
여: 네, 청재킷이랑 빨간 머리띠요.
남: 선글라스는?
여: 아니요, 저희는 그것을 안 쓰기로 결정했어요.
남: 점심 도시락을 가져가야 하지?
여: 네, 엄마가 저를 위해 싸 주실 거예요.
남: 좋아. 지금 가방에 물통을 넣어놓는 게 어때?
여: 알겠어요, 아빠.

단·어·및·표·현

jean jacket 청재킷
Why don't you ~? ~하는 게 어때?

08 할일파악(대화직후) ▶정답 ①

듣·기·대·본

M: Suji, I'm so sorry that I'm late.
W: What happened, Jiho? The movie has already started.
M: I know. I took the wrong bus, and had to take another one to get here.
W: I see. But why didn't you call me?
M: My battery died. I'm so sorry. It's all my fault.
W: Well, let's just get tickets for the next showing.
M: Sure. Let's do that.

우·리·말·해·석

남: 수지야, 늦어서 정말 미안해.
여: 무슨 일이 있었니, 지호야? 영화가 이미 시작했어.
남: 알아. 내가 버스를 잘못 타서 다시 다른 버스를 바꿔 타고 와야 했어.
여: 알겠어. 하지만 왜 나에게 전화하지 않았어?
남: 내 배터리가 방전됐어. 정말 미안해. 모두 내 잘못이야.
여: 어쨌든, 그냥 다음 상영 시간의 표를 사자.
남: 물론이지. 그렇게 하자.

단·어·및·표·현

another [ənʌ́ðər] (형) 다른
fault [fɔːlt] (명) 잘못
showing [ʃóuiŋ] (명) (영화) 상영

09 대화미언급 ▶정답 ④

듣·기·대·본

(*Telephone rings.*)
M: Hello, Barnes Books.
W: Hello, I heard Chris Bunner has a book signing this week. When is it exactly?
M: It's this Sunday at 3 p.m.
W: I see. Where is it going to be held?
M: It'll be held at the café inside our bookstore.
W: Great. How long will the event be?
M: It's scheduled to last two hours.
W: Can I take a picture with the author?
M: Of course, you can.
W: That's great. Thanks.

우·리·말·해·석

(전화벨이 울린다.)
남: 여보세요, Barnes Books입니다.
여: 여보세요, 저는 Chris Bunner가 이번 주에 책 사인회를 한다고 들었어요. 그것이 정확히 언제인가요?
남: 이번 주 일요일 오후 3시입니다.
여: 알겠어요. 어디에서 열릴 것인가요?
남: 그것은 저희 서점 내의 카페에서 열릴 것입니다.
여: 좋아요. 그 행사가 얼마나 길까요?
남: 그것은 2시간 동안 지속될 예정입니다.
여: 제가 작가와 사진을 찍을 수 있나요?
남: 물론 하실 수 있습니다.
여: 그거 좋네요. 고맙습니다.

단·어·및·표·현

be held ~이 열리다, 개최되다

10 담화화제추론 ▶정답 ①

듣·기·대·본

W: Hello, students. I am going to tell you how to access online classes, so listen carefully. Each of your accounts is already created. All you need to do is to log in. Your ID is your student email address. The password is randomly created and sent to your email. So, when you first log in, don't forget to change your password.

우·리·말·해·석

여: 안녕하세요, 학생 여러분. 온라인 수업에 접속하는 법을 알려드리려고 하니 주의 깊게 들으세요. 여러분들의 각 계정은 이미 생성되었습니다. 여러분은 로그인만 하시면 됩니다. 여러분의 ID는 여러분의 학생 이메일 주소입니다. 비밀번호는 무작위로 생성되었고 여러분의 이메일로 보내졌습니다. 그러니, 처음 로그인하실 때, 비밀번호를 바꾸는 것을 잊지 마세요.

단·어·및·표·현

access [ǽksès] (동) 접속하다
account [əkáunt] (명) 계정
randomly [rǽndəmli] (부) 무작위로

11 대화내용불일치 ▶정답 ⑤

듣·기·대·본

W: Honey, why don't we take a bike tour tomorrow?
M: Good idea. We can enjoy Barcelona in a special way.
W: According to this website, we can rent a bike for €10.
M: That's nice! A guide will take us to five different sights.
W: The tour takes three hours and it's free.

M: Wonderful! They have morning and afternoon tour times.
W: Let's take a morning tour. Do we need to make a reservation?
M: No, we just need to be at the meeting point at 9 a.m.

우·리·말·해·석

여: 여보, 우리 내일 자전거 투어를 하는 게 어때요?
남: 좋은 생각이에요. 우리는 Barcelona를 특별한 방법으로 즐길 수 있어요.
여: 이 웹사이트에 따르면, 우리는 자전거 한 대를 10유로에 빌릴 수 있어요.
남: 그거 좋네요! 가이드가 우리를 다섯 개의 다른 관광지들로 데려갈 거예요.
여: 투어는 세 시간 걸리고 무료예요.
남: 훌륭해요! 오전과 오후 투어 시간이 있어요.
여: 오전 투어를 해요. 우리가 예약을 할 필요가 있나요?
남: 아니요, 우리는 단지 오전 9시에 모이는 지점에 있어야 해요.

단·어·및·표·현

rent [rent] ⑧ 빌리다
make a reservation 예약하다

12 전화목적파악 ▶정답 ③

듣·기·대·본

(Telephone rings.)
M: Hello. Joy Community Center.
W: Hi. I signed up for the morning aerobics program, but I'd like to change it.
M: May I have your name?
W: Becky Han.
M: Okay. (Typing sound) How would you like to change it?
W: I signed up for the 10 a.m. class and I'd like to change it to the 8 p.m. class.
M: Sure. (Pause) All set. Now you're in the evening class for the aerobics program.
W: Thank you.

우·리·말·해·석

(전화벨이 울린다.)
남: 여보세요. Joy 지역주민 센터입니다.
여: 안녕하세요. 저는 아침 에어로빅 프로그램에 등록했는데 그것을 변경하고 싶어요.
남: 당신의 이름을 알 수 있을까요?
여: Becky Han입니다.
남: 알겠습니다. (타자 소리) 어떻게 변경하시겠어요?
여: 저는 오전 10시 수업에 등록했는데 오후 8시 수업으로 변경하고 싶어요.
남: 알겠습니다. (잠시 후) 다 됐습니다. 이제 당신은 에어로빅 프로그램의 저녁 수업에 들어가 있습니다.
여: 감사합니다.

단·어·및·표·현

sign up for ~ ~에 등록하다
aerobics [ɛəróubiks] ⑲ 에어로빅

13 수치파악 ▶정답 ④

듣·기·대·본

W: Welcome to the Baek Art Gallery. May I help you?
M: Hi, I'd like to buy three tickets, please.
W: Okay. The tickets are 10 dollars each.
M: Can I use these 20% discount coupons?

W: Of course you can. That'll take 2 dollars off each ticket.
M: Then, it's 8 dollars each, right?
W: Right. So, it'll be 24 dollars in total.
M: Okay. Here you are.

우·리·말·해·석

여: 백 미술관에 오신 것을 환영합니다. 도와드릴까요?
남: 안녕하세요. 입장권 세 장을 구매하고 싶어요.
여: 알겠습니다. 입장권은 장당 10달러입니다.
남: 제가 이 20% 할인 쿠폰을 사용할 수 있나요?
여: 물론 사용하실 수 있습니다. 그건 각 입장권에서 2달러씩 할인될 거예요.
남: 그러면, 장당 8달러네요, 그렇죠?
여: 맞습니다. 따라서, 총 24달러가 될 거예요.
남: 알겠습니다. 여기 있어요.

단·어·및·표·현

art gallery 미술관, 화랑
discount [diskáunt] ⑲ 할인
take ~ off (표시된 금액 등에서) ~을 빼다, 할인하다
in total 총, 모두 합하여

14 대화자관계추론 ▶정답 ②

듣·기·대·본

M: Good evening, ma'am. Can I take your order?
W: Yes. I'll have the cranberry salad and the beef steak.
M: How would you like your steak?
W: I want it medium.
M: Okay. Would you like something to drink?
W: Just water with lemon, please.
M: Alright. Anything else I can get you?
W: No, thanks. That's all.

우·리·말·해·석

남: 안녕하십니까, 손님. 주문을 받아도 될까요?
여: 네. 크랜베리 샐러드와 쇠고기 스테이크로 하겠어요.
남: 스테이크는 어떻게 익혀드릴까요?
여: 중간 정도로 익혀주세요.
남: 알겠습니다. 마실 것은 어떠신지요?
여: 그냥 레몬을 넣은 물을 주세요.
남: 알겠습니다. 제가 가져다 드릴 다른 거라도 있나요?
여: 괜찮습니다. 그게 전부예요.

단·어·및·표·현

take an order 주문을 받다

15 부탁(요청)한일파악 ▶정답 ③

듣·기·대·본

W: Honey, we should finish unpacking our stuff today.
M: Good idea. Let's start with our study then.
W: Okay. These boxes are packed with books, right?
M: Yeah. Let's start unpacking these first.
W: If you open the boxes, I'll put the books on the bookshelf.
M: Okay. These boxes are heavily wrapped with tape. Could you pass me the scissors?
W: Yes. Here you go.

우·리·말·해·석

여: 여보, 우리 오늘 짐 푸는 걸 마쳐야 해요.
남: 좋은 생각이에요. 그러면 서재부터 시작하죠.
여: 그래요. 이 상자들은 책들로 차 있죠, 맞죠?

남: 맞아요. 우리 이것들 먼저 풀어요.
여: 당신이 상자를 열면, 제가 책들을 책꽂이에 꽂을게요.
남: 알았어요. 이 상자들이 테이프로 아주 많이 싸여 있어요. 가위 좀 건네 줄래요?
여: 네. 여기 있어요.

Here you go. (상대방에게 무엇을 주면서) 여기 있어요.

16 이유파악 ▶정답 ④

듣·기·대·본

M: Ms. Choi is <u>angry at me</u> because I'm late.
W: Again? Why are you often late these days?
M: I can't sleep well at night.
W: Why? Do you <u>take a nap</u> during the daytime?
M: After school? No. You know we both don't have time. We have to study.
W: Then, what is it? Is there something that's <u>worrying</u> you?
M: No. It's my baby brother. He <u>wakes up at night and cries</u>.
W: Oh, dear.

우·리·말·해·석

남: 내가 지각했기 때문에 최 선생님이 나에게 화가 나셨어.
여: 또? 너 요즘 왜 자주 지각해?
남: 밤에 잘 잘 수가 없어.
여: 왜? 낮에 낮잠을 자니?
남: 학교 끝나고? 아니. 너는 우리 둘 다 시간이 없다는 것을 알잖아. 우리 는 공부해야 해.
여: 그러면, 뭐야? 너를 걱정하게 하는 뭔가가 있니?
남: 아니. 내 아기 동생이야. 그가 밤에 깨서 울어.
여: 아, 저런.

단·어·및·표·현

angry at ~ ~에게 화난
Dear. 저런.

17 그림상황에적절한대화찾기 ▶정답 ⑤

듣·기·대·본

① W: How are we going to get there?
　 M: Let's take the subway. It'll be fast.
② W: Music is too loud in this café.
　 M: <u>I agree</u>. Shall we speak to the waiter?
③ W: Excuse me. Is this seat taken?
　 M: No, I'm sorry. I'll <u>move my backpack</u>.
④ W: Let's sit down and listen to some music.
　 M: OK. I'll take my earphones out.
⑤ W: Can you <u>turn down</u> the music?
　 M: Of course. I'm sorry it was too loud.

우·리·말·해·석

① 여: 우리 어떻게 거기까지 가지?
　 남: 지하철을 타자. 그게 빠를 거야.
② 여: 이 카페 안의 노래가 너무 시끄러워.
　 남: 나도 동의해. 우리 웨이터한테 말할까?
③ 여: 실례합니다. 여기 자리 있나요?
　 남: 아뇨, 죄송합니다. 제 가방을 치울게요.
④ 여: 앉아서 음악 좀 듣자.
　 남: 그래. 내가 이어폰 꺼낼게.
⑤ 여: 음악 소리 좀 줄여주실 수 있나요?
　 남: 물론이죠. 너무 시끄러웠다면 죄송합니다.

단·어·및·표·현

turn down (소리·온도 등을) 줄이다

18 담화미언급 ▶정답 ④

듣·기·대·본

W: Good morning, listeners! Today I want to introduce a new book. The title is *Talking to the Moon*. The book was <u>written</u> by a best-selling writer, Sujan Lee. The story is about children's friendship and courage, just like her previous books. It's already at number five on the Amazon <u>best sellers list</u>. This book will make an excellent present for your children. So, don't <u>miss it</u>!

우·리·말·해·석

여: 좋은 아침입니다. 청취자분들! 오늘 저는 새로운 책을 한 권 소개하고 싶습니다. 제목은 "Talking to the Moon"입니다. 이 책은 베스트셀러 작가인 Sujan Lee에 의해 집필됐습니다. 이 이야기는 그녀의 이전 책 들과 마찬가지로 아이들의 우정과 용기에 관한 것입니다. 그것은 이미 아마존 베스트셀러 5위에 올랐습니다. 이 책은 당신의 아이들에게 훌 륭한 선물이 될 것입니다. 그러니, 놓치지 마세요!

단·어·및·표·현

friendship [fréndʃip] 몡 우정
courage [kə́:ridʒ] 몡 용기, 용감
previous [prí:viəs] 혱 이전의, 앞선

19 알맞은응답찾기 ▶정답 ⑤

듣·기·대·본

M: Excuse me. Are you a local here?
W: Yes, why do you ask?
M: I'm looking for a hospital. Is there a hospital near here?
W: There is. <u>Go down that road</u> and turn left when you get to the end.
M: Oh, <u>on foot</u>? How long will it take?
W: About 20 minutes. It's only <u>a few blocks away</u>.
M: Is there a bus, too?
W: Yes, but you're going to have to wait for 20 minutes for it.
M: I should walk then. Thank you.

우·리·말·해·석

① 괜찮아요. 저는 뛰는 것을 좋아해요. ② 쉽게 찾을 거예요.
③ 걱정 마세요. 멀지 않아요. ④ 알겠어요. 저는 20번을 탈게요.
⑤ 그러면 저는 걸어야겠어요. 고맙습니다.

남: 실례합니다. 여기 주민이신가요?
여: 네, 왜 물어보세요?
남: 저는 병원을 찾고 있어요. 이 근처에 병원이 있나요?
여: 있어요. 저 길을 내려가서 끝에 가면 왼쪽으로 도세요.
남: 오, 걸어서요? 얼마나 걸려요?
여: 약 20분이요. 그것은 단지 몇 블록만 떨어져 있어요.
남: 버스도 있나요?
여: 네, 하지만 20분 동안 기다려야 할 거예요.
남: <u>그러면 저는 걸어야겠어요. 고맙습니다.</u>

단·어·및·표·현

local [lóukəl] 몡 (특정 지역에 사는) 주민, 현지인
on foot 걸어서, 도보로
a few 몇, 약간의

20

20 알맞은응답찾기 ▶정답 ③

듣·기·대·본

M: Mom, can I go out to the movies with my friends?

W: Sure, you can. But have you finished your homework?

M: Of course! I finished it earlier so that I could go out.

W: Then, did you clean your room like I told you to?

M: Yes, Mom. I've done everything you told me to.

W: Good job! Well, in that case, go have fun at the movies then.

M: Thanks, Mom. I'll be leaving in a minute.

W: Okay. When will you be back home?

M: I'll be home for dinner.

우·리·말·해·석

① 저녁 식사는 7시예요.

② 저는 학교에 가야 해요.

③ 저녁 먹으러 집에 올 거예요.

④ 영화는 2시간이에요.

⑤ 아니요, 저는 숙제가 없어요.

남: 엄마, 저 친구들이랑 영화 보러 나가도 돼요?

여: 물론 가도 되지. 그런데 네 숙제는 다 끝냈니?

남: 당연하죠! 저는 외출할 수 있도록 그것을 아까 끝내놨어요.

여: 그러면 내가 너에게 말한 대로 방도 청소했니?

남: 네, 엄마. 저는 엄마가 저에게 하라고 얘기하신 것 전부 다 했어요.

여: 잘했구나! 그래. 그렇다면 영화관에 가서 재밌게 즐기렴.

남: 고마워요, 엄마. 저 바로 나갈게요.

여: 그래. 너 언제 집에 돌아올 거니?

남: 저녁 먹으러 집에 올 거예요.

단·어·및·표·현

go to the movies 영화관에 가다, 영화 보러 가다

in that case 그렇다면, 그런 경우에는

have fun 즐기다, 재미있게 놀다

Words & Expressions Review

1. 걸어서, 도보로	2. ~과 관련된	3. 우정
4. 책임, 책임감	5. 완전히 새 것인	6. 밑에
7. 이전의, 앞선	8. 긴장한, 불안한	9. (짐을) 풀다
10. 구성원, 일원	11. (특정 지역에 사는) 주민, 현지인	12. ~에게 화난
13. (소리·온도 등을) 줄이다	14. 그 밖에 다른 것	15. 독특한
16. ~에 등록하다	17. 주문하다	18. A를 꺼내다
19. 용기, 용감	20. ~이 열리다, 개최되다	21. 예약하다
22. 쉽게 찾을 거예요.	23. 잘못, 결함	24. 아주 많이, 심하게
25. 예상하다, 기대하다	26. 접속하다	27. 의상, 복장
28. 그렇다면, 그런 경우에는	29. 주문을 받다	30. 역할을 맡다
31. 감당하다, 처리하다	32. 혼자서	33. 미술관, 화랑
34. 식료품	35. 할인	36. 총, 모두 합하여
37. 다른, 또 하나의	38. ~으로 싸여 있다	39. 속상한, 마음이 상한
40. ~할 예정이다	41. 무작위로	42. 낮 (시간)
43. 계정	44. 계속하다, 지속시키다	

영어듣기 모의고사 06회

|정|답|

01 ④	02 ⑤	03 ①	04 ④	05 ②
06 ⑤	07 ③	08 ③	09 ④	10 ④
11 ④	12 ①	13 ③	14 ②	15 ①
16 ③	17 ④	18 ④	19 ③	20 ⑤

01 날씨파악-그림 ▶정답 ④

듣·기·대·본

W: Good evening. This is the weekly weather report of Sunday. Tomorrow, it will continue to rain, so don't forget your umbrella. We'll have clear skies from Tuesday to Wednesday. But on Thursday, we're expecting some heavy wind. The wind will be over by Friday morning, and it will get chilly with a bit of snow.

우·리·말·해·석

여: 좋은 저녁입니다. 일요일의 주간 일기 예보입니다. 내일은 계속해서 비가 올 예정이므로, 우산을 챙기는 것을 잊지 마세요. 화요일부터 수요일까지는 맑게 갠 하늘을 볼 수 있을 것입니다. 하지만 목요일에는 강풍이 불 것으로 예상됩니다. 바람은 금요일 아침에 멈출 것이고 약간의 눈과 함께 쌀쌀해질 전망입니다.

단·어·및·표·현

clear sky 맑게 갠 하늘

02 그림정보파악 ▶정답 ⑤

듣·기·대·본

M: Honey, I made this wooden box for Noah to store his toys.

W: Great! I can see there's a handle on top of the box.

M: Yes, the handle will make it easier to open the box.

W: Wow! You even carved his name on the front of the box!

M: Yes. I thought about putting the word 'Toys' there, but I decided to carve his name 'Noah' onto it instead.

W: I think that's better. Noah will like it.

우·리·말·해·석

남: 여보, 나는 Noah가 그의 장난감들을 보관할 이 나무 상자를 만들었어요.

여: 훌륭해요! 상자 위에 손잡이가 있는 게 보이네요.

남: 그래요, 그 손잡이는 상자를 여는 것을 더 쉽게 할 거예요.

여: 왜 당신은 상자 앞에 그의 이름을 새기기도 했어요!

남: 네. 나는 거기에 '장난감들'이라는 단어를 넣는 것에 대해 생각했었지만, 대신에 거기에 그의 이름인 'Noah'를 새기기로 결정했어요.

여: 나는 그것이 더 좋다고 생각해요. Noah가 그것을 좋아할 거예요.

단·어·및·표·현

wooden [wúdən] 형 나무로 된

carve [kɑːrv] 동 새기다, 조각하다

03 심정추론 ▶정답 ①

듣·기·대·본

M: Rita, did you hear the news about the fire?

W: What fire?

M: The diner on Bernard Street burnt down last night.

W: Oh, dear. Did anybody get hurt?

M: Thankfully, no. But, the police say the fire was not an

accident.

W: Someone set the fire? That's horrible!

M: Yeah. The house fire that happened last month could have been set by the same person.

W: That's frightening. It means there's a criminal in our town!

우·리·말·해·석

① 무서워하는　　　② 고맙게 여기는　　　③ 지루한
④ 즐거운　　　⑤ 평화로운

남: Rita, 너 화재에 대한 소식 들었어?

여: 무슨 화재?

남: 지난밤 Bernard Street에 있는 작은 식당이 불에 타버렸대.

여: 오, 저런. 누군가 다쳤니?

남: 다행히도, 안 다쳤어. 하지만, 경찰이 말하기를 그 화재는 사고가 아니었대.

여: 누군가 불을 지른 거야? 그건 너무 끔찍해!

남: 맞아. 지난달에 발생했던 주택 방화도 같은 사람이 저질렀을지도 몰라.

여: 무섭다. 그것은 우리 도시에 범인이 있다는 거잖아!

단·어·및·표·현

diner[dáinər] 명 작은 식당
burn down 타버리다, (화재로) 소실되다
set a fire 불 지르다, 방화하다
horrible[hɔ́(:)rəbl] 형 끔찍한, 소름 끼치는
could have + 과거분사 ~였을지 모른다
frightening[fráitniŋ] 형 무서운, 깜짝 놀라게 하는
criminal[krímənəl] 명 범인, 범죄자

04 한일파악　　　▶정답 ④

듣·기·대·본

M: Mindy, I heard you went to City Music Festival last weekend.

W: Yes! There were so many people dancing and taking pictures.

M: That sounds like a lot of fun. Did you see any bands playing?

W: Sadly, no. I was too busy.

M: Doing what?

W: I handed out safety flyers to people and took out trash.

M: Oh! You weren't there to enjoy. You were there to help.

W: Yeah. I volunteered weeks ago.

우·리·말·해·석

남: Mindy, 나는 네가 지난 주말에 City Music Festival에 갔다고 들었어.

여: 응! 춤추고 사진 찍는 사람들이 무척 많았어.

남: 엄청 재미있었겠다. 밴드들이 연주하는 것을 보았니?

여: 슬프게도 못 봤어. 나는 너무 바빴어.

남: 뭘 하느라고?

여: 나는 안전 전단지를 사람들에게 나눠 주고 쓰레기를 치웠어.

남: 아! 너는 거기 즐기러 간 게 아니구나. 너는 도우러 갔구나.

여: 응. 나는 몇 주 전에 자원했어.

단·어·및·표·현

hand out 나눠 주다
flyer[fláiər] 명 전단

05 대화장소추론　　　▶정답 ②

듣·기·대·본

W: May I help you?

M: Hello. I'm here for the 2 o'clock session.

W: Oh, are you Mr. Simmonds?

M: Yes. My wife and the kids are on their way.

W: Is this your first time having a family photo taken?

M: No, we've done it before.

W: Great. The photographer is experienced with kids, so it'll be a fun session.

M: That's nice. Can I go get changed? I've brought my suit.

W: Sure. The changing room is over there.

우·리·말·해·석

여: 무엇을 도와드릴까요?

남: 안녕하세요. 2시 활동(촬영) 때문에 이곳에 왔어요.

여: 오, Simmonds 씨인가요?

남: 네. 제 아내와 아이들은 오는 중이에요.

여: 가족 사진을 찍는 게 처음이신가요?

남: 아니요, 전에 해 본 적이 있어요.

여: 좋네요. 사진작가가 아이들과의 경험이 있어서 재미있는 시간이 될 거예요.

남: 그거 좋네요. 가서 갈아입고 와도 되나요? 양복을 가져왔어요.

여: 물론이죠. 탈의실은 저쪽에 있습니다.

단·어·및·표·현

session[séʃən] 명 활동, 시간
experienced[ikspí(:)əriənst] 형 경험 있는, 숙련된
changing room 탈의실

06 마지막말의도파악　　　▶정답 ⑤

듣·기·대·본

W: I'm so glad a lot of people came today.

M: Oh, a lot of people here are interested in antique exhibits.

W: It seems like it. I'm just happy my efforts paid off.

M: Did you organize this event?

W: I did. It took a lot of time and energy, but it was worth it.

M: It sure was! You did a great job.

우·리·말·해·석

여: 난 오늘 많은 사람들이 와서 정말 기뻐.

남: 아, 여기 많은 사람들이 골동품 전시물에 관심이 많구나.

여: 그런 것 같아. 난 그저 내 노력이 헛되지 않게 되어 기뻐.

남: 네가 이 행사를 준비했니?

여: 그래. 많은 시간과 에너지를 썼지만 가치 있었어.

남: 그렇고 말고! 너 정말 잘했어.

단·어·및·표·현

exhibit[igzíbit] 명 전시물
organize[ɔ́rɡənàiz] 동 (어떤 일을) 준비하다

07 특정정보파악　　　▶정답 ③

듣·기·대·본

M: Sofia, how was the volunteer work today?

W: Good. It wasn't hard at all, Dad.

M: Really? What did you do?

W: I made dolls for children in need.

M: I didn't know you could make dolls.

W: I couldn't, really. But, there was a manual and it was easy to follow.

M: That's good. Did you make anything else?

W: Not me, but the others made hats and scarves, too.

M: That sounds wonderful.

우·리·말·해·석

남: Sofia, 오늘 자원봉사 일은 어땠어?

여: 좋았어요. 그것은 전혀 어렵지 않았어요, 아빠.

남: 정말? 너는 무엇을 했니?
여: 저는 도움이 필요한 아이들을 위한 인형들을 만들었어요.
남: 나는 네가 인형들을 만들 수 있는지 몰랐어.
여: 할 수 없었어요, 정말로요. 하지만 설명서가 있었고 그것은 따라하기
　　가 쉬웠어요.
남: 그거 좋구나. 너는 그밖에 다른 것도 만들었니?
여: 저는 아니에요, 하지만 다른 사람들은 모자들과 스카프들도 만들었어요.
남: 그것은 굉장하구나.

단·어·및·표·현
in need 도움이 필요한
manual[mǽnjuəl] 명 설명서

08 할일파악(대화직후)　　▶정답 ③

듣·기·대·본
M: Mom, my running shoes are <u>worn out</u>.
W: Oh, are they?
M: Yes. Look at them. I think I need to <u>throw them away</u>.
W: You're right. Shall we go shopping after lunch?
M: Actually, I already found the perfect ones on the
　　Internet.
W: Really? Can you show them to me?
M: Here. They're even offering a <u>discount coupon</u> for
　　purchases made today.
W: They look nice. I'll <u>order</u> the shoes for you right away.

우·리·말·해·석
남: 엄마, 제 운동화가 낡았어요.
여: 오, 그러니?
남: 네. 보세요. 제 생각엔 저걸 버려야 해요.
여: 네 말이 맞구나. 점심 후에 쇼핑하러 갈까?
남: 사실, 인터넷에서 완벽한 것을 이미 찾았어요.
여: 정말이니? 그것들을 내게 보여줄 수 있을까?
남: 여기요. 심지어 그들은 오늘 구매하면 할인 쿠폰을 제공하고 있어요.
여: 좋아 보이네. 지금 바로 신발을 주문할게.

단·어·및·표·현
worn out 낡은, 닳아 해진
throw away 버리다
purchase[pə́ːrtʃəs] 명 구매, 구입

09 대화미언급　　▶정답 ④

듣·기·대·본
W: Hey, Jim. Did you watch the new show, *Love Forever*?
M: Yeah. I don't like romances, but I actually watched this
　　one.
W: If you don't like romances, why did you <u>make an</u>
　　<u>exception for</u> this one?
M: I really like the main actor in it, Park Soo Jung.
W: Oh, really? Is she your <u>type</u>?
M: Kind of? Anyway, I hope that the writer, Kim Nam Su,
　　does not <u>mess up the ending</u> like he did with his last
　　show.
W: Well, we will have to see about that.

우·리·말·해·석
여: 얘, Jim. 너 새 프로그램인 "Love Forever" 봤니?
남: 응. 난 로맨스를 좋아하지 않지만 이건 실제로 봤어.
여: 네가 로맨스를 좋아하지 않는다면, 왜 이건 예외로 한 거야?
남: 난 그것의 주인공 배우인 박수정을 정말 좋아하거든.
여: 오, 정말? 그녀가 네 타입이니?
남: 약간? 어쨌든, 난 김남수 작가가 그의 지난번 프로그램에서 했던 것처

럼 결말을 망치지 않기를 바라.
여: 음, 우린 그것에 대해서는 두고 봐야 할 거야.

단·어·및·표·현
make an exception for ~을 예외로 하다
mess up ~을 망치다, 엉망으로 만들다
ending[éndiŋ] 명 (이야기·영화 등의) 결말
last[læst] 형 지난, 가장 최근의

10 담화화제추론　　▶정답 ④

듣·기·대·본
M: Attention, everybody. <u>Before we start the test, I would</u>
<u>like to give some instructions.</u> First, all cell phones
　　must be turned off and placed inside your bags. If you
　　are <u>caught cheating or talking</u> to other people, you will
　　get an automatic zero for this test. Also, if you have a
　　question, raise your hand quietly. Thank you.

우·리·말·해·석
남: 주목하세요, 여러분. 우리가 시험을 시작하기 전에, 저는 몇 가지 지시
　　사항을 전달하겠습니다. 먼저, 모든 핸드폰은 꺼지고 가방 안에 놓여야
　　합니다. 부정 행위를 하거나 다른 사람에게 말을 하다가 걸릴 경우,
　　이 시험에 대해 자동 영점을 받게 될 것입니다. 또한, 질문이 있으면,
　　조용히 손을 드세요. 감사합니다.

단·어·및·표·현
instruction[instrʌ́kʃən] 명 지시(사항)
be caught -ing ~하다가 걸리다, 잡히다
cheat[tʃiːt] 동 부정행위를 하다, 속이다

11 대화내용불일치　　▶정답 ④

듣·기·대·본
M: Kate, do you have any plans for <u>this Saturday</u>?
W: Not really.
M: Then why don't we take a one-day Korean food cooking
　　class at the community center?
W: Sounds fun! But I'm not good at cooking. Is that okay?
M: Sure. It's a course for <u>beginners</u>. They will teach us how
　　to make *tteokbokki*.
W: Oh, I love *tteokbokki.* How much is the <u>fee</u>?
M: It's only 5,000 won. But the class is <u>limited to twenty</u>
　　people.
W: Oh, then we should hurry and register.

우·리·말·해·석
남: Kate, 이번주 토요일에 무슨 계획 있어?
여: 없어.
남: 그러면 지역 문화 회관에서 하는 한식 요리 원데이 클래스를 같이 듣
　　는 건 어때?
여: 재밌겠다! 그런데 나는 요리를 잘 못해. 괜찮을까?
남: 물론이지. 초보자를 위한 강의야. 그들은 우리에게 떡볶이를 만드는 법
　　을 가르쳐줄 거야.
여: 오, 나 떡볶이 엄청 좋아해. 요금은 얼마야?
남: 5,000원밖에 안 해. 그런데 그 강의는 20명으로 제한되어 있어.
여: 오, 그러면 우리 서둘러서 등록해야겠다.

단·어·및·표·현
community center 지역 문화 회관
be good at + 명사 ~을 잘하다
course[kɔːrs] 명 강의, 강좌
beginner[bigínər] 명 초보자, 초급자

12 전화목적파악　　　　　▶정답 ①

듣·기·대·본

(*Telephone rings.*)
W: Hello. Can I speak to Mr. Walton?
M: Sorry. He is out right now. Can I take a message?
W: Yes. This is Ms. Holmes. Please tell him that I'm going to New York this evening on business.
M: Then, you won't be able to attend his wedding this weekend, will you?
W: No. Could you tell him that I'm really sorry about that?
M: All right. I'll tell him when he gets back.

우·리·말·해·석

(전화벨이 울린다.)
여: 여보세요. Walton 씨 계세요?
남: 죄송합니다. 그는 지금 외출 중이에요. 메시지를 남기시겠어요?
여: 네. 저는 Holmes예요. 그에게 제가 사업상 오늘 저녁 뉴욕에 간다고 전해 주세요.
남: 그럼, 당신은 이번 주말 그의 결혼식에 참석하실 수 없으시겠군요, 그렇죠?
여: 네. 제가 정말 죄송해 한다고 전해 주시겠어요?
남: 알겠어요. 그가 돌아오면 이야기하겠습니다.

단·어·및·표·현

attend [əténd] 동 참석하다

👂 LISTENING ADVICE

'you won't be able to attend his wedding this weekend, will you?'에서 'won't'는 'will not'의 축약형으로 [워운ㅌ]라고 발음됩니다. 'want'와 발음이 헷갈릴 수도 있으니 주의하며 들어보세요.

● won't, want: How to pronounce [wount], [wɔːnt]
'won't'의 발음기호는 [wount]인데 여기서 'u'는 [우] 발음이 나기 때문에 'won't'는 [워운ㅌ]라고 발음하고, 'want'는 [워안ㅌ]라고 발음합니다.

---

13 수치파악　　　　　▶정답 ③

듣·기·대·본

W: Good morning. Would you like to order?
M: Yes. I'd like a ham and egg sandwich, please.
W: OK. That's 5 dollars. Would you like anything to drink?
M: Umm… How much is a coffee?
W: It's 2 dollars, but with the sandwich, you get a dollar discount.
M: Then the coffee is just 1 dollar. I'll have one, please.
W: Sure. It's 6 dollars in total. Anything else?
M: No, that's all. Here's my credit card.

우·리·말·해·석

여: 안녕하세요. 주문하시겠어요?
남: 네. 햄에그 샌드위치 하나 주세요.
여: 네. 5달러입니다. 마실 것도 드릴까요?
남: 음… 커피 한 잔은 얼마인가요?
여: 2달러인데, 샌드위치와 함께 주문하시면 1달러를 할인 받으실 수 있어요.
남: 그러면 커피가 단 1달러라는 거네요. 한 잔 주세요.
여: 그러세요. 총 6달러입니다. 더 필요하신 것 있으세요?
남: 아니요, 그게 전부예요. 여기 제 신용카드요.

단·어·및·표·현

order [ɔ́ːrdər] 동 주문하다
get a discount 할인을 받다

14 대화자관계추론　　　　　▶정답 ②

듣·기·대·본

M: Hello. What would you like today?
W: Hello. I'd like some beef for soup.
M: OK. I'll cut it up for you. How much would you like?
W: 200g, please. And can I have some pork for roasting?
M: Yes. You can choose from the packets in front of you.
W: OK. Let me see. (*pause*) I'd like this one.
M: Sure. That'll be $32 in total.
W: Here's my credit card.
M: Thank you.

우·리·말·해·석

남: 안녕하세요. 오늘은 무엇을 드릴까요?
여: 안녕하세요. 수프에 넣을 소고기 좀 주세요.
남: 알겠습니다. 제가 그것을 고객님을 위해 잘라드릴게요. 얼마나 드릴까요?
여: 200그램 주세요. 그리고 구이용 돼지고기도 좀 주시겠어요?
남: 네. 고객님 앞에 있는 (포장된) 곽 중에서 고르시면 됩니다.
여: 알겠어요. 어디 보자. (잠시 후) 이걸로 할게요.
남: 그러세요. 총 32달러입니다.
여: 여기 제 신용카드요.
남: 감사합니다.

단·어·및·표·현

cut up ~을 (잘게) 자르다
roasting [róustiŋ] 명 굽기, 복기
packet [pǽkit] 명 (포장용) 곽, 통

15 부탁(요청)한일파악　　　　　▶정답 ①

듣·기·대·본

W: Are you doing your English homework, Minho?
M: Yes, I am. It's so difficult.
W: Do you want me to help you?
M: Thanks, but I will try to do it on my own.
W: OK. Is there anything I can do for you?
M: Well, can you open the windows for me?
W: Sure. It's very hot in here.

우·리·말·해·석

여: 영어 숙제 하고 있니, 민호야?
남: 응. 그래. 되게 어렵다.
여: 내가 도와줄까?
남: 고마워. 하지만 내 스스로 하려고 노력해 볼게.
여: 알았어. 내가 다른 거 도와줄 것이 있니?
남: 음, 네가 창문 좀 열어 줄래?
여: 물론이지. 여기 정말 덥다.

단·어·및·표·현

on one's own 스스로, 혼자서

16 이유파악　　　　　▶정답 ③

듣·기·대·본

W: What did you do over the weekend?
M: I visited Jeon-ju. The weekend traffic was awful, but I love the city.
W: Yeah. There are so many things to see, right?
M: Yes. But, I wasn't there for sightseeing. My granny lives there.

W: So, you were just visiting her?
M: That's right. I do that every other month.
W: You are a good boy.

우·리·말·해·석

여: 주말 동안 뭐했어?
남: 전주에 갔다왔어. 주말 교통 상황은 끔찍했지만, 나는 그 도시가 아주 좋아.
여: 그래. 볼 게 정말 많지, 그렇지?
남: 응. 그런데 거기에 관광하러 간 건 아니었어. 우리 할머니가 거기에 사셔.
여: 그러면, 그냥 그분을 방문하러 간 거였구나?
남: 맞아. 나는 두 달에 한 번씩 그렇게 해.
여: 너 착한 아이구나.

단·어·및·표·현

granny [grǽni] 몡 할머니
every other month 두 달에 한 번씩

17 그림상황에적절한대화찾기　▶정답 ④

듣·기·대·본

① M: What happened to your leg?
　W: I fell down and broke it.
② M: What do you want to be in the future?
　W: I want to be a doctor.
③ M: Can I get a refund for this?
　W: Sure. May I see your receipt?
④ M: How can I help you?
　W: I need something for my headache, please.
⑤ M: Can I try this shirt on?
　W: Of course. The fitting room is over there.

우·리·말·해·석

① 남: 다리에 무슨 일이 있었습니까?
　여: 넘어져서 부러졌어요.
② 남: 미래에 무엇이 되고 싶나요?
　여: 의사가 되고 싶어요.
③ 남: 이거 환불 받을 수 있을까요?
　여: 물론이죠. 영수증을 볼 수 있을까요?
④ 남: 어떻게 도와드릴까요?
　여: 제 두통을 위한 뭔가가 필요해요.
⑤ 남: 이 셔츠를 입어봐도 될까요?
　여: 물론이죠. 탈의실은 저기 있습니다.

단·어·및·표·현

fall down 넘어지다
break [breik] 통 부러지다, 부서지다, 부수다
refund [rí:fʌnd] 몡 환불

18 담화미언급　▶정답 ④

듣·기·대·본

W: Green Art Center would like to invite you to our summer concert. You can meet the world-famous musician, Olivia Sharp, who will be our special guest. It will be held in our main hall. The concert is on July 2 at 7 p.m. All the profits from ticket sales will be donated to children's charities. You can buy your tickets online on our website. We hope to see you at the concert.

우·리·말·해·석

여: Green 아트 센터에서 여러분을 저희의 여름 콘서트에 초대하고자 합니다. 여러분들은 세계적으로 유명한 음악가인 Olivia Sharp를 저희의 특별 손님으로 만나실 수 있습니다. 그것은 저희의 메인 홀에서 개최될 것입니다. 그 콘서트는 7월 2일 오후 7시에 있습니다. 티켓 판매로 인한 모든 수익은 어린이 자선 단체에 기부될 것입니다. 저희 웹사이트에서 당신의 티켓을 온라인으로 구매할 수 있습니다. 저희는 여러분들을 콘서트에서 보길 바랍니다.

단·어·및·표·현

world-famous 세계적으로 유명한
profit [práfit] 몡 수익, 이익
charity [tʃǽrəti] 몡 자선 단체, 구호 단체

19 알맞은응답찾기　▶정답 ④

듣·기·대·본

M: Alice, do you have any special plans for summer vacation?
W: Well, I'm going to take a good rest at a resort in Thailand with my family.
M: Sounds like a perfect way to enjoy the vacation.
W: Yes, I'm so excited about it.
M: How long are you going to stay there?
W: I'm going to stay for a week.
M: Then, who's going to take care of your dog Max while you're gone?
W: Our neighbor will take care of him.

우·리·말·해·석

① 네가 원한다면 너는 머물 수 있어.
② 그는 우리와 같이 가지 않아.
③ 내 비행편은 오전 10시에 떠나.
④ 우리 이웃이 그를 돌볼 거야.
⑤ 태국에 좋은 식당이 있어.

남: Alice, 너는 여름 방학을 위한 어떤 특별한 계획이 있어?
여: 글쎄, 나는 나의 가족과 함께 태국의 리조트에서 푹 쉴 거야.
남: 방학을 즐기는 완벽한 방법 같다.
여: 응, 그것에 대해 무척 흥분돼.
남: 거기서 얼마나 오래 머물 거야?
여: 나는 일주일 동안 머물 거야.
남: 그러면, 네가 가버린 동안 너희 개 Max는 누가 돌보는 거야?
여: 우리 이웃이 그를 돌볼 거야.

단·어·및·표·현

take a rest 쉬다
gone [gɔ(:)n] 혱 가버린

20 알맞은응답찾기　▶정답 ⑤

듣·기·대·본

M: Hannah, what do you do in your free time?
W: I usually go swimming. How about you?
M: I play games. But I'm getting a little tired of that.
W: Maybe it's time to take up something new.
M: I think so, too. I just don't know what to do.
W: How about something active? Do you like sports?
M: I'm not sure. Can you recommend something?
W: Skateboarding could be fun.

우·리·말·해·석

① 오른쪽으로 돌아줘.
② 넌 그럴 필요가 없어.
③ 난 카페에 잠깐 들를 거야.
④ 그는 어디서 그것을 보냈니?
⑤ 스케이트보드 타기가 재밌을 것 같아.

남: Hannah, 너는 네 여가 시간에 뭐하니?

여: 나는 대개 수영하러 가. 너는 어때?

남: 나는 게임들을 해. 하지만 나는 그것에 약간 싫증이 나고 있어.

여: 어쩌면 새로운 것을 시작해야 하는 때인가 봐.

남: 나도 그렇게 생각해. 난 단지 뭘 해야 할지 모르겠어.

여: 활동적인 건 어때? 너는 운동을 좋아하니?

남: 확실하지 않아. 네가 무언가를 추천해줄 수 있어?

여: <u>스케이트보드 타기가 재밌을 것 같아.</u>

단·어·및·표·현

get tired of ~에 싫증이 나다
take up (취미, 일을) 시작하다
active [ǽktiv] ⑧ 활동적인
recommend [rèkəménd] ⑧ 추천하다
drop by 잠깐 들르다

Words & Expressions Review

1. 이웃	2. 사업상, 업무로	3. 환불
4. 가버린	5. 부러지다, 부서지다	6. ~에 싫증이 나다
7. 경험 있는, 숙련된	8. 골동품	9. 지시(사항)
10. 보관하다	11. 참석하다	12. 활동적인
13. 지난, 가장 최근의	14. (포장용) 곽, 통	15. 관광
16. ~을 예외로 하다	17. 수익, 이익	18. 끔찍한, 지독한
19. 세계적으로 유명한	20. 구매, 구입	21. 도움이 필요한
22. 범인, 범죄자	23. 작은 식당	24. ~을 망치다, 엉망으로 만들다
25. 새기다, 조각하다	26. 신용카드	27. 자선 단체, 구호 단체
28. 쉬다	29. 버리다	30. 낡은, 닳아 해진
31. 넘어지다	32. 할인을 받다	33. 타버리다
34. 스스로, 혼자서	35. 전시물, 전시하다	36. 잠깐 들르다
37. 불 지르다, 방화하다	38. 나눠주다	39. 강의, 강좌
40. 초보자, 초급자	41. ~을 (잘게) 자르다	42. ~을 예상하다, 기대하다
43. 굽기, 볶기	44. 무서운, 깜짝 놀라게 하는	

Listening Test

영어듣기 모의고사 07회

|정|답|

01 ①	02 ④	03 ②	04 ⑤	05 ④
06 ①	07 ③	08 ③	09 ③	10 ③
11 ④	12 ③	13 ①	14 ④	15 ④
16 ③	17 ③	18 ③	19 ②	20 ②

01   날씨파악-그림   ▶ 정답 ①

듣·기·대·본

W: Good morning. This is the weekly weather report. Starting on Monday, we'll see <u>bright skies</u> and beautiful sunshine for three days. On Thursday and Friday, it'll be <u>cloudy</u> all day. On Saturday, there will be <u>heavy rain</u>, which will continue through Sunday. So, I'm afraid your weekend picnic will have to wait until next week. Have a great week, everyone!

우·리·말·해·석

여: 좋은 아침입니다. 주간 일기 예보입니다. 월요일에 시작하여 3일 동안 밝은 하늘과 아름다운 햇살을 볼 수 있겠습니다. 목요일과 금요일에는 하루 종일 흐릴 것입니다. 토요일에는 폭우가 쏟아지겠고, 일요일까지 계속될 것입니다. 그래서, 여러분의 주말 소풍은 다음 주까지 기다리셔야 할 것 같습니다. 좋은 한 주 보내세요, 모두들!

단·어·및·표·현

bright [brait] ⑧ 밝은
heavy rain 폭우

02   그림정보파악   ▶ 정답 ④

듣·기·대·본

W: Tyler, what's this? Is this sign for you?

M: Yes, I made it to <u>put on</u> my car. I'm a beginner driver.

W: Oh, that's why you wrote "New Driver" in big letters in the center of the sign.

M: Yeah, I'm not used to driving yet.

W: I see. I like that you put a wing on <u>both sides</u> of the word.

M: Thanks. I hope other drivers will be <u>patient</u> with me.

W: Don't worry. Every driver knows what it is like to be a beginner on the road.

우·리·말·해·석

여: Tyler, 이게 뭐야? 이 표지판은 너를 위한 거야?

남: 응, 차에다 붙이기 위해 만들었어. 나는 초보 운전자야.

여: 오, 그래서 네가 표지판의 중앙에 큰 글씨로 "초보 운전자"라고 적었구나.

남: 응, 난 아직 운전에 익숙하지 않아.

여: 그렇구나. 나는 네가 단어의 양쪽에 날개를 달아준 게 마음에 들어.

남: 고마워. 나는 다른 운전자들이 나에게 참을성을 가지고 대했으면 좋겠어.

여: 걱정하지 마. 모든 운전자들은 도로에서 초보자라는 게 어떤 건지 알고 있어.

단·어·및·표·현

be used to + 동명사 ~하는 것에 익숙하다
patient [péiʃənt] ⑧ 참을성 있는, 인내심 있는

03   심정추론   ▶ 정답 ②

듣·기·대·본

W: Honey, did you <u>book</u> the movie tickets?

M: No, not yet.

W: Oh, you need to hurry. I don't want to see a movie sitting right <u>in front of</u> the screen like last time.

M: Don't worry. I am buying the tickets on my smart phone right now.

W: Are there any seats left?

M: Yes. There are a few seats left. We can sit in row G.

W: <u>That's great!</u>

우·리·말·해·석

① 차분한   ② 행복한   ③ 겁먹은   ④ 화난   ⑤ 실망한

여: 여보, 당신 영화 표 예매했어요?

남: 아니요, 아직이요.

여: 오, 당신 서둘러야 해요. 나는 지난번처럼 스크린 바로 앞에 앉아서 영화를 보고 싶지 않아요.
남: 걱정 마요. 내가 지금 내 스마트폰으로 표를 사고 있어요.
여: 좌석이 남아있는 게 있어요?
남: 네. 남아있는 좌석이 몇 개 있어요. 우리는 G열에 앉을 수 있어요.
여: 그거 잘됐네요!

단·어·및·표·현
row[rou] ⑲ 열, 줄

04 한일파악   ▶정답 ⑤

듣·기·대·본
W: Eric, why are you so busy in the kitchen?
M: I'm making a cake for my mom's birthday.
W: That's so sweet! Did you learn how to bake?
M: Yes. Last weekend, I took a baking class to get ready for today.
W: Wow! That's really thoughtful of you.
M: I hope she'll like it. It's my first homemade cake.

우·리·말·해·석
여: Eric, 너는 부엌에서 왜 그렇게 바쁜 거야?
남: 나는 엄마의 생일을 위한 케이크를 만들고 있는 중이야.
여: 정말 다정하다! 너는 베이킹을 배웠니?
남: 응. 지난 주말에, 나는 오늘을 준비하기 위해 베이킹 수업을 들었어.
여: 우와! 넌 정말 사려 깊구나.
남: 엄마가 그것을 좋아하시길 바라. 내가 처음으로 만든 수제 케이크거든.

단·어·및·표·현
bake[beik] ⑧ 굽다, 구워지다
get ready 준비하다, 대비하다
thoughtful[θɔ́ːtfəl] ⑲ 사려 깊은, 배려심 있는, 친절한
homemade[hóumméid] ⑲ 수제의, 손수 만든, 집에서 만든

05 대화장소추론   ▶정답 ④

듣·기·대·본
W: Wow, this place looks so real!
M: You're right. It's amazing!
W: Hey, do you recognize that school?
M: Oh, is that the setting of the movie, *Rising Youth*?
W: That's right! This is the very place that movie was filmed.
M: Cool! Let's take some pictures.
W: Wait, there's a school uniform rental shop over there. Let's borrow uniforms and then take pictures.
M: Sounds great!

우·리·말·해·석
여: 우와, 이곳은 정말 진짜 같아!
남: 네 말이 맞아. 놀라워!
여: 얘, 너는 저 학교를 알아보겠니?
남: 오, 저것은 영화 "Rising Youth"의 배경 세트이지?
여: 맞아! 여기는 그 영화가 촬영된 바로 그 장소야.
남: 멋져! 우리 사진 좀 찍자.
여: 기다려, 저기에 교복 대여점이 있어. 교복을 빌리고 나서 사진을 찍자.
남: 그거 좋아!

단·어·및·표·현
recognize[rékəgnàiz] ⑧ 알아보다
setting[sétiŋ] ⑲ 배경, 무대 장치
film[film] ⑧ 촬영하다, 찍다
take pictures 사진을 찍다

06 마지막말의도파악   ▶정답 ①

듣·기·대·본
W: Hey, Greg. I heard you are going to be on a Science Quiz Show.
M: Oh, no. It hasn't been decided yet.
W: But, you are trying out, right?
M: Yes. I have to pass the writing test first.
W: When you pass that, do I get to see you on TV?
M: On the show, yes.
W: When is the test?
M: Next week.
W: Well, good luck! Fingers crossed!

우·리·말·해·석
여: 안녕, Greg. 네가 과학 퀴즈 쇼에 나간다고 들었어.
남: 아, 아니야. 아직 결정이 안 됐어.
여: 하지만 시도하고 있는 거지, 그렇지?
남: 응. 필기시험을 먼저 통과해야 해.
여: 네가 그걸 통과하면, 너를 TV에서 볼 수 있는 거야?
남: 쇼에서, 맞아.
여: 시험이 언제야?
남: 다음 주.
여: 음, 행운을 빌어! 잘 되길 빌게!

단·어·및·표·현
Fingers crossed! 잘 되길 빌게!, 행운을 빌어!

07 특정정보파악   ▶정답 ③

듣·기·대·본
M: What are you going to buy for Daddy's birthday present?
W: I am not sure. Do you have anything in mind?
M: How about a tie or a pair of socks?
W: Well, he already has many of those.
M: How about pajamas?
W: Umm, I am not sure about his size.
M: Then, why don't we ask Mom about his size?
W: That's a good idea.

우·리·말·해·석
남: 아빠 생신 선물로 뭘 살 거니?
여: 잘 모르겠어. 생각해둔 것 있어?
남: 넥타이나 양말이 어떨까?
여: 글쎄, 그건 이미 많이 가지고 계셔.
남: 잠옷은 어떨까?
여: 음, 아빠의 치수를 잘 모르겠어.
남: 그럼, 엄마께 아빠의 치수를 물어보는 게 어때?
여: 그거 좋은 생각이다.

단·어·및·표·현
have ~ in mind ~을 생각해두다

🦻 **LISTENING ADVICE**

● **'size': How to pronounce [z]**
[z] 소리를 내기 위해서는 우선 입을 옆으로 벌리고 혀끝을 앞니 뒤쪽에 가져가야 합니다. 그 다음, 치아와 혀 사이에 작은 틈을 만들어 그곳으로 공기를 밀어내며 진동을 만들어냅니다.

08 할일파악(대화직후)   ▶정답 ③

듣·기·대·본
W: Wow, the exhibition was amazing!

M: What's the plan now, honey?

W: Let's grab some pizza at your favorite restaurant downtown.

M: That place is always crowded. Let's place a pizza order over the phone and eat at home instead.

W: Sure. Afterwards, why don't we play some board games?

M: Sounds like a plan! What kind of pizza do you want?

W: I want a pepperoni pizza. Let's order it right now.

우·리·말·해·석

여: 와, 그 전시회는 놀라웠어요!

남: 이제 계획이 뭐예요, 여보?

여: 당신이 시내에서 제일 좋아하는 식당에서 피자를 좀 먹어요.

남: 그곳은 항상 붐벼요. 피자 주문을 전화로 하고 대신 집에서 먹어요.

여: 그래요. 그 후에, 보드 게임을 좀 하는 것이 어때요?

남: 좋은 계획이네요! 당신은 어떤 종류의 피자를 원하나요?

여: 나는 페퍼로니 피자를 원해요. 지금 바로 그것을 주문해요.

단·어·및·표·현

exhibition [èksəbíʃən] 몡 전시회

grab [græb] 통 (음식, 물건 등을) 빠르게 사다, 잡다

crowded [kráudid] 혱 붐비는, 혼잡한

place an order 주문하다

afterwards [ǽftərwərdz] 뿐 그 후에

09 대화미언급 ▶정답 ③

듣·기·대·본

W: Mark, where do you work out these days?

M: I work out at the Lucky Punch boxing gym. You should come work out there, too.

W: But I've never tried boxing before.

M: Don't worry. There are classes for beginners just like you.

W: Oh, do they also offer those classes on weekends?

M: Of course. There are a lot of weekend classes.

W: Great! Do I need to buy boxing gloves right away?

M: Only if you want to. You can actually borrow them for free at the gym.

우·리·말·해·석

여: Mark, 요즘 어디서 운동해?

남: 나는 Lucky Punch 복싱 체육관에서 운동해. 너도 거기로 와서 운동해야 해.

여: 하지만 나는 전에 복싱을 해본 적이 없어.

남: 걱정하지 마. 너처럼 초보자를 위한 수업도 있어.

여: 오, 그들은 주말에도 그런 수업들을 제공해?

남: 물론이지. 많은 주말 수업이 있어.

여: 좋다! 지금 바로 복싱 글러브를 사야 할까?

남: 네가 원한다면. 체육관에서 실제로 무료로 빌릴 수 있어.

단·어·및·표·현

work out 운동하다

gym [ʤim] 몡 체육관

offer [ɔ́(ː)fər] 통 제공하다

borrow [bárou] 통 빌리다

10 담화화제추론 ▶정답 ③

듣·기·대·본

W: Hello, students. Today, I'll tell you how to participate in the survey for the new library for teenagers. First, follow the link provided on our school website. It will lead you directly to the online survey. Second, answer the questions by clicking on the answers of your choice. They will be kept completely secret. Finally, submit your answers online.

우·리·말·해·석

여: 안녕하세요, 학생분들. 오늘 제가 10대들을 위한 새로운 도서관 설문조사에 참여하는 방법을 알려드리겠습니다. 우선, 우리 학교 웹사이트에 제공된 링크를 따라가세요. 그것은 여러분을 온라인 설문조사로 바로 안내할 것입니다. 둘째, 여러분이 선택한 답변을 클릭하여 질문에 답합니다. 그것들은 완전히 비밀로 지켜질 것입니다. 마지막으로, 온라인으로 여러분의 답변을 제출하세요.

단·어·및·표·현

participate in ~에 참여하다

survey [sə́ːrvei] 몡 설문조사

teenager [tíːnèidʒər] 몡 10대, 청소년

directly [diréktli] 뿐 바로, 즉시

submit [səbmít] 통 제출하다

11 대화내용불일치 ▶정답 ④

듣·기·대·본

W: Look at this notice, Dad. There's a balcony concert in our apartment complex.

M: Oh, it's today. It's designed to allow people to listen from their own balconies.

W: Can't we watch from in front of the stage?

M: Yes, but only 15 people are allowed to watch from there.

W: It says a pianist and two violinists will play.

M: The concert lasts for an hour and a half. Do you want to go?

W: No, let's watch from our balcony. It starts at 2 p.m.

M: OK. Let's go home.

우·리·말·해·석

여: 이 공지를 보세요, 아빠. 저희 아파트 단지에서 발코니 콘서트가 있어요.

남: 오, 오늘이구나. 그것은 사람들이 자신의 발코니에서 듣는 것이 허용되도록 고안되었어.

여: 무대 앞에서 볼 수 없나요?

남: 있어, 하지만 오직 15명만 그곳에서 볼 수 있도록 허용돼.

여: 한 명의 피아니스트와 두 명의 바이올리니스트가 연주한다고 하네요.

남: 그 콘서트는 한 시간 반 동안 지속되는구나. 가고 싶니?

여: 아뇨, 우리 발코니에서 봐요. 오후 2시에 시작해요.

남: 그래. 집에 가자.

단·어·및·표·현

notice [nóutis] 몡 공지, 공고문, 안내문

complex [kámpleks] 몡 (건물) 단지, 복합 건물

be designed to + 동사원형 ~하도록 고안되다

last [læst] 통 지속되다

12 전화목적파악 ▶정답 ③

듣·기·대·본

(Telephone rings.)

W: Hello. Best Korean Restaurant. How may I help you?

M: Hi. I'd like to change my dinner reservation.

W: Certainly, sir. May I have your name?

M: Yes. Gordon Lee.

W: Okay. You reserved a table for two tonight at 6 p.m.

M: Right. Would it be possible to change my reservation to 8 p.m.?

W: Let me see. (*pause*) Yes, I can <u>arrange</u> that for you. Can I help you with anything else?
M: No, that's all. Thank you.

우·리·말·해·석

(전화벨이 울린다.)
여: 안녕하세요. 최고의 한식당입니다. 어떻게 도와드릴까요?
남: 안녕하세요. 저는 저의 저녁 예약을 변경하고 싶습니다.
여: 물론이죠, 고객님. 이름을 알려주실 수 있으신가요?
남: 네. Gordon Lee입니다.
여: 네. 당신은 오늘 밤 6시에 두 사람 자리를 예약했네요.
남: 맞아요. 저의 예약을 8시로 변경하는 게 가능할까요?
여: 잠시만요. (잠시 후) 네, 제가 조정해드릴 수 있습니다. 다른 것도 도와 드릴까요?
남: 아뇨, 그게 다입니다. 감사합니다.

단·어·및·표·현

reservation [rèzərvéiʃən] 몡 예약
arrange [əréindʒ] 동 조정하다, 해결하다

13 수치계산 ▶정답 ①

듣·기·대·본

M: Hi, would you like to order?
W: Yes. I would like this box of macaroons.
M: That's 15 dollars. Would you like <u>anything else</u>?
W: Ooh! Those egg tarts <u>look good</u>. I'll have two of those.
M: Sure, they're 2 dollars each.
W: What is <u>the total cost</u>?
M: That'll be 19 dollars in total.
W: Here's 20 dollars.
M: Thank you. Here's your <u>change</u>.

우·리·말·해·석

남: 안녕하세요, 주문하시겠습니까?
여: 네. 이 마카룬(아몬드나 코코넛으로 만든 부드러운 과자) 한 상자 주세요.
남: 15달러입니다. 그 밖에 필요한 게 있으신가요?
여: 오! 저 에그 타르트들은 맛있어 보이네요. 저것들을 두 개 주세요.
남: 알겠습니다. 그것들은 개당 2달러입니다.
여: 총 비용이 얼마인가요?
남: 총 19달러입니다.
여: 여기 20달러요.
남: 감사합니다. 거스름돈 여기 있습니다.

단·어·및·표·현

order [ɔ́ːrdər] 동 주문하다
change [tʃéindʒ] 몡 거스름돈

14 대화자관계추론 ▶정답 ④

듣·기·대·본

M: Good morning, Ms. Jackson. What can I do for you?
W: My back tooth hurts so badly.
M: Okay. Let's take a look at your tooth.
W: Oh, I'm scared. I'm always <u>afraid of</u> the dentist.
M: Take a deep <u>breath</u> first.
W: Okay. I'm ready now.
M: If you're ready, open your mouth please.

우·리·말·해·석

남: 좋은 아침입니다, Jackson 씨. 무엇을 도와드릴까요?
여: 제 어금니가 정말 아파요.
남: 알겠어요. 제가 이를 한번 보죠.

여: 오, 무섭네요. 저는 치과가 항상 두려워요.
남: 우선 심호흡하세요.
여: 좋아요. 이제 준비됐어요.
남: 준비되시면 입을 벌려 주세요.

단·어·및·표·현

take a look (한번) 보다

15 부탁(요청)한일파악 ▶정답 ④

듣·기·대·본

W: Mark, are you going to the Game Fair this Saturday?
M: Yeah, I'm <u>saving money</u> for the day. You're going as well, right?
W: I can't. I forgot my cousin's wedding is on that day.
M: But, you said you had already bought the ticket.
W: I did. So, could you <u>do me a favor</u>?
M: Sure! What is it?
W: Could you change my ticket for Sunday? You can only do it <u>on site</u>.
M: Of course! No problem.

우·리·말·해·석

여: Mark, 너는 이번 토요일에 게임 박람회에 가니?
남: 응, 나는 그날을 위해 돈을 모으고 있어. 너도 갈 거지, 맞아?
여: 나는 갈 수 없어. 나는 내 사촌의 결혼식이 그날 있다는 것을 잊었어.
남: 하지만, 너는 이미 표를 샀다고 말했잖아.
여: 그랬어. 그러니까, 내 부탁 좀 들어줄래?
남: 그럼! 뭔데?
여: 내 표를 일요일로 바꿔줄래? 너는 그것을 현장에서만 할 수 있어.
남: 물론이지! 문제없어.

단·어·및·표·현

save [seiv] 동 (돈을) 모으다, 저축하다
on site 현장에서

16 이유파악 ▶정답 ③

듣·기·대·본

W: Jaden, do you remember the Korean restaurant we went to last month?
M: Hmm… You mean the place that <u>served</u> Korean beef?
W: Yeah, I'm trying to make a dinner reservation, but they're not <u>picking up</u> the phone.
M: Maybe they're <u>closed</u> today.
W: Let me check their website. (*pause*) Oh, no!
M: What? Is something wrong?
W: It seems that the restaurant <u>went out of business</u> last week.
M: What? That's too bad.

우·리·말·해·석

여: Jaden, 지난달에 갔던 한식당을 기억하니?
남: 음… 한우를 제공한 곳 말하는 거지?
여: 응, 저녁 식사를 예약하려고 하는데 그들이 전화를 안 받네.
남: 아마 오늘은 닫았나 봐.
여: 웹사이트를 확인해볼게. (잠시 후) 오, 안 돼!
남: 뭐? 뭐가 잘못됐어?
여: 그 식당은 지난주에 폐업한 것 같아.
남: 뭐? 안됐다.

단·어·및·표·현

serve [səːrv] 동 (식당 등에서 음식을) 제공하다
reservation [rèzərvéiʃən] 몡 예약
closed [klouzd] 뎽 닫은, 마감한

07회 모의고사

go out of business 폐업하다

17 그림 상황에 적절한 대화 찾기 ▶정답 ③

듣·기·대·본

① W: Why are you up so early?
   M: I have to go to the airport.
② W: How much is this umbrella?
   M: I'm sorry, but it's not for sale.
③ W: I think it's going to rain in the afternoon.
   M: Okay, I'll take an umbrella with me.
④ W: Can we make a snowman today?
   M: Sure, put on your gloves first.
⑤ W: What sports do you like to watch?
   M: I like watching football.

우·리·말·해·석

① 여: 너 왜 이렇게 일찍 일어났니?
   남: 나 공항에 가야 해.
② 여: 이 우산은 얼마인가요?
   남: 죄송합니다, 하지만 그것은 판매하지 않습니다.
③ 여: 내 생각엔 오후에 비가 올 것 같구나.
   남: 알겠어요, 우산 가지고 갈게요.
④ 여: 저희 오늘 눈사람 만들어도 되나요?
   남: 그럼, 먼저 네 장갑부터 끼렴.
⑤ 여: 너는 어떤 스포츠 보는 것을 좋아해?
   남: 나는 축구 보는 것을 좋아해.

단·어·및·표·현

airport [ɛ́ərpɔ̀ːrt] 명 공항
not for sale 판매하지 않는, 비매품

18 담화 미언급 ▶정답 ③

듣·기·대·본

W: Hello, students. Let me tell you about the new after-school cooking class. The teacher, Mrs. Jane Parker, is an experienced cook. In the class, you'll learn how to cook Italian food. The class will be on Tuesdays from 3 p.m. to 5 p.m. Only 10 students can take the class, so sign up soon!

우·리·말·해·석

여: 안녕하세요, 학생 여러분. 새로운 방과 후 요리 교실에 대해 알려줄게요. Jane Parker 선생님은 능숙한 요리사입니다. 수업에서 여러분은 이탈리아 음식을 요리하는 법을 배울 것입니다. 수업은 화요일 오후 3시부터 5시까지입니다. 오직 10명의 학생만 수업을 들을 수 있으니, 빨리 등록하세요!

단·어·및·표·현

experienced [ikspí(ː)əriənst] 형 능숙한, 경력 있는
cook [kuk] 명 요리사 동 요리하다
sign up 등록하다, 신청하다

19 알맞은 응답 찾기 ▶정답 ②

듣·기·대·본

W: Hi, Kevin. How was your winter vacation?
M: Hi, Claire. It was great. I went on a trip to Seoul with my parents.
W: Really? I'm going there next month!
M: Oh, you'll love it. I enjoyed it a lot.
W: I should ask you about the city before I go on my trip.
M: Of course. Ask me anything.
W: What did you like the best?

M: I liked the food best.

우·리·말·해·석

① 나에게 뭐든지 물어봐.
② 나는 음식이 가장 좋았어.
③ 방학은 지루했어.
④ 나는 여름 동안 서울에 갔어.
⑤ 최고의 것들은 기다릴 가치가 있어.

여: 안녕, Kevin. 네 겨울 방학은 어땠어?
남: 안녕, Claire. 굉장했어. 나는 나의 부모님과 함께 서울로 여행을 갔어.
여: 정말? 나는 다음 달에 거기에 갈 거야!
남: 오, 너는 그것을 좋아할 거야. 나는 아주 즐거웠어.
여: 나는 내가 여행 가기 전에 그 도시에 대해 너에게 물어봐야겠다.
남: 물론이지. 뭐든지 나에게 물어봐.
여: 너는 뭐가 가장 좋았어?
남: 나는 음식이 가장 좋았어.

단·어·및·표·현

go on a trip 여행을 가다
worth -ing ~할 가치가 있는

20 알맞은 응답 찾기 ▶정답 ②

듣·기·대·본

M: Excuse me. What's the best-selling T-shirt in your store?
W: This black T-shirt with our city logo on it is the most popular.
M: I like the design. It's so unique.
W: It's especially popular with tourists.
M: Do you have it in different colors?
W: Yes. We have it in white and gray.
M: I have many black and gray T-shirts.
W: Then you should try a different color.
M: Okay, I'll buy the white one.

우·리·말·해·석

① 우리 도시로의 여행을 즐기세요.
② 알겠어요, 저는 그 흰 것을 살게요.
③ 네, 제가 가장 좋아하는 색은 검은색이에요.
④ 탈의실은 저쪽에 있어요.
⑤ 이 티셔츠는 저한테 너무 작아요.

남: 실례합니다. 이 가게에서 가장 잘 팔리는 티셔츠는 뭔가요?
여: 저희 도시 로고가 있는 이 검은색 티셔츠가 가장 인기가 많아요.
남: 저는 그 디자인이 마음에 들어요. 정말 독특하네요.
여: 그건 특히 관광객들에게 인기가 있어요.
남: 그것은 다른 색상도 있나요?
여: 네, 저희는 흰색과 회색도 있어요.
남: 저는 검은색과 회색 티셔츠가 많아요.
여: 그럼 다른 색을 시도해 보시는 게 좋겠어요.
남: 알겠어요, 저는 그 흰 것을 살게요.

단·어·및·표·현

especially [ispéʃəli] 부 특히

Words & Expressions Review

1. 수제의, 손수 만든, 집에서 만든	2. 밝은	3. 공지, 공고문
4. (음식, 물건 등을) 빠르게 사다, 잡다	5. (돈을) 모으다, 저축하다	6. 심호흡하다
7. 제공하다	8. 결정하다	9. 제출하다

10. 배경, 무대 장치	11. 운동하다	12. ~할 가치가 있는
13. 판매하지 않는, 비매품	14. 능숙한, 경력 있는	15. 10대, 청소년
16. ~에 참여하다	17. 알아보다	18. 여행을 가다
19. 전시회	20. 조정하다, 해결하다	21. ~을 (한번) 보다
22. 현장에서	23. 촬영하다, 찍다	24. 행운을 빌어!
25. 바로, 즉시	26. ~하는 것에 익숙하다	27. 지속되다
28. 굽다, 구워지다	29. 사려 깊은, 배려심 있는, 친절한	30. 특히
31. 예약	32. 주문하다	33. (건물) 단지, 복합건물
34. 시도하다	35. 열, 줄	36. 등록하다, 신청하다
37. A를 생각해두다	38. ~을 두려워하다	39. 설문조사
40. (식당 등에서 음식을) 제공하다	41. ~하도록 고안되다	42. 예약하다, 책
43. 참을성 있는, 인내심 있는	44. 폐업하다	

Listening Test
영어듣기 모의고사 08회

|정|답|

01 ④	02 ⑤	03 ⑤	04 ④	05 ②
06 ②	07 ⑤	08 ⑤	09 ④	10 ②
11 ⑤	12 ④	13 ①	14 ④	15 ⑤
16 ②	17 ③	18 ②	19 ⑤	20 ②

01　날씨파악–그림　▶정답 ④

듣·기·대·본

M: Here's this week's weather report. Everyone's wondering when this freezing weather will end. I'm afraid the snow will continue until Tuesday. On Wednesday, the temperature will be very low, but it will be sunny. On Thursday, we will have rain instead of snow, as the temperature will finally go up. This rain will continue for two days, before it starts snowing again on Saturday. On Sunday, it will be cloudy.

우·리·말·해·석

남: 이번 주 일기 예보입니다. 모든 분들이 이 무척 추운 날씨가 언제 끝날지 궁금해하시죠. 안타깝게도 화요일까지 눈이 계속되겠습니다. 수요일에 기온은 매우 낮지만, 맑을 것입니다. 목요일에는 마침내 기온이 오르면서 눈 대신 비가 올 것입니다. 이 비는 토요일에 다시 눈이 내리기 시작하기 전까지 이틀 동안 계속될 것입니다. 일요일에는 구름이 끼겠습니다.

단·어·및·표·현

I'm afraid ~ 안타깝게도 ~하다

02　그림정보파악　▶정답 ⑤

듣·기·대·본

W: How may I help you?

M: I'm looking for a watch.

W: How about this square one?

M: No, I think round ones look fancier.

W: Then, what about this digital watch?

M: Well, I wish it had hour and minute hands along with digital numbers.

W: Then, you might like this one with both digital and analog features.

M: It looks great! I'll take it.

우·리·말·해·석

여: 어떻게 도와드릴까요?

남: 전 손목 시계를 찾고 있어요.

여: 이 사각형 모양의 것은 어떠세요?

남: 아뇨, 저는 둥근 것이 더 근사해 보인다고 생각해요.

여: 그러면, 이 디지털 시계는 어떠세요?

남: 음, 저는 디지털 숫자들과 함께 시침과 분침이 있었으면 좋겠어요.

여: 그러면, 당신은 디지털과 아날로그 특징이 둘 다 있는 이것을 좋아할 거예요.

남: 좋아 보이네요! 전 그걸 살게요.

단·어·및·표·현

look for ~을 찾다, 구하다
fancy [fǽnsi] 휑 근사한
hand [hænd] 휑 (시계) 바늘, (시/분/초) 침
along with ~와 함께, 더불어
feature [fíːtʃər] 휑 특징

03　심정추론　▶정답 ⑤

듣·기·대·본

M: Shannon, I can't go to the park with you today.

W: Why not?

M: I don't have my bike. Somebody stole it.

W: Oh, no! I'm so sorry to hear that, Jake.

M: I can't believe it. I thought our neighborhood was safe.

W: Me, too. You got the bike from your parents, right?

M: Yeah, I really don't know what to tell them.

W: Cheer up. They'll understand.

우·리·말·해·석

① 수줍어하는　② 자랑스러운　③ 지루한
④ 기쁜　⑤ 속상한

남: Shannon, 나 오늘은 너와 함께 공원에 갈 수 없어.

여: 왜 안 돼?

남: 내 자전거가 없어. 누군가 그걸 훔쳐갔어.

여: 오, 안 돼! 그 얘기를 들으니 정말 안됐다, Jake.

남: 믿을 수가 없어. 난 우리 동네가 안전하다고 생각했어.

여: 나도 그래. 너 그 자전거를 너의 부모님에게서 받은 거지, 그렇지?

남: 응, 난 그분들께 뭐라고 말씀드려야 할지 정말 모르겠어.

여: 기운 내. 그분들은 이해하실 거야.

단·어·및·표·현

steal [stiːl] 통 훔치다, 도둑질하다
neighborhood [néibərhùd] 휑 동네, 이웃 사람들

04　한일파악　▶정답 ④

듣·기·대·본

M: Hi, Mina. You look happy. What's up?

W: Guess what! My parents finally got me a puppy!
M: Great! I know that you've always wanted a dog.
W: Yeah, I've got a lot to prepare, though. I actually visited the pet shop a minute ago.
M: What did you do there?
W: I bought some dog food.
M: Oh, I see. I want to see your dog.
W: Come over to my place on Saturday!
M: OK. I can't wait.

우·리·말·해·석

남: 안녕, Mina. 너는 행복해 보여. 무슨 일이야?
여: 있잖아! 내 부모님이 드디어 나에게 강아지를 사주셨어!
남: 굉장해! 나는 네가 늘 개를 원해왔던 것을 알아.
여: 응, 그렇지만 나는 준비할 것이 많았어. 나는 사실 조금 전에 반려 동물 가게를 방문했어.
남: 너는 거기서 무엇을 했어?
여: 나는 개 사료를 좀 샀어.
남: 오, 그렇구나. 나는 네 개를 보고 싶어.
여: 토요일에 내 집에 와!
남: 그래. 무척 기다려진다.

단·어·및·표·현

Guess what! 있잖아!, 이봐!
place[pleis] 몡 집, 사는 곳

05 대화장소추론 ▶정답 ②

듣·기·대·본

W: How can I help you?
M: I'd like to check in for flight 206.
W: May I see your passport, please?
M: Here it is.
W: We have only an aisle seat left. Would this be OK?
M: Sure. No problem.

우·리·말·해·석

여: 어떻게 도와드릴까요?
남: 206편 비행기를 타기 위해 탑승 수속을 밟고 싶습니다.
여: 여권을 주시겠습니까?
남: 여기 있습니다.
여: 통로 쪽 자리밖에 없는데요. 괜찮을까요?
남: 네. 괜찮습니다.

단·어·및·표·현

check in 탑승 수속을 밟다

06 마지막말의도파악 ▶정답 ②

듣·기·대·본

W: Hey, Jeff. Can I share something that's been bugging me?
M: Of course, what's up?
W: Being the older sister sucks. I'm always giving in to my little brother's demands.
M: That sounds really annoying. What happened?
W: Today, I wanted to watch my show, but he insisted on playing his game, so I gave up.
M: It seems like you're always putting his wants first.
W: Exactly! It's just too much for me.

우·리·말·해·석

여: 안녕, Jeff. 내가 나를 괴롭히고 있는 것을 공유해도 될까?
남: 물론이지, 무슨 일이야?

여: 누나가 된다는 것은 별로야. 나는 항상 내 어린 남동생의 요구를 마지 못해 받아들이고 있어.
남: 정말 짜증 나겠는걸. 무슨 일이 있었어?
여: 오늘, 나는 내 방송을 보길 원했지만, 그는 그의 게임을 하겠다고 고집 해서, 내가 포기했어.
남: 네가 항상 그의 욕구(그가 원하는 것)를 우선으로 하는 것 같네.
여: 정확해! 그건 나에게 너무 벅찬 것 같아.

단·어·및·표·현

share[ʃɛər] 통 공유하다
bug[bʌg] 통 괴롭히다
suck[sʌk] 통 별로이다, 형편없다
give in to A A를 (마지못해) 받아들이다
demand[dimǽnd] 몡 요구
insist on ~을 (강력히) 고집[요구]하다
give up 포기하다
put A first A를 우선하다, 가장 중시하다
want[wɑnt] 몡 욕구, 원하는 것

07 특정정보파악 ▶정답 ⑤

듣·기·대·본

W: Liam, what are you doing?
M: I'm looking through sports programs on the cultural complex center's website.
W: I took a swimming class there last summer and it was really good. Are you going to sign up for a class?
M: Yes, I'm thinking of taking either tennis or bowling.
W: Oh, I'm interested in tennis. Why don't we take the tennis class together?
M: That would be great!

우·리·말·해·석

여: Liam, 뭐 하고 있어?
남: 문화 복합 센터 웹사이트에서 운동 프로그램을 살펴보고 있어.
여: 나 지난 여름에 거기서 수영 수업을 들었는데 정말 좋았어. 너는 수업 을 신청할 거야?
남: 응, 테니스나 볼링 중 하나를 들을까 생각 중이야.
여: 오, 나 테니스에 관심 있어. 우리 같이 테니스 수업 듣는 거 어때?
남: 그거 좋겠다!

단·어·및·표·현

look through 살펴보다, 훑어보다
sign up for ~을 신청하다
either A or B A이거나 B

08 할일파악(대화직후) ▶정답 ⑤

듣·기·대·본

W: Our school sports day is coming soon.
M: Right. What should we do to prepare for it?
W: We need to decide on a design for our class T-shirts.
M: Let's discuss it at our class meeting tomorrow.
W: Sure, but I think we should show some sample designs to our classmates.
M: Good idea. Let's pick some designs on the Internet.
W: Then, can you find me some websites where we can buy the T-shirts?
M: No problem. I'll search for them right away.

우·리·말·해·석

여: 우리 학교 운동회가 다가오고 있어.
남: 맞아. 그것을 준비하기 위해 우리는 뭘 해야 할까?
여: 우리는 반 티의 디자인을 정해야 해.

남: 내일 학급 회의에서 그것에 대해 토의해 보자.
여: 그래, 근데 우리는 우리 반 친구들에게 디자인 샘플을 보여줘야 한다고 생각해.
남: 좋은 생각이야. 인터넷에서 디자인을 몇 개 고르자.
여: 그러면, 우리가 티셔츠를 살 수 있는 웹사이트를 찾아줄 수 있어?
남: 문제없어. 바로 찾아줄게.

단·어·및·표·현
prepare[pripéər] ⑧ 준비하다
discuss[diskʌ́s] ⑧ 토의하다, 토론하다
search[səːrtʃ] ⑧ 찾다, 검색하다

09 대화미언급　　▶정답 ④

듣·기·대·본
(Telephone rings.)
W: Hello, Jenny's Steak House. How may I help you?
M: Hello, what time do you close today?
W: We close at 11 p.m.
M: I see. Where is the restaurant located exactly?
W: It's on the second floor of the Madison Building.
M: Is there a parking lot nearby?
W: Yes, there's an underground parking lot in the same building.
M: Thanks. Do you have any discounts for birthdays?
W: If you present your ID, you'll get a 30 percent discount.

우·리·말·해·석
(전화벨이 울린다.)
여: 여보세요, Jenny's Steak House입니다. 어떻게 도와드릴까요?
남: 여보세요, 오늘 몇 시에 문을 닫나요?
여: 저희는 오후 11시에 닫습니다.
남: 알겠어요. 식당은 정확히 어디에 위치해 있나요?
여: Madison 건물의 2층에 있습니다.
남: 근처에 주차장이 있나요?
여: 네, 같은 건물에 지하 주차장이 있습니다.
남: 고맙습니다. 생일에 대한 어떤 할인이 있나요?
여: 신분증을 제시하시면, 30퍼센트의 할인을 받으실 것입니다.

단·어·및·표·현
exactly[igzǽktli] ⑨ 정확히
present[prizént] ⑧ 제시하다

10 담화화제추론　　▶정답 ②

듣·기·대·본
W: Hello, Drivers Radio listeners. Today I am going to talk about how to drive safely in a school zone. First, reduce your speed when you drive through a school zone. The speed limit is 30km/h. Second, stop and wait at crosswalks even if you don't see anyone crossing the street. Finally, stopping and parking in a school zone is not allowed.

우·리·말·해·석
여: 안녕하세요, 운전자 라디오 청취자분들. 오늘은 스쿨 존(어린이 보호 구역)에서 안전하게 운전하는 법에 대해 이야기하려고 합니다. 우선, 스쿨 존을 지나갈 때 속도를 줄이세요. 속도 제한은 30km/h입니다. 둘째, 횡단보도에서 길을 건너는 사람이 보이지 않더라도 차를 세우고 기다리세요. 마지막으로, 스쿨 존에서의 정차와 주차는 허용되지 않습니다.

단·어·및·표·현
reduce[ridjúːs] ⑧ 줄이다, 감소하다
limit[límit] ⑱ 제한, 한계

crosswalk[krɔ́(ː)swɔ̀ːk] ⑱ 횡단보도

11 대화내용불일치　　▶정답 ⑤

듣·기·대·본
M: Julie, your school newsletter says it runs a Weekend Sports Day.
W: Yes, Dad. We can enjoy sports on Saturdays.
M: You can choose from bowling and golf.
W: Those are both for beginners. I know how to bowl, so I'll take golf class.
M: Good choice! You need to register online.
W: How much does it cost to take a program?
M: It's only $10 for 15 weeks.
W: Wow! I'll sign up right away.

우·리·말·해·석
남: Julie, 네 학교 소식지에 주말 스포츠의 날을 운영한다고 쓰여 있어.
여: 네, 아빠. 우리는 토요일마다 스포츠를 즐길 수 있어요.
남: 너는 볼링과 골프 중에서 고를 수 있네.
여: 그것들은 모두 초보자를 위한 것이에요. 저는 볼링을 칠 줄 아니까, 골프 수업을 들을 거예요.
남: 좋은 선택이야! 너는 온라인으로 등록해야 해.
여: 프로그램을 듣는 데 얼마나 들어요?
남: 15주에 단지 10달러구나.
여: 와! 저는 당장 등록할 거예요.

단·어·및·표·현
register[rédʒistər] ⑧ 등록하다

12 전화목적파악　　▶정답 ④

듣·기·대·본
(Telephone rings.)
W: Doctor's office. How may I help you?
M: I'm Max Parsons. I had an appointment with Dr. Brown yesterday.
W: Hello, Mr. Parsons. Are you not feeling well again?
M: No, I'm fine, but I think I left my jacket in the waiting room yesterday.
W: Oh, yes. We found a jacket that had been left behind.
M: Does it happen to be a leather jacket?
W: Yes. Feel free to come pick it up anytime you want.

우·리·말·해·석
(전화벨이 울린다.)
여: 병원입니다. 어떻게 도와드릴까요?
남: 전 Max Parsons입니다. 전 어제 Brown 박사님과 진료예약이 있었습니다.
여: 안녕하세요, Parsons 씨. 다시 몸이 좋지 않으세요?
남: 아니요, 괜찮습니다. 그런데 제가 어제 대기실에 제 재킷을 두고 온 거 같아요.
여: 아, 맞아요. 저희가 남겨진 재킷 하나를 발견했어요.
남: 그것은 혹시 가죽 재킷인가요?
여: 네. 언제든지 편하실 때 그것을 찾으러 오세요.

단·어·및·표·현
appointment[əpɔ́intmənt] ⑱ 예약, 약속

13 수치파악　　▶정답 ①

듣·기·대·본
W: I'm so excited for the e-sports final match this Sunday!
M: Me, too! It starts at 3 p.m., right?
W: Yes, how about we meet at 2 p.m.?

M: You know what? There are <u>event booths</u> we can visit before the match. Let's <u>go earlier</u> than that.

W: Then, how about 1:30 p.m.?

M: If the match is long, we'll get hungry. <u>Let's meet at 1 p.m. and eat lunch</u> together first.

W: Sounds good.

여: 나는 이번 주 일요일에 있을 e스포츠 결승전에 대해 너무 신나!

남: 나도! 그것은 오후 3시에 시작하잖아, 맞지?

여: 응, 우리 오후 2시에 만나는 게 어때?

남: 너 그거 알아? 경기 전에 우리가 방문할 수 있는 행사 부스들이 있어. 그것보다 더 일찍 가자.

여: 그러면, 오후 1시 30분은 어때?

남: 만약 경기가 길다면, 우리는 배고플 거야. 오후 1시에 만나서 먼저 점심을 같이 먹자.

여: 좋은걸.

단·어·및·표·현

final match 결승전, 최종 경기

booth [bu:θ] 圐 부스

visit [vízit] 통 방문하다

14 대화자관계추론 ▶정답 ④

듣·기·대·본

W: How can I help you today?

M: I'm <u>looking for a book</u> on thunderstorms and lightning.

W: Do you have a particular title in mind?

M: No, not really. I just need to know how thunderstorms create lightning.

W: Well, we have <u>plenty of books</u> about weather in the Science section.

M: That's great. Thank you so much!

W: Wait, you have to leave your bag before you enter and show <u>your membership card.</u>

M: Oops. Sorry. I almost forgot.

우·리·말·해·석

여: 어떻게 도와드릴까요?

남: 전 뇌우나 번개에 관한 책을 찾고 있어요.

여: 생각하신 특정한 제목이 있나요?

남: 아니요. 저는 단지 어떻게 뇌우가 번개를 만드는지 알기만 하면 돼요.

여: 그렇다면, 저희는 과학 부문에 날씨에 관한 많은 책이 있어요.

남: 그거 잘되었네요. 정말 감사합니다!

여: 잠시만요, 당신은 들어가기 전에 가방을 두고 회원증을 보여주셔야 해요.

남: 이런. 죄송합니다. 거의 잊어버릴 뻔했네요.

단·어·및·표·현

thunderstorm [θʌ́ndərstɔ̀:rm] 圐 뇌우

15 부탁(요청)한일파악 ▶정답 ⑤

듣·기·대·본

M: Hello, Ms. Lee.

W: Hi, Minho. I <u>was about to</u> call you. Can I ask a <u>quick favor</u>?

M: Sure. What is it?

W: <u>Tomorrow's timetable</u> has changed. The second and third periods will <u>be switched.</u>

M: Oh, I see.

W: <u>Could you post that</u> in our class group chat so everyone knows?

M: Of course. I'll do it right away.

여: 안녕하세요, 이 선생님.

남: 안녕, 민호야. 너에게 막 전화하려던 참이었어. 잠깐 부탁 하나 해도 될까?

여: 물론이에요. 무엇인가요?

남: 내일의 시간표가 바뀌었어. 2교시와 3교시가 바뀔 거야.

여: 아, 알겠어요.

남: 모두가 알 수 있도록 우리 반 단체 채팅방에 그걸 올려주겠니?

여: 물론이죠. 바로 할게요.

단·어·및·표·현

be about to + 동사원형 막 ~하려는 참이다

favor [féivər] 圐 부탁, 호의

timetable [táimtèibl] 圐 시간표

switch [switʃ] 통 바꾸다

post [poust] 통 (정보·메시지를) 게시하다

16 이유파악 ▶정답 ②

듣·기·대·본

W: Mike, you look different today.

M: Maybe it's because I got a haircut yesterday.

W: Yeah, but I think something else <u>has changed</u> as well.

M: Oh, I got a new pair of glasses.

W: Ah, that's it. Why did you change your glasses?

M: I had to, because they <u>were annoying</u> me all the time.

W: <u>Your glasses?</u> What was the problem?

M: They kept <u>slipping down.</u>

우·리·말·해·석

여: Mike, 너 오늘 달라 보인다.

남: 아마 내가 어제 머리를 잘랐기 때문일 거야.

여: 맞아, 하지만 나는 다른 것 또한 바뀐 것 같다고 생각해.

남: 오, 나는 안경 하나를 새로 샀어.

여: 아, 그거구나. 너는 왜 안경을 바꿨니?

남: 나는 그래야 했어, 왜냐하면 그것이 나를 항상 짜증나게 했기 때문이야.

여: 너의 안경이? 뭐가 문제였니?

남: 그것은 계속해서 흘러내렸어.

단·어·및·표·현

get a haircut 머리를 자르다

as well 또한

a pair of glasses 안경 하나

annoy [ənɔ́i] 통 짜증 나게 하다

slip down 흘러내리다

17 그림상황에적절한대화찾기 ▶정답 ③

듣·기·대·본

① M: Do you need anything else?

　W: Yes, can I have some napkins, please?

② M: Have you finished all your food?

　W: Yes, that was <u>delicious.</u> Thank you.

③ M: How do you want your eggs?

　W: Two eggs <u>sunny side up</u>, please.

④ M: Would you like to see a dessert menu?

　W: No, thanks. <u>I'm full.</u>

⑤ M: There will be a bit of a wait. We have a lot of orders.

　W: That's okay. I'll wait.

우·리·말·해·석

① 남: 그 밖에 다른 것이 필요하세요?

　여: 네, 냅킨 좀 주시겠어요?

② 남: 음식을 다 드셨나요?

여: 네, 그것은 맛있었어요. 고마워요.
③ 남: 고객님의 달걀을 어떻게 해드릴까요?
　　여: 한 쪽만 익힌 계란 두 개요.
④ 남: 후식 메뉴를 보시겠어요?
　　여: 고맙지만 사양하겠어요. 저는 배가 불러요.
⑤ 남: 약간 기다리셔야 합니다. 주문이 많습니다.
　　여: 괜찮습니다. 저는 기다리겠어요.

단·어·및·표·현
else [els] 혱 그 밖의 다른
sunny side up 한 쪽만 익힌 계란 프라이
a bit of 약간의

18 담화미언급　　　　　　　　　　▶정답 ③

듣·기·대·본
W: Welcome to the Modern Art Gallery. I'd like to invite you to a special exhibition of paintings by the famous artist, Hillary Palmer. The exhibition will be on for 3 weeks starting today. Tickets are 10 dollars each. If you're a student, you can get a 20% discount. Don't miss this great opportunity to see the world-class artworks in person.

우·리·말·해·석
여: 현대미술관에 오신 것을 환영합니다. 유명한 화가인 Hillary Palmer의 특별 전시회에 여러분을 초대하고 싶습니다. 전시회는 오늘부터 시작하여 3주 동안 열릴 것입니다. 티켓은 각 10달러입니다. 만약 당신이 학생이라면, 20% 할인을 받을 수 있습니다. 세계적인 예술 작품들을 직접 볼 수 있는 이 좋은 기회를 놓치지 마세요.

단·어·및·표·현
discount [diskáunt] 혱 할인
opportunity [ɑ̀pərtjúːnəti] 혱 기회
world-class 세계적인, 세계 최상급의

19 알맞은응답찾기　　　　　　　　▶정답 ⑤

듣·기·대·본
M: What did you do yesterday?
W: I saw a documentary about saving water yesterday.
M: Oh, I think it's important to care for the water on our planet.
W: Yes. I learned that we can save water in many ways.
M: What ways?
W: First, turn off the water while you brush your teeth.
M: Well, that seems easy enough. What else?
W: Shorten your shower time.

우·리·말·해·석
① 그 다큐멘터리는 볼 만한 가치가 있었어.
② 매 식사 후에 이를 닦는 거야.
③ 설탕이 든 음료보다 물을 골라야 해.
④ 지구의 표면은 대부분 물이야.
⑤ 샤워 시간을 단축하는 거야.

남: 너 어제 뭘 했니?
여: 나는 어제 물을 절약하는 것에 대한 다큐멘터리를 봤어.
남: 오, 나는 우리 지구의 물에 관심을 갖는 것이 중요하다고 생각해.
여: 맞아. 나는 많은 방식으로 우리가 물을 절약할 수 있다는 것을 알게 됐어.
남: 무슨 방법들이 있어?
여: 먼저, 네가 이를 닦는 동안 수돗물을 잠가.
남: 음, 그건 충분히 쉬워 보여. 그 밖에 무엇이 있니?
여: **샤워 시간을 단축하는 거야.**

단·어·및·표·현
save [seiv] 통 절약하다, 아끼다
care for 관심을 가지다, 돌보다
turn off 잠그다, 끄다
shorten [ʃɔ́ːrtən] 통 단축하다, 짧게 하다

20 알맞은응답찾기　　　　　　　　▶정답 ②

듣·기·대·본
W: I'm going to India next month. I heard you have been there. Can you give me some advice?
M: Sure. There are some cultural differences that you should know about.
W: Can you tell me one that is important?
M: Okay. You should use your right hand when you eat a meal.
W: Really? My right hand? But I'm left-handed.
M: They use the left hand in the bathroom. So they think the left hand is dirty.
W: Oh, I see. I'll keep that in mind.

우·리·말·해·석
① 오, 너의 가방은 너무 더러워.
② 오, 그렇구나. 명심할게.
③ 인도 음식 먹어본 적 있어?
④ 얼마나 자주 손을 씻어?
⑤ 내 호텔 방에는 큰 욕실이 있어.

여: 나 다음 달에 인도에 가. 네가 거기 갔었다고 들었어. 조언 좀 해줄 수 있겠니?
남: 물론이지. 그곳에는 네가 알아야 할 문화적 차이점들이 좀 있어.
여: 중요한 거 하나만 알려줄 수 있어?
남: 알았어. 식사를 할 때는 오른손을 사용해야 해.
여: 정말? 오른손이라고? 하지만 난 왼손잡이인데.
남: 그들은 왼손을 화장실에서 사용하거든. 그래서 그들은 왼손이 더럽다고 생각해.
여: **오, 그렇구나. 명심할게.**

단·어·및·표·현
cultural difference 문화적 차이
left-handed 왼손잡이의
keep in mind 명심하다

Words & Expressions Review

1. 훔치다, 도둑질하다	2. 왼손잡이의	3. 단축하다, 짧게 하다
4. 문화적 차이	5. 제시하다	6. 괴롭히다
7. 궁금해하다	8. 살펴보다, 훑어보다	9. (시계) 바늘, (시/분/초) 침
10. 부탁, 호의	11. 준비하다	12. 사실은, 실제로
13. 줄이다, 감소하다	14. 문화와 관련된, 문화의	15. 토의하다, 토론하다
16. 등록하다	17. 부문, 부분, 구역	18. 할인
19. A이거나 B	20. 잠그다, 끄다	21. 정확히
22. 등록하다	23. 요구	24. 기온, 온도
25. 또한	26. 여권	27. 약간의
28. 동네, 이웃 사람들	29. 통로 쪽 좌석	30. 공유하다
31. 두고 가다, 남겨 두다	32. 근사한	33. 방문하다
34. 뇌우	35. 세계적인, 세계 최상급의	36. 조언, 충고

37. 부스	38. 기회	39. 관심을 가지다, 돌보다
40. 탑승 수속을 밟다	41. 명심하다	42. 예약, 약속
43. 짜증 나게 하다	44. 제한, 한계	

Listening Test

영어듣기 모의고사 **09**회

|정|답|

01 ③	02 ③	03 ④	04 ⑤	05 ④
06 ②	07 ④	08 ⑤	09 ④	10 ④
11 ④	12 ⑤	13 ③	14 ③	15 ①
16 ④	17 ④	18 ⑤	19 ③	20 ④

01 날씨파악-그림　　▶정답 ③

듣·기·대·본

M: Good morning. Here is today's world weather forecast. In New York, there will be some strong winds, so be <u>prepared</u> for it when you go outside. Shanghai will see some sunshine after many days of cloudy weather. In London, there will be <u>heavy snowfall</u>, so be careful of the <u>slippery roads</u>. Thank you.

우·리·말·해·석

남: 좋은 아침입니다. 오늘의 세계 일기예보입니다. 뉴욕에는 강한 바람이 불 예정이므로 밖에 나가실 때 이에 대비하세요. 상하이는 여러 날의 흐린 날씨 뒤에 햇빛을 좀 볼 수 있겠습니다. 런던에는 폭설이 내릴 예정이니, 미끄러운 길 조심하세요. 감사합니다.

단·어·및·표·현

weather forecast 일기예보
be prepared for ~을 대비하다
heavy snowfall 폭설
slippery [slípəri] ⑲ 미끄러운

02 그림정보파악　　▶정답 ③

듣·기·대·본

M: Sally, you <u>bought</u> a new bag.
W: Yes, I did. What do you think of it?
M: It's nice. <u>I especially like the pockets.</u>
W: They are good for <u>putting things in</u>. How about the butterfly?
M: I like it, too. You like butterflies, don't you?
W: Yes, I do.

우·리·말·해·석

남: Sally, 너 새 가방 샀구나.
여: 응, 샀어. 어떻게 생각해?
남: 좋다. 특히 주머니가 마음에 들어.
여: 이 주머니들은 물건을 넣기 좋아. 이 나비는 어때?
남: 그것도 좋아. 너 나비를 좋아하는구나, 그렇지?
여: 그래, 좋아해.

단·어·및·표·현

especially [ispéʃəli] ⑲ 특히

03 심정추론　　▶정답 ④

듣·기·대·본

M: Hey Sarah, did you see the school writing contest results?
W: I thought the results would be announced next week. Are they out already?
M: Yes! And you <u>won first place</u> with your story about friendship!
W: What? Really? I can't believe it!
M: I just saw the list. Your name is <u>at the top</u>.
W: Wow! I never thought I would win! This is amazing!

우·리·말·해·석

남: 안녕 Sarah, 너 학교 글쓰기 대회 결과 봤어?
여: 난 그 결과가 다음 주에 발표되는 줄 알았는데. 벌써 결과가 나왔어?
남: 응! 그리고 네가 우정에 관한 네 이야기로 우승했어!
여: 뭐라고? 정말? 믿을 수가 없어!
남: 내가 방금 명단을 봤어. 네 이름이 맨 위에 있어.
여: 와! 내가 상을 탈 거라고는 전혀 생각 못 했어! 놀라워!

단·어·및·표·현

announce [ənáuns] ⑧ 발표하다
win first place 우승하다, 일등을 하다
at the top 맨 위에

04 한일파악　　▶정답 ⑤

듣·기·대·본

W: Justin, how did you like my group's presentation on Korean culture?
M: I thought it was a very <u>well-put-together</u> presentation. Great job!
W: You really think so?
M: Yes. I thought your PowerPoint slides were very <u>well done</u>.
W: Right? Jane did a great job on them.
M: Also, whoever did the research really <u>put some effort into it</u>.
W: That was me!
M: Really? You are such a <u>great researcher</u>.

우·리·말·해·석

여: Justin, 한국 문화에 대한 저희 조 발표는 어땠나요?
남: 저는 그것이 매우 잘 구성된 발표라고 생각했어요. 정말 잘했어요!
여: 정말 그렇게 생각해요?
남: 네. 저는 당신들의 파워포인트 슬라이드가 아주 잘 만들어졌다고 생각해요.
여: 정말요? Jane이 그것들을 엄청 잘 해줬어요.
남: 또한, 조사한 사람이 누구든 정말 그것에 공을 많이 들였네요.
여: 그게 저였어요!
남: 정말요? 당신은 정말 훌륭한 조사원이군요.

단·어·및·표·현

well-put-together 잘 구성된, 잘 정리된
whoever [hu:évər] ⑭ 누구든 ~하는 사람(들)
put effort into ~에 공을 들이다, 노력을 기울이다

05 대화장소추론　　▶정답 ④

듣·기·대·본

M: May I help you?
W: Hi. I'd like two bicycles for adults, please.
M: Sure. How long would you like to <u>rent</u> them for?

W: Just for an hour. How much is it?
M: It's 6 dollars in total and you need to <u>leave</u> your ID card here.
W: Here you are. Do I get it back when I <u>return</u> the bicycles?
M: That's right. Take these tickets downstairs and you'll get your bicycles there.
W: Thanks.

우·리·말·해·석

남: 도와드릴까요?
여: 안녕하세요. 성인용 자전거 두 대 주세요.
남: 물론이죠. 얼마 동안 빌리고 싶으세요?
여: 딱 한 시간이요. 얼마예요?
남: 통틀어 6달러이고 당신의 신분증을 여기에 두고 가셔야 해요.
여: 여기 있습니다. 제가 자전거를 반납할 때 돌려받나요?
남: 맞습니다. 이 표들을 아래층으로 가지고 내려가시면 거기서 당신의 자전거를 받을 수 있을 거예요.
여: 감사합니다.

단·어·및·표·현

rent [rent] 동 빌리다, 대여하다
in total 통틀어, 모두 합하여
leave [liːv] 동 두고 가다[오다]
return [ritə́ːrn] 동 반납하다

06　마지막말의도파악　▶정답 ②

듣·기·대·본

W: Nick, did you ask Alice to see a movie <u>with you</u> this weekend?
M: No, I didn't.
W: Why not? You <u>met</u> her yesterday, didn't you?
M: Yes. But I was <u>afraid</u> she might say no.
W: Don't worry. I think she likes you.
M: Do you really <u>think</u> so?
W: Sure. Go and ask her now.

우·리·말·해·석

여: Nick, 너 Alice에게 이번 주말에 너랑 영화 보자고 물어봤어?
남: 아니, 안 했어.
여: 왜? 어제 그녀를 만났잖아, 그렇지 않니?
남: 응. 하지만 그녀가 싫다고 말할 것 같아서 두려웠어.
여: 걱정 마. 난 그녀가 너를 좋아한다고 생각해.
남: 정말 그렇게 생각해?
여: 물론. 지금 가서 그녀에게 물어봐.

단·어·및·표·현

afraid [əfréid] 형 두려운

07　특정정보파악　▶정답 ④

듣·기·대·본

M: Sujin, what are you having for lunch today?
W: I bought some gimbap <u>on my way</u> to work this morning.
M: Will that be enough?
W: No, that's why I also bought cup noodles. What are you having?
M: <u>I'm having a salad</u> with shrimp and avocado.
W: Wow, that sounds delicious! Where did you buy it?
M: I made it at home. It's really simple to make.
W: It sounds <u>much healthier</u> than my lunch!

우·리·말·해·석

남: 수진 씨, 오늘 점심 뭐 드실 거예요?

여: 저는 오늘 아침에 출근하면서 김밥을 좀 샀어요.
남: 그것으로 충분할까요?
여: 아니요, 그래서 컵라면도 샀어요. 당신은 뭘 드시나요?
남: 저는 새우와 아보카도가 들어간 샐러드를 먹을 거예요.
여: 와, 맛있겠네요! 당신은 어디서 그걸 사셨나요?
남: 제가 집에서 만들었어요. 그건 정말 만들기 간단해요.
여: 제 점심보다 훨씬 더 건강한 것 같네요!

단·어·및·표·현

on one's way 도중에
delicious [dilíʃəs] 형 맛있는

08　할일파악(대화직후)　▶정답 ⑤

듣·기·대·본

W: Did you hear the news? The basketball team <u>is looking for</u> players.
M: Yes, I heard about it. I'm so excited. You know how much I've wanted to join the team.
W: Yeah. You are the first one <u>who</u> I thought of when I heard the news.
M: Do you know how I can <u>try out</u>?
W: Maybe you can check the school website.
M: Oh, I can't wait. <u>I should ask</u> our gym teacher about it right now.

우·리·말·해·석

여: 너 그 소식 들었니? 농구 팀에서 선수를 구한대.
남: 응. 나 그것에 관해 들었어. 매우 신나. 넌 내가 얼마나 그 팀에 합류하고 싶어했는지 알잖아.
여: 응. 너는 내가 그 소식을 들었을 때 생각했던 첫 번째 사람이었어.
남: 내가 어떻게 지원할 수 있는지 아니?
여: 아마도 학교 홈페이지를 확인해보면 될 거야.
남: 아, 나는 못 기다리겠다. 그것에 관해 당장 체육 선생님께 여쭤봐야겠어.

단·어·및·표·현

try out (for) ~ (선발 등을 위한 경쟁에) 지원하다

09　대화미언급　▶정답 ④

듣·기·대·본

M: Hey, Suzy. Do you read any comic books?
W: Yeah. My favorite comic book is *The Thunder: Storm is Coming*.
M: Oh, I know that one. <u>That is an action comic book</u>, right?
W: Yes, that's right. The main character fights bad guys and saves the city.
M: Was the main character <u>named</u> Storm?
W: Yeah! He is <u>such a cool</u> character!
M: By the way, <u>who is the author</u> of this comic book?
W: It's by Andrew River. You should read some of <u>his works</u>.
M: Okay, I will.

우·리·말·해·석

남: 안녕, Suzy, 너는 만화책을 읽니?
여: 응. 내가 가장 좋아하는 만화책은 "The Thunder: Storm is Coming(천둥: 폭풍우가 몰려온다)"이야.
남: 오, 나 그거 알아. 그것은 액션 만화책이야, 맞지?
여: 응. 맞아. 주인공이 악당들이랑 싸워서 도시를 구해.
남: 주인공 이름이 Storm이었나?
여: 맞아! 그는 정말로 멋진 캐릭터야!
남: 그런데, 이 만화책의 작가가 누구지?

여: Andrew River야. 너는 그의 몇몇 작품들을 읽어야 해.
남: 알겠어, 그렇게 할게.
단·어·및·표·현
main character 주인공
author[ɔ́ːθər] ⑲ 작가, 저자
work[wəːrk] ⑲ (생산 결과물로서의) 작품, 일, 저작물

10 담화화제추론 ▶정답 ④
듣·기·대·본
W: Good morning, everyone! The school cheerleading team is looking for talented new members. You can learn a variety of skills on our team. We attend all our school's games. And, we won first place last year in a cheerleading competition. You can join by signing your name on the notice board. We will contact you for a tryout and interview.

우·리·말·해·석
여: 안녕하세요, 여러분! 학교 응원단에서 재능 있는 새 단원들을 찾고 있습니다. 여러분들은 저희 팀에서 다양한 기술들을 배울 수 있습니다. 저희는 학교의 모든 경기에 참석합니다. 그리고 저희는 작년 응원 대회에서 1등을 차지했습니다. 게시판에 여러분의 이름을 적어서 가입할 수 있습니다. 저희가 테스트와 인터뷰를 위해 연락 드리겠습니다.

단·어·및·표·현
talented[tǽləntid] ⑲ 재능 있는
notice board 게시판

🗣 LISTENING ADVICE
[t] 소리는 기본적으로는 우리말 [ㅌ] 소리와 비슷하지만 위치에 따라 종종 소리가 생략되거나 변형됩니다. 한 예로, 'tryout and interview'라는 구절에서 등장하는 't'는 모두 다르게 발음되지요. 단어의 끝에 오는 't'는 그 소리가 거의 생략되어 들리지 않고, 't'와 'r'이 만나면 [ㅊ] 소리로 바뀌므로 'tryout'은 [트라이아웃트]가 아닌 [츄라이아웃]으로 들립니다. 'interview'는 그대로 [ㅌ] 소리를 살려 [인터ㄹ뷰]로 발음됩니다.

11 대화내용불일치 ▶정답 ④
듣·기·대·본
W: Dustin, do you know anything about the Night with Stars Event?
M: Yeah. It's a popular school event. It's this Friday.
W: I heard it will be held on the school playground.
M: Right. Let's go together. It starts at 9 p.m.
W: Great. It will be cold, so we should bring a blanket.
M: We don't have to. Blankets are available for free.
W: Great! Do we need to sign up?
M: Yes. Only students who sign up in advance can come.
W: I see.

우·리·말·해·석
여: Dustin, 너는 'Night with Stars' 행사에 대해 아는 것이 있니?
남: 응. 그건 인기 있는 학교 행사야. 그건 이번 주 금요일이야.
여: 나는 그것이 학교 운동장에서 열린다고 들었어.
남: 맞아. 같이 가자. 오후 9시에 시작해.
여: 좋아. 날씨가 추울 거야. 그러니 우리는 담요를 가져가야 해.
남: 그럴 필요 없어. 담요는 무료로 이용할 수 있어.
여: 좋아! 우리는 신청해야 해?
남: 응. 미리 신청한 학생들만 갈 수 있어.
여: 그렇구나.

단·어·및·표·현
be held ∼이 열리다, 개최되다
available[əvéiləbl] ⑲ 이용할 수 있는
sign up 신청하다, 가입하다
in advance 미리, 사전에

12 방문이유파악 ▶정답 ⑤
듣·기·대·본
M: Hello. How may I help you?
W: I borrowed a book two weeks ago, and there's a problem.
M: Can I first have your name and membership number?
W: It's Jina Park and the number is 3342-7645.
M: OK, you borrowed *The Ten Steps* on July 10.
W: That's right. And it seems to be gone.
M: I see. If you've lost it, you must purchase the same book for us.
W: OK, I'll do that as soon as possible.

우·리·말·해·석
남: 안녕하세요. 어떻게 도와드릴까요?
여: 제가 2주 전에 책 한 권을 빌렸는데 문제가 있어요.
남: 먼저 이름과 회원 번호를 알 수 있을까요?
여: 박지나이고 번호는 3342-7645입니다.
남: 네. 7월 10일에 "The Ten Steps"를 빌리셨네요.
여: 맞아요. 그리고 그게 없어진 것 같아요.
남: 알겠습니다. 잃어버리셨다면 저희에게 같은 책을 사주셔야 합니다.
여: 네, 가능한 한 빨리 그렇게 하겠습니다.

단·어·및·표·현
as soon as possible 가능한 한 빨리

13 수치계산(거스름돈) ▶정답 ③
듣·기·대·본
M: Welcome to Mega Art Supply! What can I help you with today?
W: Hi, I'm looking to buy two sketchbooks and one paintbrush.
M: Okay. Each sketchbook costs 6 dollars and the paintbrush costs 4 dollars.
W: Then, how much does it all add up to?
M: It's 16 dollars in total. Do you need anything else?
W: That's okay, I'll just buy these three items. Here's 20 dollars.
M: Thank you. Here's your change.

우·리·말·해·석
남: Mega Art Supply(메가 미술 용품점)에 오신 것을 환영합니다! 오늘은 무엇을 도와드릴까요?
여: 안녕하세요, 저는 스케치북 두 권과 붓 하나를 사려고 해요.
남: 알겠습니다. 스케치북 한 권은 6달러이고, 붓은 4달러입니다.
여: 그럼, 모두 합해서 얼마인가요?
남: 총 16달러입니다. 그 밖에 다른 것이 필요하세요?
여: 괜찮아요, 그냥 이 세 개만 살게요. 여기 20달러요.
남: 감사합니다. 여기 거스름돈이에요.

단·어·및·표·현
art supply 미술 용품, 미술 재료
cost[kɔːst] ⑧ (값·비용이) ∼이다
add up to 총 ∼가 되다
change[tʃeindʒ] ⑲ 거스름돈

14 대화자관계추론 ▶정답 ③

듣•기•대•본

W: Hello. Can I help you?
M: I'd like to order a custom cake for my parents.
W: Do you have any special design in mind?
M: Yes. I want to put their picture on the cake.
W: Okay, anything else?
M: And write "Happy Wedding Anniversary" below the picture, please.
W: All right. Send the picture to this email address.
M: Thank you. Also, I need it next Thursday.
W: Don't worry. I'll contact you when it is ready.

우•리•말•해•석

여: 안녕하세요. 무엇을 도와드릴까요?
남: 제 부모님을 위한 맞춤 케이크를 주문하고 싶습니다.
여: 생각해 두신 특별한 디자인이 있나요?
남: 네. 저는 케이크 위에 그들의 사진을 넣고 싶어요.
여: 좋습니다. 그 밖에 또 다른 것은요?
남: 그리고 "행복한 결혼 기념일"이라고 그림 아래에 써 주세요.
여: 알겠습니다. 이 이메일 주소로 사진을 보내주세요.
남: 고맙습니다. 또한, 저는 다음 주 목요일에 그것이 필요합니다.
여: 걱정 마세요. 준비가 되면 연락을 드리겠습니다.

단•어•및•표•현

custom [kʌ́stəm] 형 맞춤의, 주문 제작한
have ~ in mind ~를 생각해 두다, 염두에 두다
picture [píktʃər] 명 사진, 그림
anniversary [æ̀nəvə́:rsəri] 명 기념일
contact [kántækt] 동 연락하다

15 부탁(요청)한일파악 ▶정답 ①

듣•기•대•본

W: Hi, Sam! Where are you going?
M: I'm going to the Math teacher's office.
W: Oh, good. Can you do me a favor?
M: What is it?
W: Could you give my homework to Ms. Kim? I have to go to the science lab now.
M: Sure. But don't forget that you owe me one!
W: Okay. Thanks a lot.

우•리•말•해•석

여: 안녕, Sam! 너 어디에 가니?
남: 나는 수학 선생님 사무실에 가는 중이야.
여: 아, 잘됐네. 내 부탁 좀 들어줄래?
남: 뭔데?
여: 내 숙제를 김 선생님께 제출해줄래? 나는 지금 과학 실험실에 가야 해서.
남: 그래. 하지만 너 나한테 신세 진 거 잊지 마!
여: 알았어. 정말 고마워.

단•어•및•표•현

owe [ou] 동 ~에게 신세 지다, 빚지다

16 이유파악 ▶정답 ④

듣•기•대•본

W: Jim, did you hear about our city marathon?
M: Yes, I did. Are you going to register?
W: Yes, and it would be nice if you signed up too.
M: Oh, I don't think that's possible.
W: Why? I thought you were a good runner.
M: I like running, but I recently injured my left ankle.
W: Really? Are you okay?
M: It's getting better, but I don't think running in a marathon is a good idea.
W: Okay, I'll find another partner, then.

우•리•말•해•석

여: Jim, 너는 우리 도시의 마라톤에 대해 들었니?
남: 응, 들었어. 너는 등록할 거니?
여: 응, 그리고 너도 등록한다면 멋질 거야.
남: 오, 나는 그것이 가능하다고 생각하지 않아.
여: 왜? 나는 네가 달리기를 잘한다고 생각했어.
남: 나는 달리기를 좋아하지만, 최근에 내 왼쪽 발목을 다쳤어.
여: 정말? 너 괜찮아?
남: 좋아지고 있지만, 나는 마라톤에서 달리는 것은 좋은 생각이라고 생각하지 않아.
여: 알았어, 그러면 나는 다른 파트너를 찾아볼게.

단•어•및•표•현

register [rédʒistər] 동 등록하다
injure [índʒər] 동 다치다, 부상을 입다

17 그림상황에적절한대화찾기 ▶정답 ④

듣•기•대•본

① M: Have you finished doing your homework?
　 W: Yes, can I go play now?
② M: Do you know where the restroom is?
　 W: It's at the end of this corridor.
③ M: Can I have a glass of water?
　 W: Sure. Here you go.
④ M: The floor is still wet, so be careful.
　 W: Okay. I'll try to watch my step.
⑤ M: This brush is too short for me.
　 W: Let's go buy a new one.

우•리•말•해•석

① 남: 너는 네 숙제 하는 것을 다 마쳤니?
　 여: 네, 이제 가서 놀아도 돼요?
② 남: 당신은 화장실이 어디 있는지 아시나요?
　 여: 그건 이 복도의 끝에 있어요.
③ 남: 물 한 잔 마실 수 있을까요?
　 여: 물론이죠. 여기 있어요.
④ 남: 바닥이 여전히 젖어있으니, 조심하세요.
　 여: 네. 조심해서 걷도록 할게요.
⑤ 남: 이 솔은 나에게 너무 짧아.
　 여: 새로운 것을 하나 사러 가자.

단•어•및•표•현

corridor [kɔ́(:)ridər] 명 복도
be careful 조심하다
try to + 동사원형 ~하도록 노력하다
watch one's step 조심해서 걷다, 조심하다

18 담화미언급 ▶정답 ⑤

듣•기•대•본

W: Hello, new students. I'd like to introduce our school library. If you want to check out books, just bring them and show your student ID to the front desk. Each student can check out ten books at one time. The due date to return the book to the library is in two weeks. Opening hours are from 10 a.m. to 6 p.m. Thanks.

우·리·말·해·석

여: 안녕하세요, 신입생 여러분. 저는 저희 학교 도서관을 소개하고 싶습니다. 만약 여러분이 책을 대출하고 싶다면, 그것들을 가져와서 안내 데스크에 당신의 학생증을 보여주세요. 각 학생은 한 번에 10권의 책들을 대출할 수 있습니다. 도서관에 책을 반납해야 하는 예정된 기한은 2주 후입니다. 운영시간은 오전 10시부터 오후 6시까지입니다. 감사합니다.

단·어·및·표·현

would like to(='d like to) + 동사 ～하고 싶다, ～하는 것을 바라다
check out (책을) 대출하다
due [dju:] 혱 예정된, ～하기로 되어 있는
return [ritə́:rn] 동 (책을) 반납하다
opening hours 운영시간

19 알맞은응답찾기　▶ 정답 ③

들·기·대·본

M: Hi, Sora! You look so <u>cheerful</u> these days.
W: Hello, Mr. Simon. I've just started a guitar class.
M: That sounds so cool.
W: I'm still a beginner, but I've always wanted to learn and finally decided to <u>give it a try</u>.
M: I'm sure you're having a lot of fun.
W: Yes. Playing music makes me feel <u>focused and creative</u>.
M: I didn't know <u>you were into</u> music. How often do you go to class?
W: <u>I take lessons three times a week.</u>

우·리·말·해·석

① 제가 그 기타를 바로 살게요.
② 저는 선생님의 수업을 놓치지 않도록 노력할게요.
③ 저는 일주일에 세 번 수업을 들어요.
④ 저는 매주 주말에 피아노 수업에 가요.
⑤ 당신은 음악을 좀 더 자주 듣는 게 좋겠어요.

남: 안녕, 소라야! 너 요즘 정말 기분이 좋아 보여.
여: 안녕하세요, Simon 선생님. 저는 이제 막 기타 수업을 시작했어요.
남: 정말 멋지다.
여: 저는 아직 초보자지만, 항상 배우고 싶었고 마침내 한번 해보기로 결심했어요.
남: 넌 정말 재미있게 보내고 있는 게 분명해.
여: 네. 음악을 연주하는 것은 저를 집중되고 창의적인 기분이 들게 해요.
남: 네가 음악에 관심이 많은 줄 몰랐어. 수업은 얼마나 자주 가니?
여: **저는 일주일에 세 번 수업을 들어요.**

단·어·및·표·현

cheerful [tʃíərfəl] 혱 기분 좋은, 쾌활한
give it a try 한번 해보다
creative [kriéitiv] 혱 창의적인
be into ～ ～에 관심이 많다

20 알맞은응답찾기　▶ 정답 ④

들·기·대·본

W: Tom, did you hear about the <u>movie shooting</u> in our neighborhood?
M: Yes! My favorite actor Daniel Park will be here.
W: You must be very excited.
M: Of course. I'm going to <u>go and watch</u> the movie shoot later.
W: Can I <u>come with</u> you? I want to see it, too.
M: Sure. I heard that they're shooting <u>all day</u> today. When do you want to go?
W: <u>How about in the afternoon?</u>

우·리·말·해·석

① 나는 코미디를 좋아해.
② 나는 택시를 타는 것을 선호해.
③ 지난 수요일 이후로.
④ 오후는 어때?
⑤ 학교 앞에서 만나자.

여: Tom, 너 우리 동네에서 하는 영화 촬영에 관해서 들었니?
남: 응! 내가 정말 좋아하는 배우 Daniel Park이 이곳에 올 거야.
여: 너 아주 신난 게 틀림없구나.
남: 물론이지. 난 가서 영화 촬영을 지켜볼 거야.
여: 내가 너와 함께 가도 될까? 나도 그걸 보고 싶어.
남: 그럼. 오늘 하루 종일 촬영을 할 거라고 들었어. 넌 언제 가고 싶어?
여: <u>오후는 어때?</u>

단·어·및·표·현

movie shooting 영화 촬영
favorite [féivərit] 혱 매우 좋아하는
excited [iksáitid] 혱 신이 난, 들뜬

Words & Expressions Review

1. 미끄러운	2. 주인공	3. 도중에
4. ～에 공을 들이다, 노력을 기울이다	5. 게시판	6. 재능 있는
7. 기분 좋은, 쾌활한	8. 누구든 ～하는 사람(들)	9. 영화 촬영
10. 잘 구성된, 잘 정리된	11. (값 · 비용이) ～이다	12. 작가, 저자
13. 거스름돈	14. 특히	15. ～을 대비하다
16. 빌리다, 대여하다	17. ～이 열리다, 개최되다	18. (선발 등을 위한 경쟁에) 지원하다
19. 다치다, 부상을 입다	20. 발표하다	21. 나비
22. ～에게 신세 지다, 빚지다	23. 매우 좋아하는	24. 작품, 일, 저작물
25. 확인하다	26. 미리, 사전에	27. 신나는, 흥분되는
28. 과학 실험실	29. ～을 생각해 두다, 염두에 두다	30. ～인 것 같다
31. 한번 해보다	32. (책을) 대출하다	33. 발목
34. 총 ～가 되다	35. 우승하다, 일등을 하다	36. 창의적인
37. 사다, 구매하다	38. 이용할 수 있는	39. 맛있는
40. ～하기로 되어 있는, 예정된	41. 통틀어, 모두 합하여	42. 기념일
43. 참석하다	44. 주문 제작한, 맞춤의	

Listening Test
영어듣기 모의고사 **10**회

|정|답|

01 ④	02 ②	03 ②	04 ③	05 ⑤
06 ⑤	07 ②	08 ⑤	09 ⑤	10 ⑤
11 ⑤	12 ④	13 ②	14 ①	15 ④
16 ④	17 ⑤	18 ④	19 ①	20 ⑤

01　날씨파악-그림　▶정답 ④

듣•기•대•본

M: Good evening! This is Tom, and I'm back with another <u>weekly</u> weather report. Monday will be clear and sunny. From Tuesday to Thursday, it will be a bit <u>cloudy</u>. Friday will be <u>windy</u>, so you might <u>need a jacket</u>. If you're planning outdoor activities, the coming weekend might not be the best time. Heavy rain is expected from Saturday morning through Sunday evening. Thank you.

우•리•말•해•석

남: 안녕하세요! 저는 Tom이고, 또 다른 주간 일기 예보로 돌아왔습니다. 월요일은 맑고 화창하겠습니다. 화요일부터 목요일은 조금 흐리겠습니다. 금요일은 바람이 불겠으니 재킷이 필요할지도 모릅니다. 여러분이 야외 활동을 계획하고 있다면, 다가오는 주말은 최적의 시기가 아닐 수도 있습니다. 토요일 오전부터 일요일 저녁까지 폭우가 예상됩니다. 감사합니다.

단•어•및•표•현

weather report 일기 예보
outdoor activities 야외 활동
heavy rain 폭우, 큰비
expect[ikspékt] ⑧ 예상하다, 기대하다

02　그림정보파악　▶정답 ②

듣•기•대•본

W: Honey, I feel like our living room floor is a bit cold these days.
M: Me, too. We should get some <u>indoor slippers</u>. Let's buy them online.
W: Hmm... (Pause) How about this furry pair?
M: I think those will make my feet <u>sweaty</u>. Let's buy a pair that isn't furry.
W: Sure. How about these ones which have <u>rabbits on them</u>?
M: Yeah, let's buy those ones with rabbits. They also <u>aren't furry</u>.

우•리•말•해•석

여: 여보, 저는 요즘 우리 거실 바닥이 약간 차가운 느낌이 있어요.
남: 저도요. 우리는 실내용 슬리퍼들을 좀 사야겠어요. 그것들을 온라인에서 사죠.
여: 음… (잠시 후) 이 털 실내화는 어때요?
남: 그것들은 제 발에 땀이 나게 할 것 같아요. 털 실내화가 아닌 것을 사죠.
여: 그래요. 그것들(실내화)에 토끼들이 달린 이것들은 어때요?
남: 네, 토끼들이 달린 그것들로 사죠. 그것들은 게다가 털로 덮여 있지 않아요.

단•어•및•표•현

feel like ~한 느낌이 있다

living room 거실
floor[flɔːr] ⑨ 바닥
these days 요즘
indoor[índɔːr] ⑩ 실내용의, 실내의
furry[fə́ːri] ⑩ 털로 덮인
pair[pɛər] ⑨ 한 쌍, 한 켤레
sweaty[swéti] ⑩ 땀나게 하는

03　심정추론　▶정답 ②

듣•기•대•본

W: Sean, why don't you eat <u>some more</u>?
M: I'm sorry, Mom, but I just can't eat any more.
W: Is there <u>something wrong</u>?
M: Well, I'm worried because I didn't study <u>enough</u> for the test today.
W: Oh, just do your best, son.
M: Yes, I will. But now I feel like <u>throwing up</u> just thinking about the test.

우•리•말•해•석

① 신이 난　② 걱정하는　③ 자랑스러운　④ 침착한　⑤ 놀란

여: Sean, 좀 더 먹는 것이 어떠니?
남: 죄송해요, 엄마, 하지만 더 이상 못 먹겠어요.
여: 무슨 일이 있니?
남: 음, 오늘 시험 공부를 충분히 하지 않았기 때문에 걱정이 돼요.
여: 오, 그냥 최선을 다하렴, 아들아.
남: 네, 그럴 거예요. 하지만 시험 생각만 해도 지금 토할 것 같아요.

단•어•및•표•현

throw up 토하다

04　한일파악　▶정답 ③

듣•기•대•본

W: Hi, Jack. Have you heard about the science fair tomorrow?
M: Yes. It's going to be a big event, isn't it?
W: Exactly. Our science club is <u>in charge of organizing</u> the fair.
M: Really? That's great! Did you plan the science events, too?
W: No, our club <u>president</u> is in charge of that.
M: Oh, then what did you do?
W: <u>I decorated</u> the auditorium.
M: I see. I'm sure the fair will be a success.

우•리•말•해•석

여: 안녕, Jack. 너는 내일 있을 과학 박람회에 대해 들어봤어?
남: 응. 큰 행사가 될 거야, 그렇지 않아?
여: 틀림없어. 우리 과학 동아리가 그 박람회 준비를 담당하고 있어.
남: 정말? 잘됐다! 과학 행사도 네가 계획한 거야?
여: 아니, 우리 동아리 회장이 그것을 담당하고 있어.
남: 아, 그럼 너는 뭘 했어?
여: 나는 강당을 장식했어.
남: 그렇구나. 나는 박람회가 성공할 거라고 확신해.

단•어•및•표•현

be in charge of ~을 담당하다, 주관하다
organize[ɔ́ːrgənàiz] ⑧ 준비하다, 조직하다
president[prézidənt] ⑨ 회장
decorate[dékərèit] ⑧ 장식하다, 꾸미다

05 대화장소추론　　　　　　▶정답 ⑤

듣·기·대·본

W: Good evening. Table for two?
M: Yes, please. Can we sit by the window?
W: Of course. How about this table?
M: It's perfect.
W: All right. Here's the menu. Take your time, and let me
　　know when you are ready to order.
M: Thank you. Um, can I use the bathroom?
W: Of course. The bathroom is right around that corner.

우·리·말·해·석

여: 안녕하세요. 두 분이신가요?
남: 네, 부탁드려요. 창가 쪽에 앉을 수 있을까요?
여: 물론이죠. 이 자리는 어떠세요?
남: 완벽하네요.
여: 알겠습니다. 여기 메뉴판입니다. 천천히 보시고, 주문할 준비가 되시면
　　저에게 알려주세요.
남: 감사합니다. 저기, 제가 화장실을 써도 될까요?
여: 물론이죠. 화장실은 저쪽 모서리를 돈 곳에 바로 있어요.

단·어·및·표·현

take one's time 천천히 하다
order[ɔ́ːrdər] ⑧ 주문하다
around[əráund] ⑳ ~를 돈 곳에

06 마지막말의도파악　　　　　▶정답 ⑤

듣·기·대·본

W: Congratulations, Marty! I saw you running. You ran
　　really fast.
M: Thanks, Celia. I'm happy that I won.
W: But, why are you limping?
M: My leg has been hurting a little since the race ended.
W: That can't be good. Did you see the doctor?
M: No. It doesn't hurt that much.
W: I really think you should see the doctor.

우·리·말·해·석

여: 축하해, Marty! 네가 뛰는 것을 봤어. 너 정말 빨리 달리더라.
남: 고마워, Celia. 내가 이겨서 나도 기뻐.
여: 그런데, 너 왜 절뚝거리니?
남: 경주가 끝난 후로 다리가 조금 아파.
여: 불길한데. 진료는 받았니?
남: 아니. 그렇게 많이 아프지는 않아.
여: 나는 정말로 네가 진료를 받아야 한다고 생각해.

단·어·및·표·현

limp[limp] ⑧ 절뚝거리다

07 특정정보파악　　　　　　▶정답 ②

듣·기·대·본

W: Alex, what will you take to the flea market?
M: I haven't decided yet, Mom.
W: How about these comic books?
M: I'm still reading them, plus these are my favorite. Can I
　　take this T-shirt?
W: Sure. I'll wash it for you.
M: Thanks. I'm also thinking of selling this basketball at the
　　market.
W: It's too old. The T-shirt will be enough.

우·리·말·해·석

여: Alex, 너는 벼룩시장에 무엇을 가져갈 거니?
남: 아직 결정하지 못했어요, 엄마.
여: 이 만화책들은 어떠니?
남: 저는 아직 그것들을 읽고 있어요, 게다가 이것들은 제가 제일 좋아하는
　　거예요. 이 티셔츠 가져가도 되나요?
여: 물론. 내가 그것을 너를 위해 빨아주마.
남: 고맙습니다. 저는 또한 이 농구공을 시장에서 팔까 생각 중이에요.
여: 그것은 너무 낡았구나. 그 티셔츠면 충분할 것 같아.

단·어·및·표·현

decide[disáid] ⑧ 결정하다

08 할일파악(대화직후)　　　　▶정답 ⑤

듣·기·대·본

W: What's your plan for today? It's the first day of our
　　vacation.
M: Yeah, we have so much to explore.
W: How about we start with a bike ride around the lake?
M: Actually, I'd like to visit the local museum.
W: That sounds interesting! Is there anything specific you
　　want to see?
M: Yes, I want to check out the exhibit on local history.
　　Want to join me?
W: Yes! Let's head to the museum now.

우·리·말·해·석

여: 오늘 네 계획은 뭐야? 우리 휴가의 첫째 날이잖아.
남: 응, 우리가 탐험할 것이 너무 많아.
여: 호수 주변에 자전거 타는 것으로 시작하는 건 어때?
남: 사실, 나는 현지 박물관을 방문하고 싶어.
여: 재밌겠는걸! 네가 보고 싶은 특정한 것이 있어?
남: 응, 나는 현지 역사에 대한 전시를 살펴보고 싶어. 나와 함께 하고 싶
　　니?
여: 응! 지금 박물관으로 가자.

단·어·및·표·현

explore[iksplɔ́ːr] ⑧ 탐험하다
actually[ǽktʃuəli] ⑭ 사실은
local[lóukəl] ⑧ 현지의, 지역의
specific[spisífik] ⑧ 특정한, 구체적인
check out ~을 살펴보다, 확인하다
exhibit[igzíbit] ⑲ 전시, 전시품
head to ~로 가다, ~로 향하다

09 대화미언급　　　　　　▶정답 ⑤

듣·기·대·본

W: Hey, George. The mid-term schedule has come out. Did
　　you see it?
M: Yes. It's from April 28 to 30.
W: I'm glad that the math test is on the last day of exams.
　　There are so many chapters to cover.
M: Tell me about it. Do we need to move to other
　　classrooms like we did last time?
W: Yes, some of us will take tests in different classrooms.
M: Oh, we need to set up the desks for the exams, as well.
W: Our teacher will tell us how to arrange the desks later.

우·리·말·해·석

여: 이봐, George. 중간고사 일정이 나왔어. 너 그거 봤니?
남: 응. 4월 28일부터 30일까지야.
여: 나는 수학 시험이 시험 마지막 날이라 기뻐. 다루는 단원이 아주 많거든.

남: 내 말이 그 말이야. 우리 지난번처럼 다른 교실로 이동해야 할까?
여: 응, 우리 중 몇 명은 다른 교실에서 시험을 볼 거야.
남: 오, 시험을 위해 책상도 준비해 놔야겠다.
여: 나중에 우리 선생님께서 어떻게 책상을 배열하는지 말씀해 주실 거야.

단·어·및·표·현

arrange[əréindʒ] ⑧ 배열하다, 정리하다

10 담화화제추론 ▶정답 ⑤

듣·기·대·본

M: Hello, *Traffic Radio* listeners. Today, I'm going to tell you how to ride an electric kickboard safely. First, <u>wear safety gear</u> including a helmet and knee pads. Second, don't ride the kickboard when it is snowing or raining. The road can be <u>too slippery</u>. Finally, when you are on a ride, hold the handle tight and don't <u>take your eyes off</u> the road.

우·리·말·해·석

남: 안녕하세요, "교통 라디오" 청취자 여러분. 오늘, 저는 전동 킥보드를 안전하게 타는 법을 여러분들께 알려드리고자 합니다. 첫 번째, 헬멧과 무릎 보호대를 포함한 안전 장비를 착용하십시오. 두 번째, 눈이 내리거나 비가 올 때는 킥보드를 타지 마십시오. 도로가 너무 미끄러울 수 있습니다. 마지막으로, 여러분이 킥보드를 탈 때, 손잡이를 꽉 잡고 도로에서 눈을 떼지 마십시오.

단·어·및·표·현

safety gear 안전 장비
slippery[slípəri] ⑱ 미끄러운
tight[tait] ⑨ 꽉, 단단히
take one's eyes off ~에서 눈을 떼다

11 대화내용불일치 ▶정답 ⑤

듣·기·대·본

M: Janet, look at this poster.
W: Oh, it's about the school <u>cartoon</u> contest.
M: Each student will <u>submit</u> one cartoon.
W: And then, the cartoons will <u>be uploaded</u> on the school website.
M: Students' names will not be posted. So, we won't know who drew what.
W: That sounds fair. So, the student who gets the most "likes" will win, right?
M: That's right. The top three will be the winners.

우·리·말·해·석

남: Janet, 이 포스터를 봐.
여: 아, 학교 만화 대회에 대한 거네.
남: 각 학생은 한 개의 만화를 제출할 거야.
여: 그러고 나서, 만화들은 학교 웹사이트에 업로드될 거야.
남: 학생들의 이름은 게시되지 않을 거야. 그래서, 우리는 누가 무엇을 그렸는지 알 수 없을 거야.
여: 공평하게 들린다. 그래서, 가장 많은 "좋아요"를 받은 학생이 우승하게 될 거야, 맞지?
남: 맞아. 상위 3명이 우승자들이 되는 거지.

단·어·및·표·현

cartoon[kɑːrtúːn] ⑱ 만화
submit[səbmít] ⑧ 제출하다
be uploaded 업로드되다
post[poust] ⑧ 게시하다
fair[fɛər] ⑱ 공평한, 공정한

12 전화목적파악 ▶정답 ④

듣·기·대·본

(*Telephone rings.*)
W: Hello?
M: Hello, Sandy. It's me, Paul. Are you busy?
W: Not really. <u>What's up</u>?
M: My cousin wants to play badminton with me today, but my racket is broken. So, I'm wondering if I could <u>borrow yours</u>.
W: Sure. Just come over here and get it.
M: Okay, thanks. I'll come there now. Bye.

우·리·말·해·석

(전화벨이 울린다.)
여: 여보세요?
남: 여보세요, Sandy. 나야 Paul. 너 바쁘니?
여: 그다지. 무슨 일이야?
남: 내 사촌이 오늘 나와 함께 배드민턴을 치고 싶어 하는데, 내 라켓이 부서졌어. 그래서 내가 네 것을 빌릴 수 있는지 궁금해.
여: 물론이지. 그냥 이리로 와서 가져가.
남: 알았어, 고마워. 지금 거기로 갈게. 안녕.

단·어·및·표·현

broken[bróukən] ⑱ 부서진, 망가진

13 수치계산(지불금액) ▶정답 ②

듣·기·대·본

M: Hello. How may I help you?
W: My 5-year-old son has <u>a mild fever</u>. Do you have anything for children?
M: Yes. We have <u>two types</u>. The powder is 6 dollars, and the liquid is 8 dollars.
W: The <u>liquid</u> type would be better.
M: OK. Here you are.
W: And can I have some <u>fine dust</u> masks for adults?
M: Sure. They're 1 dollar each. How many would you like?
W: I'd like three.
M: OK. One moment, please.

우·리·말·해·석

남: 안녕하세요. 어떻게 도와드릴까요?
여: 제 다섯 살짜리 아들에게 미열이 있습니다. 아이들을 위한 뭔가가 있나요?
남: 네. 저희에게는 두 가지 유형이 있습니다. 분말은 6달러이고, 액상은 8달러입니다.
여: 액상 유형이 더 낫겠습니다.
남: 알겠습니다. 여기 있습니다.
여: 그리고 성인용 미세 먼지 마스크를 좀 살 수 있을까요?
남: 물론입니다. 그것들은 하나에 1달러입니다. 몇 개 드릴까요?
여: 3개 주세요.
남: 알겠습니다. 잠시만 기다려주세요.

단·어·및·표·현

mild fever 미열, 가벼운 열병
liquid[líkwid] ⑱ 액체 ⑱ 액체 형태의, 액상의
fine dust 미세 먼지
adult[ədʌ́lt] ⑱ 성인, 어른

14 대화자관계추론 ▶정답 ①

듣·기·대·본

M: Hi. Welcome to Korea. May I have your <u>passport</u>,

please?
W: Sure, here it is.
M: Thank you. How long will you stay in Korea?
W: I will be here for ten days.
M: Are you here for business?
W: No. I am here on vacation.
M: I see. Enjoy your stay in Korea.
W: I will. Thank you very much.

우·리·말·해·석

남: 안녕하세요. 한국에 오신 걸 환영합니다. 여권을 주시겠어요?

여: 네, 여기 있어요.

남: 감사합니다. 한국에 얼마나 머무르실 건가요?

여: 여기 열흘 동안 있을 거예요.

남: 업무로 오셨나요?

여: 아니요. 휴가 왔어요.

남: 그렇군요. 한국에서 즐겁게 보내길 바랍니다.

여: 그럴게요. 정말 감사합니다.

단·어·및·표·현

for business 업무로

15 부탁(요청)한일파악 ▶정답 ④

듣·기·대·본

(*Cellphone rings.*)
M: Hello, Emily.
W: Hi, Alex. Remember our picnic plans for today?
M: Yes, I've packed some sandwiches and drinks.
W: That's great. I'm heading to the park near your house.
M: OK, I'll be there soon.
W: Perfect, but there's a little problem. I forgot to bring the picnic mat.
M: Oh, no worries. I'll bring one from home.
W: Thanks a lot, Alex. See you soon.
M: No problem. I'll see you shortly.

우·리·말·해·석

(휴대전화가 울린다.)

남: 여보세요, Emily.

여: 안녕, Alex. 오늘 우리의 소풍 계획 기억해?

남: 응, 나는 샌드위치들과 음료들을 좀 챙겼어.

여: 좋다. 나는 너네 집 근처의 공원으로 가고 있어.

남: 응, 나는 곧 그곳에 도착할 거야.

여: 완벽해. 하지만 약간 문제가 있어. 나는 돗자리를 가져오는 것을 잊었어.

남: 오, 걱정 마. 내가 집에서 하나 가져갈게.

여: 정말 고마워, Alex. 곧 보자.

남: 문제없어. 곧 보자.

단·어·및·표·현

pack [pæk] ⑧ (짐을) 챙기다, 싸다, 꾸리다

drink [driŋk] ⑨ 음료, 마실 것

head to ~로 가다, 향하다

forget to + 동사원형 ~할 것을 잊다

picnic mat 돗자리

shortly [ʃɔ́ːrtli] ⑨ 곧, 얼마 안 되어

16 이유파악 ▶정답 ④

듣·기·대·본

M: Hey, Melanie. What did you do over the weekend?
W: I went to a concert with my parents.
M: What kind of concert?

W: It was a concert by the city's orchestra. They played a lot of Mozart.
M: Did you like it?
W: Yes! I'm a big fan of Mozart's music.
M: I think his work is difficult to understand.
W: Maybe. But, his music is cheery and fun. That's why I like it.

우·리·말·해·석

남: 이봐, Melanie. 너 지난 주말 동안에 뭐했니?

여: 나는 부모님과 함께 콘서트에 갔어.

남: 무슨 콘서트?

여: 시립 관현악단의 콘서트였어. 그들은 모차르트의 음악을 많이 연주했어.

남: 그거 좋았니?

여: 응! 나는 모차르트 음악의 열혈 팬이야.

남: 내 생각에 그의 작품은 이해하기가 어려워.

여: 그럴 수 있어. 하지만 그의 음악은 유쾌하고 재미있어. 그게 내가 그것을 좋아하는 이유야.

단·어·및·표·현

cheery [tʃí(ː)əri] ⑲ 유쾌한, 쾌활한

17 그림상황에적절한대화찾기 ▶정답 ⑤

듣·기·대·본

① W: What is your favorite animal?
   M: I love cats! What about you?
② W: What do you want for breakfast?
   M: I would like some cereal.
③ W: How was the movie?
   M: It was really scary. I nearly jumped out of my seat!
④ W: Are you ready for your final exams?
   M: Yeah! I studied really hard.
⑤ W: Can you get that door for me? My hands are full.
   M: Sure! Here you go.

우·리·말·해·석

① 여: 네가 가장 좋아하는 동물이 뭐야?
   남: 나는 고양이가 좋아. 너는?
② 여: 아침 식사로 무엇을 원해?
   남: 나는 약간의 시리얼을 원해.
③ 여: 그 영화 어땠어?
   남: 그것은 정말로 무서웠어. 나는 거의 의자 밖으로 뛰쳐나갈 뻔했어!
④ 여: 너는 너의 기말 시험에 대해 준비가 됐니?
   남: 응! 나는 정말 열심히 공부했어.
⑤ 여: 저를 위해 저 문 좀 잡아주실 수 있어요? 내 손이 가득해요.
   남: 물론이죠! 여기요.

단·어·및·표·현

nearly [níərli] ⑨ 거의

18 담화미언급 ▶정답 ④

듣·기·대·본

W: Good morning, students. I'd like to tell you about a new documentary movie directed by Nate Young. The title is *You Are Not Alone*. This movie tells the stories of teenagers who have overcome a variety of different problems in life. It will be released on February 4. I hope that after watching this movie you will realize that you are not alone. There will always be somebody to help you out.

우·리·말·해·석

여: 안녕하세요, 학생 여러분. 저는 여러분에게 Nate Young이 감독한 새로운 다큐멘터리 영화에 대해 얘기하려고 합니다. 제목은 "당신은 혼자가 아니에요"입니다. 이 영화는 인생에서 여러 가지의 다른 문제들을 극복한 10대들의 이야기를 전해줍니다. 그것은 2월 4일에 개봉될 것입니다. 저는 여러분이 이 영화를 관람한 후에 여러분은 혼자가 아니라는 것을 깨닫길 바랍니다. 여러분을 도와줄 누군가가 항상 있을 것입니다.

단·어·및·표·현

overcome [òuvərkʌ́m] ⑧ 극복하다, 이겨내다
a variety of 여러 가지의
be released 개봉하다
realize [rí(:)əlàiz] ⑧ 깨닫다, 알아차리다
help out 도와주다

19 알맞은응답찾기 ▶정답 ①

듣·기·대·본

W: What are you doing, Clark?
M: Oh. Hi, Gina! I'm listening to music.
W: Do you like listening to music?
M: Yes, I do.
W: What music are you listening to?
M: It's Spanish music.
W: Really? Can you understand Spanish?
M: **Well, just a little bit.**

우·리·말·해·석

① 뭐, 아주 조금.
② 스페인어는 아름다운 언어야.
③ 나는 전에 스페인에 가본 적이 없어.
④ 아니, 나는 라틴 음악을 듣지 않아.
⑤ 나는 네가 스페인 출신인지 몰랐어.

여: 뭐하고 있니, Clark?
남: 아. 안녕, Gina! 나 음악 듣고 있어.
여: 너는 음악 듣는 것을 좋아하니?
남: 응, 좋아해.
여: 너는 무슨 음악을 듣고 있니?
남: 스페인 음악이야.
여: 정말? 너는 스페인어를 이해할 수 있니?
남: **뭐, 아주 조금.**

단·어·및·표·현

listen to + 명사 ~을 듣다
Spanish [spǽniʃ] ⑧ 스페인의 ⑨ 스페인어
understand [ʌ̀ndərstǽnd] ⑧ 이해하다

🦻 LISTENING ADVICE

'Really? Can you understand Spanish?'에서 문장 끝을 올려 말하는 것을 들을 수 있습니다. 이렇게 문장을 말할 때 음을 높이거나 낮추는 것을 '억양'이라고 하는데 영어는 의미에 따라 억양도 다릅니다. 보통 평서문은 문장 끝을 내려서 말하고 의문문은 문장 끝을 올려서 말합니다.

20 알맞은응답찾기 ▶정답 ⑤

듣·기·대·본

W: Hey, I heard you've been playing badminton lately.
M: Yeah, I've been playing with some friends at the park.
W: Awesome! What do you like about badminton?
M: I love how fast-paced it is, and it's a great way to stay active.
W: Is badminton hard to play?
M: Not really! It's pretty easy to learn the basics, like hitting the shuttlecock with the racket.
W: I've never played badminton before. Do you think I could learn?
M: **Definitely! I'll teach you some moves.**

우·리·말·해·석

① 난 활동적인 사람이 아니야.
② 나는 같이 배드민턴을 칠 친구들이 좀 있어.
③ 너는 어떤 종류의 운동을 좋아해?
④ 우리 배드민턴 동아리에 온 것을 환영해.
⑤ 그렇고 말고! 내가 너에게 동작들을 좀 가르쳐 줄게.

여: 안녕, 나는 네가 최근에 배드민턴을 치고 있다는 걸 들었어.
남: 응, 나는 공원에서 몇몇의 친구들과 치고 있어.
여: 좋다! 넌 배드민턴의 어떤 점을 좋아해?
남: 나는 그것이 얼마나 빨리 진행되는지를 좋아하고, 그것은 활동적이게 하는 좋은 방법이야.
여: 배드민턴은 치기 어려워?
남: 전혀! 라켓으로 셔틀콕을 치는 것과 같은 기초를 배우는 것은 꽤 쉬워.
여: 나는 전에 배드민턴을 쳐 본 적이 전혀 없어. 너는 내가 배울 수 있다고 생각해?
남: **그렇고 말고! 내가 너에게 동작들을 좀 가르쳐 줄게.**

단·어·및·표·현

lately [léitli] ⑨ 최근에
fast-paced 빨리 진행되는
stay [stei] ⑧ (특정한 상태나 상황을) 유지하다
active [ǽktiv] ⑧ 활동적인
pretty [príti] ⑨ 꽤
shuttlecock [ʃʌ́tlkàk] ⑨ 셔틀콕
racket [rǽkit] ⑨ (테니스 등의) 라켓
definitely [défənitli] ⑨ 그렇고 말고, 확실히, 분명히, 틀림없이
move [muːv] ⑨ 동작, 움직임

Words & Expressions Review

1. 깨닫다, 알아차리다	2. 게시하다	3. ~을 담당하다, 주관하다
4. 최근에	5. 사실은	6. 절뚝거리다, 기운이 없는
7. 결정하다	8. ~로 가다, 향하다	9. 공평한, 공정한
10. 궁금하다	11. 극복하다, 이겨내다	12. ~을 듣다
13. 예상하다, 기대하다	14. 주문하다	15. 탐험하다
16. 아프다	17. 개봉하다	18. (짐을) 챙기다, 싸다, 꾸리다
19. 액체	20. 거의	21. 여러 가지의
22. 곧, 얼마 안 되어	23. 장식하다, 꾸미다	24. 최선을 다하다
25. ~을 토하다	26. 관현악단	27. 지역의, 현지의
28. 땀나게 하는	29. 걱정하는, 걱정스러운	30. 빌리다
31. 그렇고 말고, 확실히, 분명히, 틀림없이	32. 제출하다	33. 휴가로
34. 미끄러운	35. ~를 돈 곳에	36. 배열하다, 정리하다
37. 꽉, 단단히	38. 야외 활동	39. 유쾌한, 쾌활한

40. 준비하다, 조직하다	41. 준비하다, 설립하다	42. 여권
43. ~에서 눈을 떼다	44. 미열	

Listening Test

영어듣기 모의고사 11^회

|정|답|

01 ④	02 ⑤	03 ⑤	04 ⑤	05 ③
06 ③	07 ②	08 ⑤	09 ④	10 ①
11 ⑤	12 ④	13 ②	14 ⑤	15 ④
16 ①	17 ③	18 ⑤	19 ②	20 ①

01   날씨파악-그림   ▶정답 ④

듣·기·대·본

M: Hello, everyone! This is your daily weather report. This morning, it is expected to be cloudy with a <u>60 percent chance</u> of rain. So, be sure to bring an umbrella. In the afternoon, the temperature will start to <u>drop</u>, and the rain will <u>turn into</u> snow. Be careful when you are driving this afternoon because the road <u>might be slippery</u>.

우·리·말·해·석

남: 안녕하세요, 여러분! 여러분의 일일 일기예보입니다. 오늘 아침에 비가 내릴 확률은 60퍼센트로 흐릴 것으로 예상됩니다. 그러니 반드시 우산을 챙기시길 바랍니다. 오후에는 기온이 떨어지기 시작하고 비는 눈으로 변할 것입니다. 길이 미끄러울 수 있으니 오후에 운전을 하실 때 조심하시기 바랍니다.

단·어·및·표·현

chance[tʃæns] 명 확률, 가능성
be sure to + 동사원형 반드시 ~하다
drop[drɑp] 동 떨어지다, 떨어뜨리다
turn into ~으로 변하다
slippery[slípəri] 형 미끄러운

02   그림정보파악   ▶정답 ⑤

듣·기·대·본

M: Judy, what are you looking at on your computer?
W: It's the final design of <u>a tumbler</u> I am ordering for my sister, Tina.
M: Wow, is it a custom order? It looks really cool.
W: Yeah, <u>I added her name</u> on it.
M: That's nice. I think <u>the handle</u> will be very useful, too.
W: That's why I chose this design. I hope Tina likes it.

우·리·말·해·석

남: Judy, 너 네 컴퓨터에서 무엇을 보고 있어?
여: 내 여동생 Tina를 위해 내가 주문하는 텀블러의 최종 디자인이야.
남: 와, 그것이 맞춤 주문이야? 그것은 정말로 멋져 보인다.
여: 응, 내가 그녀의 이름을 그 위에 추가했어.
남: 그거 멋지다. 나는 손잡이도 매우 유용할 것이라고 생각해.
여: 그것이 내가 이 디자인을 고른 이유야. 나는 Tina가 그것을 좋아하길 바라.

단·어·및·표·현

tumbler[tʌ́mblər] 명 텀블러
custom order 맞춤 주문, 주문 제작
handle[hǽndl] 명 손잡이

03   심정추론   ▶정답 ⑤

듣·기·대·본

M: Guess what, Nina. <u>I got my wallet back!</u>
W: Really? You lost it days ago!
M: Somebody found it and <u>left it</u> at the school.
W: At the school? Oh, was your student ID in the wallet?
M: Yes. I got back everything that was inside the wallet. <u>How can a total stranger</u> be so kind?
W: You are lucky.
M: I really am. <u>I want to find the stranger. I want to</u> <u>repay</u> him or her.

우·리·말·해·석

① 화난   ② 지루한   ③ 자랑스러운
④ 초조한   ⑤ 고마운

남: 있잖아, Nina. 나는 내 지갑을 되찾았어!
여: 정말? 너는 며칠 전에 그것을 잃어버렸잖아!
남: 누군가 그걸 발견해서 학교에 두고 갔어.
여: 학교에? 아, 지갑 안에 네 학생증이 있었어?
남: 응. 나는 지갑 안에 있던 모든 것들을 되찾았어. 어떻게 전혀 모르는 사람이 그렇게 친절할 수 있지?
여: 너는 운이 좋네.
남: 난 정말 그래. 나는 그 낯선 사람을 찾고 싶어. 나는 그 또는 그녀에게 보답하고 싶어.

단·어·및·표·현

Guess what. 있잖아., 맞혀 봐.
get back 되찾다
leave[liːv] 동 ~을 두고 가다[오다]
total stranger 낯선 사람, 전혀 모르는 사람
repay[ri(ː)péi] 동 보답하다, 갚다

04   한일파악   ▶정답 ⑤

듣·기·대·본

W: Hello, Yong-soo. What's up? You look angry.
M: I'm mad because somebody <u>stole my bicycle</u>.
W: What? Wasn't your bicycle brand new?
M: Yeah, my parents <u>bought it for me</u> last week.
W: I'm really sorry to hear that. Is there any way to find it?
M: I just went to the police station and <u>filed a report</u>.
W: I really hope that you get your bicycle back.
M: Thank you.

우·리·말·해·석

여: 안녕, 용수. 무슨 일이야? 너는 화나 보여.
남: 나는 누군가가 내 자전거를 훔쳤기 때문에 화났어.
여: 뭐? 네 자전거는 새 것 아니었어?
남: 맞아, 내 부모님이 지난주에 나에게 그것을 사주셨어.
여: 그 얘기를 들으니 안됐다. 그것을 찾을 어떤 방법이 있어?
남: 나는 방금 경찰서에 가서 신고를 했어.
여: 나는 정말로 네가 네 자전거를 되찾기를 바라.
남: 고마워.

단·어·및·표·현

just[dʒʌst] 부 방금, 막
file a report 신고하다

05 대화장소추론   ▶정답 ③

듣·기·대·본

W: Welcome to Ice World.

M: Hi. I bought tickets online for ice skating.

W: The rink is this way. Just scan your ticket on the way in.

M: Thanks. How many hours can we use the rink for?

W: With this ticket, up to three hours.

M: Where is the skate rental?

W: It's right inside, on your right. Just make sure you don't wear the skates outside the rink.

M: We won't. Thank you.

우·리·말·해·석

여: Ice World에 오신 것을 환영합니다.

남: 안녕하세요. 저는 스케이트 표를 온라인으로 구입했어요.

여: 스케이트장은 이쪽입니다. 들어가는 길에 고객님의 표를 스캔만 해 주세요.

남: 고마워요. 몇 시간 동안이나 우리가 스케이트장을 이용할 수 있나요?

여: 이 표로는 세 시간까지입니다.

남: 스케이트 대여소는 어디예요?

여: 그것은 바로 안쪽에, 오른편에 있습니다. 스케이트장 밖에서 스케이트를 신지 않는다는 것만 확실히 해주세요.

남: 우리는 그러지 않을게요. 고맙습니다.

단·어·및·표·현

rink[riŋk] 명 스케이트장

up to ~ ~까지

rental[réntəl] 명 대여

06 마지막말의도파악   ▶정답 ③

듣·기·대·본

M: Bye, Mom. I'm going out to play basketball with my friends.

W: Wait a minute, young man. Did you finish your homework?

M: Err… Not exactly, but don't worry. I've got it under control.

W: What do you mean that you've got it under control?

M: It means that I can finish it by today. After I come back home!

W: You'd better come back home before 9 o'clock. If you come later than that, you're grounded for a week!

우·리·말·해·석

남: 안녕, 엄마. 저 제 친구들과 농구를 하러 나가요.

여: 잠깐만, 얘야. 숙제를 끝냈니?

남: 어… 꼭 그런 것은 아니지만 걱정 마세요. 제가 잘 관리하고 있어요.

여: 네가 잘 관리한다는 것이 무슨 말이니?

남: 그 말은 제가 오늘까지 끝낼 수 있다는 거예요. 제가 집에 돌아온 후에요!

여: 너는 9시 전에 돌아오는 것이 좋을 거다. 그것보다 늦게 오면 일주일 동안 외출 금지야!

단·어·및·표·현

What do you mean that ~? ~가 무슨 말이니?

ground[graund] 동 (벌로) 외출을 금지시키다

07 특정정보파악   ▶정답 ②

듣·기·대·본

M: Hey, Jasmine. You didn't forget about our bike ride this afternoon, right?

W: No, of course not. Did you bring everything you need for the bike ride?

M: Yeah. I brought my helmet, sunglasses, gloves… Oh, I even brought a snack for us!

W: Awesome! So, meet me in front of the school at 5 o'clock.

M: Sounds good. Oh, no. I forgot to bring my water bottle with me.

W: I have two of them. You can borrow one of mine. I will bring them with me.

M: Really? Thank you so much.

우·리·말·해·석

남: 얘, Jasmine. 오늘 오후에 우리 자전거 타러 가기로 한 것 잊지 않았지, 그렇지?

여: 응, 물론 잊지 않았어. 너는 자전거를 타기 위해서 필요한 모든 것을 가져왔니?

남: 응. 나는 내 헬멧, 선글라스, 장갑을 가져왔어… 아, 나는 심지어 우리를 위한 간식도 가져왔어!

여: 아주 멋져! 그럼, 5시 정각에 학교 앞에서 만나자.

남: 좋아. 아, 이런. 나는 물병을 가져오는 것을 잊어버렸어.

여: 나 그거 두 개 가지고 있어. 너는 내것들 중 하나를 빌려도 돼. 내가 그것들을 가져올게.

남: 정말? 정말 고마워.

단·어·및·표·현

bring[briŋ] 동 가져오다, 가져다주다

awesome[ɔ́ːsəm] 형 아주 멋진, 엄청난

08 할일파악(대화직후)   ▶정답 ⑤

듣·기·대·본

W: Are you going to Jack's housewarming party?

M: Yes. It's on Saturday, right?

W: Yes. He said he's going to cook Italian dishes for the guests. He's also going to hold a barbecue party in his garden.

M: Sounds great. By the way, have you bought a gift for his housewarming party?

W: Not yet. How about going to the mall together?

M: That's a good idea, but let's ask Jack what he needs first for his new house.

W: Okay. I've got his number.

우·리·말·해·석

여: 너 Jack의 집들이에 가니?

남: 응. 토요일 맞지?

여: 응. 그가 말하기를 손님들을 위해 이탈리아 음식을 만들 거래. 또한 그의 정원에서 바비큐 파티도 열 거래.

남: 그거 좋은데. 그런데 넌 집들이 선물 샀어?

여: 아직. 우리 같이 쇼핑몰에 가는 것은 어때?

남: 좋은 생각이다, 그런데 먼저 새 집에 필요한 것이 무엇인지 Jack에게 물어보자.

여: 알았어. 내게 그의 전화번호가 있어.

단·어·및·표·현

by the way 그런데, 그나저나

09 대화미언급   ▶정답 ④

듣·기·대·본

W: Hey, Jack. Did you see the latest *Cat Hero* movie?

M: Yeah, I saw it. Oh, what was the exact title of it?

W: *Cat Hero: to the Rescue.*

M: Right! Was it directed by Jane Dickinson?

W: Yeah, I think so.

M: I heard the movie was released on February 22nd and is already a huge hit.

W: Really? How many people have seen the movie?

M: I heard that about ten million people have seen that movie!

W: That's a lot! I'd better go watch it, too.

M: Yeah, you should. It's a good movie.

우·리·말·해·석

여: 얘, Jack. 너 최신 "고양이 히어로" 영화를 봤니?

남: 응, 나는 그것을 봤어. 아, 그것의 정확한 제목이 뭐였더라?

여: "고양이 히어로: 구조대 출동"이야.

남: 맞아! Jane Dickinson이 감독했지?

여: 응, 그런 것 같아.

남: 그 영화가 2월 22일에 개봉됐고 벌써 큰 인기라고 들었어.

여: 정말? 얼마나 많은 사람들이 그 영화를 봤어?

남: 대략 천만 명의 사람들이 그 영화를 봤다고 들었어!

여: 정말 많구나! 나도 가서 보는 게 좋겠어.

남: 응, 꼭 그래야 해. 그건 좋은 영화야.

단·어·및·표·현

exact [igzǽkt] ⑱ 정확한

direct [dirékt] ⑧ 연출하다, 감독하다

release [rilíːs] ⑧ 개봉하다

10 담화주제추론 ▶정답 ①

듣·기·대·본

W: Hi, everyone. Did you know that our school's Cultural Diversity Day is next Wednesday? It's a celebration of different cultures around the world. Before the event, we'll decorate our classrooms with flags, traditional crafts, and artwork from various countries. Then, on Cultural Diversity Day, we'll share stories, music, and food from different cultures. Don't forget to wear something representing your cultural heritage, like traditional clothing or accessories.

우·리·말·해·석

여: 안녕하세요, 여러분. 여러분들은 우리 학교의 '문화적 다양성의 날'이 다음주 수요일인 것을 알고 계셨나요? 그것은 전 세계의 다양한 문화들의 기념 행사입니다. 행사 전에 우리는 우리 교실들을 다양한 국가들의 깃발들, 전통 공예품들, 그리고 미술품으로 꾸밀 것입니다. 그리고, 문화적 다양성의 날에, 우리는 다양한 문화들의 이야기들과 음악, 그리고 음식을 나눌 것입니다. 전통 의복이나 장신구 같은 여러분의 문화 유산을 상징하는 것을 입고 오는 것을 잊지 마세요.

단·어·및·표·현

cultural [kʌ́ltʃərəl] ⑱ 문화의

diversity [divə́ːrsəti] ⑲ 다양성

celebration [sèləbréiʃən] ⑲ 기념[축하] 행사

decorate [dékərèit] ⑧ 꾸미다, 장식하다

traditional [trədíʃənəl] ⑱ 전통의

craft [kræft] ⑲ 공예

artwork [άːrtwəˋːrk] ⑲ 미술품

various [vέ(ː)əriəs] ⑱ 다양한, 각양각색의

represent [rèprizént] ⑧ 상징하다, 나타내다

cultural heritage 문화 유산

11 대화내용불일치 ▶정답 ⑤

듣·기·대·본

[Telephone rings.]

W: Hello, River View Restaurant.

M: Hi, I'd like to make a lunch reservation for next Saturday.

W: Sure. May I have your name, please?

M: Kevin Park.

W: Okay. How many people will be coming?

M: Eight in total.

W: Got it. Do you have any seating preferences?

M: Yes, we'd like a table by the window. Can we bring our own cake?

W: Sure. Your reservation is set for 12 p.m. next Saturday.

우·리·말·해·석

[전화벨이 울린다.]

여: 안녕하세요, River View 식당입니다.

남: 안녕하세요, 다음 주 토요일에 점심 식사 예약을 하고 싶습니다.

여: 그러시죠. 성함이 어떻게 되시나요?

남: Kevin Park입니다.

여: 알겠습니다. 몇 분이 오시나요?

남: 총 8명입니다.

여: 알겠습니다. 좌석에 대한 선호도가 있으신가요?

남: 네, 창가 자리를 원합니다. 저희가 케이크를 (직접) 가져도 될까요?

여: 물론입니다. 당신의 예약이 다음 주 토요일 오후 12시로 정해졌습니다.

단·어·및·표·현

make a reservation 예약하다

in total 총, 전부 합쳐서

seating [síːtiŋ] ⑲ 좌석, 자리

preference [préfərəns] ⑲ 선호(도), 선호되는 것

12 전화목적파악 ▶정답 ④

듣·기·대·본

(Cellphone rings.)

M: Hello, Sarah. What's up?

W: Hi, Alex. Do you have any plans for this Saturday?

M: Not really. What's going on?

W: My cousin's wedding is this Saturday, and I need someone to water my plants while I'm away.

M: Sure, I can take care of them for you.

W: Oh, thank you so much! I really appreciate it.

M: No problem at all. I'll make sure they get plenty of water.

W: You're a lifesaver!

M: Happy to help!

우·리·말·해·석

(휴대전화가 울린다.)

남: 여보세요, Sarah. 무슨 일이야?

여: 안녕, Alex. 넌 이번 주 토요일에 일정이 있니?

남: 아니. 무슨 일인데?

여: 내 사촌의 결혼이 이번 주 토요일인데, 나는 내가 떠나 있는 동안 내 식물들에 물을 줄 누군가가 필요해.

남: 물론이지, 난 너를 위해 그것들을 돌볼 수 있어.

여: 오, 너무 고마워! 나는 정말 그것에 감사해.

남: 전혀 문제없어. 내가 그것들에게 충분한 물을 확실하게 줄게.

여: 너는 생명의 은인이야!

남: 도와줄 수 있어서 기뻐!

단·어·및·표·현

water [wɔ́ːtər] ⑧ (화초 등에) 물을 주다

be away 떠나 있다, 부재중이다

take care of ~을 돌보다
appreciate [əprí:ʃièit] 동 고마워하다
plenty of 충분한
lifesaver [láifsèivər] 명 생명의 은인

13 수치계산(거스름돈) ▶ 정답 ②

듣·기·대·본

M: Hello. How can I help you?

W: Do you have <u>any seats left</u> for the 4D movie *Hero*, starting in ten minutes?

M: Yes, but only <u>in the front row</u>. Would you still like those seats?

W: Yes, that's no problem.

M: Okay. How many seats?

W: Two, please. They're 14 dollars each, right?

M: Yes. So, it'll be 28 dollars <u>in total</u>.

W: Here is 30 dollars.

M: Thank you. Here are your tickets and change. Enjoy the movie!

우·리·말·해·석

남: 안녕하세요. 어떻게 도와드릴까요?

여: 십 분 후에 시작하는 4D영화 "영웅"에 남은 좌석이 있나요?

남: 네, 하지만 앞줄만 있습니다. 그 좌석이라도 괜찮으세요?

여: 네, 괜찮아요.

남: 알겠습니다. 몇 좌석을 원하시나요?

여: 두 자리요. 그것들은 각각 14달러죠, 맞죠?

남: 네. 그래서 총 28달러입니다.

여: 여기 30달러요.

남: 감사합니다. 여기 손님의 표와 거스름돈입니다. 즐거운 영화 관람 되세요!

단·어·및·표·현

seat [si:t] 명 좌석, 자리
row [rou] 명 줄, 열
in total 총, 모두 합해서

14 대화자관계추론 ▶ 정답 ⑤

듣·기·대·본

M: Good afternoon. How may I help you?

W: Hi. I'm <u>looking for</u> a new washing machine.

M: Okay. How about this one with a dryer?

W: I don't need the <u>drying function</u>, but I want a big washer.

M: Do you want something <u>bigger than</u> 20kg?

W: Actually, 20kg sounds perfect.

M: Then, you're lucky! That size is <u>on sale</u> this week.

W: Great! I'm glad I came today.

우·리·말·해·석

남: 안녕하세요. 어떻게 도와드릴까요?

여: 안녕하세요. 저는 새 세탁기를 찾고 있어요.

남: 네. 건조기가 있는 이것은 어떠신가요?

여: 저는 건조 기능은 필요없지만 큰 세탁기를 원해요.

남: 당신은 20kg보다 더 큰 것을 원하시나요?

여: 사실, 20kg이 완벽한 것 같아요.

남: 그러면, 당신은 운이 좋으시네요! 그 크기는 이번 주에 할인 중입니다.

여: 좋네요! 오늘 와서 다행이네요.

단·어·및·표·현

dryer [dráiər] 명 건조기
function [fʌ́ŋkʃən] 명 기능

---

on sale 할인[세일] 중인

15 부탁(요청)한일파악 ▶ 정답 ④

듣·기·대·본

(*Telephone rings.*)

W: Mango Computers.

M: Hello. I'm calling from Mr. Kim's office.

W: Yes. How may I help you?

M: I <u>ordered three new computers</u>, and tomorrow is the delivery day.

W: Do you want to change the date?

M: No. We <u>moved our office</u> this week. Can you send them to the <u>new address</u>, please?

W: No problem. Is the same date OK?

M: Yes. I'll give you the address.

우·리·말·해·석

(전화벨이 울린다.)

여: Mango 컴퓨터입니다.

남: 여보세요. 김 선생님 사무실입니다.

여: 네. 어떻게 도와드릴까요?

남: 제가 새 컴퓨터 세 대를 주문했는데, 내일이 배달일이에요.

여: 날짜를 바꾸고 싶으세요?

남: 아니요. 이번 주에 사무실을 이전했어요. 그것들을 새로운 주소로 보내주실 수 있으세요?

여: 문제없습니다. 같은 날짜가 좋으신가요?

남: 네. 주소를 알려드릴게요.

단·어·및·표·현

delivery [dilívəri] 명 배달, 배송

16 이유파악 ▶ 정답 ①

듣·기·대·본

M: Hey, Meg!

W: Hi, Milo. Where are you going?

M: I'm going to the café. I have an <u>appointment</u> there.

W: Oh, are you going to meet your friends?

M: No, I'm not. Actually, I'm going to <u>get a private lesson</u> from my tutor.

W: I see. What <u>subject</u> are you learning?

M: I study math with him. It is too hard for me to study alone.

W: I agree. Good luck to you.

우·리·말·해·석

남: 이봐, Meg!

여: 안녕, Milo. 너는 어디 가는 중이야?

남: 나는 카페에 가는 중이야. 거기서 약속이 있거든.

여: 아, 너는 네 친구들을 만날 거야?

남: 아니, 그렇지 않아. 사실, 나는 내 과외 선생님께 과외를 받을 거야.

여: 그렇구나. 너는 무슨 과목을 배우고 있어?

남: 나는 그와 수학을 공부해. 나에게 혼자서 공부하는 것은 너무 어려워.

여: 나도 동의해. 너에게 행운을 빌어.

단·어·및·표·현

appointment [əpɔ́intmənt] 명 약속
get a private lesson 과외를 받다
tutor [tjú:tər] 명 과외 선생님, 가정교사
subject [sʌ́bdʒikt] 명 과목

17 그림 상황에 적절한 대화 찾기 ▶정답 ③

듣·기·대·본

① M: This cake tastes great.
　 W: I'm glad you like it.
② M: Where should we put this painting?
　 W: Let's hang it above the sofa.
③ M: I love this music.
　 W: So do I. The pianist is amazing.
④ M: Would you like some cheese on your pasta?
　 W: Yes, I'd like a lot, please.
⑤ M: Can I pay with my credit card?
　 W: Sorry. This line is for cash only.

우·리·말·해·석

① 남: 이 케이크 정말 맛있다.
　 여: 네가 그것을 좋아해서 기뻐.
② 남: 이 그림을 어디에 두어야 할까?
　 여: 그것을 소파 위에 걸자.
③ 남: 나는 이 음악이 너무 좋아.
　 여: 나도 그래. 피아니스트가 정말 놀라워.
④ 남: 네 파스타에 치즈 좀 뿌릴래?
　 여: 응, 많이 뿌려줘.
⑤ 남: 신용카드로 계산할 수 있나요?
　 여: 죄송합니다. 이 줄은 현금 전용이에요.

단·어·및·표·현
taste [teist] ⑧ 맛이 나다
put [put] ⑧ 두다, 놓다
hang [hæŋ] ⑧ 걸다

18 담화의 언급 ▶정답 ⑤

듣·기·대·본

M: Good afternoon, students. Your favorite school event, the Talent Show is coming next month! It will be held in our school auditorium. The Talent Show is on Friday, February 21 at 7:00 p.m. Please fill out the form on the school website to register as a participant. Registration forms are due on Monday, February 10. There will be an audition for participants.

우·리·말·해·석

남: 안녕하세요, 학생 여러분. 여러분이 가장 좋아하는 학교 행사인 장기 자랑 대회가 다음 달에 열립니다! 그것은 우리 학교 강당에서 열릴 것입니다. 장기 자랑 대회는 2월 21일 금요일 저녁 7시에 있습니다. 참가자로 등록하려면 학교 웹사이트에서 양식을 작성해 주십시오. 신청서는 2월 10일 월요일에 마감합니다. 참가자들을 위한 오디션이 있을 것입니다.

단·어·및·표·현
auditorium [ɔ̀ːditɔ́ːriəm] ⑲ 강당
fill out 작성하다, 기입하다
participant [pɑːrtísəpənt] ⑲ 참가자
registration form 신청서
be due on + 특정 시점 (특정 날짜/시간까지) 마감이다

19 알맞은 응답 찾기 ▶정답 ②

듣·기·대·본

M: Hi, Mary. What are you going to do this weekend?
W: I don't have any plans.
M: Then, how about going to the newly opened Chinese restaurant?
W: You mean the restaurant near the shopping mall?
M: Yes. I heard that it is very good.
W: Well, actually I don't like Chinese food. Can we go to the Japanese restaurant instead?
M: Of course, we can.

우·리·말·해·석

① 나도 중국 음식을 좋아하지 않아.
② 물론 괜찮지.
③ 나는 일본어를 할 수 있어.
④ 응, 나는 종종 쇼핑몰에 가.
⑤ 난 다음 주에 도쿄에 가.

남: 안녕, Mary. 너 이번 주말에 무엇을 할 거니?
여: 아무 계획도 없어.
남: 그러면 새로 연 중국 음식점에 가는 게 어떠니?
여: 쇼핑몰 근처에 있는 그 음식점 말하는 거니?
남: 응. 그곳이 매우 좋다고 들었어.
여: 글쎄, 사실 난 중국 음식을 좋아하지 않아. 대신 일본 음식점에 가도 될까?
남: 물론 괜찮지.

단·어·및·표·현
actually [æ̀ktʃuəli] ⑨ 사실, 실제로

20 알맞은 응답 찾기 ▶정답 ①

듣·기·대·본

M: Melody, I heard that you're good at baking.
W: I'm not too bad.
M: Do you know how to bake a cheesecake?
W: Yes, I do. Do you want to learn?
M: Yes. My girlfriend likes cheesecake very much.
W: Well, have you ever baked bread or a cake before?
M: I've never baked anything.

우·리·말·해·석

① 난 아무것도 구워본 적이 없어.
② 난 치즈 케이크를 좋아하지 않아.
③ 난 그녀한테 그것을 배우고 싶어.
④ 그녀가 그걸 좋아하는지 몰랐어.
⑤ 초콜릿 케이크는 내가 제일 좋아하는 거야.

남: Melody, 네가 빵을 잘 굽는다고 들었어.
여: 그렇게 못하진 않아.
남: 치즈 케이크를 어떻게 굽는지 알아?
여: 응, 알아. 배우고 싶어?
남: 응. 내 여자친구가 치즈케이크를 매우 좋아해.
여: 음, 전에 빵이나 케이크를 구워본 적 있어?
남: 난 아무것도 구워본 적이 없어.

단·어·및·표·현
be good at -ing ~을 잘하다
bake [beik] ⑧ 굽다

🎧 **LISTENING ADVICE**

불규칙 동사를 제외한 모든 동사들의 과거형에는 단어의 끝에 '-ed'가 붙습니다. 하지만 동사 뒤에 붙은 모든 'ed'가 동일하게 소리 나는 것은 아니지요. [p], [k], [f], [s], [sh], [ch]와 같이 성대를 울리지 않는 소리들 뒤에 'ed'가 붙는 때에는 [t] 소리로 발음됩니다. 따라서 'Have you ever baked bread ~'에서 'baked'는 [베이크드]나 [베이키드]가 아닌 [베익ㅌ]로 들립니다.

Words & Expressions Review

1. 기능	2. 잘 관리되는	3. 공예
4. 손잡이	5. ~까지	6. 텀블러, 큰 컵
7. 총, 전부 합쳐서	8. 주소	9. 스케이트장
10. 맛이 나다	11. ~을 잘하다	12. 신고하다
13. 할인[세일] 중인	14. 배달, 배송	15. 사실, 실제로
16. 줄, 열	17. 있잖아.., 맞혀 봐.	18. 좌석, 자리
19. 다양성	20. 굽다	21. 강당
22. 반드시 ~하다	23. 뜻하다, 의미하다	24. 되찾다
25. 작성하다, 기입하다	26. 가져오다, 가져다주다	27. 정확한
28. 맞춤 주문, 주문 제작	29. ~으로 변하다	30. 연출하다, 감독하다
31. 참가자	32. 보답하다, 갚다	33. 대여
34. 신청서	35. 개봉하다	36. 건조기
37. 걸다	38. 과외 선생님, 가정교사	39. 그런데, 그나저나
40. 아주 멋진, 엄청난	41. 집들이	42. 새로, 새롭게
43. 문화의	44. 약속	

Listening Test
영어듣기 모의고사 12회

|정답|

01 ⑤	02 ④	03 ③	04 ⑤	05 ③
06 ①	07 ⑤	08 ⑤	09 ④	10 ④
11 ①	12 ②	13 ④	14 ②	15 ②
16 ⑤	17 ③	18 ③	19 ③	20 ⑤

01 날씨파악–그림　▶정답 ⑤

듣·기·대·본

W: This is the weather forecast for this week. The rain will continue with some wind today. Tomorrow, the rain will stop but it will still be cloudy. The temperature will be a little higher than today, ranging from 16 to 18 degrees Celsius.

우·리·말·해·석

여: 이번 주 일기예보입니다. 바람을 동반한 비는 오늘도 계속될 것입니다. 내일, 비는 그치겠지만 여전히 구름이 끼어 있을 것입니다. 기온은 섭씨 16도에서 18도 정도로 오늘보다 약간 높겠습니다.

단·어·및·표·현

range from A to B A부터 B까지 이르다

02 그림정보파악　▶정답 ④

듣·기·대·본

M: May I help you?

W: Oh, yes. I'm looking for a lunch box for my son.

M: Please come this way. How about the one with a dog on it?

W: Hmm... I think Fred would like the one with a dinosaur more.

M: Excellent choice. There are two types with a dinosaur. Which one do you like the best?

W: I prefer the round one to the square one. It will be easier to wash. I'll take it.

우·리·말·해·석

남: 무엇을 도와드릴까요?

여: 아, 네. 저는 제 아들에게 줄 도시락 통을 찾고 있어요.

남: 이쪽으로 오세요. 위에 개가 그려진 이것은 어떠세요?

여: 흠… 저는 Fred가 공룡이 있는 걸 더 좋아할 거라고 생각해요.

남: 탁월한 선택이세요. 공룡이 있는 건 두 종류가 있어요. 어떤 게 가장 좋으세요?

여: 저는 네모난 것보다 둥근 것이 더 좋아요. 그게 씻기도 더 쉬울 거예요. 그걸로 할게요.

단·어·및·표·현

lunch box 도시락 통
dinosaur [dáinəsɔ̀ːr] 몡 공룡
excellent [éksələnt] 혱 탁월한, 훌륭한
prefer [prifə́ːr] 통 더 좋아하다, 선호하다

03 심정추론　▶정답 ③

듣·기·대·본

W: You don't look good, Matt. Are you OK?

M: I've got a cold. I'm going to the doctor after school.

W: Oh, no. You can't come to band practice today, then.

M: Don't worry, I can. I just need the practice to start an hour later.

W: Oh, sure. We can't practice without a drummer, after all.

M: Thanks.

W: I'm glad you can come.

우·리·말·해·석

① 궁금해하는　② 피곤한　③ 안도한　④ 슬픈　⑤ 화난

여: 안색이 안 좋아 보여, Matt. 너 괜찮니?

남: 나 감기에 걸렸어. 방과 후에 병원에 갈 거야.

여: 아, 이런. 그럼 넌 오늘 밴드 연습에 올 수 없겠구나.

남: 걱정하지 마, 갈 수 있어. 그냥 연습을 한 시간 늦게 시작해야 할 뿐이야.

여: 아, 물론이지. 우리는 어쨌든 드러머 없이는 연습할 수 없으니까 말이야.

남: 고마워.

여: 네가 올 수 있다니 기뻐.

단·어·및·표·현

get a cold 감기에 걸리다

04 한일파악　▶정답 ⑤

듣·기·대·본

M: Hey, Mina. What did you do yesterday?

W: My cousin came to visit me.

M: Oh, really? Did you have fun with your cousin?

W: Yeah. I played video games with her.

M: I thought you didn't like video games.

W: I don't. I wanted to watch a movie but my cousin wanted to play games.

M: So, you just played along with her?

W: Yeah. I actually quite enjoyed playing them.

우·리·말·해·석

남: 얘, Mina야. 너 어제 뭐 했어?

여: 내 사촌이 나를 만나러 왔어.

남: 아, 정말? 네 사촌과 함께 재미있게 놀았니?

여: 응. 나는 그녀와 비디오 게임을 했어.

남: 나는 네가 비디오 게임을 좋아하지 않는다고 생각했는데.

여: 좋아하지 않아. 나는 영화를 보고 싶었지만 내 사촌이 게임을 하고 싶어 했어.

남: 그래서, 너는 그저 그녀에게 맞춰주었니?

여: 응. 나는 사실 그것들을 하는 걸 꽤 즐겼어.

단·어·및·표·현
cousin [kʌ́zən] 똉 사촌
have fun 재미있게 놀다
play along with ~ ~에 동의[동조]하는 척하다, 장단을 맞춰주다
quite [kwait] 뙤 꽤, 상당히

05 대화장소추론 ▶정답 ③

듣·기·대·본
W: When did you start feeling the pain?

M: Two weeks ago.

W: On a scale of one to ten, how would you describe how painful it is?

M: A two, I guess. It's not really that bad, but it's such a bother because it keeps on coming back.

W: I see. How long does the pain last when you get it?

M: About ten to fifteen minutes, but sometimes it lasts for an hour or so.

W: Alright, let's get started. Let me check your teeth.

우·리·말·해·석
여: 언제부터 통증을 느끼기 시작했나요?

남: 2주 전부터요.

여: 1에서 10까지를 기준으로 얼마나 고통스러운지 묘사해주겠어요?

남: 제 생각에는 2인 것 같네요. 그렇게 정말로 심하지는 않지만 계속해서 반복되기 때문에 정말 신경 쓰여요.

여: 알겠어요. 당신이 통증이 있을 때는 얼마나 오래 지속되나요?

남: 약 10에서 15분이요, 하지만 가끔은 한 시간 정도 지속됩니다.

여: 좋아요, 이제 시작하지요. 치아를 검사해 볼게요.

단·어·및·표·현
keep on -ing 계속 ~하다

06 마지막말의도파악 ▶정답 ①

듣·기·대·본
M: Laura, I have some good news for you.

W: What is it, Mr. Kennedy?

M: You've been selected to represent our school at the English debating contest.

W: Really? I can't believe it.

M: Congratulations. How do you feel?

W: I'm very happy, but I'm not sure if I'm good enough to represent our school.

M: You'll be fine. And you can always let me know if you need some advice.

W: That'll be very helpful.

M: Be confident and do your best. I'm sure you'll do a good job.

우·리·말·해·석
남: Laura, 나는 너에게 좋은 소식이 있단다.

여: 그게 뭔데요, Kennedy 선생님?

남: 네가 영어 토론 대회에서 우리 학교를 대표하도록 선발되었어.

여: 정말요? 저는 그것을 믿을 수 없어요.

남: 축하한다. 기분이 어떠니?

여: 저는 매우 기쁘지만, 제가 학교를 대표할 만큼 충분히 잘하는지 확신이 없어요.

남: 너는 잘할 거야. 그리고 조언이 필요하다면 언제든지 나에게 알려주렴.

여: 그것은 매우 도움이 될 거예요.

남: 자신감을 갖고 최선을 다하거라. 나는 네가 잘할 것이라고 확신한다.

단·어·및·표·현
select [silékt] 똥 선발하다
represent [rèprizént] 똥 대표하다
debate [dibéit] 똥 토의하다

07 특정정보파악 ▶정답 ⑤

듣·기·대·본
W: Lucas, look at this poster. Our school is having a charity event.

M: It says all the money raised will be given to local charities.

W: The charity event is this Friday in the school gym. Why don't we participate?

M: Sure! Do you have any useful items to donate?

W: I have some books that I don't need anymore. How about you?

M: Hmm... I think I'm going to donate some baseball caps I don't wear.

W: Great!

우·리·말·해·석
여: Lucas, 이 포스터를 봐. 우리 학교가 자선 행사를 할 거야.

남: 모금된 돈은 전부 지역 자선 단체들에 기부될 거라고 쓰여 있네.

여: 자선 행사는 이번 주 금요일에 학교 체육관에서 열려. 우리 참가하는 게 어때?

남: 물론이지! 너는 기부할 만한 유용한 물건이 있니?

여: 나는 더 이상 내게 필요하지 않은 책들이 좀 있어. 너는 어때?

남: 흠… 나는 안 쓰는 야구 모자들을 좀 기부할 생각이야.

여: 좋아!

단·어·및·표·현
charity [tʃǽrəti] 똉 자선, 자선 단체
raise [reiz] 똥 모금하다, 모으다
participate [pɑːrtísəpèit] 똥 참가하다
donate [dóuneit] 똥 기부하다, 기증하다

08 할일파악(대화직후) ▶정답 ③

듣·기·대·본
M: What do you want to do today? It's our last day on the island.

W: Yeah, time flies.

M: How about we go snorkeling one last time?

W: Actually, I want to explore the local market and buy some souvenirs.

M: That sounds like a fun idea! Do you need any help finding gifts?

W: Yeah, will you come with me?

M: Of course! Let's go check out the market together now.

우·리·말·해·석
남: 넌 오늘 뭐 하고 싶어? 섬에서 (보내는) 우리의 마지막 날이잖아.

여: 응, 시간이 빨라.

남: 우리 마지막으로 한 번 스노클링을 하러 가는 건 어때?

여: 사실, 나는 현지 시장을 탐험하고 기념품들을 좀 사고 싶어.

남: 재밌는 생각처럼 들리는걸! 넌 선물을 찾는 데 도움이 필요하니?

여: 응, 나와 같이 갈래?

남: 물론이지! 지금 같이 시장을 살펴보러 가자.

단·어·및·표·현
island [áilənd] 몡 섬
Time flies. 시간이 빠르다.
snorkeling [snɔ́:rkliŋ] 몡 스노클링
one last time 마지막으로 한 번
explore [iksplɔ́:r] 통 탐험하다
local market 현지 시장
souvenir [sù:vəníər] 몡 기념품, 선물
check out 살펴보다, 보다

09 대화미언급 ▶정답 ④

듣·기·대·본
W: Hello. How may I help you?
M: Yes, I'm looking for a book. It's called *The Right*.
W: Do you know who wrote it?
M: Marcus Herman. It's new. It was published just last April.
W: Okay, let me check into the computer. Mmmmh. Ahh, yeah, we have that book.
M: Great! How much is it?
W: It's $ 13, sir. It's actually our last copy. Let me get it for you.

우·리·말·해·석
여: 안녕하십니까. 무엇을 도와드릴까요?
남: 네, 저는 책을 찾고 있습니다. "The Right"라는 이름의 책입니다.
여: 누가 쓴 책인지 아세요?
남: Marcus Herman이에요. 새로 나왔어요. 그 책은 바로 지난 4월에 출판되었어요.
여: 네, 컴퓨터로 찾아보겠습니다. 음. 아, 네, 그 책이 있습니다.
남: 잘됐네요! 그것은 얼마인가요?
여: 그 책은 13달러예요, 손님. 사실은 이것이 우리 가게에 마지막 남은 한 권이네요. 제가 가져다 드릴게요.

단·어·및·표·현
publish [pʌ́bliʃ] 통 출판하다

10 담화화제추론 ▶정답 ④

듣·기·대·본
M: Hello, everyone. I'm Randy, your school librarian. Over the summer vacation, our school library went through some big changes. First, there is more room for laptops and tablets. You can easily charge your devices, too. Second, the librarian's desk was moved to the west side of the room. There are also new check-out and check-in machines. These will help improve your school life.

우·리·말·해·석
남: 안녕하세요, 여러분. 저는 학교 사서 교사인 Randy입니다. 여름방학 동안, 우리 학교 도서관은 몇 가지 큰 변화를 겪었습니다. 첫째, 노트북 컴퓨터와 태블릿을 위한 더 많은 공간이 생겼습니다. 여러분의 (전자)기기들도 쉽게 충전할 수 있습니다. 둘째, 사서 교사의 책상이 교실의 서쪽으로 이동했습니다. 또한 새로운 대출 및 반납 기계가 생겼습니다. 이것들은 여러분의 학교 생활을 개선하는 데 도움이 될 것입니다.

단·어·및·표·현
librarian [laibrέ(:)əriən] 몡 사서 (교사)
go through ~ ~을 겪다, 거치다
charge [tʃɑːrdʒ] 통 충전하다
check-out 대출
check-in 반납

improve [imprúːv] 통 개선하다, 향상시키다

11 대화내용불일치 ▶정답 ①

듣·기·대·본
W: Mr. Lee, can you give me some information on the Korea Guitar Exhibition?
M: Oh, the guitar exhibition? It starts this Thursday.
W: Will I be able to buy instruments there?
M: Yes. You'll also get a chance to meet and talk to some guitarists.
W: Great! What else will I be able to do there?
M: There's going to be a mini concert at the exhibition. You should check it out.
W: Awesome! How much is the admission price?
M: The exhibition is free for students.

우·리·말·해·석
여: 이 선생님, 제게 한국 기타 전시회에 대한 정보를 좀 줄 수 있나요?
남: 오, 기타 전시회요? 그건 이번 주 목요일에 시작합니다.
여: 제가 거기서 악기를 살 수 있을까요?
남: 네. 당신은 또한 몇몇의 기타리스트를 만나서 얘기할 수 있는 기회를 가질 수도 있어요.
여: 좋네요! 제가 거기서 또 어떤 것을 할 수 있나요?
남: 전시회에 미니 콘서트가 있을 겁니다. 꼭 확인해 보세요.
여: 멋지네요! 입장료는 얼마인가요?
남: 전시회는 학생들에게 무료입니다.

단·어·및·표·현
exhibition [èksəbíʃən] 몡 전시회
instrument [ínstrəmənt] 몡 악기, 기구, 도구
check out ~을 확인하다
free [friː] 형 무료의, 공짜의

12 전화목적파악 ▶정답 ②

듣·기·대·본
(*Telephone rings.*)
W: Hello.
M: Hello, Mrs. Jones. This is Sam, your neighbor.
W: Oh, hi. I thought you were on vacation in Busan. Have you come back?
M: No, I'm still in Busan. Actually, I'm calling to ask you a favor.
W: Okay, what is it?
M: Tomorrow, a package will be delivered to my place. Could you keep the package until I get home?
W: No problem. I'll keep it safe. Enjoy your vacation.
M: Thank you so much!

우·리·말·해·석
(전화벨이 울린다.)
여: 여보세요.
남: 여보세요, Jones 부인. 저는 당신의 이웃 Sam이에요.
여: 오, 안녕하세요. 저는 당신이 부산으로 휴가 갔다고 생각했는데요. 돌아오셨어요?
남: 아니요, 저는 아직 부산에 있어요. 사실, 부탁을 드리려고 전화하는 것입니다.
여: 그래요, 무슨 부탁이죠?
남: 내일 저희 집으로 택배가 하나 배달될 거예요. 제가 집에 갈 때까지 택배를 보관해 주시겠어요?
여: 문제없어요. 안전하게 보관할게요. 휴가 잘 보내세요.
남: 정말 감사합니다!

12 회 모의고사

단·어·및·표·현
neighbor[néibər] 몡 이웃

13 수치파악　　▶정답 ④

듣·기·대·본

M: Welcome to Grand Ice Rink. How can I help you?

W: Hi. I'd like to buy two tickets for today's show.

M: An adult ticket is $50 and a student ticket is $30.

W: One adult and one student, please. And I have a discount coupon. Can I use it now?

M: Let me take a look.

W: Here it is.

M: (Pause) Okay. You can use it now. It's a $10 discount coupon, so your total is $70.

W: Great! Here you are.

우·리·말·해·석

남: Grand Ice Rink에 오신 것을 환영합니다. 어떻게 도와드릴까요?

여: 안녕하세요. 저는 오늘 공연 티켓 두 장을 사고 싶습니다.

남: 성인 티켓은 50달러이고 학생 티켓은 30달러입니다.

여: 성인 한 명과 학생 한 명입니다. 그리고 저는 할인 쿠폰을 가지고 있습니다. 제가 그것을 지금 사용할 수 있을까요?

남: 제가 한번 보겠습니다.

여: 여기 있습니다.

남: (잠시 후) 네. 당신은 지금 그것을 사용할 수 있습니다. 10달러 할인 쿠폰이라서, 당신의 총액은 70달러입니다.

여: 좋습니다! 여기 있습니다.

단·어·및·표·현

take a look (한번) 보다

total[tóutl] 몡 총액, 합계

14 대화자관계추론　　▶정답 ②

듣·기·대·본

M: You're doing great. You look like you've lost weight.

W: Thank you. I have been working out just like you told me.

M: Good. I hope you're drinking plenty of water after.

W: Yes, I am. I'm eating what you suggested, too.

M: That's really good to hear. Keep that up and you'll soon reach your goal.

W: I'm really glad I hired you. I feel better after all those exercises you've taught me.

우·리·말·해·석

남: 당신은 잘하고 있어요. 살이 빠지신 것 같아요.

여: 감사합니다. 저는 요즘 말씀하신 것처럼 운동하고 있어요.

남: 좋아요. 저는 당신이 그 후에 충분한 물을 마시고 있기를 바랍니다.

여: 네, 그러고 있어요. 저는 또한 당신이 제안한 것들을 먹고 있어요.

남: 그런 말씀을 들으니 기분이 정말 좋네요. 계속 그렇게 하시면 곧 당신의 목표에 도달하실 거예요.

여: 전 정말 당신을 고용해서 기뻐요. 당신이 가르쳐준 이 모든 운동을 하고 나서 저는 몸이 더 좋아졌어요.

단·어·및·표·현

work out 운동하다

15 부탁(요청)한일파악　　▶정답 ②

듣·기·대·본

W: Dad, happy wedding anniversary!

M: Thank you, sweetie.

W: What shall we have for dinner tonight?

M: I'm cooking meat pie, your mom's favorite.

W: Did you get a present for Mom?

M: Yes, I bought earrings for her. But I think I'm missing something.

W: Oh, how about buying her some flowers? She'll love them.

M: Great. Then, can you go and buy some roses now? I'll give you the money.

W: Sure. No problem.

우·리·말·해·석

여: 아빠, 결혼 기념일 축하드려요!

남: 고맙구나, 얘야.

여: 우리 오늘 저녁에 뭘 먹을까요?

남: 나는 네 엄마가 가장 좋아하는 미트 파이를 요리하고 있어.

여: 아빠는 엄마에게 줄 선물을 사셨나요?

남: 응. 난 그녀를 위해 귀걸이를 샀지. 하지만 난 뭔가를 놓치고 있는 것 같아.

여: 아, 엄마에게 꽃을 좀 사주는 건 어때요? 엄마는 그것들을 좋아할 거예요.

남: 좋아. 그러면, 네가 지금 가서 장미를 좀 사다 줄 수 있니? 내가 너에게 돈을 줄게.

여: 물론이죠. 문제없어요.

단·어·및·표·현

wedding anniversary 결혼 기념일

get[get] 동 사다, 사주다

miss[mis] 동 놓치다

16 이유파악　　▶정답 ⑤

듣·기·대·본

M: Anna, good to see you. Where are you going?

W: I'm going to the rooftop of this building.

M: Oh, are you going to the new rooftop café?

W: No. My favorite singer Dave Campion is shooting his first movie here.

M: On the rooftop?

W: Yeah. It's an action film. I just want to watch him from afar.

M: I see. Can I go with you?

W: Sure.

우·리·말·해·석

남: Anna, 만나서 반가워요. 어디 가세요?

여: 저는 이 건물의 옥상으로 가고 있어요.

남: 오, 새 옥상 카페로 가고 계신가요?

여: 아니요. 제가 매우 좋아하는 가수 Dave Campion이 그의 첫 영화를 이곳에서 촬영하고 있어요.

남: 옥상에서요?

여: 네, 그것은 액션 영화예요. 저는 그냥 멀리서 그를 보고 싶어요.

남: 그렇군요. 제가 같이 가도 될까요?

여: 그럼요.

단·어·및·표·현

rooftop[rú(:)ftɑ̀p] 몡 옥상

favorite[féivərit] 형 매우 좋아하는, 아주 좋아하는

shoot[ʃuːt] 동 촬영하다

afar[əfáːr] 부 멀리

17 그림상황에적절한대화찾기　　▶정답 ③

듣·기·대·본

① M: Can you take a picture of me?

W: Sure, <u>pass</u> me your phone.
② M: How can I help you?
　　W: I want two student tickets.
③ M: <u>You are not <u>allowed to use</u> a selfie stick here.</u>
　　W: Oh, I see. I won't use it.
④ M: Excuse me. Where is the restroom?
　　W: It's <u>around</u> the corner.
⑤ M: What's your favorite painting?
　　W: I like the Mona Lisa best.

우·리·말·해·석
① 남: 내 사진 한 장 찍어 줄 수 있니?
　　여: 물론이지, 네 전화기를 내게 건네줘.
② 남: 무엇을 도와드릴까요?
　　여: 학생용 표 두 장 주세요.
③ 남: 여기서는 셀카봉을 사용하는 것이 허용되지 않습니다.
　　여: 아, 알겠어요. 저는 그것을 쓰지 않겠습니다.
④ 남: 실례합니다. 화장실이 어디에 있나요?
　　여: 모퉁이 돌아서 있습니다.
⑤ 남: 네가 가장 좋아하는 그림은 뭐야?
　　여: 나는 모나리자를 가장 좋아해.

단·어·및·표·현
pass[pæs] ⑧ 건네주다
allow[əláu] ⑧ 허용하다, 허락하다
selfie stick 셀카봉
around[əráund] ⑩ (모퉁이 따위를) 돌아서

18　담화미언급　▶정답 ③

듣·기·대·본
W: Hello, everyone. For today's lesson, I want to talk about whale sharks. Whale sharks are the largest fish in the sea. On average, they <u>grow to a length</u> between 5 and 10 meters. They can <u>weigh up to 19 tons.</u> <u>The average lifespan of whale sharks is about 70 years.</u> They like warmer areas and are <u>found in tropical waters</u> all over the world.

우·리·말·해·석
여: 안녕하세요, 여러분. 오늘의 수업으로, 저는 고래상어에 대해 얘기하고 싶어요. 고래상어는 바다에서 가장 큰 물고기예요. 평균적으로, 그것들은 5에서 10미터 사이의 길이까지 자라요. 그것들은 19톤까지 무게가 나갈 수 있어요. 고래상어의 평균 수명은 약 70년이에요. 그것들은 더 따뜻한 지역을 좋아하고 전 세계의 열대 수역에서 발견돼요.

단·어·및·표·현
on average 평균적으로, 대개
lifespan[láifspæn] ⑲ 수명
tropical waters 열대 수역

19　알맞은응답찾기　▶정답 ③

듣·기·대·본
M: What are you making for lunch?
W: I'm cooking bibimbap.
M: That sounds yummy. How do you make bibimbap?
W: First, I cook <u>some veggies</u> like carrots and spinach. Then, I make beef bulgogi and fry eggs sunny-side up.
M: Cool! What else goes in bibimbap?
W: I also make seasoned soybean sprouts and a spicy sauce with gochujang <u>to mix with</u> everything.
M: Sounds great! <u>Can you share the recipe?</u>
W: <u>Sure thing, I'll write it down for you.</u>

M: <u>Thanks! I'll give it a try.</u>

우·리·말·해·석
① 나는 매운 음식을 못 먹어.
② 나는 채소들을 좋아하지 않아.
③ 고마워! 나는 그것을 한번 해 볼게.
④ 이건 내 가족 요리법이야.
⑤ 아니, 나는 요리를 잘 못해.

남: 점심으로 무엇을 만들고 있어?
여: 나는 비빔밥을 요리하고 있어.
남: 맛있겠는걸. 넌 비빔밥을 어떻게 만들어?
여: 우선, 나는 당근과 시금치 같은 몇몇 채소들을 볶아. 그 다음, 나는 소고기 불고기를 만들고, 계란을 한쪽만 익히도록 구워.
남: 좋은데! 비빔밥에 또 무엇이 들어가?
여: 나는 또한 양념된 콩나물과 모든 것을 섞기 위한 고추장이 들어간 매운 소스도 만들어.
남: 좋은걸! 너는 요리법을 공유해줄 수 있어?
여: 물론이지, 내가 널 위해 그것을 적어줄게.
남: **고마워! 나는 그것을 한번 해 볼게.**

단·어·및·표·현
veggie[védʒi] ⑲ (= vegetable) 채소
spinach[spínitʃ] ⑲ 시금치
fry[frai] ⑧ 굽다, 튀기다, 부치다
sunny-side up 한쪽만 익힌 계란 프라이
seasoned[síːzənd] ⑲ 양념을 한
soybean sprout 콩나물
write down ~을 적다, 작성하다
give it a try 한번 해보다

20　알맞은응답찾기　▶정답 ⑤

듣·기·대·본
W: Hi, James. Are you doing anything special this weekend?
M: Yes, I'm visiting my cousin Paul for a <u>couple of days.</u>
W: Oh, that's nice! Where does he live?
M: He lives on Jeju Island and it's my first time going there.
W: Awesome! It must be really nice there this time of the year.
M: Yes, I'm really excited to see the <u>beautiful nature</u> on the island.
W: I hope you have a good trip. <u>When are you coming back?</u>
M: <u>I am flying back to Seoul on Sunday night.</u>

우·리·말·해·석
① 그녀는 배를 타고 그곳에 갈 거야.
② 우리는 저녁식사로 해산물을 먹을 거야.
③ 그 섬에는 아름다운 산들이 있어.
④ 그의 비행기는 두 시간 후에 떠날 거야.
⑤ 나는 일요일 밤에 비행기를 타고 서울로 돌아올 거야.

여: 안녕, James. 너 이번 주말에 특별한 일 할 거니?
남: 응, 난 이틀 동안 내 사촌 Paul을 방문할 거야.
여: 아, 그거 멋지다! 그는 어디 사는데?
남: 그는 제주도에 살고, 난 그곳에 가는 게 처음이야.
여: 굉장하다! 그곳은 해마다 이맘때 날씨가 정말 좋을 게 틀림없어.
남: 응, 그 섬에서 아름다운 자연을 보게 되어서 정말 신나.
여: 즐거운 여행 하길 바랄게. 너는 언제 돌아오니?
남: **나는 일요일 밤에 비행기를 타고 서울로 돌아올 거야.**

12
회
모
의
고
사

단·어·및·표·현
awesome[ɔ́:səm] 형 굉장한, 어마어마한
this time of the year 해마다 이맘때
nature[néitʃər] 형 자연

Words & Expressions Review

1. 묘사하다	2. 모금하다, 모으다	3. 굉장한, 어마어마한
4. 계속되다	5. (한번) 보다	6. ~을 확인하다
7. 결혼 기념일	8. 허용하다, 허락하다	9. (책·신문 등의) 한 부
10. 선발하다	11. 어쨌든, 결국에는	12. 자선, 자선 단체
13. 총액, 합계	14. ~을 겪다, 거치다	15. 탁월한, 훌륭한
16. 옥상	17. 고통스러운	18. A부터 B까지 이르다
19. 계속 ~하다	20. 출판하다	21. 사실은, 실제로
22. 꽤, 상당히	23. 한번 해보다	24. 평균적으로, 대개
25. 공룡	26. 기부하다, 기증하다	27. 제안하다
28. 충전하다	29. 사촌	30. 셀카봉
31. 대표하다	32. 휴가로	33. ~에 동의[동조]하는 척하다
34. 놓치다	35. 자연	36. 건네주다
37. 섬	38. (모퉁이 따위를) 돌아서	39. 수명
40. 운동하다	41. A에게 부탁을 하다	42. 이웃
43. 살이 빠지다, 살을 빼다	44. 악기, 기구, 도구	

|정|답|

01 ⑤	02 ①	03 ②	04 ③	05 ②
06 ④	07 ⑤	08 ②	09 ④	10 ②
11 ④	12 ③	13 ④	14 ②	15 ①
16 ④	17 ⑤	18 ④	19 ④	20 ⑤

01　날씨파악-그림　▶ 정답 ⑤

듣·기·대·본

M: Good morning, I'm Alan Brown. This is your weekend weather report. It's going to be mostly cloudy during the day today. Light rain showers are expected in the evening. However, on Sunday, the rain will clear and it's going to be sunny all day with no wind. The daytime temperature is going to reach 25 degrees Celsius. Thank you.

우·리·말·해·석

남: 안녕하세요, 저는 Alan Brown입니다. 여러분의 주말 날씨 예보입니다. 오늘은 낮 동안 대체로 구름이 끼겠습니다. 저녁에는 약한 소나기가 예상됩니다. 그러나 일요일에는 비가 그치고 바람 없이 하루 종일 맑겠습니다. 낮 기온은 섭씨 25도까지 오를 것으로 예상됩니다. 감사합니다.

단·어·및·표·현
mostly[móustli] 부 대체로

02　그림정보파악　▶ 정답 ①

듣·기·대·본

M: Hello. Can I help you?
W: Yes. I'm looking for a memo pad to decorate my diary.
M: Oh, look over here. These are our best sellers.
W: They all look nice. It's hard to choose just one.
M: How about this round one with a bear?
W: Well, I prefer the square ones.
M: Okay. We have two types of square memo pads.
W: I like the one with cherries. It looks cute.
M: All right. It's 3,000 won.

우·리·말·해·석

남: 안녕하세요, 무엇을 도와드릴까요?
여: 네. 저는 제 일기장을 꾸밀 메모지를 찾고 있어요.
남: 아, 여기를 살펴보세요. 이것들이 저희의 베스트셀러예요.
여: 그것들은 모두 좋아 보이네요. 딱 하나만 고르기 어렵네요.
남: 곰이 있는 이 둥근 것은 어떠세요?
여: 음, 저는 사각형의 것을 선호해요.
남: 그렇군요. 저희는 두 종류의 사각형 메모지가 있어요.
여: 저는 체리가 있는 것이 좋아요. 귀여워 보여요.
남: 알겠습니다. 3천 원입니다.

단·어·및·표·현
memo pad 메모지
decorate[dékərèit] 동 꾸미다, 장식하다
look over ~을 살펴보다, 훑어보다
prefer[prifə́:r] 동 선호하다, 좋아하다

03　심정추론　▶ 정답 ②

듣·기·대·본

W: Ugh, I can't believe this!
M: What's wrong, Emily?
W: Dad, look! I bought tickets to this concert and it got canceled at the last minute!
M: Oh, no! That's really disappointing. You were so excited about the concert.
W: I had everything planned, and now it's ruined.
M: I'm sorry, honey. Maybe you can find another event to go to?
W: It won't be the same. I have been looking forward to this for weeks!

우·리·말·해·석

여: 아, 정말 믿을 수가 없어!
남: 무슨 일이야, Emily?
여: 아빠, 봐요! 이 콘서트 티켓을 샀는데 막판에 취소됐어요!
남: 오, 이런! 그것 정말 실망스럽구나. 너 그 콘서트 엄청 기대했잖아.
여: 전 모든 것을 계획해놨는데, 이제 다 망쳤어요.
남: 유감이구나, 우리 딸. 갈 만한 다른 행사라도 찾아보는 건 어때?
여: 같지 않을 거예요. 전 몇 주 동안 이걸 기다려왔단 말이에요!

단·어·및·표·현
cancel[kǽnsəl] 동 취소하다
at the last minute 막판에, 마지막 순간에
ruin[rú(:)in] 동 망치다
look forward to ~을 기다리다, 기대하다
for weeks 몇 주 동안

듣·기·대·본

W: Jack, did you buy the baseball cap you wanted?
M: You mean the one we saw at the mall last weekend?
W: Yes, you said you would ask your mother if you could buy it.
M: Actually, I found out that I can buy it online at a much lower price.
W: Oh, really?
M: So I ordered it online yesterday.
W: Good for you! I can't wait to see you wearing it.

우·리·말·해·석

여: Jack, 너는 네가 원하던 야구 모자를 샀어?
남: 너는 우리가 지난주에 쇼핑몰에서 본 것을 말하는 거지?
여: 응, 너는 네가 그것을 사도 되는지 네 어머니께 여쭤본다고 말했잖아.
남: 사실, 나는 온라인에서 훨씬 더 저렴한 가격에 그것을 살 수 있다는 걸 알게 됐어.
여: 아, 정말?
남: 그래서 나는 어제 온라인으로 그것을 주문했어.
여: 잘됐네! 네가 그것을 쓴 것을 빨리 보고싶다.

단·어·및·표·현

baseball cap 야구 모자
find out 알게 되다, 알아내다
can't wait to + 동사 빨리 ~하고 싶다, ~하는 것이 너무 기대된다

듣·기·대·본

M: Hello, what can I do for you?
W: I'd like to fill up my car. I'll open the oil tank right away.
M: OK, coming right up. (*Pause*) All done.
W: Thank you. How much is it?
M: It'll be 80,000 won. And you can get your car washed for free.
W: That sounds good. Here is my credit card.
M: All right. Please wait for a moment.

우·리·말·해·석

남: 안녕하세요, 무엇을 도와드릴까요?
여: 저는 제 차에 (기름을) 가득 채우고 싶어요. 제가 지금 바로 기름 탱크를 열게요.
남: 네, 바로 해드리겠습니다. (잠시 후) 다 됐습니다.
여: 감사합니다. 얼마인가요?
남: 8만 원입니다. 그리고 손님은 손님의 차를 무료로 세차 받을 수 있습니다.
여: 좋아요. 여기 제 신용카드요.
남: 알겠습니다. 잠시 기다려 주십시오.

단·어·및·표·현

fill up (차의 기름 탱크를) 가득 채우다
for free 무료로

듣·기·대·본

W: Daniel, how do you like the new science teacher?
M: Well, I've only had one class with him so far.
W: He explains things so clearly and makes the class really interesting.
M: Oh, I remember he showed us some fun experiments yesterday.
W: I honestly think he's the best teacher we've had in a while.
M: That's true. I agree with you.

우·리·말·해·석

여: Daniel, 새 과학 선생님 어때?
남: 음, 아직까지 그 선생님 수업을 한 번밖에 안 들어봤어.
여: 그분은 아주 명확하게 설명해 주시고 수업을 정말 흥미롭게 만들어 주셔.
남: 아, 어제 그분이 우리에게 몇몇 재미있는 실험들을 보여주셨던 거 기억나.
여: 솔직히 나는 그분이 우리가 한동안 만나 본 중에 최고의 선생님이라고 생각해.
남: 맞아. 나도 동의해.

단·어·및·표·현

How do you like ~? ~은 어때?
so far 지금까지
experiment [ikspérəmənt] 명 실험
in a while 한동안, 오랜만에

듣·기·대·본

M: Hey, today is Heesoo's birthday. How about a surprise party?
W: Sounds great! What should we prepare?
M: Jaemin said he'll buy a cake and candles. Do we need anything else?
W: I think a couple of balloons would be good.
M: Good idea! Then you bring the balloons.
W: What about you?
M: I have a board game that everyone can play together. I'll bring that.
W: Okay. See you after school then.

우·리·말·해·석

남: 이봐, 오늘은 희수의 생일이야. 깜짝 파티 하는 거 어때?
여: 좋아! 우리가 뭘 준비해야 해?
남: 재민이는 그가 케이크와 초들을 살 거라고 말했어. 우리 더 필요한 거 있어?
여: 난 몇 개의 풍선들이 있으면 좋을 것 같아.
남: 좋은 생각이다! 그러면 네가 풍선들을 가져와.
여: 너는?
남: 나는 모두가 함께 놀 수 있는 보드게임이 있어. 난 그걸 가져올게.
여: 알겠어. 그러면 방과 후에 보자.

단·어·및·표·현

How about ~? (제안) ~은 어때?
prepare [pripέər] 동 준비하다, 대비하다
anything else 그 밖에 또 무엇인가
a couple of 몇 개의, 두서너 개의
bring [briŋ] 동 가져오다, 데려오다

듣·기·대·본

M: Grace, thanks for inviting me to this music concert.
W: You're welcome. I'm glad you could join me.
M: Many of my favorite bands are performing tonight. Shall we go in?
W: Actually, I'm hungry. Can we grab a bite to eat before we go in?
M: Of course. What do you feel like eating?
W: How about some pizza? There's a pizzeria just around

13
회
모
의
고
사

the corner.

M: Sounds good. Let's go grab some pizza.

남: Grace, 이 음악 콘서트에 나를 초대해줘서 고마워.

여: 천만에. 난 네가 나와 함께할 수 있어서 기뻐.

남: 내가 좋아하는 밴드들 중 많은 밴드들이 오늘 밤 공연해. 들어가 볼까?

여: 사실, 나는 배고파. 우리 들어가기 전에 간단하게 먹을까?

남: 물론이지. 너는 뭐가 먹고 싶어?

여: 피자는 어때? 코너를 돌면 바로 피자 전문점이 있어.

남: 좋아. 가서 피자를 좀 먹자.

단·어·및·표·현

invite [inváit] ⑧ 초대하다

perform [pərfɔ́ːrm] ⑧ 공연하다, 연주하다

grab a bite 간단히 먹다

pizzeria [pìːtsəríːə] ⑲ 피자 전문점

09 대화미언급 ▶ 정답 ④

들·기·대·본

W: Roy, have you checked out the volunteer program on our school website?

M: Not yet. What are the details?

W: Volunteers will be helping senior citizens at the community center.

M: I see. When does the volunteer program take place?

W: It is every Saturday from 2 to 4 p.m.

M: Do you know how to apply?

W: Yes. You should download the form and return it by email.

M: That's easy.

W: The deadline for applications is June 29th. So, you should hurry and apply if you are interested.

우·리·말·해·석

여: Roy, 넌 우리 학교 웹사이트에 있는 자원봉사 프로그램을 확인해봤어?

남: 아직. 세부 사항들이 뭐야?

여: 자원봉사자들은 주민 센터에서 어르신들을 도울 거야.

남: 그렇구나. 자원봉사 프로그램은 언제 해?

여: 매주 토요일 오후 2시부터 4시까지야.

남: 너는 어떻게 지원하는지 알아?

여: 응. 넌 양식을 다운받고, 이메일로 그것을 답신 보내야 돼.

남: 그거 쉽네.

여: 지원 마감일은 6월 29일이야. 그러니, 너는 만약 관심이 있다면, 서둘러서 지원해야 해.

단·어·및·표·현

check out 확인하다, 보다

volunteer [vὰləntíər] ⑲ 자원봉사(자)

detail [ditéil] ⑲ 세부사항

senior citizen 어르신, 노인

take place (행사 등을) 하다, 열리다

deadline [dédlàin] ⑲ 마감

application [æ̀pləkéiʃən] ⑲ 지원, 신청

10 담화화제추론 ▶ 정답 ②

들·기·대·본

M: Hello, class! Let me explain how to play the game, *Blind Square.* You will divide into groups of four. I will give each group a long rope and four blindfolds. Put on a blindfold, hold onto the rope, and try to make a square within 5 minutes with your group members. When your

group agrees you've made a square, put the rope down on the floor. The group that makes a square first within the given time wins!

우·리·말·해·석

남: 안녕하세요, 학생 여러분! 제가 어떻게 "Blind Square(눈 가리고 정사각형 만들기)" 게임을 하는지 설명드리겠습니다. 여러분은 네 명이 한 조로 나뉠 것입니다. 제가 각 조에게 긴 줄 한 개와 눈가리개 4개를 드릴 겁니다. 눈가리개를 쓰고, 줄을 잡고, 5분 안에 여러분의 조원들과 정사각형을 만들어보세요. 여러분이 정사각형을 만들었다고 여러분의 조가 동의할 때, 줄을 바닥에 내려놓으세요. 주어진 시간 안에 가장 먼저 정사각형을 만든 조가 이깁니다!

단·어·및·표·현

square [skwɛər] ⑲ 정사각형

blindfold [bláindfòuld] ⑲ 눈가리개

put on ~을 쓰다

try to + 동사원형 ~하려고 해보다, 노력하다

put down 내려놓다

11 대화내용불일치 ▶ 정답 ④

들·기·대·본

M: Martha, do you have any special plans for this summer?

W: Not really.

M: Then, why don't we take a Korean course at City Cultural Center?

W: Oh, I would like to learn Korean. Are there any courses for beginners?

M: Yes, there is one in the morning. And there's no level test.

W: Great! How many people can enroll in the class?

M: The class is limited to ten people. I guess we should hurry.

W: Okay, let's sign up.

우·리·말·해·석

남: Martha, 이번 여름에 어떤 특별한 계획이 있어?

여: 별일 없어.

남: 그러면, 시립 문화 센터에서 한국어 강좌를 듣는 게 어때?

여: 오, 나는 한국어를 배우고 싶어. 초보자를 위한 강좌가 있어?

남: 응, 아침에 하나 있어. 그리고 수준 테스트도 없어.

여: 좋아! 그 반에 얼마나 많은 사람이 등록할 수 있어?

남: 그 반은 10명까지로 제한되어 있어. 나는 우리가 서둘러야 한다고 생각해.

여: 알았어, 등록하자.

단·어·및·표·현

Not really. 별일 없어. 꼭 그렇지는 않아.

enroll in ~ ~에 등록하다

12 전화목적파악 ▶ 정답 ③

들·기·대·본

(*Cell phone rings.*)

M: Hello?

W: Hello, this is Cherry.

M: Oh, hi, Cherry. I'm already on my way to the mall. How about you?

W: Me too, but I got stuck in traffic. I called to say I cannot make it on time.

M: It's okay, I understand. See you in a while!

W: Thanks!

(휴대전화가 울린다.)

남: 여보세요?

여: 여보세요? 나 Cherry야.

남: 오, 안녕, Cherry. 나 벌써 쇼핑몰에 가는 중이야. 넌 어때?

여: 나도 그래, 그렇지만 난 교통 체증에 옴짝달싹 못하고 있어. 내가 시간에 맞춰 갈 수 없다고 이야기하려고 전화했어.

남: 괜찮아, 이해해. 조금 이따가 보자!

여: 고마워!

단·어·및·표·현

get stuck 옴짝달싹 못하다, 갇히다

in a while 이따가, 곧

🦻 LISTENING ADVICE

문장 내에서 자음과 모음(a, e, i, o, u)이 만나면 마치 한 단어처럼 연결되어 발음됩니다. 따라서 'stuck in'은 [스터킨]으로, 'make it'은 [메이킷]으로 자연스럽게 이어져 들립니다.

13 수치계산(지불금액) ▶ 정답 ④

듣·기·대·본

M: Welcome to our flower shop.

W: Hello. Do you have purple tulips?

M: Yes, ma'am. Purple tulips cost $25 for 15.

W: Okay, I'll buy 30 tulips.

M: Would you like a vase to match the flowers? We have a pink vase available for $13. We also sell a red vase for $16.

W: Hmm... Okay, I'll take one red vase. Here's my payment.

우·리·말·해·석

남: 우리 꽃집에 오신 걸 환영해요.

여: 안녕하세요. 자주색 튤립이 있나요?

남: 네, 부인. 자주색 튤립은 15송이에 25달러입니다.

여: 좋아요, 저는 튤립 30송이를 사겠어요.

남: 꽃과 어울리는 꽃병은 어떠세요? 저희에게는 13달러에 살 수 있는 분홍색 꽃병이 있습니다. 저희는 또한 16달러에 빨간색 꽃병을 팔고 있어요.

여: 음… 좋아요, 저는 빨간색 꽃병 하나를 사겠어요. 여기 돈이요.

단·어·및·표·현

vase[veis] 명 꽃병

14 대화자관계추론 ▶ 정답 ②

듣·기·대·본

W: Welcome to Suzie's Garden. What can I do for you?

M: Hi. I want to buy some flowers for my mom.

W: How about this basket? It's filled with popular flowers.

M: Good. Do you make deliveries, too?

W: Of course. When do you want it?

M: Can you deliver it on May 8th?

W: Sure. The total will be 35 dollars.

M: Here you are.

우·리·말·해·석

여: Suzie의 정원에 오신 것을 환영합니다! 무엇을 도와드릴까요?

남: 안녕하세요. 저는 엄마를 위한 꽃을 좀 사고 싶어요.

여: 이 바구니는 어떠세요? 그것은 인기 있는 꽃들로 가득 차 있어요.

남: 좋네요. 배달도 해주시나요?

여: 물론이죠. 언제 그것을 원하시나요?

남: 당신은 그것을 5월 8일에 배달해주실 수 있나요?

여: 물론이죠. 총액은 35달러예요.

남: 여기 있어요.

단·어·및·표·현

basket[bǽskit] 명 바구니

be filled with ~ ~로 가득 차다

make a delivery 배달하다

total[tóutl] 명 총액, 총계, 합계

15 부탁(요청)한일파악 ▶ 정답 ①

듣·기·대·본

W: Dad, I'm leaving for the trip now.

M: All right. Did you change your train ticket like you planned?

W: Yes, I changed it to 10 a.m.

M: Good. Then, is everything ready?

W: I guess so. Would you do me a favor?

M: Of course. What is it?

W: Could you book a taxi for me?

M: No problem. I'll take care of it right away.

우·리·말·해·석

여: 아빠, 저 이제 여행 떠나요.

남: 그래. 계획했던 대로 기차표는 바꿨니?

여: 네, 오전 10시로 바꿨어요.

남: 잘했어. 그럼 모든 준비가 된 거니?

여: 그런 것 같아요. 부탁 하나 들어주실 수 있어요?

남: 물론이지. 뭔데?

여: 저를 위해 택시를 예약해 주실 수 있나요?

남: 문제없어. 지금 바로 처리할게.

단·어·및·표·현

do ~ a favor ~의 부탁을 들어주다

book[buk] 동 예약하다

take care of ~을 처리하다. ~을 돌보다

16 이유파악 ▶ 정답 ④

듣·기·대·본

M: Mom, I'm home.

W: Jeff, you're later than usual. Why are you sweating so much?

M: Oh, I walked here from school.

W: Why didn't you take a bus? Did you miss the bus?

M: No, I didn't.

W: Then, why did you walk home? Our home is quite far from your school.

M: I had to stop by the library to return some books on my way home.

W: I see. Next time, call me if you're going to be late.

우·리·말·해·석

남: 엄마, 저 집에 왔어요.

여: Jeff, 너는 평소보다 더 늦었구나. 넌 왜 그렇게 땀을 많이 흘리고 있니?

남: 아, 저는 학교에서부터 여기까지 걸어왔어요.

여: 너는 왜 버스를 타지 않았니? 버스를 놓쳤니?

남: 아뇨, 안 놓쳤어요.

여: 그러면, 왜 너는 집에 걸어왔니? 우리 집은 네 학교에서 꽤 멀잖아.

남: 저는 집에 오는 길에 책 몇 권을 반납하기 위해서 도서관에 잠시 들러야 했어요.

여: 그렇구나. 다음 번에는 늦을 예정이면 나에게 전화해.

단·어·및·표·현

than usual 평소보다

sweat[swet] 동 땀을 흘리다

miss [mis] 동 (탈것을) 놓치다
quite [kwait] 부 꽤, 상당히
stop by ~ ~에 잠시 들르다
on one's way home 집으로 오는 길에

17 그림상황에적절한대화찾기 ▶정답 ⑤

듣•기•대•본

① M: I've baked this cake for you.
　W: Thank you so much! It looks delicious.
② M: How may I help you?
　W: I'd like to buy an air conditioner.
③ M: This is not what I ordered.
　W: I'm sorry. I'll check your bill.
④ M: I'm so hot and tired.
　W: Then let's go to a café and have a drink.
⑤ M: Could you turn off the air conditioner?
　W: Sure. No problem.

우•리•말•해•석

① 남: 내가 너를 위해서 이 케이크를 만들었어.
　여: 정말 고마워! 맛있어 보여.
② 남: 무엇을 도와드릴까요?
　여: 에어컨을 한 대 사고 싶습니다.
③ 남: 이건 제가 주문한 게 아닙니다.
　여: 죄송합니다. 제가 고객님의 계산서를 확인해 보겠습니다.
④ 남: 나는 너무 덥고 피곤해.
　여: 그러면 카페에 가서 음료를 한 잔 마시자.
⑤ 남: 에어컨을 꺼 주실 수 있나요?
　여: 그럼요. 문제 되지 않아요.

단•어•및•표•현

air conditioner 에어컨
bill [bil] 명 계산서, 청구서
have a drink (음료 등을) 한 잔 마시다
turn off (전원을) 끄다

18 담화미언급 ▶정답 ④

듣•기•대•본

W: Hello, class. Before you leave for home, I want to give you some important information about Sports Day tomorrow. You should come to the Central Field by 9:30 a.m. The events will start at 10 a.m., and will be finished around 4 p.m. You don't have to bring your lunch. Hamburgers will be provided. According to the weather forecast, tomorrow will be very hot, so bring your hat and cold water. See you tomorrow.

우•리•말•해•석

여: 안녕하세요, 학생 여러분. 여러분이 귀가하기 전에, 내일 운동회에 대한 몇 가지 중요한 정보를 전달하고 싶어요. 여러분은 오전 9시 30분까지 Central Field로 와야 합니다. 행사는 오전 10시에 시작할 것이고, 오후 4시쯤에 끝날 것입니다. 여러분은 점심을 가져올 필요가 없습니다. 햄버거가 제공될 예정입니다. 일기예보에 따르면, 내일은 매우 더울 것이니 모자와 차가운 물을 가져오세요. 내일 봐요.

단•어•및•표•현

leave for ~ ~로 떠나다
according to ~ ~에 따르면

19 알맞은응답찾기 ▶정답 ④

듣•기•대•본

M: Hi, Selena. Science Day is this Friday.

W: Hi, Nick. Did you decide which contest you are going to enter on Friday?
M: Not yet. There is a drawing contest and a writing contest, right?
W: Yes. How about entering the drawing contest with me?
M: Hmm… What do I need to do for the drawing contest?
W: You need to draw a picture about a science principle and provide an explanation for it.
M: I can do that. Is there anything I should bring to the contest?
W: You need your paints.

우•리•말•해•석

① 나는 과학책 몇 권을 반납해야 해.
② 나는 3시에 그 선생님을 만나야 해.
③ 과학실로 가 봐.
④ 너는 네 물감이 필요해.
⑤ 포스터를 만들자.

남: 안녕, Selena. 과학의 날이 이번 주 금요일이야.
여: 안녕, Nick. 너는 금요일에 어느 대회에 참가할 건지 결정했니?
남: 아직 안 했어. 그림 그리기 대회와 글쓰기 대회가 있지, 맞지?
여: 응. 나랑 같이 그림 그리기 대회에 참가하는 게 어때?
남: 흠… 그림 그리기 대회를 위해서 내가 무엇을 해야 하니?
여: 너는 한 가지 과학 법칙에 대해 그림을 그리고 그것에 대해 설명해야 해.
남: 그건 할 수 있지. 내가 대회에 가져가야 하는 무언가가 있니?
여: 너는 네 물감이 필요해.

단•어•및•표•현

decide [disáid] 동 결정하다, 결심하다
enter [éntər] 동 (대회 등에) 참가하다, 출전하다
principle [prínsəpl] 명 (물리·자연의) 법칙
provide an explanation 설명하다

20 알맞은응답찾기 ▶정답 ⑤

듣•기•대•본

W: Hey, Drake! You play the game Underclock, right?
M: Yeah. Why? Do you play it?
W: Yes. I am a newbie that just started playing.
M: Oh, really? Did you know that they are making Underclock 2?
W: I didn't know that. Will it be different from the original?
M: Yes. I heard it will be more difficult to play than the first one.
W: I am already having trouble with the first one… I wish I were good at playing games.
M: Do you want to go to the PC room with me? I can teach you.
W: Yeah, I would love that!

우•리•말•해•석

① 게임을 하는 데에 시간제한을 걸어.
② 그건 팀 기반의 온라인 게임이야.
③ 나는 두 번째 것을 잘해.
④ 나는 PC방에 가본 적이 있어.
⑤ 응. 무척 그러고 싶어!

여: 야, Drake! 너 "Underclock" 게임을 하지, 그렇지?
남: 응. 왜? 너도 그걸 하니?
여: 응. 나는 갓 게임을 시작한 초보야.
남: 아, 정말? 너는 그들이 "Underclock 2"를 만들고 있다는 걸 알고 있었

니?
여: 그건 몰랐어. 그건 원작과 다를까?
남: 맞아. 첫 번째 것보다 게임을 하기가 더 어려울 거라고 들었어.
여: 나는 이미 첫 번째 것을 하는 데 어려움을 겪고 있는걸⋯ 내가 게임을 잘한다면 좋을 텐데.
남: 나와 함께 PC방에 갈래? 내가 가르쳐 줄게.
여: 응, 무척 그러고 싶어!

단·어·및·표·현

newbie[njúːbiː] ⑲ 초보자
be different from ~ ~와는 다르다
have trouble with ~ ~하는 데 어려움을 겪다
be good at -ing ~을 잘하다
would love ~ 무척 ~하고 싶다

Words & Expressions Review

1. 지불, 금액	2. 계산서, 청구서	3. 초대하다
4. ~하는 데 어려움을 겪다	5. 선호하다, 좋아하다	6. 망치다
7. (음료 등을) 한 잔 마시다	8. 구할[이용할] 수 있는	9. 빨리 ~하고 싶다, ~이 너무 기대된다
10. ~로 떠나다	11. ~에 잠시 들르다	12. 공연하다, 연주하다
13. 배달하다	14. (~로) 가는 길에	15. (물리·자연의) 법칙
16. ~에 따르면	17. 땀을 흘리다	18. 눈가리개
19. (차의 기름 탱크를) 가득 채우다	20. ~과 다르다	21. (제안) ~은 어때?
22. 대체로	23. ~으로 가득 차다	24. 알게 되다, 알아내다
25. 지금까지	26. 취소하다	27. 마감
28. 실험	29. 예상하다	30. 기온, 온도
31. 평소보다	32. 몇 개의, 두서너 개의	33. 이따가, 곧
34. 초보자	35. 무료로	36. 세부사항
37. ~을 살펴보다, 훑어보다	38. (탈것을) 놓치다	39. 명확하게, 분명히
40. (대회 등에) 참가하다, 출전하다	41. 지원, 신청	42. ~의 부탁을 들어주다
43. 옴짝달싹 못하다, 갇히다	44. ~에 등록하다	

Listening Test
영어듣기 모의고사 14회

|정|답|

01 ①	02 ④	03 ③	04 ③	05 ②
06 ②	07 ⑤	08 ①	09 ③	10 ④
11 ④	12 ⑤	13 ③	14 ④	15 ③
16 ⑤	17 ④	18 ⑤	19 ④	20 ②

01 날씨파악-그림 ▶정답 ①

듣·기·대·본

M: Here is the weather forecast for Seoul. Tonight will be wet and windy. However, the rain will stop before tomorrow morning. There will be clear and beautiful skies tomorrow. But the day after tomorrow, you should be careful when you go out. Yellow dust will come to Seoul with strong winds.

우·리·말·해·석

남: 서울의 일기예보입니다. 오늘 밤은 비가 오고 바람이 불겠습니다. 하지만 비는 내일 아침 전에 그칠 것입니다. 내일은 맑고 쾌청한 하늘이 될 것입니다. 그러나 내일모레에는 외출하실 때 조심하셔야 합니다. 서울에 강한 바람과 함께 황사가 있을 예정입니다.

단·어·및·표·현

yellow dust 황사

02 그림정보파악 ▶정답 ④

듣·기·대·본

W: How can I help you?
M: I'd like to buy a shirt to wear when I go for a run.
W: This T-shirt here is quite popular.
M: It's getting cold these days, so I'd like one with long sleeves.
W: Okay, what about this one which has stripes?
M: Well, I'd like something more simple.
W: Then how about this one which has a triangle on the chest?
M: That looks great! I'll take it.

우·리·말·해·석

여: 어떻게 도와드릴까요?
남: 저는 제가 달리기를 할 때 입을 셔츠를 사고 싶어요.
여: 여기에 있는 이 티셔츠는 꽤 인기 있어요.
남: 요즘 날씨가 추워져서 긴 소매가 좋겠어요.
여: 알겠어요, 줄무늬가 있는 이건 어떠세요?
남: 음, 저는 더 단순한 것이 좋아요.
여: 그러면 가슴에 삼각형이 있는 이건 어떠세요?
남: 좋아 보이네요! 저는 그걸 살게요.

단·어·및·표·현

go for a run (운동으로) 달리다
quite[kwait] ⑨ 꽤, 상당히
sleeve[sliːv] ⑲ 소매
stripe[straip] ⑲ 줄무늬

03 심정추론 ▶정답 ③

듣·기·대·본

W: Junha, why are you smiling?
M: Hi, Mina. I'm searching for information about Tokyo Disneyland.
W: Why? Are you planning to go there?
M: Yes! Guess what? I won a free flight there.
W: Really? How did you win it?
M: Well, I won the Japan Introduction Video Contest. I didn't even know I could do it.
W: You're amazing!

우·리·말·해·석

① 지루한 ② 무서워하는 ③ 신난 ④ 편안한 ⑤ 초조한

여: 준하야, 왜 웃고 있어?

남: 안녕, 미나. 나는 도쿄 디즈니랜드에 대한 정보를 검색하고 있어.

여: 왜? 너 거기에 갈 계획이야?

남: 응! 있잖아, 내가 거기 가는 공짜 항공편을 얻었어.

여: 정말? 그것을 어떻게 얻었어?

남: 그러니까, 내가 일본 소개 동영상 대회에서 우승했어. 나는 내가 우승할 줄은 정말 몰랐어.

여: 너 대단하다!

단·어·및·표·현
search for ~ ~을 검색하다
introduction [ìntrədʌ́kʃən] 몡 소개

04　한일파악　　　　　　　　　▶정답 ③

듣·기·대·본

W: Look, Dad. My classmates and I put together this newspaper.

M: It looks great! Was it a school project?

W: Yeah. Elly came up with the theme of Korean history.

M: Nice. Which article did you write?

W: I didn't write any.

M: Then, what did you do?

W: I drew the pictures. They help the reader understand the articles.

M: Oh, really? You drew them so well! I think you could be an artist someday.

우·리·말·해·석

여: 보세요, 아빠. 저희 반 친구들과 제가 이 신문을 만들었어요.

남: 그건 멋져 보이는구나! 그게 학교 과제였니?

여: 네. Elly가 한국사를 주제로 생각해 냈어요.

남: 좋구나. 넌 무슨 기사를 썼니?

여: 전 아무것도 쓰지 않았어요.

남: 그럼, 넌 무엇을 했니?

여: 전 삽화를 그렸어요. 그것들은 독자가 기사를 이해하는 것을 도와줘요.

남: 오, 정말? 그것들을 정말 잘 그렸구나! 난 네가 언젠가 예술가가 될 수도 있다고 생각한다.

단·어·및·표·현
put together (이것저것을 모아) 만들다
come up with ~을 생각해 내다, 제안하다
theme [θiːm] 몡 주제, 테마

05　대화장소추론　　　　　　　▶정답 ②

듣·기·대·본

M: Excuse me. Can you tell me where the books about space science are?

W: You can find them on the fourth floor.

M: Thank you. How many books can I check out?

W: Four at a time. You can keep them for five days. After that, you will be fined if you don't return the books on time.

M: How much is the fine?

W: 200 won a day per book.

우·리·말·해·석

남: 실례합니다. 우주 과학에 관한 책이 어디에 있는지 알려주시겠습니까?

여: 4층에서 찾으실 수 있습니다.

남: 감사합니다. 책은 몇 권을 대출할 수 있나요?

여: 한 번에 네 권이요. 책은 닷새 동안 가지고 계실 수 있어요. 그 후에는, 제시간에 반납하지 않으면 벌금을 물게 됩니다.

남: 벌금이 얼마인데요?

여: 한 권당 하루에 200원이요.

단·어·및·표·현
fine [fain] 통 벌금을 과하다 몡 벌금

06　마지막말의도파악　　　　　▶정답 ②

듣·기·대·본

M: Hey, Jane! You have a long face. What's wrong?

W: Hi, Mike. I was scolded by my mom because I didn't get a good grade.

M: Oh, I'm sorry to hear that. You can do better next time!

W: Thanks, Mike. I don't have any energy to take the classes.

M: Did you have lunch?

W: No, I have no appetite so I didn't eat anything.

M: No way! You should eat something! Let's grab some sandwiches.

W: Thank you, but I don't feel like eating right now.

우·리·말·해·석

남: 안녕, Jane! 우울해 보여. 뭐가 문제야?

여: 안녕, Mike. 좋은 성적을 받지 못해서 엄마에게 꾸중들었어.

남: 오, 그렇다니 안됐어. 너는 다음에 더 잘할 수 있어!

여: 고마워, Mike. 나는 수업을 들을 기운이 없어.

남: 점심 먹었어?

여: 아니, 식욕이 없어서 아무것도 먹지 않았어.

남: 안 돼! 너는 뭘 먹어야 해! 샌드위치 먹자.

여: 고맙지만 지금 당장은 먹고 싶지 않아.

단·어·및·표·현
long face 우울한 얼굴
appetite [ǽpətàit] 몡 식욕

07　특정정보파악　　　　　　　▶정답 ⑤

듣·기·대·본

M: Sarah, we should go camping over the holiday weekend.

W: I'm not sure. How about we relax at home or go to the movies instead?

M: I was hoping we could spend time outdoors and have a barbecue.

W: It's too hot outside and what if there are bugs?

M: Then what about going to the water park? It will be cool and there won't be bugs.

W: That does sound like a good idea. Let's go!

M: Good.

우·리·말·해·석

남: Sarah, 우리는 주말 연휴 동안 캠핑을 가야 해.

여: 잘 모르겠네. 우리는 대신 집에서 쉬거나 영화를 보러 가는 게 어때?

남: 나는 우리가 야외에서 시간을 보내고 바비큐를 할 수 있길 바랐어.

여: 밖은 너무 덥고 벌레가 있으면 어쩌지?

남: 그러면 워터파크에 가는 건 어때? 시원할 거고 벌레도 없을 거야.

여: 그건 정말 좋은 생각처럼 들려. 가자!

남: 좋아.

단·어·및·표·현
outdoors [àutdɔ́ːrz] 튀 야외에서, 야외로
What if ~? ~이면 어쩌지?

08　할일파악(대화직후)　　　　▶정답 ①

듣·기·대·본

M: Now, the party decorations are done. What shall I do next?

W: Thank you for being so helpful, Matt.

M: You're welcome. Do you want me to set the tables?

W: We can do that later. Why don't you take a break?

M: It's okay. I'm not tired.

W: Then could you pick up the birthday cake from the bakery?

M: No problem. I can go now.

우·리·말·해·석

남: 이제 파티 장식이 다 됐어. 난 그 다음에 무엇을 하면 돼?

여: 많은 도움을 줘서 고마워, Matt.

남: 아니 뭘. 이제 내가 식탁을 차릴까?

여: 우리는 그건 나중에 해도 돼. 너 잠시 휴식을 취하지 그래?

남: 괜찮아. 난 피곤하지 않아.

여: 그럼 빵집에서 생일 케이크를 좀 찾아 줄래?

남: 문제없어. 난 지금 갈 수 있어.

단·어·및·표·현

take a break 잠시 휴식을 취하다

09   대화미언급   ▶정답 ③

듣·기·대·본

M: Ms. Wilson, I want to join the Science Camp this year.

W: Sure. I think that's a good idea.

M: How long is the Science Camp?

W: It will be from August 8 to August 15.

M: Can anyone participate in the Science Camp?

W: Only second-year students can participate this year.

M: I see. What kind of activities are done at the camp?

W: You will do various science experiments.

M: That sounds fun. How much is the fee?

W: The total fee is 150 dollars.

우·리·말·해·석

남: Wilson 선생님, 저는 올해 과학 캠프에 참가하고 싶어요.

여: 그래! 좋은 생각인 것 같구나.

남: 과학 캠프는 기간이 얼마나 되나요?

여: 그것은 8월 8일부터 8월 15일까지란다.

남: 과학 캠프에 누구나 참가할 수 있어요?

여: 올해에는 2학년 학생들만 참가할 수 있어.

남: 알겠습니다. 캠프에서 어떤 종류의 활동들이 이루어지나요?

여: 넌 여러가지 과학 실험들을 할 거야.

남: 재미있을 것 같아요. 요금은 얼마죠?

여: 총 요금은 150달러야.

단·어·및·표·현

participate in ~에 참가하다

fee[fiː] ⑲ 요금, 가입비

10   담화화제추론   ▶정답 ④

듣·기·대·본

W: Good afternoon, students. I'm here to tell you about a new after-school program we are starting at our school. It's called the Reading Buddies Program. This program pairs older students with younger students to help improve their reading skills. This will be a great opportunity for everyone to learn and grow together. If you are interested, please sign up at the library by Friday.

우·리·말·해·석

여: 안녕하세요, 학생 여러분. 저는 우리 학교에서 시작하는 새로운 방과후 학교 프로그램에 대해 말씀드리기 위해 여기 있습니다. 그건 "독서 친구 프로그램"이라고 불립니다. 이 프로그램은 읽기 능력을 향상시키는 것을 돕기 위해 고학년 학생들과 저학년 학생들이 둘씩 짝을 짓습니다. 이것은 모두가 함께 배우고 성장할 수 있는 좋은 기회입니다. 만약 관심이 있다면, 금요일까지 도서관에 등록해주십시오.

단·어·및·표·현

buddy[bʌ́di] ⑲ 친구

pair[pɛər] ⑧ (둘씩) 짝을 짓다

improve[imprúːv] ⑧ 향상시키다, 개선하다

opportunity[ɑ̀pərtjúːnəti] ⑲ 기회

sign up 등록하다

11   대화내용불일치   ▶정답 ④

듣·기·대·본

M: Sandra, do you know Green Park Campground? It just opened last month.

W: Yes. I heard it's on a beautiful lake.

M: Right. My family and I went there last week. We enjoyed a barbeque.

W: Did you bring your dogs, too?

M: No. You can't bring pets there.

W: I see. Did you rent a tent?

M: Yes, there is no cost to rent a tent. They even have free wi-fi.

W: That's great.

우·리·말·해·석

남: Sandra, 너는 Green Park 캠핑장을 알아? 그건 지난달에 막 개장했어.

여: 응. 나는 그게 아름다운 호수에 있다고 들었어.

남: 맞아. 내 가족과 나는 지난주에 거기에 갔었어. 우리는 바비큐를 즐겼어.

여: 너는 네 개들도 데려갔어?

남: 아니. 너는 거기에 반려동물을 데려갈 수 없어.

여: 그렇구나. 너는 텐트를 빌렸어?

남: 응, 텐트를 빌리는 데 비용이 들지 않아. 그들은 심지어 무료 와이파이도 있어.

여: 그거 좋다.

단·어·및·표·현

campground[kǽmpgràund] ⑲ 캠핑장, 야영장

rent[rent] ⑧ 빌리다, 대여하다

cost[kɔ(ː)st] ⑲ 비용

free wi-fi 무료 와이파이

12   전화목적파악   ▶정답 ⑤

듣·기·대·본

(*Telephone rings.*)

M: Hello, Comet Clothing. How may I help you?

W: Hi, I ordered a jacket through your store last week, and I'm wondering when it will be in stock.

M: Sure, may I have your name, please?

W: Yes, it's Hannah Kim.

M: (*Typing sound*) I found your order. Your jacket should be in stock this Saturday.

W: Great! Then can I pick it up at the store that day?

M: Sure. We'll notify you as soon as it arrives.

W: Okay. Thank you.

우·리·말·해·석

(전화벨이 울린다.)

남: 여보세요, Comet 옷 가게입니다. 무엇을 도와드릴까요?

여: 안녕하세요, 저는 지난주에 당신의 가게를 통해 재킷 하나를 주문했는

데, 그것이 언제 입고될지 궁금합니다.

남: 네, 성함이 어떻게 되시나요?

여: 네, 김한나입니다.

남: (타자 소리) 저는 당신의 주문을 찾았습니다. 당신의 재킷은 이번 주 토요일에 입고될 것입니다.

여: 좋아요! 그러면 제가 그날 가게에서 그것을 찾을 수 있나요?

남: 네, 저희가 그것이 도착하는 대로 알려드리겠습니다.

여: 네, 감사합니다.

단·어·및·표·현

should [ʃəd] 图 (아마) ~일 것이다
pick ~ up (어디에서) ~을 찾다
notify [nóutəfài] 图 알리다
as soon as ~하자마자

13 수치계산(거스름돈)　　▶정답 ③

듣·기·대·본

W: Hi, welcome to Minute Mini Golf.

M: Hi, I would like to play one round of mini golf, please.

W: Sure, it's 9 dollars for a round of mini golf. Anything else?

M: I need to borrow two golf clubs as well.

W: Okay, it's 4 dollars per golf club.

M: Great, how much is that in total?

W: Your total comes to 17 dollars.

M: Okay, here's a 20-dollar bill.

W: Thank you. Here's your change.

우·리·말·해·석

여: 안녕하세요, Minute Mini Golf에 오신 것을 환영합니다.

남: 안녕하세요, 미니 골프 한 라운드를 치고 싶습니다.

여: 네, 미니 골프는 한 라운드당 9달러입니다. 그 밖에 필요한 게 있으신가요?

남: 저는 골프채 두 개도 빌려야 합니다.

여: 네, 골프채는 한 개당 4달러입니다.

남: 좋네요, 총 얼마인가요?

여: 총 17달러입니다.

남: 네, 여기 20달러짜리 지폐입니다.

여: 감사합니다. 여기 거스름돈입니다.

단·어·및·표·현

round [raund] 图 (골프 등에서) 라운드(코스 전체를 한 바퀴 도는 것)
golf club 골프채
as well ~도, 또한
come to (총계가) ~이 되다
change [tʃeindʒ] 图 거스름돈, 잔돈

14 대화자관계추론　　▶정답 ④

듣·기·대·본

M: Hello. Can I help you?

W: Hi. I live in apartment 305, and I think I have a problem.

M: What kind of problem?

W: I didn't get any hot water all morning.

M: Really? I'm so sorry. Is the problem in the kitchen or bathroom?

W: Both. Can you send someone to look into it?

M: Of course. I'll send up a repair person as soon as possible.

우·리·말·해·석

남: 안녕하세요. 제가 도와드릴까요?

여: 안녕하세요. 저는 아파트 305호에 살고 있는데, 문제가 있는 것 같아요.

남: 어떤 종류의 문제요?

여: 오전 내내 온수가 전혀 나오지 않았어요.

남: 정말요? 정말 죄송해요. 그 문제가 부엌에 있나요, 아니면 욕실에 있나요?

여: 둘 다요. 그것을 살펴봐줄 사람을 보내줄 수 있나요?

남: 물론이죠. 제가 되도록 빨리 수리공을 보내겠습니다.

단·어·및·표·현

all morning 오전 내내
look into ~ ~을 조사하다, 주의 깊게 살펴보다
repair person 수리공
as soon as possible 되도록 빨리

15 부탁(요청)한일파악　　▶정답 ③

듣·기·대·본

(Cellphone rings.)

M: Hello, Emma.

W: Hi, James. Remember our plan to go jogging in the park?

M: Yes, I've already put on my running shoes and stretched.

W: That's great. I'm on my way to the park near your house.

M: OK, I'll be there in a few minutes.

W: Perfect, but there's a minor problem. I forgot my sunglasses at home.

M: No worries, I'll bring an extra pair for you.

W: Thanks a lot, James. See you soon.

우·리·말·해·석

(휴대전화가 울린다.)

남: 여보세요, Emma.

여: 안녕, James. 공원에 조깅하러 가기로 한 우리의 계획 기억해?

남: 응, 난 이미 운동화를 신었고 스트레칭을 했어.

여: 좋은걸. 나는 너네 집 근처에 있는 공원으로 가는 길이야.

남: 알겠어, 나는 몇 분 안에 그곳에 도착할 거야.

여: 완벽해, 하지만 작은 문제가 하나 있어. 나는 집에서 내 선글라스를 (챙기는 것을) 잊었어.

남: 걱정 마, 내가 널 위해 여분의 것을 가져갈게.

여: 너무 고마워, James. 곧 보자.

단·어·및·표·현

go jogging 조깅하러 가다
put on ~을 신다
running shoes 운동화
stretch [stretʃ] 图 스트레칭하다
on one's way to ~로 가는 길[도중]에
in a few minutes 몇 분 안에, 곧
minor [máinər] 图 작은, 가벼운

16 이유파악　　▶정답 ⑤

듣·기·대·본

(Telephone rings.)

W: Hello. Coach Roberts? It's me, Jane.

M: Hello, Jane. How are you?

W: I am all right. But my brother has a bad cold and my mom is very busy. So, I'll have to take him to the doctor.

M: I am sorry to hear that. So, you can't come to the training session this afternoon, can you?

W: No, I am afraid I can't.

우·리·말·해·석

(전화벨이 울린다.)

여: 여보세요. Roberts 코치님? 저예요, Jane이에요.

남: 안녕, Jane. 잘 지내니?

여: 저는 잘 있어요. 그런데 동생이 독감에 걸렸는데 엄마는 매우 바쁘세요. 그래서 제가 동생을 의사 선생님께 데리고 가야 할 것 같아요.

남: 그런 말을 듣게 되어 유감스럽구나. 그러면 오늘 오후 연습 시간에는 못 오겠네, 그렇지?

여: 네, 죄송하지만 못 가겠어요.

단·어·및·표·현
bad cold 독감

17 그림상황에적절한대화찾기 ▶정답 ④

듣·기·대·본

① W: Do you want to go grocery shopping with me?
　　M: Okay! Let's go to the hardware store afterwards.
② W: Do you like eating cereal?
　　M: Not really. I prefer pancakes over cereal.
③ W: Remind me to buy some cereal later.
　　M: Okay, I will try not to forget.
④ W: Excuse me, where can I find the cereal?
　　M: Oh, that would be in aisle number 5.
⑤ W: Do you want to eat steak for dinner?
　　M: Of course! I will never say no to steak!

우·리·말·해·석

① 여: 너는 나랑 장 보러 가고 싶니?
　　남: 응! 그 후에 철물점에 가자.
② 여: 너는 시리얼 먹는 것을 좋아해?
　　남: 별로. 나는 시리얼보다 팬케이크를 더 좋아해.
③ 여: 나에게 나중에 시리얼을 좀 사라고 상기시켜줘.
　　남: 알겠어, 잊지 않도록 노력할게.
④ 여: 실례합니다, 제가 시리얼을 어디서 찾을 수 있나요?
　　남: 아, 그것은 5번 통로에 있을 거예요.
⑤ 여: 너는 저녁으로 스테이크를 먹고 싶어?
　　남: 물론이지! 나는 절대 스테이크를 거절하지 않을 거야!

단·어·및·표·현
go grocery shopping 장 보러 가다
hardware store 철물점
prefer A over B A를 B보다 더 좋아하다
remind A to + 동사 A에게 ~할 것을 상기시키다, 생각나게 하다
aisle[ail] 명 통로
say no to ~ (제안, 제의 등) ~을 거절하다, 거부하다

18 담화미언급 ▶정답 ⑤

듣·기·대·본

W: Hello, students. Our school field trip is tomorrow. As you know, we will visit Newton Science Center. We will use our school buses for the trip. The buses will leave at 9 a.m., so I expect you to be here by 8:30. You don't need to bring your lunch, but please don't forget to bring your parent approval slip. See you tomorrow, then!

우·리·말·해·석

여: 안녕하세요, 학생 여러분. 우리의 학교 현장 학습이 내일입니다. 아시다시피, 우리는 Newton 과학 센터를 방문할 것입니다. 우리는 여행을 위해 학교 버스를 이용할 것입니다. 버스들은 오전 9시에 떠날 것이기 때문에 여러분들이 8시 30분까지 여기로 오시길 바랍니다. 여러분은 점심 식사를 가져올 필요가 없지만, 여러분들의 부모님의 승인 쪽지를 가져오는 것을 잊지 마세요. 그러면, 내일 봅시다!

단·어·및·표·현
approval[əprúːvəl] 명 승인
slip[slip] 명 쪽지

19 알맞은응답찾기 ▶정답 ④

듣·기·대·본

W: Henry, what are you searching on the Internet?
M: I'm looking for information on the use of plastic, Mom.
W: Is it for homework?
M: Yes. I need to find ways to reduce the use of plastic.
W: Right. How about bringing a food container from home when taking out food from a restaurant?
M: Yes. I've discovered that's one of the ways to avoid using plastic.
W: What other things can we do?
M: We can bring our own shopping bags.

우·리·말·해·석

① 이 식당은 어때요?
② 플라스틱이 더 싸고 가벼워요.
③ 죄송해요. 저는 제 숙제를 해야 해요.
④ 우리는 우리의 쇼핑백을 가져갈 수 있어요.
⑤ 플라스틱은 환경에 좋지 않아요.

여: Henry, 너 인터넷으로 무엇을 검색하고 있니?
남: 저는 플라스틱의 사용에 대한 정보를 찾고 있어요, 엄마.
여: 숙제를 위한 것이니?
남: 네. 저는 플라스틱 사용을 줄이는 방법을 찾아야 해요.
여: 그렇구나. 식당에서 음식을 포장해 올 때 집에서 음식 용기를 가져가는 건 어떠니?
남: 네. 저는 그것이 플라스틱 사용을 피하는 방법 중 하나라는 것을 알아냈어요.
여: 우리가 할 수 있는 다른 게 무엇이 있을까?
남: 우리는 우리의 쇼핑백을 가져갈 수 있어요.

단·어·및·표·현
reduce[ridjúːs] 동 (규모 · 크기 · 양 등을) 줄이다, 축소하다
container[kəntéinər] 명 용기, 그릇
discover[diskʌ́vər] 동 알아내다, 찾다
avoid[əvɔ́id] 동 피하다, 방지하다

20 알맞은응답찾기 ▶정답 ②

듣·기·대·본

W: Oh, the printer is out of ink.
M: Let's replace the empty cartridge with a new one.
W: Isn't that difficult? Do you know how to do it?
M: It's a piece of cake. Open the cover and pull the cartridge out.
W: All right, and then?
M: Remove the protective strip from the new cartridge and insert it.
W: All done. What next?
M: Let's print a test page.

우·리·말·해·석

① 그것은 노란 버튼이야.
② 테스트 페이지를 인쇄하자.
③ 우리는 종이를 다 써버렸어.
④ 우리는 기술자를 불러야 해.
⑤ 프린터는 옆 방에 있어.

여: 이런, 프린터 잉크가 다 떨어졌어.
남: 빈 카트리지를 새것으로 교체하자.
여: 그것은 어렵지 않니? 너는 그것을 하는 방법을 알고 있니?
남: 식은 죽 먹기야. 덮개를 열고 카트리지를 당겨서 꺼내.

여: 그렇구나, 그러고 나서?

남: 새로운 카트리지의 보호용 테이프를 제거하고 그것을 끼우면 돼.

여: 다 했어. 다음은 뭘 하지?

남: **테스트 페이지를 인쇄하자.**

단·어·및·표·현

be out of ~이 다 떨어지다, ~를 다 써서 없다

replace [ripléis] ⑧ 교체하다, 대신하다

cartridge [káːrtridʒ] ⑲ 카트리지(프린터의 잉크 용기)

a piece of cake 식은 죽 먹기

protective strip (새 제품에 부착되어 있는) 보호용 테이프

use up 다 써버리다

call in 부르다, 전화하다

Words & Expressions Review

1. 대단한, 놀라운	2. 식욕	3. 기회
4. 내일모레	5. 식탁을 차리다	6. 승인
7. (어디에서) ~을 찾다	8. 친구	9. 알리다
10. ~을 검색하다	11. ~이 다 떨어지다, ~을 다 써서 없다	12. (이것저것을 모아) 만들다
13. 벌금을 과하다, 벌금	14. ~하자마자	15. (도서관 등에서) 대출하다
16. 수리공	17. 반납하다	18. (총계가) ~이 되다
19. 황사	20. 통로	21. 잠시 휴식을 취하다
22. 비용	23. ~에 참가하다	24. 소개
25. 다 써버리다	26. 인기 있는	27. 캠핑장, 야영장
28. 주제, 테마	29. 일기 예보	30. 알아내다, 찾다
31. ~을 조사하다, 주의 깊게 살펴보다	32. ~이면 어쩌지?	33. 야외에서, 야외로
34. ~하게 되어 유감이다	35. 꾸짖다	36. 꽤, 상당히
37. 용기, 그릇	38. 철물점	39. 빌리다, 대여하다
40. ~을 생각해 내다, 제안하다	41. 시간, 기간	42. 요금, 가입비
43. 쪽지	44. 작은, 가벼운	

Listening Test

영어듣기 모의고사 15회

|정|답|

01 ②	02 ③	03 ①	04 ②	05 ④
06 ④	07 ③	08 ⑤	09 ⑤	10 ③
11 ⑤	12 ④	13 ②	14 ①	15 ②
16 ⑤	17 ⑤	18 ⑤	19 ⑤	20 ④

01   날씨파악-그림   ▶정답 ②

듣·기·대·본

M: It's time for the weather forecast. Tomorrow, Seoul will have its <u>first snow of the season</u>. Daejeon will be rainy. In Gangneung, there will be a lot of snow <u>along with</u> strong winds, so when you drive, be extra cautious. And in Daegu, it will be clear and sunny, but it will be cold, so <u>dress warmly.</u>

우·리·말·해·석

남: 일기예보 시간입니다. 내일, 서울에 첫눈이 내리겠습니다. 대전은 비가 내릴 것입니다. 강릉에는 강한 바람과 함께 많은 눈이 내릴 것이니, 운전할 때 각별히 조심하셔야겠습니다. 그리고 대구는 맑고 화창하겠지만 추울 것으로 예상되니 따뜻하게 입으시기 바랍니다.

단·어·및·표·현

along with ~와 함께

extra [ékstrə] ⑨ 각별히, 특별히

cautious [kɔ́ːʃəs] ⑩ 조심스러운, 신중한

dress [dres] ⑧ 옷을 입다

02   그림정보파악   ▶정답 ③

듣·기·대·본

M: May I help you?

W: Yes, I'd like to buy a cake.

M: Sure. What do you have <u>in mind</u>?

W: I'd like one with flowers <u>on top</u>. But, I don't want any writing on it.

M: Then, <u>how about</u> this heart-shaped cake? It's very <u>popular</u> these days.

W: It's nice. I'll take it.

우·리·말·해·석

남: 도와드릴까요?

여: 네, 케이크를 하나 사고 싶어요.

남: 그러시군요. 어떤 걸 마음에 두고 계시죠?

여: 위에 꽃이 있는 걸 원해요. 하지만 위에 아무 글씨도 없는 걸 원해요.

남: 그렇다면, 이 하트 모양 케이크는 어떠세요? 요새 아주 인기 있어요.

여: 좋네요. 이걸로 살게요.

단·어·및·표·현

-shaped ~ 모양의

03   심정추론   ▶정답 ①

듣·기·대·본

M: Bad news, Ava. Dad can't take us to the beach. He has to work.

W: I heard. Well, it <u>can't be helped</u>.

M: But you really wanted to go there this weekend.

W: I did. But you and I can't go <u>on our own</u>, can we?

M: True. <u>You seem pretty relaxed about this.</u>

W: <u>Why not?</u> There's always another day.

M: All right. If you say so.

우·리·말·해·석

① 평온한   ② 속상한   ③ 신난   ④ 감사하는   ⑤ 실망한

남: 나쁜 소식이야, Ava. 아빠가 우리를 해변에 데려다 줄 수 없어. 일을 하셔야 한대.

여: 나도 들었어. 글쎄, 어쩔 수 없지.

남: 하지만 너는 이번 주말에 거기에 정말 가고 싶어 했잖아.

여: 그랬지. 하지만 너와 내가 단독으로 갈 수는 없잖아, 그렇지?

남: 맞아. 너는 이것에 대해 꽤 진정되어 보인다.

여: 왜 아니겠어? 항상 다른 날이 있는걸.

남: 좋아. 네가 그렇게 말한다면야.

단·어·및·표·현

It can't be helped. 어쩔 수 없다.

on our own 단독으로, 우리끼리

seem [siːm] ⑧ ~처럼 보이다
pretty [príti] ⑨ 꽤, 상당히
relaxed [rilǽkst] ⑱ 진정된, 평온한

04 한일파악 ▶정답 ②

듣•기•대•본

M: Jasmine, I've brought some apples for you.
W: Oh, thanks. Where did you get them?
M: <u>I went to my grandparents' farm yesterday</u> and <u>picked them myself</u>.
W: Wow! That's cool!
M: It was hard <u>at first</u>, but I had so much fun.
W: That sounds very exciting.
M: It's not <u>far from here</u>. Why don't you join me next weekend?
W: Great! I'd love to go there and try it.

우•리•말•해•석

남: Jasmine, 나는 너를 위해 사과를 좀 가져왔어.
여: 아, 고마워. 너는 그것들을 어디에서 얻었니?
남: 나는 어제 내 조부모님 댁의 농장에 가서 직접 그것들을 땄어.
여: 우와! 그거 멋진데!
남: 처음에는 어려웠지만 엄청 재미있었어.
여: 그거 아주 신나게 들린다.
남: 여기에서 멀지 않아. 다음 주말에 너도 나와 함께 하는 게 어때?
여: 좋아! 나는 그곳에 가서 그것(사과 따는 것)을 해보고 싶어.

단•어•및•표•현

pick [pik] ⑧ (과일 등을) 따다
at first 처음에는

05 대화장소추론 ▶정답 ④

듣•기•대•본

M: Hello. How may I help you?
W: <u>I'd like to send this package to Korea.</u>
M: OK. Can you put it here, please?
W: Sure. I'd like to send it <u>by air mail</u>.
M: OK. Then it will be 17 dollars. <u>What's in</u> the package?
W: Some toys for my cousins in Korea.
M: I see.

우•리•말•해•석

남: 안녕하세요. 어떻게 도와드릴까요?
여: 이 소포를 한국에 보내고 싶어요.
남: 알겠습니다. 그것을 여기에 놓으시겠어요?
여: 네. 이걸 항공 우편으로 보내고 싶어요.
남: 알겠습니다. 그러면 17달러가 될 겁니다. 소포에는 무엇이 들었죠?
여: 한국에 있는 제 사촌들을 위한 몇 개의 장난감이요.
남: 그렇군요.

단•어•및•표•현

air mail 항공 우편

06 마지막말의도파악 ▶정답 ④

듣•기•대•본

M: Mom, I have something to tell you. Please don't <u>get mad at</u> me.
W: What happened, my dear? Why do you look so worried?
M: I was watching TV and I <u>accidentally spilled</u> grape juice on the new carpet.
W: Oh no! That carpet was a gift from your aunt!

M: I know, Mom. I'm really sorry.
W: <u>It's all right.</u> I'm glad you told me. Just be more careful next time.

우•리•말•해•석

남: 엄마, 저 엄마께 드릴 말씀이 있어요. 부디 제게 화내지 마세요.
여: 무슨 일이니, 얘야? 너 왜 그렇게 걱정스러워 보이니?
남: 저는 TV를 보고 있었는데 실수로 새 카펫에 포도 주스를 엎질렀어요.
여: 오, 이런! 그 카펫은 너의 고모가 준 선물인데!
남: 저도 알아요, 엄마. 정말 죄송해요.
여: 괜찮다. 네가 말해 주어 나는 기쁘구나. 다음번에는 좀 더 조심하렴.

단•어•및•표•현

get mad at ~ ~에게 화내다
accidentally [æ̀ksidéntəli] ⑨ 실수로, 우연히
spill [spil] ⑧ 엎지르다, 쏟다

07 특정정보파악 ▶정답 ③

듣•기•대•본

M: Jimin, your jeans <u>look a little tight</u> on you.
W: You're right, Dad. Maybe I should put them in the recycling bin.
M: Can't you get them <u>altered</u>?
W: I think it's better to just buy a new pair. These ones are too old.
M: Well, why don't I make something out of them?
W: Great! What can you make?
M: Hmm…You already have many bags. So, <u>I'll make you a skirt</u>.
W: That's fantastic!

우•리•말•해•석

남: 지민아, 네 청바지가 너에게 좀 꽉 껴 보인다.
여: 맞아요, 아빠. 아마 저는 그것을 재활용함에 넣어야 할 것 같아요.
남: 그것을 수선하면 되지 않을까?
여: 그냥 새 것을 사는 게 더 나을 것 같아요. 이것은 너무 낡았어요.
남: 음, 내가 그것으로 뭔가 만들어 보는 건 어떨까?
여: 좋네요! 아빤 뭘 만드실 수 있어요?
남: 음… 너는 이미 가방이 많이 있지. 그러니, 내가 너에게 치마를 만들어 줄게.
여: 너무 좋아요!

단•어•및•표•현

tight [tait] ⑱ (옷이 몸에) 꽉 끼는, 딱 붙는
recycling bin 재활용함
alter [ɔ́ːltər] ⑧ (옷을) 고치다
out of (수단 · 재료) ~로, ~에 의해

08 할일파악(대화직후) ▶정답 ⑤

듣•기•대•본

W: Phew, that gym class was <u>exhausting</u>!
M: Tell me about it, Emma. I'm ready to relax.
W: What do you want to do after school, Jack?
M: Let's go to the basketball court and <u>shoot some hoops</u>.
W: It's a bit far. How about we play some board games in the cafeteria instead?
M: Okay. Then, how about we invite Sarah and Matt <u>to join us</u>?
W: That sounds like fun! <u>Let's go ask them now.</u>

우•리•말•해•석

여: 휴, 그 체육 수업은 진을 빼게 했어!
남: 내 말이, Emma. 나는 쉴 준비가 됐어.

15
회
모
의
고
사

여: 너는 방과 후에 무엇을 하고 싶어, Jack?
남: 우리 농구장에 가서 농구공을 좀 던져 넣자(농구하자).
여: 좀 먼데. 우리 대신 식당에서 보드게임을 좀 하는 건 어때?
남: 그래. 그러면, 우리 Sarah와 Matt도 함께 하자고 초대하는 건 어때?
여: 재밌겠는걸! 지금 그들에게 가서 물어보자.

단·어·및·표·현
gym class 체육 수업
exhausting [igzɔ́:stiŋ] ⑱ 진을 빼는, 기진맥진하는
Tell me about it. 내 말이 (그 말이야).
be ready to + 동사 ~할 준비가 되다
relax [rilǽks] ⑧ 쉬다, 휴식을 취하다
court [kɔːrt] ⑲ (테니스 등의) 코트, 경기장
shoot some hoops 농구하다
instead [instéd] ⑨ 대신에

09 대화미언급 ▶정답 ⑤

듣·기·대·본
W: Peter, what are you watching on your laptop?
M: I'm watching a documentary. It's narrated by my favorite actor, Ben Parker.
W: Oh, I love his voice. It's perfect for narrating documentaries. What's the title?
M: The title is *The World's Deadliest Spiders*.
W: Ah, let me guess. The documentary is about venomous spiders, isn't it?
M: You're right. Spiders are fascinating creatures.
W: That sounds like a nature documentary.
M: Yes, it is. Actually, nature documentaries are my favorite.

우·리·말·해·석
여: Peter, 너는 네 노트북으로 뭘 보고 있어?
남: 나는 다큐멘터리를 보고 있어. 내가 가장 좋아하는 배우인 Ben Parker가 내레이션을 했어.
여: 아, 나는 그의 목소리를 정말 좋아해. 그것(그의 목소리)은 다큐멘터리를 내레이션하기에 완벽해. 제목이 뭐야?
남: 제목은 '세상에서 가장 치명적인 거미들'이야.
여: 아, 맞춰볼게. 그 다큐멘터리는 독거미에 대한 거구나, 그렇지 않니?
남: 맞아. 거미는 매력적인 생명체야.
여: 자연 다큐멘터리처럼 들린다.
남: 응, 맞아. 사실, 자연 다큐멘터리는 내가 가장 좋아하는 것이야.

단·어·및·표·현
narrate [nǽreit] ⑧ 내레이션을 하다
deadly [dédli] ⑱ 치명적인, 생명을 앗아가는
venomous [vénəməs] ⑱ 독이 있는
creature [krí:tʃər] ⑲ 생물, 동물

10 담화화제추론 ▶정답 ③

듣·기·대·본
M: Hello, travelers. Today, I want to give you some tips on using translation apps during your trip abroad. First, download the app and check if it works without the Internet. Second, try speaking into the app so it can translate your voice. Third, save some useful sentences before your trip. That way, you can find them quickly. These apps can really help you communicate in a foreign country.

우·리·말·해·석
남: 안녕하세요, 여행자 여러분. 오늘은 해외여행 중 통역 앱 사용에 관한

몇 가지 요령을 알려드리겠습니다. 첫째, 앱을 다운로드한 후 인터넷 없이도 작동하는지 확인하세요. 둘째, 그것(앱)이 여러분의 음성을 통역할 수 있도록 앱에 말을 한번 해보세요. 셋째, 여행 전에 유용한 문장 몇 개를 저장해 두세요. 그렇게 하면, 그것들을(유용한 문장들을) 빨리 찾을 수 있습니다. 이러한 앱들은 당신이 외국에서 의사소통하게 도울 수 있습니다.

단·어·및·표·현
traveler [trǽvələr] ⑲ 여행자
translation [trænsléiʃən] ⑲ 통역, 번역
abroad [əbrɔ́ːd] ⑨ 해외로
translate [trænsléit] ⑧ 통역[번역]하다
save [seiv] ⑧ 저장하다

11 대화내용불일치 ▶정답 ⑤

듣·기·대·본
M: Tiffany, have you been to the Mega Shopping Mall? It opened last Saturday.
W: Not yet. I heard it's now the biggest shopping mall in the city.
M: That's right. It only takes 10 minutes by subway to get there from our school.
W: Wow! It's near our school.
M: I heard that one of the major hot spots is Aquafield, a combination of a spa and waterpark.
W: Great! We should go check it out.
M: Sure. There's an opening event that offers a gift with purchases over $100 until next week.
W: That's great.

우·리·말·해·석
남: Tiffany, 너는 메가 쇼핑몰에 가봤니? 지난주 토요일에 개장했어.
여: 아직 안 가봤어. 그건 이 도시에서 현재 가장 큰 쇼핑몰이라고 들었어.
남: 맞아. 우리 학교에서 거기까지 가는 데 지하철로 10분밖에 걸리지 않아.
여: 우와! 우리 학교 근처에 있네.
남: 나는 주요 핫스팟 중 하나가 스파와 워터파크가 합쳐진 아쿠아필드라고 들었어.
여: 좋네! 우리는 가서 확인해 봐야 해.
남: 물론이지. 다음 주까지 100달러 이상 구매 시 사은품을 증정하는 개장 이벤트가 있어.
여: 좋다.

단·어·및·표·현
combination [kàmbənéiʃən] ⑲ 결합, 조합
check out ~을 확인하다, 조사하다
purchase [pɔ́ːrtʃəs] ⑲ 구매, 구입
over [óuvər] ⑳ (시간·비용 등이) ~ 이상의, ~이 넘는

12 전화목적파악 ▶정답 ④

듣·기·대·본
(*Telephone rings.*)
W: Hello. Noah's Restaurant.
M: Hi. I made a reservation for three people this Saturday. My name is Harry Wilson.
W: Let me see... Yes, I have your name here, sir. How may I help you?
M: I booked Dinner Course A. Can I change it to Course B?
W: Sure. So, Dinner Course B for three people, right?
M: That's right.
W: I've made the change. Is there anything else?

M: No, that's all. Thank you.

우·리·말·해·석

(전화벨이 울린다.)

여: 안녕하세요. Noah의 레스토랑입니다.

남: 안녕하세요. 저는 이번 주 토요일에 3명을 예약했습니다. 제 이름은 Harry Wilson입니다.

여: 확인해 볼게요… 네, 여기 당신의 이름이 있습니다. 고객님. 어떻게 도 와드릴까요?

남: 저는 저녁 코스 요리 A를 예약했습니다. 제가 코스 요리 B로 바꿀 수 있을까요?

여: 네. 그럼, 저녁 코스 요리 B 3명 맞으시죠?

남: 맞습니다.

여: 변경했습니다. 다른 게 있을까요?

남: 아니요, 그게 다예요. 감사합니다.

단·어·및·표·현

make a reservation 예약하다
book[buk] ⑧ 예약하다
make a change 변경하다, 수정하다
else[els] ⑨ 그 밖에, 달리

13 수치파악 ▶정답 ②

듣·기·대·본

M: I'm really looking forward to the movie premiere this Friday.

W: Me, too! It's at 6 p.m., isn't it?

M: Yes, how about we meet at 5 p.m.?

W: That's a bit early for me. What about 5:30 p.m.?

M: There's a red carpet event before the premiere. Wouldn't you like to see the celebrities?

W: Oh, absolutely! Let's meet at 5:15 p.m.

M: Sounds good. See you outside the theater!

우·리·말·해·석

남: 난 이번 주 금요일에 (있을) 영화 시사회가 정말 기대돼.

여: 나도! 오후 6시잖아, 그렇지 않아?

남: 응. 우리 오후 5시에 만나는 게 어때?

여: 그건 나에겐 좀 이르다. 오후 5시 30분은 어때?

남: 시사회 전에 레드카펫 행사가 있어. 너는 유명인들을 보고 싶지 않니?

여: 오, 물론이지(물론 보고 싶지)! 우리 오후 5시 15분에 만나자.

남: 좋아. 영화관 밖에서 보자!

단·어·및·표·현

look forward to ~을 기대하다. 고대하다
movie premiere 영화 시사회
a bit 조금, 약간, 다소
celebrity[səlébrəti] ⑨ 유명인, 유명인사
Absolutely. 물론이지. 그럼.

14 대화자관계추론 ▶정답 ①

듣·기·대·본

W: Hello, Mr. Kim. Thank you for coming.

M: No problem, Mrs. Han. So, how is my son doing?

W: He's doing great, especially in English, but he finds math a little difficult.

M: I see. How is he in your class?

W: He's very good. He likes history, and he's a great student.

M: That's good to hear. He also said that he likes your class very much.

W: Thank you. I'm glad to hear that.

우·리·말·해·석

여: 안녕하세요, 김 선생님. 와 주셔서 감사해요.

남: 천만에요, 한 선생님. 그래서, 제 아들은 어떤가요?

여: 그는 잘하고 있어요, 특히 영어를요. 하지만 그는 수학을 조금 어려워 해요.

남: 알겠습니다. 그가 선생님의 수업에서는 어떤가요?

여: 그는 아주 잘하고 있어요. 그는 역사를 좋아하고, 훌륭한 학생이에요.

남: 다행이네요. 그는 선생님의 수업을 아주 좋아한다고도 말했어요.

여: 감사합니다. 그 말을 들으니 기쁘네요.

단·어·및·표·현

find[faind] ⑧ ~라고 생각하다

15 부탁(요청)한일파악 ▶정답 ②

듣·기·대·본

W: Giho, can you turn off the TV? You have to do your homework.

M: Mom, this is my favorite soccer team. Can I watch a little longer?

W: OK. But you must do your homework later.

M: I promise. And I'll also do the dishes.

W: I've already done that. Can you take out the trash instead?

M: Of course. Come and watch, Mom.

W: OK. Oh, your favorite player is playing.

M: Yes! I'm so excited.

우·리·말·해·석

여: 기호야, TV 좀 꺼줄래? 너는 숙제를 해야 하잖아.

남: 엄마, 이건 제가 가장 좋아하는 축구팀이에요. 조금만 더 봐도 돼요?

여: 좋아. 하지만 나중에 숙제를 꼭 해야 해.

남: 약속할게요. 그리고 설거지도 할게요.

여: 그건 이미 내가 했어. 대신에 쓰레기를 좀 내다 버려 줄래?

남: 물론이죠. 와서 보세요, 엄마.

여: 그래. 오, 네가 가장 좋아하는 선수가 경기를 하고 있구나.

남: 네! 저는 너무 신나요.

단·어·및·표·현

do the dishes 설거지하다

16 이유파악 ▶정답 ⑤

듣·기·대·본

W: Dad, I'm going to Jenny's.

M: Jenny? Who is Jenny?

W: I've told you about her, Dad. She is my new friend.

M: Oh, I see. But it's almost 5 p.m. Why are you going to Jenny's now?

W: We have to do some research together for a science report.

M: Okay. Do you want me to give you a ride?

W: It's okay. I will just ride my bike.

M: Will it take long?

W: No, Dad. I'll be back before dinner.

우·리·말·해·석

여: 아빠, 저는 Jenny네 집에 갈 거예요.

남: Jenny? Jenny가 누구니?

여: 제가 그녀에 대해 말했잖아요, 아빠. 그녀는 제 새로운 친구예요.

남: 아, 그렇구나. 하지만 거의 오후 5시야. 너는 왜 지금 Jenny네 집에 가 는 거니?

여: 저희는 과학 보고서를 위해 같이 조사를 좀 해야 해요.

남: 알겠어. 너는 내가 너를 차로 태워주길 원하니?
여: 괜찮아요. 저는 그냥 제 자전거를 탈게요.
남: 오래 걸리니?
여: 아뇨, 아빠. 저는 저녁 식사 전에 돌아올 거예요.

단·어·및·표·현
do research 조사를 하다
give ~ a ride ~를 태워주다
take long (시간이) 오래 걸리다
be back 돌아오다

17 그림상황에적절한대화찾기 ▶정답 ⑤

듣·기·대·본

① M: Do you want some more cake?
  W: Yes, please. It's delicious.
② M: Place a seashell to your ear.
  W: It seems like I'm hearing the sea.
③ M: I'd like two tickets to Busan, please.
  W: Okay. That will be 20 dollars.
④ M: Would you help me carry these bags?
  W: Sure. No problem.
⑤ M: Isn't it peaceful here, honey?
  W: Yes, it is. I love the sound of the waves.

우·리·말·해·석

① 남: 당신은 케이크를 좀 더 먹고 싶나요?
  여: 네, 부탁해요. 맛있네요.
② 남: 당신의 귀에 조개껍데기를 갖다 대봐요.
  여: 내가 마치 바다 소리를 듣고 있는 것 같아요.
③ 남: 부산행 티켓 두 장 주세요.
  여: 네. 20달러입니다.
④ 남: 제가 이 가방들을 나르는 것을 도와주시겠어요?
  여: 물론이죠. 문제없어요.
⑤ 남: 여기는 평화롭지 않나요, 여보?
  여: 네, 맞아요. 저는 파도 소리를 정말 좋아해요.

단·어·및·표·현
carry [kǽri] ⑧ 나르다, 들고 있다
peaceful [píːsfəl] ⑩ 평화로운

18 담화미언급 ▶정답 ⑤

듣·기·대·본

W: Hello, everyone. Let me introduce myself to you. My name is Vicki Johnson. I live in London, England. Since childhood, I've always wanted to work in the field of fashion and beauty. So, I studied jewelry design at university. I'm a metal jewelry designer now. I design rings, earrings, and necklaces out of gold, silver, and bronze. Today, I'm going to tell you how to become a jewelry designer.

우·리·말·해·석

여: 안녕하세요, 여러분. 여러분께 제 소개를 하겠습니다. 제 이름은 Vicki Johnson입니다. 저는 영국 런던에 삽니다. 어린 시절부터 저는 늘 패션과 미용 분야에서 일하고 싶었습니다. 그래서, 저는 대학에서 보석 디자인을 공부했습니다. 저는 현재 금속 보석 디자이너입니다. 저는 금, 은, 그리고 동으로 반지, 귀걸이, 그리고 목걸이를 디자인합니다. 오늘, 저는 여러분들께 보석 디자이너가 되는 법을 말씀드리겠습니다.

단·어·및·표·현
childhood [tʃáildhùd] ⑩ 어린 시절
field [fiːld] ⑩ 분야
out of (재료·수단) ~으로, ~에 의해

19 알맞은응답찾기 ▶정답 ⑤

듣·기·대·본

M: Monica, we should decide where to do volunteer work.
W: I know. Have you found anything?
M: Look at this website for volunteer work at an animal shelter.
W: An animal shelter? What are we supposed to do there?
M: We help to feed the cats and dogs and clean up.
W: That's interesting. But we only have time on weekends. Are they open on Saturdays?
M: Let me check. (Pause) Yes, they are.
W: Wonderful. Let's start this weekend.

우·리·말·해·석

① 나는 개 두 마리를 입양하고 싶어.
② 우리는 자원 봉사자들이 좀 필요해.
③ 너는 지난 토요일에 뭐 했니?
④ 응. 나는 수의사가 되고 싶어.
⑤ 잘됐네. 이번 주말에 시작하자.

남: Monica, 우리는 어디서 자원봉사를 할지 결정해야 해.
여: 맞아. 너는 뭐 좀 찾았어?
남: 동물 보호소에서 자원 봉사를 하려면 이 웹사이트를 봐.
여: 동물 보호소? 우리는 거기서 뭘 해야 돼?
남: 우리는 고양이들과 개들에게 먹이를 주고, 치우는 것을 도와.
여: 흥미롭네. 하지만 우리는 주말에만 시간이 있잖아. 그들은 토요일에 열어?
남: 확인해볼게. (잠시 후) 응, 열어.
여: **잘됐네. 이번 주말에 시작하자.**

단·어·및·표·현
volunteer work 자원봉사
animal shelter 동물 보호소
be supposed to + 동사 ~해야 한다, ~할 의무가 있다
feed [fiːd] ⑧ 먹이를 주다
clean up ~을 치우다, 청소하다
adopt [ədápt] ⑧ 입양하다

20 알맞은응답찾기 ▶정답 ④

듣·기·대·본

W: I heard that there's going to be a fire drill at school today.
M: What's a fire drill?
W: It's when you practice getting out of the building in case a fire breaks out.
M: Oh, is that really necessary? I don't feel like running around.
W: It's to help prepare for an actual fire, so we should take it seriously.
M: Okay. When is the drill going to start?
W: I heard that it's going to start at 3 o'clock.

우·리·말·해·석

① 오늘 밤에 저녁으로 피자를 먹자.
② 내 꿈은 소방관이 되는 거야.
③ 나는 적어도 7시 정각까지 집에 도착해야 해.
④ 나는 그것이 3시 정각에 시작할 거라고 들었어.
⑤ 화재가 발생했을 때 너는 무엇을 해야 해?

여: 나는 오늘 학교에서 소방 훈련이 있을 거라고 들었어.
남: 소방 훈련이 뭐야?
여: 그것은 화재가 발생했을 때를 대비해서 네가 건물 밖으로 나가는 것을

연습하는 시간이야.

남: 오, 그것이 정말 필요해? 나는 이리저리 뛰어다니고 싶지 않아.

여: 그것은 실제 화재에 대비하는 것을 도와, 그래서 우리는 그것을 진지하게 받아들여야 해.

남: 알았어. 언제 훈련이 시작해?

여: 나는 그것이 3시 정각에 시작할 거라고 들었어.

단·어·및·표·현
drill [dril] 명 훈련
break out (화재·전쟁·전염병 등이) 발생하다

Words & Expressions Review

1. 소포	2. (과일 등을) 따다	3. 물론이지., 그럼.
4. ~처럼 보이다	5. 쓰레기	6. 각별히, 특별히
7. 조심스러운, 신중한	8. 해외로	9. 분야
10. 처음에는	11. 저장하다	12. 평화로운
13. 설거지하다	14. 어쩔 수 없다.	15. 내 말이 (그 말이야).
16. 독이 있는	17. 어린 시절	18. ~ 모양의
19. 발생하다	20. A를 마음에 두다	21. ~해야 한다, ~할 의무가 있다
22. ~을 확인하다, 조사하다	23. 내놓다, 꺼내다	24. (시간이) 오래 걸리다
25. 예약하다	26. 어려운	27. (옷을) 고치다
28. 훈련	29. 대신에	30. ~를 태워주다
31. 통역, 번역	32. 실제의	33. 치명적인, 생명을 앗아가는
34. (수단·재료) ~로, ~에 의해	35. 단독으로, 우리끼리	36. 입양하다
37. ~과 함께	38. 진을 빼는, 기진맥진하는	39. ~에게 화내다
40. 유명인, 유명인사	41. (행위 등을) 함께 하다	42. 항공 우편
43. 실수로, 우연히	44. 나르다, 들고 있다	

Listening Test
영어듣기 모의고사 16회

|정|답|

01 ④	02 ②	03 ④	04 ①	05 ②
06 ③	07 ③	08 ④	09 ④	10 ③
11 ⑤	12 ④	13 ④	14 ②	15 ⑤
16 ⑤	17 ④	18 ④	19 ①	20 ④

01 날씨파악-그림　▶정답 ④

듣·기·대·본
W: Good morning. Here's today's weather. Today will start off with thick clouds in the sky. Over time, the temperature will drop, and there will be snow in the afternoon. The snow is expected to last until midnight, and then the sky will clear up tomorrow morning. So, if you are out this afternoon, you'll have to watch out for snow on the roads.

우·리·말·해·석
여: 좋은 아침입니다. 오늘의 날씨입니다. 오늘은 하늘에 두꺼운 구름이 끼면서 시작하겠습니다. 시간이 지나면서, 기온은 떨어지고, 오후에는 눈이 올 것입니다. 눈은 자정까지 지속될 것으로 예상되며, 하늘은 내일 아침에 맑아지겠습니다. 그러니, 만약 오늘 오후에 밖에 계신다면 도로 위 눈을 조심하셔야겠습니다.

단·어·및·표·현
start off (~하는 것으로) 시작하다
over time 시간이 지나면서
last [læst] 동 (특정한 시간 동안) 지속되다
watch out for ~을 조심하다

02 그림정보파악　▶정답 ②

듣·기·대·본
W: Excuse me, I'm looking for a coaster.
M: Oh, they're here. These are the popular ones.
W: They're all cute. I don't know which one to choose.
M: How about the one with a whale?
W: Well, I prefer pandas more than whales.
M: Okay. There are two coasters with a panda. Which one do you like more?
W: I like the round coaster. I'll take that one.

우·리·말·해·석
여: 실례합니다, 저는 컵받침을 찾고 있어요.
남: 오, 그것들은 여기 있어요. 이것들이 인기 있는 것들이에요.
여: 그것들은 모두 귀엽네요. 저는 어떤 것을 골라야 할지 모르겠어요.
남: 고래가 있는 것은 어떠세요?
여: 음, 저는 고래보다는 판다를 더 선호해요.
남: 알겠습니다. 판다가 그려진 컵받침은 두 개가 있어요. 어떤 것이 더 좋으세요?
여: 저는 둥근 컵받침이 더 좋아요. 저걸로 살게요.

단·어·및·표·현
coaster [kóustər] 명 컵받침
prefer [prifə́:r] 동 ~을 더 선호하다, 좋아하다

03 심정추론　▶정답 ④

듣·기·대·본
W: You look happy, Andy. What's up?
M: I'm going to go *sea walking next week. I can't wait!
W: Sea walking? But you can't even swim, can you?
M: No, but it doesn't matter. I'll wear a special air helmet.
W: Are you sure it will be safe?
M: Of course! Just imagine walking around at the bottom of the sea!
W: But that sounds pretty dangerous to me.
M: I'll be fine. There will be lifeguards around, too.
W: OK, just make sure you remember all the safety rules and follow them.

*sea walking: 산소 공급 호스가 달린 헬멧을 쓰고 바닷속을 걷는 여가 활동

우·리·말·해·석
① 자랑스러운　　② 신난　　③ 부러워하는
④ 걱정하는　　⑤ 실망한

여: 너 행복해 보여, Andy. 무슨 일이야?
남: 나 다음 주에 바닷속 걷기를 하러 갈 거야. 무척 기다려져!
여: 바닷속 걷기? 하지만 너는 수영조차도 못 하잖아, 그렇지 않아?
남: 응, 하지만 문제없어. 나는 특수한 공기 헬멧을 쓸 거야.
여: 그것이 안전할 거라고 확신해?

남: 물론이지! 바다 바닥에서 이리 저리 걷는 것을 상상해봐!
여: 하지만 그것은 꽤 위험하게 들리는데.
남: 나는 괜찮을 거야. 주위에 안전 요원들도 있을 거야.
여: 그래. 꼭 모든 안전 규칙을 기억하고 따르도록 해.

단·어·및·표·현
What's up? 안녕?, 무슨 일이야?
lifeguard [láifgɑ̀ːrd] 명 안전 요원

04 한일파악 ▶ 정답 ①

듣·기·대·본
W: Do you want to go to the movies?
M: I can't. I have to save money.
W: Why?
M: I want to buy a bicycle. And I promised my dad I would pay for half of it.
W: That's nice of you! It'll take some time to save that much money, though.
M: So, I started a part-time job last weekend.
W: Maybe I should look for a job, too. I want a new backpack, but I don't want to ask my parents for money.

우·리·말·해·석
여: 영화 보러 갈래?
남: 난 갈 수 없어. 난 돈을 저축해야 해.
여: 왜?
남: 난 자전거를 사고 싶어. 그리고 그것의 절반을 내가 지불하겠다고 아빠와 약속했어.
여: 너 멋지다! 하지만 그렇게 많은 돈을 저축하려면 시간이 좀 걸릴 거야.
남: 그래서, 난 지난 주말에 아르바이트를 시작했어.
여: 어쩌면 나도 일자리를 찾아야 할 것 같아. 난 새 배낭을 원하지만 부모님께 돈을 달라고 요구하고 싶지 않아.

단·어·및·표·현
save [seiv] 동 저축하다, 절약하다
pay for ~의 값을 지불하다
though [ðou] 부 하지만, 그렇지만
look for ~을 찾다
ask A for B A에게 B를 요구하다

05 대화장소추론 ▶ 정답 ②

듣·기·대·본
M: Hey, Maggie. Glad to see you here.
W: Hi, Jim. Where are you going?
M: I'm on my way to my piano lesson. It's three stops away.
W: Yeah? I'm on my way home. Whoa, the ride is bumpy today.
M: The driver looks mad. I hope he doesn't run into anything.
W: Maybe it's just the road. Can you push that button? I'm getting off at the next stop.
M: Sure. See you tomorrow.

우·리·말·해·석
남: 안녕, Maggie. 여기서 널 보다니 반갑다.
여: 안녕, Jim. 너는 어디 가고 있니?
남: 나는 피아노 교습을 받으러 가는 길이야. 그곳은 세 정거장 거리에 있어.
여: 그래? 나는 집에 가는 길이야. 와, 오늘은 차가 덜컹거리네.
남: 운전기사가 화나 보여. 나는 그가 무언가를 들이받지 않길 바라.
여: 어쩌면 그건 그냥 길 때문일 수도 있어. 저 버튼을 눌러줄 수 있어? 나는 다음 정거장에서 내리거든.
남: 물론이지. 내일 보자.

단·어·및·표·현
on one's way to ~로 가는 길에
stop [stɑp] 명 정거장, 정류장
bumpy [bʌ́mpi] 형 덜컹거리는, 울퉁불퉁한
run into ~ ~에 들이받다, 충돌하다
get off 내리다, 하차하다

06 마지막말의도파악 ▶ 정답 ③

듣·기·대·본
W: What are you doing, Harry?
M: I'm searching for information on dental clinics for children.
W: Is it for your daughter?
M: Yes. She needs to get a dental check-up, but she hates going to the dentist.
W: So, you're looking for a place that will be more comfortable for her?
M: Yes. It would be nice to find a clinic that is child-friendly.
W: Then how about posting a question about it on the community website?

우·리·말·해·석
여: 뭐 하고 있어, Harry?
남: 나는 아이들을 위한 치과 병원에 대한 정보를 찾는 중이야.
여: 네 딸을 위한 거야?
남: 응. 그녀는 치과 검진을 받아야 하는데 그녀는 치과에 가는 것을 싫어해.
여: 그래서, 너는 그녀를 위해 더 편안한 곳으로 찾는 중이니?
남: 응. 어린이에게 친절한 병원을 찾으면 좋을 것 같아.
여: 그러면 커뮤니티 웹사이트에 그것에 대한 질문을 올려보는 건 어때?

단·어·및·표·현
search for ~을 찾다
dental clinic 치과 병원
go to the dentist 치과에 가다
comfortable [kʌ́mfərtəbl] 형 편안한, 편한
child-friendly 어린이에게 친절한, 아동 친화적인

07 특정정보파악 ▶ 정답 ③

듣·기·대·본
W: How was your weekend? What did you do?
M: I spent some time with my nephews. It was a lot of fun.
W: Really? What did you do with them?
M: We went to the park. I cooked *tteokbokki* for lunch, too.
W: I didn't know you could cook. What else did you do?
M: We also played a board game and watched a film together at home.
W: What a nice uncle you are!
M: We played a new video game, too. It was so much fun.

우·리·말·해·석
여: 주말은 어땠어? 넌 무엇을 했니?
남: 난 조카들과 시간을 보냈어. 그건 매우 즐거웠어.
여: 정말? 넌 그 아이들과 무엇을 했는데?
남: 우리는 공원에 갔어. 난 점심으로 떡볶이도 만들었어.
여: 난 네가 요리를 할 수 있는지 몰랐어. 그 밖에 다른 것은 뭐했어?
남: 우리는 보드게임도 하고 집에서 함께 영화도 봤어.
여: 넌 정말 좋은 삼촌이구나!
남: 우리는 새로 나온 비디오 게임도 했어. 정말 재미있었어.

단·어·및·표·현
what else 그 밖에 다른 것

08 할일파악(대화직후) ▶정답 ④
듣·기·대·본

W: Jake, this picnic spot is so nice! It's so beautiful and quiet here.
M: Yeah, I'm glad we found this place.
W: But the ground is a little wet.
M: Should we just sit on the grass?
W: No, I'll get the picnic mat from the car.
M: Do you want me to come with you?
W: It's fine. I'll be right back with it.

우·리·말·해·석

여: Jake, 이 소풍 장소 정말 좋다! 여기는 너무 아름답고 조용해.
남: 응, 우리가 이곳을 찾아서 기뻐.
여: 그런데 땅이 좀 젖어 있어.
남: 그냥 잔디에 앉을까?
여: 아니, 내가 차에서 소풍용 돗자리 가져올게.
남: 내가 같이 가길 원하니?
여: 괜찮아. 내가 그걸 가지고 금방 돌아올게.

단·어·및·표·현

spot [spɑt] 圀 (특정한) 곳, 장소
ground [graund] 圀 땅, 지면

09 대화미언급 ▶정답 ④
듣·기·대·본

W: Hey, David! Do you know the photographer named Tommy Shipman?
M: I do! Didn't he publish a new photograph collection?
W: He did! It came out two days ago on June 3rd.
M: Really? So, what's the overall theme of it?
W: It is a collection of photos of fashionable people from all around the world!
M: Cool! I bet a lot of people want to see this collection.
W: Definitely! I heard 25,500 copies have been sold already!

우·리·말·해·석

여: 이봐, David! 너 Tommy Shipman이라는 이름의 사진작가가 아니?
남: 알아! 그가 새로운 사진집을 출판하지 않았니?
여: 그랬어! 그것은 이틀 전인 6월 3일에 나왔어.
남: 정말? 그래서, 그것의 전반적인 주제가 뭐니?
여: 그것은 전 세계의 패션 감각이 있는 사람들의 사진 모음집이야!
남: 멋지다! 나는 많은 사람들이 이 사진집을 보고 싶어 할 것이라고 확신해.
여: 틀림없어! 나는 벌써 25,500부가 팔렸다고 들었어!

단·어·및·표·현

publish [pʌ́bliʃ] 圐 출판하다, 발행하다
overall [òuvərɔ́:l] 휑 전반적인, 종합적인
theme [θi:m] 圀 주제, 테마
bet [bet] 圐 ~이 틀림없다(무엇에 대해 거의 확신함을 나타냄), (돈 등을) 걸다
definitely [défənitli] 휞 틀림없이[분명히]

10 담화화제추론 ▶정답 ③
듣·기·대·본

(Chime bell rings.)
M: Hello, everyone. The school festival is coming up next

Friday! We need forty volunteers for that day. Everyone is welcome. If you're interested, please sign up. You can register either on the list in the school office or school website. You must sign up by next Tuesday. Don't miss your chance to become a volunteer!

우·리·말·해·석

(종소리가 울린다.)
남: 안녕하세요, 여러분. 학교 축제가 다음 주 금요일로 다가왔습니다! 우리는 그날을 위한 40명의 자원봉사자가 필요합니다. 모든 사람을 환영합니다. 만약 관심이 있으시면, 등록해주세요. 당신은 학교 사무실에 있는 목록 혹은 학교 홈페이지에서 등록할 수 있습니다. 다음 주 화요일까지 반드시 등록해야 합니다. 자원봉사자가 될 기회를 놓치지 마세요!

단·어·및·표·현

volunteer [vɑ̀ləntíər] 圀 자원봉사자

11 대화내용불일치 ▶정답 ⑤
듣·기·대·본

W: Matt, what's that big yellow building?
M: The one next to City Hall? It's a new convention center called Power Center.
W: Ah, that's the one! I heard a famous architect designed it.
M: Yes, it was designed by Erica Johnson.
W: Right. It's really beautiful.
M: Isn't it? It also won a design award.
W: That's amazing. Look! There's an international food fair going on right now.
M: Do you want to go check it out?
W: Yes!

우·리·말·해·석

여: Matt, 저 큰 노란 건물은 무엇이니?
남: 시청 옆에 있는 거? 그것은 Power Center라고 불리는 새로운 컨벤션 센터야.
여: 아, 저게 그거구나! 나는 유명한 건축가가 그것을 설계했다고 들었어.
남: 응, 그것은 Erica Johnson에 의해 설계되었어.
여: 맞아. 그것은 정말 아름답다.
남: 그렇지 않니? 그것은 디자인 상도 수상했어.
여: 그거 놀랍다. 봐! 지금 국제 음식 박람회가 진행 중이야.
남: 가서 확인해 보고 싶니?
여: 응!

단·어·및·표·현

architect [ɑ́:rkitèkt] 圀 건축가
international [ìntərnǽʃənəl] 휑 국제적인
fair [fɛər] 圀 박람회

12 전화목적파악 ▶정답 ④
듣·기·대·본

(Telephone rings.)
W: Hello. Nature Hotel.
M: Hi, I booked four nights in a suite starting on August 8th, but I'd like to change my reservation.
W: Sure, may I have your name, please?
M: It's Eddie Carpenter.
W: All right. How would you like to change your reservation?
M: I would like to stay until the 15th instead of the 12th.
W: Okay, your reservation has been extended. Anything

else?
M: No, that's all. Thank you.

(전화벨이 울린다.)
여: 안녕하세요. Nature 호텔입니다.
남: 안녕하세요. 저는 8월 8일을 시작으로 스위트룸 4박을 예약했는데, 예약을 변경하고 싶어요.
여: 알겠습니다. 성함을 알려주시겠어요?
남: Eddie Carpenter입니다.
여: 네. 당신의 예약을 어떻게 변경하고 싶으신가요?
남: 전 12일 대신에 15일까지 머물고 싶어요.
여: 알겠습니다, 당신의 예약은 연장되었습니다. 그 밖에 필요한 것이 있으신가요?
남: 아뇨, 그게 다예요. 감사합니다.

단·어·및·표·현
suite[swiːt] 명 (특히 호텔의) 스위트룸(연결된 몇 개의 방으로 이루어진 공간)
reservation[rèzərvéiʃən] 명 예약
instead of ~ ~ 대신에
extend[iksténd] 동 연장하다

13 수치계산(거스름돈) ▶정답 ④

듣·기·대·본
W: Welcome to Burger House. How may I help you?
M: Could I get one chicken burger combo?
W: That will be 11 dollars. What kind of drink would you like?
M: Coke, please. Oh, can I upsize my fries as well?
W: Yes. That will be a dollar more. Is that okay?
M: Yes. It's fine.
W: Your total is 12 dollars.
M: Here is a 20-dollar bill.
W: Here is your change. Thank you.

우·리·말·해·석
여: Burger House에 오신 것을 환영합니다. 어떻게 도와드릴까요?
남: 치킨 버거 콤보 하나 주시겠어요?
여: 11달러입니다. 어떤 종류의 음료를 원하십니까?
남: 콜라로 주세요. 아, 제 감자튀김도 양을 늘릴 수 있나요?
여: 네. 그것은 1달러가 추가될 것입니다. 괜찮으신가요?
남: 네. 괜찮습니다.
여: 총 12달러입니다.
남: 여기 20달러짜리 지폐입니다.
여: 거스름돈 여기 있습니다. 감사합니다.

단·어·및·표·현
upsize[ʌ́psaiz] 동 양을 늘리다
as well ~도, 또한
change[tʃeindʒ] 명 거스름돈, 잔돈

14 대화자관계추론 ▶정답 ②

듣·기·대·본
M: How can I help you, ma'am?
W: I picked up this wallet on the street across from the police station.
M: Oh, that's kind of you. Did you look inside the wallet?
W: No, I trust that you will find the owner.
M: Of course. Could I have your name, please?
W: It's Violet Carter.

M: Thank you. Could you also fill in this form?
W: Sure! I hope you find the owner soon.

우·리·말·해·석
남: 무엇을 도와드릴까요, 부인?
여: 저는 이 경찰서 건너편 거리에서 이 지갑을 주웠어요.
남: 오, 친절하시네요. 당신은 지갑 안쪽을 보셨나요?
여: 아니요. 저는 당신이 주인을 찾을 거라고 믿어요.
남: 물론이죠. 당신의 이름을 알 수 있을까요?
여: Violet Carter입니다.
남: 감사합니다. 그리고 이 양식을 작성해 주시겠어요?
여: 그럼요! 나는 당신이 주인을 곧 찾기를 바라요.

단·어·및·표·현
across from ~ ~의 건너편에
fill in (서식을) 작성하다

15 부탁(요청)한일파악 ▶정답 ⑤

듣·기·대·본
M: Honey, hurry up! The movie's starting.
W: OK. Have you ordered the pizza?
M: Yes, I have. Do you want me to turn off the light?
W: No, let's leave it on. Thanks for setting the plates on the table. Oh, but we don't have any cups for the Coke.
M: I'll go get some. Is there anything else you need?
W: I forgot my glasses. Can you bring them from the bedroom?
M: No problem.

우·리·말·해·석
남: 여보, 서둘러요! 영화 시작해요.
여: 알았어요. 당신 피자 주문했어요?
남: 네, 했어요. 불을 끌까요?
여: 아니요, 그대로 켜 둬요. 테이블에 접시를 놔 줘서 고마워요. 오, 하지만 콜라를 따를 컵이 하나도 없네요.
남: 제가 가져올게요. 더 필요한 것 있어요?
여: 제 안경을 깜빡했어요. 침실에서 그것을 좀 가져다줄래요?
남: 문제없어요.

단·어·및·표·현
turn off ~ ~을 끄다

16 이유파악 ▶정답 ⑤

듣·기·대·본
W: Ben, you got home late today.
M: I'm sorry, Mom. I didn't know how much time had passed.
W: Did you play with your friends?
M: Not today. I left school right after class.
W: Then, did the bus break down again?
M: No. I saw people filming a movie on the way home.
W: Oh, did you watch them?
M: Yes. I watched the actors for almost two hours. It was fun.

우·리·말·해·석
여: Ben, 넌 오늘 집에 늦게 도착했네.
남: 죄송해요, 엄마. 전 시간이 얼마나 흘렀는지 몰랐어요.
여: 너는 네 친구들과 놀았니?
남: 오늘은 아니에요. 저는 수업 후 바로 학교를 떠났어요.
여: 그러면, 버스가 또 고장 났니?
남: 아뇨, 전 집에 오는 길에 사람들이 영화 촬영하는 것을 봤어요.
여: 오, 넌 그들을 봤니?

남: 네. 저는 거의 두 시간 동안 배우들을 봤어요. 재밌었어요.

단·어·및·표·현

pass [pæs] ⑧ (시간이) 흐르다, 지나가다
leave [liːv] ⑧ 떠나다, 출발하다
break down 고장 나다
film [film] ⑧ 촬영하다
on the way home 집에 오는[가는] 길에
almost [ɔ́ːlmoust] ⑨ 거의

17 그림상황에적절한대화찾기 ▶정답 ④

듣·기·대·본

① M: I fell off my bike.
　　W: Let me put some medicine on the wound.
② M: Can I open the window?
　　W: Sure, go ahead.
③ M: How long does it take to get to the hospital?
　　W: It takes about 10 minutes by car.
④ M: It's going to hurt, isn't it? I hate getting shots.
　　W: I'll do my best to reduce the pain.
⑤ M: What is your favorite ice cream flavor?
　　W: I like vanilla the best.

우·리·말·해·석

① 남: 제가 제 자전거에서 떨어졌어요.
　　여: 제가 상처에 약간의 약을 바를게요.
② 남: 제가 창문을 열어도 될까요?
　　여: 그럼요, 그러세요.
③ 남: 병원에 가는 데 얼마나 걸려요?
　　여: 차로 약 10분 걸려요.
④ 남: 그것은 아플 거예요, 그렇지 않아요? 저는 주사 맞는 것이 싫어요.
　　여: 제가 통증을 줄이도록 최선을 다할게요.
⑤ 남: 당신이 가장 좋아하는 아이스크림 맛은 무엇이에요?
　　여: 저는 바닐라를 가장 좋아해요.

단·어·및·표·현

fall off ~ ~에서 떨어지다
get a shot 주사를 맞다
reduce [ridʒúːs] ⑧ 줄이다
flavor [fléivər] ⑨ 맛, 풍미

18 담화미언급 ▶정답 ⑤

듣·기·대·본

W: Hello, everyone. Today, I'd like to tell you about a new opera written by the composer Hilda Woo. It's called *My Luck* and it is about the lives of six people who win the lottery. The characters will be played by a fantastic cast, including the famous baritone, Sebastian Vale. The opera will be playing at Star Art Center starting in November. Buy your tickets online now!

우·리·말·해·석

여: 안녕하세요, 여러분. 오늘 저는 여러분께 작곡가 Hilda Woo에 의해 작곡된 새로운 오페라에 대해 말씀드리려고 합니다. 그것은 "My Luck" 이라고 불리며 복권에 당첨된 여섯 사람의 삶에 대한 이야기입니다. 등장인물들은 유명한 바리톤 가수인 Sebastian Vale을 포함한 환상적인 출연진에 의해 연기될 겁니다. 이 오페라는 11월에 시작하여 스타 아트 센터에서 공연될 것입니다. 지금 온라인으로 표를 구매하십시오!

단·어·및·표·현

composer [kəmpóuzər] ⑨ 작곡가
win the lottery 복권에 당첨되다
character [kǽriktər] ⑨ (책·영화 등의) 등장인물

play [plei] ⑧ 연기하다, 공연되다
cast [kæst] ⑨ 출연진, 출연자

19 알맞은응답찾기 ▶정답 ①

듣·기·대·본

M: What are you doing, Jessica?
W: I'm looking for a book on modern art.
M: Modern art? Why?
W: I'm planning to go to a modern art gallery in New York this weekend. So I want to study about it first.
M: Wow! What a wonderful idea! Are you going there with your family?
W: No. I'm going there alone. Do you want to come with me?
M: I'd love to, but I have other plans.

우·리·말·해·석

① 그러고 싶지만, 난 다른 계획이 있어.
② 난 너의 가족을 만나고 싶어.
③ 뉴욕에는 미술 전시관들이 많아.
④ 멋진 계획이 있구나.
⑤ 뉴욕은 큰 도시야.

남: 뭐 하고 있니, Jessica?
여: 현대 미술에 관한 책을 찾고 있어.
남: 현대 미술? 왜?
여: 이번 주말에 뉴욕에 있는 현대 미술 전시관에 갈 계획이야. 그래서 먼저 그것에 대해 공부하고 싶어.
남: 와! 아주 멋진 생각이구나! 거기 너희 가족과 함께 갈 거니?
여: 아니. 난 혼자 갈 거야. 나랑 같이 갈래?
남: 그러고 싶지만, 난 다른 계획이 있어.

단·어·및·표·현

wonderful [wʌ́ndərfəl] ⑩ 멋진

20 알맞은응답찾기 ▶정답 ④

듣·기·대·본

W: What are you doing?
M: I'm playing a mobile game. It's called *The Next Kingdom*.
W: Really? Did you read the novel as well?
M: What do you mean?
W: The game is based on a fantasy novel titled, *The Next Kingdom*.
M: I didn't know that! I wonder if the book is as good as the game.
W: Oh, I'm sure it is. I enjoyed reading it.
M: Then, I will read the novel, too.

우·리·말·해·석

① 나는 모바일 게임들을 좋아하지 않아.
② 응, 그 이야기는 아주 좋아.
③ 정말? 그건 내가 가장 좋아하는 책이야.
④ 그러면, 나도 그 소설을 읽어봐야겠다.
⑤ 나는 너에게 왕국에 대해 얘기해줄 수 있어.

여: 넌 뭐 하고 있니?
남: 나는 모바일 게임을 하고 있어. 그건 "The Next Kingdom(다음 왕국)" 이라고 불려.
여: 정말? 너는 그 소설도 읽었어?
남: 무슨 뜻이야?
여: 그 게임은 "The Next Kingdom(다음 왕국)"이라는 제목의 판타지 소설을 바탕으로 한 거야.
남: 난 그걸 몰랐어! 나는 그 책이 게임만큼 좋은지 궁금해.

여: 오, 난 그럴 거라고 확신해. 나는 그것을 읽는 것을 즐겼어.
남: 그러면, 나도 그 소설을 읽어봐야겠다.

단·어·및·표·현

be called ~로 불리다
novel [návəl] 명 소설
as well ~도, 또한, 역시
be based on ~을 바탕으로 하다, ~에 기초하다
title [táitl] 통 제목을 붙이다
wonder if ~인지 아닌지 궁금하다

Words & Expressions Review

1. 그대로 두다	2. ~에 기초하다, ~을 바탕으로 하다	3. 주제, 테마
4. A에게 B를 요구하다	5. 전시관	6. ~에 들이받다, 충돌하다
7. 자원봉사자	8. 박람회	9. ~을 찾다
10. ~이 틀림없다, (돈을) 걸다	11. (특정한) 곳, 장소	12. 내리다, 하차하다
13. 땅, 지면	14. (서식을) 작성하다	15. (강좌 등에) 등록하다
16. 양을 늘리다	17. 줄이다	18. 연장하다
19. (~하는 것으로) 시작하다	20. 영화를 보다	21. 컵받침
22. ~으로 불리다	23. 고장 나다	24. (특정한 시간 동안) 지속되다
25. 등록하다, 기록부	26. 작곡가	27. 그 밖에 다른 것
28. 바닥	29. ~의 건너편에	30. ~로 가는 길에
31. 출판하다, 발행하다	32. 정거장, 정류장	33. 시간이 지나면서
34. 전반적인, 종합적인	35. ~에서 떨어지다	36. ~을 찾다
37. 문제가 되다, 중요하다	38. ~을 끄다	39. 건축가
40. ~도, 또한	41. 흐르다, 지나가다	42. 저축하다, 절약하다
43. 남자 조카	44. 맛, 풍미	

Listening Test
영어듣기 모의고사 17회

|정|답|

01 ②	02 ⑤	03 ⑤	04 ⑤	05 ①
06 ②	07 ⑤	08 ③	09 ④	10 ①
11 ③	12 ①	13 ④	14 ⑤	15 ④
16 ②	17 ④	18 ④	19 ①	20 ④

01 날씨파악-그림 ▶정답 ②

듣·기·대·본

W: Today, in Macao, we had partly cloudy skies. The temperature reached 21 degrees Celsius. Tomorrow's forecast will be sunny with clear skies. The temperature will be around 25 degrees. It should be a great day to go to the beach.

우·리·말·해·석

여: 오늘 마카오는 부분적으로 구름이 끼었습니다. 기온은 21도에 달했습니다. 내일의 예상되는 날씨는 햇빛이 나고 하늘이 맑겠습니다. 기온은 25도 안팎이 되겠습니다. 해변으로 가기에 매우 좋은 날일 것입니다.

단·어·및·표·현

partly [pá:rtli] 부 부분적으로

02 그림정보파악 ▶정답 ⑤

듣·기·대·본

W: May I help you?
M: I want to buy a ball for my nephew.
W: How about this one with the bear on it? It's popular.
M: Well, my nephew isn't that young. I like that thunder design.
W: Boys like it. This one has Pele's name, too.
M: It's nice, but I'll take this ball with no text on it.
W: Sure.

우·리·말·해·석

여: 무엇을 도와드릴까요?
남: 제 조카에게 줄 공을 사고 싶습니다.
여: 곰이 있는 이것은 어떠세요? 인기가 있습니다.
남: 글쎄요, 제 조카는 그렇게 어리지 않아요. 저는 저 천둥 디자인이 좋네요.
여: 남자아이들이 그것을 좋아합니다. 이것은 Pele의 이름도 있습니다.
남: 멋지네요. 하지만 글자가 없는 이 공으로 하겠습니다.
여: 네.

단·어·및·표·현

nephew [néfju:] 명 남자 조카

LISTENING ADVICE

● **thunder: How to pronounce [θ]**

[θ]는 흔히 번데기 발음이라고 말하는 발음입니다. 윗니와 아랫니로 혀 앞부분을 살짝 물고 성대를 울리지 않고 [쓰]라고 발음합니다.

'I like that thunder design.'에서 'thunder'의 [θ] 발음을 잘 들어보세요.

---

03 심정추론 ▶정답 ⑤

듣·기·대·본

M: Mom, Uncle Dennis sent you a letter.
W: Oh, really? Let me see it.
M: What does it say?
W: It's an invitation.
M: To what?
W: To a baby shower.
M: Really? I'm gonna have a baby cousin?
W: Yes. That's why Aunt Wendy's belly keeps growing. She's pregnant.
M: I can't wait to play with my little cousin! I wonder if it will be a boy or a girl.

우·리·말·해·석

① 실망한　　② 화난　　③ 질투하는
④ 긴장한　　⑤ 신난

남: 엄마, Dennis 이모부가 편지를 보냈어요.

여: 아, 정말? 어디 보자.
남: 뭐라고 써 있어요?
여: 초대장이구나.
남: 뭐에 대한 건데요?
여: 베이비 샤워에 초대한 거야.
남: 정말이요? 저 아기 사촌 동생이 생기는 거예요?
여: 응. 그래서 Wendy 이모의 배가 자꾸 커지는 거야. 임신을 하셨거든.
남: 빨리 어린 사촌 동생이랑 놀고 싶어요! 남자일지 여자일지 궁금해요.

단·어·및·표·현
belly[béli] 명 배
pregnant[prégnənt] 형 임신한

04 한일파악　　　　▶정답 ⑤

듣·기·대·본
M: Mom, I'm home from school.
W: You're home early. I thought you <u>were going to</u> play basketball after school today.
M: Logan <u>hurt</u> his ankle at school, so we couldn't play.
W: Oh, did he get <u>badly</u> hurt?
M: No, but he had trouble walking on his own so I helped him to the hospital.
W: Ah, that's sweet of you. Good job!
M: It wasn't a big deal.

우·리·말·해·석
남: 엄마, 저 학교 다녀왔어요.
여: 너는 집에 일찍 왔구나. 나는 오늘 네가 방과 후에 농구를 할 거라고 생각했단다.
남: Logan이 학교에서 그의 발목을 다쳐서, 우리는 놀 수 없었어요.
여: 오, 그는 심하게 다쳤니?
남: 아니요, 하지만 그는 혼자서 걷는 데 어려움이 있어서 제가 병원에 가는 걸 도와주었어요.
여: 아, 정말 다정하구나. 잘했어!
남: 별일 아니었는걸요.

단·어·및·표·현
ankle[ǽŋkl] 명 발목
badly[bǽdli] 부 심하게, 몹시
have trouble -ing ~하는 데 어려움이 있다
on one's own 혼자서, 단독으로, 자력으로

05 대화장소추론　　　　▶정답 ①

듣·기·대·본
M: Good afternoon. How may I help you?
W: Hi, I <u>have a reservation</u> for today. My name is Julie Kim.
M: Let me check. Can you show me your passport, please?
W: Sure, here you go.
M: Mrs. Kim, <u>we've reserved</u> a standard room for you for two nights. Is that correct?
W: Yes, it is.
M: We've upgraded your room so it now has an ocean view. Here's your key card to room 701.
W: That's great! Thank you very much.
M: You're welcome. Please <u>enjoy your stay</u>!

우·리·말·해·석
남: 안녕하세요. 제가 어떻게 도와드릴까요?
여: 안녕하세요, 저는 오늘로 예약을 했어요. 제 이름은 Julie Kim이에요.
남: 확인해보겠습니다. 저에게 당신의 여권을 보여주시겠어요?
여: 그럼요, 여기 있습니다.
남: 김 씨, 저희는 2박으로 당신을 위한 일반실을 예약을 해 두었습니다.

이것이 맞나요?
여: 예, 맞습니다.
남: 저희는 당신의 방을 업그레이드해서 그것은 이제 바다 전망을 갖고 있습니다. 여기 701호실 키카드가 있습니다.
여: 잘됐군요! 매우 감사합니다.
남: 천만에요. 여기에 머무는 것을 즐기세요!

단·어·및·표·현
reservation[rèzərvéiʃən] 명 예약
reserve[rizə́:rv] 동 예약하다

06 마지막말의도파악　　　　▶정답 ②

듣·기·대·본
M: Wow, what happened to you, Avery?
W: I <u>fell down the stairs</u> and broke my leg.
M: That must have hurt. How long do you have to <u>keep the cast on</u>?
W: The doctor said to keep it on for a month.
M: So, you have to be on crutches for a month?
W: Unfortunately, yes. I guess this is what I get for <u>not paying attention</u> on the stairs.
M: No, don't say that. Does your leg still hurt?
W: Yeah, a little bit.
M: I hope you feel better soon.

우·리·말·해·석
남: 저런, 네게 무슨 일이 있었니, Avery?
여: 나는 계단에서 넘어져서 다리가 부러졌어.
남: 아팠겠다. 너는 얼마나 오랫동안 그 깁스를 해야 하니?
여: 의사 선생님은 그것을 한 달 동안 하라고 하셨어.
남: 그럼, 너는 한 달 동안 목발을 짚어야 하니?
여: 불행하게도 그래. 내가 계단에서 조심하지 않아서 이렇게 됐나 봐.
남: 아냐, 그렇게 말하지 마. 아직도 네 다리가 아프니?
여: 응, 조금.
남: 빨리 낫길 바랄게.

단·어·및·표·현
fall down 넘어지다
keep the cast on 깁스를 하다
crutch[krʌtʃ] 명 목발
unfortunately[ʌnfɔ́:rtʃənətli] 부 불행하게도, 유감스럽게도
pay attention 조심하다, 주의를 기울이다

07 특정정보파악　　　　▶정답 ⑤

듣·기·대·본
W: Did you know that our school is <u>taking suggestions</u> for a new club?
M: Yes, I've heard that someone suggested a video games club or a fashion design club.
W: I don't think the teachers will choose <u>either of them</u>.
M: Do you have an idea for one?
W: I was thinking about a cooking club. How about you?
M: I'm <u>going to suggest</u> a swimming club.
W: Oh, that's nice!

우·리·말·해·석
여: 너 우리 학교가 새 동아리를 위한 제안을 받고 있다는 거 알고 있었니?
남: 응, 나는 누군가 비디오게임 동아리나 패션 디자인 동아리를 제안했다고 들었어.
여: 내 생각에 선생님들은 그것들 중 어떤 것도 선택하시지 않을 것 같아.
남: 너는 그것에 대한 아이디어가 있니?
여: 나는 요리 동아리를 생각하고 있었어. 너는 어때?

남: 나는 수영 동아리를 제안할 거야.

여: 오, 그거 좋다!

단·어·및·표·현

take a suggestion 제안을 받아들이다

either [íːðər] ⑭ (둘 중) 어느 한쪽

08 할일파악(대화직후) ▶정답 ③

듣·기·대·본

W: Honey, let's go jogging.

M: Sorry, but I can't go out today. I'm not <u>feeling well</u>.

W: Why don't you see a doctor?

M: Well, I think I just need to <u>get some rest</u> at home.

W: Okay. I'll make chicken soup for you. What do you think?

M: I like chicken soup. Thank you, honey.

W: <u>I'm going to the grocery store now</u>. Get some sleep, then.

우·리·말·해·석

여: 여보, 우리 조깅하러 가요.

남: 미안한데, 난 오늘 못 나가겠어요. 몸 상태가 좋지 않아요.

여: 병원에 가는 것이 어때요?

남: 그게, 내 생각에 집에서 약간의 휴식을 취하는 것이 좋겠어요.

여: 알았어요. 당신을 위해 닭고기 수프를 만들어 줄게요. 어떻게 생각해요?

남: 난 닭고기 수프를 좋아해요. 고마워요, 여보.

여: 전 지금 식료품점에 갈게요. 그럼 잠 좀 자요.

단·어·및·표·현

get some rest 약간의 휴식을 취하다

09 대화미언급 ▶정답 ④

듣·기·대·본

W: Jaehoon, <u>have you seen</u> this video clip?

M: Oh, is this the one that's been popular online recently?

W: Yes! It's a trailer for <u>a new TV show</u>, *The Prize*.

M: I haven't seen it yet. Is it good?

W: It's <u>beyond good</u>. The beloved actor, Kim Sung Hyun, stars as the main character, Namsoo.

M: Oh, I love him, too. What is it about?

W: It seems like <u>a survival story of some kind</u>.

M: Sounds interesting. Where is it going to be aired?

W: <u>It will be aired on ONBC.</u>

우·리·말·해·석

여: 재훈아, 너 이 영상 클립 본 적 있어?

남: 오, 이게 최근에 온라인에서 인기 있는 그거니?

여: 응! 그것은 새로운 TV 프로그램, 'The Prize'의 예고편이야.

남: 나는 그것을 아직 안 봤어. 그것은 재미있니?

여: 그것은 엄청 재미있어. 인기 많은 배우 김성현이 주인공 남수로 출연해.

남: 오, 나도 그를 너무 좋아해. 그것은 무엇에 관한 거니?

여: 그것은 일종의 생존 이야기 같아 보여.

남: 흥미롭게 들린다. 어디서 방송되니?

여: 그것은 ONBC에서 방송될 거야.

단·어·및·표·현

video clip 비디오 클립(판촉용으로 짧게 제작한 비디오)

trailer [tréilər] ⑲ (영화·텔레비전 프로그램의) 예고편

beyond good 엄청 재미있는

beloved [bilʌ́vd] ⑲ 인기 많은, 사랑받는

star [staːr] ⑧ (영화·연극 등에서) 주연[주역]을 맡다, 출연하다

of some kind 일종의

air [ɛər] ⑧ 방송하다, 방송되다

10 담화화제추론 ▶정답 ①

듣·기·대·본

W: May I have your attention, please? We have a lost boy here named Jimmy Mulligan and he is looking for his father. He was found at the toy section this afternoon. He is six years old and he is wearing a striped white and blue shirt, black pants and a red baseball cap. If you know this child, please come to the customer service office. Thank you.

우·리·말·해·석

여: 주목해 주시겠습니까? 저희는 Jimmy Mulligan이라는 이름의 길 잃은 남자아이를 데리고 있고 아이가 아버지를 찾고 있습니다. 이 아이는 오늘 오후 장난감 코너에서 발견되었습니다. 아이는 6살이며 흰색과 파란 줄무늬 셔츠, 검정바지와 빨간 야구 모자를 착용하고 있습니다. 이 아이를 아신다면, 고객서비스 사무실로 와주십시오. 감사합니다.

단·어·및·표·현

attention [ətén∫ʌn] ⑲ 주목, 집중

striped [straipt] ⑲ 줄무늬의

11 대화내용불일치 ▶정답 ③

듣·기·대·본

M: Maggie, have you heard about the Spring Flower Festival that's taking place in Orion Park?

W: Yes. Actually, I went to the festival last weekend. It started on May fifth.

M: Is there an entrance fee?

W: It's only $2 per person and children under 8 are free.

M: I heard they are having a photo contest!

W: Yes, you can submit the photos that you take at the festival online to be entered in the contest.

M: Sounds fun!

W: Oh, you should know it's closed on Tuesdays.

M: I see. Thanks for the information.

우·리·말·해·석

남: Maggie, 너는 Orion 공원에서 열리는 봄꽃 축제에 대해서 들어봤니?

여: 응. 사실, 나는 지난 주말에 그 축제에 다녀왔어. 그것은 5월 5일에 시작했어.

남: 입장료가 있니?

여: 그것은 인당 2달러밖에 안 하고 8살 미만의 어린이는 무료야.

남: 나는 그들이 사진 대회를 연다고 들었어!

여: 응, 축제에서 찍은 사진을 온라인으로 제출하는 것으로 대회에 참가할 수 있어.

남: 재미있겠다!

여: 오, 그것이 매주 화요일에는 열지 않는다는 걸 알아야 해.

남: 그렇구나. 정보 고마워.

단·어·및·표·현

take place 열리다, 개최되다

entrance fee 입장료

submit [səbmít] ⑧ 제출하다

enter [éntər] ⑧ (대회 등에) 참가하다[시키다], 출전하다[시키다]

12 전화목적파악 ▶정답 ①

듣·기·대·본

(*Telephone rings.*)

M: Hello.

W: Hello, Travis. Are we still meeting at two o'clock?

M: Yes. Why do you ask?

W: I don't think I can make it.
M: Are you busy? Do you want to cancel?
W: No, I have some extra work to do, but I really want to
   see a movie. How about meeting at five o'clock?
M: Okay. Five o'clock in front of the theater, right?
W: Yes. See you then.

우·리·말·해·석

(전화벨이 울린다.)
남: 여보세요.
여: 안녕, Travis. 우리 여전히 두 시에 만나는 거지?
남: 응, 너는 왜 물어보는데?
여: 나 그 시간에 못 갈 것 같아.
남: 너 바쁘니? 취소하길 바라니?
여: 아니, 난 추가로 할 일이 있지만 영화가 정말 보고 싶어. 다섯 시에 만
   나는 건 어떨까?
남: 좋아, 다섯 시 영화관 앞, 맞지?
여: 응. 그때 보자.

단·어·및·표·현

cancel [kǽnsəl] ⑧ 취소하다

13 수치계산(지불금액) ▶ 정답 ④

듣·기·대·본

W: Hello, I'd like to rent some bicycles.
M: Okay. How many do you need?
W: I want one for me and one for my 10-year-old son.
M: The price is the same for adults and children.
W: Okay. How much is it?
M: It's $5 per hour. How long do you need them?
W: I think we need them for 3 hours.
M: If you rent them for a half day, you will only pay $10 for
   each.
W: That's great. Then, I'd like to rent two bikes for a half
   day.
M: Sure! I'll get your bikes. One moment, please.

우·리·말·해·석

여: 안녕하세요, 저는 자전거를 몇 대 대여하고 싶어요.
남: 좋습니다. 몇 대가 필요하세요?
여: 저는 제 거 하나와 10살 아들을 위한 거 하나를 원해요.
남: 가격은 어른과 아이들에 대해 같아요.
여: 그래요. 얼마예요?
남: 시간당 5달러입니다. 얼마나 오래 그것들이 필요하세요?
여: 저는 우리가 세 시간 동안 그것들이 필요할 거라고 생각해요.
남: 반일 동안 대여하신다면, 각각 10달러만 지불하시게 됩니다.
여: 그거 좋네요. 그러면, 저는 두 대의 자전거를 반일 동안 대여하고 싶
   어요.
남: 알겠습니다! 자전거들을 가져올게요. 잠시만 기다리세요.

단·어·및·표·현

rent [rent] ⑧ 대여하다, 빌리다

14 대화자관계추론 ▶ 정답 ⑤

듣·기·대·본

M: Hi, what can I help you with?
W: My cell phone battery dies too quickly.
M: Let me see. How long have you been using this phone?
W: Around three years. What can I do about it?
M: Well, if you don't want to get a new phone, I think it's
   best to replace the battery.

W: How much will that cost?
M: It costs $49 for this model.
W: Okay. Please change it for me.
M: No problem. Please fill out this form.

우·리·말·해·석

남: 안녕하세요, 무엇을 도와드릴까요?
여: 제 휴대폰 배터리가 너무 빨리 꺼져요.
남: 제가 (한번) 볼게요. 이 휴대폰은 얼마나 오래 쓰신 건가요?
여: 약 3년 정도요. 제가 무엇을 하면 될까요?
남: 글쎄요, 새 휴대폰을 원하는 게 아니시면 제 생각엔 배터리를 교체하는
   게 최선일 것 같네요.
여: 그건 얼마 정도가 드나요?
남: 이 모델은 49달러가 듭니다.
여: 알겠습니다. 부디 그것을 교체해주세요.
남: 문제없습니다. 이 서식을 작성해주세요.

단·어·및·표·현

die [dai] ⑧ 꺼지다, 없어지다
replace [ripléis] ⑧ 교체하다, 대체하다
cost [kɔ(:)st] ⑧ (비용이) 들다
fill out ~을 작성하다, 기입하다

15 부탁(요청)한일파악 ▶ 정답 ④

듣·기·대·본

(Telephone rings.)
M: Charlie's Cupcakes.
W: Hello. This is Hollie Jenkins. I placed an order yesterday.
M: Let me see. You ordered twelve vanilla cupcakes.
W: Yes. Can I make a change?
M: Would you like to change the original order?
W: No, I want to add five more cupcakes. Mint chocolate,
   this time.
M: No problem. When do you want to pick them up?
W: At 2 p.m. Thank you.

우·리·말·해·석

(전화벨이 울린다.)
남: Charlie 컵케이크입니다.
여: 여보세요. Hollie Jenkins입니다. 저는 어제 주문을 했어요.
남: 확인해 보겠습니다. 바닐라 컵케이크 12개를 주문하셨네요.
여: 네. 변경을 할 수 있을까요?
남: 원래의 주문을 변경하시겠어요?
여: 아니요, 저는 컵케이크 5개를 추가하고 싶어요. 이번에는 민트 초콜릿
   으로요.
남: 문제없습니다. 언제 가져가시겠어요?
여: 오후 2시에요. 감사합니다.

단·어·및·표·현

place an order 주문하다

16 이유파악 ▶ 정답 ②

듣·기·대·본

M: Karen, you look excited. What's up?
W: I'm actually on my way to the animal shelter to
   volunteer.
M: That sounds exciting! What kind of work do you do
   there?
W: I usually walk the dogs and clean their cages.
M: Wow, that's amazing. I love animals, too.
W: Why don't you come along this weekend?
M: I wish I could, but I have to visit my sick grandmother.

W: No problem. Family always comes first.

우·리·말·해·석

남: Karen, 너 신나 보여. 무슨 일이야?

여: 난 사실 자원봉사를 하기 위해 동물 보호소에 가는 길이야.

남: 그거 재밌겠다! 넌 거기서 어떤 종류의 일을 하니?

여: 난 보통 개들을 산책시키고 그들의 우리를 청소해.

남: 와, 굉장하다. 나도 동물들을 아주 좋아해.

여: 이번 주말에 함께 가는 게 어때?

남: 그럴 수 있으면 좋겠지만, 난 편찮으신 할머니를 뵈러 가야 해.

여: 괜찮아. 항상 가족이 가장 먼저지.

단·어·및·표·현

animal shelter 동물 보호소

volunteer [vàləntíər] ⑧ 자원봉사 하다

cage [keidʒ] ⑲ (쇠창살이나 철사로 만든 짐승의) 우리, 새장

come along 함께 가다[오다]

come first 가장 먼저다, 최우선 고려 사항이다

17 그림상황에적절한대화찾기　▶정답 ④

듣·기·대·본

① M: How much is this bag?
　 W: I'll go and check the price for you.

② M: It looks delicious! Did you do all the cooking?
　 W: Yes, I did. Help yourself.

③ M: The sun is strong. Why don't you wear a hat?
　 W: Okay, I will. Thanks.

④ M: He's speaking so loudly on the phone.
　 W: Yes. Let's move to another table.

⑤ M: It's so cold.
　 W: Right. Let's go inside and drink something warm.

우·리·말·해·석

① 남: 이 가방은 얼마인가요?
　 여: 당신을 위해 제가 가서 가격을 확인해 볼게요.

② 남: 맛있어 보여요! 모든 요리를 당신이 했나요?
　 여: 네, 제가 했어요. 맘껏 드세요.

③ 남: 햇빛이 강하네요. 모자를 쓰는 게 어때요?
　 여: 네, 그럴게요. 고마워요.

④ 남: 그는 너무 큰 소리로 통화하고 있어요.
　 여: 그러게요. 다른 테이블로 이동합시다.

⑤ 남: 너무 추워요.
　 여: 맞아요. 안에 들어가서 따뜻한 것을 마십시다.

단·어·및·표·현

price [prais] ⑲ 가격

Help yourself. 마음껏 드세요.

speak on the phone 통화하다

loudly [láudli] ⑭ 큰 소리로, 크게

18 담화미언급　▶정답 ④

듣·기·대·본

W: Hello, students. The grade two class field trip will be held this Saturday, August 9. The meeting place is the front yard of the school. Boarding time is 7 a.m. and the bus will leave promptly at 7:15 a.m. Please don't be late so that we can depart on time. Make sure to wear your school shirt and jogging pants. I hope everyone enjoys the trip!

우·리·말·해·석

여: 안녕하세요, 학생 여러분. 2학년 현장학습이 이번 주 토요일, 8월 9일에 실시될 예정입니다. 모임 장소는 학교 앞의 운동장입니다. 탑승 시간은 오전 7시이며 버스는 7시 15분에 정확히 출발할 것입니다. 우리가 정시에 출발할 수 있도록 부디 늦지 마세요. 여러분의 학교 셔츠와 조깅 바지를 꼭 입고 오세요. 저는 모두가 현장학습을 즐기길 바랍니다!

단·어·및·표·현

promptly [prάmptli] ⑭ 정확히, 즉각

depart [dipάːrt] ⑧ 출발하다, 떠나다

on time 정시에

19 알맞은응답찾기　▶정답 ①

듣·기·대·본

M: Hello. Welcome to Juice Wonderland! How can I help you?

W: Hi. What's the most popular drink in this store?

M: The strawberry smoothie is our best seller.

W: Does it have any milk in it?

M: Yes, it's made with milk and yogurt.

W: Milk gives me a stomachache. Do you have a drink without any milk in it?

M: Yes. We have orange juice. It's made with oranges only.

W: Then I'll have that.

우·리·말·해·석

① 그럼 저는 그걸로 할게요.

② 당신은 우유를 주문할 수 있어요.

③ 지금 이 약을 드세요.

④ 이 오렌지들은 신선해 보여요.

⑤ 제가 가장 좋아하는 과일은 딸기예요.

남: 안녕하세요. Juice Wonderland에 오신 걸 환영합니다! 어떻게 도와드릴까요?

여: 안녕하세요. 이 가게에서 가장 인기 있는 음료는 뭐예요?

남: 딸기 스무디가 저희의 가장 잘 팔리는 제품이에요.

여: 그 안에 우유가 들어 있나요?

남: 네, 우유와 요구르트로 만들어져요.

여: 저는 우유를 마시면 배가 아파요. 우유가 전혀 들어 있지 않은 음료도 있나요?

남: 네. 오렌지 주스가 있어요. 오렌지만으로 만들어졌어요.

여: 그럼 저는 그걸로 할게요.

단·어·및·표·현

be made with ~으로 만들어지다

20 알맞은응답찾기　▶정답 ④

듣·기·대·본

M: Hey, I didn't expect to meet you at the book store.

W: Hi, Pierce. I'm here to buy some books for my friends.

M: Oh, is it someone's birthday?

W: No, I'm going to give books as a gift for World Book Day.

M: That's a good idea. Maybe I'll buy a poetry book for my mom, too.

W: Good for you. Does she like poetry?

M: Yes, but I don't know much about it. Can you recommend one?

W: Sure, let me show you some.

우·리·말·해·석

① 그녀의 생일을 축하해!

② 편지 쓰는 것을 잊지 마.

③ 그것은 우체국 옆에 있어.

④ 물론이지, 몇 권 보여 줄게.

⑤ 목걸이를 사는 것이 어때?

남: 안녕, 나는 서점에서 너를 만날 것을 예상하지 못했어.
여: 안녕, Pierce. 나는 내 친구들을 위한 책을 몇 권 사러 여기에 왔어.
남: 오, 누군가의 생일이니?
여: 아니, 나는 세계 책의 날을 맞아 책들을 선물로 줄 거야.
남: 좋은 생각이야. 나도 엄마를 위한 시집을 한 권 사야겠어.
여: 잘됐네. 그녀는 시를 좋아하니?
남: 응, 하지만 나는 그것에 대해 많이 알지 못해. 네가 하나 추천해줄 수 있니?
여: **물론이지, 몇 권 보여 줄게.**

단·어·및·표·현
expect[ikspékt] ⑧ 예상하다, 기대하다
poetry[póuitri] ⑲ 시
recommend[rèkəménd] ⑧ 추천하다

Words & Expressions Review

1. 정확히, 즉각	2. 일반적인, 보통의	3. 예약
4. 주문하다	5. 취소하다	6. 복통
7. 방송하다, 방송되다	8. 임신한	9. 교체하다, 대체하다
10. 남자 조카	11. 부분적으로	12. 약간의 휴식을 취하다
13. 천둥	14. 가장 먼저다, 최우선 고려 사항이다	15. 큰 소리로, 크게
16. 줄무늬의	17. 배	18. 통화하다
19. 열리다, 개최되다	20. ~을 작성하다, 기입하다	21. (영화, 텔레비전 프로그램의) 예고편
22. 제안을 받아들이다	23. 글, 문서	24. 목발
25. 출발하다, 떠나다	26. ~으로 만들어지다	27. 혼자서, 단독으로
28. 함께 가다[오다]	29. 마음껏 드세요.	30. 시
31. 변경하다	32. (둘 중) 어느 한쪽	33. 넘어지다
34. 심하게, 몹시	35. 식료품점	36. 정시에
37. 주목, 집중	38. 추천하다	39. ~에 달하다, 이르다
40. 초대장, 초대	41. 건강 상태가 좋다	42. 불행하게도, 유감스럽게도
43. 대여하다, 빌리다	44. 제출하다	

Listening Test
영어듣기 모의고사 18회

|정|답|

01 ③	02 ③	03 ②	04 ⑤	05 ③
06 ④	07 ④	08 ①	09 ⑤	10 ④
11 ④	12 ②	13 ③	14 ①	15 ③
16 ④	17 ③	18 ④	19 ②	20 ①

01 날씨파악-그림 ▶정답 ③

듣·기·대·본
W: Good morning! You are listening to Everyday Weather. We are expecting snow this morning along with a huge temperature drop. Also, it will be quite windy. So, remember to dress warmly. Looking ahead, tomorrow morning, it is expected to be sunny. Stay tuned for any new weather updates!

우·리·말·해·석
여: 좋은 아침입니다! 여러분은 매일의 일기예보를 듣고 계십니다. 오늘 아침에는 급격한 기온 하락과 함께 눈이 내릴 것으로 예상됩니다. 또한, 바람이 상당히 많이 불겠습니다. 그러니 따뜻하게 챙겨 입으시길 바랍니다. 앞을 내다보면, 내일 아침에는 맑을 것으로 예상됩니다. 새로운 날씨 정보를 위해 채널을 고정해 주시기 바랍니다!

단·어·및·표·현
expect[ikspékt] ⑧ 예상하다, 예측하다
drop[drɑp] ⑲ (수량·정도의) 하락, 감소
look ahead (앞일, 미래 등을) 내다보다
stay tuned 채널을 고정하다
update[ʌ́pdèit] ⑲ 최신 정보, 소식

02 그림정보파악 ▶정답 ③

듣·기·대·본
W: Danny, do you want to look at these umbrellas on my screen?
M: Sure, Mom. You're going to get me an umbrella, right?
W: Yes. I think the polka-dotted one looks nice.
M: Hmm. I don't want polka dots on my umbrella.
W: Okay. Then, how about these ones with sea animals on them?
M: They're cool. I'll go for the one with the shark.
W: Great. I'll order that one.

우·리·말·해·석
여: Danny, 내 화면에 있는 이 우산들 좀 볼래?
남: 네, 엄마. 저에게 우산 하나 사주실 거죠, 그렇죠?
여: 그래. 나는 물방울무늬가 있는 게 먼저 보이는 것 같아.
남: 음. 저는 제 우산에 물방울 무늬는 싫어요.
여: 알았어. 그럼 바다 동물이 그려진 이것들은 어때?
남: 멋져요. 저는 상어가 있는 걸로 할게요.
여: 좋아. 내가 그것을 주문할게.

단·어·및·표·현
polka-dotted 물방울무늬의

03 심정추론 ▶정답 ②

듣·기·대·본
W: You look happy today. What's up?
M: I'm going on a picnic with my family tomorrow.
W: That sounds like a lot of fun.
M: Yes. And the weather forecast said that it would be a beautiful day.
W: Oh, really? I hope you have a great time.
M: Thanks.

우·리·말·해·석
① 걱정되는   ② 신난   ③ 긴장된   ④ 지루한   ⑤ 화난

여: 너 오늘 행복해 보이는데. 무슨 일이야?
남: 우리 가족들이랑 내일 소풍 가.
여: 그거 정말 재미있겠다.
남: 응. 그리고 일기예보에서 그러는데 날씨도 아주 좋을 거래.
여: 오, 정말? 멋진 시간이 되길 바라.
남: 고마워.

단·어·및·표·현
go on a picnic 소풍 가다

04 한일파악 ▶정답 ⑤

듣·기·대·본

M: Mary, you are nicely tanned!
W: Thanks. I went to the beach last weekend.
M: Good. Did you go swimming?
W: No, I didn't swim. The water was still too cold.
M: Then, what did you do? Oh, let me guess. You collected clams?
W: Actually, there was a movie shooting on the beach.
M: Wow, you went there just to see the shoot?
W: Yes! I watched my favorite actor preparing and acting for three hours!

우·리·말·해·석

남: Mary, 피부가 보기 좋게 탔다!
여: 고마워. 나는 지난 주말에 해변에 갔었어.
남: 좋았겠다. 수영하러 갔었니?
여: 아니, 수영은 안 했어. 물이 아직도 너무 차갑더라.
남: 그러면, 뭘 했어? 오, 내가 한번 맞혀 볼게. 너 조개 모았지?
여: 사실, 해변에서 영화 촬영이 있었어.
남: 와, 그럼 단지 촬영하는 것을 보러 간 거야?
여: 응! 나는 세 시간 동안 내가 가장 좋아하는 배우가 준비하고 연기하는 것을 봤어!

단·어·및·표·현

clam [klæm] 명 조개
movie shooting 영화 촬영

05 대화장소추론 ▶정답 ③

듣·기·대·본

M: Hello, how can I help you?
W: Hi, I'd like to buy two tickets for *Toy Adventures*.
M: Sure! For what time?
W: 6:30, please.
M: Let me check. (*pause*) Um… We only have front row seats left. Is that okay with you?
W: Hmm… Can we at least get seats that are in the center?
M: Sure! I'll get you seats that are in the center. That will be 30 dollars, please.
W: Here's my credit card.
M: Please wait for a minute while I print out your tickets.

우·리·말·해·석

남: 안녕하세요, 제가 어떻게 도와드릴까요?
여: 안녕하세요, 저는 "Toy Adventures"에 대한 표 2장을 사고 싶어요.
남: 그러세요! 몇 시로요?
여: 6시 30분이요.
남: 확인해보겠습니다. (잠시 후) 음… 저희는 앞 줄 좌석만 남아있습니다. 괜찮으신가요?
여: 흠… 적어도 가운데에 있는 좌석을 얻을 수 있나요?
남: 물론이죠! 제가 가운데에 있는 좌석을 드리겠습니다. 그것은 30달러입니다.
여: 여기 제 신용카드요.
남: 제가 당신의 표를 인쇄하는 동안 잠시 기다려주세요.

단·어·및·표·현

row [rou] 명 줄, 열

06 마지막말의도파악 ▶정답 ④

듣·기·대·본

W: I'm so happy that the exam is over!

M: Yes. I really want to sleep all day.
W: Didn't you sleep well? So, it wasn't just me.
M: Of course not! I studied science until late, but the exam was still very hard.
W: I think I did science all right, but English was very difficult for me.
M: Tell me about it. It was hard for me, too.

우·리·말·해·석

여: 시험이 끝나다니 너무 기뻐!
남: 응. 난 정말로 하루 종일 자고 싶어.
여: 잠을 잘 못 잤니? 그렇다면, 나만 그런 게 아니었구나.
남: 당연히 못 잤지! 나는 늦게까지 과학 공부를 했는데, 그래도 시험이 너무 어려웠어.
여: 나는 과학은 잘 본 것 같은데, 영어가 나에게는 어려웠어.
남: 내 말이 그 말이야. 나도 어려웠어.

단·어·및·표·현

be over 끝나다

07 특정정보파악 ▶정답 ④

듣·기·대·본

W: I'm getting tired of my hairstyle. I want to try a different look.
M: What do you have in mind?
W: Hmm… Do you think blonde hair will look good on me?
M: No, I don't think so. Your hair will look like a wig.
W: Okay. I'll just get a perm at the salon then.
M: That's a good idea. You'll look cute with curly hair.

우·리·말·해·석

여: 나 내 머리 스타일이 지겨워지고 있어. 나는 다른 모습을 해 보고 싶어.
남: 생각해 둔 것이 있니?
여: 흠… 너 금발이 내게 잘 어울릴 것이라고 생각하니?
남: 아니, 나는 그렇게 생각하지 않아. 네 머리는 가발처럼 보일 거야.
여: 좋아. 그럼 난 미용실에서 그냥 파마를 하겠어.
남: 그거 좋은 생각이야. 너는 곱슬거리는 머리를 하면 귀여워 보일 거야.

단·어·및·표·현

get tired of ~ ~에 지겨워지다, ~에 싫증나다
look good on ~ ~와 잘 어울리다

08 할일파악(대화직후) ▶정답 ①

듣·기·대·본

W: Hi, Kevin. Did you finish the survey for your project?
M: Yes, Ms. Park. I prepared the survey questions last night.
W: Good job! Did you bring enough copies for the class?
M: Oh! I only brought one copy with me.
W: You'll need to hand out copies to everyone.
M: Right. Can I use the copy machine now?
W: Sure. It's in the teachers' room.
M: Okay. I'll go and make copies of my survey right now.

우·리·말·해·석

여: 안녕, Kevin. 네 프로젝트를 위한 설문지 마무리했니?
남: 네, 박 선생님. 어젯밤에 설문지 질문들을 준비했어요.
여: 잘했어! 학급 전체를 위해 충분한 복사본을 가져왔니?
남: 아! 한 부만 가져왔어요.
여: 네가 모두에게 복사본을 나눠줘야 할 거야.
남: 맞아요. 지금 복사기를 써도 될까요?
여: 물론이지. 교무실에 있어.

남: 알겠어요. 지금 바로 가서 제 설문지를 복사할게요.

단 · 어 · 및 · 표 · 현
survey [sə́ːrvei] 명 설문조사
prepare [pripɛ́ər] 동 준비하다
copy [kάpi] 명 복사본, 사본 동 복사하다
hand out 나눠주다
teachers' room 교무실

09 대화미언급　　　　　▶ 정답 ⑤

듣 · 기 · 대 · 본
W: Daniel, what are you listening to?
M: It's a song by a new singer, Paula Dawson. Do you want to hear it?
W: Yes, I do! (*pause*) Oh, it's good. She just debuted the song this month, right?
M: That's right. This song is titled "Crash."
W: Strong name. And it sounds like a rock ballad.
M: Yes, it is. I like rock ballads very much.
W: I like them, too. I should download this song.
M: Yeah, you should.

우 · 리 · 말 · 해 · 석
여: Daniel, 무엇을 듣고 있니?
남: Paula Dawson이라는 신인 가수의 노래야. 넌 그것을 듣고 싶니?
여: 응, 듣고 싶어! (잠시 후) 오, 좋다. 그녀가 이번 달에 막 최초로 공개한 곡이지, 그렇지?
남: 맞아. 이 곡의 제목은 "Crash"야.
여: 강렬한 이름이다. 그리고 그것은 록 발라드처럼 들려.
남: 응, 맞아. 난 록 발라드를 무척 좋아해.
여: 나도 그것들을 좋아해. 난 이 곡을 다운로드 해야겠어.
남: 응, 꼭 그렇게 해.

단 · 어 · 및 · 표 · 현
debut [déibjùː] 동 ～을 최초로 공개하다
title [táitl] 동 제목을 붙이다

10 담화화제추론　　　　　▶ 정답 ③

듣 · 기 · 대 · 본
W: Hello, students. Future Career Week has finally arrived! The event will be held between 3 and 5 p.m. for five days starting next Monday. After class, go to the gym and participate in as many programs as possible. You will be amazed at how many exciting future jobs there are, and you can explore them all with your friends. For more information, check out the school website. Have fun!

우 · 리 · 말 · 해 · 석
여: 안녕하세요, 학생 여러분. Future Career Week(미래 직업 주간)가 드디어 다가왔습니다! 행사는 다음 주 월요일부터 시작해서 5일간 오후 3시부터 5시 사이에 열릴 것입니다. 수업 후에 체육관에 가서 가능한 한 많은 프로그램에 참여하세요. 여러분은 얼마나 많은 흥미진진한 미래 직업이 있는지 놀라게 될 것이고, 그 모든 직업을 친구들과 함께 탐색할 수 있습니다. 자세한 내용은 학교 홈페이지를 확인하세요. 재미있게 보내세요!

단 · 어 · 및 · 표 · 현
be held 열리다, 개최되다
participate in ～에 참여하다
be amazed at ～에 깜짝 놀라다
explore [ikspló:r] 동 탐색하다

11 대화내용불일치　　　　　▶ 정답 ④

듣 · 기 · 대 · 본
M: Amy, do you have any plans for the summer?
W: Yes! I'm going to take a dance class. It'll begin on July 1.
M: That's cool. What kind of dance?
W: Hip-hop. Are you interested?
M: Yeah, I've always wanted to learn hip-hop. When is the class held?
W: Every Saturday at 10 a.m. It's an hour long.
M: All right. I'll sign up for it.
W: Great! You need to sign up at the community center.

우 · 리 · 말 · 해 · 석
남: Amy, 너 여름에 어떤 계획이 있니?
여: 응! 나는 댄스 수업을 들을 거야. 그것은 7월 1일에 시작할 거야.
남: 그거 멋지다. 무슨 종류의 댄스야?
여: 힙합이야. 너 관심 있니?
남: 응. 나는 늘 힙합을 배우고 싶었어. 수업이 언제 열려?
여: 매주 토요일 오전 10시야. 그것은 한 시간 길이야.
남: 좋아. 나는 그것에 등록할 거야.
여: 훌륭해! 너는 주민센터에서 등록해야 해.

단 · 어 · 및 · 표 · 현
sign up for ~ ～에 등록하다

12 방문이유파악　　　　　▶ 정답 ②

듣 · 기 · 대 · 본
M: Hello. Can I help you?
W: Yes. I bought this electric fan here this morning.
M: I see. Is there a problem with it?
W: No, the fan works fine. I just want to cancel the payment I made and pay with a different credit card.
M: Sure. Do you have your receipt and the card you used?
W: Yes, I brought both.
M: Great. I'll help you with that.

우 · 리 · 말 · 해 · 석
남: 안녕하세요. 도와드릴까요?
여: 네. 저는 오늘 아침에 여기에서 이 전기 선풍기를 샀어요.
남: 그렇군요. 그것에 문제가 있나요?
여: 아니요, 선풍기는 잘 작동해요. 저는 단지 제가 했던 결제를 취소하고 다른 신용 카드로 결제하고 싶어서요.
남: 물론이죠. 당신은 당신의 영수증과 당신이 사용했던 카드를 가지고 있나요?
여: 네, 저는 둘 다 가져왔어요.
남: 좋네요. 제가 그것을 도와드릴게요.

단 · 어 · 및 · 표 · 현
electric [iléktrik] 형 전기의, 전기를 이용하는
fan [fæn] 명 선풍기
work [wəːrk] 동 (기계 · 장치 등이) 작동하다, 기능하다
cancel [kǽnsəl] 동 취소하다, 무효화하다
payment [péimənt] 명 결제, 지불
receipt [risíːt] 명 영수증
bring [briŋ] 동 가져오다, 가져다 주다

13 수치계산(거스름돈)　　　　　▶ 정답 ③

듣 · 기 · 대 · 본
M: Welcome to Juice World. May I take your order?
W: Yes. I would like to order one ABC juice.

M: Okay. What size would you like? If you <u>upsize</u>, it will cost one dollar more.
W: I'll upsize, please.
M: Okay, that will be 5 dollars. <u>Will that be all</u> for today?
W: Oh, could I also get <u>a bag of</u> rice crisps?
M: Including the rice crisps, your total will be 7 dollars.
W: Here is 10 dollars for you.
M: Thank you. Here is your change.

우·리·말·해·석

남: Juice World에 오신 것을 환영합니다. 주문하시겠습니까?
여: 네. 저는 ABC주스 한 잔을 주문하고 싶어요.
남: 알겠습니다. 어떤 용량을 원하세요? 만약 용량을 늘리시면, 1달러 더 비용이 듭니다.
여: 용량을 늘려주세요.
남: 알겠습니다. 5달러입니다. 오늘 더 주문할 것은 없으신가요?
여: 오, 쌀과자 한 봉지도 살 수 있을까요?
남: 쌀과자를 포함해서, 고객님의 총액은 7달러입니다.
여: 여기 10달러입니다.
남: 감사합니다. 여기 거스름돈입니다.

단·어·및·표·현
take an order 주문을 받다
ABC juice ABC 주스(사과, 비트, 당근을 갈아 만든 주스)
total [tóutl] 몡 총액, 합계
change [tʃeindʒ] 몡 거스름돈

14 대화자관계추론 ▶정답 ①

듣·기·대·본

W: Excuse me. Why hasn't boarding started? The ferry is supposed to leave in a minute.
M: I'm sorry. The captain has <u>delayed departure</u>. The waves are too high right now.
W: Oh, no. I really have to cross the channel tonight.
M: It <u>depends on</u> the weather, but I'm sure we will be able to leave tonight.
W: Are you one of the crew?
M: Yes. I'll <u>let you know</u> as soon as we are ready to leave.
W: Thank you.

우·리·말·해·석

여: 실례합니다. 왜 탑승이 시작되지 않았나요? 연락선은 곧 출발하기로 되어 있어요.
남: 죄송합니다. 선장님께서 출발을 연기하셨어요. 지금 당장은 파도가 너무 높아요.
여: 아, 안돼요. 저는 오늘 밤에 꼭 해협을 건너야 해요.
남: 그건 날씨에 달려 있지만, 전 우리가 오늘 밤에 출발할 수 있을 거라고 확신해요.
여: 당신은 선원 중 한 명인가요?
남: 네. 제가 저희가 출발할 준비가 되자마자 당신께 알려드릴게요.
여: 감사합니다.

단·어·및·표·현
ferry [féri] 몡 (사람, 차량 등을 운반하는) 연락선, 여객선
be supposed to ~하기로 되어있다
in a minute 잠시 후에, 곧
delay [diléi] 통 지연시키다, 지체하게 하다
departure [dipáːrtʃər] 몡 출발
channel [tʃǽnəl] 몡 해협
depend on ~에 달려있다, ~에 의존하다
crew [kruː] 몡 선원, 승무원

15 부탁(요청)한일파악 ▶정답 ③

듣·기·대·본

W: Fred, you look tired.
M: I <u>spent the whole day</u> trying to write a song.
W: The music homework? But, you are good at playing the piano.
M: Well, writing a song is a <u>totally different thing</u>.
W: Oh… I know what you mean. Well, I know a website that might help.
M: What kind of website is it?
W: It shows simple steps to song writing.
M: Can you give me the website address?
W: Sure. I'll <u>text</u> it to you.

우·리·말·해·석

여: Fred, 너 피곤해 보여.
남: 나는 작곡하는 데 하루를 다 보냈어.
여: 음악 숙제? 하지만 너는 피아노 연주를 잘하잖아.
남: 글쎄, 작곡하는 것은 완전히 다른 일이야.
여: 오… 나는 네가 무슨 말을 하는지 알아. 그런데, 나는 도움이 될지도 모르는 웹사이트를 알아.
남: 무슨 종류의 웹사이트인데?
여: 그것은 작곡에 대한 간단한 단계들을 보여줘.
남: 나한테 그 웹사이트 주소를 줄 수 있어?
여: 물론이지. 너한테 그것을 문자로 보낼게.

단·어·및·표·현
whole [houl] 몡 전체의, 온전한
text [tekst] 통 문자를 보내다

16 이유파악 ▶정답 ④

듣·기·대·본

M: Hey, Jenny. Where are you <u>headed</u>?
W: I'm going to Central Park.
M: Why are you going there at this hour? It's <u>getting dark</u>.
W: There's going to be a free concert there tonight.
M: You mean at Central Park?
W: Yeah. The concert will be featuring the Korea Symphony Orchestra.
M: Oh, so it's a classical music concert. Can I <u>come with you</u>?
W: Of course! Let's go.

우·리·말·해·석

남: 이봐, Jenny. 어디에 가고 있니?
여: 난 Central 공원에 가는 중이야.
남: 왜 이 시간에 거기에 가는 거야? 어두워지고 있어.
여: 오늘 밤 거기서 무료 콘서트가 있을 거야.
남: Central 공원에서 말이니?
여: 응. 그 콘서트에는 한국 교향악단이 출연할 거야.
남: 오, 그러니까 그건 클래식 음악 콘서트구나. 내가 너와 같이 가도 될까?
여: 물론이지! 가자.

단·어·및·표·현
be headed (for) (~로) 향하다
feature [fíːtʃər] 통 ~을 출연시키다, ~에 출연하다
come with ~와 같이 가다

17 그림상황에적절한대화찾기 ▶정답 ③

듣·기·대·본

① W: Can I borrow your bicycle on the weekend?

M: I'm sorry, but mine is broken.

② W: Excuse me. Where can I find cereal?

M: That would be in aisle 3, ma'am.

③ W: I think the steak is undercooked. Could you cook it more?

M: Certainly. I'll have the chef cook it more.

④ W: How would you like your one thousand dollars, sir?

M: In fifties, please.

⑤ W: How often should I take this medicine?

M: Take it once a day after a meal.

우·리·말·해·석

① 여: 주말에 내가 너의 자전거를 빌릴 수 있을까?

남: 미안하지만 내 거 고장났어.

② 여: 실례합니다. 시리얼을 어디서 찾을 수 있나요?

남: 그것은 통로 3에 있을 것입니다, 부인.

③ 여: 저는 스테이크가 덜 익혀졌다고 생각해요. 그것을 더 익혀주시겠어요?

남: 물론입니다. 제가 요리사가 그것을 더 익히도록 하겠습니다.

④ 여: 당신의 천 달러를 어떻게 원하세요, 손님?

남: 50달러짜리로 부탁합니다.

⑤ 여: 제가 이 약을 얼마나 자주 먹어야 하나요?

남: 하루에 한 번 식후에 드세요.

단·어·및·표·현

aisle [ail] ⑱ 통로

undercook [ʌ̀ndərkúk] ⑧ 덜 익히다

18 담화미언급 ▶정답 ④

듣·기·대·본

W: Hello, students! For art lovers, Washington Middle School holds an art contest. It will be held next month, on the 21st at the school. First prize will be a tablet PC. There are other prizes for winners, so sign up now! Students' work will be judged by local artists. Your art teachers are expecting many talented students to enter the contest!

우·리·말·해·석

여: 안녕하세요, 학생 여러분! 미술을 사랑하는 사람들을 위해, Washington 중학교가 미술 대회를 개최합니다. 그것은 다음 달 21일에 학교에서 열립니다. 일등상은 태블릿 PC가 될 것입니다. 우승자들을 위한 다른 상들도 있으니, 지금 등록하세요! 학생들의 작품은 지역 화가들에 의해 심사될 것입니다. 여러분의 미술 선생님들이 많은 재능 있는 학생들이 대회에 참여하기를 기대하고 있습니다!

단·어·및·표·현

judge [dʒʌ́dʒ] ⑧ 심사하다, 평가하다

local [lóukəl] ⑲ 지역의

19 알맞은응답찾기 ▶정답 ②

듣·기·대·본

M: Angela, we need to get things ready.

W: What's going on, Dad?

M: Don't you remember that we have guests today? They will be here soon.

W: Oh, right. I've already cleaned up my room like you asked.

M: You have? Great! Then, can you give me a hand with the living room?

W: Sure. What do you need me to do?

M: Please open the curtains and arrange the cushions on the sofa.

W: Okay, I'll take care of it right away.

우·리·말·해·석

① 죄송해요, 저는 지금 바빠요.

② 알겠어요. 제가 바로 처리할게요.

③ 방을 치워 줘서 고마워요.

④ 커튼과 쿠션을 좀 주문해요.

⑤ 제가 손님께 전화해서 만남을 취소할게요.

남: Angela, 우리는 준비를 해야 해.

여: 무슨 일이에요, 아빠?

남: 우리 오늘 손님이 있다는 거 기억 안 나니? 그분들이 곧 여기 도착할 거야.

여: 아, 맞다. 아빠가 시키신 대로 제 방은 이미 치워놨어요.

남: 그랬니? 잘했구나! 그럼 거실 치우는 것 좀 도와줄 수 있겠니?

여: 물론이죠. 제가 무엇을 하면 될까요?

남: 커튼을 열고 소파에 쿠션들을 정리해 주렴.

여: 알겠어요. 제가 바로 처리할게요.

단·어·및·표·현

give ~ a hand ~에게 도움을 주다

arrange [əréindʒ] ⑧ 정리하다, 배열하다

20 알맞은응답찾기 ▶정답 ①

듣·기·대·본

W: How was your trip, Mike?

M: Not so good.

W: Why? What happened?

M: Most of the time, I stayed at the hotel.

W: Why? Were you sick?

M: No, I wasn't. It was because of the bad weather. It rained a lot.

W: Oh, that's too bad.

우·리·말·해·석

① 오, 정말 안됐구나. ② 천만에.

③ 만나서 반가워. ④ 좋은 생각이야.

⑤ 정말 멋진 시간을 보낸 것처럼 들려.

여: 여행 어땠어, Mike?

남: 그다지 좋지 않았어.

여: 왜? 무슨 일 있었니?

남: 대부분의 시간은 호텔에서 머물렀어.

여: 왜? 아팠어?

남: 아니, 아프지 않았어. 안 좋은 날씨 때문이었어. 비가 많이 내렸거든.

여: 오, 정말 안됐구나.

단·어·및·표·현

bad weather 안 좋은 날씨, 흐린 날씨

Words & Expressions Review

1. (기계·장치 등이) 작동하다, 기능하다	2. ~을 최초로 공개하다	3. 행사
4. 앞의	5. 개최하다, 열다	6. 소풍을 가다
7. 줄, 열	8. ~에게 도움을 주다	9. 정리하다, 배열하다
10. 결제, 지불	11. 모으다, 수집하다	12. 채널을 고정하다
13. (수량·정도의) 하락, 감소	14. 안 좋은 날씨	15. 바라다, 희망
16. ~에 등록하다	17. 통로	18. 적어도, 최소한

19. 단계	20. 물방울무늬의	21. 설문조사
22. 주문을 받다	23. 심사하다, 평가하다	24. 덜 익은
25. 조개	26. ~이 지겨워지다	27. 머무르다
28. ~와 잘 어울리다	29. 출발	30. (특정 방향으로) 가다, 향하다
31. 제목을 붙이다	32. ~와 같이 가다	33. ~에 깜짝 놀라다
34. 전기의, 전기를 이용하는	35. 완전히, 전적으로	36. 영화 촬영
37. 끝나다	38. 지연시키다, 지체하게 하다	39. ~을 출연시키다, ~에 출연하다
40. 약을 먹다	41. 인쇄하다	42. 탐색하다
43. (앞일, 미래 등을) 내다보다	44. 화면	

영어듣기 모의고사 19회

|정답|

01 ③	02 ④	03 ②	04 ⑤	05 ②
06 ③	07 ⑤	08 ⑤	09 ③	10 ④
11 ⑤	12 ④	13 ④	14 ③	15 ②
16 ⑤	17 ④	18 ④	19 ①	20 ③

01 날씨파악–그림　▶ 정답 ③

듣·기·대·본

M: Good morning. This is the Friday weather report. Today, it will be cloudy in the afternoon, and it's going to rain at night. On Saturday, it will be colder, and the rain will change to snow. The snowy weather will continue until Monday. Thank you.

우·리·말·해·석

남: 좋은 아침입니다. 금요일 날씨 보도입니다. 오늘은 오후에 구름이 끼겠으며, 밤에는 비가 올 것입니다. 토요일에는 더 추워질 것이며, 비가 눈으로 변할 것입니다. 눈 오는 날씨는 월요일 전까지 계속될 것입니다. 감사합니다.

단·어·및·표·현

continue [kəntínju(:)] ⑤ 계속되다, 지속하다

02 그림정보파악　▶ 정답 ④

듣·기·대·본

M: Which one of these mats do you like most for our bathroom?

W: I like the bright, heart-shaped mat.

M: But the bright one will get dirty easily.

W: You're right. Then, which mat do you like?

M: I think a dark mat would be best. Let's choose one of these cloud-shaped ones.

W: Okay. How about the dark, cloud-shaped mat with a smiley face?

M: The smiley face looks cute. Let's buy that one.

우·리·말·해·석

남: 우리 욕실을 위해서 이 매트들 중 어떤 게 가장 마음에 들어요?

여: 난 밝은 하트 모양의 매트가 마음에 들어요.

남: 하지만 밝은 건 쉽게 더러워질 거예요.

여: 맞아요. 그러면, 당신은 어떤 매트가 좋아요?

남: 내 생각에는 어두운 색 매트가 가장 좋을 것 같아요. 이 구름 모양의 것들 중 하나를 골라봅시다.

여: 좋아요. 웃는 얼굴이 있는 어두운 색의 구름 모양 매트는 어때요?

남: 웃는 얼굴이 귀여워 보이네요. 그걸로 삽시다.

단·어·및·표·현

bright [brait] ⑧ 밝은
smiley face 웃는 얼굴

03 심정추론　▶ 정답 ②

듣·기·대·본

M: This painting is amazing! What a little artist our daughter is!

W: I know. She's improved her skills a lot lately.

M: No one will believe this is the work of a 10-year-old.

W: You're right. She's pretty good for her age.

M: Let me take a picture of her painting.

W: What are you going to do with it?

M: I want to show everyone how talented our daughter is.

우·리·말·해·석

① 수줍은　② 자랑스러운　③ 걱정하는　④ 감사하는　⑤ 실망한

남: 이 그림은 놀라워요! 우리 딸은 정말 어린 예술가예요!

여: 맞아요. 그녀는 최근에 그녀의 기술을 많이 향상시켰어요.

남: 이게 10살짜리의 작품이라는 것을 아무도 믿지 않을 거예요.

여: 맞아요. 그녀는 그녀의 나이에 비해서 꽤 잘했어요.

남: 그녀의 그림을 사진 찍을게요.

여: 그것으로 뭘 할 거예요?

남: 우리 딸이 얼마나 재능이 있는지 모두에게 보여주고 싶어요.

단·어·및·표·현

improve [imprúːv] ⑤ 향상시키다
skill [skil] ⑧ 기술, 기량
lately [léitli] ⑨ 최근에
work [wəːrk] ⑧ (생산 · 결과물로서의) 작품, 일
for one's age 나이에 비해
talented [tǽləntid] ⑧ (타고난) 재능이 있는

04 한일파악　▶ 정답 ⑤

듣·기·대·본

W: I really want a dog, but I can't afford one.

M: You can still play with dogs even if you don't own one.

W: How can I do that?

M: I volunteered at an animal shelter last weekend and played with the dogs there. You can do the same.

W: Really? Volunteer work sounds like a great idea.

M: Yes, and it's good for the dogs, too. They need love and attention.

W: I'll definitely check it out.

우·리·말·해·석

여: 난 정말 개를 키우고 싶지만 여유가 안 돼.

남: 네가 개를 키우지 않더라도 개들과 놀 수 있어.

여: 내가 어떻게 그렇게 할 수 있어?

남: 난 지난 주말에 동물 보호소에서 자원 봉사를 했는데 거기에서 개들과 놀았어. 너도 똑같이 할 수 있어.

여: 정말? 자원 봉사는 정말 좋은 생각인 것 같아.

남: 응, 그리고 그건 개들에게도 좋아. 그들은 사랑과 관심이 필요해.

여: 난 반드시 그것을 확인해볼거야.

단·어·및·표·현

afford [əfɔ́ːrd] 통 (~을 살·할 금전적·시간적) 여유가 되다
animal shelter 동물 보호소
attention [əténʃən] 명 관심, 주의
definitely [défənitli] 부 반드시, 분명히

05 대화장소추론 ▶정답 ②

듣·기·대·본

M: Welcome. How may I help you?

W: I'm here to pick up my earrings.

M: Did you pre-order a new pair?

W: No. I left my old earrings here for repair. The hooks had fallen off.

M: Right. Are you Amanda Peet? Here they are.

W: That's right. (*pause*) Oh, they are shining like new!

M: The cleaning service is included.

W: Thanks a lot. I'll drop by to buy new ones some other time.

우·리·말·해·석

남: 어서 오세요. 어떻게 도와드릴까요?

여: 저는 여기에 제 귀걸이를 찾으러 왔어요.

남: 새 귀걸이를 선주문 하셨나요?

여: 아뇨. 전 여기에 제 오래된 귀걸이를 수리하기 위해 맡겼어요. 고리가 떨어졌거든요.

남: 그렇군요. 당신이 Amanda Peet이신가요? 여기 있습니다.

여: 맞아요. (잠시 후) 오, 그것들이 새것처럼 반짝이네요!

남: 세척 서비스가 포함되어 있습니다.

여: 정말 고맙습니다. 다음에 새것들을 사러 들를게요.

단·어·및·표·현

pre-order 선주문하다
repair [ripɛ́ər] 명 수리, 보수, 수선
fall off 떨어지다
drop by 잠깐 들르다, 방문하다

06 마지막말의도파악 ▶정답 ③

듣·기·대·본

W: Why do you look so down?

M: My dog is missing.

W: I'm so sorry. How did it happen?

M: I think she left when the door was open.

W: Why was the door open?

M: I guess I left it open when I went to the convenience store.

W: Oh, no! Well, did you check the animal shelter?

M: I did. She wasn't there.

W: Then, why don't you make some flyers?

우·리·말·해·석

여: 너 왜 그렇게 기운이 없어 보이니?

남: 내 개가 없어졌어.

여: 너무 안됐다. 어쩌다 그런 일이 생겼어?

남: 문이 열려 있을 때 나간 것 같아.

여: 왜 문이 열려 있었어?

남: 내가 편의점에 갔을 때 그것을 열어두었나 봐.

여: 아, 이런! 음, 너 동물 보호소는 확인해봤니?

남: 했어. 거기에 없었어.

여: 그럼, 전단지를 좀 만드는 게 어때?

단·어·및·표·현

missing [mísiŋ] 형 없어진, 실종된
leave ~ open ~을 열린 채로 두다
animal shelter 동물 보호소
flyer [fláiər] 명 (광고) 전단지

07 특정정보파악 ▶정답 ⑤

듣·기·대·본

W: You look so down today. What's the matter?

M: I'm worried.

W: What is it, Steve?

M: Next Friday is my parents' wedding anniversary. But I don't have enough money to buy them a nice present.

W: Don't worry too much. Your parents will like whatever you give them.

M: Do you really think so?

W: Sure. A small gift from your heart will make them happy.

우·리·말·해·석

여: 너 오늘 너무 기운 없어 보여. 무슨 일이니?

남: 걱정거리가 있어.

여: 그게 뭔데, Steve?

남: 다음 주 금요일이 부모님의 결혼기념일이야. 그런데 좋은 선물을 사드릴 충분한 돈이 없어.

여: 너무 걱정하지 마. 너희 부모님은 네가 무엇을 드려도 좋아하실 거야.

남: 너 정말 그렇게 생각해?

여: 물론이지. 네 마음에서 우러나온 작은 선물이 그분들을 행복하게 할 거야.

단·어·및·표·현

look down 기운이 없어 보이다, 의기소침해 보이다
enough [inʌ́f] 형 충분한

LISTENING ADVICE

'gh'는 두 가지 발음으로 소리 납니다. 위의 본문에서와 같이 'enough'와 같은 단어는 [f]로 발음하여 [이너프]로 소리 납니다. 하지만 'dough', 'through', 'although'와 같은 단어는 묵음 처리되어 'gh' 앞의 모음까지만 발음하여 각각 [도우], [뜨루], [올도우]로 소리 납니다.

---

08 할일파악(대화직후) ▶정답 ⑤

듣·기·대·본

W: Ben, the zoo is bigger than I thought!

M: Yeah, it's really sunny today, too. You'd better put on your hat.

W: You're right. I should've brought my hat from the car.

M: Do you want me to get it for you?

W: No, it's okay. I'll go get it myself.

M: Are you sure?

W: Yes, I'll be right back with my hat.

우·리·말·해·석

여: Ben, 동물원이 내가 생각했던 것보다 크네!

남: 응, 오늘 날씨도 정말 화창해. 너는 네 모자를 쓰는 게 낫겠어.

여: 네 말이 맞아. 나는 차에서 내 모자를 가져왔어야 했어.

남: 내가 너에게 그것을 가져다주길 원하니?

여: 아니, 괜찮아. 내가 직접 가지러 갈게.

남: 정말 괜찮아?

여: 응, 모자 가지고 금방 돌아올게.

19
회
모
의
고
사

단·어·및·표·현
had better ~하는 것이 낫다
put on ~을 쓰다/입다/신다
should have p.p. ~했어야 했다

09 대화미언급 ▶정답 ③

듣·기·대·본

(Telephone rings.)

W: Hello, Blue Swimming Center. How may I help you?

M: Hi, I want to learn to swim. Do you have classes for beginners?

W: Yes. We offer a beginner's class every morning.

M: Oh, good. How many students are in each class?

W: We take up to six people in each class.

M: Do I need to bring my own towel?

W: No, we have towels for you here.

M: Can I use the lockers?

W: Sure. It's 10 dollars per month.

M: Okay. Thank you.

우·리·말·해·석

(전화벨이 울린다.)

여: 여보세요, Blue Swimming Center입니다. 어떻게 도와드릴까요?

남: 안녕하세요, 저는 수영을 배우고 싶어요. 초보자를 위한 반들이 있나요?

여: 네. 저희는 매일 아침 초급자 반(수업)을 제공합니다.

남: 오, 잘됐네요. 각 반에 몇 명의 학생들이 있나요?

여: 저희는 각 반에 6명까지 받습니다.

남: 제 수건을 가져가야 하나요?

여: 아니요, 여기에 당신을 위한 수건이 있습니다.

남: 제가 사물함을 사용할 수 있나요?

여: 그럼요. 그것은 한 달에 10달러입니다.

남: 좋아요. 감사합니다.

단·어·및·표·현

beginner [bigínər] 명 초보자, 초급자

up to ~ ~까지

locker [lákər] 명 사물함

10 담화화제추론 ▶정답 ④

듣·기·대·본

W: Hello, students. Today, I'm going to tell you how to stay healthy in extreme heat. First, try to keep out of the sun between 11 a.m. and 3 p.m. Second, drink plenty of water often. Lastly, apply sunscreen frequently and wear a hat, if you have to go out in the heat. Please be careful in hot weather.

우·리·말·해·석

여: 안녕하세요, 학생 여러분. 오늘, 저는 폭염 속에서 어떻게 건강하게 지낼 수 있을지에 대해 여러분에게 말할 것입니다. 첫째, 오전 11시에서 오후 3시 사이에는 햇빛을 피하도록 하세요. 둘째, 많은 물을 자주 마시세요. 마지막으로, 여러분이 더위 속에서 밖에 나가야 한다면, 자외선 차단제를 자주 바르고 모자를 쓰세요. 부디 더운 날씨에 (건강) 유의하세요.

단·어·및·표·현

extreme [ikstríːm] 형 극도의

keep out of ~ ~을 피하다

plenty of 많은

apply [əplái] 동 바르다

sunscreen [sánskrìːn] 명 자외선 차단제

11 대화내용불일치 ▶정답 ⑤

듣·기·대·본

M: Emily, look at this website. They're holding auditions for a singing contest.

W: It's for a TV program.

M: Yes. The winners will star in a famous musical. Why don't you try out? It would be your dream come true!

W: They only select 100 people from the whole country.

M: You just have to send a video clip of your singing to apply. There's nothing to lose.

W: When is the deadline?

M: It's December 1.

W: That's three days from today.

M: That's plenty of time!

우·리·말·해·석

남: Emily, 이 웹사이트를 봐. 그들이 노래 대회의 오디션을 열고 있어.

여: 그것은 TV 프로그램을 위한 거야.

남: 그래. 우승자들은 유명한 뮤지컬에서 주연을 맡을 거야. 네가 해보는 것이 어때? 그것은 네 꿈이 실현되는 것일 수 있어!

여: 그들은 전국에서 100명의 사람들만 뽑아.

남: 너는 신청하기 위해 네가 노래한 것의 짧은 비디오를 보내기만 하면 돼. 잃을 게 없어.

여: 기한이 언제야?

남: 12월 1일이야.

여: 그것은 오늘로부터 3일 후야.

남: 그 정도면 충분한 시간이야!

단·어·및·표·현

star [staːr] 동 주연을 맡다

deadline [dédlàin] 명 기한

plenty of 많은

12 전화목적파악 ▶정답 ④

듣·기·대·본

(Cellphone rings.)

M: Hello?

W: Hello! It's Ruth. Are you busy this weekend?

M: No, not really. Why?

W: Mark and I are volunteering this Saturday. Do you want to join us?

M: Cool! What kind of volunteer work are you guys thinking of doing?

W: Well, we were thinking about volunteering for a river clean-up group. The members of the group pick up trash by the riverside.

M: Sounds great. Can you sign me up as well?

W: Sure.

우·리·말·해·석

(휴대폰이 울린다.)

남: 여보세요?

여: 안녕! 나 Ruth야. 너 이번 주말에 바쁘니?

남: 아니, 그다지 바쁘지 않아. 왜?

여: Mark와 나는 이번 토요일에 자원봉사를 할 예정이야. 너도 우리와 함께 할래?

남: 멋지다! 너희들은 어떤 종류의 자원봉사를 하려고 생각하고 있어?

여: 음, 우리는 강 정화 작업 단체에서 자원봉사를 할까 생각하고 있었어. 그 단체의 회원들은 강변에서 쓰레기를 주워.

남: 좋은 생각이디. 나도 신청해줄래?

여: 물론이야.

단·어·및·표·현
clean-up 정화 (작업)
riverside [rívərsàid] 몡 강변
sign up 신청하다, 등록하다

13 수치파악 ▶정답 ④

듣·기·대·본
M: May I take your order?
W: Yes. I'd like to have an egg sandwich, please.
M: That will be 5 dollars. Do you want a bag of potato chips, too?
W: Yes, please. Can I have a bottle of orange juice as well?
M: Sure. The orange juice is 3 dollars. And the potato chips are 2 dollars.
W: Okay. How much is the total?
M: Your total is 10 dollars. Do you want to pay by cash?
W: Yes. I'll pay in cash.

우·리·말·해·석
남: 주문하시겠습니까?
여: 네. 계란 샌드위치 하나 주세요.
남: 5달러입니다. 감자칩도 한 봉지 원하세요?
여: 네, 주세요. 오렌지 주스도 한 병 주시겠어요?
남: 물론이죠. 오렌지 주스는 3달러입니다. 그리고 감자칩은 2달러입니다.
여: 네. 총액이 얼마인가요?
남: 손님의 총액은 10달러입니다. 현금으로 지불하시겠어요?
여: 네. 저는 현금으로 지불할게요.

단·어·및·표·현
as well (~뿐만 아니라/~은 물론) …도

14 대화자관계추론 ▶정답 ③

듣·기·대·본
M: Hello, Ms. Davidson. I'm Jinsu Han from *The Monthly Pianist* magazine.
W: It's nice to meet you, Mr. Han.
M: Thank you for giving your time for this interview.
W: My pleasure.
M: So, are you here in Korea for your concert tomorrow?
W: That's right. This is my second visit.
M: I guess you enjoyed performing here the last time you came.
W: Yes. Korean audiences are very enthusiastic.
M: Tell me more about it.

우·리·말·해·석
남: 안녕하세요, Davidson 씨. 저는 "The Monthly Pianist" 잡지의 한진수입니다.
여: 만나서 반갑습니다, 한 기자님.
남: 이 인터뷰를 위해 당신의 시간을 내주셔서 감사합니다.
여: 저의 기쁨입니다.
남: 그러니까, 당신은 내일 당신의 콘서트를 위해 여기 한국에 오셨나요?
여: 맞아요. 이것은 저의 두 번째 방문이에요.
남: 당신이 지난번에 왔을 때 여기서 연주하는 것을 즐기셨던 것 같아요.
여: 네. 한국 청중들은 매우 열광적이에요.
남: 그것에 대해 더 말씀해 주세요.

단·어·및·표·현
perform [pərfɔ́ːrm] 통 연주하다
audience [ɔ́ːdiəns] 몡 청중, 관중
enthusiastic [inθjùːziǽstik] 휑 열광적인

15 부탁(요청)한일파악 ▶정답 ②

듣·기·대·본
M: Mom, I'm a bit hungry. Can I have a snack?
W: Sure, what do you want? We can make some pancakes, if you'd like.
M: That sounds great! Let's make pancakes, then.
W: Okay. We'll need milk, flour, and some eggs.
M: I'll go check. (*pause*) I only see milk and flour.
W: Then, can you go and buy some eggs now?
M: Okay. I'll be back in a few minutes.

우·리·말·해·석
남: 엄마, 저 조금 배고파요. 간식을 먹어도 될까요?
여: 물론이지, 뭘 원하니? 네가 원하면 우린 팬케이크를 좀 만들 수 있단다.
남: 그거 좋아요! 그럼 우리 팬케이크를 만들어요.
여: 그래. 우린 우유, 밀가루, 그리고 계란이 좀 필요해.
남: 제가 가서 확인해 볼게요. (잠시 후) 우유와 밀가루만 보여요.
여: 그러면, 지금 네가 가서 계란을 좀 사올 수 있니?
남: 알겠어요. 금방 다녀올게요.

단·어·및·표·현
a bit 조금, 약간
flour [fláuər] 몡 밀가루

16 이유파악 ▶정답 ⑤

듣·기·대·본
M: Hello, Lisa. Where are you heading?
W: I'm on my way to the shopping mall.
M: Oh, do you have something to buy?
W: No. I'm going to meet my favorite boy group there. I got picked for their fan signing event.
M: Wow! Lucky you. That's why you look so awesome today.
W: Thank you. I even brought some dolls as presents for them.
M: Good for you. I hope you have a wonderful time there.
W: Thank you so much.

우·리·말·해·석
남: 안녕, Lisa. 너 어디 가고 있어?
여: 나는 쇼핑몰로 가는 길이야.
남: 아, 너 뭐 살 게 있니?
여: 아니. 나는 거기서 내가 가장 좋아하는 남자 아이돌 그룹을 만날 거야. 나는 그들의 팬 사인회에 뽑혔거든.
남: 우와! 운 좋다. 그게 네가 오늘 멋져 보이는 이유구나.
여: 고마워. 나는 심지어 그들을 위한 선물로 몇몇 인형들을 가져왔어.
남: 잘했네. 나는 네가 거기서 멋진 시간을 보내길 바라.
여: 정말 고마워.

단·어·및·표·현
head [hed] 통 (특정 방향으로) 가다, 향하다
on one's way to ~ ~로 가는 길[도중]에

17 그림상황에적절한대화찾기 ▶정답 ④

듣·기·대·본
① W: I'm looking for a guitar for beginners.
　 M: How about this one? It's $100.
② W: Are you going to participate in the talent show?
　 M: Yes, I'm going to play the piano.
③ W: Could you turn down the music, please?
　 M: Oh, sorry. I'll turn it down.

④ W: Look! That guy is busking over there.
　M: Let's go and take a look.
⑤ W: It's so crowded in here. All the benches are full.
　M: We should have come earlier.

우·리·말·해·석
① 여: 저는 초보자를 위한 기타를 찾고 있어요.
　남: 이것은 어때요? 100달러예요.
② 여: 너는 장기자랑에 참가할 거니?
　남: 응, 나는 피아노를 칠 거야.
③ 여: 음악 소리 좀 줄여 주실 수 있나요?
　남: 오, 죄송합니다. 줄이겠습니다.
④ 여: 봐! 저 남자는 저기서 길거리 연주를 하고 있어.
　남: 가서 구경하자.
⑤ 여: 여기 너무 붐빈다. 모든 벤치가 꽉 찼어.
　남: 우리는 더 일찍 왔어야 했어.

단·어·및·표·현
participate in ~에 참가하다
turn down (소리·온도 등을) 줄이다, 낮추다
busk[bʌsk] ⑧ 길거리에서 연주하다
crowded[kráudid] ⑨ (사람들이) 붐비는, 복잡한

18　담화미언급　▶ 정답 ④

듣·기·대·본
M: Hello, everyone. Friday, May 19 is the grand opening of Yellow Waffles, our new store. Our store will have more than 20 sorts of delicious waffles, coffees, and many other ice drinks. Anyone who buys a waffle-coffee combo will get a tumbler as a welcome gift. We also make deliveries for orders of 30 dollars or more. Please download our app for more information.

우·리·말·해·석
남: 안녕하세요, 여러분. 5월 19일 금요일에 저희의 새 가게인 Yellow Waffles가 개점합니다. 저희 가게는 20가지 이상의 맛있는 와플, 커피, 그리고 많은 다른 차가운 음료가 있을 것입니다. 와플-커피 콤보를 사시는 분은 누구든지 환영 선물(개업 사은품)로 텀블러를 받으실 것입니다. 저희는 또한 30달러 이상의 주문에 대해 배달을 합니다. 더 많은 정보를 위해 저희의 앱을 다운로드하세요.

단·어·및·표·현
sort[sɔːrt] ⑨ 종류
make deliveries 배달하다

19　알맞은응답찾기　▶ 정답 ①

듣·기·대·본
W: Hey, Anthony. Can I ask you a favor?
M: Sure! What is it?
W: Can you teach me how to throw free throws?
M: Yeah, no problem. You're preparing for your PE exams, right?
W: You're right. I've practiced a lot, but I don't seem to get any better.
M: I see... Then, how about meeting at the school basketball court at 8 p.m.?
W: Okay, I'll see you then.

우·리·말·해·석
① 좋아, 그때 보자.
② 우리는 저녁 먹으러 나갈 거야.
③ 아니, 나는 농구하는 것을 좋아하지 않아.
④ 나에게 네 책을 빌려줘서 고마워.
⑤ 나는 농구보다 테니스를 더 좋아해.

여: 안녕, Anthony. 부탁 하나 해도 될까?
남: 그럼! 뭐야?
여: 나에게 자유투 하는 법을 가르쳐 줄 수 있어?
남: 응, 문제없어. 너는 체육 시험에 대비하고 있구나, 맞지?
여: 맞아. 나는 많이 연습했지만, 조금도 나아지는 것 같지 않아.
남: 알겠어… 그러면, 학교 농구 코트에서 오후 8시에 만나는 게 어때?
여: 좋아, 그때 보자.

단·어·및·표·현
get better 나아지다, 좋아지다

20　알맞은응답찾기　▶ 정답 ③

듣·기·대·본
W: Where are you going, Peter?
M: I'm going out to ride my bike, Mom.
W: Look out the window. It's raining hard.
M: Oh, no! I promised to meet my friends at the park.
W: Well, maybe you should call them and change your plans.
M: Will it rain for long? I really want to hang out with them.
W: The rain isn't going to stop anytime soon.

우·리·말·해·석
① 너무 오랫동안 어울려 다니지 마라.
② 그 공원은 여기서 꽤 멀어.
③ 비는 곧 멈추지 않을 거야.
④ 너와 네 친구들은 좋은 계획을 만들었구나.
⑤ 요즘 자전거를 타는 것은 위험해.

여: 어디 가니, Peter?
남: 저는 제 자전거를 타러 나가고 있어요, 엄마.
여: 창 밖을 봐. 비가 심하게 내리고 있어.
남: 오, 안 돼요! 저는 공원에서 친구들을 만나기로 약속했어요.
여: 글쎄, 아마도 너는 그들에게 전화를 해서 계획을 바꿔야 할 거야.
남: 오랫동안 비가 내릴까요? 저는 정말로 그들과 같이 어울려 시간을 보내고 싶어요.
여: 비는 곧 멈추지 않을 거야.

단·어·및·표·현
hang out 어울려 시간을 보내다, 놀다

Words & Expressions Review

1. (타고난) 재능이 있는	2. 수리, 보수, 수선	3. (특정 방향으로) 가다, 향하다
4. 열광적인	5. 조금, 약간	6. 떨어지다
7. 밀가루	8. 어울려 시간을 보내다	9. 주연을 맡다
10. 밝은	11. (사람들이) 붐비는, 복잡한	12. 극도의
13. 구름	14. 관심, 주의	15. 많은
16. 현금	17. 신청하다, 등록하다	18. 나아지다, 좋아지다
19. 초보자, 초급자	20. 선물	21. ~을 피하다
22. 연주하다	23. (소리·온도 등을) 줄이다, 낮추다	24. 반드시, 분명히
25. 전단지	26. 정보	27. 바르다
28. ~까지	29. 편의점	30. 청중, 관중
31. 사물함	32. 기한	33. 배달하다
34. 나이에 비해	35. 충분한	36. 날씨 보도

<table>
<tr><td>37. 동물 보호소</td><td>38. 강변</td><td>39. 기운 없어 보이다</td></tr>
<tr><td>40. 종류</td><td>41. 없어진, 실종된</td><td>42. 향상시키다</td></tr>
<tr><td>43. 최근에</td><td colspan="2">44. 길거리에서
연주하다</td></tr>
</table>

Listening Test
영어듣기 모의고사 20회

|정|답|

01 ③	02 ④	03 ④	04 ③	05 ③
06 ③	07 ⑤	08 ③	09 ④	10 ③
11 ④	12 ⑤	13 ②	14 ①	15 ③
16 ④	17 ①	18 ③	19 ⑤	20 ①

01 　날씨파악-그림　▶정답 ③

듣·기·대·본

W: Good morning. Here is the weather forecast for today. Beijing will have a sunny day, while Tokyo will have cloudy skies. Melbourne will have rain showers. While Athens will experience snow, it will be sunny in London.

우·리·말·해·석

여: 안녕하세요. 오늘의 일기 예보입니다. 도쿄는 흐린 하늘을 보이는 반면 베이징은 맑을 것입니다. 멜버른은 소나기가 올 것입니다. 아테네에 눈이 올 반면, 런던은 맑을 것입니다.

단·어·및·표·현

while [*h*wail] 접 반면에, ~지만

02 　그림정보파악　▶정답 ④

듣·기·대·본

W: Excuse me. I'm looking for a curtain for my children's room.

M: Oh, look over here. These styles are popular for children.

W: Oh, they all look so cute!

M: How about this one with a whale on it?

W: Well, my children love dogs.

M: All right. There are two curtains with a dog. Which one do you prefer?

W: I like the one with the checkered pattern. I'll take it.

우·리·말·해·석

여: 실례합니다. 저는 제 아이들 방을 위한 커튼을 찾고 있어요.

남: 아, 여기를 보세요. 이 스타일들이 아이들에게 인기가 있습니다.

여: 오, 그것들은 모두 매우 귀여워 보여요!

남: 커튼에 고래가 있는 이것은 어떠세요?

여: 글쎄요, 제 아이들은 강아지를 좋아해요.

남: 좋습니다. 강아지가 있는 커튼이 두 개 있습니다. 당신은 어느 것을 더 좋아하세요?

여: 저는 체크무늬가 있는 것이 좋아요. 저는 그것으로 할게요.

단·어·및·표·현

prefer [prifə́ːr] 동 ~을 더 좋아하다
checkered [tʃékərd] 형 체크무늬의

03 　심정추론　▶정답 ④

듣·기·대·본

M: Hi, Susan. What did you do yesterday?

W: I attended a dance competition.

M: How did it go?

W: Not great. I didn't make it to the final round.

M: Oh, I'm sorry to hear that. What happened?

W: I stumbled during my routine and lost my rhythm.

M: You practiced so hard for this competition.

W: Yes, I did. I had expected to do better.

우·리·말·해·석

① 안심한　② 수줍은　③ 지루한　④ 실망한　⑤ 고마운

남: 안녕, Susan. 넌 어제 뭐 했어?

여: 나는 춤 대회에 참석했어.

남: 그건 어떻게 됐어?

여: 좋지 않았어. 난 결승전에 진출하지 못했어.

남: 오, 그것 안됐다. 무슨 일이 있었어?

여: 나는 내 (춤) 루틴(정해진 동작) 중에 발을 헛디뎠고, 박자를 놓쳤어.

남: 넌 이 대회를 위해 엄청 열심히 연습했잖아.

여: 응, 그랬지. 나는 더 잘할 거라고 기대했었어.

단·어·및·표·현

attend [əténd] 동 참석하다
competition [kàmpətíʃən] 명 대회, 경연, 시합
make it (바라던 일을) 해내다, 성공하다
stumble [stʌ́mbl] 동 발을 헛디디다
lose the rhythm 박자를 놓치다

04 　한일파악　▶정답 ③

듣·기·대·본

W: Jake, how's your school promotion video project going?

M: It's finished, Mom. Mr. Park will upload the video on the school website today.

W: Great. Did your project group do all the filming and editing yourselves?

M: Yes, we did.

W: Wow. What was your role in the project?

M: I wrote the subtitles.

W: Oh, transcribing all the words people say in the video must have been hard work.

M: Yes, it was. But it was fun.

우·리·말·해·석

여: Jake, 학교 홍보 영상 프로젝트는 어떻게 되고 있니?

남: 그건 끝났어요, 엄마. 박 선생님께서 오늘 학교 웹사이트에 영상을 올리실 거예요.

여: 잘했구나. 네 프로젝트 조는 모든 촬영과 편집을 직접 했니?

남: 네, 직접 했어요.

여: 우와. 프로젝트에서 네 역할을 뭐였니?

남: 저는 자막을 썼어요.

여: 아, 영상에서 사람들이 하는 모든 말을 (키보드로 입력하여) 문자화하는 건 틀림없이 어려운 일이었을 거야.

남: 네, 그랬어요. 하지만 재밌었어요.

단·어·및·표·현

promotion [prəmóuʃən] 명 홍보[판촉] (활동)
subtitle [sʌ́btàitl] 명 자막
transcribe [trænskráib] 동 (연설 등을) 문자화하다, 필기하다

20회 모의고사

듣·기·대·본

W: Wow, you got a strike! Good job!
M: Thanks. It's your turn now. Try to focus on the pins at the end of the lane!
W: Okay, but I think this ball is too heavy for me.
M: Try using this ball instead.
W: Thank you. (*pause*) Did you see that? I knocked down nine pins!
M: Good job!

우·리·말·해·석

여: 와, 너 스트라이크야! 잘했어!
남: 고마워. 이제 네 차례야. 레인 끝에 있는 핀에 집중하려고 애써 봐.
여: 알았어, 하지만 이 공은 나한테 너무 무거운 것 같아.
남: 대신에 이 공을 써 봐.
여: 고마워. (잠시 후) 봤어? 내가 핀 아홉 개를 쓰러뜨렸어!
남: 잘했어!

단·어·및·표·현

try to + 동사원형 ～하려고 애쓰다, 노력하다

> 🎧 LISTENING ADVICE
> 'I knocked down nine pins!'에서 'knock'은 [낙]이라고 발음됩니다. 'k'는 'n' 앞에서 소리가 나지 않는 묵음이 됩니다. 다른 예로는 'knife', 'know'가 있습니다.

듣·기·대·본

M: Emily, what are you doing?
W: I'm filling in this online form to participate in a recycling event.
M: A recycling event? What's that all about?
W: You wash used plastic bottles and return them, and then you might get a prize.
M: Wow. I want to participate, too. Does everyone get a prize?
W: No, they'll pick 100 people randomly. But you should try it.
M: Would you send me the link to the online event?

우·리·말·해·석

남: Emily, 뭐 하고 있어?
여: 난 재활용 행사에 참여하기 위해서 이 온라인 서식을 작성하고 있어.
남: 재활용 행사? 그게 다 무엇에 관한 거야?
여: 사용한 플라스틱 병을 씻어서 그것들을 돌려주면 상을 받을지도 몰라.
남: 와. 나도 참여하고 싶어. 모든 사람이 상을 받니?
여: 아니, 그들이 100명을 무작위로 뽑을 거야. 하지만 한번 해봐.
남: 그 온라인 행사에 대한 링크를 나에게 보내줄래?

단·어·및·표·현

fill in a form 서식을 작성하다
participate in ~ ～에 참여하다
get a prize 상을 받다
randomly [rǽndəmli] ⓟ 무작위로

듣·기·대·본

M: Are you planning to come to Yumi's birthday party?
W: Yes, I am.

M: I'm thinking of buying a teddy bear for her. What about you?
W: I don't buy presents. I usually make them.
M: Then shall we make a gift together?
W: Let's see. Maybe we can make her a necklace.
M: A necklace will be perfect!

우·리·말·해·석

남: 너 유미 생일파티에 갈 계획이니?
여: 응, 갈 거야.
남: 난 그녀를 위해 곰 인형을 살까 생각 중이야. 넌 어때?
여: 난 선물을 사지 않아. 보통 만들지.
남: 그럼 함께 선물을 만들까?
여: 어디 보자. 그녀에게 목걸이를 만들어줘도 될 것 같아.
남: 목걸이라니 완벽해!

단·어·및·표·현

think of -ing ～하는 것을 생각하다

> 🎧 LISTENING ADVICE
> 'Maybe we can make her a necklace.'에서 대명사인 her는 문장 중간에 올 경우 [h] 소리가 나지 않습니다. 'her' 이외에도 'h'로 시작하는 대명사 'he', 'him', 'his' 등도 문장 중간에 오면 [h] 소리가 탈락되어 발음됩니다. 단, 첫머리에 올 경우에는 [h]가 탈락되지 않습니다.

듣·기·대·본

W: We've finally finished filming the videos for our school website.
M: Yes. Now we need to edit them.
W: I can do that, but can you help me with something else?
M: Sure. What is it?
W: I need some photos of our teachers to add to the videos.
M: OK. What do you want me to do?
W: Can you take photos of the teachers in their classrooms?
M: No problem. I'll go and do it right away.

우·리·말·해·석

여: 우리는 드디어 우리 학교 웹사이트를 위한 동영상 촬영을 끝냈어.
남: 응. 우리는 이제 그것들을 편집해야 해.
여: 내가 그건 할 수 있는데, 네가 다른 것을 도와줄 수 있니?
남: 물론이지. 그게 뭐야?
여: 나는 영상들에 추가할 우리 선생님들의 사진들이 좀 필요해.
남: 그래. 너는 내가 뭘 해줬으면 해?
여: 너는 교실에 있는 선생님들의 사진을 찍어줄 수 있니?
남: 문제없어. 내가 당장 가서 그것을 할게.

단·어·및·표·현

film [film] ⓥ 촬영하다, 찍다
edit [édit] ⓥ 편집하다, 수정하다
add [æd] ⓥ 추가하다, 더하다
take a photo of ~ ～의 사진을 찍다, ～을 촬영하다

듣·기·대·본

W: Wow! Fred, how did you get a perfect score on our math quiz?
M: I got a lot of help by using Math Master.
W: Oh, isn't that a mobile application?

M: Yes. It <u>recommends</u> daily math problems for you to study.
W: Oh, really? Is it helpful?
M: Of course! It also provides lots of video content which is <u>helpful as well</u>.
W: Wow! I think I should download it.
M: You really should! <u>The best thing</u> about it is that it's free!

우·리·말·해·석

여: 왜! Fred, 어떻게 우리 수학 퀴즈에서 만점을 받았어?
남: 난 Math Master를 이용해서 많은 도움을 받았어.
여: 오, 그거 모바일 앱이 아니니?
남: 맞아. 그건 네가 공부할 수 있도록 날마다 수학 문제들을 추천해줘.
여: 오, 정말? 그게 도움이 되니?
남: 물론이지! 그건 도움이 되는 많은 동영상 자료도 또한 제공해줘.
여: 왜! 나 그걸 다운로드 해야겠어.
남: 넌 정말 그래야 해! 그것의 가장 좋은 점은 무료라는 거야!

단·어·및·표·현

get a perfect score 만점을 받다
recommend [rèkəménd] ⑧ 추천하다
helpful [hélpfəl] ⑲ 도움이 되는
provide [prəváid] ⑧ 제공하다

10 담화화제추론　　▶정답 ③

듣·기·대·본

M: Hi, everyone. As the Best Man, I want to thank you for coming today. It was a beautiful wedding. I've never seen my friend Matthew so happy. <u>Ever since</u> we were rookie basketball players, he has helped me <u>through a lot</u>. I'm sure his kind, generous heart will make his bride very happy. <u>Please join me in wishing the couple the best of luck</u>, health, and joy.

우·리·말·해·석

남: 안녕하세요, 여러분. 신랑 들러리로서, 오늘 와주신 것에 대해 감사드립니다. 아름다운 결혼식이었습니다. 저는 제 친구 Matthew가 그렇게 행복해하는 것을 본 적이 없습니다. 저희가 새내기 농구 선수였을 때부터, 그는 저를 많이 도와줬습니다. 저는 그의 친절하고 넉넉한 마음이 그의 신부를 매우 행복하게 해줄 것이라고 확신합니다. 저와 함께 이 부부에게 최고의 행운과 건강, 기쁨이 있기를 빌어주세요.

단·어·및·표·현

generous [dʒénərəs] ⑲ 넉넉한, 관대한
bride [braid] ⑲ 신부

🔊 **LISTENING ADVICE**

● **How to pronounce [θ]**

[θ] 소리는 윗니와 아랫니 사이에 혀끝을 위치시킨 상태에서 힘주어 공기를 밀어내며 우리말 [ㄸ]와 비슷한 소리가 나도록 합니다. 다음 단어들의 [th] 소리에 집중하며 10번 문제를 다시 들어보세요. 'Thank you', 'Matthew', 'through', 'health'. 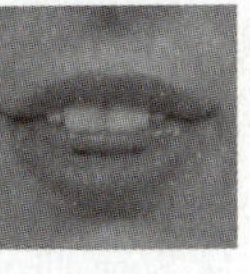

---

11 대화내용불일치　　▶정답 ④

듣·기·대·본

M: Hey, check out this new backpack. It's <u>on sale</u>.
W: Oh, that's a good price. And it has so many pockets and sections!
M: Yeah, it's <u>got space</u> for everything I need.

W: And it's spacious. It can hold up to 15 liters.
M: Plus, they're including a <u>free rain cover</u> with it.
W: That's awesome. It <u>comes in</u> two colors, blue or gray.
M: I think I prefer the gray one.

우·리·말·해·석

남: 이봐, 이 새로운 배낭을 봐봐. 이거 할인 중이야.
여: 오, 그건 좋은 가격이네. 그리고 이건 매우 많은 주머니들과 구획이 있어!
남: 응, 이건 내가 필요한 모든 것을 위한 공간을 갖고 있어.
여: 그리고 널찍해. 15리터까지 담을 수 있어.
남: 게다가, 그것들은 그것에 무료 비가림막을 포함하고 있어.
여: 굉장한걸. 그건 파란색이나 회색 두 가지 색으로 나와.
남: 나는 회색인 것이 더 좋다고 생각해.

단·어·및·표·현

check out (살펴)보다, 확인하다
on sale 할인 중인
section [sékʃən] ⑲ 구획, 부분, 부문
spacious [spéiʃəs] ⑲ 널찍한
hold [hould] ⑧ 담다
up to ~까지
include [inklú:d] ⑧ 포함하다
rain cover 비가림막
come in (제품 등이) 나오다

12 전화목적파악　　▶정답 ⑤

듣·기·대·본

(*Telephone rings.*)
M: Hello?
W: Hi, Mike. It's Jenny. Is this <u>a bad time</u> to call?
M: Hi, Jenny. Not at all. What's going on?
W: I was hoping you could help me with my laptop.
M: What's wrong with it?
W: I'm not sure. <u>It keeps crashing</u>. And all these errors come up.
M: I see. Well, sure, <u>I can take a look</u> at it.

우·리·말·해·석

(전화벨이 울린다.)
남: 여보세요?
여: 안녕, Mike. 난 Jenny야. 전화하기 나쁜 때니?
남: 안녕, Jenny. 전혀. 무슨 일이야?
여: 네가 내 노트북 컴퓨터에 대해 도와주었으면 해.
남: 무슨 문제가 있는데?
여: 잘 모르겠어. 자꾸 다운이 돼. 그리고 이 모든 오류들이 떠.
남: 알겠어. 음, 물론이지. 내가 그것을 봐 줄 수 있어.

단·어·및·표·현

error [érər] ⑲ 오류

13 수치계산(지불금액)　　▶정답 ②

듣·기·대·본

M: Hi, are you <u>ready to order</u>?
W: Yes, I want a large popcorn and a hotdog, please.
M: It's 11 dollars. Anything else?
W: Um… I'd like two Diet Cokes, please.
M: Okay. <u>The total comes to 15 dollars.</u>
W: Oh, I got this free popcorn coupon for my birthday. Can I use it now?
M: Of course. <u>The popcorn is 8 dollars so I'll deduct that from your total.</u>

W: All right. Here's my credit card.

남: 안녕하세요, 주문할 준비가 되셨나요?

여: 네, 저는 큰 팝콘과 핫도그를 원해요.

남: 11달러입니다. 다른 것은요?

여: 음… 다이어트 콜라 둘 주세요.

남: 알겠습니다. 총액은 15달러입니다.

여: 오, 저는 제 생일을 위한 이 공짜 팝콘 쿠폰이 있어요. 제가 그것을 지금 사용할 수 있나요?

남: 물론이죠. 팝콘은 8달러이니까 제가 총액에서 그것을 뺄게요.

여: 좋아요. 여기 제 신용카드가 있습니다.

단·어·및·표·현

The total comes to ~ 총액은 ~이다

deduct[didʌ́kt] 통 빼다, 제하다

14 대화자관계추론 ▶ 정답 ①

듣·기·대·본

W: Hello, I made a reservation yesterday.

M: Yes, come in. What can I do for you?

W: I would like to change my hair color.

M: Have a seat and we'll take a look.

W: Will I look good in black?

M: Yes, you are very fair. Black would look good on you.

W: My hair has grown so long. I also want to have it cut.

M: Okay. What do you have in mind?

W: I would like it to be shorter.

M: Hmm… a shoulder-length cut would be better for the shape of your face.

우·리·말·해·석

여: 안녕하세요, 저 어제 예약했는데요.

남: 네, 들어오세요. 무엇을 해드릴까요?

여: 머리색을 바꾸고 싶어요.

남: 여기 앉으세요, 한번 보죠.

여: 검은색이 제게 잘 어울릴까요?

남: 네, 당신은 매우 흰 피부를 가지셨네요. 검은색은 당신에게 잘 어울릴 거예요.

여: 제 머리가 너무 길었어요. 머리도 자르고 싶어요.

남: 좋아요. 생각해 두신 게 있나요?

여: 더 짧게 하고 싶어요.

남: 흠… 당신의 얼굴형에는 어깨 길이 컷이 더 좋겠네요.

단·어·및·표·현

fair[fɛər] 형 흰 피부의, (피부·머리카락이) 옅은 색의

look good on ~ ~와 잘 어울리다

15 부탁(요청)한일파악 ▶ 정답 ③

듣·기·대·본

(Cellphone rings.)

M: Hello.

W: Hi, Junho. It's Dabin. How's your preparation going for the school concert?

M: Not too bad. I was just practicing the piano.

W: Have you finished designing the posters?

M: Yes. It was really hard, and took a lot of time.

W: I see. Is there anything I can do to help?

M: Can you put up the posters at school? Then I can practice some more.

W: Sure. I'll come to your practice room later.

우·리·말·해·석

(휴대전화가 울린다.)

남: 여보세요.

여: 안녕, 준호야. 나 다빈이야. 학교 콘서트 준비는 잘 돼 가니?

남: 나쁘지 않아. 방금 피아노를 연습하는 중이었어.

여: 너 포스터 디자인은 마쳤니?

남: 응. 그것은 정말 어려웠고, 시간도 오래 걸렸어.

여: 그렇구나. 내가 도와줄 일이 뭐라도 있니?

남: 학교에 포스터를 붙여줄 수 있니? 그러면 내가 연습을 좀 더 할 수 있을 것 같아.

여: 물론이지. 나중에 내가 너의 연습실로 갈게.

단·어·및·표·현

preparation[prèpəréiʃən] 명 준비

16 이유파악 ▶ 정답 ④

듣·기·대·본

M: Leona, how was the amusement park?

W: Oh, I didn't go.

M: Were you too tired to drive?

W: No. I was going to take the shuttle bus anyway.

M: Then, why didn't you go? It wasn't raining, was it?

W: No. There was a big fire near the park. I heard about it on the morning news.

M: What? I didn't know that. So, the traffic was bad.

W: Really bad. I didn't want to arrive late. So, I just stayed home. Maybe next time.

우·리·말·해·석

남: Leona, 놀이공원은 어땠어?

여: 아, 나 안 갔어.

남: 너는 너무 피곤해서 운전할 수 없었니?

여: 아니. 어차피 셔틀버스를 타려고 했어.

남: 그러면 왜 가지 않았어? 비가 오지 않았지, 그렇지?

여: 안 왔어. 공원 근처에서 큰 화재가 있었어. 난 아침 뉴스에서 그 소식을 들었어.

남: 뭐라고? 난 그걸 몰랐어. 그래서 교통(상황)이 안 좋았구나.

여: 정말 안 좋았어. 난 늦게 도착하고 싶지 않았어. 그래서 그냥 집에 있었어. 다음에 갈래.

단·어·및·표·현

amusement park 놀이공원

too ~ to... 너무 ~해서 …할 수 없다

shuttle bus 셔틀버스

anyway[éniwèi] 부 어차피, 어쨌든

traffic[trǽfik] 명 교통(량)

17 그림상황에적절한대화찾기 ▶ 정답 ①

듣·기·대·본

① W: I don't think he should eat here.

　　M: You're right. Everyone can smell his food.

② W: Do you have this shirt in a smaller size?

　　M: Sure. I'll go get it for you.

③ W: Dinner's ready.

　　M: Wow. Everything looks so delicious.

④ W: It's raining so heavily.

　　M: Yes. I think we should get inside.

⑤ W: Are you ready to order?

　　M: Not yet. Do you have any recommendations?

우·리·말·해·석

① 여: 저는 그가 여기서 먹으면 안 된다고 생각해요.

남: 맞아요. 모든 사람들이 그의 음식 냄새를 맡을 수 있어요.
② 여: 이 셔츠 더 작은 사이즈로 있나요?
　남: 물론이죠. 제가 당신을 위해 가져다드릴게요.
③ 여: 저녁 식사 준비 다 됐어요.
　남: 우와. 모든 게 너무 맛있어 보여요.
④ 여: 비가 너무 많이 와요.
　남: 그러게요. 우리는 안으로 들어가야 할 거 같아요.
⑤ 여: 주문하실 준비가 되셨어요?
　남: 아직 안 됐어요. 추천해주실 게 있나요?

단·어·및·표·현
heavily [hévili] ⊕ 많이, 심하게
recommendation [rèkəməndéiʃən] ⑲ 추천

18　담화미언급　▶정답 ③

듣·기·대·본
W: Hello, everyone. Let me introduce myself to you. My name is Chelsea Collins. I'm from California, USA. I've been <u>interested in medicine</u> since childhood. So, I studied nursing science at university. I'm a nurse now. I <u>work</u> at a big university hospital, and help many sick people there. Today, I'm going to tell you about <u>a typical day</u> in the life of a nurse.

우·리·말·해·석
여: 안녕하세요, 여러분. 여러분에게 제 소개를 하겠습니다. 제 이름은 Chelsea Collins입니다. 저는 미국 캘리포니아에서 왔습니다. 저는 어렸을 때부터 의학에 관심이 있었습니다. 그래서 저는 대학에서 간호학을 공부했습니다. 저는 지금 간호사입니다. 저는 큰 대학 병원에서 일하고, 거기서 많은 아픈 사람들을 돕습니다. 오늘 저는 여러분에게 간호사의 삶의 전형적인 일상에 대해 말씀드리려고 합니다.

단·어·및·표·현
medicine [médisin] ⑲ 의학
childhood [tʃáildhùd] ⑲ 어린 시절
nursing science 간호학
typical [típikəl] ⑲ 전형적인, 보통의

19　알맞은응답찾기　▶정답 ⑤

듣·기·대·본
M: Shannon, I can't find my <u>wallet</u>.
W: What? Did you check <u>your pockets</u>?
M: Yes, but it's not there.
W: You used it when we were at the coffee house.
M: No, you paid for the coffee.
W: Right. Where did you go before we met?
M: Umm… I went to a clothing store and <u>bought a belt</u>.
W: You should call that store now.

우·리·말·해·석
① 저녁은 내가 살게.
② 그것은 멋진 벨트야.
③ 나는 쇼핑을 좋아하지 않아.
④ 나는 커피보다 차를 좋아해.
⑤ 너는 지금 그 가게에 전화해야 해.

남: Shannon, 난 내 지갑을 찾을 수가 없어.
여: 뭐라고? 네 주머니들을 확인했어?
남: 응, 하지만 거기엔 없어.
여: 우리가 커피숍에 있었을 때 네가 그것을 사용했어.
남: 아니야, 네가 커피 값을 지불했어.
여: 맞아. 너 우리가 만나기 전에 어디 갔었어?

남: 음… 난 옷가게에 가서 벨트를 샀어.
여: 너는 지금 그 가게에 전화해야 해.

단·어·및·표·현
pay for ~의 값을 지불하다
clothing store 옷가게
Dinner is on me. 저녁은 내가 살게.

20　알맞은응답찾기　▶정답 ①

듣·기·대·본
M: Hi, Dahyun. What are you looking at?
W: Hey, Minwoo. I'm <u>checking out</u> the website for the Teen Invention Contest.
M: Teen Invention Contest? Tell me more about it.
W: At the contest, you need to <u>make something new</u>.
M: Something new? Can I make anything?
W: No, you will be given materials. You can use only <u>the materials provided</u>.
M: Oh, then it will not be easy.
W: It's all about creativity.

우·리·말·해·석
① 창의력이 핵심이야.
② 학생은 5달러야.
③ 그는 대회에서 우승하지 못했어.
④ 난 지금 매우 피곤해.
⑤ 넌 일찍 자야 해.

남: 안녕, 다현아. 넌 무엇을 보고 있니?
여: 안녕, 민우야. 난 십대 발명 대회 웹사이트를 확인하고 있어.
남: 십대 발명 대회? 나에게 그것에 대해 더 말해줘.
여: 그 대회에서 넌 뭔가 새로운 것을 만들어야 해.
남: 뭔가 새로운 것? 내가 무엇이든 만들어도 돼?
여: 아니, 너에게 재료가 주어질 거야. 넌 제공된 재료들만 사용할 수 있어.
남: 오, 그럼 그건 쉽지 않겠다.
여: 창의력이 핵심이야.

단·어·및·표·현
teen [tiːn] ⑲ 십대(나이가 13~19세인 사람)
invention [invénʃən] ⑲ 발명
material [mətí(ː)əriəl] ⑲ (물건의) 재료
It's all about ~ ~이 핵심이다, 가장 중요하다

Words & Expressions Review

1. 서식을 작성하다	2. 신부	3. ~까지
4. 교통(량)	5. ~에 참여하다	6. ~의 값을 지불하다
7. 저녁은 내가 살게.	8. 추천하다	9. 어린 시절
10. 총액은 ~이다	11. 전형적인, 보통의	12. 편집하다, 수정하다
13. ~하는 것을 생각하다	14. ~이긴 하지만, 반면에	15. 자막
16. 많이, 심하게	17. 예약하다	18. ~을 더 좋아하다
19. 의학	20. (물건의) 재료	21. 쓰러뜨리다
22. 체크무늬의	23. 기대하다	24. 소나기
25. 구획, 부분, 부문	26. 널찍한	27. 전혀.
28. (연설 등을) 문자화하다, 필기하다	29. 발을 헛디디다	30. 도움이 되는
31. 붙이다, 게시하다	32. ~할 계획이다	33. ~에 집중하다
34. 무작위로	35. 빼다, 제하다	36. 홍보[판촉] (활동)
37. ~의 사진을 찍다, ~을 촬영하다	38. ~이 핵심이다, 가장 중요하다	39. 발명

40. 넉넉한, 관대한 　41. 모양, 형태 　42. 준비
43. ~을 확인하다 　44. ~와 잘 어울리다

Listening Test
영어듣기 모의고사 21^회

|정|답|

01 ②	02 ②	03 ④	04 ④	05 ②
06 ①	07 ⑤	08 ⑤	09 ④	10 ③
11 ③	12 ②	13 ①	14 ③	15 ②
16 ④	17 ②	18 ⑤	19 ②	20 ②

01 날씨파악-그림　▶정답 ②

듣·기·대·본

M: Good morning. Today is Monday, March 4, and here is the weather forecast for this week. It will be sunny today and tomorrow, Tuesday. The weather will be partly cloudy from Wednesday until Friday. Finally, there will be rain showers on Saturday and Sunday.

우·리·말·해·석

남: 안녕하세요. 오늘은 3월 4일 월요일이고 이번 주 날씨 예보입니다. 오늘과 화요일인 내일은 맑을 것입니다. 수요일부터 금요일까지 날씨는 일부 구름이 낄 것입니다. 마지막으로, 토요일과 일요일에는 소나기가 올 것입니다.

단·어·및·표·현

cloudy [kláudi] 형 구름 낀

> ### 🎧 LISTENING ADVICE
> 'Wednesday'에서 [d] 발음은 소리가 나지 않습니다. 'd'는 'n' 앞이나 뒤에서 소리가 나지 않는 경우가 있습니다. 다른 예로는 'handsome', 'handkerchief'가 있습니다.

02 그림정보파악　▶정답 ②

듣·기·대·본

M: Allison, what's this? Is it a pencil case?
W: Yes, I made it at school. I took sewing lessons.
M: Wow, nice work! I like the striped pattern.
W: Thanks. I picked the cloth myself.
M: There's even a tag with your name on it! Did you make the tag, too?
W: Yeah, I wanted to mark it as mine.
M: I see. You are really good with your hands.

우·리·말·해·석

남: Allison, 이건 뭐야? 필통이니?
여: 응, 내가 학교에서 그걸 만들었어. 나는 바느질 수업을 들었어.
남: 와, 잘 만들었다! 줄무늬가 마음에 든다.
여: 고마워. 내가 직접 천을 골랐어.
남: 심지어 그 위에 네 이름이 적힌 이름표도 있어! 네가 이름표도 만들었니?
여: 응, 나는 그것을 내 것이라고 표시하고 싶었어.
남: 그렇구나. 너는 손재주가 정말 좋아.

단·어·및·표·현

sewing [sóuiŋ] 명 바느질, 재봉
striped pattern 줄무늬
cloth [klɔ:θ] 명 천, 옷감
tag [tæg] 명 (어떤 표시를 하기 위해 붙인) 이름표[태그]
be good with one's hands 손재주가 좋다

03 심정추론　▶정답 ④

듣·기·대·본

M: Hey, my brother and I are going to the soccer match.
W: Wow, that's great. Have you ever been to a soccer match before?
M: No. Actually, this is my first time.
W: I'm sure you will like it.
M: Yes, I'm really looking forward to it.
W: Oh, I envy you. Let's go together next time.

우·리·말·해·석

① 슬픈　② 시기하는　③ 놀란　④ 신난　⑤ 긴장된

남: 야, 나 형이랑 축구 경기 보러 갈 거야.
여: 와, 멋지다. 예전에 축구 경기를 보러 간 적 있어?
남: 아니. 사실, 이번이 처음이야.
여: 나는 네가 좋아할 거라고 확신해.
남: 응. 진짜 기대돼.
여: 오, 부럽다. 다음에는 함께 가자.

단·어·및·표·현

actually [ǽktʃuəli] 부 사실

04 한일파악　▶정답 ④

듣·기·대·본

M: Chloe, what are you carrying in that big bag?
W: Some old clothes. I'm taking them to the donation center.
M: That's nice of you. What made you decide to do that?
W: Last weekend, I cleaned out my closet and found so many clothes I don't wear anymore.
M: Good idea! I should do that, too.
W: Yeah, it feels good to give clothes to people who need them.

우·리·말·해·석

남: Chloe, 그 큰 가방 안에 뭐 들고 가는 거야?
여: 헌 옷이야. 그것들을 기부 센터에 가져가려고.
남: 너 참 착하다. 왜 그렇게 하기로 결심했어?
여: 지난 주말에 내 옷장을 정리했는데, 더 이상 입지 않는 옷들이 정말 많이 나왔어.
남: 좋은 생각이네! 나도 그렇게 해야겠다.
여: 맞아. 그것들이(옷들이) 필요한 사람들에게 옷을 주는 것은 기분을 좋게 해.

단·어·및·표·현

carry [kǽri] 동 들고 가다, 나르다
donation [dounéiʃən] 명 기부, 기증

05 대화장소추론　▶정답 ②

듣·기·대·본

W: Hello. How can I help you?
M: I'd like to buy some flowers for my daughter's graduation ceremony.
W: Okay. Let me see. How about this rose bouquet?

M: I don't think my daughter likes roses. What else do you have?
W: This tulip bouquet is also popular for that kind of ceremony.
M: I like that bouquet. How much is it?
W: It's 50 dollars.

우·리·말·해·석

여: 안녕하세요. 어떻게 도와드릴까요?
남: 저는 제 딸의 졸업식을 위해 꽃을 좀 사고 싶어요.
여: 알겠습니다. 한번 보죠. 이 장미 꽃다발은 어떠세요?
남: 제 생각에 제 딸은 장미를 안 좋아하는 것 같아요. 다른 건 뭐가 있나요?
여: 이 튤립 꽃다발도 그런 종류의 행사에 인기가 있어요.
남: 저는 그 꽃다발이 마음에 들어요. 그것은 얼마인가요?
여: 50달러입니다.

단·어·및·표·현

graduation ceremony 졸업식
bouquet [boukéi] 圀 꽃다발, 부케

06 마지막말의도파악　▶정답 ①

듣·기·대·본

W: What are you doing, Jake?
M: Hi, Luna. I'm packing to go away for a while.
W: Are you going on a family trip? You did that last year for summer vacation.
M: No. I'm going to a two-week training program for the school cycling team.
W: Oh, you made the team! I know how much you wanted to be a member.
M: I know! I still can't believe I'm on the team.
W: It's great news. I'm so happy for you.

우·리·말·해·석

여: 너 뭐 하고 있니, Jake?
남: 안녕, Luna. 나는 잠시 떠나려고 짐을 싸고 있어.
여: 너는 가족여행을 가니? 작년 여름 방학 동안에도 갔었잖아.
남: 아니. 나는 학교 사이클링 팀을 위한 2주간의 훈련 프로그램에 가.
여: 오, 너 팀에 들어갔구나! 나는 네가 얼마나 팀원이 되고 싶어했는지 알아.
남: 맞아! 난 아직도 내가 그 팀에 있다는 게 믿기지 않아.
여: 좋은 소식이다. 네가 잘 돼서 기뻐.

단·어·및·표·현

pack [pæk] 圐 (짐을) 싸다, 꾸리다
go away 짐을 떠나다, 어디를 가다
make the team 팀에 들어가다

07 특정정보파악　▶정답 ⑤

듣·기·대·본

M: Good evening. What can I get you?
W: What are the special dishes tonight?
M: Well, we have chicken stew and beef curry as our specials.
W: I've had them before. Do you have any seafood?
M: Yes, we do. We also have clam chowder or fish fillet, if you like.
W: On second thought, can you just get me a beef steak with plenty of onions, please?
M: How do you want your steak cooked?

W: Medium will be fine, thanks.

우·리·말·해·석

① 치킨 스튜　　② 소고기 카레　　③ 조개 수프
④ 생선 살코기　　⑤ 소고기 스테이크

남: 좋은 저녁입니다. 무엇을 가져다 드릴까요?
여: 오늘 밤의 특별 요리가 무엇이죠?
남: 음, 특별식으로 치킨 스튜와 소고기 카레가 있습니다.
여: 전에 그것들을 먹었어요. 해산물 요리 있나요?
남: 네, 있습니다. 손님이 좋아하신다면 저희는 또한 조개 수프와 뼈를 바른 생선 살코기도 있습니다.
여: 다시 생각해 보니, 그냥 소고기 스테이크를 충분한 양파와 함께 가져다 주시겠어요?
남: 스테이크는 어떻게 요리해 드릴까요?
여: 중간으로 익히는 게 괜찮겠네요. 감사합니다.

단·어·및·표·현

dish [diʃ] 圀 요리, 접시

08 할일파악(대화직후)　▶정답 ⑤

듣·기·대·본

W: What are you doing today? It's our last day before our summer vacation.
M: Yeah, we're finally taking a break from school.
W: Do you want to grab some snacks at the cafeteria?
M: No, I actually need to go to the school library.
W: Do you have some books to return?
M: Yes, the books I borrowed are due today. Want to come along?
W: Sure, let's head there now.

우·리·말·해·석

여: 오늘 뭐 할 거야? 우리 여름 방학 전 마지막 날이잖아.
남: 그래, 드디어 학교로부터(학교를 떠나) 쉬게 됐네.
여: 매점에서 간식을 좀 먹을래?
남: 아니, 사실 학교 도서관에 가야 해.
여: 반납할 책 있어?
남: 응, 내가 빌린 책들이 오늘 반납 기한이야. 같이 갈래?
여: 좋아, 지금 거기로 가자!

단·어·및·표·현

grab a snack 간단히 뭐 좀 먹다, 간식을 먹다
return [ritə́ːrn] 圐 반납하다
borrow [bárou] 圐 빌리다
due [djuː] 圀 반납일이 ~인
come along 함께 가다
head [hed] 圐 ~로 향하다

09 대화미언급　▶정답 ④

듣·기·대·본

W: Woosung, are the preparations for your trip to China going well?
M: Yes. I am listening to the radio to practice speaking Chinese these days.
W: What's the name of the program?
M: *Chinese Exploration*! It is broadcast at 6 a.m. every morning.
W: I'd like to listen to it. Where can I hear the program?
M: On 95 FM.
W: Cool! But it's on too early. I'm not a morning person.
M: Don't worry! It's being rerun twice every afternoon.

W: That's great. I'll definitely check it out!

우·리·말·해·석

여: 우성아, 네 중국으로의 여행 준비는 잘 되어 가니?

남: 응. 나는 요즘 중국어 말하기를 연습하기 위해 라디오를 듣고 있어.

여: 그 프로그램의 이름이 뭐니?

남: "중국어 탐험"이야! 그것은 매일 아침 6시에 하는 방송이야.

여: 나도 그것을 들어보고 싶어. 내가 어디서 그 프로그램을 들어볼 수 있니?

남: 95 FM에서.

여: 좋아! 하지만 그것은 너무 이른 시간에 해. 나는 아침형 인간이 아니야.

남: 걱정하지 마! 그것은 매일 오후에 두 번씩 재방송되고 있어.

여: 잘됐다. 나는 반드시 그것을 확인해볼 거야!

단·어·및·표·현

preparation [prèpəréiʃən] 몧 준비
broadcast [brɔ́:dkæst] 통 방송하다 몧 방송
morning person 아침형 인간
rerun [rí:rʌ̀n] 통 재방송하다
definitely [défənitli] 뫼 반드시, 틀림없이

10 담화화제추론 ▶정답 ③

듣·기·대·본

M: Welcome to Little Forest Campsite! For everyone's convenience, please remember these rules when using the campsite. First, do not make a fire directly on the ground without fire tools. Between 11 p.m. and 7 a.m., keep the noise down so everyone can have a peaceful night. Finally, no pets are allowed in the campsite. Thank you.

우·리·말·해·석

남: Little Forest 캠핑장에 오신 것을 환영합니다! 모두의 편의를 위해, 캠핑장을 이용할 때 이 규칙들을 기억하시길 바랍니다. 첫째, 소방 도구 없이 땅에 직접 불을 지피지 마십시오. 오후 11시에서 오전 7시 사이에, 모든 사람들이 평화로운 밤을 보낼 수 있도록 소음을 줄이십시오. 마지막으로, 캠핑장에는 반려동물이 허용되지 않습니다. 감사합니다.

단·어·및·표·현

convenience [kənví:njəns] 몧 편의, 편리
make a fire 불을 지피다
fire tools 소방 도구
keep ~ down ~을 줄이다, 낮추다

11 대화내용불일치 ▶정답 ③

듣·기·대·본

M: Esther, look! There's going to be a Nature Walk at Central Forest this weekend.

W: Oh, it's a guided walk where you can learn about different plants and animals.

M: Doesn't it sound fun?

W: Yeah, they will lend us binoculars so we can observe the wildlife up close.

M: Great! It's this Saturday at 2 p.m.

W: Good. We'll need to sign up online.

M: Okay. Is there anything else we need to know?

W: Yes, they will provide us with a map of the forest.

우·리·말·해·석

남: Esther, 봐! 이번 주말에 Central 숲에서 Nature Walk가 있을 거야.

여: 아, 그건 다양한 식물과 동물들에 대해 배울 수 있게 안내를 받으며 하는 산책이야.

남: 재밌을 것 같지 않아?

여: 응, 그들이 우리에게 쌍안경을 빌려줄 거라서 우리는 야생 생물을 바로 가까이에서 관찰할 수 있어.

남: 좋다! 이번 주 토요일 오후 2시야.

여: 좋아. 우리는 온라인으로 등록해야 해.

남: 알겠어. 우리가 더 알아야 할 것이 있을까?

여: 응, 그들은 우리에게 숲 지도를 제공해 줄 거야.

단·어·및·표·현

guided walk 안내를 받으며 하는 산책
binoculars [bainɑ́kjulərz] 몧 쌍안경
observe [əbzə́:rv] 통 관찰하다, 관측하다
up close 바로 가까이에(서)
sign up 등록하다
provide A with B A에게 B를 제공하다

12 전화목적파악 ▶정답 ②

듣·기·대·본

(*Telephone rings.*)

W: Hello. Dr. Kim's Dental Clinic.

M: Hi. I have an appointment on May 7th, but I'd like to change it.

W: May I have your name?

M: It's Kevin Park.

W: Please hold. (*Pause*) Your appointment is at 2 p.m. Would you like to come at a different time?

M: No, 2 p.m. is good, but can I come on the 8th instead of the 7th?

W: Sure. I'll change your appointment to the next day.

M: Thank you.

우·리·말·해·석

(전화벨이 울린다.)

여: 안녕하세요. 닥터 김 치과입니다.

남: 안녕하세요. 저는 5월 7일에 예약했는데 그것을 변경하고 싶어요.

여: 성함을 알려주시겠어요?

남: Kevin Park입니다.

여: 잠시만 기다려주세요. (잠시 후) 예약은 오후 2시로 되어있네요. 다른 시간에 오시기를 원하시나요?

남: 아뇨, 오후 2시는 좋은데 7일 대신 8일에 가도 될까요?

여: 물론이죠. 예약을 다음 날로 변경해드리겠습니다.

남: 감사합니다.

단·어·및·표·현

dental clinic 치과 병원
appointment [əpɔ́intmənt] 몧 (진찰 등의) 예약
hold [hould] 통 (전화를 끊지 말고) 기다리다
instead of ~ ~ 대신에

13 수치계산(거스름돈) ▶정답 ①

듣·기·대·본

W: Good morning. How may I help you today?

M: The sandwiches look great. How much are they?

W: They are usually $7 each, but we are having a sale today. Every sandwich is $6 before noon.

M: That's great. I'd like two tuna sandwiches and one bacon sandwich please.

W: Is it for here or to go?

M: To go please.

W: Okay. It's $18 in total.

M: Here's a 20 dollar bill.

W: Here's your change.

여: 좋은 아침입니다. 오늘 어떻게 도와드릴까요?

남: 샌드위치가 정말 맛있어 보이네요. 그것들은 얼마인가요?

여: 그것들은 보통 개당 7달러지만, 저희는 오늘 세일을 하고 있습니다. 낮 12시 전까지 모든 샌드위치는 6달러입니다.

남: 정말 좋네요. 참치 샌드위치 두 개와 베이컨 샌드위치 한 개 주세요.

여: 여기서 드실 건가요, 아니면 가져가실 건가요?

남: 가져갈게요.

여: 알겠습니다. 총 18달러입니다.

남: 여기 20달러짜리 지폐 드릴게요.

여: 거스름돈 여기 있습니다.

단·어·및·표·현

noon[nuːn] 몡 낮 12시, 정오
tuna[túːnə] 몡 참치
bill[bil] 몡 지폐
change[tʃeindʒ] 몡 거스름돈

14 대화자관계추론 ▶ 정답 ③

듣·기·대·본

W: Hi. I want to send this package to Singapore.

M: Okay. Do you want to send it by air or ship?

W: The ship takes much longer, doesn't it?

M: Yes, much longer.

W: Then, please send it by air.

M: Okay. If you pay the postage on the post office app, you'll get a 10% discount.

W: That's great! I'll pay on my phone now.

M: Take your time.

우·리·말·해·석

여: 안녕하세요. 저는 이 소포를 싱가포르에 보내고 싶어요.

남: 알겠습니다. 당신은 그것을 항공편으로 보내고 싶나요, 아니면 배편으로 보내고 싶나요?

여: 배는 훨씬 더 오래 걸리죠, 그렇지 않나요?

남: 네, 훨씬 더 오래요.

여: 그러면, 항공편으로 보내주세요.

남: 알겠습니다. 만약 당신이 우체국 앱에서 우편 요금을 지불하시면, 당신은 10% 할인을 받을 것입니다.

여: 좋아요! 저는 지금 제 핸드폰에서 지불할게요.

남: 천천히 하세요.

단·어·및·표·현

package[pǽkidʒ] 몡 소포, 포장물
postage[póustidʒ] 몡 우편 요금
discount[diskáunt] 몡 할인
take one's time 천천히 하다, 여유를 가지다

15 부탁(요청)한일파악 ▶ 정답 ②

듣·기·대·본

M: Hi, Betty. Do you want to watch a movie with me?

W: Of course. I'm free on Friday.

M: Me, too. Let's book tickets now. [Pause] How about this action movie?

W: I'd like to see it. I have a membership at the theater, so I'll book the tickets.

M: Okay. The movie starts at 8 p.m. How about having dinner before watching the movie?

W: That's a good idea. Can you find a restaurant around the theater?

M: Sure.

우·리·말·해·석

남: 안녕, Betty. 너는 나랑 영화를 보고 싶니?

여: 물론이지. 나는 금요일에 한가해.

남: 나도. 지금 표들을 예매하자. [잠시 후] 이 액션 영화는 어때?

여: 난 그거 보고 싶어. 나에게 극장 회원권이 있으니 내가 표들을 예매할게.

남: 좋아. 그 영화는 오후 8시에 시작해. 영화 보기 전에 저녁 먹는 건 어때?

여: 좋은 생각이야. 네가 극장 주변의 식당을 찾아줄 수 있어?

남: 물론이지.

단·어·및·표·현

free[friː] 혱 한가한, 다른 계획[약속]이 없는
book[buk] 통 예매하다, 예약하다

16 이유파악 ▶ 정답 ④

듣·기·대·본

M: Let's try that Italian restaurant in town!

W: I want to, but I can't.

M: Why not? I thought you liked Italian food.

W: I heard the food there is expensive. I don't have enough money right now.

M: How about that seafood restaurant nearby? I heard their crab dish is delicious.

W: Sorry, I don't eat crabs.

M: Oh, I forgot. You are allergic to seafood.

W: Let's just eat at my place. I'm not very hungry now anyway.

우·리·말·해·석

남: 시내에 있는 이탈리아 식당에 가보자!

여: 그러고 싶지만 안 돼.

남: 왜? 난 네가 이탈리아 음식을 좋아한다고 생각했는데.

여: 나는 거기 음식이 비싸다고 들었어. 지금은 돈이 충분히 없어.

남: 근처의 해산물 식당은 어떠니? 나는 거기 게 요리가 맛있다고 들었어.

여: 미안, 나 게 안 먹어.

남: 오, 내가 잊었네. 너 해산물 알레르기가 있지.

여: 우리 집에서 그냥 먹자. 나 지금은 어쨌든 배가 고프지 않아.

단·어·및·표·현

be allergic to ~ ~에 알레르기가 있다

17 그림상황에적절한대화찾기 ▶ 정답 ②

듣·기·대·본

① M: What do you think of my tie?
　W: Pink suits you very well.

② M: What would you like to have?
　W: One burger and a Coke, please.

③ M: Would you like to watch a movie?
　W: Yes, that would be great!

④ M: We have an earlier flight to Brazil.
　W: Thank you, I'll take that then.

⑤ M: Would you like me to gift-wrap these?
　W: No, thank you.

우·리·말·해·석

① 남: 내 넥타이 어때?
　여: 분홍색이 아주 잘 어울린다.

② 남: 무엇을 드시겠습니까?
　여: 햄버거 하나랑 콜라요.

③ 남: 영화 보는 거 괜찮겠니?
　여: 응, 그거 좋은데!

④ 남: 브라질로 가는 더 이른 항공편이 있어요.
　여: 고마워요, 그럼 그걸 탈게요.
⑤ 남: 이거 선물 포장 해드릴까요?
　여: 아니요, 괜찮습니다.

단·어·및·표·현
suit [suːt] ⑧ 어울리다

18 담화미언급　▶정답 ⑤
듣·기·대·본
W: Hello, everyone. Today, I'd like to tell you about a play. The title is *A Man Next Door*. The story is about a small neighborhood and the people with an interesting past who live there. It is written by Nora Jung, and the main role will be played by Dan Nolan. It will be shown at Blue Art Center. You can buy tickets both online and offline. Students get a discount on their tickets.

우·리·말·해·석
여: 안녕하세요, 여러분. 오늘, 저는 여러분께 한 연극에 대해 알려드리려고 합니다. 제목은 "옆집 남자"입니다. 작은 동네와 그곳에 사는 흥미로운 과거를 가진 사람들에 대한 이야기입니다. Nora Jung 씨에 의해 쓰여졌으며, 주인공은 Dan Nolan 씨에 의해 연기될 것입니다. 그것은 Blue Art Center에서 공연될 것입니다. 티켓은 온라인과 오프라인 둘 다에서 구매하실 수 있습니다. 학생들은 표를 할인받습니다.

단·어·및·표·현
play [plei] ⑨ 연극, 극
neighborhood [néibərhùd] ⑨ 동네, 근방, 이웃
role [roul] ⑨ (배우의) 역할, 배역
get a discount 할인을 받다

19 알맞은응답찾기　▶정답 ②
듣·기·대·본
M: Cathy, you don't look so good. Are you feeling alright?
W: I feel sick. I think I have a cold.
M: Oh, no! Do you want to go see the school nurse?
W: No, I think I should go to the hospital.
M: Okay. Is there anything that I can help you with?
W: Well, can you go get my bag for me, please? I have to call my mom.
M: **Okay. Wait here while I get your bag.**

우·리·말·해·석
① 너는 너의 가방을 어디서 샀니?
② 알았어. 내가 네 가방을 가져오는 동안 여기서 기다려.
③ 아니, 나는 엄마에게 전화하지 않았어.
④ 응, Hudson 씨가 우리 학교 보건 선생님이야.
⑤ 가장 가까운 병원이 어디에 있는지 나에게 말해 줄 수 있니?

남: Cathy, 너 좋아 보이지 않아. 너 괜찮니?
여: 나 아파. 나는 내가 감기에 걸린 거라고 생각해.
남: 오, 안 돼! 너는 학교 보건 선생님에게 가보길 원하니?
여: 아니, 나는 내가 병원에 가야 한다고 생각해.
남: 알았어. 내가 너를 도울 수 있는 뭔가가 있니?
여: 글쎄, 가서 내 가방을 나를 위해 가져다 줄 수 있어? 나는 엄마에게 전화를 해야 해.
남: **알았어. 내가 네 가방을 가져오는 동안 여기서 기다려.**

단·어·및·표·현
go get 가서 가져오다

20 알맞은응답찾기　▶정답 ②
듣·기·대·본

W: Matt, you're not dressed up. Why?
M: I'm afraid I can't go to Mary's birthday party. My grandfather is sick. I have to stay home with him.
W: Really? That's too bad. Does he have a serious illness?
M: No, he's just not feeling well today.
W: I see. Then, I guess I'll have to go alone.
M: **Please say hello to her for me.**

우·리·말·해·석
① 걱정하지 마. 그녀는 괜찮을 거야.
② 그녀에게 나 대신 안부를 전해줘.
③ 내 생일 파티에 올 수 있겠니?
④ 난 그녀에게 생일 선물을 사주지 않았어.
⑤ 그녀는 어릴 때 나와 함께 놀았어.

여: Matt, 너 옷을 차려 입지 않았구나. 왜 그래?
남: 유감이지만 Mary의 생일 파티에 못 갈 것 같아. 할아버지께서 편찮으셔. 같이 집에 있어드려야 해.
여: 정말? 너무 안됐다. 심각한 병이라도 있으신 거야?
남: 아니, 그냥 오늘 몸이 좋지 않으신 거야.
여: 알겠어. 그럼, 난 혼자 가야겠네.
남: **그녀에게 나 대신 안부를 전해줘.**

단·어·및·표·현
dress up (옷을) 차려 입다

Words & Expressions Review

1. (짐을) 싸다, 꾸리다	2. 우편 요금	3. 천천히 하다, 여유를 가지다
4. 쌍안경	5. ~에 알레르기가 있다	6. (옷을) 차려 입다
7. 들고 가다, 나르다	8. 선물용으로 포장하다	9. 가서 가져오다
10. 예매하다, 예약하다	11. 방송하다	12. 기부, 기증
13. 팀에 들어가다	14. (진찰 등의) 예약	15. ~로 향하다
16. 낮 12시, 정오	17. 심각한, 진지한	18. 편의, 편리
19. 줄무늬	20. ~을 줄이다, 낮추다	21. ~ 대신에
22. (배우의) 역할, 배역	23. 한가한, 다른 계획[약속]이 없는	24. 다시 생각해보니
25. 비행기, 항공편	26. 근처에, 가까이에	27. 소포
28. 간단히 뭐 좀 먹다, 간식을 먹다	29. 거스름돈	30. ~을 기대하다
31. 결심하다, 결정하다	32. 졸업식	33. 요리, 접시
34. 집을 떠나다, 어디를 가다	35. 사실, 실제로	36. 어울리다
37. 부분적으로	38. 충분한, 많은	39. 반납일이 ~인
40. 바로 가까이에(서)	41. 소나기	42. 과거
43. 바느질, 재봉	44. 재방송하다	

|정|답|

01 ②	02 ③	03 ①	04 ④	05 ③
06 ③	07 ①	08 ④	09 ⑤	10 ⑤
11 ④	12 ④	13 ②	14 ④	15 ②
16 ⑤	17 ⑤	18 ④	19 ②	20 ②

01   날씨파악-그림   ▶정답 ②

듣·기·대·본

W: Good evening! This is Peggy with your three-day weather report. Monday will be mainly <u>sunny</u> and hot, but it will be <u>cloudy</u> in the evening. On Tuesday, the temperature will go down and <u>strong winds</u> are expected. On Wednesday, there is a strong chance of showers. So, don't forget to <u>take an umbrella</u> with you on Wednesday. Thank you.

우·리·말·해·석

여: 안녕하세요! 저는 여러분의 3일 일기예보의 Peggy입니다. 월요일은 주로 맑고 덥겠지만 저녁에는 구름이 끼겠습니다. 화요일에는, 온도가 내려갈 것이고 강한 바람이 예상됩니다. 수요일에는, 소나기의 강한 가능성이 있습니다. 그러니, 수요일에 우산을 가져가는 것을 잊지 마세요. 감사합니다.

단·어·및·표·현

mainly [méinli] 🕭 주로
chance [tʃæns] 📖 가능성
shower [ʃáuər] 📖 소나기

02   그림정보파악   ▶정답 ③

듣·기·대·본

M: May I help you?
W: Hi, I'm looking for gloves to wear for the winter.
M: We have <u>gloves and mittens</u>.
W: <u>I like mittens better.</u>
M: Okay. How about these <u>checkered mittens</u>?
W: <u>I don't like checkered designs.</u>
M: Then, what about these mittens with hearts?
W: They look pretty. I'll buy <u>those heart mittens</u>.

우·리·말·해·석

남: 도와드릴까요?
여: 안녕하세요, 저는 겨울에 낄 장갑을 찾고 있어요.
남: 저희는 일반장갑과 벙어리장갑이 있습니다.
여: 저는 벙어리장갑이 더 좋아요.
남: 알겠습니다. 이 체크무늬 벙어리장갑은 어떠세요?
여: 저는 체크무늬 디자인을 안 좋아해요.
남: 그러면, 이 하트가 있는 벙어리장갑은요?
여: 그것들은 예뻐 보여요. 저는 그 하트 벙어리장갑을 살게요.

단·어·및·표·현

mitten [mítən] 📖 벙어리장갑
checkered [tʃékərd] 🕭 체크무늬의

03   심정추론   ▶정답 ①

듣·기·대·본

W: When is your student concert at the community center?

M: It was yesterday.
W: Oh, no! I missed it. I really wanted to see you play the piano.
M: Don't worry. You didn't <u>miss much</u>.
W: What do you mean?
M: I made a <u>big mistake</u> at the beginning and played <u>terribly</u> afterwards.
W: Oh, I see. Are you okay?
M: Not really. <u>I still feel like crying.</u>

우·리·말·해·석

① 슬픈   ② 자랑스러운   ③ 불안한
④ 안도하는   ⑤ 기분 좋은

여: 주민 센터에서 하는 당신의 학생 콘서트는 언제인가요?
남: 그건 어제였어요.
여: 아, 이런! 전 그걸 놓쳤네요. 저는 당신이 피아노를 연주하는 걸 정말 보고 싶었어요.
남: 걱정 마요. 당신은 많이 놓치지 않았어요.
여: 무슨 뜻인가요?
남: 전 처음에 큰 실수를 했고 그 뒤에는 형편없게 연주했어요.
여: 아, 그렇군요. 당신은 괜찮아요?
남: 사실 안 괜찮아요. 저는 아직도 울고 싶어요.

단·어·및·표·현

make a mistake 실수하다
terribly [térəbli] 🕭 형편없이, 몹시, 심각하게
afterwards [æftərwərdz] 🕭 그 뒤에, 나중에

04   한일파악   ▶정답 ④

듣·기·대·본

M: Are you going to the flea market tomorrow, Jia?
W: Yes. I will be <u>selling some stuff</u> there.
M: Really?
W: Yes. I want to <u>earn some extra money</u> and buy a new bicycle.
M: Great. What are you selling?
W: Some clothes I don't wear anymore and some books. I <u>priced</u> all of them yesterday.
M: You labeled all your things with the prices?
W: Right. I have some books you might like, so come and <u>have a look</u>!

우·리·말·해·석

남: 지아야, 너는 내일 벼룩시장에 갈 거야?
여: 응. 나는 거기서 물건을 좀 팔 거야.
남: 정말?
여: 응. 나는 여분의 돈을 좀 벌어서 새로운 자전거를 사고 싶어.
남: 좋네. 넌 무엇을 팔 거야?
여: 더 이상 입지 않는 옷 몇 벌과 책 몇 권. 나는 어제 그것들 모두에 가격표를 붙였어.
남: 너는 너의 모든 물건에 가격을 붙였어?
여: 맞아. 네가 좋아할 만한 책이 몇 권 있으니 와서 구경해!

단·어·및·표·현

flea market 벼룩 시장
stuff [stʌf] 📖 물건, 물질
price [prais] 🕭 가격표를 붙이다, 값을 매기다 📖 가격
label [léibəl] 🕭 라벨을 붙이다
have a look 구경하다, (한번) 보다

05 대화장소추론 ▶정답 ③

듣·기·대·본

M: Honey, this place is huge!

W: It is. Why don't we check out the floor plan first?

M: Good idea. We are here at the counter… Oh, the classic novels are on the second floor.

W: Let's go there and find the book you're looking for.

M: Aren't you going to buy anything?

W: I'll buy a cookbook. That section is on the second floor, too.

우·리·말·해·석

남: 여보, 이곳은 거대해요!

여: 그래요. 우리는 먼저 평면도를 확인하는 게 어때요?

남: 좋은 생각이에요. 우리는 여기 판매대에 있어요… 오, 고전 소설들은 2 층에 있어요.

여: 거기 가서 당신이 찾고 있는 책을 찾아보아요.

남: 당신은 아무 것도 사지 않을 거예요?

여: 나는 요리책을 살 거예요. 그 구역도 2층에 있어요.

단·어·및·표·현

huge[hjuːdʒ] 휑 엄청난, 거대한
floor plan 평면도
counter[káuntər] 몡 판매대, 계산대

06 마지막말의도파악 ▶정답 ③

듣·기·대·본

W: Excuse me. May I ask what you're doing here?

M: We're unpacking a new refrigerator.

W: Well, I live next door and it's a little noisy.

M: Oh, I'm sorry. There wasn't enough room in the kitchen to unpack it.

W: So, you're doing it in the corridor?

M: Yes. We'll try to be as quiet as possible.

W: How long do you think it'll take?

M: About 5 more minutes. Is it OK if we carry on here?

W: Only 5 minutes? Then you can take your time.

우·리·말·해·석

여: 실례합니다. 여기서 무엇을 하고 있는 중인지 여쭤봐도 될까요?

남: 저희는 새 냉장고를 상자에서 꺼내고 있어요.

여: 음, 저는 옆집에 사는데 조금 시끄럽네요.

남: 오, 죄송합니다. 그것을 풀기에는 부엌에 충분한 공간이 없었어요.

여: 그래서, 그것을 복도에서 하고 계신 거예요?

남: 네. 저희는 가능한 한 조용하도록 노력하겠습니다.

여: 얼마나 시간이 걸릴 거라고 생각하세요?

남: 대략 5분 더요. 저희가 여기서 계속해도 괜찮을까요?

여: 5분만요? 그러면 천천히 하셔도 돼요.

단·어·및·표·현

unpack[ʌnpǽk] 동 (짐을) 풀다
corridor[kɔ́(ː)ridər] 몡 복도
carry on ~을 계속하다
take one's time 천천히 하다, 서두르지 않다

07 특정정보파악 ▶정답 ①

듣·기·대·본

M: Helen, have you finished packing for camping tomorrow?

W: Yes, Dad. I remembered to pack a flashlight and a warm jacket.

M: Good! By the way, I found the camping chairs that we thought we had lost.

W: Cool! We're all set.

M: One little problem. I can't find the camping knife, so I'm heading out to buy one.

W: Oh, I see. Do you want me to come with you?

M: No need. Why don't you help your mom with her packing?

W: Okay, I will.

우·리·말·해·석

남: Helen, 내일 캠핑을 위한 짐을 싸는 것을 끝냈니?

여: 네, 아빠. 저는 손전등과 따뜻한 재킷을 챙기는 것을 기억했어요.

남: 좋아! 그나저나, 나는 우리가 잃어버린 줄 알았던 캠핑 의자를 찾았 단다.

여: 멋져요! 우리는 준비가 다 됐어요.

남: 작은 문제가 하나 있단다. 나는 캠핑용 칼을 찾을 수가 없어서 하나 사 러 갔다 올 거야.

여: 오, 알겠어요. 제가 같이 갈까요?

남: 그럴 필요 없단다. 네 엄마가 짐 싸는 것을 돕는 게 어떠니?

여: 네, 그럴게요.

단·어·및·표·현

all set 준비가 다 된

08 할일파악(대화직후) ▶정답 ④

듣·기·대·본

W: Honey, those shoes look really good on you.

M: Thanks. This is the last pair they have. I think I'll buy them.

W: But they are quite expensive.

M: If I don't buy them now, they could be sold out.

W: Why don't you search the product online first? The price could be lower.

M: Good idea. I'll search on the Internet with my phone right now.

우·리·말·해·석

여: 여보, 그 신발들은 당신에게 정말 잘 어울려요.

남: 고마워요. 이것은 그들에게 있는 마지막 한 켤레예요. 저는 그것들을 살까 해요.

여: 하지만 그것들은 꽤 비싸요.

남: 만약 제가 지금 그것들을 사지 않는다면, 그것들은 품절될 거예요.

여: 우선 온라인으로 그 상품을 검색해보는 건 어때요? 가격이 더 낮을 수 도 있어요.

남: 좋은 생각이에요. 제가 지금 당장 제 전화기로 인터넷에서 검색해볼게요.

단·어·및·표·현

look good on ~ ~와 잘 어울리다
quite[kwait] 튀 꽤, 상당히
search[səːrtʃ] 동 검색하다
product[prádəkt] 몡 상품, 제품
price[prais] 몡 가격

09 대화미언급 ▶정답 ⑤

듣·기·대·본

W: Jinho, have you heard about the Global Science Fair Competition?

M: Yes, I have. Google hosts that international competition, right?

W: Yeah. I made it through to the final competition.

M: Really? Congratulations! When is it?

W: It's from March 1st to May 15th.

M: Oh, it lasts a long time. Do you have to qualify for the competition?

W: Yes. Only students who won the regional science competition can apply for it.

M: I see. I'm sure you will do well.

여: 진호야, 너는 세계 과학 경진 대회에 대해 들어봤니?

남: 응, 들어봤어. 구글이 그 국제 대회를 주최하지, 맞지?

여: 맞아. 나 결승전까지 진출했어.

남: 정말? 축하해! 그건 언제야?

여: 3월 1일부터 5월 15일까지야.

남: 오, 그거 오래 하는구나. 그 대회에 참가하려면 자격이 있어야 하니?

여: 응. 지역 과학 대회에서 우승한 학생들만이 지원할 수 있어.

남: 그렇구나. 나는 네가 잘 해낼 거라고 확신해.

host[houst] 통 주최하다
international[ìntərnǽʃənəl] 형 국제적인
make it through 진출하다, 통과하다
last[læst] 통 오래가다, (특정한 시간 동안) 계속되다
qualify[kwάləfài] 통 (대회에) 참가할 자격이 있다, ~할 자격[권리]이 있다
regional[rí:dʒənəl] 형 지역의, 지방의
apply[əplái] 통 지원하다, 신청하다

10 담화화제추론 ▶ 정답 ⑤

들·기·대·본

W: Hello, students. I'm Ms. Kim, your head teacher. Before using the cafeteria, please remember to follow these rules. First, your safety is very important, so do not run. Stay in line and don't push others. Second, again for your safety, wash your hands before eating. Third, help yourself to the food, but try not to waste it. I hope you enjoy your lunch.

여: 안녕하세요, 학생 여러분. 저는 여러분의 교장 선생님인 김 선생님입니다. 급식실을 이용하기 전에 다음과 같은 규칙들을 따르는 것을 기억하세요. 첫째, 여러분의 안전은 매우 중요하니, 절대 뛰지 마세요. 줄을 서고, 다른 사람들을 밀지 마세요. 둘째, 다시 한번 여러분의 안전을 위해, 먹기 전에 손을 씻으세요. 셋째, 음식을 마음껏 먹되 낭비하지 않도록 노력하세요. 즐겁게 점심 식사하길 바랍니다.

head teacher 교장
cafeteria[kæ̀fətíəriə] 형 급식실, 구내식당
stay in line 줄을 서다
Help yourself. 마음껏 드세요.

11 대화내용불일치 ▶ 정답 ④

들·기·대·본

M: Kelly, I have two tickets to a musical. Do you want to go?

W: I'd love to! Which musical is it?

M: *The Lion King*. It's playing at Lakewood Theater.

W: Great. When is the show?

M: This Sunday at 7 p.m. And the running time is two hours.

W: I see. Are we going to sit close to the stage?

M: Yeah, our seats are in the second row.

W: That's awesome! I can't wait to see it.

남: Kelly, 나는 뮤지컬 표가 두 장 있어. 너 (보러) 가고 싶어?

여: 가고 싶어! 그것은 어느 뮤지컬이야?

남: "The Lion King"이야. Lakewood 극장에서 공연되고 있어.

여: 좋아. 공연이 언제야?

남: 이번 일요일 오후 7시야. 그리고 상연 시간은 2시간이야.

여: 알겠어. 우리는 무대 가까이에 앉을 거야?

남: 응. 우리 자리는 두 번째 줄에 있어.

여: 그거 굉장하다! 나는 그것을 빨리 보고 싶어.

can't wait to + 동사원형 빨리[매우] ~하고 싶어 하다

12 전화목적파악 ▶ 정답 ④

들·기·대·본

(*Telephone rings.*)

W: Hello.

M: Hi, Mrs. Morris. I'm Hank Moore, John's homeroom teacher.

W: Oh, hi, Mr. Moore. Thanks again for bringing my son to the hospital earlier today.

M: No problem. I called to check in on John. How is he doing?

W: He's doing fine. The doctor discharged him. He's resting in his room now.

M: I'm glad to hear it. So, was it a stomach flu?

W: Yes. Nothing serious. He'll be up and running around soon.

M: That's good news.

(전화벨이 울린다.)

여: 여보세요.

남: 안녕하세요, Morris 부인. 저는 John의 담임 교사인 Hank Moore입니다.

여: 오, 안녕하세요, Moore 선생님. 오늘 (아까) 저희 아들을 병원으로 데려가 주셔서 다시 한번 감사드려요.

남: 천만에요. 저는 John의 안부를 확인하려고 전화드렸습니다. 그는 좀 어떻습니까?

여: 그는 괜찮아요. 의사가 그를 퇴원시켰어요. 지금 자기 방에서 쉬고 있어요.

남: 반가운 소리네요. 그럼, 장염이었나요?

여: 네. 심각한 건 아니에요. 그는 곧 일어나서 뛰어다닐 거예요.

남: 그거 좋은 소식이네요.

homeroom teacher 담임 교사
check in on ~ ~의 안부를 확인하다, 상태를 살피다
discharge[distʃáːrdʒ] 통 (병원에서) 퇴원시키다
stomach flu 장염
run around (이리저리) 뛰어다니다

13 수치계산(거스름돈) ▶ 정답 ②

들·기·대·본

W: Hello, are you ready to order?

M: Yes. I want two cups of black coffee, please.

W: Okay, it's 4 dollars for each cup. Anything else?

M: Um, I would like a piece of strawberry cake, please.

W: Okay, that will be 5 dollars.

M: How much is the total?
W: The total will be 13 dollars. For here or to go?
M: To go. Here's 15 dollars.
W: Thank you. Here is your change.

우·리·말·해·석

여: 안녕하세요. 주문하실 준비가 되셨나요?
남: 네. 블랙 커피 두 잔 주세요.
여: 네, 한 잔에 4달러입니다. 그 밖에 필요한 게 있으신가요?
남: 음. 딸기 케이크 한 조각 주세요.
여: 네, 5달러입니다.
남: 총 얼마인가요?
여: 총 13달러입니다. 드시고 가시나요, 아니면 가져가실 건가요?
남: 가지고 갈 거예요. 여기 15달러요.
여: 감사합니다. 여기 거스름돈입니다.

단·어·및·표·현

For here or to go? 드시고 가시나요, 아니면 가져가실 건가요?
change [tʃeindʒ] 몡 거스름돈, 잔돈

14　대화자관계추론　▶정답 ②

듣·기·대·본

W: Can you tell me what time we'll leave?
M: We'll leave in a few minutes, ma'am, but we're still
　　waiting for the other members of the group to arrive.
W: I wonder why they're late.
M: They're probably tired and overslept at the hotel.
W: You can say that again! Do you think our tour today will
　　be as tiring as yesterday's?
M: Well, I'll be taking your group to some historical places.
　　However, since you'll be viewing them mostly from the
　　bus, I don't think it will be too tiring.
W: That's good news! I'm looking forward to today's tour.

우·리·말·해·석

여: 우리가 몇 시에 출발하는지 말해 주시겠어요?
남: 우리는 몇 분 후에 출발합니다. 부인, 하지만 우리는 여전히 그룹의 다
　　른 멤버들이 도착하길 기다리고 있는 중입니다.
여: 저는 그들이 왜 늦는지 궁금하군요.
남: 그들은 아마도 피곤해서 호텔에서 늦잠 잤을 것 같아요.
여: 저도 그렇게 생각해요! 오늘 관광이 어제만큼 피곤할까요?
남: 글쎄요, 저는 오늘 이 그룹을 역사적인 장소에 데려갈 것입니다. 그렇지
　　만 대부분 버스에서 볼 것이기 때문에 그렇게 피곤하지는 않을 거예요.
여: 그거 좋은 소식이네요! 저는 오늘의 관광이 기대돼요.

단·어·및·표·현

oversleep [òuvərslíːp] 몡 늦잠 자다

15　제안파악　▶정답 ②

듣·기·대·본

M: Candice, what are you going to do this Sunday?
W: I'm going to stay at home. What about you?
M: I'm volunteering at the soup kitchen.
W: Oh, I didn't know you volunteered. What do you do
　　there?
M: I clean the kitchen and throw out the garbage.
W: How kind of you!
M: Will you join me? They need more volunteers.
W: Okay, I'll join you.

우·리·말·해·석

남: Candice, 너 이번 주 일요일에 뭐 할 거니?

여: 나는 집에 있을 거야. 너는 뭐 할 거야?
남: 나는 무료 급식소에서 자원봉사할 거야.
여: 오, 나는 네가 자원봉사를 했는지 몰랐어. 너는 거기서 무엇을 하니?
남: 나는 주방을 청소하고 쓰레기를 버려.
여: 정말 마음씨가 곱구나!
남: 나와 함께 할래? 그들은 자원봉사자가 더 필요해.
여: 알겠어, 너와 함께 할게.

단·어·및·표·현

volunteer [vὰləntíər] 몡 자원봉사하다 몡 자원봉사자
soup kitchen 무료 급식소
throw out the garbage 쓰레기를 버리다

16　이유파악　▶정답 ⑤

듣·기·대·본

W: Hi, Derek. Long time no see. How have you been?
M: Great. Thank you. And you?
W: I'm fine. Are you still taking tennis lessons on
　　Saturdays?
M: No, I'm not. I can't take lessons because I'm busy
　　working at my brother's store.
W: The grocery store near your school?
M: Yes. I usually help him on Saturdays.

우·리·말·해·석

여: 안녕, Derek. 오랜만이야. 어떻게 지냈어?
남: 좋아. 고마워. 너는?
여: 잘 지내. 너 아직도 토요일마다 테니스 강습 받니?
남: 아니, 안 받아. 우리 형의 가게에서 일하느라 바빠서 강습을 받을 수가
　　없어.
여: 학교 근처의 그 식료품 가게 말이야?
남: 응. 난 보통 토요일마다 형을 돕거든.

단·어·및·표·현

be busy -ing ~하느라 바쁘다

17　그림상황에적절한대화찾기　▶정답 ⑤

듣·기·대·본

① M: Can you take the trash out for me?
　　W: Sure. No problem.
② M: Excuse me, where is the Hanjin apartment building?
　　W: It's that tall building you see right there.
③ M: It's so hot today.
　　W: Right. Let's get something to drink.
④ M: Do you need help with that box?
　　W: Oh, it's fine. I can handle it myself.
⑤ M: This bottle goes in with the plastics, right?
　　W: Yes, but take the label off first.

우·리·말·해·석

① 남: 저를 위해 쓰레기를 버려주실 수 있나요?
　　여: 물론이지. 문제없어.
② 남: 실례합니다. 한진 아파트가 어디 있나요?
　　여: 바로 저기 보이는 저 높은 건물이란다.
③ 남: 오늘은 너무 더워요.
　　여: 맞아. 마실 것을 사자.
④ 남: 그 상자에 대해 도움이 필요하시나요?
　　여: 아, 괜찮아. 혼자서 처리할 수 있어.
⑤ 남: 이 병은 플라스틱에 들어가죠, 맞죠?
　　여: 맞아, 하지만 먼저 라벨을 떼야 해.

단·어·및·표·현
take the trash out 쓰레기를 버리다
handle [hǽndl] ⑧ 처리하다, 다루다
take ~ off ~을 떼다, 벗기다

18 담화미언급 ▶정답 ④

듣·기·대·본

W: Hello, All About Games subscribers! Today, I will introduce a fun game to you. The title is *Story of Seasons*. It is a role-playing simulation game. In this game, you must manage your grandfather's farm after his death, so you need to grow crops and raise animals. The price is 20 dollars. If you are a fan of these kinds of games, I'm sure you will enjoy this game, too!

우·리·말·해·석

여: 안녕하세요, '게임에 대한 모든 것' 구독자 여러분! 오늘, 저는 여러분께 재미난 게임 하나를 소개할 겁니다. 제목은 "계절들의 이야기"입니다. 이것은 롤플레잉 시뮬레이션 게임입니다. 이 게임에서, 여러분은 여러분의 할아버지가 돌아가신 후 할아버지의 농장을 관리해야 하며, 그래서 여러분은 농작물을 기르고 동물을 키워야 합니다. 가격은 20달러입니다. 만약 여러분이 이런 종류의 게임의 팬이라면, 이 게임도 좋아할 것이라고 저는 확신합니다!

단·어·및·표·현

subscriber [səbskráibər] ⑲ 구독자
manage [mǽnidʒ] ⑧ 관리하다, 운영하다
crop [krɑp] ⑲ 농작물

19 알맞은응답찾기 ▶정답 ②

듣·기·대·본

M: Honey, I think we got all the gifts on our list for Christmas.
W: Let's see… We didn't buy a present for your mother.
M: What should we get for her?
W: How about this sweater? It looks warm and comfortable.
M: Didn't we buy one for her last Christmas?
W: Oh, you're right. Then, how about giving her a scarf?
M: Okay. Should we buy this red scarf or that white one?
W: I think the white one is better.

우·리·말·해·석

① 그것은 우리에게 30달러가 들어요.
② 나는 하얀 것이 더 좋다고 생각해요.
③ 크리스마스 케이크를 주문합시다.
④ 우리는 모든 선물들을 포장해야 해요.
⑤ 나는 나 자신을 위해 검은색 코트를 사고 싶어요.

남: 여보, 우리는 크리스마스 목록에 있는 모든 선물들을 산 것 같아요.
여: 봅시다… 우리는 당신의 어머니를 위한 선물을 사지 않았어요.
남: 우리가 그녀를 위해 무엇을 사야 할까요?
여: 이 스웨터는 어때요? 그것은 따뜻하고 편해 보여요.
남: 우리가 지난 크리스마스에 그녀에게 하나 사드리지 않았어요?
여: 오, 당신이 맞아요. 그러면 그녀에게 스카프를 드리는 것은 어때요?
남: 좋아요. 우리가 이 빨간 스카프를 사야 할까요? 아니면 저 하얀 것을 사야 할까요?
여: 나는 하얀 것이 더 좋다고 생각해요.

단·어·및·표·현

comfortable [kʌ́mfərtəbl] ⑱ 편한, 안락한
wrap [ræp] ⑧ 포장하다, 싸다

20 알맞은응답찾기 ▶정답 ②

듣·기·대·본

W: Did you join any clubs this semester?
M: I joined the school newsletter club.
W: School newsletter club? That sounds interesting. How do you like it?
M: It's mostly fun. But, there is one problem.
W: What is it?
M: Sometimes it takes too much of my time. Meetings, interviews, writing…
W: Oh, I'm sorry to hear that.
M: Maybe I'll just drop it next semester.
W: Think it over before quitting.

우·리·말·해·석

① 나는 동아리에 관심이 없어.
② 그만두기 전에 그것을 심사숙고해 봐.
③ 나는 네가 곧 낫길 바라.
④ 너무 많은 회의들이 있어.
⑤ 너는 수학 강의들을 듣는 게 어때?

여: 너는 이번 학기에 어떤 동아리에 가입했니?
남: 나는 학교 신문부에 가입했어.
여: 학교 신문부? 흥미로운걸. 어때?
남: 대부분 재밌어. 하지만, 한 가지 문제가 있어.
여: 그게 뭔데?
남: 때때로 그건 내 시간을 너무 많이 소모해. 회의, 인터뷰, 집필…
여: 아, 그거 안됐다.
남: 어쩌면 난 다음 학기에 그것을 그냥 그만둘 것 같아.
여: 그만두기 전에 그것을 심사숙고해 봐.

단·어·및·표·현

semester [siméstər] ⑲ 학기
mostly [móustli] ⑨ 대부분, 주로
drop [drɑp] ⑧ (하던 일, 논의를) 그만두다, 중단하다
think over (결정을 내리기 전에) ~을 심사숙고하다
quit [kwit] ⑧ 그만두다
be interested in ~에 관심이 있다

Words & Expressions Review

1. 줄	2. 주로	3. 평면도
4. 학기	5. 복도	6. 무료 급식소
7. 체크무늬의	8. (짐을) 풀다	9. 강습, 수업
10. 엄청난, 거대한	11. 그 뒤에, 나중에	12. 그만두다, 중단하다
13. 구경하다, (한번) 보다	14. ~을 계속하다	15. 포장하다, 싸다
16. 그만두다	17. 준비가 다 된	18. 지역의, 지방의
19. ~와 잘 어울리다	20. 구독자	21. 도착하다
22. 줄을 서다	23. 형편없이, 몹시, 심각하게	24. 주최하다
25. 교장	26. 관리하다, 운영하다	27. 쓰레기를 버리다
28. 식료품점	29. ~하느라 바쁘다	30. ~의 안부를 확인하다, 상태를 살피다
31. 판매대, 계산대	32. 벙어리장갑	33. 벼룩 시장
34. 늦잠 자다	35. 편한, 안락한	36. ~을 기대하다

37. 빨리[매우] 　～ 하고 싶어 하다	38. 농작물	39. ～로 향하다
40. 가능성	41. 진출하다, 통과하다	42. 처리하다, 다루다
43. (병원에서) 퇴원시키다	44. (이리저리) 뛰어다니다	

Listening Test
영어듣기 모의고사 **23**회

|정|답|

01 ④	02 ②	03 ③	04 ①	05 ④
06 ①	07 ②	08 ⑤	09 ⑤	10 ③
11 ⑤	12 ④	13 ③	14 ③	15 ④
16 ④	17 ④	18 ⑤	19 ⑤	20 ②

01　날씨파악-그림　▶정답 ④

들·기·대·본

W: Hello. Here's today's weather report for cities around the world. In Seoul, there will be thunderstorms and the temperature will drop. On the other hand, it will get warmer in Hong Kong as the sunshine continues through this week. Tokyo will be very cloudy. In New York, showers are expected as the temperature rises and days of heavy snow end. London will be windy and cold. Thank you very much.

우·리·말·해·석

여: 안녕하세요. 전 세계 도시들의 오늘 일기 예보입니다. 서울에는 뇌우가 있을 것이고 기온이 떨어질 것입니다. 반면에 홍콩은 이번 주 내내 햇빛이 계속되면서 따뜻해질 전망입니다. 도쿄는 매우 흐릴 것입니다. 뉴욕에는 기온이 오르면서 여러 날 내리던 폭설이 멈추고 소나기가 예상됩니다. 런던은 바람이 불고 추울 것입니다. 대단히 감사합니다.

단·어·및·표·현

through this week 이번 주 내내
heavy snow 폭설

02　그림정보파악　▶정답 ②

들·기·대·본

M: Leah, what are you looking at on the Internet?
W: I think we need a picture frame as a decoration in the living room.
M: That's a great idea! [Pause] How about these double photo frames?
W: Well, I think single frames are much better to look at.
M: I see. Then, check out this square one. It looks simple and nice.
W: I love it. Let's buy that single square photo frame.

우·리·말·해·석

남: Leah, 너는 인터넷에서 무엇을 보고 있니?
여: 우리는 거실에 장식품으로 (둘) 사진 액자가 필요한 것 같아.
남: 좋은 생각이다! [잠시 후] 이 두 개로 된 사진 액자는 어때?

여: 음, 단일 액자가 보기에 훨씬 더 좋은 것 같아.
남: 그렇구나. 그러면, 이 정사각형의 것을 살펴봐 봐. 그것은 단순하고 좋아 보여.
여: 난 그것이 좋아. 저 단일 정사각형의 사진 액자를 사자.

단·어·및·표·현

frame[freim] 몡 액자
as[æz] 전 ～로(서)
decoration[dèkəréiʃən] 몡 장식품
check out 살펴보다, 보다

03　심정추론　▶정답 ③

들·기·대·본

M: That's amazing! When did our daughter learn to skateboard like that?
W: She picked it up about four months ago.
M: Did you know about this?
W: Yeah, but she asked me to keep it quiet. She wanted to surprise you.
M: She's unbelievable! Everyone here is clapping and shouting for her cool moves.
W: She practiced every day after school.
M: I want everyone to know she's our daughter.

우·리·말·해·석

① 긴장한　　② 불안한　　③ 자랑스러운
④ 느긋한　　⑤ 화가 난

남: 놀랍네요! 우리 딸이 언제 저렇게 스케이트보드를 배웠나요?
여: 그녀는 약 4개월 전에 익히게 되었어요.
남: 당신은 이것에 대해 알았어요?
여: 네, 하지만 그녀는 제게 그것을 비밀로 하길 부탁했어요. 그녀는 당신을 놀라게 해주고 싶어 했어요.
남: 그녀는 놀랍네요! 여기 (있는) 모두가 그녀의 멋진 동작들에 박수치고 환호하고 있어요.
여: 그녀는 매일 방과 후에 연습했어요.
남: 전 그녀가 우리 딸이라는 것을 모두가 알기를 원해요.

단·어·및·표·현

pick up (습관 · 재주 등을) 익히게 되다
keep quiet 비밀로 하다
unbelievable[ʌ̀nbilíːvəbl] 혱 놀랄 만한, 믿을 수 없는
clap[klæp] 동 박수를 치다
shout[ʃaut] 동 환호하다
move[muːv] 몡 동작, 움직임

04　한일파악　▶정답 ①

들·기·대·본

W: Dong-hyun, you look very tired.
M: Yeah, I didn't get enough sleep last night.
W: Did you play computer games again?
M: No, I stayed up late doing my homework.
W: Really? What homework?
M: Our math homework. Aren't we supposed to hand it in today?
W: No, I'm sure it's not due until next week.
M: Oh… That means I stayed up late for nothing!
W: Look on the bright side. At least you finished your homework.

우·리·말·해·석

여: 동현아, 너는 매우 피곤해 보여.

남: 응, 나는 지난밤에 충분한 잠을 자지 못 했어.

여: 너 또 컴퓨터 게임 했어?

남: 아니, 나는 내 숙제를 하면서 늦게까지 깨어 있었어.

여: 정말? 무슨 숙제?

남: 우리 수학 숙제. 우리는 오늘 그것을 제출하기로 되어 있지 않아?

여: 아니, 다음 주 전까지는 마감이 아닌 것이 확실해.

남: 오… 그것은 내가 괜히 늦게까지 깨어 있었다는 뜻이네!

여: 긍정적으로 생각해. 적어도 너는 너의 숙제를 끝냈잖아.

단·어·및·표·현
hand ~ in ~을 제출하다
for nothing 괜히, 헛되이

05 대화장소추론 ▶정답 ④

들·기·대·본
M: Hi, Lucy. What can I get you?

W: Hi, Tim. I'm not here to buy anything.

M: Is something wrong?

W: No, no. You see, I bought a cup of coffee and some cookies here this morning.

M: Yes, I remember.

W: I found that you gave me a dollar more for change.

M: Oh, so you came back?

W: Yeah, here's a dollar. Sorry I didn't come back right away.

M: I know how busy you are with your clothing shop. Thank you for this. You are so kind.

W: You are welcome. See you tomorrow!

우·리·말·해·석
남: 안녕하세요, Lucy. 무엇을 드릴까요?

여: 안녕하세요, Tim. 저는 뭘 사려고 온 게 아니에요.

남: 뭐가 잘못됐나요?

여: 아니, 아니에요. 아시다시피, 저는 오늘 아침에 여기에서 커피 한 잔과 쿠키를 좀 샀어요.

남: 네, 기억해요.

여: 당신이 거스름돈으로 1달러를 더 준 것을 발견했어요.

남: 아, 그래서 돌아오신 거예요?

여: 네, 여기 1달러요. 바로 돌아오지 않아서 미안해요.

남: 당신이 옷 가게 일로 얼마나 바쁜지 알아요. 이것에 대해 감사해요. 당신은 무척 친절하네요.

여: 천만에요. 내일 봐요!

단·어·및·표·현
get A B A에게 B를 주다
change[tʃeindʒ] 몡 거스름돈
busy with ~ ~으로 바쁜

06 마지막말의도파악 ▶정답 ①

들·기·대·본
M: Sia, what are you building?

W: These are model airplanes.

M: Model airplanes? What do you do with them?

W: Some people collect them, others enjoy building and painting them.

M: That sounds interesting. Do you collect them?

W: No, I build them as a hobby. It's fun and challenging.

M: Can you show me how to build one?

우·리·말·해·석
남: Sia, 너는 무엇을 만들고 있니?

여: 이것들은 모형 비행기야.

남: 모형 비행기? 그것들로 무엇을 해?

여: 어떤 사람들은 그것들을 수집하고, 다른 사람들은 그것을 만들고 칠하는 것을 즐겨.

남: 그거 흥미롭게 들리네. 너는 그것들을 수집하니?

여: 아니, 난 그것들을 취미로 만들어. 그건 재미있고 도전의식을 불러일으켜.

남: 너는 그것을 어떻게 만드는지 나에게 보여줄 수 있니?

단·어·및·표·현
build[bild] 통 만들다, (기계류를) 조립하다
model[mádəl] 몡 (보통 실물보다 작게 만든) 모형
collect[kəlékt] 통 수집하다
challenging[tʃælindʒiŋ] 톙 도전의식을 불러일으키는, 도전적인

07 특정정보파악 ▶정답 ②

들·기·대·본
W: Can you come here and help me out?

M: Sure thing. What's up?

W: I'm trying to choose between these two souvenirs for my friends back home.

M: The refrigerator magnet and the local artwork?

W: Yeah, I like both of them, but I can't decide which one to buy.

M: Hmm... I think the local artwork would be a unique and memorable gift.

W: Do you really think so? Okay, then I'll buy it.

우·리·말·해·석
여: 너는 여기로 와서 나를 도와줄 수 있어?

남: 물론이지. 무슨 일이야?

여: 나는 고국에 있는 내 친구들을 위해 이 두 가지 기념품들 중에서 고르려고 하고 있어.

남: 냉장고 자석과 현지 예술품?

여: 응, 나는 그것들 둘 다 마음에 들지만, 어떤 것을 살지 결정 못 하겠어.

남: 음… 난 현지 예술품이 특별하고 기억할 만한 선물이 될 것 같아.

여: 넌 정말 그렇게 생각해? 그래, 그럼 난 그것을 사야겠다.

단·어·및·표·현
help out 도와주다
souvenir[sùːvəníər] 몡 기념품
local[lóukəl] 톙 현지의
artwork[áːrtwəːrk] 몡 예술품
both of ~ 둘 다
decide[disáid] 통 결정하다
unique[juːníːk] 톙 특별한, 독특한
memorable[mémərəbl] 톙 기억할 만한

08 할일파악(대화직후) ▶정답 ⑤

들·기·대·본
M: Matt, today is Grandma's 80th birthday.

W: Right. I knitted a scarf for her.

M: That's thoughtful. We can give her the scarf at the party.

W: What else can we do to celebrate?

M: Let's bake some cookies before the party.

W: Good idea. What type of cookies should we make?

M: How about chocolate chip cookies? Grandma loves them.

W: Sounds perfect. Let's search for a recipe.

우·리·말·해·석
남: Matt, 오늘은 할머니의 80번째 생신이야.

여: 맞아. 나는 그녀를 위해 목도리를 떴어.
남: 사려 깊은걸. 우리는 파티에서 그녀에게 목도리를 드릴 수 있어.
여: 축하하기 위해 우리가 무엇을 더 할 수 있을까?
남: 파티 전에 쿠키들을 좀 굽자.
여: 좋은 생각이야. 우린 어떤 종류의 쿠키를 만들어야 할까?
남: 초콜릿칩 쿠키는 어때? 할머니는 그것들을 좋아하셔.
여: 완벽한걸. 요리법을 찾아보자.

단·어·및·표·현

knit [nit] 동 (실로 옷을) 뜨다, 짜다
scarf [skɑːrf] 명 목도리, 스카프
thoughtful [θɔ́ːtfəl] 형 사려 깊은
celebrate [séləbrèit] 동 축하하다, 기념하다
bake [beik] 동 굽다
search for ~을 찾다, 검색하다
recipe [résəpì:] 명 요리법, 레시피

09 대화미언급 ▶정답 ⑤

듣·기·대·본

W: Carl, are you going to participate in the photography contest?
M: I haven't made up my mind yet.
W: Don't forget the deadline for submission is October 20th.
M: I know. And the theme of the photo contest is family.
W: Yes. Do you have the email address?
M: Of course. I'm supposed to submit my photo with a short introduction by email, right?
W: Right! Do you know the prize for the winner?
M: Sure. The winner will receive a gift certificate.

우·리·말·해·석

여: Carl, 너는 사진 콘테스트에 참가할 거야?
남: 나는 아직 결정하지 못했어.
여: 제출 마감일이 10월 20일이라는 것을 잊지 마.
남: 알아. 그리고 사진 콘테스트의 주제는 가족이야.
여: 응. 넌 그 이메일 주소가 있니?
남: 물론이야. 이메일로 간단한 소개와 함께 나의 사진을 제출해야 해, 그렇지?
여: 맞아! 우승자에게 주는 상이 뭔지 아니?
남: 물론이지. 우승자는 상품권을 받을 거야.

단·어·및·표·현

participate in ~에 참가하다
make up one's mind 결정하다, 결심하다
deadline [dédlàin] 명 기한, 마감 시간[일자]
submission [səbmíʃən] 명 (서류 등의) 제출
theme [θi:m] 명 주제, 테마
be supposed to + 동사원형 ~해야 한다
submit [səbmít] 동 제출하다
gift certificate 상품권

10 담화화제추론 ▶정답 ③

듣·기·대·본

W: Class, please settle down. I have some important announcements to make, so listen carefully. As you are all aware of, tomorrow we will be going on a school trip. We will be leaving at 8 o'clock tomorrow morning, so everybody must be on board the school bus by 7:50 a.m. Please, don't be late! We will be staying there for two nights, so don't forget to bring your spare clothes

and toiletries. Lastly, at all times please be safe.

우·리·말·해·석

여: 학급 학생 여러분, 정숙해주세요. 중요한 공지사항이 있으니 주의해서 들으세요. 여러분 모두가 알고 있듯이 내일 우리는 수학여행을 갑니다. 우리는 내일 아침 8시에 떠나니 모두들 오전 7시 50분까지 학교 버스에 탑승해야 합니다. 늦지 마세요! 우리는 거기서 이틀 밤을 묵을 것이니 잊지 말고 여벌의 옷과 세면용품을 가져오세요. 마지막으로, 항상 안전(에 유의)하세요.

단·어·및·표·현

announcement [ənáunsmənt] 명 공지, 발표

11 대화내용불일치 ▶정답 ⑤

듣·기·대·본

W: Mark, you should come join me at the school book club. You'll love it.
M: Hmm… I'm not sure. How many members are there?
W: Currently, we have 10 members, and you can join for free.
M: Okay, how many books do you read?
W: We read one book every two weeks.
M: So, you have gatherings every two weeks after reading the book?
W: You're right. We also don't write any book reports. So, no pressure.
M: That sounds okay. Count me in, then.

우·리·말·해·석

여: Mark, 네가 학교 독서 클럽에 나와 같이 합류했으면 좋겠어. 너는 그것을 좋아할 거야.
남: 흠… 나는 잘 모르겠어. 몇 명의 회원이 있어?
여: 현재 우리는 10명의 회원이 있고, 너는 무료로 가입할 수 있어.
남: 알았어. 너는 얼마나 많은 책을 읽어?
여: 우리는 2주마다 한 권의 책을 읽어.
남: 그러니까, 너희는 책을 읽은 후 매 2주마다 모임이 있는 거야?
여: 맞아. 우리는 또한 어떤 독후감도 쓰지 않아. 그러니까, 압박이 없어.
남: 그것은 좋은 것 같다. 그러면, 나도 끼워줘.

단·어·및·표·현

gathering [gǽðəriŋ] 명 모임
Count me in. 나도 끼워줘.

12 전화목적파악 ▶정답 ④

듣·기·대·본

(Telephone rings.)
W: Good morning, Grand Hotel. How may I assist you?
M: Hi, I have a reservation for a room tomorrow night, but I need to cancel it.
W: I'm sorry to hear that. May I have your name and reservation number, please?
M: It's Brandon Lee and my reservation number is 3672.
W: Thank you. May I know why you are cancelling?
M: There was a sudden change of plans.
W: I see. Your reservation has been cancel(l)ed.
M: Thank you.

우·리·말·해·석

(전화벨이 울린다.)
여: 좋은 아침입니다, Grand 호텔입니다. 어떻게 도와드릴까요?
남: 안녕하세요, 저는 내일 밤으로 방을 예약했는데 그걸 취소해야 해요.
여: 안타깝네요. 예약자 분의 성함과 예약 번호를 알 수 있을까요?

남: Brandon Lee이고 제 예약 번호는 3672입니다.
여: 감사합니다. 취소 사유를 여쭤봐도 되겠습니까?
남: 계획이 갑자기 변경되었어요.
여: 알겠습니다. 예약이 취소되었습니다.
남: 감사합니다.

단·어·및·표·현
assist [əsíst] ⑧ 돕다
have a reservation 예약하다
cancel [kǽnsəl] ⑧ 취소하다
sudden [sʌ́dən] ⑱ 갑작스러운

13 　수치파악　▶정답 ③

듣·기·대·본
M: Good morning. Welcome to Central Museum.
W: Good morning. I would like two tickets, please.
M: Sure. The tickets are 13 dollars per person.
W: Oh, I heard there's a discount for students.
M: Yes, there's a 3-dollar discount if you show me your student card.
W: Here are two student cards. That means it's 10 dollars each, right?
M: Yes. Your total comes to 20 dollars.
W: Here's my credit card.

우·리·말·해·석
남: 좋은 아침입니다. 중앙박물관에 오신 걸 환영합니다.
여: 좋은 아침이에요. 표 두 장 주세요.
남: 네. 표는 한 사람당 13달러입니다.
여: 오, 저는 학생들에게 할인이 있다고 들었어요.
남: 맞아요, 만약 당신의 학생증을 제게 보여주시면 3달러 할인됩니다.
여: 여기 학생증 두 개요. 이러면 그것은 각자 10달러라는 거죠, 맞죠?
남: 네. 손님의 총액은 20달러입니다.
여: 여기 제 신용카드요.

단·어·및·표·현
each [iːtʃ] ⑨ 각자, 각각
total [tóutl] ⑲ 총액, 합계
come to (합계가) 되다, (정도, 범위 등에) 이르다

14 　대화자관계추론　▶정답 ③

듣·기·대·본
W: Excuse me, sir. You can't have that drink here.
M: What do you mean?
W: Drinks in disposable containers are not allowed on the bus.
M: Oh, I didn't know. Why is that?
W: If a drink gets spilt, it can be dangerous.
M: I see. But can't I bring it just this once?
W: I'm afraid not. It's the rule. I can't start the bus unless you get off.
M: OK, it looks like I have no choice.

우·리·말·해·석
여: 실례합니다. 선생님. 여기서 그 음료수를 드실 수 없습니다.
남: 무슨 말씀이시죠?
여: 버스에서 일회용 용기에 들어 있는 음료는 허용되지 않습니다.
남: 오, 몰랐습니다. 왜 그런 거죠?
여: 만약 음료가 쏟아지면 위험할 수 있기 때문입니다.
남: 알겠습니다. 하지만 이번 한 번만 가지고 타면 안 될까요?
여: 죄송하지만 안 됩니다. 규칙이라서요. 선생님이 내리지 않으시면 제가

출발할 수가 없습니다.
남: 알겠습니다. 저에게 선택의 여지가 없는 것 같네요.

단·어·및·표·현
be allowed 허용되다
have no choice 선택의 여지가 없다, 대안이 없다

15 　부탁(요청)한일파악　▶정답 ④

듣·기·대·본
M: Jessica, let's go eat lunch.
W: I'm sorry, but I think you should go alone today.
M: Why? Are you feeling all right?
W: Actually, I'm still working on the materials for the meeting at 2 p.m. this afternoon.
M: Oh, do you need any help? Like making copies or something?
W: That's okay. Instead, can you buy me something to eat?
M: Sure! What about a sandwich?
W: That sounds great. Thank you.
M: No problem.

우·리·말·해·석
남: Jessica, 우리 점심 먹으러 가자.
여: 미안하지만, 오늘은 너 혼자 가야 할 것 같아.
남: 왜? 너 괜찮아?
여: 사실, 나는 아직도 오늘 오후 2시에 있을 미팅을 위한 자료들을 작업 중이거든.
남: 오, 무슨 도움이 필요하니? 그것들을 복사하는 것 같은 거?
여: 괜찮아. 대신에, 나를 위해 먹을 것을 좀 사다 줄 수 있니?
남: 물론이지! 샌드위치는 어때?
여: 그거 참 좋겠다. 고마워.
남: 그 정도 가지고.

단·어·및·표·현
be still working on ~ ~을 아직도 작업하고 있다
material [mətí(ː)əriəl] ⑲ 자료, 재료

16 　이유파악　▶정답 ④

듣·기·대·본
M: Hi, Rachael. Are you still taking that Spanish conversation class?
W: Oh, I thought I told you. I'm not taking it anymore.
M: Really? Why? I thought you really liked it. Was the textbook too difficult?
W: No, the materials were fine.
M: Then what happened?
W: I'm going on a long business trip overseas, so I had to stop going to the class.
M: I see. Are you planning to join the class again when you return?
W: Yes, definitely.

우·리·말·해·석
남: 안녕, Rachael. 넌 아직 그 스페인어 회화 수업을 듣고 있니?
여: 아, 나는 너에게 말한 줄 알았어. 난 더 이상 그거 안 들어.
남: 정말? 왜? 난 네가 그걸 정말 좋아했다고 생각했는데. 교재가 너무 어려웠어?
여: 아니, 자료들은 괜찮았어.
남: 그럼 무슨 일이 있었어?
여: 나는 해외로 장기 출장을 가게 되어서 그 수업에 가는 것을 그만둬야 했어.
남: 그렇구나. 넌 돌아올 때 그 수업에 다시 참여할 계획이니?

여: 응, 물론이지.

단·어·및·표·현

conversation [kὰnvərséiʃən] 몡 회화, 대화
material [mətí(ː)əriəl] 몡 (수업 등 특정 활동에 필요한) 자료
overseas [óuvərsìːz] 倒 해외로, 해외의
definitely [défənitli] 倒 (강조의 의미로 쓰여) 절대(로),
분명히[틀림없이]

17 그림상황에적절한대화찾기 ▶정답 ④

듣·기·대·본

① M: Excuse me, where is the bank?
  W: It's next to the police office.
② M: Hi, I'd like to order a coffee, please.
  W: Of course! For here or to go?
③ M: Look at the waiting line.
  W: Why don't we go somewhere else?
④ M: What do you want to drink?
  W: I'll have a soda.
⑤ M: This music is so good.
  W: Right? I love every song of theirs.

우·리·말·해·석

① 남: 실례합니다, 은행이 어디에 있나요?
  여: 그것은 경찰서 옆에 있어요.
② 남: 안녕하세요, 커피 하나 주문할게요.
  여: 물론이죠! 드시고 가실 건가요, 아니면 가져가실 건가요?
③ 남: 대기 줄 좀 봐.
  여: 우리 다른 데로 가는 게 어때?
④ 남: 너는 무엇을 마시고 싶니?
  여: 나는 탄산음료를 마실게.
⑤ 남: 이 음악 진짜 좋다.
  여: 그렇지? 난 그들의 모든 노래를 좋아해.

단·어·및·표·현

order [ɔ́ːrdər] 통 주문하다
waiting line 대기 줄
soda [sóudə] 몡 탄산 음료

18 담화미언급 ▶정답 ⑤

듣·기·대·본

M: Hello, everyone. Welcome to Central History Museum.
Our museum introduces our country's history through
pictures, art works, and many other items from the
past. We also have a special exhibit on the second
floor. We are open from 10 a.m. to 6 p.m. on Tuesday
and Thursday through Sunday, and to 7 p.m. on
Wednesdays. Please be aware that we are closed on
Mondays. Please check our website for more details.

우·리·말·해·석

남: 안녕하세요, 여러분. 중앙 역사 박물관에 오신 것을 환영합니다. 저희
박물관은 우리나라 역사를 사진, 미술품, 그리고 과거에서 온 많은 다
른 물품들을 통해 소개합니다. 저희는 또한 2층에 특별 전시가 있습니
다. 저희는 매주 화요일과 목요일부터 일요일까지는 오전 10시부터 오
후 6시까지 열며, 매주 수요일에는 오후 7시까지 엽니다. 저희는 월요
일에는 닫는다는 것을 알아두세요. 더 많은 세부 사항에 대해서는 저희
웹사이트를 확인해주세요.

단·어·및·표·현

exhibit [igzíbit] 몡 전시, 전시품
aware [əwέər] 몡 알고 있는

19 알맞은응답찾기 ▶정답 ⑤

듣·기·대·본

W: Hi, Tim. Did you watch the nature documentary on TV
last night?
M: No, what was it about?
W: It was about interesting animal facts.
M: Can you tell me one?
W: Sure. Do you know what animal sleeps the most?
M: I don't know. Is it the bat?
W: No. It's koalas!
M: Really? How much time do they spend sleeping?
W: They sleep up to 22 hours a day.

우·리·말·해·석

① 그들은 동굴 안에 사는 것을 좋아해.
② 그들은 호주가 원산지야.
③ 그들은 잎을 먹는 것으로 알려졌어.
④ 그들은 천적이 없어.
⑤ 그들은 하루에 22시간까지 잠을 자.

여: 안녕, Tim. 너 어젯밤에 TV에서 자연 다큐멘터리 봤니?
남: 아니, 무엇에 관한 거였는데?
여: 그것은 동물의 흥미로운 사실에 관한 거였어.
남: 하나 말해줄래?
여: 그래. 너는 어떤 동물이 잠을 가장 많이 자는지 아니?
남: 모르겠어. 그것은 박쥐니?
여: 아니. 코알라야!
남: 정말? 그들은 잠자는 데 시간을 얼마나 쓰니?
여: 그들은 하루에 22시간까지 잠을 자.

단·어·및·표·현

fact [fækt] 몡 사실
spend [spend] 통 (시간을) 보내다
native to A A가 원산지인, A 고유의
natural predator 천적, 자연적 포식자

20 알맞은응답찾기 ▶정답 ②

듣·기·대·본

W: Hi, Somin. How was your trip to Jeju-do?
M: It was fantastic. I had so much fun.
W: How did you get there, on a ferry or by plane?
M: I went there by plane. Then my parents rented a car and
drove us around.
W: What is the most memorable thing from your trip?
M: It's seeing dolphins in the sea. We were so lucky.
W: Wow. Did you go on a boat to see them?
M: No. We were in our car and suddenly, we spotted
dolphins out in the sea.
W: That sounds unbelievable.

우·리·말·해·석

① 정말 슬픈 얘기다!
② 믿기 어렵게 들려.
③ 내 눈을 믿을 수 없었어.
④ 네가 다음에는 돌고래를 보기를 바라.
⑤ 네가 배를 타고 있었다니 운이 좋았다.

여: 안녕, 소민아. 제주도 여행은 어땠어?
남: 환상적이었어. 엄청 재미있었어.
여: 거기에 어떻게 갔어, 여객선 아니면 비행기?

남: 비행기로 거기에 갔어. 그러고 나서 부모님이 차를 렌트해서 우리를 태우고 다니셨어.

여: 네 여행에서 가장 기억할 만한 것이 뭐야?

남: 바다에 있는 돌고래들을 본 것이야. 우리는 무척 운이 좋았어.

여: 와. 그것들을 보기 위해 배를 탔니?

남: 아니. 우리는 차에 있었는데 갑자기 바다에 나와있는 돌고래들을 발견했어.

여: **믿기 어렵게 들려.**

단·어·및·표·현

memorable [mémərəbl] 형 기억할 만한

suddenly [sʌ́dnli] 부 갑자기

Words & Expressions Review

1. 돕다	2. 도전의식을 불러일으키는, 도전적인	3. (서류 등의) 제출
4. (습관·재주 등을) 익히게 되다	5. 액자	6. A에게 B를 주다
7. 세부 사항	8. 취소하다	9. 예술품
10. 갑자기	11. 공지, 발표	12. 장식품
13. (합계가) 되다, (정도, 범위 등에) 이르다	14. 기념품	15. 자료, 재료
16. 특별한, 독특한	17. 기억할 만한	18. 반면에
19. 작업하다	20. (실로 옷을) 뜨다, 짜다	21. 나도 끼워줘.
22. 갑작스러운	23. 주의하여, 신중히	24. 놀랄 만한, 믿을 수 없는
25. 긍정적으로 생각해.	26. 수집하다	27. ~을 아는
28. 만약 ~하지 않는다면	29. 모임	30. 해외로, 해외의
31. 결정하다, 결심하다	32. 일회용의	33. 사실
34. 거스름돈	35. 각자, 각각	36. ~으로 바쁜
37. 제출하다	38. ~으로(서)	39. (강조의 의미로 쓰여) 절대(로), 분명히[틀림없이]
40. 회화, 대화	41. (건물의) 층, 바닥	42. 사려 깊은
43. A가 원산지인, A 고유의	44. 천적, 자연적 포식자	

영어듣기 고난도 모의고사  High Level **24**회

|정|답|

01 ①	02 ②	03 ②	04 ②	05 ②
06 ②	07 ①	08 ④	09 ②	10 ②
11 ①	12 ③	13 ④	14 ⑤	15 ③
16 ③	17 ③	18 ④	19 ④	20 ④

01 날씨파악-그림 ▶정답 ①

듣·기·대·본

M: Good morning. Let's take a look at the weather for this week. On Monday, it will be sunny all day. But on Tuesday, some rain is likely. So, get your umbrella ready. It will be cloudy on Wednesday. Again, you will see some rain on Thursday. But on Friday, you will have a sunny day.

우·리·말·해·석

남: 안녕하세요. 이번 주 날씨에 대해 알아봅시다. 월요일에는 하루 종일 화창할 것입니다. 하지만 화요일에는 약간의 비가 올 것 같습니다. 그러니, 당신의 우산을 준비하세요. 수요일에는 흐릴 것입니다. 또다시, 목요일에는 약간의 비가 올 것입니다. 하지만 금요일에는 화창할 것입니다.

단·어·및·표·현

get ~ ready ~을 준비하다

02 그림정보파악 ▶정답 ②

듣·기·대·본

W: Welcome to Ocean Gift Shop. How can I help you?

M: Hi. I'm looking for a keychain for my friend.

W: Sure. We have seashell and starfish-shaped keychains. Both are quite popular.

M: I'll choose the starfish-shaped keychain.

W: Good choice. They come in two styles, plain and polka-dotted. Which do you prefer?

M: I think the polka-dotted one looks nice.

W: All right. Then, how about this one with the word "SEA" on it? It reminds you of the endless ocean.

M: Great! I'll take it.

우·리·말·해·석

여: Ocean 선물 가게에 오신 걸 환영합니다. 어떻게 도와드릴까요?

남: 안녕하세요. 전 친구에게 줄 열쇠고리를 찾고 있어요.

여: 물론이죠. 저희는 조개 모양과 불가사리 모양 열쇠고리가 있어요. 둘 다 꽤 인기있어요.

남: 전 불가사리 모양 열쇠고리를 고를게요.

여: 좋은 선택이에요. 그것들은 무늬 없는 것과 물방울무늬, 두 가지 종류로 나옵니다. 어떤 게 좋으세요?

남: 물방울무늬가 예쁜 것 같아요.

여: 알겠습니다. 그럼 "SEA"라는 글자가 쓰여 있는 이건 어때요? 그건 당신이 끝없는 바다를 떠올리게 해요.

남: 좋아요! 그걸로 할게요.

단·어·및·표·현

seashell [síːʃel] 명 조개껍데기

starfish [stáːrfiʃ] 명 불가사리

polka-dotted 물방울무늬의

prefer [prifə́ːr] 동 ~을 더 좋아하다, 선호하다

remind [rimáind] 동 떠올리게 하다
endless [éndlis] 형 끝없는

03 심정추론　　　　　　　　　▶ 정답 ②

듣·기·대·본

M: Mom, can we leave now?
W: Not yet, honey. We need some onions.
M: We've already bought so much stuff, though.
W: Not that much. What's wrong? Are you feeling unwell?
M: No. I just want to get out of here. This market is not fun.
W: You promised to help me, Dave.
M: Yeah, but we've stayed here too long.
W: It's only been twenty minutes. You really need to learn some patience.

우·리·말·해·석

① 자랑스러운　　　　　② 지루한　　　　　③ 긴장한
④ 슬픈　　　　　　　　⑤ 기쁜

남: 엄마, 우리 지금 출발할 수 있을까요?
여: 아직 아니야, 얘야. 우리는 양파가 좀 필요해.
남: 하지만 우리는 이미 아주 많은 것들을 샀잖아요.
여: 그렇게 많지 않아. 무슨 일이야? 몸이 안 좋아?
남: 아니요. 전 그냥 여기서 나가고 싶어요. 이 시장은 재미없어요.
여: 너는 날 돕겠다고 약속했어, Dave.
남: 네, 하지만 우리는 여기서 너무 오래 머물렀어요.
여: 겨우 20분 됐어. 너는 정말 인내심을 배워야 해.

단·어·및·표·현

stuff [stʌf] 명 것, 물건
feel unwell 몸이 안 좋다
promise to + 동사원형 ~하기로 약속하다
patience [péiʃəns] 명 인내심, 참을성

04 한일파악　　　　　　　　　▶ 정답 ②

듣·기·대·본

W: Alex, what's that smell?
M: I baked a chocolate cake. I just took it out of the oven.
W: It smells really good! I've never baked one. Can I have a slice?
M: Sure, but I'm not sure if it turned out well.
W: Thanks. (*Pause*) It tastes amazing!
M: Thanks. I actually attended a baking class last weekend.
W: That's interesting. Maybe I should join one, too.

우·리·말·해·석

여: Alex, 저게 무슨 냄새야?
남: 나는 초콜릿 케이크를 구웠어. 나는 방금 그것을 오븐에서 꺼냈어.
여: 그거 냄새가 정말 좋다! 난 그걸 한 번도 구워본 적이 없어. 한 조각 먹어도 될까?
남: 물론이지. 그런데 그게 잘 되었는지는 나는 확신 못 하겠어.
여: 고마워. (잠시 후) 이거 정말 맛있다!
남: 고마워. 사실 나는 지난 주말에 베이킹 수업에 참석했어.
여: 그거 흥미롭네. 어쩌면 나도 참여해야 할 것 같아.

단·어·및·표·현

take out of ~에서 꺼내다
bake [beik] 동 (음식을) 굽다
slice [slais] 명 조각
turn out (결과가) ~으로 되다, 되어 가다
attend [əténd] 동 참석하다

05 대화장소추론　　　　　　　　▶ 정답 ②

듣·기·대·본

M: Hello. How may I help you?
W: I'd like to get a passport photo taken.
M: Okay. Here is a mirror so you can check your appearance before I take the picture.
W: Do I have to take off my glasses?
M: They are allowed as long as your eyes are clearly visible and there is no glare on the lenses.
W: All right. Then, I'll just wear them.
M: Tuck your hair behind your ears so that the ears can be seen.
W: Okay. Now, I am ready.
M: Keep your mouth closed and face the camera!

우·리·말·해·석

남: 안녕하세요. 어떻게 도와드릴까요?
여: 저는 여권 사진을 찍고 싶어요.
남: 좋습니다. 여기 거울이 있으니 제가 사진을 찍기 전에 당신은 당신의 외모를 확인할 수 있습니다.
여: 제가 제 안경을 벗어야 하나요?
남: 당신의 눈이 분명하게 보이고 렌즈에 번쩍임이 없는 한 그것들은 허용됩니다.
여: 좋아요. 그러면, 그냥 쓸게요.
남: 귀가 보이도록 머리를 귀 뒤로 넘기세요.
여: 알겠어요. 이제, 저 준비되었어요.
남: 입을 다무시고 카메라를 바라보세요!

단·어·및·표·현

appearance [əpí(:)ərəns] 명 외모
as long as ~ ~하는 한
tuck [tʌk] 동 밀어넣다
face [feis] 동 바라보다, 향하다

06 마지막말의도파악　　　　　　　▶ 정답 ②

듣·기·대·본

W: Oh, no! It's almost my turn to perform! Can we just leave?
M: Don't even think of backing out. Just relax, okay?
W: I'm sorry, Coach, but I can't do this.
M: I don't understand why you're so nervous, Megan.
W: The other contestants are so good! I don't stand a chance!
M: That's not true. You have what it takes to win this contest.
W: Do you really think so?
M: I'm positive. Believe in yourself.

우·리·말·해·석

여: 오, 안 돼! 이제 거의 제가 공연할 차례가 다 됐어요! 우리 그냥 가면 안 돼요?
남: 내뺄 생각은 하지도 마. 그냥 침착해, 알겠니?
여: 죄송해요, 코치님, 하지만 저는 이것을 할 수가 없어요.
남: 네가 이렇게 긴장하는 이유를 이해 못하겠어, Megan.
여: 다른 참가자들이 너무 잘해요! 저는 가능성이 없어요!
남: 그건 사실이 아니야. 너는 이 대회에서 이길 수 있는 자질을 가지고 있어.
여: 정말 그렇게 생각하세요?
남: 확실해. 스스로를 믿어.

단·어·및·표·현

back out 내빼다, 철회하다
stand a chance 가능성이 있다
I'm positive. 확실해.

듣·기·대·본

W: Robin, could you help me?

M: Of course. How can I help you?

W: What should I bring to the potluck party? I'm trying to choose between pasta and tacos with assorted fillings.

M: Both of them are good options.

W: Yes. That's why I can't decide.

M: Hmm… I think tacos would be better. They are convenient to eat, and people can customize them according to their preferences.

W: You're right. I'll make sure to bring different fillings like meat, beans and veggies.

우·리·말·해·석

여: Robin, 너는 날 도와줄 수 있니?

남: 물론이지. 어떻게 도와줄까?

여: 내가 포틀럭 파티에 무엇을 가져가야 할까? 나는 파스타와 여러 가지 속재료를 곁들인 타코 중에 고르려고 해.

남: 그것들은 둘 다 좋은 선택지들이네.

여: 응. 그게 내가 결정할 수 없는 이유야.

남: 음… 나는 타코가 더 나을 것 같아. 그것들은 먹기 간편하고, 사람들은 그들의 선호에 따라 그것들을 원하는 대로 만들 수 있어.

여: 맞아. 나는 고기, 콩, 그리고 채소같은 다른 속재료들을 꼭 가져가야겠어.

단·어·및·표·현

potluck [pátlʌk] 몡 포틀럭(여러 사람들이 각자 음식을 조금씩 가져와서 나눠 먹는 식사)

assorted [əsɔ́:rtid] 혱 여러 가지의, 갖은

filling [fíliŋ] 몡 (파이 등 음식의) 소[속]

convenient [kənvíːnjənt] 혱 간편한, 편리한

customize [kʌ́stəmàiz] 통 원하는 대로 만들다, 바꾸다

according to ~에 따라

preference [préfərəns] 몡 선호

veggie [véʤi] 몡 채소

듣·기·대·본

M: Mia, can you come to the kitchen and give me a hand?

W: Sure, Dad. What do you need me to do?

M: Can you bring me some chocolate chips from the cupboard?

W: Okay. Oh! Are you baking cookies? Can I help you make them?

M: Sure! Why don't you take this dough and shape it into a cookie?

W: Okay. (pause) Hmm… This is harder than I thought.

M: You did a great job! Now, I'll put these in the oven for you.

우·리·말·해·석

남: Mia, 부엌으로 와서 나를 도와줄 수 있니?

여: 네, 아빠. 제가 무엇을 해야 할까요?

남: 찬장에서 초콜릿칩을 좀 가져다줄 수 있니?

여: 좋아요. 아! 쿠키를 굽고 계세요? 제가 도와드릴까요?

남: 물론이지! 이 반죽을 가져가서 쿠키 모양으로 만드는 게 어때?

여: 좋아요. (잠시 후) 흠… 이것은 제가 생각했던 것보다 더 어려워요.

남: 너는 정말 잘했어! 이제, 내가 너를 위해 이것들을 오븐에 넣을게.

단·어·및·표·현

give ~ a hand ~를 돕다

do a great job 잘 해내다, 정말 잘하다

듣·기·대·본

W: Hey, Max. Have you heard about the science fair next month?

M: No, I didn't know about it. When is it?

W: It's on February 15th. It's open to all middle schoolers.

M: Cool! What kind of projects can we do?

W: Anything related to science — from biology to physics!

M: Awesome! How long do we have to present our projects?

W: Each presentation should be about 5 minutes long.

M: Sounds fun! I'll start thinking of ideas now!

우·리·말·해·석

여: 안녕, Max. 다음 달 과학 박람회 소식을 들었니?

남: 아니, 난 그것에 대해 몰랐어. 그게 언제야?

여: 2월 15일이야. 모든 중학생에게 열려 있어.

남: 멋지다! 우리는 어떤 종류의 프로젝트를 할 수 있어?

여: 생물학부터 물리학까지 과학과 관련된 어떤 것이든지!

남: 굉장한데! 우리 프로젝트를 얼마나 길게 발표해야 해?

여: 각 발표는 약 5분 정도 길이여야 해.

남: 재미있겠다! 이제부터 아이디어를 생각해볼게!

단·어·및·표·현

science fair 과학 박람회

project [prάʤekt] 몡 연구 프로젝트, 과제

related to ~과 관련 있는

biology [baiάləʤi] 몡 생물학

physics [fíziks] 몡 물리학

present [prizént] 통 발표하다

presentation [prìːzəntéiʃən] 몡 발표

듣·기·대·본

W: Hello, students. Our school football team's final game is tomorrow. I know a lot of you want to see the game. So, the school has booked a bus. If you want to catch the bus to the stadium, please tell your teacher. The bus will leave the school at 5 p.m. Come to the game, and show your support. See you tomorrow!

우·리·말·해·석

여: 안녕하세요. 학생 여러분. 우리 학교 축구 팀의 결승 경기가 내일입니다. 나는 많은 여러분들이 경기를 보고 싶어 한다는 것을 압니다. 그래서, 학교가 버스를 예약했습니다. 여러분이 경기장으로 가는 버스를 타고 싶다면, 여러분의 선생님에게 얘기하세요. 버스는 오후 5시에 학교를 떠납니다. 경기에 와서 여러분의 지지를 보여주세요. 내일 봅시다!

단·어·및·표·현

final game 결승 경기

support [səpɔ́:rt] 몡 지지, 응원

듣·기·대·본

W: Honey, look at this website! This toy scooter is on sale.

M: Yeah, and it's for preschool children aged 6 and under.

W: Right. It's perfect for Billy. And it's three-wheeled for safety.

M: That's nice! It comes in two colors. Which color do you like?

W: I prefer the blue one. Is the price okay?

M: It's only 30 dollars. That's good.

W: Yeah, it's also delivered for free.
M: Okay. Let's order it now.

우·리·말·해·석
여: 여보, 이 웹사이트를 봐요! 이 장난감 스쿠터를 세일하고 있어요.
남: 네, 그리고 그것은 6세 이하의 미취학 아동들을 위한 것이에요.
여: 맞아요. 이것은 Billy에게 완벽해요. 그리고 이것은 안전을 위해 바퀴가 세 개 달렸어요.
남: 그것 좋네요! 이것은 두 가지 색으로 나와요. 당신은 어느 색이 좋아요?
여: 나는 파란 것이 더 좋아요. 가격은 괜찮아요?
남: 이것은 30달러밖에 안 해요. 좋아요.
여: 네, 그것은 또한 무료로 배송돼요.
남: 좋아요. 지금 이것을 주문합시다.

단·어·및·표·현
deliver [dilívər] ⑧ 배송하다, 배달하다
for free 무료로

12 전화목적파악 ▶정답 ③

듣·기·대·본
(Telephone rings.)
W: Hello, this is Jolly Bistro.
M: Hi. I'm planning to dine at your restaurant tonight, but I have some questions regarding your menu.
W: Yes, how may I help you?
M: So, my daughter is a vegetarian. Do you have any vegetarian options on the menu?
W: Oh, yes, we do. We have vegetarian burgers, mushroom pasta, and various salad choices.
M: That's great. Thank you so much.
W: Is there anything else I can help you with?
M: No. That will be all. Thanks.

우·리·말·해·석
(전화벨이 울린다.)
여: 안녕하세요, Jolly Bistro입니다.
남: 안녕하세요. 저는 오늘 밤 당신의 식당에서 식사를 할 계획인데 메뉴에 관해서 질문이 좀 있어요.
여: 네, 어떻게 도와드릴까요?
남: 그러니까, 제 딸은 채식주의자예요. 메뉴에 채식주의자가 선택할 수 있는 게 있나요?
여: 오, 네, 있습니다. 채식 버거, 버섯 파스타, 그리고 선택 가능한 다양한 샐러드들이 있습니다.
남: 그거 잘됐네요. 정말 감사합니다.
여: 제가 도와드릴 수 있는 게 더 있나요?
남: 아뇨. 그게 다예요. 감사합니다.

단·어·및·표·현
bistro [bístrou] ⑲ (편안한 분위기의) 작은 식당
dine [dain] ⑧ (잘 차린) 식사를 하다, 만찬을 들다
regarding [rigá:rdiŋ] ⑳ ~에 관하여
vegetarian [vèdʒité(:)əriən] ⑲ 채식주의자 ⑱ 채식(주의자)의
choice [tʃɔis] ⑲ 선택 가능한 수[범위]

13 수치파악(시각) ▶정답 ④

듣·기·대·본
M: I have good news, Wanda. A new Mexican restaurant is opening soon.
W: Wow, I love Mexican food! When do they open?
M: This Saturday. Do you want to go there together?
W: Sure! Can we meet at 12 p.m. on Saturday?
M: I'm sorry. I have a tennis lesson until 1 p.m.

W: Then, how about meeting at 1:30?
M: If a late lunch is okay with you, it's okay with me.
W: Alright. I'll see you at the restaurant, then. I hope there's a grand opening event!

우·리·말·해·석
남: 나는 좋은 소식이 있어, Wanda. 새로운 멕시코 식당이 곧 문을 열어.
여: 우와, 나는 멕시코 음식을 좋아해! 그들은 언제 열어?
남: 이번 주 토요일. 너는 그곳에 함께 가길 원하니?
여: 그럼! 우리 토요일 낮 12시에 만날 수 있어?
남: 미안해. 나는 오후 1시까지 테니스 레슨이 있어.
여: 그러면, 1시 30분에 만나는 것은 어때?
남: 늦은 점심 식사가 너에게 괜찮다면, 나도 괜찮아.
여: 좋아. 그때 너를 식당에서 만날게. 나는 성대한 개업 이벤트가 있기를 바라!

단·어·및·표·현
then [ðen] ⑲ 그때

14 대화자관계추론 ▶정답 ⑤

듣·기·대·본
M: Excuse me. Is the subway on Line 4 running now?
W: I'm afraid not. It is temporarily out of service due to a signal problem.
M: Oh no. I need to get to City Hall Station soon.
W: In that case, take Line 3 to Union Station and transfer to a bus there.
M: Got it. Thanks for the information.
W: You're welcome. Let me know if you need any more help.

우·리·말·해·석
남: 실례합니다. 지금 지하철 4호선이 운행하고 있나요?
여: 유감스럽게도 아니에요. 신호 문제로 인해 서비스가 일시적으로 중단됐어요.
남: 아, 안돼요. 저는 곧 시청역에 가야 해요.
여: 그런 경우, 3호선을 타고 유니언 역으로 가서 거기에서 버스로 환승하세요.
남: 알겠어요. 정보 감사합니다.
여: 천만에요. 도움이 더 필요하시면 제게 말씀해주세요.

단·어·및·표·현
run [rʌn] ⑧ (버스·기차 등이 특정 노선으로) 운행하다, 다니다
temporarily [tèmpəré(:)rəli] ⑳ 일시적으로
out of service 서비스가 중단된, 사용이 중지된
due to ~로 인해, ~때문에
signal [sígnəl] ⑲ 신호
transfer [trænsfər] ⑧ 환승하다, 갈아타다
information [ìnfərméiʃən] ⑲ 정보

15 부탁(요청)한일파악 ▶정답 ③

듣·기·대·본
M: Mom, can you come here for a minute?
W: Sure. What's the matter?
M: You know how much I hate cockroaches, right?
W: Yeah, I know that you're terrified of them.
M: Well, I managed to capture one underneath that paper cup over there.
W: Good job! I'm proud of you! Is it still alive?
M: Yes, Mom. Could you throw away that paper cup for me? I'm too scared to touch it again.
W: Okay, leave it to me.

우·리·말·해·석

남: 엄마, 여기로 잠깐 와주실래요?
여: 그래. 무슨 일이니?
남: 엄마는 제가 바퀴벌레를 얼마나 싫어하는지 아시죠, 그렇죠?
여: 그래, 나는 네가 그것들을 엄청 무서워하는 것을 알아.
남: 그런데, 제가 (바퀴벌레) 한 마리를 저기 종이컵 속에 간신히 잡아 넣었어요.
여: 잘했다! 네가 자랑스럽구나! 그것이 아직 살아있니?
남: 네, 엄마. 저 대신 저 종이컵을 버려주시겠어요? 저는 너무 무서워서 그것을 다시 만질 수가 없어요.
여: 알았다. 내게 맡기렴.

단·어·및·표·현

be terrified of ~ ~을 매우 무서워하다
manage to + 동사원형 간신히 ~하다
capture [kǽptʃər] 동 포획하다
throw away 버리다

16 이유파악 ▶정답 ③

듣·기·대·본

W: Dad, I'm going swimming. I need to get some exercise.
M: Honey, is that a good idea? I thought you had a cold.
W: No need to worry. I feel fine today.
M: Okay, but don't exercise too hard.
W: Thanks, I'll be home before dinner.
M: Come to think of it, isn't the swimming pool closed for repairs?
W: Err… I'm not sure.
M: Yes, it says here on their website.
W: Oh, it seems that they aren't open until next month.
M: I guess you should just go for a run instead.

우·리·말·해·석

여: 아빠, 저 수영하러 갈 거예요. 저는 운동을 좀 할 필요가 있어요.
남: 얘야, 그것이 좋은 생각이니? 나는 네가 감기에 걸렸다고 생각했어.
여: 걱정할 필요가 없어요. 저는 오늘 상태가 좋아요.
남: 좋아, 하지만 너무 심하게 운동하지 마라.
여: 고마워요, 저는 저녁 식사 전에 집에 올 거예요.
남: 그러고 보니, 수영장이 수리를 위해 문을 닫지 않았니?
여: 어… 잘 모르겠어요.
남: 맞아, 여기 웹사이트에 쓰여 있다.
여: 오, 그들은 다음 달 전까지 열지 않는 것 같네요.
남: 대신에 너는 그냥 달리기하러 가야겠구나.

단·어·및·표·현

come to think of it 그러고 보니
repair [ripɛ́ər] 명 수리

17 그림상황에적절한대화찾기 ▶정답 ③

듣·기·대·본

① W: You look so excited. What's up?
　 M: I've bought a new cell phone.
② W: It's chilly. Can I close the window?
　 M: Sure. Go ahead.
③ W: Get up now, or you will be late for school.
　 M: OK, Mom. I will.
④ W: Would you like some more spaghetti?
　 M: No, thank you. I'm full.
⑤ W: It's going to rain according to the weather forecast.
　 M: I'd better not forget to take an umbrella, then.

우·리·말·해·석

① 여: 너 정말 신나 보인다. 무슨 일이야?

남: 나는 새로운 휴대폰을 샀어요.
② 여: 쌀쌀하네. 내가 창문을 닫아도 될까?
　 남: 그럼요. 그렇게 하세요.
③ 여: 지금 일어나지 않으면 너는 학교에 늦을 거야.
　 남: 알겠어요, 엄마. 일어날게요.
④ 여: 스파게티 좀 더 먹을래?
　 남: 아니요, 괜찮아요. 저는 배불러요.
⑤ 여: 일기예보에 따르면 비가 올 거야.
　 남: 그럼 저는 우산을 가져가는 것을 잊지 않아야겠네요.

단·어·및·표·현

chilly [tʃíli] 형 쌀쌀한, 추운
go ahead (승인, 인가) ~하세요
full [ful] 형 배부른
according to ~에 따르면, ~에 의하면

18 담화미언급 ▶정답 ④

듣·기·대·본

W: Dear musical fans, our musical company is glad to announce the opening of the musical *Hide* playing at the Roseville Theater. The musical is about the tragic love between a doctor called Hide and his fiancée Emma. We are proud to introduce the talented actor, David Choi who will be playing the main character. The musical will be on stage from September 14th to December 21st. You can purchase tickets starting on August 20th. We hope you don't miss it!

우·리·말·해·석

여: 뮤지컬 팬 여러분, 저희 뮤지컬 회사는 Roseville 극장에서 공연하는 뮤지컬 "Hide"의 개막을 발표하게 되어 기쁩니다. 그 뮤지컬은 Hide라 불리는 박사와 그의 약혼녀 Emma 사이의 비극적 사랑에 대한 것입니다. 저희는 주인공을 연기하게 될 재능 있는 배우 David Choi를 소개하게 되어 자랑스럽습니다. 뮤지컬은 9월 14일부터 12월 21일까지 공연될 것입니다. 8월 20일부터 표를 구입하실 수 있습니다. 놓치지 않으시길 바랍니다!

단·어·및·표·현

announce [ənáuns] 동 발표하다

19 알맞은응답찾기 ▶정답 ④

듣·기·대·본

(*Telephone rings.*)
M: Hello, Mrs. Hudson? This is Michael.
W: Hi, Michael. How are you?
M: Not so great. I'm actually calling to tell you that I won't be able to make it to my piano lesson this week.
W: Oh, I hope nothing's wrong!
M: I sprained my finger yesterday while playing basketball, so I can't play the piano this week.
W: I'm sorry to hear that. I hope you get better soon.
M: Thank you. So, may I reschedule my lesson to next week?
W: Of course! Thanks for giving me the heads up.

우·리·말·해·석

① 걱정하지 말아요. 당신은 뛰어난 피아노 연주자예요.
② 미안하지만, 나는 점심시간을 갖는 중이에요.
③ 좋은 소식이네요! 당신이 새 피아노를 사서 기뻐요.
④ 물론이죠! 미리 알려줘서 고마워요.
⑤ 문제없어요. 나는 클래식 음악 듣는 것도 즐겨요.

(전화벨이 울린다.)
남: 안녕하세요, Hudson 선생님? Michael입니다.

여: 안녕하세요, Michael. 어떻게 지내요?

남: 그렇게 좋지는 않아요. 저 실은 이번 주 피아노 수업에 갈 수 없다는 것을 말씀드리려고 전화했어요.

여: 오, 아무 일 아니기를 바라요!

남: 농구를 하다가 어제 손가락을 삐어서 이번 주에는 피아노를 칠 수 없어요.

여: 그 말을 들으니 안됐네요. 곧 호전되기를 바라요.

남: 고맙습니다. 그래서, 제 수업을 다음 주로 일정을 변경해도 될까요?

여: **물론이죠! 미리 알려줘서 고마워요.**

단·어·및·표·현

sprain[sprein] ⑧ 삐다
get better 호전되다

20 알맞은응답찾기 ▶정답 ④

듣·기·대·본

M: Jane, is it true that you're going to Sok-cho?

W: Yes. My family will stay there for two weeks.

M: That long? Where will you stay?

W: My parents rented a house. I can't wait to try all the famous food there.

M: Will you go sea bathing, too? That's a beach area.

W: No, I don't like water. But, there's a big traditional market!

M: Right, you like shopping.

W: I think I'll go there every day.

우·리·말·해·석

① 나는 수영을 잘해.

② 그것은 아름다운 해변이야.

③ 그것에 대해서는 정말 미안해.

④ 난 내가 거기에 매일 갈 거라고 생각해.

⑤ 우리는 매 여름마다 캠핑을 가.

남: Jane, 네가 속초에 간다는 게 사실이니?

여: 응. 우리 가족은 2주 동안 그곳에서 지낼 거야.

남: 그렇게 오래? 어디에서 묵을 거야?

여: 우리 부모님이 집을 빌리셨어. 난 어서 빨리 거기서 모든 유명한 음식을 먹어보고 싶어.

남: 너는 해수욕도 하러 갈 거야? 그곳은 해변 지역이잖아.

여: 아니, 나는 물을 좋아하지 않아. 하지만, 큰 전통시장이 있어!

남: 맞아, 너는 쇼핑을 좋아해.

여: 난 내가 거기에 매일 갈 거라고 생각해.

단·어·및·표·현

rent[rent] ⑧ (사용료를 내고 단기간) 빌리다
can't wait to + 동사원형 어서 빨리 ~하고 싶다, ~가 기대된다
sea bathing 해수욕
traditional[trədíʃənəl] ⑱ 전통적인

Words & Expressions Review

1. 실은	2. 확실해.	3. 참석하다
4. 인내심, 참을성	5. ~에 따르면, ~에 의하면	6. 포획하다
7. 미취학 아동	8. 간편한, 편리한	9. (승인, 인가) ~하세요
10. (결과가) ~으로 되다, 되어 가다	11. 채식주의자, 채식(주의자)의	12. 결승 경기
13. 참가자	14. 그러고 보니	15. 흐린
16. 발표하다	17. (편안한 분위기의) 작은 식당	18. 떠올리게 하다
19. 버스를 (잡아) 타다	20. ~에 관하여	21. ~과 관련 있는
22. 발표하다	23. 가능성이 있다	24. ~를 돕다
25. 놓치다	26. ~을 (한번) 보다	27. ~하는 한
28. 원하는 대로 만들다, 바꾸다	29. 서비스가 중단된, 사용이 중지된	30. 쌀쌀한, 추운
31. 것, 물건	32. 지지, 응원	33. 감기에 걸리다
34. 일시적으로	35. 외모	36. 해수욕
37. 삐다	38. 전통적인	39. 안전, 안전성
40. 달리다	41. 몸이 안 좋다	42. 선택 가능한 수 [범위]
43. 비극적인	44. 내빼다, 철회하다	

중학영어듣기 필수 표현

중요도 최상 ★★★ 상 ★★ 중 ★

길 안내하기

중요도	주요표현	해석
★★	(In fact) It's ~	(사실) 그것은 ~에 있습니다.
★★	(In that case,) Go(Cross, Turn, Follow)~.	(그럴 경우엔,) ~가십시오. (~건너십시오, ~도세요, ~따라가십시오.)
★	(Excuse me.) Can you tell me the way ~	(실례합니다.) ~가는 길 좀 알려주시겠어요?
★	Can you tell me where ~ is?	~가 어디인지 알려주시겠어요?
★	Excuse me. Where's the ~?	실례합니다. ~가 어디 있죠?
★	Where can I find ~?	~를 어디에서 찾을 수 있죠?
★	How can I get there?	어떻게 거기에 갈 수 있죠?
★	Is this the right way to ~?	이 길이 ~가는 길 맞죠?
★	It's (just) down the road.	그것은 (바로) 길 아래에 있습니다.
★	That road leads you to ~	저 길로 가면 ~에 도착합니다.
★	Let's go straight. We can walk across ~	직진합시다. 우리는 ~를 건너갈 수 있습니다.
★	You can see it on your ~	당신의 ~에서 그것을 볼 수 있습니다.
★	You have to go straight ~	직진하셔야 합니다.

기억/경험 묻고 말하기

중요도	주요표현	해석
★★	Do you remember ~?	~기억납니까?
★★	I'll never forget ~	나는 ~를 결코 잊지 않을 거야.
★★	I've (actually) never p.p. ~	(사실) 나는 ~한 적이 결코 없습니다.
★	Is that really true?	그게 정말 사실입니까?
★	Have you forgotten ~?	~잊으셨습니까?
★	Sure.	물론이야.
★	I forgot about that.	나 그거 잊어버렸어.
★	I didn't know that. That's amazing!	나는 그거 몰랐어. 놀라워라!
★	I find it hard to believe ~.	나는 ~을 믿기 어렵습니다.
★	Have you ever ~ p.p.?	~한 적이 있습니까?
★	I've (actually) p.p. ~	(사실) 나는 ~한 적이 있습니다.
★	(Actually,) I have had (done) the same experience (before).	(사실,) 나는 똑같은 경험이 있습니다.

마더텅 100%실전대비 MP3 중학영어듣기 24회 모의고사 2학년

정답표

1회

1	2	3	4	5	6	7	8	9	10
④	③	②	②	②	①	④	⑤	⑤	③

11	12	13	14	15	16	17	18	19	20
④	④	③	②	②	③	③	③	②	③

2회

1	2	3	4	5	6	7	8	9	10
⑤	①	①	③	④	⑤	④	①	④	②

11	12	13	14	15	16	17	18	19	20
③	⑤	③	③	②	⑤	①	④	②	⑤

3회

1	2	3	4	5	6	7	8	9	10
③	⑤	①	⑤	①	③	③	①	③	④

11	12	13	14	15	16	17	18	19	20
④	⑤	②	③	③	④	⑤	⑤	③	③

4회

1	2	3	4	5	6	7	8	9	10
②	③	③	④	⑤	④	④	③	⑤	①

11	12	13	14	15	16	17	18	19	20
④	①	③	⑤	①	⑤	④	③	⑤	①

5회

1	2	3	4	5	6	7	8	9	10
③	⑤	②	⑤	②	⑤	③	①	④	①

11	12	13	14	15	16	17	18	19	20
⑤	③	④	②	③	④	⑤	④	⑤	③

6회

1	2	3	4	5	6	7	8	9	10
④	⑤	①	④	②	⑤	③	③	④	④

11	12	13	14	15	16	17	18	19	20
④	①	③	②	①	③	④	④	④	⑤

7회

1	2	3	4	5	6	7	8	9	10
①	④	②	⑤	④	①	③	③	③	③

11	12	13	14	15	16	17	18	19	20
④	③	①	④	④	③	③	③	②	②

8회

1	2	3	4	5	6	7	8	9	10
④	⑤	⑤	④	②	②	⑤	⑤	④	②

11	12	13	14	15	16	17	18	19	20
⑤	④	①	④	⑤	②	③	③	⑤	②

9회

1	2	3	4	5	6	7	8	9	10
③	③	④	⑤	④	②	④	⑤	④	④

11	12	13	14	15	16	17	18	19	20
④	⑤	③	③	①	④	④	⑤	③	④

10회

1	2	3	4	5	6	7	8	9	10
④	②	②	③	⑤	⑤	②	⑤	⑤	⑤

11	12	13	14	15	16	17	18	19	20
⑤	④	②	①	④	④	⑤	④	①	⑤

11회

1	2	3	4	5	6	7	8	9	10
④	⑤	⑤	⑤	③	③	②	⑤	④	①

11	12	13	14	15	16	17	18	19	20
⑤	④	②	⑤	④	①	③	⑤	②	①

12회

1	2	3	4	5	6	7	8	9	10
⑤	④	③	⑤	③	①	⑤	③	④	④

11	12	13	14	15	16	17	18	19	20
①	②	④	②	②	⑤	③	③	③	⑤

13회

1	2	3	4	5	6	7	8	9	10
⑤	①	②	③	②	④	⑤	②	④	②

11	12	13	14	15	16	17	18	19	20
④	③	②	④	①	④	⑤	④	④	⑤

14회

1	2	3	4	5	6	7	8	9	10
①	④	③	③	②	②	⑤	①	③	④

11	12	13	14	15	16	17	18	19	20
④	⑤	④	④	③	⑤	④	④	④	②

15회

1	2	3	4	5	6	7	8	9	10
②	③	①	②	④	④	③	⑤	⑤	③

11	12	13	14	15	16	17	18	19	20
⑤	④	②	①	②	⑤	③	⑤	⑤	④

16회

1	2	3	4	5	6	7	8	9	10
④	②	④	①	②	③	③	④	④	③

11	12	13	14	15	16	17	18	19	20
⑤	④	④	②	⑤	⑤	④	⑤	①	④

17회

1	2	3	4	5	6	7	8	9	10
②	⑤	⑤	⑤	①	②	⑤	③	④	①

11	12	13	14	15	16	17	18	19	20
③	①	④	⑤	④	②	④	④	②	④

18회

1	2	3	4	5	6	7	8	9	10
③	③	②	⑤	④	④	④	①	⑤	③

11	12	13	14	15	16	17	18	19	20
⑤	②	④	③	①	③	④	③	②	①

19회

1	2	3	4	5	6	7	8	9	10
③	④	②	⑤	⑤	②	⑤	⑤	③	④

11	12	13	14	15	16	17	18	19	20
⑤	④	②	④	③	①	⑤	③	⑤	④

20회

1	2	3	4	5	6	7	8	9	10
③	④	③	④	⑤	⑤	④	②	③	③

11	12	13	14	15	16	17	18	19	20
④	⑤	④	②	⑤	④	⑤	⑤	②	③

21회

1	2	3	4	5	6	7	8	9	10
②	②	④	④	⑤	⑤	⑤	⑤	③	③

11	12	13	14	15	16	17	18	19	20
③	②	⑤	④	④	①	③	④	⑤	④

22회

1	2	3	4	5	6	7	8	9	10
①	②	③	①	④	③	④	⑤	⑤	⑤

11	12	13	14	15	16	17	18	19	20
④	④	②	②	②	⑤	⑤	④	②	②

23회

1	2	3	4	5	6	7	8	9	10
④	②	④	①	④	④	④	④	⑤	②

11	12	13	14	15	16	17	18	19	20
⑤	④	③	③	③	④	④	⑤	⑤	②

24회

1	2	3	4	5	6	7	8	9	10
①	②	②	②	②	⑤	③	④	②	②

11	12	13	14	15	16	17	18	19	20
②	③	④	⑤	③	③	③	④	④	④

중학영어듣기 필수 표현 📝

중요도 최상 ★★★ 상 ★★ 중 ★

질문/대답하기

중요도	주요표현	해석
★★★	I'm(We're) planning to + 동사원형	나는(우리는) ~할 계획이야.
★★★	I'm going to + 동사원형	나는 ~할 계획이야.
★★★	Have you heard of/about ~?	~에 대해 들어본 적 있어?
★★★	What are you planning to do?	무엇을 할 생각이야? (계획이 뭐야?)
★★★	Could/Can you (please) tell me ~?	~에 대해 말해 줄 수 있어?
★★	What would you like to + 동사원형?	너 무엇을 ~하고 싶어?
★★	Have you (ever) p.p. ~?	너 ~해본 적 있어?
★	What are you going to do?	너 뭐 할거야?
★	Do you know ~?	너 ~에 대해 알아?
★	Do you want to + 동사원형?	너 ~하고 싶어?
★	Are you planning to + 동사원형?	너 ~할 계획이야?
★	Do you have any plans?	어떤 계획이라도 있어?
★	I've never p.p. ~	나는 ~해본 적이 없어.
★	I have to ~	나는 ~해야만 해.
★	How did you + 동사원형?	어떻게 ~했어?
★	What is ~?	~는 무엇이야?
★	Who + 과거동사 ~?	누가 ~했어?
★	What did he + 동사원형 ~?	그가 무엇을 ~했어?
★	When + 동사 ~?	언제 ~야?
★	Why ~?	왜 ~야?
★	Did you + 동사원형 ~?	너 ~했어?
★	What do you do to + 동사원형 ~?	~하기 위해 너는 무엇을 해?
★	What do you call + 명사 ~?	너는 ~를 뭐라고 불러?
★	What A do you want to + 동사원형?	어떤 A를 ~하기 원해?
★	Which A do you like most?	어떤 A를 너는 가장 좋아해?
★	Which A would you like to + 동사원형?	어떤 A를 ~하고 싶어?
★	What do you want to be in the future?	너는 커서 무엇이 되고 싶어?
★	Would you like to + 동사원형 ~?	너 ~하고 싶어?
★	What kind of A do you prefer?	어떤 종류의 A를 너는 선호해?

 **중학영어듣기 필수 표현**

중요도 최상 ★★★ 상 ★★ 중 ★

감사/칭찬

중요도	주요표현	해석
★	I couldn't have p.p. without you.	네가 없었다면 나는 ∼할 수 없었을 거야. (정말 고마워.)
★	Thanks (so much).	(매우) 감사합니다.
★	Thank you for + 명사	∼에 대해 감사드립니다.
★	I appreciate it.	그것에 대해 감사드립니다.
★	It's (very) nice of you to + 동사원형	∼를 해주셔서 (매우) 감사드립니다.
★	Terrific!	정말 멋졌어! (정말 잘했어!)
★	Excellent!	정말 멋졌어! (정말 잘했어!)
★	You did a good(great) job!	너 정말 훌륭했어!
★	I like(liked) your + 명사	나는 너의 ∼가 좋아(좋았어).
★	You are such a friendly person.	너는 매우 친절하구나.
★	I'm glad you like it.	네가 그것을 좋아하니 기쁘다.
★	Don't mention it.	별말씀을요. (그렇게 말해 주니 고마워요.)

불가능 표현하기

중요도	주요표현	해석
★★★	I have no idea how ~	나는 어떻게 ∼ 하는지 잘 모르겠어. (못하겠어.)
★	It's/That's/A is (almost) impossible!	그것은(A는) 불가능해!
★	I can't.	나는 할 수 없어.
★	That won't be possible.	그것은 불가능해.
★	I don't think I can.	내가 할 수 있다고 생각하지 않아. (못해.)
★	I /We won't be able to + 동사원형	나는(우리는) ∼ 할 수 없어요.
★	I'm not good at ~	나는 ∼를 잘하지 못해요.
★	There is no/a chance ~	∼ 인 가능성은 없어. (있어.)
★	I have no time to + 동사원형	나는 ∼ 할 시간이 없어.